GLOBAL TERRORISM

Global Terrorism, second edition, continues to provide students with the most comprehensive introduction to terrorism as a global phenomenon. It introduces students to history, politics, ideologies, and strategies of both contemporary and older terrorist groups.

Written in a clear and accessible style, each chapter explains a different aspect of terrorism and illustrates this with a wide variety of detailed case studies from across the world. Although the focus is on the contemporary, the book also includes discussion of older terrorist groups.

Building on the strengths of the first edition, this edition includes new material on:

- July 7 attacks in London
- Bali bombings
- Domestic terrorism in Columbia
- Attacks in Iraq
- Al Qaeda, the Tamil Tigers, the IRA
- Animal rights extremism

The unique combination of a genuinely historical focus and truly global coverage makes this an ideal introductory textbook for anyone studying terrorism.

James M. Lutz is Professor of Political Science at Indiana University-Purdue University at Fort Wayne. He has long been interested in various types of political violence.

Brenda J. Lutz is a PhD candidate at the Department of Politics, University of Dundee, Scotland, focusing on the animal rights movement and factory farming.

GLOBAL TERRORISM

Second edition

James M. Lutz and Brenda J. Lutz

Routledge
Taylor & Francis Group

LONDON AND NEW YORK

First published 2004

Second edition 2008
by Routledge
2 Park Square, Milton Park, Abingdon, Oxon, OX14 4RN

Simultaneously published in the USA and Canada
by Routledge
270 Madison Avenue, New York, NY 10016

Reprinted 2009

Routledge is an imprint of the Taylor & Francis Group, an informa business

© 2008 James M. Lutz and Brenda J. Lutz

Typeset in Garamond by Swales & Willis Ltd, Exeter, Devon
Printed and bound in Great Britain by the MPG Books Group

British Library Cataloguing in Publication Data
A catalogue record for this book is available from the
British Library

Library of Congress Cataloging in Publication Data
A catalog record for this book has been requested

ISBN10: 0–415–77246–X (hbk)
ISBN10: 0–415–77247–8 (pbk)
ISBN10: 0–203–89503–7 (ebk)

ISBN13: 978–0–415–77246–4 (hbk)
ISBN13: 978–0–415–77247–1 (pbk)
ISBN13: 978–0–203–89503–0 (ebk)

For Carol Hoover and Byron Hoover,
our daughters Cara and Tessa,
and our St Bernards, Bessie and Barnaby.

CONTENTS

List of illustrations   *xi*
Preface to second edition   *xiii*

1 Terrorism in the World Today and Yesterday   **1**
Terms   6
Further reading   6

2 What Is Terrorism? Definition and Classification   **7**
Defining terrorism   7
Classification and categories   14
Causes of terrorism   16
Prevalence of terrorism   20
Summary   23
Terms   24
Further reading   24

3 Tactics, Weapons, and Targets   **25**
Techniques   26
Weapons   28
Targets   35
Summary   47
Terms   48
Further reading   48

4 State Sponsors and Supporters of Terrorism   **49**
True state control   49
State support of foreign terrorists   51
Case studies   54
    4.1   Italy and Hungary in Yugoslavia   54
    4.2   Iran   57
    4.3   The United States and the Contras in Nicaragua   60
    4.4   The cold war between India and Pakistan   63
Summary   66

Terms 67
Further reading 68

5 Religious Justification for Terrorism **69**
Terrorism and the world's religions 70
Case studies 79
    5.1   The Zealots in Judea 80
    5.2   The Sikhs and Khalistan 81
    5.3   Algeria in the 1990s 86
    5.4   Aum Shinrikyo (Supreme Truth) 89
    5.5   Anti-abortion activities in the United States 91
    5.6   Osama bin Laden and the Al Qaeda network 93
Summary 98
Terms 100
Further reading 101

6 Ethnic and National Bases of Terrorism **102**
Modernity and ethnic conflict 103
Case studies 108
    6.1   The Boston Tea Party 108
    6.2   Basque nationalists in Spain 110
    6.3   Dayaks and migrants in Borneo 114
    6.4   Albanians in Kosovo and Macedonia 117
    6.5   The Palestinian Liberation Organization and the struggle with Israel 121
Summary 126
Terms 128
Further reading 128

7 Terrorism and Ideologies of the Left **129**
Ideology and beliefs 130
Dissatisfaction from the left 130
Case studies 138
    7.1   The Baader–Meinhof Gang in West Germany 139
    7.2   The Italian Red Brigades 142
    7.3   The Montoneros in Argentina 146
    7.4   Naxalites in India 150
    7.5   The Animal Liberation Front and the Animal Rights Militia 153
Summary 157
Terms 159
Further reading 160

8 Terrorism and Ideologies of the Right **161**
Right-wing dissatisfaction: Marxism and minorities 162
Case studies 166
    8.1   Stormtroopers in Weimar Germany 166

8.2   The Ku Klux Klan (1920s and 1930s)   169
8.3   Neo-fascism in postwar Italy   171
8.4   The American Militia/Patriot Movement   174
8.5   Neo-Nazis and Skinheads in Europe   180
Summary   185
Terms   188
Further reading   188

9 Terrorism and Multiple Motivations   **189**
Terrorist campaigns with complex causes   189
Case studies   195
9.1   Leftists and indigenous populations in Peru   195
9.2   Irish republicanism   199
9.3   Colombia: regionalism, ideology, and narcotics   205
9.4   Nigeria: religion and region, ethnicity and environmentalism   208
Summary   212
Terms   214
Further reading   214

10 State Use of Domestic Terrorism and Repression   **216**
Government induced fear and compliance   217
Government complicity in terrorism by non-state groups   218
Genocide and ethnic cleansing   221
Case studies   223
10.1   Terror in the first years of the French Revolution   224
10.2   Paramilitary militias in East Timor   226
10.3   Farm invasions in Zimbabwe   228
10.4   Ethnic cleansing in Bosnia and Herzegovina   230
10.5   Ethnic cleansing in the Sudan   234
10.6   Genocide in Rwanda   237
Summary   241
Terms   243
Further reading   244

11 Countries with Multiple Crises of Terrorism   **245**
The prevalence of multiple crises   245
Waves of violence and terrorism in Sri Lanka   248
Terrorism and insurgency in Iraq   254
Summary   258
Terms   260
Further reading   260

12 Counterterrorism   **261**
Techniques of counterterrorism   261
Weapons of mass destruction and mass casualties   277

Summary   278
Terms   281
Further reading   282

13 Terrorism: A continuing phenomenon   283
Why terrorism continues   284
What we know from the historical experience   289

Glossary   291
Bibliography   308
Index   336

ILLUSTRATIONS

MAPS

1	India and South Asia	83
2	Indonesia	115
3	Former Yugoslavia	118
4	Peru	198
5	The Sudan	235
6	East Africa	239

TABLES

2.1	Casualties in international terrorist incidents, 1980–2006	22
3.1	Number of international terrorist incidents by region, 1980–2006	42
3.2	Number of injuries due to international terrorist incidents by region, 1980–2006	43
3.3	Number of deaths due to international terrorist incidents by region, 1980–2006	44
5.1	Number of suicide attacks, 1980–2003	76
8.1	Number of deaths in left-wing and right-wing attacks in West Germany and Italy, 1968–87	187

PREFACE TO SECOND EDITION

When we prepared the first edition of this textbook, we were concerned that too much emphasis in terrorism studies was being placed on Islamic terrorist groups and on terrorism in the Middle East. With the appearance of the global jihadist movement and the escalating violence in the Middle East and elsewhere in the world, Islamic terrorism is an important issue that needs to be covered, but not to the exclusion of other examples of terrorism. As part of this continuing need to provide a broad framework and appropriate context for the study of terrorism, the second edition of *Global Terrorism* is significantly different from the first edition. The materials in all of the chapters have been extensively updated. While the total number of case studies remains the same, some of them have been changed to reflect recent events. This edition includes more material on Islamic groups and events in the Middle East because these topics have indeed become more important. The situation in Iraq, for example, is now covered extensively in Chapter 11 along with terrorism in Sri Lanka because both countries demonstrate how different groups with different objectives can be operating at the same time in the same country. While Islamic groups have received more attention, this edition stills uses both historical and contemporary examples and includes case studies from many parts of the world. It is indeed a study of global terrorism.

This edition, like its predecessor, attempts to limit one of the major problems that anyone teaching terrorism has to face. The inclusion of anything but the most recent cases in a text runs into the difficulty that not all the students will be familiar enough with world history (even recent world history) or geography to place the terrorist movement in an appropriate context. The case study approach in this volume provides enough background to alleviate this difficulty for most of the examples. If the students have read the material, they will have the necessary context for the analysis and comparison of particular cases or series of cases. The cases are amenable to comparison and analysis in a variety of ways. The background in the chapters should permit an instructor to incorporate additional cases that she or he considers important, either from the historical past or from new events that have occurred. There are, of course, other cases that could have been included and covered in greater depth. This edition, however, makes it possible for an instructor to incorporate others topics of interest. The text is designed to be flexible in this regard.

In writing this text we owe much to many different people. Foremost on the list would be the students who have taken the class on terrorism at Indiana University-Purdue University at Fort Wayne since it was first taught in 1999. Their questions and comments have influenced the material that has been included in many ways. Some of the case studies are the direct result of questions they have raised about particular events or groups. At other times, their uncertainty about some issues has suggested greater coverage in the pages that follow. Although general readers would hopefully find this book enlightening, it was written principally for students. Current students will benefit from the insights, the questions, the doubts, and the interests of other students who have gone before.

A number of people deserve our thanks. Many colleagues at Indiana University-Purdue University at Fort Wayne and elsewhere have drawn our attention to various materials and happenings. They may notice their suggestions incorporated directly or indirectly in the pages that follow. These suggestions have been very much appreciated and welcome. A special note of thanks is due to Barbara Blauvelt, the Secretary of the Department of Political Science at Indiana University-Purdue University at Fort Wayne. Administrative duties as Chair could have been overwhelming while this edition was being written, but her expertise and skill meant that bureaucratic duties, teaching, and writing could all proceed at the same time. Without her able assistance with the necessary and essential administrative tasks, it would have taken much longer for this edition to be completed.

We would like to thank the people at Routledge for their continued support. Craig Fowlie has worked with us from the beginning with the first edition. He led us throughout the process and made excellent suggestions for improvements. We would also like to extend our appreciation to Carol and Byron Hoover, Betty Lutz, Joanne Kendregan, David Power, and Donald and Susan Sinclair for their friendship, personal interest in the book, and support throughout this entire project.

Finally, a word of direct acknowledgment for those who are mentioned on the dedication pages is in order. Our beautiful daughters, Carol (aka Cara, now thirteen) and Tessa (now twelve), have been a constant inspiration to us. They have blessed our lives and given us an important incentive to work on this edition just as for the first edition. They have provided a balance in our personal and professional lives. In much the same way our St Bernards have provided enjoyment and diversion for us on many occasions. They are indeed magnificent animals. We would like to say that quiet walks with them have helped us to formulate our thoughts, but the walks were too infrequent and seldom quiet enough for reflection and contemplation. Their playfulness, their loyalty, and their interactions with the girls, however, helped to invigorate us so that we have been able to return to the blank pages with a clearer focus and reinforced purpose.

CHAPTER 1

Terrorism in the World Today and Yesterday

The attacks on September 11th, 2001 on the World Trade Center and the Pentagon dramatically demonstrated the importance that terrorist acts can have for citizens and residents of the United States. These deadly attacks reinforced the fact that terrorism had been a significant problem for the rest of the world for a long time. While the 9/11 attacks were exceptional, it is important to recognize that terrorism has had a long history (F. Schulze 2004: 183). The attacks in 2001 were followed by other major attacks, including the one against the tourist facilities on Bali in 2002, the siege of a middle school in Breslan, Russia in 2003, the attacks against the Spanish commuter trains in Madrid in 2004, the London transit system in 2005, and others. These attacks resulted in major casualties and have provided ongoing evidence that terrorism is a continuing problem for many societies around the world.

In the case of the attacks on 9/11, the use of airliners to destroy the World Trade Center was the single most deadly terrorist act known to have happened. The nature of the weapon used and timing of the attacks made it very clear that the terrorists intended to cause as many casualties as possible on the ground (in addition to the passengers in the airplanes). The airliner that crashed into the Pentagon was not as deadly in terms of the results, but the intent in this case was to cause massive casualties as well, and many did die in this assault. The fourth airliner that was hijacked did not reach its target, which was somewhere in the Washington DC area. Its delayed departure from the Newark airport meant that it was taken over later than the other three flights, and passengers on this plane became aware of their likely fate. The plane crashed when the passengers attempted to recapture the aircraft and prevent the hijackers from using it as a weapon as had been the case with the other three aircraft.

This coordinated attack on September 11th was very sophisticated in terms of conceptualization and execution. The planning involved indicated that dedicated and determined terrorists were capable of inflicting great damage on targets in the United States. Four aircraft from three different airports were hijacked pretty much simultaneously soon after they took off. The hijackers of the four aircraft knew how to get past airport security in at least three airports with relatively crude, but effective, weapons. They were also aware of the standard operating procedures for airline crews, which specified that they should cooperate with the hijackers. The organization provided by Al Qaeda made sure that the hijackers included persons who were able to pilot the planes into their targets. There had to be someone with sufficient skills to navigate and fly the planes well enough to approach New York and Washington and strike the target buildings since there would be no way that the hijackers could force a pilot at the controls of the airliner to commit suicide by flying into a building filled with people. The one failure in this relatively sophisticated plan was the absence of any contingency procedures providing options for the hijackers on any one of the aircraft if their flight was behind schedule. The fourth aircraft that crashed in western Pennsylvania could have done considerable damage somewhere in the United States if the hijackers on board had attempted to take over the craft sooner or had opted to change targets once it became obvious that the authorities and people on the ground knew what was happening.

As deadly as the September 11th attacks were, they have not been the only significant attacks made against targets involving the United States in recent years. The truck bomb detonated at the Murrah federal office building in Oklahoma City in 1995 has been the most deadly attack linked to domestic terrorists in the history of the United States. This attack demonstrated the type of damage that could be done against a relatively vulnerable target and the types of casualties that could result. It also clearly demonstrated that there was a wide range of potential targets for terrorist attacks that existed within the United States. The bombings of the US embassies in Nairobi in Kenya and Dar-es-Salaam in Tanzania in 1998 were clearly attacks directed against the interests of the United States, even if the hundreds of dead and thousands of wounded were mostly residents of these two African countries. The casualty figures were still high and demonstrated what was possible if mass casualties were desired. The suicide attack on the US destroyer *Cole* in the harbor at Aden in 2000 was significant as well because it was an attack on a US warship, indicating that even military targets could be attacked successfully. Violent attacks directed against the United States have now been ongoing for years, and there clearly has been a problem requiring attention. The 9/11 attacks led to the launching of a global war on terrorism. The invasion of Afghanistan was a direct consequence of the devastation of these attacks. One of the rationales for the US-led invasion of Iraq in 2003 was the possibility that lethal Iraqi resources, including chemical or biological weapons, could end up in the hands of terrorist groups. Even if the nature and extent of the threats that Iraq represented were exaggerations, the presence of major terrorist actions with significant casualties in the immediate past provided an important background that made fears of such weapons more believable.

These examples of attacks directed against the United States and other attacks have only been part of the global pattern of terrorism in the twentieth and now the twenty-first century. Terrorism in the final analysis is a technique that is available to many groups dissatisfied with some government somewhere—terrorism is a means, not an end (Betts 2002: 20). Terrorism has been a tool used with great regularity by many organizations. Terrorist assaults on targets in many countries have occurred and continue to occur with depressing regularity. The world's remaining superpower has not been immune to these attacks. Palestine and Israel have been the sites of numerous acts of violence in the twentieth century. There have been the attacks by Palestinians or other Arabs against Israel since the creation of that state. In addition, there have been violent actions by Jewish extremists seeking to promote their own political objectives in the country. Sri Lanka has been wracked by a deadly civil war for years. Bombings and other kinds of attacks have been present in Chechnya in the former Soviet Union, in Northern Ireland, in Algeria (most recently against the prime minister), in India, and in Indonesia. Iraq has now seen outbreaks of terrorist violence within the country from multiple sources. This conflict, sometimes with a confusing cast of characters, has included a large number of deadly terrorist actions by the groups involved. The political violence, terrorism, and atrocities in some cases have claimed thousands and tens of thousands of lives. The high death tolls in some of these countries have been cumulative ones rather than the result of just one deadly attack, but the casualties are still just as high. Of the other countries in the world, some have suffered from violence and terrorism for decades while others have had only brief periods during which they have had to deal with terrorism. Other countries have avoided being the victims of any acts of terrorism so far, but any country could experience such acts in the future.

What is obvious from the above very incomplete list of places where terrorism has been occurring is that the violence has affected many other countries in the world, and in fact, it has heretofore been a more serious problem in a number of other countries than it has been for the United States. What should also be obvious from the list of countries mentioned above or any list of countries that have dealt with major terrorist violence in the last quarter of a century is the fact that terrorism has not just been a problem involving actors from the Middle East. Terrorist violence has occurred widely, including in places that have no connection with problems originating in the Middle East. Many different groups in many places have relied on political violence in attempts to achieve their goals. Great care must be taken to avoid stereotyping terrorists as persons from the Middle East who are determined to destroy the West. There are other problems, other causes, and other objectives that organizations have sought to resolve or achieve through the use of political violence. Osama bin Laden has been one important terrorist but he is not the only one who has been active in recent years. There have been many others, and it is important to be aware of them as well.

Some of the recent terrorist attacks have involved the use of potentially deadly new techniques designed to inflict mass casualties. Suicide attacks by fanatic pilots in hijacked airliners are just one example that displays the scope of the damage that is possible. The attacks with nerve gas in the subway system of Tokyo by a domestic Japanese group are another recent use of potential weapons of mass destruction that have become available to terrorists. The use of anthrax inside letters mailed in the United States in the aftermath of September 11th provides another example of the use of a new kind of deadly weapon. There has also been the fear that nuclear weapons could fall into the hands of terrorists. To date this possibility has been a plot for novels and Hollywood movies, but even as an unlikely possibility it is still quite frightening. Of course, more traditional means of terrorizing populations remain and can be deadly as indicated by ethnic cleansing in what used to be Yugoslavia, in Rwanda, and in the Sudan.

Analysis of terrorism has often focused on recent events. One observer suggested that the attack on Israeli athletes at the 1972 Munich Olympics was the beginning of modern terrorism (Deutch 1997: 11). While this attack may have introduced some new elements into terrorist practices, it is hardly a major threshold between non-occurrence and the occurrence of this type of political violence. In point of fact, terrorism had been ongoing in many areas of the world long before 1972. What made the 1972 attack noteworthy in some respects is that it managed to capture world attention. Today, there is greater awareness of the phenomenon because of the capabilities of modern mass communications. Violent terrorism, however, is quite ancient. Some of the most notable examples go back centuries or even a millennia or more. It is important to put the current terrorists activities in both a historical and geographical perspective. The current political culture of a country or society, which can reflect events and conflicts centuries old, influences the style of confrontation and the type of violence used. It is important to realize that terrorism is not something new under the sun, and its long history as a political tool by various groups suggests that it will not quickly disappear in the immediate future. The attacks on September 11th are one especially deadly example of a continuing phenomenon, one that occurred within existing geographical or historical perspectives. Without these perspectives, however, it is more difficult to understand events such as September 11th, and an appropriate perspective can also suggest actions that are relevant to dealing with terrorism. Governments in the past have ignored terrorists at their own peril at times. In other cases, the governments have made the wrong decisions or played into the hands of the terrorist dissidents. Government policies have created the conditions in which terrorists have prospered and in other cases policies have weakened whatever support terrorists might have had. Thus, what governments do—and do not do—can be very important for the success or failure of terrorist movements. The knowledge of terrorism becomes important for understanding and dealing with terrorism when and where it appears.

Many theories seeking to explain terrorism have been put forward over the years. Of course, there is no one cause for such a widely occurring phenomenon and anyone who suggests that there is only one cause should be regarded with great care and considerable skepticism. If there were one simple solution to terrorism it would have been discovered by now. Governments have not determined the conditions that lead people to resort to violence so that they can avoid them, and appropriate security measures that will always work have not been discovered. The examples of terrorist movements that will be provided in the following chapters will supply some indications of some of the reasons why dissident political movements form and decide to use violence in their efforts to change the political circumstances in which they find themselves, their groups, or their societies. In general, some group has to think that the government is being manifestly unfair in some way. The key is the perception of unfairness. Things may actually turn out not to be better with different laws or leaders or with different boundaries, but if groups think things can be better, demands for change will occur and if these demands are not met, the potential for violence exists. Similarly, things may be much better than the perceptions of the dissidents indicate, but again it is the perceptions that could provoke recourse to violence. Generally, it is true that terrorist groups that constitute real threats to a society cannot be created in countries where there are no major causes for complaint and no dissident groups have appeared. There have been too many attempts to establish dissident guerrilla movements or terrorist organizations that have quickly failed for such activities to be created out of thin air. Of course, as noted above, events such as recessions, globalization and modernization, and wars will generate sufficient dissatisfaction for some residents of many societies and potential dissidents can then find ample persons to draw upon for recruits and support in attacks upon governments.

Terrorism as a topic is complex, but it is clearly important in today's world and will continue to be important. One way to better understand the prevalence of terrorism is to compare different groups and their tactics and analyze the circumstances under which organizations willing to use terror appeared. While not all groups and circumstances are similar, there are common patterns that can be found. Most of the following chapters include case studies that provide some detail on particular terrorist groups and their activities. The case studies also provide enough detail so that the appearance of dissident organizations willing to use terror as a means of achieving objectives can be understood in the context of local circumstances. Some grievance, real or imagined, had to be present to trigger the violence. The case studies make clear what these grievances of the dissidents were, what kinds of actions they attempted, and how successful they were in their efforts. In some cases it will also be readily apparent how governments were able to deal with the terrorist groups or why they failed to be effective in dealing with the challenge. These case studies in some depth are essential to comparing, contrasting, and understanding what terrorism is and how it can appear within a political system.

The case studies have been drawn from a wide variety of times and places. A conscious effort has been made to include some historical examples that indicate that terrorism as a form of political violence has been around for a long time. More importantly, the most historical of the case studies provide some examples of very successful uses of terrorism, successful at least in the sense of achieving or coming close to achieving the goals of the group responsible for the political violence. Of course, less successful terrorist undertakings from the past are not as well known. Any quick failures of dissidents willing to use terrorism usually do not make it into the history books, especially when the victors write history. Notwithstanding the importance of cases from the past, the focus in the choice of the case studies was on more recent events. In addition to selecting examples from across time, a very conscious effort has also been made to discuss terrorists and dissident organizations that have operated in many parts of the world. Europe, North America, South America, Africa, the Middle East, and the rest of Asia have all been the scenes of important terrorist movements and bloody terrorist attacks. It is important to realize that terrorism has its roots in many societies around the world and the first step in understanding its prevalence is to realize its extent.

The following chapters will thus provide a rather comprehensive introduction into the phenomenon of terrorism. Chapters 2, 3, and 4 will deal with some necessary definitions, broad concepts, and ways of categorizing particular dissident organizations. The basic groundwork will be laid in these chapters for Chapters 5 through 11 that deal with specific types of terrorist groups. These chapters will all include detailed case studies of particular terrorist groups that have operated in the world, including organizations that have been condoned by governments in power. Chapter 12 deals with a variety of counterterrorist strategies that have been proposed or adopted. Chapter 13 contains some conclusions and a summary of what governments can do and why terrorism persists. The world changes, political activities change, weapons change, and so does terrorism. An understanding of terrorism in the past, and especially in the recent past, will help us all to better understand terrorism when it occurs in the future.

A list of terms and some suggested further reading will be presented at the end of each chapter. The key terms will be provided as a means of reinforcing the information contained in each of the chapters. Terms will also be contained in the glossary at the end of the book for easy reference. The list of materials for further reading will provide a starting point to acquire more in-depth information relevant for the case studies that are included in the chapters. Some of the books, articles, and chapters will also provide additional information on the general topics covered in each of the chapters. The additional readings listed at the end of this chapter, for example, deal with some books that provide useful general introductions to the topic of terrorism or even compilations of valuable material. All of these materials will be useful supplements for what is discussed in the chapters. Occasionally films are listed as well if they are particularly good demonstrations of key points. While such films are few in number, they are worth viewing if they can be found. These suggested readings, of course, are only a starting point. The references used in each of the chapters and the bibliography at the end of the book provide a great deal more sources from which to start to gather additional information. Further, there will be additional materials coming out in the future, so a search of the tables of contents for journals and library catalogs will be essential as well.

TERMS

Breslan	Murrah Federal Office Building
Munich Olympics (1972)	USS *Cole*

FURTHER READING

Crenshaw, M. and Pimlott, J. (eds) (1997) *Encyclopedia of World Terrorism*, Armonk, NY: M. E. Sharpe.

Hoffman, B. (2006) *Inside Terrorism*, revised and expanded edition, New York: Columbia University Press.

Kegley, C. W., Jr (ed.) (2003) *The New Global Terrorism: Characteristics, Causes, Controls*, Upper Saddle River, NJ: Prentice Hall.

Laqueur, W. (1999) *The New Terrorism: Fanaticism and the Arms of Mass Destruction*, New York: Oxford University Press.

Lutz, J. M. and Lutz, B. J. (2005) *Terrorism: Origins and Evolution*, New York: Palgrave.

CHAPTER 2

What is Terrorism? Definition and Classification

"One person's freedom fighter is another person's terrorist."

The above statement occurs in a variety of forms that all say much the same thing—that terrorism, like beauty, is in the eye of the beholder. But, having a useable definition of terrorism is essential for any valid consideration of its occurrence in the world. How do you distinguish a terrorist group from a non-terrorist group? What kinds of terrorism have existed and continue to exist in the world? What are some of the underlying causes of terrorism? How prevalent is terrorism—has it been increasing or has it been on the decline? The current chapter will consider these very contentious issues.

DEFINING TERRORISM

Terrorism as a word in its usual usage has a connotation of evil, indiscriminate violence or brutality. Someone has been terrorized! Thus, to label a group or action as terrorist is to seek to imply that the actors or the violence is immoral, wrong, or contrary to obvious basic ethical principles that any reasonable human being might hold. To use different terms for the violence that may occur such as freedom fighter, revolutionaries, rebels, resistance fighters, members of the democratic opposition, or national liberation soldiers, however, implies that the group undertaking the violence is motivated by some greater good or higher moral principle. The choice of terms to describe persons undertaking political violence often contains underlying assumptions about the goals of the group. To call a group freedom fighters or resistance soldiers suggests a positive evaluation of the goals of the organization. The victims of the violence are usually supporters of a political system that denies freedom and that seeks to oppress and repress at least part of the population. Innocent bystanders—collateral damage in the new parlance of violence—may be killed or wounded. Of course, the losses among innocents are ultimately the fault of the repressive government that refuses to grant the people their rights. It might indeed be possible to argue that a truly repressive government kills or harms more people, especially the innocent, than all the attacks by the groups fighting for freedom or democracy. Better to undergo some loss of life in the short term in order to avoid the greater and continuing loss of life in the future.

Terrorists, on the other hand, attack governments that are legitimate and accepted by the people they govern. They seek to undermine and destroy a political system and even a way of life that is desirable or good. Their attacks are frequently directed against innocent civilians and designed to cause indiscriminate casualties among them. The terrorists in some cases may even be labeled cowardly since they sneak about targeting innocent civilians or unarmed members of the government rather than undergoing the risks that would come with attacks on armed police or military troops who would fight back. In the case of suicide bombings the terrorists have convinced perhaps gullible supporters to give up their lives for the cause. These evil terrorists are seeking to overthrow democratic governments or at least reasonably democratic governments in some cases. In other cases, they are seeking to replace less than democratic dictatorial systems with one that is far worse. A relatively benign military dictator or king would be supported in order to avoid radical communists or fanatical religious groups from coming to power—that is, provide support for the lesser of two evils.

The difficulty with this approach lies in deciding who gets to decide how to define good government and bad government. Different people value different political goals or have different priorities. For some, it is economic equality. Others may find anything more than the most limited government to be oppressive. Yet others may feel that a good political system must support morality and natural rights. All of these groups, and others as well, will categorize the same political systems differently. Thus, a definition of terrorism needs to be separated as much as possible from evaluations of the groups using violence and their targets. This is not to say, however, that value judgments about governments and groups should not be made. Any thinking person has to weigh the good and bad of a political system and its opponents. Are the actions of some groups attacking governments so evil or so unrelated to the good that they seek that they have to be opposed—even to the point of sending military aid and even troops to support the government under attack? Alternatively, is the government so bad or evil that all external support should be withdrawn giving the opposition a greater chance of winning, even with violent attacks? Terrorist attacks by the groups being victimized by the Nazis, for example, would hardly have deserved any negative evaluations (Crenshaw 1983: 3–5). Governments and populations must make decisions about right and wrong in such cases. These decisions, however, can be made without the need to apply different terms to persons who have undertaken basically the same action.

When faced with a definition that is so value-laden and used by governments or others to apply negative labels, social scientists frequently like to create new words that are more value free. Since terrorism as a word is so widely used, such an option is really not available. No special vocabulary is necessary. What is necessary is to provide a working definition, as neutral as possible. What is also necessary is to read and evaluate with care how others use the word. A clear, workable definition of terrorism should cover both groups that individuals agree with and groups that they disagree with. The need for neutral definitions does not preclude the necessity

causes

of making political judgments and evaluating political organizations on the basis of whatever principles and priorities are most important.

It is not surprising that there have been a multitude of definitions provided for terrorism. Many definitions are exceedingly complex or have far too many elements (Schmid 1983). With such complex and all-inclusive definition, terrorism could involve individuals, groups, or states; attacks could be random or selective; intimidation or propaganda could be the goal; and the goals themselves could be eccentric, political, or criminal. Definitions to be useful need to exclude as well as include different kinds of violence. Laqueur (1987) considered terrorism the illegitimate use of force to achieve political objectives. This definition has the virtue of being simple, but it too involves far too many types of activities. It also avoids a definitional problem with terrorism by shifting the definition problems to a determination of what is legitimate use of force and what is illegitimate! Governments provide definitions, but they often are self-serving to at least some degree. Opponents of the government are defined as terrorists while irregular allies of the government fail to meet the definitional standards as terrorists. Over the years, the United States has had a list of countries that have been considered to be state supporters of terrorism. Cuba has remained on the list long after it stopped supporting terrorist groups in Latin America. The list, however, ignored countries supporting terrorist groups that were allies or potential allies, because their inclusion would have created problems, or because their actions did not especially concern the United States. South Africa aided groups in Angola and Mozambique that practiced terror, but it was never included. The Soviet Union never made the list, primarily because its inclusion would have greatly complicated US diplomatic activities and US foreign policies. The United States and the United Kingdom both had lists of organizations. Thirteen different dissident groups were on both lists, but the United Kingdom had eight groups not on the US list, and the United States had fifteen not on the British list (Silke 2004: 5). Not even close allies could agree, and the most obvious difference was the fact that the US list did not ever include the IRA, although it did include a splinter Irish group. The obvious point is that governments make definitions fit their own needs.

Rather than provide a discussion of some of the possible definitions, it will be simpler to provide a working definition that will be reasonably inclusive and to specify the various elements that are part of the definition. This definition will apply to all practitioners of this type of political violence, regardless of the political goals of the terrorists or the political views of the individuals targeted by the terrorists. The definition that will be used throughout this book is one that is derived from the works of Crenshaw (1983), Hoffman (2006), and Claridge (1996), that have definitions incorporating most of what will be included in the definition for this volume. They approached the issue of terrorism from somewhat different perspectives, but between them they cover the key ingredients involved in terrorist activities. Combining the issues raised by these three works results in the following definition, which has six major components:

> Terrorism involves political aims and motives. It is violent or threatens violence. It is designed to generate fear in a target audience that extends beyond the immediate victims of the violence. The violence is conducted by an identifiable organization. The violence involves a non-state actor or actors as either the perpetrator, the victim of the violence, or both. Finally, the acts of violence are designed to create power in situations in which power previously had been lacking (i.e., the violence attempts to enhance the power base of the organization undertaking the actions).

The first key element of this definition is that the violence is undertaken primarily for political reasons. In fact, terrorism has been considered uniquely political in nature, with terrorism even being considered "the continuation of politics by other means" (Sick 1990: 51). Political goals are a key element that separates terrorist acts from other forms of violence (Long 1990: 5). The violence is not undertaken for financial reasons or because of personal issues. Kidnappings of prominent political leaders or corporate executives to make political statements are different from those kidnappings that serve as criminal ventures to raise money for the abductors. The use of fear to extort money from businesses (the protection rackets of American gangster fame or infamy) is criminal, not political. Sometimes, of course, opposition groups have used kidnapping or bank robberies to finance their organizations, and they have been known to levy "revolutionary taxes" on groups that could be forced to pay. In these cases, the goals are still generally political because the money received is used to fund subsequent political activities, including possibly more violence, rather than leading to gains in personal wealth. While political objectives are a key for defining terrorism, the goals that are sought by terrorists can fall into a number of categories. The terrorists may be seeking to have a government change its policies— to stop a particular program from being continued or to force the adoption of some new policy. The political objectives may involve an effort to change leaders or the political elite, regarded as corrupt or illegitimate. Goals may go further, seeking to bring about a complete change in the framework of the government—changing from a monarchy to a republic or from a strongly centralized system to a more decentralized one or from a military dictatorship to a theocratic state run by religious leaders. Finally, the terrorists may be seeking to change national boundaries—to detach a region to create a new state, to attach some territory to another state, or to amalgamate existing states into a new country.

The second element of a terrorist action is that violence or the credible threat of violence is present (Badey 1998: 93). Requests for changes, demonstrations, and petitions are not terrorism, no matter how disconcerting they may be to a government. Although massive demonstrations may make a government apprehensive about the future, there is no direct threat of violence. Actual violence is fairly obvious to detect and recognize. The threat of violence is only likely to be effective as a technique with a group that has already demonstrated that it is able and willing to be violent. A political organization that has never undertaken any type of political violence is unlikely to be credible in its threats. Once violence has been used, however, the threat of additional violence may generate the necessary fear that the dissident group desires and lead to the government giving in to the specific demands of the group, whatever those demands might be. Hoaxes can, as a consequence, be part of a terrorist campaign, especially when they follow upon actual earlier violent actions.

Third, for violence, and even political violence, to qualify as terrorism, it must also affect a target audience beyond the immediate victims and influence such audiences as part of the attempt to gain the political objectives of the organization. The violent acts are intended to have effects beyond the immediate events (B. Jenkins 1990: 29). Terrorism is a form of psychological warfare that intends to influence governments and general publics (Chalk 1996: 13). If a political leader is assassinated with the goal of removing that individual in order to permit the next in line to move up, the death is political violence, but it has no target audience. For an assassination to be a terrorist action, it must involve parties beyond the assassin or assassins and the immediate victim (Schmid 1992a: 10). On the other hand, if a political leader is assassinated in order to send a message to other members of the political elite that they need to change policies or make concessions in order to avoid a similar fate, then that assassination is a terrorist act. Bombings of buildings (with or without casualties) or car bombs in crowded areas are often intended to demonstrate to general publics that they are vulnerable. The resulting fear may lead the public to put pressure on the government to change policies or weaken public support for the leaders in power who clearly are unable to protect the citizens from a small band of dissidents. If the initial attacks do not generate the expected fear, groups may find it necessary to escalate the violence in a lengthy campaign of attacks (Neumann and Smith 2005: 588). The need to reach a target audience is one reason why terrorist groups seek publicity. If no one knows of a terrorist act, the goals have not been achieved. If the deaths of government personnel are ascribed to a plane crash rather than a bomb on the aircraft, the target audience will draw the wrong conclusion about threats to the state or to the safety of individuals. The need for publicity is also why some organizations have established pre-set code words with the media so that they can authenticate the claims for the organization when they provide a warning that a bomb is about to go off. It will not be necessary in all cases for particular organizations to claim credit for particular terrorist actions. The local situation and the target will often make it clear that the cause of a particular group of dissidents is behind the activity. If swastikas are painted on a Jewish synagogue, the anti-Semitic message is obvious. If a car bomb goes off at the headquarters of the ruling party, the general population is likely to know whether it is a local minority group or whether it is the political opposition that is behind the attack.

Some definitions of terrorism include the specification that the targets of terrorist violence are civilians (Schmid 2004: 204). Guerrilla groups are more likely to target police or the military, setting them apart from their terrorist counterparts. Insurgent attacks on military personnel in Iraq, for example, are not normally considered terrorist attacks. Civilians are often the targets for terrorism, and when guerrilla groups begin to target civilians they usually cross over into terrorism. Adding this component to the definition, however, adds complexity. Are off-duty police or reserve military personnel civilians acceptable targets? What about civilian employees working on military bases? When attacks result in the deaths of both civilians and military personnel, are the civilians considered the targets or acceptable collateral damage? To include this component in the definition also may require knowledge of the intentions of those launching the attacks. As a consequence, it does not seem necessary to include the targeting of civilians as a key component of the definition, but it is useful to recognize that civilian populations are often the intended targets of terrorist attacks, if for no other reason than to increase the resulting fear among a target population.

Fourth, for political violence to be terrorism there must be an identifiable organization. An individual is unable to carry out the actions, reach the target audience, and present the political demands for the changes that are necessary to end the violence. An effective campaign to create change also requires enough actions to be credible, an effort beyond a single individual over time. Effective terrorism rests on the potential for repetition and the systematic use of violence (Badey 1998: 93). Terrorist actions almost inevitably lead to casualties or arrests among the dissidents; thus, a single individual is likely to be captured or killed too. The organization is necessary to continue the political battle. Theodore Kaczynski, the Unabomber, is a classic example of the limitations inherent with campaigns by one individual. His bombings over the years inspired fear, but the target audience was unclear, and it was not obvious what actions the target audience was expected to take. The FBI and other police agencies knew that the bombings were related due to forensic analyses, but they were unable to establish the linkages between the victims, nor were they were able to identify the political agenda of the person behind them. The linkages were present in Kaczynski's mind in terms of being a protest against modern society. Kaczynski himself did not issue any statements for a long time, further reducing any influence on target audiences. While the US government and the general public would not have given into any demands by Kaczynski, it was impossible to undertake any policy changes since the demands were not known. Interestingly enough, once Kaczynski did attempt to present his political agenda, he was identified and arrested, thus ending the bombing campaign.

While organization is a key element of terrorism, the nature of the way in which dissidents are organized has changed with modern technology. Not all terrorist groups have a constant organization. Different members may coalesce temporarily for a specific attack and then go their separate ways rather than being permanent members of an organization (Cameron 1999: 283). In other cases the terrorists become in essence part-time activists. They may accept central direction in how they proceed, but they are not centrally controlled (Hoffman 1995: 281). Individuals may even participate in what has been termed leaderless resistance where their actions are in accord with a dissident organization, but they are not directly part of the group. Individual hate crimes against minorities would not normally qualify as terrorism (P. Jenkins 2003: 29). If the attackers, however, see their actions as part of a larger campaign against the particular minority that derives from an implied unity with other biased individuals, it can become terrorism. With internet capabilities and instantaneous communication, such terrorist actions within a network or loosely coordinated group are not only possible, but they can also be very effective (Kushner 1998b: 82–3). These kinds of loosely coordinated groups exist in addition to the more conventionally organized groups; they do not replace them completely. These groups have some advantages for the dissidents. Their amorphous nature means that they are more difficult to detect, to infiltrate, and to destroy (Chalk 1999: 159). The persons actually undertaking the actions will also have relative freedom in making tactical decisions regarding the attacks (Hoffman 2001: 418). The lack of central direction may limit the constraints that normally come with an organizational structure. Without central control, loosely aligned individuals who are not concerned about the long term effects of their actions or about the best way to use terror to achieve political objectives may be more willing to inflict higher casualties and more willing to use exotic weapons than the conventional dissident groups using political violence (Parachini 2001: 403).

The fifth component of the definition specifies the targets and perpetrators of the violence. For purposes of the present volume, terrorism will be defined as situations in which either the perpetrators of the political violence, the victims, or both are not states or governments. Actions between states, including war, will not be included. During wartime or cold war confrontations, governments and/or their militaries may consciously seek to generate terror in the enemy's ranks or among the civilian population. The Mongols massacred populations of cities that resisted them in order to convince other cities to surrender and avoid a similar fate. The bombings of Rotterdam and London by the Germans and Hamburg, Tokyo, and Hiroshima by the Allies during World War II were all designed to create terror as well. Of course, if both state and non-state actions are defined as terrorism, equality is established between dissident groups and governments. Such arguments, of course, have some legitimacy, but they confuse the issue, and they are often raised to promote the cause of the dissidents. Eliminating state actors from consideration in terrorism may suit a particular political agenda, but including state actors will serve a different political agenda. Limiting a definition of terrorism to exclude actions between states, however, does not excuse or ignore the violence that states undertake. As a consequence, the role of states in furthering terrorist actions will indeed be considered and will be part of the case studies. Governments do use terror against segments of their own populations in order to achieve some political goal. Frequently such political violence will involve paramilitary groups or death squads permitting the government to officially deny any role in the actions but to still benefit from the terror created in a target audience. The government can always disclaim culpability and maintain plausible (or even implausible) deniability (Campbell 2000). Sometimes vigilante groups will appear to attack fellow citizens. These groups may be supported by the government, but they often appear precisely because the government is too weak to govern effectively (Abrahams 1988: 4). In other cases vigilante groups may appear because the members think that the government is unable to protect their interests (Pedahzur and Perliger 2003: 12). It is important to note, however, that government repression is not necessarily the same as terrorism. Even in a repressive state, individuals have an opportunity to know what the law is and to avoid actions that would lead to punishment (Sproat 1991: 24). Governmental use of terrorism against its own citizens, however, creates situations in which individuals cannot avoid becoming victims.

The last part of the definition depends on the fact that the terrorist actions are used to improve the power situation of the organization that is using this form of political violence. While the specific agendas of groups using terrorism are quite different, they all share this characteristic. They are attempting to improve their power situation—to increase their probability of being able to influence political decisions. Terrorist campaigns are frequently mounted by organizations that have failed to bring about their desired changes by other means, i.e., they are politically weak. They have failed in democratic elections to gain enough power to bring about change, governments have ignored peaceful protests and appeals, or they have been met by government repression that prevents further efforts at peaceful change. Since they are relatively powerless in the conventional political setting of their own society due to limited electoral appeal or limited support in the face of government repression, they resort to unconventional means in an effort to improve their power base. Terrorism is appealing to weaker groups because it can be undertaken with limited resources and the possible rewards are high (Crenshaw 2003a: 97). Groups will rationally make terrorism the technique of choice because others methods may not work or will take too long, especially when calculations of the superior resources of governments are taken into account (Crenshaw 1998: 16). Groups can also use terrorism as a force multiplier—most effectively through the fear that is generated, making the use of limited resources more effective (Vinci 2005).

While all six of the above characteristics are necessary for an action to be considered a terrorist act, they are interrelated. Political aims are clearly linked with organizations that choose violence given their relative weaknesses. Political goals and aims also generally involve actions designed to affect either the government or other actors in the political systems, and in order for this effect to take place a target audience is obviously necessary for persuasion or influence. Note also that the definition applies to all groups using political violence to induce fear in an effort to bring about political change in any direction. Terrorism "is primarily an extremism of means, not one of ends" (Bjorgo 2005b: 2). The definition is not specific to any one group nor does it exclude others.

The above six-part definition is basically one for academic use. It is designed to help in understanding the terrorist phenomenon. It cannot serve as an appropriate definition in a court of law. Governments usually need a more precise legal definition if they are going to use their courts and legal systems to try, convict, and punish individuals who are involved in terrorist actions, and it may be essential for a government that had to decide whether or not a person accused of terrorism elsewhere should be extradited (Schmid 1992a: 9). In many cases, however, national legal systems will not require any special definition of terrorism. Hijacking an airplane, setting off a bomb, and killing people are already crimes under national laws, even when the crimes are undertaken for political purposes. If a state wishes to impose stiffer penalties for crimes associated with terrorism, however, then some sort of legal definition becomes important. Similarly, if a national legislature desires to prohibit financial contributions to terrorist groups, then the government has to provide some system for designating which groups are prohibited. This latter option may introduce arbitrary elements, but it usually provides a flexible procedure permitting governments to avoid choices that alienate domestic groups. The definition used by US Department of State, for example, is ambiguous, giving officials a great deal of flexibility in its application (Badey 1998: 92).

International definitions of terrorism and terrorists may also be necessary, and such definitions will undoubtedly be different from the one suggested above as well as the definitions used in different countries. An international definition would be useful for purposes of extradition and return of fugitives. Ideally, it would match national definitions or even an analytical definition. Realistically, it will need to be some minimal definition that most countries will accept. It would probably have to include specific actions and would leave some areas of activity uncovered; some coverage under international law is better than none at all. Countries that wished to cooperate in the elimination of some other terrorist actions would be free to do so if they wished—guaranteeing extradition and cooperation in a wider variety of areas. Of course, for such definitions to work, governments would have to risk the possibility that what they see as freedom fighters might be extradited and convicted along with terrorists. The state may, more awkwardly, have to decide when violent political acts do not constitute terrorism and when persons involved in these actions will not be tried or, more importantly, not extradited. Governments will have to make the distinction between freedom fighter and terrorist—when the same action is acceptable and when it is not. Politicians will have to decide, and local public opinion will be important in that decision. Public opinion is not necessarily a negative factor to be considered in such a situation, but governments will always be caught between choosing consistent approaches and taking into account special circumstances.

CLASSIFICATION AND CATEGORIES

A working definition of terrorism is an essential first step for studying this type of political violence. Also necessary is some classification scheme for presenting and discussing different terrorist organizations that have been present in the world. Similar organizations need to be considered together. The discussion could be organized geographically, chronologically, or thematically. In this volume, the last approach will be taken. The categories utilized will include groups pursuing religious goals, national/ethnic/linguistic/regional goals, left-wing ideological goals, right-wing ideological objectives, groups whose goals have involved a clear mixture of objectives to the extent that no one predominates, and the use of terrorism by governments, especially in contexts where "unofficial" groups undertake the action rather than government agencies.

Religious dissidents will be the first type to be discussed. This discussion will include groups that use terrorist attacks to attempt to achieve their goals in terms of creating religious freedom for their groups or bringing groups that are more theologically correct to power. Virtually all the major religions in the world have at times provided the justifications for terrorist violence by some adherents (as well as providing justifications for many wars over the centuries). Many active terrorist organizations have sought objectives related to a particular ethnic group, or linguistic group, or region of the country. These groups seek to liberate themselves and their co-nationals from what they perceive to be a colonial situation or a repressive government. What is essential for the nationalist perspective to dominate the dissident group is this perception of colonialism or domination. The actual levels of differences present between the two groups may in some sense be "objectively" small (the languages are related, and geneticists would find it difficult to separate members of the two groups on the basis of DNA samples), but it is the perceptions of the members of the organization that drive the actions, not the results of some academic research or debate. Such national situations can obviously include cases of overseas colonialization, but some groups will feel colonialized by being included as part of a neighboring country. Others may see a foreign minority controlling their own country. Ideologies have also served to define the political objectives of organizations using terror. There have been both left-wing and right-wing groups that have used terrorist tactics. They will be considered separately in different chapters since the goals and objectives between the two types of groups are so dissimilar, even though at times they have shared the goal of destroying the existing states. They appear in different contexts in many cases with leftist groups opposing one kind of regime or government and rightist groups opposing a different kind of regime or government. Both groups have at times operated in the same countries, even at the same time, however, when they have generally been opposed to a middle-of-the-road government.

It is not possible for some groups that practice terrorism to specify a dominant cause that has fueled their opposition activities. In an ideal typology, every terrorist movement that ever existed or would exist could be easily categorized. But in the real world this is often not possible. In some cases that will be discussed in the earlier chapters, the dominant cause underlying the dissident movement will be easily identifiable. Even where one objective dominates, any terrorist organization can reflect other concerns. The ethnic dissidents may practice a different religion or the ideological dissidents have greater appeal for some minority group. For example, a national liberation movement will usually be ethnically distinct from the colonial power, and the inhabitants of the colony may overwhelmingly be of a different religion. The religious differences may reinforce the national feelings, but the struggle against the colonial power with associated terrorist activities will be national rather than religious. The religious differences simply reinforce the national ones. There are cases, however, where it is difficult to choose a dominant underlying cause for the terrorist organization given the great significance of more than one group of objectives. These complex cases also involve some of the more interesting and more important cases of active terrorist organizations.

The final type of terrorism in this is terrorism undertaken essentially by or on behalf of the government. Generally it will involve unofficial groups that use terror to reinforce governmental policies or deal with dissident groups. Governments will frequently use death squads or other such groups to instill the necessary fear rather than relying on the police or the armed forces for the necessary repression. What will be discussed with this type of terrorism are activities supported by the government that are similar to the activities of terrorist groups in that violence is used for political objectives, that it is directed against not only the victims but also a target audience within the country, and that the objective is to enhance the power position of the government.

The above definition and typology does not take into account one distinction that is frequently used with analyses of terrorism. Terrorist actions are often divided between domestic terrorism and international terrorism. International terrorism usually will include situations that involve a target in another country attacked by a group from another, thus creating a situation in which more than one government has an interest. Domestic terrorism is an internal affair of country and at least in theory less open to the involvement of other states. This distinction between domestic and international terrorism, however, can often be a false one. It has even been suggested that in today's interconnected world that ultimately all domestic terrorism has international implications and that all international terrorism has domestic implications (B. Jenkins 2003). Domestic terrorist actions may only be possible with foreign support and aid, yet the presence of that support and assistance may not be known for some time, leading to a misclassification of the act. A dissident organization may seek to attack a foreign ally of the government that it opposes in order to have the foreign support reduced. Such an attack would clearly be international in scope, but generally domestic in the objective it seeks. In yet other cases, what passes for an international terrorist act is less distinctive. If Kurdish separatists in Turkey attempt to attack the office of a provincial governor, it is domestic terrorism. If the same separatist group attacks Turkish offices in Europe, as they have frequently done, then the attack is considered international terrorism since it took place on foreign soil. In both cases, however, the attack represents actions by the same organization against the same government. Whether the attack occurred in Turkey or France is a matter of convenience for the separatists; it does not reflect a significantly different type of action. Similarly, the 1934 assassination of King Alexander of Yugoslavia in France by a Bulgarian in the pay of Croat nationalists was ultimately a domestic terrorist action that arose from the regional and ethnic disunity that plagued Yugoslavia between World War I and World War II (not to mention later years). The assassination occurred in France because the terrorists correctly assumed the king would be more vulnerable in that country. The Bulgarian assassin was wanted in Bulgaria on criminal charges related to his attempt to detach portions of Yugoslavia so that they could be united to Bulgaria, and thus despite his nationality he was linked with the Croat nationalists. He also had Croat collaborators in his attack on King Alexander (Havens *et al.* 1975: Chap. 9). Even the fact that Prime Minister Barthou of France was killed did not make the incident international in scope since Barthou was not the target. He was simply an innocent bystander, albeit a very high ranking one. The assassination was indeed a terrorist attack. King Alexander represented the ruling elite. His death did not lead to the end of the dissident activities of this group of Croats— it was simply one action among many.

CAUSES OF TERRORISM

Since terrorism is simply one violent technique that dissident groups (or the government) can use, there is unlikely to be any unique cause for terrorism (Tilly 2004: 12). The same factors that lead to other forms of political violence, such as guerrilla warfare, rebellions, riots, and civil wars, can lead to terrorism (Bjorgo 2005b: 4). Terrorism, as noted above, will be adopted because it may be the only technique available for groups with limited resources. Guerrilla tactics, like those of terrorism, however, are a weapon of the weak. Guerrilla warfare usually has military objectives whereas terrorism does not (Wilkinson 2000b: 13). Thus, outbreaks of terrorism may occur as a result of some of the same underlying causes as other forms of political violence. Circumstances such as the weakness of the groups or the balance of forces between one group and another or one group and the government may determine the choice of technique.

Virtually every dissident organization has specific reasons relatively unique to the group and its circumstances that led to the decision to rely on violence to achieve the political objectives of the group. There are, however, some general underlying factors that have been theorized to contribute to the appearance of terrorism in different places and different groups. Initially many thought that terrorists suffered from psychological disabilities, but the stereotype from popular culture is untrue. It has been generally found that individuals with psychological problems have not normally been present in terrorist organizations. Efforts to come up with psychological profiles of terrorists have ultimately not been very productive. Terrorists are not normally crazy or suffering from mental problems (Horgan 2003). In fact, terrorist groups frequently avoid such individuals because they are unreliable and thus dangerous to the organization (Bjorgo 2005b: 7). Even if psychological patterns could identify one type of individual who joins a terrorist groups (ideological, ethnic, or religious) it would be unlikely to hold true for individuals who join other types of groups or even for similar kinds of groups in different geographical regions (Reich 1998: 270). Further, even if there might be some discernible characteristics of terrorists, the vast majority of people in such categories do not join terrorist groups (Crenshaw 1998: 250–1).

Other explanations for the appearance of terrorism include the possibilities that government structures and exploitative economic systems exist, that repression and discrimination are present, that there is relative deprivation wherein a group sees its position in society slip in regard to other groups even if all groups are raising their standards of living, that rapid change disrupts the social and political systems, imperialism and colonialism, and that disasters—natural or otherwise—overwhelm the political society. All of these explanations have at least some validity in some circumstances, but terrorism is such a complex phenomenon that no one theory can be sufficient as an explanation for all occurrences (Laqueur 2001: 143). Regardless of the underlying causes in a social or political system, one factor is virtually universal. Violence is likely when some subgroup in the population has major grievances. The problems can be real or perceived. The basis of problems can be grounded in religious beliefs, ethnic concerns, ideological issues, or a mixture of these factors. In fact, many persons implicitly identify the causes of terrorism in ethnic, religious, and ideological terms when they use the objectives of the terrorist to categorize the causes of the violence.

In a number of cases it is obvious that disparities in economic well being play a role in the grievances (Howell 2003: 177). Marxist theories in its many variations would clearly accept class differences and economic structures as one key in the appearance of violence. One economic factor that has not been associated with terrorism in any consistent fashion, however, has been poverty. There is no evidence that poverty is linked with terrorism in any systematic way even though it obviously is a factor in some circumstances (Horgan 2003; Maleckova 2005). It has been suggested that the upper-class individuals who have joined terrorist groups are socially marginal (Apter 1997: 27). That suggestion, however, is not very helpful since their social marginalization only becomes obvious after it is discovered that they have joined terrorist groups. Individuals in groups that see their position in society decline relative to other groups—a sense of relative deprivation—may resort to violence (Gurr 1970). Another possibility is that poverty or relative deprivation may not be a direct cause of terrorism. Instead, groups in society that face a major loss of status or position in absolute or relative terms may resort to various kinds of political violence in an effort to preserve their position. A second group that could provide individuals willing to use violence could include groups that see opportunities to make major gains in status or position. Members of these two groups, which need not be lower-class groups or composed of the poor, may adopt risky behavior such as participation in terrorist organizations because the potential gains are great (Kuznar and Lutz 2007). Ultimately, the adoption of terrorism is a conscious choice for a course of action, it is not an automatic response to economic deprivation (Gurr 2006: 85). Of course, the groups facing potential losses in status or tempted by the prospects of major gains need not be the same in every society. What is perhaps more important is that dissidents see their religious, ethnic, or class group suffering from such disparities. This situation is taken as one indication of the presence of a discriminatory and unfair political system that needs to be changed, by violence if all else fails.

Not only do the dissidents believe that problems exist, but that violence is the solution to the problems. The dissidents can view the structure of the state, the form of government, or its policies as illegitimate. A resort to violence is seen either as the solution to the problems or as one means of forcing a government to deal more quickly with the problems. Terrorism can, for example, place political change on the agenda (Crenshaw 1998: 17). Violence may also be fueled by a lack of opportunity for political participation in a society (Crenshaw 2003a: 95). Participation opportunities may be lacking because of government repression or the existence of an authoritarian political system. Overreactions by the authorities to protests and other forms of participation can help to promote further outbreaks of terrorism (Weinberg and Richardson 2004: 158). Of course, if there are enough protests or other activities by dissidents, the chances of such overreaction will increase. At the extreme government repression can be so severe that it directly generates violent struggles to overthrow a dictatorial regime or colonial administration. In other cases the dissidents may simply be unable to mobilize political support, even in a democracy, through the existing political processes. The failure to mobilize support through existing channels or in the absence of channels for participation can then lead the dissidents to use violence to overcome the disadvantages that they have in the system.

There are some factors that can contribute to the occurrence of terrorist violence in many contexts. What governments do or do not do may be important in some circumstances, but there are times when government policies and practices may not be the key factors that account for the appearance of terrorist actions. Economic globalization has caused inequality among states as well as within countries (S. Hoffmann 2002: 108). The resulting inequalities have fueled frustrations within states and helped set the stage for appeals for violence by dissident groups. It has been suggested that the spread of market capitalism that accompanies globalization has often destroyed the structure of local economies, further contributing to the conditions that support the appearance of violent responses to change (M. Mousseau 2002/3). Globalization may be generally advantageous for a country, but not every group will gain or gain equally (the issue of relative deprivation). Entering the global economy will mean that some groups face income losses or job losses. In addition, even if the globalization process yields new jobs, it is not necessarily true that the persons who lose their jobs are the same ones as the persons who are able to fill the new jobs. Earlier periods of globalization have seen increases in terrorism (Enders and Sandler 2006: 36).

Economic recessions and depressions generate economic anxiety and dissatisfaction that in turn can breed terrorism. When economic problems occur, some groups in a society will lose ground while others may stay at the same level or even prosper. The groups that suffer may think that government favoritism is responsible for the faulty distribution of resources and may ultimately resort to violence when government policies fail to reinstate gains for them. Unfortunately for countries facing disgruntled citizens, individual governments are not normally the cause of recessions even when their policies can have some effect on the severity of economic problems. Some countries are even likely to be victims, often unintentional ones, of economic policies in other countries that contribute to recessions. These countries can do little to mitigate the recessions and can only deal with the consequences of economic dislocation. Virtually all the countries of the world suffered during the Great Depression. In a variety of ways the policies of the United States, the United Kingdom, and France helped set the stage for the economic collapse that affected everyone. Germany was one of the countries hardest hit by the economic dislocations, and popular dissatisfaction with the economic problems led to an increase in support for the Nazi Party and Adolf Hitler. Unfortunately for the democratic government and parties in Germany in 1930, there was little that the German government could do about the Great Depression.

In addition to direct economic problems, globalization and modernization can place great stresses on societies in other ways. Globalization also leads to significant challenges to local cultures and generates strains within society (Leiber and Weisberg 2002). Societies dealing with changes are inherently vulnerable to the displacement of groups and popular dissatisfaction. Modernization can also disrupt social structures by de-emphasizing old patterns of respect and social interaction as new economic and social elites develop. Modernization will leave people isolated and marginalized, and radical groups in many countries will be able to attract recruits as a consequence (Abuza 2003b: 13–14). Countries undergoing rapid modernization, in fact, may be more prone to outbreaks of terrorism (Bjorgo 2005a: 256). Not everything that comes with modernization is inherently good, and even the good effects can have adverse consequences for portions of society. It is quite likely that life patterns will be disrupted; some groups will gain and others will lose, not just economically but in terms of status or place in a structured social environment. Modernization and globalization will also affect the structure of values and norms. Belief patterns, including religions, will be faced with the challenges that come with changes. Western culture and values are seen as threatening to local religions and cultures (S. Hoffmann 2002: 112). Other groups will see their cultures or subcultures threatened by the centralization of national cultures (Justice 2005: 297–8). The importance of modernization and globalization in contributing to terrorism has been demonstrated by the fact that any symbol of modernization becomes a legitimate target for attack (Klare 2003: 30). Political violence can be one reaction to these challenges and changes, especially if the values or beliefs under attack are important ones to the community or a portion of the community. Finally, modernization also has contributed to terrorism by making economies and societies more vulnerable than they had been in the past (Crenshaw 2003a: 93). The terrorism of the late twentieth century has in fact often been a manifestation of and a reaction to the process of globalization (Wilkinson 2003: 124).

Wars, like economic problems and globalization, have bred situations that have contributed to terrorism in later years. Wars from the past have effects that carry over into later years. There are groups that are unhappy with some aspect of the peace settlements following wars. Lost territories, new boundaries, different government structures, new ruling elites, and other changes can create problems for future governments. Governments inherit these problems, which can include populations predisposed to distrust the government and rulers in power. Governments of states may even be held responsible for changes that did not occur in the aftermath of a conflict (an ethnic or religious group did not get to found an independent state). Even the continuation of the status quo can lead to discontent. Those opposed to the government may be willing to use violence, including terrorism, to redress what they see as past wrongs. The current government then has to deal with the problems from the past. At some level, of course, the policies of individual countries are responsible for wars, but the long-term consequences of warfare will often fall upon different states. Refugees have often appeared as a consequence of war, and the numbers of displaced persons may overwhelm some countries. The refugees may also become virtually permanent residents and create a minority population where none existed before. At the very least refugee populations cause a temporary economic strain that can lead to political problems down the road.

Conflict often breeds more conflict. The Napoleonic Wars helped to lead to the rise of modern nationalism, which in turn contributed to national insurrections and additional conflicts— the War of 1812, the wars against the colonial administrations in the Spanish colonial empire, and the wars of German and Italian unification, and the Balkan Wars. Each of these conflicts in turn led to more violence, both domestic and international. Similarly, World War I led to the overthrow of the Russian monarchy by a war-weary population. That change in government then permitted Lenin and the Bolsheviks to seize power, and the creation of a Communist system that in turn played a role in generating many later conflicts. World War I also resulted in the break up of the German, Austro-Hungarian, Russian, and Ottoman Empires leading to political violence and terrorism among the successor states and populations dissatisfied with the new boundaries. It remains to be seen what Iraq's future is and what problems may (or may not) appear down the road in this area. Thus, the outbreak of wars, in both good causes and bad ones, will have consequences years later, and governments have to deal with these consequences. Ending the causes of war may be a major step toward the elimination of terrorism at some point in time, but political leaders in the present will still have to deal with problems inherited from a past that they cannot change. Thus, for the immediate future the world will still have to deal with the consequences of previous international conflicts, even if no new ones appear in the future.

A final possible factor involved in outbreaks of terrorism is the presence of weak states or governing bodies. Weak states mean ineffective law enforcement and such circumstances make it easier for terrorists and guerrillas to operate (Schmid 2005: 232). These groups may be domestic organizations that target their own governments or could be foreign groups that simply use the territory of a weak state as a base for attacks on their home governments. Rampant terrorism in sub-Saharan Africa, for example, has been facilitated by the present of weak governments and failed states (Cilliers 2003: 102). While such weak states are not a cause of terrorism, they clearly facilitate the operation of terrorist groups.

The underlying causes for outbreaks of terrorism could be different in different time periods. Rapoport (2003) has suggested that there is a link with the historical era and therefore the causes of terrorism. He posits four waves of violence. The first was the anarchist, beginning in the 1880s; the second was anticolonial, beginning in the 1920s; the third was violence associated with the new left, beginning in the late 1960s; and the fourth was a religious wave that began in 1979. While this series of waves does not cover all the terrorist groups that have been active (J. Lutz and B. Lutz 2005: 159–61), there is evidence to support the model. This evidence, of course, also supports the idea that historical factors could be a factor involved with differing causes of terrorism in different time periods.

PREVALENCE OF TERRORISM

One of the more important issues regarding terrorist attacks involves whether or not terrorism has been on the increase. It is a rare day that the newspaper in any medium-sized US city does not contain information about a violent attack somewhere in the world. The news media in larger cities and those with national audiences that cover events in foreign countries more extensively invariably have information on more than one instance of such violence. Even before September 11th, there was clearly the perception (at least in the United States) that the world was becoming a more dangerous place, and that terrorists could be anywhere. Of course, the definition of terrorism is an important issue in this regard since different authors and the various groups collecting data use different definitions making precise comparisons more difficult. Trends within data accumulated by the same author or organization, however, can be more reliable for purposes of detecting trends and general patterns. Over the centuries we clearly have much better information on recent times and especially the most recent half-century than in earlier centuries or millennia. While massive campaigns that involved the use of terror would be more obvious in existing historical materials, more isolated instances would be lost. As a consequence, discussions of changing frequencies of terrorist acts of necessity have to be limited to more recent times.

In considerations of all kinds of terrorism, there clearly was an increase between the 1970s and the 1980s in the number of incidents. There were almost four times as many acts in the 1980s (Stern 1993: 393–4). The impression that the West is the frequent target of terrorism is probably at least somewhat misleading. With a free press, the attacks that do occur are widely covered in the media (Schmid 1992b: 16). In other circumstances there may be few reliable media sources for collecting data, as has been the case for the former Soviet Union (Pluchinsky 1998: 121). The media in many parts of sub-Saharan Africa are also relatively weak, and information on activities may not be as well known. Even if it is assumed that there was better reporting of such actions as terrorism became a phenomenon more worthy of watching and analyzing, the increase has still been obvious. When terrorism does occur, it can be for a variety of causes. Many acts are domestic, and by far the majority of terrorist acts that do occur are domestics ones (Wilkinson 2000b: 45). Of course, whether or not to define an attack as a terrorist act can become very political since some governments will proclaim any act of opposition to be terrorist violence.

Another way to view terrorism has been to focus on acts that are defined as international terrorism. Even though only a small portion of all terrorist attacks can be classified as international, the classification is somewhat arbitrary since many international acts are part of domestic campaigns. A focus on such actions, however, can still prove useful for detecting trends. There have been suggestions that many of these international acts of terrorism were related to the struggles that were part of the Cold War. From the late 1960s to the mid-1980s authoritarian regimes including the Soviet Union frequently resorted to terrorism in response to foreign policy defeats at the hands of democratic states (O'Brien 1996). Of course, this approach assumes that there was some kind of network involving local groups and outside supporters or that the CIA and KGB were quite active in promoting actions across borders. With the break up of the Soviet Union there was a decline in Soviet support for terrorism and thus a decrease in the level of international acts of terrorism (Enders and Sandler 2000). While the end of the Cold War may have played a role in the reduction of such violent incidents, countermeasures in Western states could have been a factor as well (Enders and Sandler 1999). But not all terrorism in the world resulted from conflict among nations as was obvious on September 11th, and not even all terrorist actions that have been supported by state governments were part of the Cold War.

What is probably more important than the sheer number of terrorist attacks that occur is how deadly they are. Not only have the number of attacks increased, but they have also become much more lethal (Chalk 1999: 164). The numbers of dead and injured increased for international incidents of terrorism in the 1980s and 1990s. While there were somewhat fewer attacks, those that did occur were more deadly (Enders and Sandler 2000: 327–8). Table 2.1 contains a summary of casualties inflicted in international terrorist incidents from 1980 to 2006. The number of such incidents was usually higher in the 1980s than in later years and actually peaked in 1985. The highest number of deaths occurred in 2001 with the September 11th attacks but other years after 1990 also had high totals of deaths or injuries. Overall, it is clear that casualties per incident were higher for most years in the 1990s and the first years of the twenty-first century, even if there were a few years with relatively few deaths and injuries in the international attacks. Terrorist attacks did indeed become more lethal. Singular incidents at the

TABLE 2.1   CASUALTIES IN INTERNATIONAL TERRORIST INCIDENTS, 1980–2006

Year	Incidents	Dead	Injured	Total	Dead/ Year	Injured/ Year	Total/ Year
1980	235	161	317	478	0.69	1.35	2.03
1981	300	320	1138	1458	1.08	3.78	4.86
1982	356	111	737	848	0.32	2.07	2.38
1983	279	600	838	1438	2.16	3.00	5.15
1984	326	165	450	615	0.51	1.38	1.89
1985	434	733	1167	1900	1.69	2.69	4.38
1986	377	351	1236	1587	0.93	3.28	4.21
1987	361	375	1165	1540	1.04	3.23	4.27
1988	369	702	1832	2534	1.90	4.96	6.87
1989	359	347	468	815	0.97	1.30	2.27
1990	285	122	320	442	0.42	1.12	1.55
1991	420	192	236	428	0.46	0.56	1.02
1992	272	145	556	701	0.53	2.04	2.58
1993	272	471	2677	3148	1.73	9.84	11.58
1994	310	435	1082	1517	1.40	3.49	4.89
1995	266	293	6007	6300	1.10	22.58	23.68
1996	237	570	2957	3527	2.40	12.48	14.88
1997	171	246	871	1117	1.44	5.09	6.53
1998	161	377	5350	5727	2.55	33.23	35.57
1999	125	65	121	186	0.53	0.97	1.49
2000	106	47	95	142	0.44	0.90	1.34
2001	205	3184	3373	6557	15.53	16.45	31.99
2002	298	970	2957	3927	3.26	9.92	13.18
2003	276	470	1766	2236	1.70	6.40	8.10
2004	395	732	2023	2755	1.85	5.12	6.97
2005	308	551	864	1415	1.79	2.80	4.60
2006	216	296	438	734	1.37	2.03	3.40

Source: National Memorial Institute for the Prevention of Terrorism (MIPT), Terrorism Knowledge Base, online at http://www.tkb.org (accessed 2007)

international level can influence the casualty figures. The 2001 figures clearly represent the many dead in the World Trade Center towers. While the 1993 figures for injured are high because of the people injured in the first attack on the World Trade Center. The patterns for the international attacks do provide some evidence of increasingly lethal incidents. It is true that international incidents are becoming more deadly, but the largest number of deaths and injuries still occur in domestic situations. In 1995, for example, more people died in the Oklahoma City bombing than in all the recorded international incidents. Ongoing terrorist campaigns have also resulted in cumulative death tolls in the thousands or tens of thousands. Since 9/11, the United States has been focused on international terrorism and a global war on terrorism, but for many countries, domestic terrorism remains the major threat (de Castro 2004: 194). It has been suggested that the increasingly deadly nature of terrorism, both domestic and international, results from three factors. More terrorist groups are motivated by religious views and values, more amateurs operating alone have launched attacks, and the more professional terrorists have greater knowledge and sophistication in using weapons (Hoffman 1997: 3). This increase in the level of casualties is more important than number of incidents. Clearly, terrorism has not been on the decline with the end of the Cold War or with other changes in the international system. While there would appear to be variations over time and no consistent trend and the relative contribution of different kinds of terrorist activities (religious, ethnic, ideological, mixed, or state repression) may change from period to period, the overall level of terrorist violence remains high.

SUMMARY

It is essential to reiterate that terrorism is not a new phenomenon. The infliction of death and misery by violent groups seeking to achieve political ends has been going on for millennia as will be demonstrated in at least some of the following chapters. If precise information is not always present, enough indications are available to have an idea of past and present occurrences. Religious differences and ethnic differences have long been sources of conflict. Ideological groups of both the left and the right engaged in the use of terror before and after World War II. The following chapters will help to make clear whether terrorism has been on the increase, not just over the centuries but in terms of trends in the recent decades as well. The working definition provided at the beginning of this chapter is a key for all the material to follow. It provides a clear summation of what constitutes terrorism—political objectives, violence or the threat of violence, a target audience, an organization, the involvement of non-state actors, and an effort to increase the power of the terrorist group. Individuals may feel in their own minds that other groups qualify. Individual students will also have to make value judgments as to whether the levels of violence utilized are justified by the target government or policies where change is sought. As stated above, the neutral definition of terrorism is not intended to suggest that persons ignore the contexts in which the violence occurs. Terrorist actions can be undertaken in the pursuit of worthwhile causes as well as objectionable ones. It can even be argued in at least some cases that the death and terror in the present will be less than that which would occur were no dissident violence to take place. The neutral definition simply removes the necessary value judgments from the basic analysis of the phenomenon of terrorism. Similarly, the classification, imperfect as it must be since it deals with real world situations, facilitates understanding the complexity of terrorist organizations and their goals—whether these goals are religious, national or ethnic, based on left-wing or right-wing ideologies, composed of more than one major element, or designed to support the government. The first steps in terms of beginning to understand these organizations will begin in the next two chapters where the tactics and weapons used by terrorist groups will be discussed and where the issue of foreign support or control of terrorist groups will be dealt with. Discussions of these elements will help to set the stage for the cases studies in the other chapters.

TERMS

CIA	leaderless resistance
globalization	terrorism
KGB	Unabomber
King Alexander of Yugoslavia	

FURTHER READING

Badey, T. J. (1998) "Defining International Terrorism: A Pragmatic Approach," *Terrorism and Political Violence*, 10, 1: 90–107.

Bjorgo, T. (2005a) "Conclusions," in T. Bjorgo (ed.), *Root Causes of Terrorism: Myths, Reality and Ways Forward*, London: Routledge, 256–64.

Claridge, D. (1996) "State Terrorism? Applying a Definitional Model," *Terrorism and Political Violence*, 8, 3: 47–63.

Crenshaw, M. (2003a) "The Causes of Terrorism," in C. W. Kegley, Jr (ed.) *The New Global Terrorism: Characteristics, Causes, Controls*, Upper Saddle River, NJ: Prentice Hall, 92–105.

Gurr, T. R. (2006) "Economic Factors," in L. Richardson (ed.) *The Roots of Terrorism*, New York: Routledge, 85–101.

CHAPTER 3

Tactics, Weapons, and Targets

The definition and typology from Chapter 2 provide an essential starting point for understanding terrorism. There are other elements that can be common to various kinds of organizations that practice political violence, regardless of their religious, ethnic/national, or ideological orientation. The ends may be different, but frequently the means can be similar—not just with the initial decision to resort to the use of terrorism but in terms of the types of attacks that are undertaken and the broad strategies. Different groups can follow the same broad strategies. Groups can seek to intimidate target audiences. They can also follow strategies of attrition against a state, seek to provoke countermeasures, to spoil negotiations, or to seek to increase support at the expense of other competing groups (Kydd and Walter 2006: 51). Dissident organizations may be similar in the techniques they employ, the types of weapons that they use, and the targets that are selected. Local conditions and circumstances, however, are more likely to determine choices rather than the goals of the dissident group using violence. Available resources (financial and otherwise) may be more important in determining which weapons, tactics, or targets are preferred rather than the political goals of the organization. All of the selections ultimately are made from possibilities that almost any group with sufficient planning skills, funding, weapons, and personnel may attempt to undertake. Techniques will be discussed first. The weapons that can be used will be discussed next, including a consideration of the possibility of groups using weapons of mass destruction such as nuclear bombs, chemical poisons, or biological agents. Clearly concerns about the possibilities for the use of these weapons in the twenty-first century have increased. Finally, the possible types of targets that can be chosen and which are chosen will be discussed. Included in this discussion will be a consideration of the possibility that democratic countries are more vulnerable to terrorist attacks than non-democratic ones.

TECHNIQUES

The same techniques are generally available to all dissident organizations, regardless of the type of government they are fighting or the political goals they seek. Of course, some techniques might be more effective against one government and less effective against another. A brutally repressive government may be less concerned about attacks on civilians than one that is trying to fairly represent its population. Personal attacks on individuals can take place with a variety of weapons, but the goal is to indicate to the public and to specific groups that are supporting the government that there is a level of vulnerability or risk present. These attacks do not need to involve sophisticated weapons; very simple weapons may suffice. In some cases the personal assault need not be deadly. The terrorist may only wound their chosen targets, as might occur with breaking bones or shooting people in the legs or kneecaps. Choosing to wound rather than kill targets demonstrates to the population at large that the dissidents are not out to kill people. Such attacks show that the terrorists could kill since it is more difficult to get close enough to successfully wound a target. The technique of wounding is thus a display of greater abilities and can demonstrate that the terrorist group has an even greater potential to disrupt the political life of the society than if it had simply killed an individual.

Personal assaults are not the only possibility. Kidnappings are another tactic available to any dissident group with sufficient resources to capture and hide the victim. The kidnapping may be designed to embarrass the government by demonstrating the ease with which some prominent individual may be taken. The kidnapping also demonstrates how vulnerable persons in the country may be to the political dissidents. The kidnapping may also be designed to raise funds for the group by ransoming the victim. The government, family, or business may be pressured to exchange money for the victim. In other cases the group may offer to release the kidnapped individual in exchange for imprisoned comrades or for government policy concessions. The publicity, financial gain, or political concessions can all be very beneficial to any dissident organization. Success demonstrates the capabilities of the dissidents and the weaknesses of the government.

Other techniques are similarly available to all kinds of groups. Bank robberies are commonly used to finance dissident movements in many countries. Not only do they raise money, but they may embarrass the government as well. The robberies will qualify as terrorism when the funds are devoted to the organization rather than to the private luxuries of the dissidents. Extortion (revolutionary confiscations) may occur when groups have the opportunity to do so during temporary occupations of buildings or villages. Such action may have a short-term advantage in that necessary finances are generated but could have negative long-term costs if the population is alienated from the dissident movement. If the money is taken from groups that are not likely to ever support the dissidents, the cost in terms of alienated segments of the population will be negligible. Financial support can also come from involvement in smuggling or in drug trafficking.

Hijackings and the associated taking of hostages have been used by a wide variety of groups. Airliners have become frequent targets for hijackings. Hijackings are not a new phenomenon. The first recorded instance was in 1930 when Peruvian revolutionaries used a hijacked plane to drop propaganda leaflets (Piszkiewicz 2003: 2). Skyjackings became quite common for a period of time. Skyjackings as a technique was quickly adopted by other groups, culminating, of course, in the attacks of 9/11. The key to the takeover is usually not the vehicle in question but the crew and passengers that are on board. These individuals become hostages that can be used in the political struggle between the dissidents and the government they are targeting. They are bargaining chips in any negotiations. For example, the release of the hostages is offered in exchange for the release of imprisoned members of the organization. Many governments, however, have been very hesitant to make such trades since it might encourage further hostage-taking efforts or make the government appear to be weak. Hijackers also frequently are willing to exchange hostages for the publication of demands or manifestoes. These demands have normally been met lest the government appear to be indifferent to the lives of the hostages. This publicity is frequently a goal of the groups as they seek to make their cause known. Such publicity may be invaluable in attracting support for the dissident cause or weakening support for the government. Hijackings in the past usually ended with the release of the hostages and some agreement to permit the hijackers to be transported to some other country. The hijackers have gained their immediate goal by publicizing their cause and demonstrating their ability to successfully undertake a political action.

The occupations of government offices or other buildings with the taking of hostages, such as the situation in Breslan, Russia, have also occurred. Such occupations can provide an indication of the strength of the dissidents and the weaknesses of the government. The dissidents can then negotiate with the government for publication of demands or release of persons in prison. Arranging for the safe escape of the terrorists may also be part of the negotiations. While the circumstances are generally analogous to hijacking aircraft or ships, occupying buildings is more difficult. On an aircraft or ship, the hostages are naturally concentrated, and a few terrorists can control access. Buildings have more exits, and they are more difficult to control. Thus, the occupation will require a larger number of activists, risking a larger portion of the human assets of the dissident group. Embassies or consulates are targets at times because the occupation generates greater publicity, but such buildings, *once occupied*, may be easier to control since they are frequently designed for greater security with limited access. Seizing an embassy may also introduce international complications for a government. A repressive government may be indifferent to the fate of its own citizens, whereas when foreign citizens are held hostage the government may have to be at least somewhat more open in terms of what actions are taken or at least have some willingness to negotiate.

It should be re-emphasized that all the above techniques are available to any dissident organization that chooses to use them. There may be good terrorist tactics, or at least tactics that can be judged to be less evil (kidnapping instead of death; hijacking a plane rather than blowing it up), but these tactics remain available to freedom fighters and terrorists alike. No one type of group has a monopoly on any particular technique. Terrorism as a general technique can be emulated by different, unrelated groups (Enders and Sandler 2006: 15). The spread of techniques to different groups around the world has been facilitated by the availability of rapid means of communication and transmission of information (Weinberg 2006: 46). Once a particular technique proves to be effective, it is quickly copied by groups elsewhere, including those that have nothing in common with the group originating the technique. Many techniques used by terrorists are copied once they prove to be successful (B. Jenkins 1981: 7). Campaigns of assassinations as a technique spread in the later nineteenth century (Enders and Sandler 2006: 15). Today, modern technology and communications can speed up the emulation process. Car bombs, for example, have rapidly spread as a technique. Hijacking airliners to publicize a cause became quite common, and groups used them with a wide variety of political interests. There were even civilian airliners from behind the Iron Curtain that were hijacked and flown to "freedom" in the West. The hijackers in these cases were then considered refugees, and heroes, rather than international criminals. One consequence of widely different groups using the same type of tactic is that it becomes more difficult for any country to actually enforce absolute rules about never granting landing rights to hijackers or refusing to grant them asylum. Political reality and public opinion can require that countries treat individual hijackers differently, depending upon their political values and the goals that are sought.

WEAPONS

Weapons and techniques are related, of course, and weapons availability will influence what kinds of actions a terrorist group can even attempt. A dissident group that wanted to eliminate the top leadership in a country all at once would like to have a cruise missile or other type of smart bomb that it could direct to the opening session of parliament or to a meeting of the ruling military council. Such a strike would create the chaos that would give the dissidents greater opportunities to take power or otherwise influence government policy. Of course, dissident organizations do not have access to such weapons, forcing them to find other weapons for carrying out their attacks. The consideration of weapons that might be used will first deal with more conventional weapons that are available to dissident organizations. Then, weapons that have come to be termed weapons of mass destruction will be considered. The possibility that terrorist organizations would gain access to such weapons and use them to inflict mass casualties has been of increasing concern in recent years.

Conventional weapons

Most weapons used by dissident organizations are designed to inflict casualties or disruption on a small scale. Terrorist groups normally have little difficulty acquiring personal weapons. A terrorist could attempt to kill a chosen target with a pistol or knife. Since such weapons are only accurate at close range, the apprehension of the attackers will be easy unless the attack takes place in an isolated location away from other people. Rifles are also readily available in many countries and could be used with precision by a marksman from a distance. Various kinds of automatic weapons and assault rifles have also become increasingly easy to obtain. Use of such assault weapons could lead to higher casualties if the attack occurs where many people are present. The advantage of these automatic weapons is that they require less precision to use and that the intent of the dissidents to attack the government can be readily demonstrated. The cause is publicized and a target audience may become aware of the goals of the terrorist organization. These kinds of weapons can be purchased, stolen from the security forces or police, or captured in raids on armories. Increasing lethal weapons have also become available with the stockpiles of "surplus" arms left over after the end of the Cold War (Chalk 1999: 158). Personal weapons will be necessary not only for attempts to inflict casualties but also for activities such as kidnappings, extortion, and bank robberies.

Various kinds of bombs have been a mainstay of terrorist groups for many years. Approximately half of all terrorist attacks involve bombs (Enders and Sandler 2006: 7). Typical cartoons from the latter part of the nineteenth and into the twentieth century portrayed the terrorist as a bearded, scruffy individual with a lighted bomb in hand. Bombs can range from simple devices such as a grenade or a Molotov cocktail that is thrown at targets to more sophisticated devices that can be detonated by remote control or by timers. The more sophisticated devices can be used more selectively against particular targets. A mine that can be detonated by remote control, for example, can be used against a particular vehicle, whereas a regular land mine will detonate when the first vehicle of sufficient weight passes over it. Terrorists, of course, can still use the normal type of land mine since the intent might be used to disrupt the transport system, to demonstrate to the general population that the government is unable to provide protection, or to target a particular region or particular group. With increasingly compact explosives, letter bombs and package bombs can be used to attack individuals. If all the letters or packages in the national mail system become suspect, the terrorists have already had one of their desired effects on behavior by inducing widespread fear.

Some kinds of bombs can be especially deadly. Bombs that are intended to go off in planes in the air are obviously designed to kill people. In the past, these bombs usually involved timers, but the bombs had sometimes detonated prematurely on the ground due to rough handling. In other cases because of flight delays or because the luggage had been misdirected (i.e., lost), the bomb exploded while still on the ground, causing minimal damage. With access to modern technology, the bombers came up with newer methods. The bombs that were built were pressure sensitive so that they would go off when the air pressure in the cargo hold of the airliner had decreased to a particular level. Such pressure sensitive devices would even be linked to timing devices so that the process started at a particular altitude but the plane would be over the ocean before detonation. Security agencies for airliners or airports, in turn, developed machinery to simulate this reduced pressure level so that luggage with suspicious materials could be tested on the ground. The development of bombs and detection mechanisms is an ongoing contest between terrorists (and criminals) and the security agencies. As one type of potential attack is rendered ineffective, a new weapon is developed. The battle between bombers and security will go on. As technology provides more opportunities to inflict damage, it will also provide better mechanisms to detect explosives before they can kill and destroy.

Car bombs have been a relatively recent addition to the armory of terrorist groups. Vehicles packed with explosive can do considerable damage and kill and wound many people. Thirteen vehicle bombs that were set off in Bombay (now Mumbai), India in February 1993 killed more than 400 people and injured over a thousand people (Hoffman 2001: 421). In other cases car bombs have been driven into targets on suicide missions, as happened in Lebanon to US marines and French paratroopers trying to end the Lebanese civil war. Vehicles have also been left to go off with a timer or to be detonated by remote control. The first bombing of the World Trade Center in New York City in 1993 utilized such a bomb with a timer, as did the bomb used against the federal building in Oklahoma City. Car and truck bombs had previously have been used with some regularity in the Middle East and Northern Ireland for many years. Their use increased when the techniques for using large amounts of fertilizer to produce a massive blast became available and widely known. Terrorists no longer needed to access high-grade explosives when a ton of fertilizer could be easily obtained. Car bombs have one advantage for terrorists in that one vehicle can easily blend into a large number of similar vehicles on a street, in a parking facility, or in a parking area. It will be impossible for local authorities to continuously check all such vehicles. Using civilian airliners as flying bombs has increased the potential for casualties (see Box 3.1).

Suicide bombings have become prevalent for some terrorist groups. They are in some respects an extreme form of psychological warfare (Moghadam 2003: 75). They increase the credibility

BOX 3.1 CIVILIAN AIRLINERS AS BOMBS IN SUICIDE ATTACKS

The use of airliners as suicide vehicles in peacetime was seen as a unique occurrence when it happened on September 11th, 2001. The plans for the attack were well thought out. Four airliners were hijacked at virtually the same time. All four were chosen because they were flying from the East Coast to the West Coast and thus their fuel tanks were full given the distances involved. The additional fuel was intended to add to the destruction when they were crashed into the buildings. The total destruction of the World Trade Center towers was much more than bin Laden had apparently anticipated, although he was not upset by the more extensive damage (Robbins 2002: 357–7). There had been earlier indications that hijacked airliners might be used in this fashion. In 1986 a TWA plane was seized in Pakistan. The hijackers reportedly intended to have the plane fly to Israel where it would be crashed in the center of Tel Aviv (Hoffman 2002b: 306). The plane never had the opportunity of leaving the ground after refueling, but it is unlikely that it could have successfully made the long flight to Israel to launch the attack. In 1994 Algerian dissidents hijacked an Air France flight. They intended to crash the plane in Paris, perhaps with the Eiffel Tower as a specific target. The goal of the attack was to force the French to stop supporting the Algerian government. The effort was short circuited when French commandos recaptured the plane while it was on the ground in Marseille (Shapiro and Suzan 2003: 81). It not known at present how much information Al Qaeda might have had about these earlier operations, but it is quite likely that the group was aware of the plan.

of future attacks since it is obvious that they cannot be deterred (Pape 2005: 29). They have resulted in increased casualties as well whether it be by driving a car into a building, by crashing an airplane, or by an individual exploding a bomb on his or her person in a crowded street. Suicide attacks provide an advantage over other bombs since the explosives can more readily be delivered to a location that might otherwise be inaccessible while the timing of the detonation can be more effectively controlled (Dolnik 2003: 20). Suicide bombings also are a relatively low cost method (except for the bomber or driver or pilot) of inflicting damage on opponents. Activists can even consider suicide attacks to be an effective method of providing a better life for their children or relatives (Azam 2005). Suicide attacks have other functions too. They can mobilize supporters and build solidarity among groups that may support the terrorist organization (Hoffman and McCormick 2004: 246, 250). In some cases the reliance on suicide attacks represents efforts by competing groups to gain greater support (Bloom 2004). The persons involved in suicide missions often are retaliating against the enemy for the injury to or the death of family members of friends (Moghadam 2003: 72). While such personal motivations will lead people to join terrorist organizations, their actions are part of the larger campaign directed against a target audience.

Modern technology has also provided potential terrorists with many more weapons options. Surface-to-air missiles can be used against commercial aircraft as well as military ones. The roof of any building along the flight path for an airport could become a site for the launching of such missiles. The successful firing of such a missile is not as simple as it may appear, but the necessary training can be acquired; consequently, such an attack remains a dangerous possibility. There have been at least twenty-five attacks against aircraft with these missiles, usually with military aircraft as the targets. About 60 percent of the attacks have been successful (Wilkinson 2000b: 214). A Russian missile brought down a civilian airliner in Sri Lanka (Hoffman 2002b: 312). A surface-to-air missile was also used in a failed attempt to bring down an Israeli airliner in Kenya in 2003 (Cilliers 2003: 101). Civilian airliners have also been brought down by guerrillas in Zimbabwe and the Sudan. The United States attempted to reacquire the Stinger missiles that it had channeled to the Afghan rebels to minimize future uses of such weapons. In 1982, Italian police found four powerful ground-to-air missiles when they raided a terrorist hideout (R. Drake 1989: 145). Security forces in Turkey also found Stinger rockets in an arms cache of a Kurdish dissident group (Criss 1995: 29). The biggest disadvantage of these weapons for the terrorists is that while opportunities to acquire them do appear, it is difficult to get them in sufficient quantities to permit members of the terrorist group to practice by actually firing the weapons.

The use of sophisticated devices to launch attacks has been increasing. In 1991 the Irish Republican Army (IRA) used remote control mortars to attack Number 10 Downing Street, the residence of the British prime minister. John Major, prime minister at the time, and the rest of the cabinet were in a meeting when the attack occurred. The mortar tubes had been hidden in a van parked in the vicinity. The shells landed harmlessly in a courtyard, but the attack had demonstrated what was possible, and it might have killed or wounded the British prime minister and many cabinet ministers. The persons involved in the attack were able to escape undetected. Formulas for explosives, directions for building bombs with fertilizer, instructions for creating remote control devices, and materials on other ways of creating havoc are all readily available in books and on the internet. The spread of knowledge has also included the spread of the necessary information for creating terror.

There are some additional possible weapons that reflect technical sophistication. Computer systems have become more central in modern states. Breaking into a computer system and changing commands or introducing a virus could create havoc, and such attacks might even lead to a loss of life. These kinds of weapons have been referred to as weapons of mass disruption given the scope of dislocations that could occur. Computers programmed to provide incorrect information could not only create economic difficulties but could also take a great deal of time to fix. Interference with computers or other electronic elements of the modern world could become a very effective terrorist weapon (Bunker 2000).

Weapons of mass destruction

There has been increasing concern recently that terrorists might begin to use weapons of mass destruction to inflict large numbers of casualties on the targets as a means of attempting to obtain their political objectives. Such weapons have generally included biological and chemical weapons, radiological bombs, and even nuclear devices. To date there has been no evidence that any terrorist organization has gained access to nuclear devices or to weapons grade uranium or plutonium. One fear has been that with the break up of the old Soviet Union such weapons were more readily available since there are doubts about the quality of security measures and safeguards at Soviet nuclear stockpiles (B. Jenkins 1998: 234). There was a fear that some well-funded organization might purchase a nuclear device from one of the successor states. The security guards, currently underpaid—if paid at all—might be susceptible to bribes to let a nuclear device "disappear" (Schmid 2000). The rumors that terrorist groups obtained nuclear weapons from the old Soviet stockpiles have proven to be false so far (Cameron 1999: 289). As knowledge of how to construct nuclear weapons has spread, the danger of some sort of nuclear device making its way into the hands of a terrorist organization has increased. For the present, the greatest nuclear danger might be an assault on a nuclear power facility that is designed to create conditions that would lead to a meltdown or a heat explosion similar to the Chernobyl disaster in the old Soviet Union. In point of fact, nuclear hoaxes or contamination with radioactive materials seems much more likely than the use of nuclear weapons by terrorists (B. Jenkins 1998: 233). There is also the danger of a radiological weapon or a "dirty bomb" where a conventional bomb is loaded with materials contaminated by radiation so that that the death and destruction from the blast is increased. This is the easiest weapon of mass destruction that terrorists could construct and use (Cameron 2004: 83).

Chemical and biological weapons have generated even more concern. Some observers have considered these emerging weapons to be the weapons of the future for terrorists. Terrorists using such weapons would be able to spread fear and chaos and cause massive casualties. This fear has been particularly great among policy-makers who would have to deal with such attacks (Dishman 2001: 304). This concern has increased since there have now been recent cases of both biological and chemical attacks. In 1995 there was a chemical attack on the Japanese subway with a chemical nerve agent, which resulted in a few fatalities and many more hospitalized. In 2001, in the aftermath of the September 11th attacks in the United States, letters containing anthrax were sent to members of Congress and to persons involved in the news media. Less than a dozen people died in these attacks, but more could have been potentially affected. The source of the anthrax and the purpose behind the attacks has yet to be determined. While it was initially presumed that the mailings were from someone associated with the Osama bin Laden group, analyses of the anthrax used indicated that the material was likely to have originated in the United States.

While the use of nerve gas and anthrax demonstrates the possibilities of biological and chemical weapons, it also has demonstrated the limitations. Chemical weapons may not be especially lethal. For example, it would take a ton of sarin nerve gas released by aircraft under ideal weather conditions to kill 3,000 to 8,000 people in an urban area (Sokolski 2000: 211). Disseminating a ton of the gas, however, would be difficult even under ideal circumstances. Similarly, biological agents or chemicals released into water systems are unlikely to work because of existing filtration systems and chlorination (Tucker 1996: 174). Tons of chemicals or biological agents would be required to effectively contaminate a municipal water supply given the dilution that would occur in the lake or reservoir (Gurr and Cole 2000: 65). Anthrax is actually quite limited as a biological weapon because it is not contagious. It cannot be spread by human contact, so even though it can be deadly in some forms, it cannot start an epidemic. The more deadly type of biological weapon would be one that was both deadly *and* contagious. The 2001 anthrax attacks did lead to disruptions in mail delivery, and they shut down government offices for various periods of time, and they spread fear throughout the United States, particularly coming so soon after the attacks on New York City and Washington DC. The loss of life, however, was no greater than might have occurred with letter bombs or package bombs left in corridors of government offices or other places. Letter bombs might even have had a similar effect in terms of generating fear, but the anthrax scare was probably more effective in terms of spreading fear since it was a new weapon and less well understood by the general public.

In actual fact, the threat of chemical and biological weapons may well be exaggerated. Tucker (2000b) collected cases dealing with various efforts or presumed efforts to use biological or chemical weapons by persons knowledgeable about the individual efforts. Out of fifteen cases of presumed or possible attacks using these weapons, in only three instances were such weapons actually used on targets. One was the case of the use of nerve gas in Japan that has already been mentioned. A second involved the use of a biological weapon in a very localized setting. The followers of a cult in Oregon attempted to spread food poisoning among the local population to incapacitate enough voters so that the members of the cult living in the religious compound could dominate the election, but they still lost the election (Carus 2000). The group abandoned the scheme when it became clear that their candidate was not going to win in any event (Stern 1999: 66). Members of the group were eventually caught and convicted for their initial use of the biological weapons. The final case of an actual attack with biological weapons occurred even earlier. Immediately after World War II, a group of Jewish Holocaust survivors tried to poison the bread that was given to members of the German SS being held in a prisoner-of-war camp. The goal was to kill as many of the prisoners as possible in retaliation for the death camps run by the Nazis. The attack was carried out and led to illnesses for many prisoners and some deaths. The authorities were not even aware that the illnesses were intentional since many former soldiers were suffering from the long-term effects of malnutrition, wounds suffered during the war, and other physical weaknesses (Sprinzak and Zertal 2000). The attack was successful up to a point. There were deaths, but they were not in the large numbers that the Holocaust survivors had hoped to achieve. The attack does not really qualify as a terrorist act since there was no target audience since it was in revenge for Nazi atrocities during the war. The limited success of the effort does demonstrate the limitations of biological and chemical weapons such as the use of poisons.

Tucker's collection of fifteen cases of possible chemical and biological weapons is very informative in other ways. It is clear that in twelve cases groups either never reached the stage of actively pursuing the production of chemical or biological weapons or if they did they failed in the efforts. Such weapons have been considered easy to create, but the evidence would suggest otherwise (Rosenau 2001: 297). In these three cases where such weapons were used, mass casualties did not result. In the case of Oregon, the cult was not seeking to kill people. The food poisoning scheme was actually a very appropriate weapon to attempt to use to dominate a local election. In the Japanese case there was intent to cause mass casualties, but it failed. The groups responsible might have been better off to use conventional weaponry in their attacks. In the case of the prisoner-of-war camp, mass casualties also did not result as desired. The recent anthrax attacks in the United States similarly have not led to mass casualties. As a consequence, it is easy to agree with the assessment that known uses of chemical and biological weapons have been infrequent, and none of the ones intended to be weapons of mass destruction have been successful (Tucker 2000a: 253). As is the case with nuclear weapons, credible hoaxes rather than actual use may be the greatest threat with biological and chemical weapons (Veness 2001: 409).

While biological weapons have not been effective weapons of mass destruction in the past, their lethal potential exists. The use of a biological agent that is contagious raises its own set of problems. The biological agent may be slow acting. This may make it easier for the terrorists to escape detection (Tucker 2000a: 264), but such slow acting weapons also do not generate the media attention that terrorists often desire. The greatest difficulty with a biological weapon is that it can quickly get beyond the control of the dissident group that used it, and the dissidents could become victims as well. Handling such weapons is also dangerous, and the terrorists could become victims before the rest of the population if there were an accident or ineffective isolation mechanisms. Such weapons might become more deadly if they were used as part of a suicide attack. There is also some thought that biological weapons could be used in economic attacks on agricultural systems or livestock in a target country. The disruption of the food system could result in significant economic losses rather than immediate mass casualties (Foxell 2001: 113–14).

Any attempt to use biological and chemical weapons faces other difficulties as well. The political demands of the terrorist organization must be communicated to a government or a public audience, yet doing so means facing possible retaliation. A government facing a rampant plague might be willing to take extreme measures to punish the dissidents and is unlikely to compromise. A group that has caused massive casualties in the population is likely to be in a poor bargaining position to achieve its objectives since public anger at the group would make it difficult for a government to make any concessions (Claridge 2000b: 142). If, however, the attack is intended to paralyze, disrupt, and disorient the government and general population so that some other political goals can be achieved more readily, then a group need not specifically acknowledge its role in causing large number of deaths. In such circumstances, a group might well be tempted to use a biological or chemical weapon if it is available. Organizations that are seeking or willing to accept a large number of dead or even intent on causing mass casualties might use such weapons. Groups that have been willing to use conventional weapons to cause many deaths might be tempted to use biological or chemical weapons, especially if the weapon could be controlled.

Pragmatic concerns probably provide the most important reasons why terrorists have refrained from using biological and chemical weapons (Laqueur 1998: 50). Efforts to acquire such weapons may come at a significant cost since key operatives of the organization may be more susceptible to capture by the authorities (Ivanova and Sandler 2006: 424). The use of chemical or biological weapons has not spread because terrorists frequently prefer the familiar, tried-and-true weapons (Cameron 1999: 279). The knowledge for building bombs, simple or sophisticated, is known. If the bomb explodes, anywhere—with or without casualties—it is a success since the government and the public will not know whether the intended target was actually destroyed (B. Jenkins 1998: 243). The terrorists can claim success even if the attack miscarried in some fashion. There is little incentive to try to develop new weapons, which may or may not be effective and which may or may not be controllable. Investing in new unproven weaponry could stretch the resources of many dissident organizations (Claridge 2000b: 143), although some groups have been willing to invest in labs to try to produce biological and chemical weapons, albeit not very successfully. The use of hijacked airliners in the destruction of the World Trade Center towers and the assault on the Pentagon has demonstrated that terrorist groups caused mass casualties with familiar techniques used in a new way.

While the use of biological and chemical weapons of mass destruction is not as likely as some have predicted, the threat is still present (Geiger 2001: 709). Efforts to make such weapons have occurred. A wide variety of terrorist organizations has apparently sought to acquire such weapons, including Al Qaeda, the PLO, the Red Army Faction in West Germany, Hizballah in Lebanon, the Kurdistan Workers' Party in Turkey, and neo-Nazi groups in Germany (Cronin 2002/3: 48). The danger that a terrorist organization can successfully manufacture or acquire such weapons is likely to increase. The focus on the possible use of such weapons of mass destruction may even have encouraged terrorists to think about obtaining them (Merari 2005: 64). Terrorist groups may be unwilling to use these weapons because of technical difficulties or expense, but clearly some groups are willing to inflict mass casualties. Thus, while gaining operating weapons remains difficult, there are groups that will be more willing to use them once they are acquired (O'Neil 2003: 110). With the passage of time there will be a learning curve, which will probably lead to greater knowledge of the problems involved with the development and use of such weapons—and solutions to these problems. Any such weapons will become more effective as terrorist groups learn from their own past mistakes and the mistakes of others and as the knowledge and technology for the use of such weapons diffuse even further. Since terrorists do emulate each other, and the successful use of weapons of mass destruction by one group could trigger similar attacks by others (Stern 1999: 74). There is also a continuing possibility that some governments might make effective biological or chemical weapons available to a dissident organization. Governments are unlikely to supply such weapons to terrorist groups because of a fear of retaliation if the weapons can be traced to them. Doing so might generate significant risks for the country, but if the country or its government is facing a major crisis or the threat of defeat in war, it might be willing to gamble on being able to avoid retaliation for providing the weapons.

TARGETS

One of the most significant choices that any dissident group has to make is the selection of targets for a terrorist attack. Targets can be chosen in order to cause the greatest damage, generate the most fear, or to attract recruits (Heymann 2003: 52). Where will the attack take place? Should the targets be human or simply physical objects? Should the targets include buildings or people associated with foreign countries? Should the targets be chosen on the basis of their symbolic value or because they are representative units of a larger group defined in political, social, or economic terms by the terrorists? While the appearance of randomness increases anxiety in target audiences (Enders and Sandler 2006: 3), what is very rare is the situation in which targets are really random despite the common misperception that terrorists do not care who or what the targets are. Terrorist groups are very rational in their choice of targets, evaluating strengths and weaknesses, costs and benefits (Long 1990: 139). Target choice is rarely indiscriminate (C. Drake 1998: 53). The targets that are chosen have at least some linkage with the goals and objectives of the terrorist groups. Dissident groups can also strategically use terror as a force multiplier. No matter how barbaric the actions may appear, they serve a rational purpose (Vinci 2005).

Structures and people as targets

Terrorist organizations will at times restrict themselves to efforts to damage property. In fact, the vast majority of terrorist incidents are not directed at people. Between 1968 and 2001, there were either no fatalities or only one fatality in almost 96 percent of international incidents (Stohl 2003: 86). Bombs will be set off in buildings at times when it is expected that they will be unoccupied. The building may have a very specific connection with the political concerns of the dissident group. It could be a government office or a party headquarters in a one party state or even in a democracy where the party in question is considered to be closely tied to the establishment. It could be a religious building associated with the dominant group or a minority religion that is seen to be a threat. The offices of a particular business could be the target because of its links to a group or party in power. Newspapers, labor union offices, radio stations, professional associations, and other buildings could all be potential targets in a particular national context. The target possibilities with buildings are legion, but they will vary according to local circumstances and the political goals of the organization that has opted to use violence. The numbers involved will usually be far too many to be effectively guarded by police, troops, or private security personnel.

Some targeted buildings or structures could have symbolic value. National monuments would be a case in point. Their damage or destruction would indicate that any part of a society is vulnerable. If a highly regarded national monument can be successfully attacked, then almost any property or building would be in danger. If a government cannot protect obvious targets, it is not likely that it will be able to guard the less obvious ones. Of course, attacks on symbolic national monuments are not equally likely with all kinds of terrorist groups. A separatist group or a national liberation movement would have the most incentive since likely supporters would be indifferent to the loss of someone else's national monument. A non-separatist group, however, would be less likely to attack such a symbolic target since it would alienate potential supporters.

A terrorist group concerned with global or national capitalism or simply globalization in general could target a particular corporate office or regional headquarters that is a symbol of the free enterprise system (Ford, Coca-Cola, British Petroleum, IBM, Microsoft, Volkswagen, Phillips, or Nestlé). Any government building might be bombed to indicate the vulnerability of such offices. A stadium, statue, or other building project associated with a particular ruling party, leader, or group would have such high salience that the symbolism would be obvious. The two attacks on the World Trade Center in New York, even though designed to cause large numbers of human casualties, also represented a symbolic target. The World Trade Center served as a symbol of American economic might, the global importance of US capitalism, and of all the changes that come with modernization. The symbolism was even greater for the second attack in 2001 since the first attack was largely a failure. The second attack demonstrated that even if a building survived one attack, it could succumb to a second. Similarly, the attack on the Pentagon targeted an important symbol of the United States. Most other countries also have structures with similar symbolic values as targets—Westminster Abbey, the Eiffel Tower, the Taj Mahal, the Colosseum in Rome, the Acropolis in Athens, the Imperial Palace in Japan, or the Hermitage in St Petersburg. Attacks on such symbolic buildings would spread the fear that many terrorist groups seek and generate the media attention that is often so essential for broadcasting their message to the world.

While terrorist organizations may restrict their attacks to property as a means of demonstrating their concern for the population and to try to maintain popular support, many organizations will eventually move on to attacks on people. It is a rare circumstance in which property attacks alone will be sufficient to force a government to change policies, to create a new political system, or to allow a region to become independent. If a dissident group perceives conditions to be so oppressive that attacks on property are required, graduation to attacks on people is likely. The human targets can be specific, symbolic, and more general, just as property attacks can be.

Specific attacks on individuals may be undertaken because of their particular action as individuals. Assassinations of especially unpopular individuals may also serve the positive benefit of creating support for the terrorists and reaffirming the support of members of the organization (C. Drake 1998: 54). Of course, eliminating an extremely unpopular individual may be counterproductive since one source of popular irritation with the government has been removed. A judge will be killed or wounded because he or she sentenced members of the group to death or to long prison terms. A member of the security forces with a reputation for torture is killed as punishment for his activities. For the assassination to be terrorism, however, there does have to be a target audience, which could include other judges or police officials. A police official or judge may be targeted because of their positions supporting the (oppressive) legal system of the states. Any police official or judge can be chosen as a representative of the group. Similarly, a member of the national legislature could be the victim because he or she is a member of a class of politicians who are refusing to make the appropriate changes in government policy. Business executives, labor leaders, journalists, government workers and teachers, and officials of political parties could also be chosen if they are perceived to be representatives of groups that are supporting or collaborating with the government. The wide range of potential targets provides dissidents with a major advantage. There are far too many individuals to be effectively protected. Some attacks will be successful sooner or later, although effective security agencies may be able to track down the persons involved once they have struck. Human targets may be chosen for their symbolic value. Members of a royal family may have no political power or influence, but they may symbolize the nation or institutions under attack. High-ranking clerics or media personnel, actors or musicians, or others may also have similar symbolic value. When an IRA bomb killed Lord Mountbatten near his country home in the Republic of Ireland, it was a symbolic attack. Mountbatten was a hero from World War II, and a cousin of Queen Elizabeth II. He played no role in policy-making in the United Kingdom, and he was actually retired. He did, however, symbolize the long-standing British presence in Ireland.

The potential target group can be even larger. If ethnic, linguistic, or religious differences separate a society, any members of groups that the terrorists oppose may be considered targets. The attacks could be intended to eliminate group support for disliked policies or government leaders or even to convince members of these groups to leave a particular region of the country or even the country altogether as part of a policy of ethnic cleansing. The general population can serve as potential targets for the terrorists to publicize their goals and to seek to change the government. Actions causing significant casualties and disruptions will be intended to indicate to the population at large that the existing government cannot protect them. The government will have failed to provide security, a primary function of government (Chalk 1998b: 376). Even if dissidents set off the bombs, the government could be held doubly responsible for the carnage. First, the government either created the situation that led to the creation of the terrorist group or allowed a situation to continue that led to the violence. Second, the government will have been unable to prevent the violence. The end to the violence will require that the general population stops supporting the government in power, requiring that government to change policies or permitting the dissidents to establish a new government.

None of the above situations involve random violence. The attacks are designed to inflict casualties on a particular group, and the group may indeed be an entire national population. The violence and death is not undertaken to inflict pain for the pleasure of doing so but to send specific messages to target audiences. If an entire population begins to fear, the goals of the terrorist may have been achieved. At times they will simply be average citizens in the wrong place at the wrong time when a car bomb explodes in a shopping area. If average citizens are the chosen targets, it would indicate that the terrorists are seeking to induce fear in as large a portion of the population as possible to indicate that virtually no one will be safe. Compromise by the government or even surrender becomes more credible to the population if fear becomes widespread. Since many terrorist groups have failed in their political objective, the loss of life may indeed be pointless, but these circumstances do not mean that the attacks were random.

Attacks on foreign interests can also be part of a logical campaign to undermine a domestic government. Like other terrorist attacks, these attacks will not be random but part of a planned effort. External countries may be providing significant support to the government in power, perhaps even making it possible for the regime to survive (Byman 1998: 161). The aid might be as direct as providing arms, anti-terrorist equipment for the police, training in interrogation techniques, and the gathering of intelligence data on dissidents living abroad. Attacks against the foreign interests may persuade the foreign government to cease support because they realize there is real domestic opposition or simply because it thinks its local ally is incompetent. Personnel involved in the provision of economic aid could also be likely targets for two reasons. First, economic aid is likely to strengthen the government in its struggles with dissidents by increasing its capacities to offer resources to wavering groups or to appease the population in general with items such as subsidized food or fuel prices, increased wages, or new infrastructure projects in a politically volatile region. Thus, economic aid can be a direct threat to the dissident organization. It can also be an indirect threat as well. Some foreign countries will not supply military aid to a government; they limit aid to economic projects in an effort to avoid increasing the military or repressive capacity of the government. Every million dollars of economic aid, however, may permit a government to divert a million dollars of locally raised revenues to buy arms or increase the size of the security forces. As a consequence, economic aid projects that simply seek to help the people may, in fact, provide benefits to the government in terms of its ability to coerce or defeat internal dissidents. When the hand of the government security forces is strengthened in this fashion, it is much more difficult for the internal dissidents to achieve their goals.

For similar reasons, foreign economic activity may become a target for terrorists (J. Lutz and B. Lutz 2006b). Terrorist attacks can lead to reductions in foreign investment, especially when attacks are directed at foreign facilities (Enders and Sandler 1996). Terrorist efforts to limit US foreign investment abroad have had different effects in different countries but have generally been an effective tactic (Enders *et al.* 2006). Foreign workers in key industries may be targets as well. If selective attacks on technicians or other workers can disrupt key industries or the extraction of natural resources, then the tax base of the government and the revenues available will be reduced. Tourists have become targets in some countries. The attacks on tourists have sometimes been seen as random and to be a reflection of the fact that the terrorists enjoy violence. These attacks, however, have a clear purpose. Any successful attack, and even unsuccessful ones, severely hurts the tourist industry. In some countries tourism brings in badly needed foreign exchange and provides additional revenue. A successful attack leads to tour cancellations and a drop off in revenues (Enders *et al.* 1992). The resource base of the government is hurt and a political message is sent to the world at large. The bombing in Bali in Indonesia clearly had such an effect, even if the principal reason for the attack was anti-Western. Tourism clearly declined in the aftermath of the bombings. There were shocks throughout the Indonesian economy (Putra and Hitchcock 2006: 160). The Jakarta stock exchange lost 10 percent of its value and the loss to the Indonesian economy was approximately 1 percent of total GDP (Abuza 2003b: 3). There was even some expectation that the economic downturn from the drop in tourism revenues would increase recruitment for violent dissident groups since individuals are more susceptible to joining in hard times (Abuza 2003b: 166). Attacks against tourists by Muslim groups in Egypt have had exactly these kinds of effects on government revenues (Shultz 1994: 295). Tourism in Egypt declined by 53 percent in the wake of such attacks with the obvious negative consequences for obtaining foreign currency (Gurr and Cole 2000: 88). In Corsica, bombing campaigns have hurt the local tourist earnings (Soeters 2005: 2). The frequency of such attacks rather than their severity has so far had the greatest negative impact on tourism (Pizam and Fleischer 2002: 339).

It has also been logical for groups to launch attacks abroad in many cases—to internationalize the terrorism. In national liberation struggles it makes sense to carry the battle to the colonial power whenever possible. Attacks in other countries may be logical in other circumstances. When a foreign government is supporting the local domestic regime, attacks abroad as well as in one's own country can be part of the effort to change polices. Such attacks could be upon government offices, commercial targets, or the population in general. The violence sends a message to a target population, in this case a general audience in the foreign country. It is also possible for the attacks against the foreign supporter of the domestic regime to be undertaken in third, "neutral" countries. Thus, a dissident movement in Country A may regard Country B as an important supporter of the domestic elite in power in Country A. It may then launch an attack against a corporate office of a company from Country B or a consulate of Country B in Country C to send the message to the target audience that Country B is vulnerable around the world and will be forced to pay a price for supporting the regime in Country A. Country C may be chosen for the attack because of the presence of local supporters, because of limited security for the target, because of the minimal security and intelligence forces in Country C, or other factors. The choice of Country C for the attack is simply a matter of convenience for the dissidents. Dissidents in exile could also provide a local support network and local information for attacks in a foreign country, or the terrorist group may also have established links with a like-minded group in that country.

Vulnerability of democratic countries

Terrorist attacks may be launched in some countries more frequently than others, either by groups of domestic dissidents or by foreign groups seeking to attack their regime in more convenient locations. It has been suggested that democratic countries are more vulnerable to terrorist attacks than other kinds of political systems (Posen 2001/2: 41). Democratic countries with a commitment to civil liberties and basic rights find it more difficult to gather intelligence on citizens, to arrest, to interrogate, and to extract information. The effectiveness of the courts can also be undermined by the intimidation of witnesses or other illegal actions (Schmid 1992b: 19). The whole range of protections generally available in democracies makes both prevention of terrorist actions and the apprehension of terrorists after the fact more difficult. Even when alleged terrorists are arrested, convictions are not automatic. Rights accorded to the accused may mean that there will be insufficient evidence for a conviction. Democracies also provide legal proceedings for any terrorists who are caught. Conviction is not guaranteed, although it may be likely. The courtroom can also provide a valuable platform for the terrorists to publicize their cause (P. Jenkins 2003: 72). It is also possible that it may be easier to acquire the weapons or explosives needed for a terrorist action in a democracy, although the international market in weapons is often sufficient to supply the needs of many groups.

Democracies face other difficulties when dealing with terrorist threats. The limited possibilities for surveillance and detention all combine to encourage terrorist actions on their soil. In dealing with terrorist threats, democratic societies have to be careful to maintain the essence of their system—the rights of individuals. There are dangers of overreaction in democracies since publics will want their governments to take actions against the terrorists (Kydd and Walter 2006: 71). A society facing terrorist attacks may develop a siege mentality and permit actions that are contrary to the whole democratic system. A desire for expedited justice can lead to the creation of military tribunals with lesser standards for convicting terrorists (Chalk 1998b: 377). The country may also adopt procedures to provide for detention of suspects for lengthy periods of time without the filing of formal charges and overreactions by the government may even increase support for the dissidents (Reinares 1998: 363, 368–9). There can also be cases of rushes to judgment where suspects are poorly treated and confessions are coerced and other rights bypassed (Lutz *et al.* 2002). Even with problems such as these, however, the legal systems in democracies give suspected terrorists more rights than other systems. All of these factors may make democracies a more suitable setting for groups initiating violence. New democracies that lack strong political institutions may be especially vulnerable (Cronin 2006: 43).

In non-democratic countries, dissident organizations are more constrained. The least democratic governments with the most limited participation have been the least bothered by terrorism (Laqueur 2001: 220). In a totalitarian system where the government has comprehensive security agencies and informers everywhere, opposition is much more difficult to organize. Once suspicion focuses on an individual or a group of individuals, their activities can be monitored, mail opened, phone lines tapped, etc. Persons can be arrested on suspicion and questioned indefinitely. Searches can be arbitrary and undertaken at any time. Torture and drugs can be used to extract information from persons in custody. The investigation and arrest of suspects can proceed with relatively few limitations. Once the official agencies become convinced of the guilt of a particular individual, a conviction will be arranged (unless the state sees no need for a trial). In fact, the greatest threat to totalitarian rulers will come from attempted coups by fellow elite members rather than from domestic groups that rely on terrorism (Wilkinson 1975: 108–9). If the dissidents themselves cannot be readily caught, the government has other options. It can retaliate against family members and friends or hold them hostage or use other similar measures to convince terrorists to surrender or go into exile (Chalk 1998b: 386). Such regimes can also launch attacks abroad against the dissidents or their family members. Groups considering political violence will be limited under these circumstances, and the likelihood of surviving to conduct a long campaign of political violence is very low. The casualties among the group members are likely to be very high as well.

The deterrence that is present with totalitarian systems is fairly obvious in a number of cases. In the old Soviet Union, ethnic tensions such as those present in Chechnya today were not possible. The desires for autonomy and independence were clearly present, but the Soviet system had the capabilities to deal with any dissent quickly and effectively. Many of the successor states to the old Soviet Union are now dealing less effectively with dissident groups that are organized on the basis of nationality and ethnic differences or in terms of a different religious background from the regime elite or the majority of the state. Similarly, the violence in what used to be Yugoslavia did not occur until after the national Communist regime collapsed. Prior to that time ethnic differences had been contained by the power of the central government and the security apparatus at its disposal.

Authoritarian governments may have similar state capacities to control dissidents. If the security forces are active and well run, it will be difficult for opponents of the regime to use violent actions successfully. If they do so, they are likely to be caught. But not all authoritarian systems have the resources to detect and capture terrorists with ease. In a poor country, there may simply be too few resources to fund an effective security apparatus. Poverty, however, is no guarantee against efficient security forces. Haiti while governed by François Duvalier ("Papa Doc") was one of the poorest countries in the world and one in which dissidents and opponents were never permitted to organize (or to live). In poorer countries dissidents may have one advantage in that there are likely to be relatively isolated areas or limited transport and communications facilities available. Thus, a terrorist group might be able to retreat into the countryside and survive for at least a period time to mount attacks against the government. In other cases, the authoritarian regimes may be unwilling to use sufficiently harsh measures to control dissidents, and thus they will open themselves up to terrorist attacks. Authoritarian regimes, as a consequence, may be very capable of dealing with potential terrorist threats in some cases, and less effective in others. Egypt would qualify as a mildly authoritarian system that has been unable to eliminate Islamic domestic opponents. Syria, a somewhat more repressive authoritarian system, has been more effective in dealing with disgruntled domestic opponents.

It turns out that democracies have been more likely to be countries where terrorist attacks occur (Weinberg and Eubank 1998). The terrorists will also frequently gain the necessary attention if democratic governments maintain constant alerts or broadcasts information about threats, terrorist groups will have achieved both publicity and perhaps increased the psychological effects of their operations. Pape (2005) noted in a variety of contexts that suicide attacks have only occurred in democracies. While there may be some exceptions (Lebanon during its civil war, Pakistan in 2007), it is clearly a phenomenon most prevalent in democracies. It would also appear that while weapons of mass destruction have problems in terms of their usage, they are more likely to be used in democratic states (Ivanova and Sandler 2006: 433). Thus, not only are democracies more likely to be the scene of terrorist attacks, they are perhaps likely to be more deadly.

A geographic breakdown of incidents of international terrorism indicates that some democratic areas are prone to terrorist incidents while others have been normally immune. While the majority of terrorist incidents are domestic, the databases for domestic terror attacks are incomplete. For example, the overwhelming majority of deaths from terrorism in sub-Saharan Africa are domestic (Cilliers 2003), yet few incidents are reported, and these few tend to be ones that have international elements. Databases often rely on media reports, and such reports for this region are limited. A review of the information on international terrorism indicates that North America has the fewest such incidents among the various regions. There has only been an average of six per year (see Table 3.1). Western Europe, on the other hand, often has a large number of incidents. From 1980 to 1986 there were more incidents in Western Europe than any other region (Chalk 1996: 174). Many Middle Eastern dissident groups have found it easier to achieve publicity by launching their attacks in Western Europe (Weinberg and Richardson 2004). Since 1987 the region has often had large numbers of incidents. Latin America and the Middle East have been the other regions that often have had more incidents than Western Europe. The East European countries (the former Communist countries of Eastern Europe and the successor states of the Soviet Union) have had relatively few incidents but more in recent years. Figures for Asia and Africa have shown greater variability. These figures demonstrate the relative immunity of strong authoritarian states and the greater vulnerability of countries in transition.

When injuries in these incidents are considered, Asia most consistently had high levels, although it is obvious that any region could have high levels in a given year (see Table 3.2). The total casualty figures can be somewhat misleading. Western Europe had moderate numbers of casualties in most years while in North America it was either massive casualties or virtually none. A breakdown of casualties between dead and wounded between 1998 and 2002 indicates that fatalities are more likely in some areas. Western Europe, Latin America, and East Europe generally have fewer deaths, while North America has virtually none with the obvious exception

TABLE 3.1   NUMBER OF INTERNATIONAL TERRORIST INCIDENTS BY REGION, 1980–2006

YEAR	REGION							
	Africa	Asia	East Europe	Latin America	Europe	Middle East	North America	Total
1980	8	6	2	48	97	44	30	235
1981	6	7	2	68	133	58	26	300
1982	21	14	2	49	190	41	33	356
1983	20	26	2	56	98	64	13	279
1984	47	13	1	62	135	60	8	326
1985	30	16	3	74	154	151	5	433
1986	23	32	1	107	107	103	9	377
1987	28	53	0	88	91	95	6	361
1988	23	87	1	91	85	78	4	369
1989	20	47	2	133	83	65	9	359
1990	20	58	7	91	61	46	2	285
1991	13	43	10	122	126	102	4	420
1992	33	20	7	81	70	59	2	272
1993	57	26	19	47	55	65	3	272
1994	85	22	21	55	51	73	3	310
1995	48	21	18	22	118	39	0	266
1996	39	42	13	40	58	44	2	238
1997	16	33	20	40	22	27	13	171
1998	22	22	31	15	37	34	0	161
1999	21	10	8	7	59	20	2	125
2000	9	14	1	15	38	29	0	106
2001	8	31	5	16	24	118	3	205
2002	8	59	13	20	24	173	1	298
2003	15	52	5	24	39	142	0	277
2004	7	50	12	12	26	288	0	395
2005	10	54	8	15	20	203	1	311
2006	19	55	1	4	15	147	0	241

Source: National Memorial Institute for the Prevention of Terrorism (MIPT) website at http://www.tkb.org/ (accessed 2007)

of 2001 (see Table 3.3). While terrorists may often stage attacks in the democratic countries of Western Europe to generate publicity for their causes, they normally do not seek to kill large numbers of people. In the case of North America, the attacks have been different. The figures for North America (which in this case means the United States) are the most deceptive of all in these tables. In most years there are no international incidents. In 1993, there was only one incident (the first attack on the World Trade Center) with many injuries, but of these there were only a few deaths. In 2001, however, there were many deaths but the figures understate the number of wounded in the attacks against the World Trade Center and the Pentagon. It needs to be remembered, of course, that none of these tables include domestic terrorism. Deaths from

TABLE 3.2 NUMBER OF INJURIES DUE TO INTERNATIONAL TERRORIST INCIDENTS BY REGION, 1980–2006

YEAR	REGION							
	Africa	Asia	East Europe	Latin America	West Europe	Middle East	North America	Total
1980	85	27	3	19	117	56	27	317
1981	3	4	3	18	327	780	3	1,138
1982	5	28	0	17	307	354	26	737
1983	1	59	2	26	164	583	3	838
1984	36	48	0	45	191	179	29	528
1985	9	4	0	16	634	421	1	1,085
1986	22	260	0	63	522	347	22	1,236
1987	91	782	0	69	110	112	1	1,165
1988	83	1,363	0	89	222	73	2	1,832
1989	3	96	5	110	28	224	2	468
1990	37	43	0	58	40	142	0	320
1991	3	86	12	41	36	58	0	256
1992	136	8	13	284	58	56	1	556
1993	146	1,237	3	101	29	116	1,045	2,677
1994	108	20	62	250	49	590	3	1,082
1995	52	5,207	30	5	229	485	0	6,007
1996	125	1,581	18	19	280	934	111	3,068
1997	60	339	3	7	3	455	4	871
1998	5,185	47	11	6	1	100	0	5,350
1999	113	0	0	0	2	6	0	121
2000	2	31	10	0	10	52	0	95
2001	6	78	0	1	2	949	2,337	3,373
2002	100	569	661	36	6	1,582	3	2,957
2003	5	284	0	80	1	1,396	0	1,766
2004	227	482	34	1	614	6,14	0	2,023
2005	234	73	3	4	2	548	0	864
2006	114	95	0	19	0	245	0	473

Source: National Memorial Institute for the Prevention of Terrorism (MIPT) website at http://www.tkb.org (accessed 2007)

domestic terrorism in a number of democracies have been high, exceeding any damage done resulting from international incidents. The 1995 truck bombing in Oklahoma City was much more deadly than the first attack on the World Trade Center, but it does not appear in the statistics since it was a domestic terrorist act. The areas with consistently high casualties, both dead and injured, include the Middle East in most years and Asia or Africa in many years.

The figures in the various tables actually understate the importance of the United States as a target. While incidents on American soil have been rare, US interests abroad are often targeted. The attacks against the US embassies in Kenya and Tanzania in 1998 are a prime example. These car bombings explain the large casualty figures and number of deaths for Africa in 1998, yet

TABLE 3.3   NUMBER OF DEATHS DUE TO INTERNATIONAL TERRORIST INCIDENTS BY REGION, 1980–2006

YEAR	REGION							
	Africa	Asia	East Europe	Latin America	West Europe	Middle East	North America	Total
1980	51	2	0	48	38	17	5	161
1981	3	3	0	16	22	274	2	320
1982	11	7	1	15	32	39	6	111
1983	10	26	2	8	25	526	3	600
1984	25	38	1	10	53	49	4	180
1985	26	36	2	25	113	183	330	715
1986	19	72	1	25	27	207	0	351
1987	43	261	0	8	17	45	1	375
1988	35	263	0	25	310	69	0	702
1989	183	69	0	31	14	50	0	347
1990	19	46	0	24	8	22	3	122
1991	6	46	2	49	18	69 2	192	
1992	35	20	2	43	12	33	0	145
1993	56	342	5	10	13	35	10	471
1994	126	15	17	122	7	146	2	435
1995	83	92	2	8	21	87	0	293
1996	197	171	11	26	23	142	1	571
1997	89	82	12	10	6	45	2	246
1998	305	36	4	2	0	30	0	377
1999	51	4	0	3	1	6	0	65
2000	15	7	0	3	2	20	0	47
2001	10	50	10	2	1	129	2,982	3,184
2002	89	321	163	19	0	375	3	970
2003	42	92	0	8	1	327	0	470
2004	39	89	6	3	192	403	0	732
2005	79	54	1	1	0	416	0	551
2006	39	81	0	6	0	168	0	294

Source: National Memorial Institute for the Prevention of Terrorism (MIPT) website at http://www.tkb.org (accessed 2007)

the target of the attacks was clearly the United States and not the local African countries. Terrorism has negatively affected Americans abroad for many years. In the 1980s and the 1990s there were 666 Americans killed in incidents of international terrorism—most of them in attacks launched abroad, while 190 died from domestic terrorism (Pillar 2001: 19).

The fact that democracies are more frequently the sites where terrorist attacks do occur does not necessarily mean that the democracy itself is the target. A terrorist group from another country could choose to mount an attack in a democratic society against its home government that is authoritarian or totalitarian because security is weaker in the democracy. Western Europe has served as a convenient site in this regard. Embassies, businesses connected to the home government such as national airlines, or persons from the home country would all be potential targets. Bombing a building, kidnapping a business leader, or the assassination of a diplomat will occur in the democracy because it is easier to make the attack there than it would be in the home country. The same logic can hold true for mounting attacks on targets in weaker authoritarian systems. The bombing of the two US embassies in Kenya and Tanzania reflected such calculations. Tanzania was partially democratic while a single party with a pretense of democracy governed Kenya. Neither country has special ties with the United States or would be considered an ally, nor was either one of them on bad terms with the Muslim world. In fact, Tanzania has a substantial Muslim population of its own. Both, however, had relatively limited security services available, making any early detection of the bombing operations very unlikely. Both countries also had citizens of Middle Eastern descent in their populations, making it easier for the persons involved in the attacks to blend in with the population. In effect, these two countries were chosen for attacks because they were convenient for the terrorist organization in question. Some other terrorist group with a grudge against the United States or with a desire to bring about a change in US policy could just as easily have chosen embassies in some other country with limited security and intelligence services.

Other political systems can face greater dangers as well. Long-established authoritarian regimes where control mechanisms begin to loosen may be especially susceptible (Schreiber 1978: 28). Another type of political system that might be more likely to be chosen as the location for attacks, at least in the short term, would be a country in transition—one in which one type of ruling group is being replaced by another (Weinberg and Eubank 1998: 114). Protest against policies or government personnel can become more radicalized for countries undergoing a democratic transition (Bjorgo 2005b: 9). Even a transition from one type of authoritarian regime to another could leave a country temporarily vulnerable. Once the changeover is complete, however, the new authoritarian regime may be quite capable of dealing with challenges to its legitimacy. An authoritarian system shifting toward becoming a new democracy could be subject to attacks as well. While democracies have indeed been more vulnerable to some types of terrorism, the newest democracies have been the most vulnerable (D. Mousseau 2001). In any of the cases of a political system in the process of changing, if the old security forces have been discredited and eliminated with the fall of the old system, terrorists could have some important temporary advantages. Even if these weaker authoritarian system or systems undergoing transformation are not the targets of terrorist attacks as such, they could still be chosen for attacks against embassies or symbolic targets of other countries since their security apparatuses could be quite weak. Ineffective security arrangements in democracies and weaker authoritarian systems have, in fact, been considered to be a permissive cause (rather than an underlying cause) of increased terrorism (Crenshaw 2003a: 94).

There are some additional reasons why democracies or weaker authoritarian systems might be chosen for attacks. Terrorist groups seek an audience, and it is imperative that knowledge of the actions reaches that audience. If the group is attempting to reach potential supporters among citizens living aboard in exile or the population of the home country, information on the attack has to be disseminated. A totalitarian or strong authoritarian system might be able to repress or control the news if the attack occurs within its own boundaries, limiting the effective influence of even successful terrorist actions. Activities by anti-Soviet groups in the USSR after World War II were not broadcast, and the dissidents operated in isolation and were eventually eliminated. Thus, the attacks never reached the audience they sought to mobilize. In some countries, the news of the assassination of a local official in a state where news is controlled can officially become a traffic fatality or a heart attack. Other incidents can be ascribed to a variety of causes rather than political violence, effectively limiting the public attention that the terrorist action was designed to gain. The government will know the truth, but potential supporters of the dissident organization will remain in the dark. If the action is undertaken in a democratic society, however, the media attention will not be controlled since freedom of the press is present (Schmid 1992b: 16). The incident may only be minor news—hence the tendency of groups to undertake more noteworthy actions—but it will not be suppressed. If the action is spectacular enough, the media attention is likely to bring the political goals or the demands of the dissidents to public attention. With increased press attention groups may be able to raise funds abroad and to begin to pressure the government back home to change policies, at least by threatening to create global embarrassment or to indicate to the world at large that not all citizens are happy to live in a controlled, non-democratic setting. In the world of today with fax machines, the internet, and 24-hours news broadcasts via satellites in orbit, it is even possible that potential dissidents within the authoritarian or totalitarian state will become aware of the presence of like-minded people and what appears to be the existence of an effective dissident group.

Democratic states provide one more advantage for the dissidents. Fundraising opportunities may be more easily undertaken there. Civil rights and liberties will often make it difficult for the government to restrict such efforts, especially if the fundraising is undertaken in conjunction with supposed charitable operations. If funds are being raised locally, symbolic attacks may be launched in that country as well to spur the effort. If the dissident groups continue to be successful, it will receive funds from exiles, as it becomes the centerpiece to opposition to the regime at home. If the organization is successful, a democracy (or weak authoritarian system) may provide a situation in which the group can levy "taxes" on exiles to fund the effort back home. Funds could even be extorted by selective kidnappings to send a warning to other exiles. The kidnappings themselves can only be marginally considered terrorist activities, but they are being undertaken in the democratic society to pursue the political violence at home. For these efforts to succeed, publicity would again be a key.

While all democracies may be particularly good targets for attacks by terrorists, the United States is particularly appealing to a wide variety of dissidents. The United States has the dubious distinction of being the most favored target of international attacks (Wilkinson 2003: 110). Most of these attacks have been undertaken outside the United States since they are easier to undertake in those locales, but there is no doubt that the United States and its interests are the targets (Enders and Sandler 2006: 7). There are a variety of reasons for the targeting of the United States. It is a media center, so if publicity is important the effect is greater if US interests are somehow involved than in the case of an attack on smaller democracies. The United States is also symbolic of the West, modernization, democracy, capitalism, and multinational corporations. The United States with its long-standing tradition of distrusting government has meant that tracking "suspicious" individuals is difficult, even in the wake of the attacks of September 11th. There is no national ID card, and while social security numbers have been used in that capacity, Americans are not typically required to present their social security card. National government agencies are limited by law in their ability to exchange information among themselves. Literally, the right hand does not know what the left hand is doing much of the time, nor can the right hand legally find out. The CIA and the FBI, as the most important national investigatory agencies (Homeland Security could perhaps now be added), lack any institutional base for working together. While many governments separate the tasks of domestic counter-espionage from foreign operations, the two are generally linked more closely than the CIA and

FBI. In the United Kingdom there are similar problems. The Security Service (MI5) deals with domestic threats while the Secret Intelligence Service (MI6) (think "M" and James Bond) undertakes foreign operations. The two agencies may disagree and have different agendas. Further, even the American systems of federalism limits the effective responses that can be undertaken in some cases. A handful of national agencies, the state police of the fifty states, and countless thousands of local police forces must cooperate, a process that can be difficult at best and tremendously inefficient at worst.

The United States as the only superpower also becomes a more appealing target for some terrorists. Attacking the only surviving superpower in the world is a means of demonstrating the potential of the dissident organization and its abilities. The threat to target audiences is greater as a consequence. The United States as a superpower becomes a target because it is involved in political situations throughout the world. Terrorist organizations will attack because of US foreign policy decisions. In some regions the antagonism towards the United States as the symbol of the West is so high that any US activity is seen as having some malignant purpose (M. Mousseau 2002/3: 23). What terrorists believe the United States is doing is very important, and mistaken beliefs are not easily changed by modifications in US policy (Pillar 2001: 67). In other cases, terrorist organizations will target the United States because it failed to take any action. In effect, whatever the United States does or does not do can make it a target. Not all decisions of the US government in any given time period are always the best, but even decisions to undertake an action that is appropriate or decisions to stay uninvolved that are wise can generate adverse reactions by a dissident group. Groups that the United States fails to aid may target US interests, even if the United States does nothing to help the opposing side. The question as to whether the US government made the right decision is, of course, tremendously important, but equally important is the view of dissident groups abroad. If they disagree with US actions, for good reasons or bad, they can choose to launch attacks against the country.

SUMMARY

Clearly the tactics, targets, and weapons available to terrorists can be highly variable. An organization that is willing to risk its existence and its members in attacks will always be able to attempt violence. Sophisticated weaponry is not essential to begin a struggle, even if it would be of great value. The range of potential targets is very great. The resources of the terrorist organization and existing security measures will often influence the choice (C. Drake 1998: 54). Ultimately, "terrorists always have the advantage. They can attack anything, anywhere, at any time. We cannot possibly protect everything all of the time" (B. Jenkins 2001: 323). If the weapons available are limited, if the planning is poor, or if the security and intelligence forces are on their toes, the initial attempts will fail and the organizations will be crushed. If the attacks succeed, then the organization may gain strength, gaining additional funds and adherents to strike again. Many more terrorist efforts fail than succeed, for terrorism is a weapon of the weak, and acts of terrorism are designed to change the balance of power between the government and the challengers. If the dissident organizations were stronger, they would be able to try to utilize other avenues to create change. Some groups have been successful in bringing about changes, while others ultimately failed when the state opted for repression rather than compromise. A terrorist group that has some initial successes will have more scope to make choices. The choice of targets will have to continue to be non-random if the group is going to continue to be successful. Choices about weapons, techniques, and targets will become important in these contexts. Poor choices could result in the organization losing its momentum and eventually failing, even after a promising start.

TERMS

anthrax

Osama bin Laden

Chechnya

dirty bombs

Francois Duvalier

Lord Mountbatten

weapons of mass destruction

weapons of mass disruption

FURTHER READING

Enders, W., Sachsida, A., and T. Sandler, T. (2006) "The Impact of Transnational Terrorism on U.S. Foreign Direct Investment," *Political Research Quarterly*, 59, 4: 517–31.

Ivanova, K. and Sandler, T. (2006) "CBRN Incidents: Political Regimes, Perpetrators, and Targets," *Terrorism and Political Violence*, 18, 3: 423–48.

Kydd, A. H. and Walter, B. F. (2006) "The Strategies of Terrorism," *International Security*, 31, 1: 49–80.

Lutz. J. M. and Lutz, B. J. (2006b) "Terrorism as Economic Warfare," *Global Economy Journal*, 6, 2: 1–20.

O'Neill, A. (2003) "Terrorist Use of Weapons of Mass Destruction: How Serious Is the Threat?" *Australian Journal of International Affairs*, 57, 1: 99–112.

Weinberg, L. B. and Eubank, W. L. (1998) "Terrorism and Democracy: What Recent Events Disclose," *Terrorism and Political Violence*, 10, 1: 108–18.

CHAPTER 4

State Sponsors and Suporters of Terrorism

One area of contention that has surfaced in regard to terrorism has been the extent to which foreign countries have sponsored such activities. In many cases it is foreign governments that have been considered responsible for the bombings, hijackings, and assassinations. It is argued that without the involvement of these foreign sponsors, the terrorist threats to domestic peace and security in another country would disappear. The definition of the problem presupposes the answer. The solution to the problem would be a foreign policy issue. Diplomatic pressure, economic threats, or even military force might be used to encourage the foreign government to do the right thing. If one of these methods fails, then another can be tried if the international situation is conducive to some other action. In addition, counterintelligence agencies can be used to deal with the foreign operations in a particular country and to deal with their local collaborators. Ultimately, if foreign sponsorship is the cause of domestic terrorism, it can be defeated abroad. If foreign sponsorship is not responsible for domestic terrorism, however, then efforts directed against foreign nations will be much less successful. Foreign support of terrorist organizations can be direct, but much more often it is indirect.

TRUE STATE CONTROL

The truest form of state sponsorship of violence in other countries for political ends would be situations in which intelligence agencies actively plan the actions, train the operatives, issue orders, and then send them off to carry out these orders. This kind of state sponsorship of violence is part of ongoing conflicts between states that occurs at the covert level. These kinds of violent actions really do not meet the definition of terrorism as provided in Chapter 2 since the activities are state to state ones. Most actions by national security services are designed for intelligence gathering purposes, but activities can also include sabotage, economic disruption, bombings, and assassinations. Governments have accepted this type of activity by themselves and their foes or potential foes as one of the normal consequences of being involved in international policies.

Some violent activity is carried out by state agencies. During the Cold War the CIA and KGB were quite active in violent activities. Sometimes, the actions involved agents of allied states. Radio Free Europe relied on refugees and dissidents from Eastern Europe to serve as analysts and broadcasters for sending news and propaganda to various parts of Eastern Europe and the Soviet Union behind the Iron Curtain. In 1978 in London, members of the Bulgarian secret service assassinated a number of these employees in the finest James Bond tradition. Special umbrellas with deadly poison (ricin) in the tips were used to jab these individuals in the leg on crowded London streets or in the subways. These attacks were clearly state sanctioned and directed, and not just by Bulgarian authorities. Any special operations such as these using special poisons had to be approved by the KGB advisors who ran the Bulgarian secret service. The use of Bulgarian personnel as surrogates, however, technically distanced the Soviet Union from the attacks in case of exposure (and the British authorities did determine what was occurring).

Israel has been active in both direct and indirect use of violence to achieve objectives through the use of violence. The Israelis have undertaken foreign assassinations against selected targets. Israeli agents tracked down most of the members of Black September involved in the 1972 Munich Olympic attacks and killed them (Silke 2003b: 220). Israel even used "false flag" operations. In 1954 sympathetic Jews in Egypt used bombs and arson against US installations. The objective was for local Arab radicals to receive the blame for the attacks in order to prevent improved US–Egyptian relations (Arian 1998: 111). In 1978 Israel was alarmed at Iraq's efforts to build a nuclear reactor. After diplomatic efforts failed to deter firms from supplying parts to Iraq, Israel resorted to more direct measures. Parts bound for Iraq were sabotaged. Attacks were made on Italian and French companies that were providing the parts for the reactor, and their employees were threatened—all as part of an effort to stop shipments. When both diplomacy and covert operations have failed, Israeli aircraft launched a surprise raid on the reactor in 1981, destroying it only months before it was due to become operational (Stern 1999: 115). Israel also assassinated a member of the Iraqi Atomic Energy Commission and Gerald Bull, an English munitions expert, who was attempting to develop a super long-range gun for Iraq (Richelson 2002: 249). The kinds of operations undertaken by Israel are typical of the actions that governments can undertake. The targeting of the private companies and their employees clearly was an effort not only to disrupt the supply of parts to Iraq but also to intimidate and terrorize a target audience into compliance with the wishes of the Israeli government. Another example of such direct state sponsorship would be the bombing of Pan Am Flight 103 over Lockerbie, Scotland in 1988. It was planned and carried out under the orders of the Libyan government, and the bombing would not have occurred without the action of a government. Using the camouflage of a terrorist attack was important for deniability by the government since open acknowledgment of the attack was not possible.

While some activity is directly undertaken by the intelligence agencies of various countries, more frequently state sponsorship has been used to refer to situations where a country trains, funds, and controls domestic groups that are involved in political violence in another country. The groups in these circumstances are indirect agents of a foreign power. This type of sponsorship implies that if the foreign country withdraws its support, either because of policy changes, shifting alliances, or a threat of retaliation, the domestic terrorist group would collapse. Both direct and indirect state sponsorship has important implications for the domestic terrorist activities. If the groups are indeed funded and controlled from the outside, the government has not failed to serve its own citizens. Such presumed foreign sponsors, however, can serve as convenient scapegoats for domestic violence that could be the direct consequence of ill-considered government programs or policies.

There are examples of situations where foreign support has been highly important for the continued existence of opposition groups that have resorted to violence. There are other cases where a foreign government effectively controlled political groups that were willing to undertake violent activities even when the groups had a base in their local societies. The National Socialist (Nazi) parties in Austria and Czechoslovakia in the late 1930s were prominent examples. In the case of these parties, they were reflections of right-wing discontent with the Austrian and Czech governments and policies. They were clearly not an invention of the Nazi Party of Germany, nor did they exist solely due to external support. On the other hand, they did respond to directives from the Nazi Party in Germany and, after 1933, the German government. Protests, political activity, and violence increased or decreased in response to outside directions. In these cases the local terrorist activities did reflect outside sponsorship in a fairly clear way.

Similarly, in the period before and after World War II various national Communist parties around the world took their cues directly from the Soviet Union while that country existed, even though very real national domestic problems and concerns for the plight of the working class led to their formation in many countries. After World War II, local Communist parties frequently underwent contortions in terms of changing their policies to support or attack different governments on the basis of their relationships with the Soviet Union. The Egyptian Communist Party, for example, was called upon to support the government of Nasser when Egypt became an ally of the Soviet Union, even though Nasser was in the process of eliminating the Egyptian Communist Party and arresting its members. These Communist parties were clearly accepting foreign direction and foreign support, and they undertook at least some violent actions at foreign direction. These parties, however, would have continued to survive without foreign support, even if they would have been less effective in some cases.

STATE SUPPORT OF FOREIGN TERRORISTS

Most charges of state involvement in terrorist activities have involved situations in which foreign governments had aided terrorist groups that already existed in some other country. Such state support can be very important in increasing the capacity of terrorist groups, expanding the geographical range of possible actions, and making their attacks more lethal (Veness 2001: 409). Governments have been quick to take advantage of opportunities to weaken their enemies or potential enemies, including the provision of support to dissident political movements. If a political movement appeared that caused problems for an enemy or potential enemy, then it was appropriate to assist and encourage that political movement. If the dissident political group resorted to violent attacks and terrorism, then it made sense to provide weapons, money, and a safe refuge. Governments will also train members of dissident groups in the use of weapons and provide expert training for the construction and detonation of bombs. The United States tolerated the activities of anti-Castro Cuban exile groups in the United States and supported their activities abroad. These groups attacked Cuban interests in a number of countries and targeted companies that did business with Cuba (Gurr 1989: 221–2). They also attacked Cuban exiles who were regarded as being in insufficiently zealous in opposing Castro (Hewitt 2000: 5). State aid to such dissident groups can take other forms, including the use of diplomatic pouches for communications or arms or the provision of false passports, or even diplomatic passports (Rathmell 1997b: 655–6). Such support would be a relatively inexpensive foreign policy tool. In addition, from the government perspective, these groups were expendable and support could be stopped with little disadvantage if governmental foreign policy should change. Even so, it is important to note that these groups existed and would continue to exist without the foreign support. Any dissident political group capable of undertaking an extended political campaign of terror must be grounded in its own society (Rubenstein 1987: 63). The external aid is useful and even important, but it is not essential. Further, foreign governments did not control these groups. The groups themselves determined their political agendas. They might consult with their foreign allies, and even take their interests into account, but they did not take orders from them. This lack of control is another factor that clearly sets state support for terrorist groups that have been recipients of weapons or money from abroad apart for state terrorism or state sponsorship.

Examples of foreign governments "fishing in troubled waters" in the above fashion abound through the ages. During the long Peloponnesian Wars, Sparta and Athens regularly intervened in the internal politics of other Greek city states. Sparta supported aristocratic factions against more popular groups in efforts to separate allies or satellites from Athens, while Athens supported more democratic factions against aristocrats in an effort to convert Spartan allies to its side. Intervention in supporting royal pretenders, separatists, and potential heirs was practiced by many states and empires in later eras as well. In other cases, governments have supported violent groups in states that they have sought to weaken. The Black Hand and the Serbian government were linked in the early 1900s. The goal of the Black Hand was independence for Slavs located in other states. The group was especially interested in detaching areas inhabited by Serbs from Austro-Hungarian rule and uniting them with Serbia. The Black Hand, and indirectly the government of Serbia, supported political dissidents in their violent attacks, the most important case being the aid that was present for the assassination of Archduke Franz Ferdinand, heir to the Austro-Hungarian throne, in Sarajevo in 1914. This assassination triggered the outbreak of World War I, a conflict in which Serbia itself was defeated and occupied, paying the price for attempting to weaken a threatening neighbor. Notwithstanding the presence of support from Serbia, the opposition to Austrian or Hungarian states by dissident Slavic groups within the Empire was a result of domestic situations and would have been present even in the absence of external Serbian support. While governments may prefer to support dissident terrorists with similar religious values or ideologies, it is not essential that there be any compatibility in terms of shared values (J. Lutz and B. Lutz 2006a: 91).

One other type of foreign involvement should be mentioned in passing before discussing the case studies in detail. Dissident political organizations that have resorted to the use of violence have often had support in diaspora communities. Diaspora groups can prolong violence by dissidents in their home country by contributing funds (Fair 2005). In addition, to giving moral support and financial aid to dissident groups, supporters abroad have applied pressure on other governments to support the dissident causes. If the diaspora community is important enough, foreign governments may find it difficult to interfere with fundraising, recruitment, sheltering of key figures involved in the violent movements, or even the purchase of arms. For example, the IRA has been able to more or less openly raise funds in the United States, and the PLO has maintained widespread support among the Palestinian community worldwide (Byman

BOX 4.1 KOREA: NORTH VERSUS SOUTH

Beginning a few years after World War II, North Korea began to launch numerous terrorist attacks against the Republic of Korea (South Korea), sandwiched around the invasion of the South. The North Koreans often relied on their own agents or spies for these actions, but at times they used South Korean dissident groups as well. In addition to sabotage and other forms of terrorism, there were a series of assassination attempts against South Korean presidents. In 1974 President Park Chung-hee survived an attack that killed his wife (Nahm 1988: 414–15). In 1983 five cabinet ministers were killed in explosion during a state visit to Rangoon (Yangoon) in Burma (Myanmar), but the president survived the attack (Kirkbride 1994: 73). In 1987 North Korea was behind a bomb explosion that killed 115 persons on a South Korean airliner. The destruction of the aircraft was part of a concerted effort to undermine the Seoul Olympics and to put South Korea in a bad light (Harmon 2000: 158–9, 213). During the Cold War, North Korea was also active in providing training facilities for a wide variety of terrorist groups that operated in Western countries. With the break up of the Soviet Union and the end of the Cold War, however, North Korea repudiated the use of terrorism and support for terrorist groups in 1995 (Richardson 2000: 210). While North Korea did stop the overt support for terrorist groups, its continued efforts to develop nuclear weapons, even if not a concern in the struggle against terrorism, remains a major concern for neighboring countries and the United States.

1998: 161). In the case of the IRA and the United States, no president was ever willing to put the IRA on the official list of terrorist organizations. Had the group received this designation, fundraising would have been more difficult. The failure to do so provided indirect assistance to the group. Of course, the primary reason for not officially branding the IRA as a terrorist group was the voting strength of Irish-Americans in the United States. Other groups have received significant financial support from abroad as well (Fair 2005; Mohan 1992: 304). Diaspora communities with wealthy and better-educated members willing to support violence have usually been the most effective ones (Sheffer 2006: 126). In these types of cases the support by foreign governments resulted more indirectly from their reluctance or inability to interfere with the support activities of the communities supporting the dissidents. Inaction can sometimes be as helpful as action. The diaspora community was not responsible for the dissidence or the violence, but the continued assistance may be important for a more successful struggle.

The above examples of state support are very clear cut, but there are other ways in which states may be supportive of terrorist organizations. Countries have managed to avoid arresting a wanted terrorist on their own territory to avoid becoming a target for terrorist acts (Long 1990: 9). Prior to the 1980s, for example, France had a doctrine of neutrality in regard to international terrorist groups. As long as there were no attacks on France, the members of the groups would be left alone (Shapiro and Suzan 2003: 69). In 1977 French intelligence agents arrested Abu Daoud, a PLO leader implicated in the planning of the attack at the Munich Olympics. He was wanted in a number of countries, including West Germany and Israel. He was released, however, and quickly left France. The French government facilitated his release since his trial in France or his extradition to some other country would have disrupted French diplomatic and economic links with Arab states and exposed France to the danger of possible retaliation (Schreiber 1978: 55–8). Italy for a long time had a similar arrangement with the PLO. In exchange for Italian non-interference, the PLO agreed not to launch attacks in Italy or to target Italian citizens (Chalk 1996: 11). Obviously, a wide variety of actions and non-actions by a government can contribute aid in some sense for dissident organizations abroad that have used violence or which may use violence, and questions involving state sponsorship or aid can be quite complicated.

It has been generally conceded that active assistance by foreign governments for terrorist groups has declined since the end of the Cold War (Schmid 2005: 200). Without the counterbalancing superpowers in competition with each other, a country actively aiding terrorist organizations could become an obvious target for military retaliation. As a consequence, governments have usually had to become much more circumspect in providing any support to violent dissidents. The resulting reduction in access to foreign resources may have weakened some terrorist groups and made them less dangerous. Diaspora groups, however, could continue to provide important assistance for some groups. In addition, there is the possibility that groups with similar goals in different countries could cooperate with each other and provide mutual support.

CASE STUDIES

There are many examples of countries supporting or sponsoring terrorist groups in addition to the examples mentioned above. Four will be discussed in some detail below to indicate that almost any country may at times use such support or even sponsorship of domestic groups in other countries as part of their foreign policies, even when they ultimately do not control the groups. The first case is the most historical and deals with the support given by Italy and Hungary to opposition and separatists groups in Yugoslavia in the period between World War I and World War II. The second case involves the support given by Iran to various groups involved in terrorist activities, not only in the Middle East but also in Europe and elsewhere. A third case is the US support for the insurgent Contras in Nicaragua. While the Contras were more involved in a guerrilla insurgency, there were times when they relied more on terrorist actions. Finally, the assistance given by India and Pakistan to dissidents in the other's territory will be discussed.

CASE STUDY 4.1   ITALY AND HUNGARY IN YUGOSLAVIA: FISHING IN TROUBLED WATERS

Yugoslavia was created after World War I by the combination of a number of rather disparate territories. The old kingdom of Serbia served as the core of the new state, which expanded to include other territories, and the royal family of Serbia became the royal family for Yugoslavia. In 1918, Serbia included the Macedonian territories that had been acquired in the First and Second Balkan Wars, as well as some additional territory in this area acquired from Bulgaria in the peace settlements after World War I. The small kingdom of Montenegro was forcibly united with Serbia in the new state, although not without some opposition in the region (Banac 1984: 285–91). The new kingdom also acquired major territories from the old Austro-Hungarian Empire that disintegrated in the aftermath of World War I. Slovenia, Bosnia, Dalmatia, Croatia, Slavonia, and the Banat had been part of the dual monarchy. The disparate nature of the new country was indicated by its first name—the Kingdom of the Serbs, the Croats, and the Slovenes, which was changed only in 1929 to the Kingdom of Yugoslavia (Kingdom of South Slavs).

Internally, Yugoslavia reflected the many differences in the territories that made up the new kingdom. Serbia and Montenegro were both largely inhabited by Serbs who were Greek Orthodox and who used the Cyrillic alphabet. There were also Macedonians (South Serbs was the official terminology) in the southern part of the country in the areas acquired in the Balkan Wars and after World War I. The Macedonians were also Greek Orthodox, used the Cyrillic alphabet, and spoke a Slavic dialect that was linguistically closer to Bulgarian than to Serbian. There was also an Albanian minority in portions of Yugoslavia bordering on Albania who spoke Albanian (a non-Slavic language at its base) and were largely Muslims in terms of religious background. In the northern parts of the new country the Croats and Slovenes were Roman Catholic, reflecting their history as part of the Austro-Hungarian Empire, and they used the Latin alphabet. Croat was linguistically similar to Serbian, while Slovenian was more distant. In the Bosnian region there was a mixture of Serbs, Croats, and those who had converted to Islam centuries earlier when the region was part of the Ottoman Empire. The Banat region (Vojvodina) north of Belgrade, the capital, was acquired from Hungary. While a majority of the inhabitants were Greek Orthodox Serbs, there were significant German and Hungarian minorities in this area. Thus, the new state was a collection of differing languages, religions, alphabets, and governing traditions.

The new state was built upon the Serbian royal family and on the government institutions that had existed in the old Serbia. The Serbs were also the single largest group in the new country, although not a majority. The constitution for the new country created centralized institutions that favored the Serbs as the largest group in the states, and institutions of local government that would have been dominated by local majorities were abolished (Havens *et al.* 1975: 87). Serbian officials held most of the key positions in the government, and Serbs dominated the officer corps in the military. The officials of the new state used repression against non-Serb groups such as the Bulgarians, Macedonians, Albanians, and Muslims in Bosnia and Herzegovina (Banac 1984: 320, 367). As a consequence, there were tensions between the Serbs and the other groups in the country, and there was a perception that Serbs were inordinately powerful in the new country. Parties and politicians from other groups in the country boycotted elections or government institutions at different times to protest against Serbian influences, further disrupting the new state. There was overt opposition to the new government in Macedonia, and Croatian leaders began to seek greater autonomy and even independence from Yugoslavia in reaction to the perceptions of Serb dominance. Opposition in other parts of the country included violence and terrorist attacks. The assassination of Croatian parliamentary leaders in 1928 completely disrupted the political system and directly led to the establishment of a royal dictatorship in 1929 (Hoptner 1962: 7–8).

While there were real difficulties that appeared within the state, the dissension within Yugoslavia was exacerbated by disputes over borders with neighboring countries and claims by these neighbors to portions of Yugoslav territory. Serbia had acquired territory in Macedonia in the First Balkan War that Bulgaria hoped to gain and had taken additional territory at Bulgarian expense in the Second Balkan War and World War I. Yugoslavia had also gained territory in Dalmatia from the Austro-Hungarian Empire that Italy had expected to receive in return for joining the Allies in 1915. These territories were given to the new country instead to strengthen it, notwithstanding an earlier British and French promise to Italy. Similarly, Hungary sought to regain at least some of the territories that it had lost to the new state after World War I. Consequently, at various times, all three of these countries supported the internal dissidents when they could as part of their efforts to weaken the Yugoslav state. They all hoped to eventually acquire the disputed territories when Yugoslavia could not resist or when it collapsed.

Bulgarian efforts at supporting dissidents were largely confined to support for Macedonians seeking to unite their regions with that state. Hungary and Italy, on the other hand, supported various dissident groups throughout Yugoslavia (Poulton 2000: 92). Assistance was given to groups that were not linked to any territorial claims. The ultimate goal of this support was to weaken Yugoslavia and to make it more vulnerable. These two governments provided important support to Croat nationalist groups seeking autonomy or independence. Ante Pavelich, was the leader of a local Croat fascist party (Utashe)—one of the major dissident groups and one that was willing to use terrorist tactics. After fleeing the country, he established his headquarters in Italy, protected by Mussolini's regime. Hungary's authoritarian government also supported Pavelich and other Croat nationalist groups as part of efforts to destabilize Yugoslavia. Italy and Hungary provided funds and arms to the Croat nationalists groups and supported their terrorist attacks. They offered safe havens for individuals who had to leave Yugoslavia. They provided training camps for potential terrorists, and the Hungarian and Italian intelligence agencies passed along information to the Croat nationalists as well, and helped in the planning of some of their activities (Havens *et al.* 1975: 89–90). Fascist Italy in the 1930s was probably the country most involved in supporting terrorist groups in other countries. The Italian secret service was very active in clandestine operations and the prototype for providing assistance to violent dissidents in other countries (P. Jenkins 2003: 163). The assassination of King Alexander mentioned in the previous chapter took place with the direct involvement of these two countries, including the provision of funds and intelligence information.

Hungary and Italy did not create, control, or direct the domestic oppositions groups. They aided them because it was in their perceived national interests to do so. Such assistance was critical for weakening the Yugoslav state and was important in the successful assassination of King Alexander in France. Without Italian and Hungarian support, however, such an attempt on the monarch's life could have occurred elsewhere. There had been an attempt in 1921 that failed and at least one planned attempt earlier in 1933 that miscarried when the assassin lost his nerve (Havens *et al.* 1975: 89–90). The Croat nationalists benefited from the external support, perhaps especially in their terrorist attacks, but they were not dependent upon that external support to persist in their efforts to gain greater control of at least local political affairs. The Italian and Hungarian efforts were eventually successful in achieving their goals. The efforts to destabilize Yugoslavia weakened resistance to the German invasion that occurred in 1940. The country was overrun and partitioned. Italy and Hungry (and Bulgaria) acquired much of the Yugoslav territory that they had wanted. The Italian, Hungarian, and Bulgarian gains proved to be short lived since they were on the losing side in World War II and had to return the territories. The Croat opposition groups also initially benefited. After the Axis invasion, an independent Croatia was established under Pavelich, including not only Croatia and Dalmatia but also large portions of Bosnia. This state was allied to the Germans under these Croat nationalists, but its life as an independent state was limited. It disappeared in 1945 with the defeat of Germany in World War II.

CASE STUDY 4.2   IRAN

When the Shah was in power, Iran was not a supporter of terrorist groups, although the Iranian government did support Kurdish insurgents in neighboring Iraq as a means of weakening various regimes in that country. It is likely that the Shah would have supported terrorist dissidents in Iraq if such had been available, but the political violence by the Kurds was more in the nature of guerrilla activities and small-scale battles. Eventually the Shah stopped aid to the Kurds in return for Iraqi concessions in other areas. When the Islamic Republic was established in Iran, the government became more involved in supporting terrorist groups. Iran has even been considered to be the most active or among the most active sponsors of terrorist groups in other countries. Iranian involvement has taken a number of forms. The Republic attacked domestic exiles abroad. It has provided support to groups whose activities might in some way facilitate Iranian foreign policy objectives, and it has aided both fellow Shia co-religionists in other parts of the Middle East and more generally other Islamic groups seeking to force their governments to adopt a more decidedly Islamic form of governance. Training camps in Iran have been open both to Iranians training for battle and to members of many terrorist and guerrilla organizations. Iranian charitable organizations and funds for cultural groups have also helped Iran to develop linkages in various countries and to recruit allies and even members for terrorist organizations (Harmon 2000: 118–20).

The attacks on dissidents and former members of the Shah's regime would seem to have been undertaken by agents of the Iranian government. Much like the United States, Iran has maintained members of its intelligence services in its embassies abroad. And they have coordinated the assassinations of dissidents (Harmon 2000: 118–19). Iranian agents have eliminated a variety of dissidents abroad, including Shahpur Bakhtiar, who was a former prime minister when the Shah was in power. Attacks against opponents or potential opponents of the Islamic Republic have occurred in Europe and the Middle East by agents of the state or persons hired for the purpose (Hoffman 1998: 190–4).

Iran has also supported dissident groups in neighboring states in the region, partially in an attempt to increase the strength of Iran and to weaken neighbors, and partially in an attempt to establish governments based on the Shia version of Islam. A special coordinating office, the Islamic Revolutionary Council, was formed and training was provided to Iranians and others (Shultz 1994: 284–5). Iran expected that if such Islamic regimes were established, the governments would likely be allies of Iran. Iraq, some of the smaller monarchies in the Persian Gulf, and parts of Saudi Arabia are particularly vulnerable to this type of activity because of significant Shia minorities or even majorities. Iran has supported groups such as the Organization of the Islamic Revolution in the Arabian Peninsula, the Islamic Front for the Liberation of Bahrain, the Islamic Call Party, and the Supreme Council for the Islamic Revolution in Iraq. These kinds of support for various groups reflect state support for particular groups that have goals that are complementary to the state. There has been no doubt that Iran has provided funding and support for these groups in the Persian Gulf area, but it would appear that the dissatisfaction that Shia residents in these states have with their governments was already present, and Iran has simply taken advantage of the opportunity to further its own interests. Like many other states, Iran was supporting terrorism when it thought it could benefit by doing so (Green 1995: 594).

Iran almost from the outset of the establishment of the Islamic Republic supported the Shia Muslims in Iraq. The fear by the government of Saddam Hussein that Shia groups might undermine the legitimacy of his government was one factor in the Iraqi decision to invade Iran. It probably was not the dominant factor since Iraq has demonstrated its ability to deal with domestic opposition without too much difficulty on numerous occasions. Iranian support for Shia groups was clearly an irritant rather than a grave threat. Once actual war occurred between Iran and Iraq, support for such groups clearly became an element of direct state policy as one means for weakening a military opponent. As it turns out, the Shia dissidents did not prove to be a very effective military weapon against Iraq, but they were a relatively cheap weapon to employ. Iran's support of Shia dissidents elsewhere in the Gulf region, however, explains much of the Arab support for Iraq in its long war with Iran.

Iranian involvement with terrorist groups went further afield. The Iranians clearly supported a variety of groups involved in the conflicts in Israel and Lebanon. The Islamic Republic took a very hard line in the Israeli–Arab struggles, strongly supporting the Palestinians as fellow Muslims. Iran provided funds and weapons to various Palestinian groups including Hamas, Palestinian Islamic Jihad, and the Popular Front for the Liberation of Palestine-General Command (PFLP-GC). These groups have all rejected at some point in time the idea of recognition of the state of Israel, and they all have been involved in terrorist activities in Israel and the Occupied Territories of Gaza and the West Bank (Combs 2000: 80–1). The Islamic Jihad and PFLP-GC predated the appearance of the Islamic Republic, and they represented groups among the Palestinians who wanted to continue the struggle against Israel. Iranian funding and weapons strengthened their capabilities, but they did not depend upon Iran for their continued existence. Hamas appeared later and became more prominent after the Islamic Republic had been formed, but it drew its strength from support in the Palestinian community in the Occupied Territories and from Palestinians abroad. Iranian support was welcome, but hardly essential for the continuation of the organization.

Hizballah represented the Shia community that had long been the group at the economic bottom of Lebanese society. The Shia community of Lebanon had clear grievances with other groups in their own country. Iran became one of the most important supporters of the Hizballah organization in Lebanon. In fact, Iran's ambassador to Lebanon at the time was important in the creation of the organization, and Hizballah has been a major recipient of Iranian weapons and funds (Hoffman 2006: 265). Iran funded the training camps for Hizballah in Lebanon, and Iran was the principal source of weapons as well. Iranian diplomatic relations with Syria, which have tended to be good, have also been important since Syrian military units have been in control of the Bekaa Valley where the training camps have been located. Iran has also sent thousands of its paramilitary Revolutionary Guards to these camps where they supply support, staff, and training personnel (Harmon 2000: 118). Hizballah was much more effective with Iranian support, and it in turn supported Iran. After the Iraqi invasion of Iran, a car bomb destroyed the Iraqi embassy in 1981 and killed the Iraqi ambassador and seventy-one others; this attack was a Hizballah action (Kostiner 1989: 116). While Hizballah has acted at times in direct accordance with Iranian wishes as it did with the attack on the Iraqi embassy, at other times it has followed its own priorities. Iranian support for groups such as Hizballah and Hamas in Palestine has made them more lethal, but these groups are not controlled by Iran and follow their own agendas (Richardson 2005: 193).

Iran has also cooperated with the Islamic regime established in the Sudan. Sudan, like Iran, followed Islamic doctrines. The Islamic credentials of the government in power since 1989 have been impeccable. Although Sudanese follow Sunni Islam rather than the Shia version, the relationship has indicated Iran's willingness to work with other Islamic countries, notwithstanding theological differences. Sudan has had training camps for a variety of terrorist groups, including Egyptian groups opposed to the relatively secular government of that country, and Iran has provided funds and Revolutionary Guards to help run these camps (Shultz 1994: 286). Iran has also actively supported Sunni Islamic movements in Turkey, Egypt, and Algeria (Rathmell 1997a), indicating that Iranian support for Islamic groups at odds with their secular governments can be wide-ranging. In all these cases Iranian support is important to the groups in question, but such support is not essential to their survival.

Eventually Iran began to take a lower profile in terms of supporting terrorist groups abroad. By the 1990s the Iranian leadership had recognized that it had failed to export its Islamic revolution to neighboring states and began to use radical groups abroad more selectively to further its national foreign policy (Burke 2003: 109). There has been a softening of Iranian attitudes toward various countries and an apparent desire to move back into the mainstream of international relations and contacts. While such support has lessened, there continue to be many cases of Iranian support for groups abroad, and collaboration with regimes, such as Syria and Sudan, which themselves have been accused of sponsoring, supporting, or controlling terrorist organizations. The invasion of Iraq by the United States and its allies has led to increased tensions between these countries and Iran. Iran has been accused of aiding more militant groups in Iraq that have been involved on attacks on the government or Western forces (Hoffman 2006: 265). There is no reason to expect Iran to forgo the advantages of cooperating with terrorist groups whose actions may help weaken Iranian enemies, provide the government with opportunities, or otherwise facilitate the achievement of other governmental or national goals. Iran is likely to continue to support groups with an anti-Western orientation given its own conflicts with the West and concerns about Western influences and the continued presence of the state of Israel in the lands of Islam. Many Iranians would even like to see a massive Islamic state, the bringing together of the peoples of Islam under one government, as is seen to be the ideal for an Islamic society. Iran has consequently utilized groups that have been available because of the dissatisfaction of its members with policies, leaders, or the forms of government in their own societies.

Iranian support for terrorist organizations abroad has had both costs and benefits. The elimination of dissidents abroad has probably most directly benefited Iran since potential centers for opposition disappeared and others were cowed into silence. Support for dissident groups in Iraq during the long war with that country at best offset the disadvantages created by Iraqi support for Iranian dissidents. In other cases, Iran's support probably generated greater costs than benefits. The efforts to establish friendly Islamic governments in the Persian Gulf with Shia leaders in key positions failed. Not only was Iran not able to help these regimes establish themselves, but also Iran antagonized the ruling elites that remained in power. Support for terrorists in other countries resulted in international isolation; however, this support may have helped to consolidate the new government in Iran itself (Crenshaw 1995b: 23). Iran's connections with attacks on Westerners, including hostage taking by Hizballah in Lebanon, meant that Iraq received support from other countries as well. Concern expressed by the administration of George W. Bush about Iranian support for terrorism is evidence of the continuing costs of these policies.

CASE STUDY 4.3 THE UNITED STATES AND THE CONTRAS IN NICARAGUA

In July of 1979 the Somoza regime in Nicaragua was overthrown. The broad-based opposition had been led by the Sandinistas, a group with a leftist orientation that took its name from a guerrilla leader who fought against the regime put into place by an earlier US involvement in Nicaragua in the 1920s. The Sandinistas gradually eased the other groups that had participated in the struggle against the Somoza regime out of power, concentrating leadership into their own hands. The United States increasingly came to see the regime in power as a leftist authoritarian regime with links to the Soviet Union and its allies. One disturbing indicator was the fact that the military forces in Nicaragua were linked to the Sandinista party, not the state. Thus, the armed forces were organized as the Sandinista Popular Army, not the Nicaraguan Army, indicating that the primary loyalty of the military would be to the party. Many in the Sandinista leadership had determined that a neutral, apolitical army was not possible—the armed forces had to be politically controlled in order to avoid a situation in which the military could threaten the government (Pastor 1987: 199–200). As a consequence, doubts developed about the likelihood that there could be a peaceful transition of power from the Sandinistas to opposition groups should they win an election. In fact, the Sandinistas did win a majority in elections that had been held somewhat later than promised in 1984, after being postponed. The government used various means in its power in that election to make it difficult for opposition parties to field candidates, mount campaigns, and have an effective chance of winning.

All of the above characteristics did not really distinguish the Sandinistas when in power from any of the other authoritarian regimes in power in Latin America. US concern was present because the regime clearly had a leftist tinge, and the government in fact proceeded to develop close ties with Cuba and the Soviet Union and its allies. The United States also charged the regime in Nicaragua (with justification) with providing aid to the leftist forces in El Salvador that were fighting against the government of that country. Thus, there appeared to be a danger that the creation of an antagonistic, leftist regime in Nicaragua would lead to increased leftist rebellions and the establishment of more such regimes elsewhere in Central America. As a consequence, the United States was predisposed to support groups attempting to bring about the end of the Sandinista regime.

The initial opposition forces drew heavily upon members of the military under Somoza (Barry *et al* 1988: 89). As such, they suffered from linkages to the old regime that had become increasingly brutal and generated such widespread opposition that the effort to remove the regime had tremendous popular support. Their military activities against the Sandinistas were few and largely ineffective. Somoza himself provided the necessary leadership for these forces to undertake any action at all. His assassination in Paraguay in 1980, probably by leftist groups in South America rather than by Sandinista operatives (Pastor 1987: 217), removed a key leader from these forces. The opposition forces were thus in some disarray when President Reagan began his administration. The United States through the CIA began to supply increasing support to the opposition forces, counter-revolutionaries from the Sandinista perspective—hence Contras. Arms, training, food, medicine, and general funding came to the remaining forces in neighboring Honduras. Events in Nicaragua led to additional groups at least tacitly supporting armed opposition to the government in Nicaragua, and even some persons prominent in the initial uprising against Somoza came over to the Contra side. With increasing US support the Contras did become a more effective military force. US support was very important for the Contras, but the members of the units drew upon some real dissatisfaction with the Sandinistas, especially from peasants in the countryside (Barry *et al.* 1988: 89; Landau 1993: 61). The Contras engaged in both guerrilla attacks and terrorist activities. In effect, their incursions into the country were a combination of such actions, a fairly common situation in such insurgencies. The incursions proved to be relatively unsuccessful, notwithstanding major US support.

While the Contras were able to draw upon some real opposition to the Sandinistas in Nicaragua, they ultimately hurt their cause by the types of activities they undertook. The military incursions were frequently ineffective, and the Contras were never able to establish a safe base area within Nicaragua. Contra movements into the country increasingly focused on undermining the Sandinista political structure and on terrorizing the population. They murdered villagers with any connection to the Sandinistas or who appeared to support the government. Government officials, including teachers, doctors, relief personnel, and other officials attempting to follow through with reforms in the countryside were killed, while torture and rape were routinely used against civilians (Landau 1993: 39–46). The Contras were attempting to demonstrate that the government was incapable of protecting its citizens. The murder of government officials would make it more difficult for the Sandinistas to control the countryside or to rally support by the effective implementation of policies that were popular. Ultimately, these terror tactics failed. The Sandinistas proved to be strong enough to prevent the Contras from controlling the countryside, and news of the atrocities created adverse public opinion in the United States to such an extent that the US Congress enacted laws limiting aid to the Contras.

In the fighting between the Contras and the Sandinista Popular Army and local defense forces, the Contras had one advantage that is normally not present for insurgents fighting against regular military forces. The Contras were provided with sophisticated weapons and in many cases they were better armed than the Sandinista forces (Kornbluh 1987: 25). Although the better weaponry did not permit the Contras to win many battles, it did mean that it was also very difficult for the government forces to defeat them. The US support created a military stalemate, at least in the short term, where neither side was likely to win. The guerrilla insurgency by the Contras, and the terror associated with it, did destabilize the Sandinista regime. The economic reforms that had been promised with the overthrow of Somoza were in many cases never started or in other cases undercut by the fighting (Conroy and Pastor 1988: 220). The government had to divert resources to the military, and government officials attempting the reforms were often the targets of the Contras. As a consequence, the government suffered a loss of support due to its inability to deliver on its promises. The reforms may or may not have been productive in the long term, but they never had a chance to succeed or fail. When a reasonably fair election took place in 1990, the Sandinistas fell from power. Their electoral defeat was also due to a variety of other factors. There had remained groups opposed to the Sandinistas from the beginning and other groups that turned to opposition after the Sandinistas consolidated power in their own hands. Some were willing to vote for a change of government since so many Sandinista programs had not worked. It was clear to many voters that if the Sandinistas were defeated, US support for the insurgency would end, the Contras would de-mobilize, and US aid would be available to repair much of the damage of the war. Another factor of major importance was the decline of the Soviet Union as a major power. With the Soviet withdrawal from Eastern Europe and the manifest problems the Soviet Union was facing, it was unlikely that the Soviet Union could continue to serve as a counterweight to the United States.

The support provided by the United States to the Contras was eventually effective. They remained a military force and a threat to the Nicaraguan regime. Even when they were not launching attacks or when the attacks were defeated, the Sandinistas had to divert resources from other areas of government activity to deal with them. It is also evident that without such US support the Contras would have been much less of a threat to the government in Nicaragua. Since the Contras drew upon concerns and dissatisfaction with the Sandinista government from people in Nicaragua, the Contras were not a group that was created by the United States. Without US support, however, the Contras could have faded into relative insignificance since the Sandinistas had sufficient resources to deal with an unsupported insurgency. They had the goodwill and support of much of the population for the overthrow of Somoza, and they also received sufficient external aid from Cuba and the Soviet Union as additional resources. The US support was clearly sponsorship, and US "advisers" had tremendous influence with the Contras (planning some of the missions for them), but the movement fell short of being a US creation (Kornbluh 1987: 25). At a case before the International Court of Justice in The Hague in which Nicaragua brought charges against the United States, a majority of judges ruled in 1986 that the United States was guilty of breaches of international law for its support of attacks against Nicaragua. The court also ruled, however, that the Contras were not just an instrument of US policy (i.e., they had a domestic base in Nicaragua) and that the Sandinistas had indeed been aiding the insurgents in El Salvador (Pastor 1987: 257, 376n).

CASE STUDY 4.4   THE COLD WAR BETWEEN INDIA AND PAKISTAN

While great power conflicts explain much of the past state support for terrorist groups in other countries, states can develop animosities toward their neighbors that are independent of such larger conflicts. India and Pakistan have been in this type of situation since they became independent countries. The break up of colonial British India into two independent states involved a tremendous amount of violence and led to efforts at ethnic cleansing by Muslims against Hindus and by Hindus and Sikhs against Muslims. Massacres on one side of the new border led to retaliation on the other, resulting in a spiral of violence. When the attacks ended, at least half a million were dead and millions more had been driven out (Bell-Fialkoff 1999: 41). The violence inside the two countries in turn contributed to the outbreak of fighting between the two new countries. These two states have since fought a number of wars, including the one that led to East Pakistan successfully breaking away from the Pakistani state and forming the independent country of Bangladesh. Both Pakistan (i.e., the old West Pakistan) and India have since developed nuclear weapons capabilities, increasing the stakes and the dangers involved in the conflict between them. The conventional wars that have occurred between the two countries have been largely inconclusive; neither participant has gained any major advantages. The war that led to the creation of an independent Bangladesh was, of course, more conclusive, but while East Pakistan may have been an economic asset for a unified Pakistan, it was a military liability. The continual tension between the two countries and their wars (and skirmishes) makes it easy to understand why both have been willing to support dissident groups inside the other.

Local circumstances in both India and Pakistan have provided more than a few opportunities for the intelligence agencies on each side. The main intelligence services in both Pakistan and India are the Inter-Services Intelligence (ISI) units formed out of the intelligence services of the British Indian army. Pakistan has been an artificial state with relatively heterogeneous population groups that have relatively little in common. The differences between West Pakistan and East Pakistan, separated by thousands of miles of

Indian territories, were among the most obvious. The Muslim Bengalis and the population of the western part of the country had little in common beyond their religion. West Pakistan was also a diverse region with different ethnic or tribal groups. As a consequence of the communal violence at independence, Pakistan has been overwhelmingly Muslim. There is a Shia minority in the country, however, that has been at odds with the Sunni majority at times. Sunni terrorism against the Shia population has resulted in Shia retaliation and an overall increase in violence. The level of violence has been further increased by the arrival of Shia refugees from Afghanistan, who fled from the harsh policies of the Sunni Taliban regime (Laqueur 2003: 181). There have also been tensions between the original inhabitants of what is now Pakistan and the refugees who fled from what is now India (Singh 2002: 90). India, in turn, is also quite diverse. English is the only common language, and there are many different languages used for administrative and educational purposes. There are major linguistic differences between Hindu and related Indo-European languages in the north and the Dravidian languages in the south. While many Muslims were forced out of India in the violence at independence, many were unwilling or unable to flee and remained as Indian citizens. Today Muslims are the largest religious minority in a largely Hindu country, numbering approximately 140 million individuals (Bajpai 2003: 120). There are other religious, linguistic, or ethnic minorities in India as well.

The Indian intelligence services have been active at various times in aiding dissident groups in Pakistan. Pakistan suspected that Indian intelligence operations in Afghanistan were ultimately intended to weaken Pakistan's control of border areas, and the Indians have been at least partly effective with efforts to destabilize Pakistan by increasing the tensions between Shia and Sunni and between the original inhabitants and the refugees (Laqueur 1999: 153). Pakistanis were convinced that India was involved in supporting the dissidents in East Pakistan and providing clandestine assistance for the rebels. There is actually little doubt that India took advantage of this opportunity to weaken its traditional enemy. After the attacks of 9/11, Pakistan became important for the campaign led by the United States against the Taliban regime in Afghanistan and al Qaeda. The alliance of the government with the United States, however, generated disagreements within Pakistan. Some groups have been vehemently opposed to their government siding with the West against an Islamic government. This situation has provided additional opportunities for Indian intelligence operations that would encourage opposition to the government. Of course, a destabilized Pakistan with nuclear weapons may not actually be in India's long-term best interests.

Pakistan has clearly assisted groups that have used violence to challenge Indian rule in the state of Kashmir (Jammu and Kashmir). In 1947 Kashmir was a largely Muslim state (the much smaller Jammu is largely Hindu and has not been a center of contention). The ruler of the state, however, was a Hindu. He initially tried to make Kashmir an independent state that would not be part of either Pakistan or India. When he was faced with an armed Muslim insurgency, however, he opted to call upon India for support, a process that effectively led over time to the incorporation of Kashmir into India (S. Bhatt 2003: 217). Kashmir was one scene of heavy fighting in the first war between India and Pakistan. Pakistani and Muslim irregular forces occupied parts of Kashmir, but much of the province remained under Indian control. Muslim dissidents using guerrilla and terrorist tactics have been active in Kashmir. Some of the local political organizations have supported the idea of an independent Kashmiri state. Other Muslim groups have favored union with Pakistan. Over the years, Pakistan has consistently provided support to various dissident organizations, but especially to those groups that favored union (Mohan 1992: 299). Tensions and fighting in the state have increased in the 1990s and into the twenty-first century. The withdrawal of Soviet troops from Afghanistan and then the defeat of the Communist regime in Kabul had consequences for Kashmir. India anticipated the possibility that Islamic militants might redirect their attention to this area by clamping down on the dissidents, and rigging the state elections to guarantee victory for a pro-Indian political leadership (Burke 2003: 90). Militant Muslim organizations in turn began to look for other opportunities to fight a holy war on behalf of fellow Muslims. Groups such as Lashkar-I-Taiba and Harkat-ul-Mujahideen sent forces into Kashmir to help liberate it from Indian rule. Veterans of the Afghan wars and other Muslim volunteers from many countries began to filter into Kashmir with the toleration of the Pakistani government (S. Bhatt 2003: 220). By one calculation, 40 percent of the active militants in Kashmir in the late 1990s were foreign, and they outnumbered the native Kashmiris that were seeking an independent state instead of the union with Pakistan (Stern 2000b: 118). The influx of foreign groups has meant that groups favoring union with Pakistan have predominated in the struggle. The terrorist activities of these groups have spilled over into other areas of India. Kashmiri terrorists were responsible for the December 13th attack on the Indian parliament that left five terrorists and nine others dead (Wirsing 2002: 94). The Pakistani intelligence services and Kashmiri groups have also been blamed for the 2007 bombs that went off on commuter trains serving Mumbai (Bombay) in northwestern India. Even if Pakistan has not necessarily supported these groups or their attacks, the government has tolerated training camps in the country. In fact, it would have been very difficult for the government to crack down upon these groups without generating significant, and perhaps unmanageable, domestic opposition. Pakistani support for these groups may ultimately be a mixed blessing for the country. While the militant groups have been focusing their attention on the struggle in Kashmir, they ultimately also hope to turn Pakistan into a real Islamic state (Stern 2000b: 118).

Pakistan has supported dissident groups elsewhere in India as well. The government has clearly looked the other way or tolerated the activities of groups that have used the proceeds from drug sales to purchase weapons for attacks inside India (Feldman 2006: 358). India has faced a series of problems with ethnic groups and minorities in Assam and neighboring provinces. Pakistan, in some case with assistance from Bangladeshi intelligence agencies, has been involved in providing support for many of these groups (Saikia 2002: 191–2). There is always the suspicion that Pakistan has been supporting other dissident organizations in India and at times there has been some evidence of such external assistance.

Given the continuing level of conflict between India and Pakistan, it is not surprising that they have supported domestic terrorists on each other's soil. Any activity that would weaken their potential enemy could be useful. Since there has often been a danger of another conventional military confrontation, prudent defense policy would favor weakening the potential adversary by any means possible. India has larger armed forces than Pakistan, but the Kashmir insurgency has been a relatively cheap way for Pakistan to tie down a significant portion of India's military forces (Stern 2000b: 116). It is important to note, however, that neither India nor Pakistan has created the terrorist groups involved, nor do they control them. "Pakistan could not have sustained the current level of violence in Kashmir if there were not substantial local resentment to exploit" even though India could have more easily contained the violence minus the Pakistani support (Bajpai 2003: 115). While the internal dissent is real, foreign support has made the various dissident groups on both sides more dangerous.

SUMMARY

The above case studies illustrate the range of state support for terrorism that is possible. While non-state actors are involved in an overwhelming percentage of significant terrorist attacks, state involvement in terrorism can still be important (Badey 1998: 102). North Korea has most clearly involved itself in state directed and controlled terrorist activities. The kinds of actions undertaken were similar to the activities of the CIA, the KGB, and MI6, and other agencies during the Cold War. Terrorism became a common aspect of foreign policy during the Cold War. India and Pakistan have been involved in their own cold war with both countries aiding terrorist groups in the other. Israeli efforts to track down and assassinate individuals targeted as terrorists fit into this category as well. Support for terrorist groups in these kinds of struggles can result in unintended consequences, or what Johnson (2003) refers to as "blowback." For example, the United States provided support for Islamic militants in Afghanistan. Their victory over the Soviet Union ultimately resulted in the Taliban coming to power. The Taliban regime in turn facilitated the terrorist activities of Al Qaeda that are discussed in Chapter 5. Pakistan facilitated the training of militants in a variety of groups for the fighting in Afghanistan. The government has then had to face militant Islamic groups that are unhappy with some of its policies—another example of blowback. As noted in the discussion of the Kashmir insurgency, these kinds of problems could escalate in the future.

Many other nations, including Iran, have also used state agents to attack dissidents abroad as part of strengthening the domestic regime. Some of the support for various terrorist groups abroad was designed to further foreign policy goals. Syrian aid for groups during the Lebanese civil war and Libyan support for attacks in Europe, including the bombing of Pan Am flight over Lockerbie, are examples of countries using their own agents or surrogates to pursue policy objectives. It is important to note that such foreign policy objectives can be wide-ranging and include a wide variety of goals, increasing the possibility that state support might be available.

The United States with its support for the Contras provides an example of state sponsorship that was important to the continuation of a dissident organization. It is possible that the Contras would have faded into insignificance; the assistance from the United States made them more dangerous and probably prolonged their existence. The US foreign policy goal of establishing a friendlier regime in Nicaragua was ultimately achieved by its support of the Contras. The examples of Italy and Hungary in Yugoslavia and Iran in the Middle East are typical of the willingness of governments to use existing dissident groups to further their foreign policy aims. Dissident groups in Yugoslavia and the Shia organizations in Iraq already existed, but they obviously benefited such foreign aid. Most of the Arab countries of the Middle East have supported the PLO or other Palestinian groups at times. Iran has now become a supporter as well. This support in terms of funding, arms, and safe havens has been important in many cases, but Palestinian opposition to Israel was never dependent on foreign support for its existence or continuation.

Support by Iran for Shia groups in the Gulf area has been religiously motivated in terms of helping co-religionists. While it is true that Shia Islamic republics in the Gulf area would have some benefit to Iran as a country, the assistance seems to have been determined more by religious solidarity than by hopes of any immediate benefits for Iran. Support for the Shi'ites in Lebanon would seem to have been based on the same kind of religious linkage since greater power for Shi'ites in a state as small as Lebanon would unlikely be able to provide any significant foreign policy advantage for Iran. Further, support for the Islamic government in the Sudan and for political parties rooted in Islam in many other countries in the Middle East would seem to be religiously motivated rather than grounded in any perception of specific Iranian national interests although Iran has also been willing to pursue national interests as well.

In none of the above cases was state sponsorship or support associated with the use of weapons of mass destruction. Car bombs, bombs on airplanes, and other kinds of attacks do cause high casualties, but the state supporters would appear to have avoided providing terrorist groups with biological or chemical weapons. Clearly countries do have such capabilities, much more so than dissident or terrorist groups. North Korea has been developing a nuclear capability, and Iran is at least threatening to move in that direction. To provide a dissident organization with such weapons, however, would invite world condemnation of the supporting country and make retaliation possible. The benefits of doing so would normally be outweighed by the costs. As a consequence, to some extent it is possible that state sponsorship can provide a check on the worst kinds of attacks by terrorist groups. At the same time, however, lesser types of attacks might still be aided.

TERMS

Assam	
Shahpur Bakhtiar	KGB
Bekaa Valley	Lashkar-I-Taiba
Black Hand	Macedonia
blowback	Ante Pavelich
CIA	Popular Front for the Liberation of
Contras	Palestine-General Command (PFLP-GC)
false flag attacks	Rangoon bombing
Hamas	Revolutionary Guards
Harkat-ul-Mujahideen	Sandinistas
Hizballah	Shia
Inter-Services Intelligence (ISI)	Anastacio Somoza
Islamic Jihad (Palestine)	Sunni
Kashmir	Utashe

FURTHER READING

Bhatt, S. (2003) "State Terrorism vs. Jihad in Kashmir," *Journal of Contemporary Asia*, 33, 2: 215–24.

Green, J. D. (1995) "Terrorism and Politics in Iran," in M. Crenshaw (ed.) *Terrorism in Context*, University Park, PA: Pennsylvania State University Press, 553–94.

Hoptner, J. B. (1962) *Yugoslavia in Crisis: 1934–1941*, New York: Columbia University Press.

Kornbluh, P. (1987) "The Covert War," in T. W. Walker (ed.) *Reagan versus the Sandinistas: The Undeclared War on Nicaragua*, Boulder, CO: Westview, 21–38.

Shultz, R. H., Jr (1994) "Iranian Covert Aggression: Support for Radical Political Islamists Conducting Internal Subversion Against States in the Middle East/Southwest Asia Region," *Terrorism and Political Violence*, 6, 3: 281–302.

CHAPTER 5

Religious Justification for Terrorism

With the turmoil and conflict based in the Middle East and attacks against the United States at home and abroad, religiously based terrorist organizations have been in the spotlight. Religious justifications for violence, however, are among the oldest ones in the world. Religion is one important source of group identity that can provide for unity in a community (Juergensmeyer 1996: 5). Given its ancient roots, it will be discussed first in the typology based on the objectives of the dissident groups resorting to terrorism. Religious justifications for violence, including terrorism, were the most frequent before the nineteenth century (Rapoport 1984: 659). Religious justifications for terrorism, of course, is not only ancient but also contemporary, meaning that such causes underlying the use of violence have been very long-lasting in the history of humanity. Religious wars and crusades have been among the most devastating and costly conflicts in history in part because those believing in a different religion would be killed whereas members of the same religion would often be better treated. In some religious wars the clear intent was to eliminate the other religious group. Conquest or conversion was not seen as real options.

Any list of religious wars would be very lengthy indeed, and there has also been domestic political violence resulting from religious differences. A minority might fear that a centralizing state could undermine their beliefs and the cohesion of the community (Nandi 1996: 180). Religious discrimination by majority populations could very easily result in the violent defense of the minority's beliefs (Fox 1998: 46). In some cases a government could initiate the violence to repress a religious minority that might be seen to be unreliable or a community that could revolt in the future or join with a foreign enemy. In other circumstances minorities could seek to defend their status or even their opportunities to practice their beliefs by launching attacks against adherents of the majority religion in a state. This kind of violence could be designed to secure rights for the minority or to lead to separation of the group from the parent state. In rare cases the violence may even be directed at establishing or re-establishing the minority religion as the dominant one for a society. In England after the establishment of the Church of England, Catholics were viewed as an untrustworthy group likely to serve foreign (i.e., papal) interests and re-establish the former dominant religion.

Terrorism can also involve groups that are part of the dominant or majority religion in a country. Such groups may resort to violence in efforts to reinforce or reinvigorate the purity of the religion or force the government to base domestic laws and actions on religious precepts. While legal systems in virtually all countries reflect the cultural effects of the dominant religious affiliations of their people or their elites, some members of the dominant religion may want to imbed their values more forcefully and more deeply in society. As such, these types of groups are most frequently seeking to change the policies of their political leaders. Sometimes these types of groups desire a change of leadership from the ungodly to the more spiritually worthy as well. Much less frequently, major changes in the form of government to correspond to religious standards may be the key objective of the groups. They may, for example, seek to create a theocratic state where religious leaders have the final word on what is permissible and possible within the country.

TERRORISM AND THE WORLD'S RELIGIONS

More extreme forms of religious attitudes have appeared in many religions, and frequently the phrase religious fundamentalism is used and misused to identify terrorists. Many people in the world would quality as religious fundamentalists. They follow the precepts of their religions with devotion, they attempt to avoid sin, and they practice virtue according to their religious values. They may also take a literal interpretation of their particular set of holy scriptures. They may seek to convert by example or to be more active in their efforts to spread their faith. They may choose to vote for or support "virtuous" persons in the government or political elite. These religious individuals would qualify as fundamentalists, and they might accept that label, but they would not use violence to bring about the imposition of their religious values in society. Among religious groups, the leaders and institutions often actually promote inactivity rather than activism among their followers (Fox 1999). Obviously, not all fundamentalists are terrorists or even potential terrorists. Similarly, not all terrorists fighting under a religious banner would need to be fundamentalists. Dissidents seeking to defend their religion from state repression may resort to violence in self-defense. The persons involved in the Warsaw Ghetto uprising against the Germans in 1943 were not all fundamentalists, and it would be difficult to regard their revolt as anything other than justified. Extremist—although a word with a negative connotation— might be a more precise term to use with regard to religious terrorists instead of fundamentalist since they are the individuals willing to go to extremes for their beliefs, although violence in self-defense is not really extremism.

Fundamentalist groups opposed to a variety of practices and modern attitudes have appeared within the Christian community. Many of the right-wing groups active in the United States, which will be discussed in Chapter 8, have elements of religious fervor that help to explain their activities. Christian groups in the United States and other countries have been concerned about the dangers that are represented by the concept of secular humanism, which denies the validity of any Supreme Being. Christian religious beliefs have been used to justify racism, anti-gay attitudes and violence, and xenophobia in a number of countries. This fear of contamination by outside influences is not restricted to non-Western religions. Some of the more violent attitudes have appeared in the efforts to prevent abortions, as will be discussed in one of the case studies.

Extremist violence has appeared within Judaism. Jewish groups in the British mandated territory of Palestine utilized terrorism in their independence struggle, but this struggle was much more of an effort at state creation (i.e., national liberation struggle) than religious terrorism. In Israel today there are political parties that seek to incorporate religious ideas into the government and legal system and even to create a theocracy based on Jewish religious practices (Pedahzur 2001b). More extreme groups have appeared opposing the secular nature of Israeli society (Rapoport 1998: 104). Members of these organizations see themselves as God's Chosen People with a duty to implement God's law (at least according to their interpretations). This worldview permits them to use a wide range of actions since their goals are in keeping with a divine plan (Hanauer 1995: 251–2). They were involved in plots to blow up the Muslim mosques and shrines in Jerusalem (Rapoport 1998: 193–4). Control of the lands in the region that corresponded to the Biblical Kingdom of Israel are seen as part of this plan since God gave the Jewish People all of the lands, including Judea and Samaria (the West Bank) and the Gaza Strip (Hoffman 2006: 98). As a consequence, they are opposed to any arrangements to create a Palestinian state in the territories controlled by Israel. Extremists in the settler movement launched terrorist attacks against Arabs in the Occupied Territories, and some even hoped to stop the Israeli withdrawal from the Sinai Peninsula in return for peace with Egypt (Sandler 1997: 144). Violence by Jewish groups increased in response to the Oslo Accords as settler groups and other militants sought to derail the compromise (Pedahzur and Perliger 2003: 19). Gush Emunim, one of the settler groups, has long practiced vigilante violence against Palestinians in an effort to intimidate them or drive them away, efforts that are justified as part of new conquest of the land of Canaan (Sprinzak 2000: 219). In other cases, the violence by settlers was in retaliation for attacks by Palestinians (Pedahzur and Perliger 2003).

There was also the attack in 1994 by Baruch Goldstein, a Jewish extremist, on Muslim worshippers in Hebron. Goldstein, who was religiously motivated in his desire to make sure that Israel included the West Bank, killed twenty-nine Muslims and wounded many others before he was killed. Rabbi Meir Kahane, an Orthodox American rabbi from Brooklyn, has found political support in Israel for his extreme views. He justified violence against both Israeli Arabs and Palestinians since the Arabs were eventually likely to attack Jewish citizens in Israel. He argued for driving all Arabs out of Israel and the Occupied Territories (Hoffman, 2006: 98). His views also have a clear racist tinge since he feared that Arabs would sleep with Jews and defile the Jewish nation as a consequence (Pedahzur 2001b: 29). He formed a political party and won two seats in the Israeli parliament. Baruch Goldstein was a member of the party and a student of Kahane, and he was a candidate on the party list in 1983 (Brownfield 2000: 111). Kahane's views were so extreme that he was eventually denied his seat in the Israeli parliament. While back in the United States a Palestinian resident in the country murdered him, but parties espousing his extremist views have continued to be represented in the Israeli parliament. Other groups have resorted to violence and terrorism against fellow Israelis in their efforts to preserve the state and to secure it from any possible threat. Israeli protesters against their country's involvement in Lebanon became targets for violent attacks by supporters of the invasion (Sprinzak 2000: 223). The assassination of Yitzak Rabin in 1995 for making concessions to the Palestinians is the most prominent example of such religiously based terrorism. His assassin used religious views to justify the attack. He believed that he could stop the peace process by the assassination (Pedahzur and Perliger 2003: 27). His supposition was not wrong since any resolution of Palestinian–Israeli problems did become more difficult. Both Goldstein and Rabin's assassin have been regarded as heroes by some of the extremist Jewish groups (Ranstorp 1996: 41–2).

Before he went to Israel Kahane had been active in the United States. He helped to found the Jewish Defense League (JDL) to defend Jews against anti-Semitism. The JDL, however, did not restrict itself to self-defense actions. It launched terrorist attacks against the Soviet Union

BOX 5.1 THE ASSASSINS

One early Islamic group that practiced political terrorism as a matter of policy was the Assassins. The Assassins, an unorthodox Shia sect (the Nizari), appeared in the eleventh century and flourished into the thirteenth century. The Nizari sought to purify Islam in order to set the stage for a better religious and political system (Rapoport 1998: 121). As an unorthodox minority in an era where religion was a defining characteristic of individuals they faced periodic repressions due to their beliefs. Given their precarious position, the sect used assassination as a weapon against the rulers who represented the Sunni majority. Rulers or governors that sought to suppress the sect would be targeted for political murder to dissuade the continued attacks. The assassination was essentially a defensive response to protect the members of the sect (Rapoport 1990: 150). The Assassins were almost always successful in killing their targets because escape for the individual committing the act was not an issue. The Assassin believed that his death in the act of political murder would result in immediate entrance into paradise. The deaths of the rulers, governors, or military officers proved to be very effective, especially with the obvious target audience—other political leaders who might seek to repress the sect. Sometimes the potential target was even publicly warned of his impeding death. If the targeted official changed policy, so much the better. If the target persisted in the attacks on the sect, he was assassinated and the Assassins appeared to be that much more powerful. It has been suggested that the Assassins also used hashish (assassin was originally a word derived from the term for hashish eater) to bolster their resolve in the assassination attempt. While normally considered to be fact, such a policy would be unlikely since any individuals under the influence of a narcotic were unlikely to be effective attackers.

The Assassins are an important example because they were so effective. They preserved their sect against a much larger body of more orthodox Muslims for centuries by the selective use of violence and terror. The public as well as leaders and high officials knew the extent and successes of the assassination campaigns, even in a time when there was no mass communication. The assassinations usually occurred in public places—not only demonstrating how powerful the group was but ensuring that news of the event would spread (Rapoport 1984: 663). Mass media outlets were not essential for the successful communication of fear to appropriate audiences (Wilkinson 2000b: 174). Religious doctrine was important in strengthening the resolve of the individual members, and religion provided them with a reward in the next world for their sacrifice in protecting their religious community. The power base of the Assassins was eventually undermined by the Mongol invasions, which also disrupted or destroyed many conventional states throughout the Middle East.

and its interests in the 1970s and 1980s. The JDL was protesting the policies that made it extremely difficult for Soviet Jews to emigrate to Israel. The organization was responsible for a number of bombings directed against the Soviet Union, and its members were implicated in a number of murders as well (George and Wilcox 1996: 306–12). The group has become less prominent with the end of the Cold War and the death of Kahane.

Within the Muslim community religious violence has occurred as well. The division between Shia and Sunni within Islam has led to some violence (see Boxes 5.1 and 5.2). It also has been responsible for terrorist violence between Sunnis and Shias in Pakistan (Laqueur 2003: 181). Much attention has been on the religious extremism of the Muslim community today directed against the West and the concept of jihad or holy war invoked by various leaders. The focus on jihad as a special form of warfare has obscured the real meaning of the word for Muslims. A more accurate translation of jihad is that of striving. First and foremost, it refers to personal striving to achieve the ideals of Islam as a way of life. Second, it means striving in the sense of improving the religious situation for the community of believers. Finally, it refers to striving in the sense of converting non-Muslims and carrying the word of God to the unbelievers. This last striving can refer to the necessity of using force to convert those who do not believe. Of course, there are those within Islam that focus on conversion by the sword and selectively use the Quran to justify what they are already predisposed to do. The frequent appearance of jihad in the name of their organizations clearly is intended to indicate their support of violence to achieve their ends not their support of personal reflection. Thus, while jihad has many meanings, dissident organizations do use it to mean holy war. There are some militants among Muslim clerics who have gone so far as to ague that holy war against non-Muslims is an essential tenet of the practice of Islam (Bouchat 1996: 343). The majority of theologians in both branches of Islam, however, do not agree that such violence is justified, either between Sunni and Shia or against Christians or Jews. Many Muslim groups, including those that would be considered fundamentalist, do not subscribe to these views and do not participate in the violence. Of course, it is not necessary for all Muslims or a majority of Muslims to subscribe to the idea that violence is essential or justified. A minority of believers is all that is necessary to supply the recruits for the violent groups that practice terrorism. One of the factors that has led people to see a connection between Islam and violence is that Muslim societies were more likely to be in the Third World and to be conducting national liberation struggles. These liberation struggles, either against colonial powers or by governments perceived to be in alliance with the outside world led to greater violence (Kennedy 1999: 17). The mobilization of Muslims from around the world to battle the Soviet troops in Afghanistan was also a spur to Islamic radicalism and the spread of violence as the volunteers returned to their countries after the Soviet withdrawal. The volunteers were encouraged by their victory over what the perceived to be one Western ideology (Communism) and thus were more willing to battle against others (parliamentary democracy, capitalism).

Difficulties in Islamic societies have risen when Muslim groups have sought to install the Sharia as the basis of the legal system in the country. The Sharia is based on the Quran and the life and examples of the Prophet Muhammad and the early Muslim community of believers. The more fundamentalist political groups seeking to have strict adherence to the Sharia serve as the basic law of the land. All other laws must be in accord with the holy scripture and cannot contradict it. The Sharia has been established as the precise basis for law in the Islamic Republic of Iran, the Sudan, and Afghanistan when it was under the rule of the Taliban. Large elements of the Sharia have been directly included in the legal system of Pakistan as well. While it is a significant portion of the law in many other Muslim countries, many governments in power in the Middle East, have frequently relied on legal systems based in part on Western or secular principles. Conflict has thus been created between Muslims who are in favor of strict interpretations of their scriptures and more modern groups in society. These conflicts have resulted in the repression of those out of power (either secular or religious) and violence and terrorism against those in power (either secular or religious).

The religious fervor of Islam has also been associated with suicide bombings, especially by Palestinians and by other Muslims as well. Islam does not directly condone suicide, but it accepts self-martyrdom in the right cause. There has been a tradition of suicidal assaults in the Muslim communities of Southeast Asia. As Muslim territories were incorporated into non-Muslim colonial empires, attacks by individuals occurred in an effort to achieve better treatment for other Muslims at the hands of the foreign occupiers. To some extent these tactics were successful in leading the colonial government and prominent individuals to treat local Muslims more fairly (Dale 1988). Hamas in its struggle with Israel has found suicide bombings to be a very effective weapon given the resources available to the organization (Dolnik and Bhattacharjee 2002). Muslim clerics have argued that this kind of attack is justified because the targets are members of a foreign occupation (Malka 2003: 22). Given the prominence of suicide attacks against non-Muslims today, it is ironic that the first suicide car bombing in Lebanon involved an attack by Muslims against other Muslims (Dolnik 2003: 23).

Most societies glorify heroic exploits of small groups undertaking military missions against great odds—the aptly named suicide missions. The Spartans at Thermopylae are honored for their bravery in covering the retreat of the other Greeks, even though their decision to stand and fight amounted to suicide. In other armies and other wars the sacrifices of individuals or small units to save comrades are honored rather than being denounced as suicide. Suicide attacks by militant dissidents have appeared in many cultures. Baruch Goldstein surely did not expect to survive his attack on the worshippers at the mosque; furthermore, he left a farewell note (Gorenburg 2000: 204). Early Russian anarchists expected to be killed by their dynamite bombs. Their deaths demonstrated to the public that the attacks were political and not criminal (Rapoport 2003: 39). Buddhist and Shinto Japanese militants sacrificed themselves in attacks against Westerners and government officials when the country was opening up to outsiders (Silke 2003a: 102). In Romania in the 1930s select members of the fascist Iron Guard were part of a group that launched suicidal attacks on those considered as enemies, including opposition political leaders (Berend 1998: 337). They formed death squads that vowed to carry out their missions regardless of the costs (Iordachi 2004: 29). Suicidal attacks are not unique to Islamic societies. Modern-day examples of suicide attacks are not limited to religious groups. Between 1980 and 2000 more than half of the suicide attacks were launched by the nationalist rebels in Sri Lanka (see Table 5.1). Suicide terrorism has been on the increase because different groups have learned that it works (Pape 2005: 61). It has proven to "be one of the most efficient and least expensive tactics ever to be employed by terror and guerrilla groups" (Pedahzur and Perliger 2006: 1). More recently, elements of secular, nationalist Palestinian groups have begun to use suicide attacks (Dolnik 2003: 25). The secular Palestinian nationalists also were pushed to use suicide attacks to keep pace with Hamas and to maintain their popular appeal (Bloom 2004). These secular groups have even been willing to use female bombers whereas the Islamic religious organizations have not (Nacos 2003: 2). Like other activities, suicide bombings are a technique open to many different types of terrorist groups. One interesting aspect of the suicide bombing campaigns has been that regardless of the background of the groups (secular or religious), the majority of the targets have inevitably been democracies.

BOX 5.2 HIZBALLAH

Hizballah (Party of God) is both a conventional political organization and a terrorist group. It appeared in Lebanon to represent the Shia community in that country. The Shia constitute the largest single religious group in the country competing with Sunnis, Druze, and various Christian denominations. All of these groups were Arab, so there were no ethnic differences involved in the domestic conflicts in Lebanon between the various groups; it was the religious differences that were most important. While the Shia became the largest group in the country, they were also the poorest. Hizballah, as a consequence, was able to mobilize support by promising to deal with the grievances of this community. Hizballah was quite willing to use terrorist attacks and more conventional military means in its efforts to support and advance the status of the Shia community. It has been relatively successful in becoming the political representative of the Shia Arabs in Lebanon after the country recovered from its long civil war, and it has focused many of its efforts on domestic politics.

The group has also engaged in terrorist actions with international characteristics. The group developed a positive relationship with the clerical regime in Iran which provided financial support and training. The group was responsible for the car bombing of the Iraqi embassy with the outbreak of the war between Iraq and Iran. It also was behind the bombing of the barracks for US marines and French paratroopers in 1983. It has supported terrorist operations by Palestinians in Israel as well, even though the Palestinian struggle has not usually been the primary focus of the organization. The group has frequently used its activities in opposition to Israel as a way of establishing its credentials as a good Arab party so as to be able to maintain its electoral support in Lebanon. The 2006 capture of Israeli military personnel and the subsequent rocket attacks from Lebanon against targets in Israel seem likely to have been undertaken to further enhance the domestic status of the party. In this case the leaders of Hizballah were guilty of miscalculation and underestimating the Israeli response.

Extreme views have also appeared within Hinduism, and religiously motivated violence has resulted. Violent defenders of the Hindu culture go back to the 1920s when the Rashtriya Swayamsevak Sangh (RSS—National Patriotism Organization) began training paramilitaries. An RSS member assassinated Mohandas Gandhi because he was willing to compromise with non-Hindus on the new state of India (Juergensmeyer 2000: 95). There have been Hindu groups and political parties that have sought to have Hindu practices (Hinduvata) incorporated into national law since a large majority of the population of India is Hindu. The Bharatiya Janata Party that promotes Hindu practices has become the largest religious and nationalist movement in the world (Juergensmeyer 1996: 6). While the party moderated its use of Hindu themes in the election campaign of 1998, it did not offer any real assurances to the religious minorities of increased tolerance (Chandra 1999: 65–6). They feel that the members of the minority religions should be reabsorbed into the Hindu community (Greenway 2001: 91). These efforts correspond to the attempts by Muslims to have the Sharia as the basis of national law or of groups in the United States to have Christian principles more directly incorporated into national

TABLE 5.1   NUMBER OF SUICIDE ATTACKS, 1980–2003

Group/Type	Location	Number of Attacks	
		1980–2000	2001–3
Liberation Tigers of Tamil Eelam (ethnic)	Sri Lanka/India	168	6
Hizballah and pro-Syrian Lebanese (religious)	Lebanon, Kuwait, Argentina	52	0
Hamas (religious)	Israel	22	39
Kurdish Workers Party (ideological/ethnic)	Turkey	15	0
Palestinian Islamic Jihad (religious)	Israel	8	22
Al Qaeda (religious)	East Africa, United States, Europe	2	17
Egyptian Islamic Jihad (religious)	Croatia	1	0
Islamic Group (religious)	Pakistan	1	0
Barbar Khalsa International (religious)	India	1	0
Islamic Army Group (religious)	Algeria	1	0
Chechen groups (nationalist/religious)	Russia	4	15
Palestinian Front for the Liberation of Palestine (nationalist)	Israel	0	6
Fatah (nationalist)	Israel	0	27
Kashmir (nationalist/religious)	Kashmir and India	1	4
Iraq (various groups)	Iraq	0	20

Source: Radu (2002: 280) for 1980–2000 and Pape (2005: 270–5) for 2001–3 and some additions to the data from Radu.

and state laws. To them, secularism and equal treatment of all religious groups effectively denies equal treatment for Hindus who are the majority. The cow is a sacred animal for Hindus, and one of their goals has been to have national law prohibiting the slaughtering of cows or the eating of beef. Incorporation of this belief and other practices into national law would clearly have effects on other religious communities in India.

Efforts at promoting the Hindu religion have gone further than pushing for incorporation of religious practices into national legislation. There have also been violence against Christians, and Christian missionaries have been murdered because they were attempting to convert Hindus (Oommen 2005: 117). Efforts have also been made to reclaim sacred sites on which other religious groups have established mosques or worship centers. More extreme Hindu groups such as the RSS have organized efforts where the buildings of other groups have been torn down and Hindu temples erected in their place. Efforts to demolish the existing buildings have at times generated violence between the Hindu and other religious communities. Confrontations at Ayodhya in northern India have been among the most violent. The Hindu extremists wanted to reclaim this holy site for a new Hindu temple. In order to do so, they needed to demolish a mosque located there. The militants were eventually successful in doing so with the help of local authorities. The events at Ayodhya also sparked outbreaks of fighting between Hindus and

Muslims elsewhere in India (C. Bhatt 2001: 196–201). For the Hindu extremists this violence is a positive outcome since it leads many Hindus in the region to identify with the Hindu majority and support the religious position of the political leaders (Austin and Gupta 1990: 8). These religious extremists have carried their actions even further. They have fomented communal violence directed at the religious minorities, sometimes with the support of local authorities. Not only Muslims have been affected by these actions. The intent has clearly been to indicate to members of at least some religious minorities that they are not necessarily free to practice their religion or that overt community religious practices are not necessarily going to be permitted. Migration or conversion, rather than persistence in the minority religious practices, would appear to be the goals desired by these Hindu groups.

Pressures from religious extremists can generate communal violence in other circumstances. Fighting has broken out between Christians and Muslims in Indonesia. Internal migration led to Muslims moving to largely Christian areas of Sulawesi. The Christian communities, faced with increases in Muslim immigration to the island, attacked Muslims in an effort at ethnic cleansing. Muslims than began to retaliate (Abuza 2003b: 69). Local extremists who have hoped to gain by the dominance of their religious community have stoked competition between the religious groups. The end result has been fighting, massacres, and terrorist attacks. The violence has actually been exacerbated by the appearance of more democratic processes in Indonesia since officials, who have now been elected locally rather than centrally appointed, control significant government resources that can be important for the different religious communities. At least some individuals on each side have sought to use the attacks to drive out members of the other religious community (Rohde 2001). Local politicians and businessmen organized the gangs terrorizing the other side as part of the effort to gain political control (Mann 2005: 494). There has been corresponding violence between Muslims and Christians in the Moluccas Province as well. Some Christians organized a separatist movement, but many of the local Christians did not support such an effort (Sholeh 2007: 156–7). At least some Muslim organizations elsewhere in Indonesia have sent armed supporters and assistance to the local Muslims (Veitch 2007: 136–7). Their arrival turned the tide in the favor of local Muslims in at least some cases (Abuza 2002: 447).

From the above examples it is clear that extreme or fringe groups within many religious communities have used violence. These religious extremists do have some common attributes that go beyond the use of violence and the religious justifications that they draw upon. Many of the more extreme movements and groups have appeared as a consequence of change in their respective societies. Globalization and changing world conditions have generated stress within societies and led people to place a greater reliance on religion to provide mental and psychological support in a changing world (Fox 1998: 51–2). "[P]oliticized religion can be seen as a response to modernity" (Sandler 1997: 134). A greater commitment to religious values is one means of dealing with the threats and dangers that come with changes, and violence is a method that can be used to deal with the forces that the religious communities and others have come to see as the causes of such unwelcome change.

The perception that change brings threats can be seen in the pronouncements of virtually all religions. Groups hark back to a time in the past when religion played a greater role in society and a time when the values of the dominant religion defined what was and what was not permissible in society. The past times are often seen as "golden ages" or better times than the present, and change has not been to the benefit of society. Such groups also define nationality in religious terms rather than ethnic or geographical ones (Hanauer 1995: 248–9). The terrorists will see themselves as soldiers in a spiritual army (Juergensmeyer 1997: 16). Most extreme religious groups see themselves to be battling with secularism (Pillar 2001: 65). The battles against "secular humanism" in the West and efforts to make the Sharaiat (Islamic religious principles) the foundation of law in Muslim countries are an example of such efforts. For many Muslims, Western ideas, including Marxism, seem to reflect a different kind of secular humanism that is designed to undermine the religious and moral values of Islamic society. For Jewish extremists, there is the call for the recreation of a Jewish state within the boundaries established by the Kingdom of Israel in the Old Testament days, combined in many cases with efforts to makes the laws of Israel more closely correspond to the religious precepts of Orthodox Judaism. In the case of the Hindu groups there has been the effort to limit foreign influences, represented especially by Islam and Christianity, and to purify the country by officially establishing Hinduism as the state religion or incorporating distinctly Hindu traditions into state law.

The mobilization of groups to practice violence in reaction to the threat of change from the outside may result in terrorist actions being carried out in third countries or for attacks against foreign targets in their own countries. Foreign actors being in the outside "contamination" are often associated with the changes that threaten the local religious values. If the foreign support can be removed, and then it will be much easier to force the local, godless elites from power (Juergensmeyer 1997: 181). Much of the reaction by Muslim groups in many countries has been a reaction against the intrusion of secular Western values (Ousman 2004: 69). Foreign elements may even be seen as groups that are attempting to proselytize and convert locals to a foreign religion, thus destroying the position of the domestic religion. Western interactions with countries in the Middle East and India have introduced changes, some of which have conflicted with local religious traditions and practices. Western countries have also frequently been more comfortable with the more secular, "modern" political elites that are in power. Not surprisingly, they have frequently supported the leaders who are bringing their countries "into the twentieth century." Further, Western countries have brought missionaries who seek to convert local populations to Christianity. As a consequence, foreign targets will frequently seem to be very appropriate to many religious groups in non-Western parts of the world when they resort to political violence. The resulting violence is a reaction to globalization and modernization processes. It is not even necessarily a product of successful modernization but can be a reaction to its failure to deliver jobs, education, and development (Almonte 2003: 237–8).

It has been suggested that religiously based groups that resort to terrorism may be more willing to inflict mass casualties with their attacks, especially when the population is composed of unbelievers. An analysis of terrorist attacks that resulted in twenty-five or more fatalities in the 1980s and 1990s found that over half of the attacks were undertaken by groups with religious motivations (Quillen 2002). Since 2001 attacks with large numbers of casualties have increased at the same time that terrorists campaigns by religious groups have proliferated (Dolnik and Gunaratna 2006: 80). There has also been concern that religious groups would be willing to use biological, chemical, or radiological weapons (Cronin 2004: 314). Religious terrorists may also see themselves as following a higher law that they see as superseding normal rules or behavior (Fox 1998: 49). The unbelievers have placed themselves outside the boundaries of the protected community, and may even be considered potential sources of unbelief. Members of these types of groups see themselves engaged in a struggle between good and evil, and any outsider is evil (Cronin 2002/3: 41). Religiously motivated terrorists may also be less likely to appeal to an uncommitted audience; thus, they may be less restrained than other groups (Hoffman 1995: 272–3). If the religious terrorists see God as being the audience for their actions, they may be less interested in public reactions to a large number of deaths (Crelinsten 2000: 186). Religious dissident groups may also have beliefs that call for the purification of their society. These rites of purification necessary to re-establish the ideal society *may* lead to actions that are designed to cause a large number of casualties as part of the process of purification. Such apocalyptical views may require massive rather than selective casualties. While groups with clear religious motivations have undertaken some attacks resulting in mass casualties, not all such attacks have been launched by religious groups; furthermore, not all religious terrorist groups seek to inflict mass casualties (Parachini 2001: 399).

Huntington (1996) has suggested that the world may be facing a "clash of civilizations." The possibility that religiously based terrorism might be especially deadly could result from the fact that the great conflicts of the future could occur between different cultures since the major religions help to culturally define the dominant civilizations in the world. The current civilizations are based in Western Christianity (West and Central Europe, North America, and Australasia), Latin Christianity (South and Central America), Orthodox Christianity (Russia and Slavic Europe), Confucianism (China and other Asian countries), Shintoism (Japan), Hinduism (India), and Islam (Middle East, and parts of Asia and Africa). Clashes at the borders of these civilizations (fault lines) are more likely than clashes within any one civilization. Further, clashes between civilizations are more likely to be sustained in time and more costly than the clashes that occur within a given civilization. While the clashes between the cultural areas are not strictly religious, different religious values underlay the cultures and civilizations of the world. Militant Islamic rhetoric emphasizes these differences when it proclaims that Islam's value is higher than Western ideas (Khashan 1997: 8). Many (but not all) of the recent conflicts with religious elements can be seen in the regions where two or more civilizations or cultural areas meet—Bosnia (Muslim and Orthodox and Western), Israel (Western and Muslim), Nigeria and the Sudan (Muslim and others), and the Indian subcontinent (Hindu and Muslim among others). Once conflict has broken out in areas where religions and cultures meet, there have been local leaders willing to mobilize populations on the basis of their religions and associated cultures. There have even been some indications that terrorism has shifted from being within the same general cultural area to occurring along the fault lines and between such cultural areas (Weinberg and Eubank 2000: 98–9). These cultural divides have become more important with the end of the Cold War as religion has become a more important source of identification (Ellingsen 2005). Other studies, however, have found limited support for Huntington's main thesis (Fox 2004; Rajendran 2002). While the clash of civilizations argument may not always hold true as explaining terrorist outbreaks and can only serve as a partial explanation, it does provide important insights and seems relevant as an explanation for some cases (J. Lutz and B. Lutz 2005: 166).

CASE STUDIES

Five case studies are presented dealing with religiously based terrorist activities. The activities of the Jewish Zealots in the Roman Province of Judea before the revolt in CE (AD) 66 is one of the earliest examples of a focused campaign of terror directed toward particularly political ends. The other examples are more recent and include the outbreak of religious based violence in Algeria in the 1990s, the terrorist and guerrilla campaign of the Sikhs in India to gain greater autonomy or even an independent state, the activities of the Aum Shinrikyo sect in Japan, violent anti-abortion activism in the United States, and the activities of the Al Qaeda network associated with Osama bin Laden.

CASE STUDY 5.1   THE ZEALOTS IN JUDEA

Zealot has come to refer to those who are fanatically committed to a particular cause. The term goes back to the first century of the current era when members of the Jewish community in the province of Judea in the Roman Empire sought to liberate their country from alien rule. These efforts eventually resulted in the Jewish Revolt that lasted from CE (AD) 66 to 71. Although Judea was a small province in a large empire, an earlier revolt under the Maccabees, while Israel was part of the Greek state founded by the successors of Alexander the Great, had succeeded. The intent of the Jewish rebels, who came to be known as the Zealots, was to repeat this victory and to force out the Romans, as well as the Greeks who had come in their wake. The Zealots saw the uprising as a necessary preliminary step to divine redemption. They were "profoundly religious patriots" (Applebaum 1971: 169). The Jewish community had to be mobilized for the revolt to pave the way for a new religious state that would follow (Rapoport 1990: 152–3). The religious, rather than the national, character of the uprising was obvious when the Idumeans, Jewish by religion but not one of the tribes of Israel, were brought in as allies against the Romans (Josephus 1981: 252–63).

The Zealots, as well as other militants known as the Sicarri (daggermen) for one of their weapons of choice when dealing with opponents, first had to convince the Jewish community to support their intended rebellion. They had to intimidate those who opposed the idea of rebellion or who sought to compromise with Rome. Compromise was in fact quite possible since the Romans were quite willing to defer to local religious sensibilities in this period of time. To achieve the objectives of a unified community in favor of revolt, the militants mounted a *campaign* of assassinations. Moderates in the Jewish community, which included priests, merchants, and other members of the elite who had benefited from Roman rule, were assassinated, usually in broad daylight. One of the first victims was the High Priest (Reich 1998: 263). The choice of open attack, often in crowded surroundings, demonstrated the capabilities of the militants and the vulnerability of those who disagreed with them. The assassins were often able to escape, but they were also willing to suffer the consequences if they were caught. Potential opponents were targets, but the entire Jewish population of the region was the target as well. As Josephus (1981: 147), who was an observer on the scene at the time, noted: "More terrible than the crimes themselves was the fear they aroused." The rebels also used tactics that would be associated with more modern groups. They kidnapped prominent individuals, including at one point the son of the High Priest (a pro-Roman sympathizer) in order to exchange them for captured comrades (Allegro 1972: 278).

The Roman response to the campaign of assassinations was initially subdued as the local provincial authorities sought to avoid inflaming local religious sensitivities. Eventually, however, confrontations between crowds of demonstrators and Roman troops resulted in heightened tensions. Riots and panic resulted, and many Jews lost their lives, further inflaming local opinion (Rapoport 1990: 154–5). Eventually, the rebellion that was sought by the Zealots broke out. The opposition had been silenced and support for the revolt was solidified. When the fighting broke out, there was virtually no opposition from the population or pro-Roman elements. The rebels quickly gained control of Jerusalem and much of Judea, and even defeated the initial Roman force sent against them. The rebellion, however, was eventually crushed. Jerusalem was captured by the Roman legions in CE 70, and the last strongholds of the militants were taken in CE 71. Judea was then reabsorbed into the Roman Empire. The defeat of the rebels did not end the Roman problems. There were later revolts—one from CE 115 to CE 117 that began in Cyrene (modern Cyrenaica in Libya) that spread to Egypt and other provinces before being contained and one in CE 132 in Judea that the Romans were only able to put down with difficulty (Eck 1999).

The revolt, based in the religious values of the Zealots and the population in general, ultimately failed even though the terror campaign to generate the revolt was quite successful. The rebels could not maintain the independence of the region in the face of the Roman legions. Had the revolt been assured of success, there probably would have been very little opposition among the Jewish population. As it was, the issue was in doubt for at least the first years of the revolt. The relative weakness of Jewish military resources vis-à-vis the Empire eventually became obvious when Rome mobilized sufficient resources to deal with the uprising. Even so, it took a major campaign and a long siege of Jerusalem before the revolt was broken. During this time Rome was experiencing its own internal difficulties. In CE 68 a revolt by the legionary commander in Spain resulted in his overthrow of the Emperor Nero. This new emperor himself was overthrown in CE 69, and finally Vespasian became the generally accepted emperor. He was in command of the Roman forces subduing Judea and besieging Jerusalem when the troubles began, but his departure for Rome did not disrupt the campaign (Grant 1974: Chap. 7). Had his task been more difficult or had he faced possible defeat, the forces in Judea might have been withdrawn (leaving Judea to be re-conquered at some future time). In later centuries, the civil wars and succession struggles in the Roman Empire or pressures on the imperial frontiers made it possible for provinces to break away permanently or for periods of time. Unfortunately for the Zealots, Roman politics were not sufficiently chaotic at the time of the revolt to permit success.

CASE STUDY 5.2   THE SIKHS AND KHALISTAN

India is a very diverse country with numerous religious, linguistic, ethnic, and regional groups in the state. When independence came in 1948, British India was divided into Pakistan and India. Communal violence broke out between Muslims and Hindus, resulting in the relocation of many Muslims to Pakistan while virtually all Hindus residents in areas that became part of Pakistan left. In the new, smaller India, there were still significant numbers of Muslims, who constitute the single largest religious minority in the country. Religious tensions between Muslims and Hindus have been present through the decades, and there have been outbreaks of communal violence between members of the two groups. In addition, there are other religious minorities in the countries, including the relatively small (in percentage terms) Sikh and Christian communities. The many linguistic groups in India have caused problems as well. There are over twenty languages that have at least a million speakers. In the northern part of the country, much of the population speaks Hindi or related dialects and languages. In the southern part of the country, moreover, the local languages are Dravidian, a completely different language group that is unrelated to Hindi. There have been efforts to promote Hindi as a national language, and these efforts have naturally generated tensions among the speakers of the other languages. English remains as an important de facto national language that is understood by elites from the different regions, and has the advantage of not providing special advantages to any of the language groups in the country.

Given the tremendous diversity of groups that exists in India, it is not surprising that the country has had to deal with communal tensions and violence. Various groups have provided the personnel for attacks against the government, and in some cases the communities have targeted each other. The Sikhs have been one of the religious groups that for a time presented serious problems for the central government and the preservation of national unity. While the Sikh religion draws heavily upon Hinduism, it has other elements included as well. Most, but not all Sikhs, consider their religion to be distinctive from Hinduism rather than simply a variation within that rather broad religious community. Sikhism is monotheistic, and it never accepted the Hindu caste system (Nandi 1996: 180). Under British rule and the early years of independence, there was little conflict between the Sikh and Hindu communities. In the 1970s, however, problems began to develop, especially in the province of the Punjab (see Map 1). While Sikhs are present in many areas of India, they were geographically concentrated in this province. The cities contained Hindu majorities, but the countryside was overwhelmingly Sikh. Elements of the Sikh community came to see themselves as being marginalized in their own land. Part of the reason for concern among the Sikhs was the increasing demands by some political parties to have Hinduism play a more important part in the country. While this drive to implant Hinduism in the state generated tensions principally between the Muslim and Hindu communities, the pattern was disturbing for the Sikhs as well (Unnithan 1995).

Sikh concerns led to political protests. The Indian government did make some concessions to Sikh feelings. Provincial boundaries were redrawn so that a new, smaller Punjab province had a clear Sikh majority. The Sikhs, however, remained divided amongst themselves—sometimes on the basis of the old caste lines, so the government and other parties were able to divide the Sikh vote to prevent the Sikhs from controlling the province (Nandi 1996: 184). For example, the government headed by Indira Gandhi and her Congress Party covertly supported Sant Jarnail Singh Bhindranwale who created a new party to challenge the dominant Akali Dal party. Support for this party weakened the Akali Dal, which had cooperated with other parties in opposing the Congress Party (Long 1990: 60). This effort to divide and conquer failed when Bhindranwale became the leader of one of the more important terrorist groups.

In the early 1980s, after he failed to achieve a dominant position in the province through electoral politics, Bhindranwale advocated political violence. He especially attracted the young and educated as his followers who hoped to recreate the former Sikh periods of glory (Yaeger 1991: 227). Bhindranawale was able to rally Sikh militants as a reaction to modernization. He felt that foreign influences were undermining religious norms in the Punjab (Wallace 1995: 361). His followers began to engage in terrorist actions. A large number of other groups (well over a hundred) appeared and also became involved in terrorist actions in the 1980s and the 1990s (Wallace 1995: 357). Many of the groups sought to achieve an independent Sikh Khalistan ("Land of the Pure"), while some appeared willing to accept a decentralized Indian state in which the Punjab would be dominated by the Sikhs and would have great control over domestic policies. The various groups engaged in typical

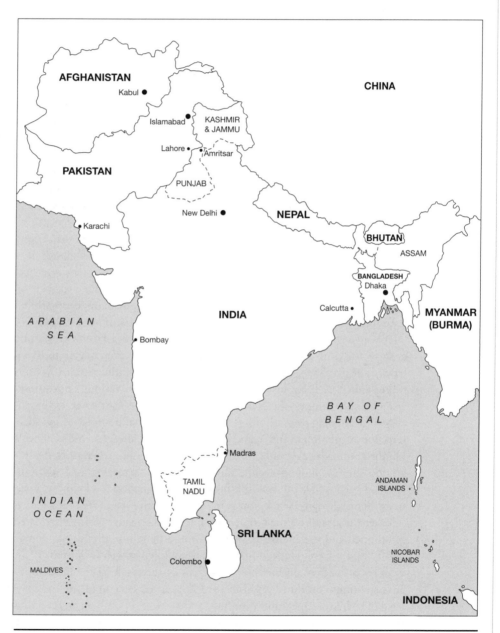

Map 1   India and South Asia

terrorists operations, including bombings, kidnapping, assassinations, and attacks on the security forces. Among the targets were Hindu inhabitants in the Punjab. The attacks were designed to force other Hindus to flee the area, and in this effort they were somewhat successful, although the terrorist groups were never successful in instigating full-scale communal violence between the two religious communities. Various terrorist groups also attacked moderate Sikhs who were willing to compromise with the government. Bhindranwale and his followers established their headquarters in the compound containing the Golden Temple of Amritsar, the most holy site for the Sikh religion. While Indian authorities knew that members of the terrorist group were present, action against the dissidents was deferred given the religious significance of the temple to all Sikhs. Eventually, after the failure of negotiations Prime Minister Indira Gandhi ordered a military attack (Operation Blue Star) on the temple compound in 1984. After much fighting and destruction the compound was captured. More than a thousand persons were killed, including Indian troops, guerrillas, Bhindranwale and members of his organization, and hundreds of Sikh pilgrims who happened to be present at the time of the assault. While the assault was a military success since it eliminated many guerrillas and terrorists and a key leader of the militants, it was a political disaster since it alienated many members of the Sikh community who had previously been neutral or even favorably disposed toward the central government.

The assault on the Golden Temple led to additional complications. Later in 1984 Prime Minister Gandhi was assassinated by two of her Sikh bodyguards in retaliation for Operation Blue Star and the sacrilege that it represented. In the aftermath of Gandhi's death, riots broke out in northern India in which Hindus attacked Sikhs and their businesses. Thousands of Sikhs died in the rioting, in many cases while the police did nothing and the military remained in their barracks (Pettigrew 1995: 8–9). These deaths further increased the antagonisms between the Sikh and Hindu communities and drove more recruits into the ranks of the various independence organizations that were practicing terror. The death of Gandhi had another, somewhat indirect effect. With her demise, the ruling Congress Party lost some of its cohesion, and various opposition parties gained ground. The Congress Party had generally tried to at least some extent to generate mass appeal by crossing over ethnic, religious, and regional boundaries. As such it was often a force for integration in India, and it usually, but not always, avoided appeals to specifically Hindu nationalist elements. In the troubled times after Gandhi's death, the party lost ground, and the more parochial Hindu nationalist parties gained strength. The presence of these parties that promoted Hinduism as the national religion in government led to many Sikhs seeing their religion being placed in an even more precarious position.

After the assault on the Golden Temple attacks against Hindus escalated. Buses would be stopped and the Hindu passengers would be removed and massacred (Yaeger 1991: 228). Hindus were removed from trains and killed as well (Hoffman 1995: 279). Bombs were set off in New Delhi and other areas of India taking the battle outside of Punjab. Assassinations continued and included the retired general of the Indian Army who had been in charge of Operation Blue Star. Sikhs placed a bomb on an Air India flight in 1985 that exploded over the Atlantic Ocean, killing more than 300 persons. The terrorist attacks in the Punjab continued to target Sikhs who did not support the dissident organizations and who favored compromise with the government of India. The targets also included family members of Punjab police, both Sikh and Hindu. In fact, by the 1990s the targets of the terrorist more frequently included other Sikhs rather than Hindus (Wallace 1995: 355, 399). The leader of the Akali Dal, the large Sikh party favoring "collaboration" with the government was one of the casualties. The fact that the groups had shifted their targets to Sikhs in an effort to mobilize support within their own community was one indication of declining support among the very group that they claimed to represent.

The government of India was eventually able to control and contain the worst of the violence in the Punjab. A number of factors came into play in accounting for the eventual success of the government forces. One factor undoubtedly was a certain amount of weariness with the unending violence and uncertainty on the part of the population in general. The government also committed more regular troops and police units to the Punjab, and paramilitary forces were raised to provide some protection against the guerrilla and terrorist forces. Government counterterrorist techniques also improved. The government relied increasingly on the use of former members of the resistance movements to supply information on their colleagues by offering either rewards or threatening severe punishments. There was also some effort to be more aware of the sensibilities of the Sikh population. A second operation to clear the Golden Temple of new concentrations of resistance fighters (Operation Black Thunder) was undertaken with more care and minimal damage and loss of life to innocent bystanders (Wallace 1995: 398). The government also employed less praiseworthy methods of dealing with the dissidents. There is considerable evidence that the government relied on murders and assassinations (i.e., death squads) to remove leaders and members of the dissident organizations, avoiding the necessity of supplying proof in any judicial setting. There were even questionable deaths among many human rights activists and others who queried the government methods for dealing with the dissident movements in the Punjab (Pettigrew 1995: Chap. 1).

The government also attempted to maintain better control on the border with Pakistan. Punjab Province borders on Pakistan, and the Indian government long claimed that Pakistan was supplying arms to the organizations opposing the central government (thereby explaining the persistence of the dissident Sikh groups). There was relatively little evidence to indicate that Pakistan consistently supplied arms or major support to the various movements in the Punjab as a matter of policy. On the other hand, looking the other way when Sikhs acquired arms in Pakistan was an effective and inexpensive way of discomforting a potential enemy. A number of Sikh separatist organizations in exile also currently have headquarters in Pakistan (Chima 2002: 33). A more important source of aid for the dissidents over the years came from the Sikh communities in Europe and North America. Sikhs in these areas have provided funds and other aid for the groups opposed to the central government (Fair 2005). Such support, while important in the armed struggle, was insufficient to achieve victory or to make continuation of the battle an attractive alternative.

By the mid-1990s the Sikh insurrection and attacks had largely been contained. The violence and efforts to create an independent Khalistan had failed. While immensely disruptive of the ordinary routine of government of the Punjab province, little was ultimately accomplished. Sikh parties returned to the political arena and participated in the usual political exchanges. They bargained with the other large parties, trading their support in the national legislature for projects and other benefits for the Punjab. It was politics as usual with vote trading and efforts at gaining more national dollars for local projects that is often the core of political compromise in democracies. Some armed groups still remain, but they largely become bandits rather than groups of political dissidents (Chima 2002: 33). Dissident Sikhs assassinated Punjab's chief minister in 1995, but the attack did not trigger a new outbreak of violence (Juergensmeyer 2000: 91). Many or most Sikhs could again become concerned about their future or the future of their religion in India. The rise in strength of Hindu nationalist parties, seeking to impose national policies that would limit the practices of the religious minorities in the country, or increase in violence by Hindu fundamentalists could create the necessary concern and foster new violence. Should some dynamic leader arise to unite the frequently divided Sikhs in order to achieve short-term goals such as greater local control of provincial resources or long-term goals such as autonomy or even independence, violence could erupt again.

CASE STUDY 5.3   ALGERIA IN THE 1990S

Algeria has suffered from political violence and terrorism on two occasions in its recent history. During the struggle for independence from France in the late 1950s and early 1960s, the Algerian National Liberation Front engaged in both guerrilla warfare and terrorism in its efforts to become independent. By 1962 independence was achieved, and a civilian government was installed. In 1965, the military intervened to establish an authoritarian system of government that continued to be dominated by the officer corps. Until 1989, Algeria was officially a one party system under a series of presidents, all of whom had been former officers. During this period the higher-ranking officers as a group were really the key decision-makers in the country. By the late 1980s, economic problems led to increasing domestic unrest, and Islamic movements appeared that gained support among the groups left behind by modernization. Prices were increasing and there was significant unemployment in the country. Declining prices for petroleum products had led to an economic downturn, and there were also problems with corruption and inadequate provision of services for the population (Fuller 1996: 24–6). In an effort to open the political system to greater input, the government permitted the formation of opposition parties and scheduled elections, first for municipal councils and then a two-stage election for the national legislature. One of the more important opposition parties formed to contest the election was the Islamic Salvation Front (FIS). The FIS mobilized support on the basis of structuring the legal system on Islamic principles and promoting an Islamic form of government in contrast to the clearly secular regime of the military and the governing party. The FIS was not unified on all issues. Some leaders adopted a moderate stance on tolerating non-Islamic parties and activities, while others advocated establishing the Quran as the state constitution, limiting the role of women in society, and limiting non-Islamic political activity (Willis 1997: 198–200). The FIS held together, however, and did quite well in the municipal elections. The FIS and its allies put many of the more clearly Islamic practices and beliefs into practice when they won control of these local institutions of government (Stone 1997: 167–8). The government then began to pull back from its commitments to open up the political system, and it began to harass the FIS and even arrest some of the leaders. Confrontations between the government and the FIS led to a postponement of the elections until 1992. When the elections were held the FIS did so well in the first round that it was virtually assured of winning an absolute majority of the seats in the legislature by winning runoffs in the second stage where no candidate had received a majority (Takeyh 2003: 68). The government proceeded to annul the results of the first round of elections, cancel the second stage of the elections, declare martial law, and ban the FIS.

The crackdown on the FIS was counterproductive. The government destroyed the credibility of the moderate leaders who had pursued an electoral strategy, and further arrests made it easier for hard-liners to take over the movement (Takeyh 2003: 69). Faced with government repression and the refusal of the ruling party to abide by the election results, supporters of the FIS and others resorted to violence. The Muslim militants adopted many of the same tactics that were used against the French in the national liberation struggle (P. Jenkins 2003: 82). The political groups that favored abiding by the election results and a more Islamic form of government came together in the Islamic Army Group (GIA) and the Islamic Movement Army (MIA). While the MIA and later successor groups were linked with the FIS, the FIS did not directly control the violent dissidents. The GIA shared the Islamic view of the FIS but was an independent organization that at times came into direct conflict with the FIS. These groups that resorted to violence and terrorism recruited members of earlier Islamic movements, and drew upon Algerian veterans of the Afghan war against the Soviet Union (Takeyh 2003: 69–70). The dissident movements used both guerrilla warfare and terrorism. The guerrilla portion of the struggle occurred in the countryside and consisted of targeting the police, security forces, and the military in an effort to defeat the government in power.

The terrorist campaign that was launched had a number of components. The Islamic groups targeted government leaders, members of the governing party, and individuals working for the government. The president of Algeria was assassinated in June 1992. One view was that it was the Islamic dissidents who planned the attack, while another view is that the Algerian military took advantage of the unrest to eliminate a leader who was not vigorous enough in maintaining the system of government (Willis 1997: 263–6). Other attacks were designed to paralyze the government and to make it impossible for the government to provide services in the country. Other groups quickly became targets. Any individuals seen to be supporting the existing system, including journalists who published accounts favorable to the government, might be killed. In fact, Algeria in the 1990s became the most dangerous country in the world for journalists (Van Atta 1998: 70). Academics and schoolteachers who continued to go to work and perform their duties became victims. Liberal and secular members of society became targets, including women who were in positions of some authority or who were public figures. Women in Western dress could be beaten or killed on the streets (Maddy-Weitzman 1997: 182). Even schoolgirls who did not cover their heads in approved Islamic fashion were killed as a warning to others (Crenshaw 1994: 278). A point was even reached where family members of personnel in the security forces were targeted (Stone 1997: 192). Even moderates in the FIS became targets because they were willing to negotiate with the military government (Lesch 2002: 83).

The terrorism widened to include other groups that were considered to be providing challenges to the vision of an Islamic government and society in Algeria. Priests and other members of the Christian clergy became victims (Weinberg and Eubank 2000: 103). Anyone working for foreign companies or foreign technicians employed by the government also became targets (Willis 1997: 282–4). The attacks against foreign workers threatened key sectors of the economy and made it even more difficult for the government to provide goods and services to the population in general. If economic hardships on the population could be increased, the Islamic groups could gain even greater support. The violence and terrorism spread beyond Algeria itself. The opponents of the government launched attacks in France in an effort to convince the French to end their support of the government in Algeria. The attacks include a plan to use the hijacked Air France plane in a suicide attack on Paris. The attacks did force a debate about the French policies towards Algeria and about the policies of the Algerian government, but the French continued to support the Algerian government (Fuller 1996: 46–7). This shift to attacks on targets outside of Europe was evidence that the efforts of the Algerian government to deal with the rebellion were succeeding (Lesch 2002: 83).

The terrorist attacks in Algeria soon included the general population as targets. Car bombs and other attacks have taken place in the cities to demonstrate the weakness of the government and to indicate that the opposition could strike anywhere. The violence now included large numbers of everyday Algerians residing in the countryside. Rebel groups attacked villages with some regularity, massacring the inhabitants. These attacks were carried out with extreme brutality, involving torture, rape, and death. Frequently, women and children were not spared in the attacks. The victims were seen as an offering to God (Chalk 1999: 160). The rationale for the villages that were chosen is often obscure. At times the attacks appeared to be designed to draw military units into ambushes. In other cases there was the possibility that the village was regarded as being pro-government. In at least some cases the massacres occurred in villages where the GIA suspected that the people were shifting their allegiance to the government (Kydd and Walter 2006: 67). More generally, the attacks seem to have been designed to indicate to the population at large that the government could not protect them. The only choices for the population were death or active cooperation with the insurgents. The massacres of villagers often involved cutting of the throats of the victims in order to create even greater fear in the rest of the population (Laqueur 1999: 130). It is possible that the tactics, which involved such extreme violence, were due to a mixture of a conscious desire to spread fear among the general population and the effects of religious zeal (Stone 1997: 191). One factor that makes it difficult to discern the particular goals of any one set of attackers is the fact that the opposition forces are not a single unified group, and different groups were following different strategies. Particularly violent attacks seem to have been undertaken at times to sabotage any chance of negotiations between the government and some of the rebel groups (Roberts 1995: 242).

As a consequence, the reason for one extremely violent attack on a village would not necessarily be the same as the reasons for other attacks. There have been some claims that the government staged the massacres to discredit the insurgents. There is no clear evidence of such a government policy, although there have been some instances of overreaction and active repression by the government forces that have contributed to the death toll in Algeria. In the first five years of fighting over 100,000 Algerians have died, a death toll as high as it is because of these kinds of attacks by the dissidents (Testas 2002: 161).

There have been some indications that the Islamic extremists have been receiving some foreign support. Iran and the Sudan and foreign groups in other Arab countries provided some aid. Al Qaeda initially provided some support for the GIA, but the attacks on the villages had negative effects on Muslim opinion, leading Al Qaeda to reduce its ties with the GIA (Rabasa *et al.* 2006: 125–6). Algerians who have been living in Europe provided some assistance as well. The nature of the violence and the attacks on foreign workers and the population in general, however, tended to solidify support for the government from countries in the West. The actions of the GIA and other groups have clearly played into the hands of those groups that argue about the dangers presented by Islamic groups. To date the government seems to have weathered these attacks. With external support the Algerian government has been able to survive, and to even hold a number of reasonably fair elections. The government, however, has been unable to defeat the insurgents totally. Negotiations between the government and the FIS leadership have reduced the violence, and Islamic parties have won seats in elections for the national legislature. Continuing economic difficulties have made the achievement of lasting peace more difficult (Testas 2002: 179). In addition, the GIA has still refused to enter into any negotiations with the government and continues the armed struggle.

CASE STUDY 5.4   AUM SHINRIKYO (SUPREME TRUTH)

Japanese domestic terrorism hit the world news in March 1995 when it was discovered that a religious sect had released sarin nerve gas in the Japanese subway system in an effort to cause mass casualties. Members of Aum Shinrikyo undertook this attack, resulting in a handful of deaths and the need for medical care for thousands. Had the materials used been more potent and the delivery system better controlled, the death toll could have easily been in the hundreds and might even have been in the thousands. The sect had undertaken earlier attempts at chemical warfare, but they had not been noticeably successful. The authorities had not even been aware that chemical attacks had been launched.

Shoko Asahara founded Aum Shinrikyo in 1987. It was one of many such sects in Japan, and as a consequence it initially received relatively little attention. Religious sects in Japan are given a great deal of latitude with few restrictions on how they operate. In fact, Aum Shinrikyo was actually the first such sect to undergo rigorous investigation (Szykowiak and Steinhoff 1995: 294). The sect, which claimed more than 40,000 members—most of them in Japan and Russia, was dominated by its founder, who basically made all the rules and set the policy for the group (Schmid 2000: 124). Asahara saw himself as the religious leader who had been sent to save the world and who had acquired the supreme truth necessary to do so (Hoffman 2006: 121–2). Asahara hoped to reinvigorate Japanese society and establish a pure and holy society, and he foresaw a world war that would occur as a necessary form of purification. The world must be destroyed in order to be renewed (Lifton 2000: 203). The use of the chemical weapons and the possibilities of a large number of casualties fit within this framework of ideas, which called for apocalyptic actions and sacrifices to create the new pure society of the future. For Asahara it was necessary to destroy the present government and to create a theocratic state that he would lead in order to save Japan (Watanabe 1998: 95).

The potential for violence by the group increased for a variety of reasons. Asahara ran for a seat in parliament in 1990. When he lost, he believed the government had rigged the results to deny him the victory he deserved (Tucker 2006: 330). While the cult was flourishing and attracting new members, it also began to face problems with former members, including legal action, and disputes related to some of its business practices. The members of the cult began to see themselves as victims of persecution by the government and general population because they had found the supreme truth; they eventually came to see non-members as dangerous to the group and its religious mission (Watanabe 1998: 87–9). The sect dealt with former members and other threats to the group by murdering the individuals in question (Raufer 2000: 38). Facing the apparent persecution, the group increased its efforts to develop chemical weapons, and it also sought to acquire a variety of both conventional weapons and biological agents abroad, especially in Russia (Harmon 2000: 97). Such activities eventually led to government interest in the sect. Legal difficulties multiplied, and the group was in danger of being prosecuted for a variety of illegal activities. Violence was chosen as one means of deflecting government investigations. The group attempted to incapacitate judges who were hearing a case against the group. Wind-borne chemicals were carried to the hotel and caused illness to the judges, one of whom died. There were unintended casualties totalling seven deaths and even more illnesses that resulted from the attack (Tucker 2006: 338). The attack was successful in the sense that it disrupted the trial, although the authorities did not realize at the time that a chemical attack had been launched. There were other unsuccessful efforts to use biological weapons and to launch chemical attacks, which may have been tests of the materials available (Lifton 2000: 39–40, 208–9). The failures kept the movement from being detected as the source of the health problems. Once an attack was reasonably successful, however, the source of the violence was traced and the group was shut down. While these attacks were part of a political agenda, they had a practical goal as well—to deflect government attention away from the activities of the sect. The sarin attacks on the subways occurred at a time when government investigations were beginning to bring unwanted publicity to the activities of the group (Crelinsten 2000: 186). Since the gas was released in the subway system in the heart of Tokyo's government district, it is likely that government bureaucrats were the targets (Tucker 1996: 167). If large numbers of bureaucrats had been killed, the government could have found it difficult to cope with everyday issues as well as an investigation of the cult.

The Aum sect was noteworthy in that it was an organization that commanded significant resources. The group had sufficient funds, some of which were attained because members turned over their assets to the organization. The availability of financial resources meant that the sect could create laboratories and undertake the necessary research to create chemical weapons. The group also attracted a significant number of members who had the appropriate scientific or educational training at the graduate or post-graduate level to operate the labs. While Aum was able to produce the chemical weapons that it used with these resources, the materials were not of sufficiently good quality to make them very effective (Leitenberg 2000: 156). It is possible that Asahara was forced to use the low-quality materials before he was ready because of the government investigations. With more time the researchers might have been able to come up with much more deadly materials. Even so, with major resources and a period of time during which it did not face government scrutiny Aum Shinrikyo was unable to come up with effective chemical or biological weapons. One problem for the group was that it did not focus on just one project. Instead, resources were shifted from one area to another without achieving truly useful results in any one (Rosenau 2001: 296). The use of the nerve gas by the Aum group remains important, however, because it was the first use of chemical weapons in an attack by an organization in a domestic setting as opposed to open warfare.

While Asahara remains in prison for his role in the subway attacks, the cult has not collapsed. Many secondary leaders of Aum could only be convicted of minor offenses since there was no evidence linking them to involvement in the subway attacks or other acts of violence. The sect is currently regrouping, and there is little evidence that the members feel remorse for the attacks (D. Kaplan 2000: 225). It remains possible, as a consequence, that the group could again resort to the use of biological or chemical weapons in an effort to achieve its goals. The factors that made Aum Shinrikyo dangerous in the past were its wealth and its belief system that accepted and even promoted violence. These circumstances have not changed (Cameron 1999: 301). It is likely that faced with internal dissention or opposition from outside the sect could resort to the use of conventional weapons to deal with the disloyal or the unbelievers.

CASE STUDY 5.5   ANTI-ABORTION ACTIVITIES IN THE UNITED STATES

Many Christian groups have supported anti-abortion protests in the United States. The anti-abortion movement is unusual in that it brought together members of religious denominations that generally do not share similar values. In fact, individuals would actually disagree on many other points of theology, but they came together in a rather ad hoc coalition of individuals who cooperate in this one area (B. Lutz and J. Lutz 2007: 122). These groups have usually practiced passive resistance and demonstrated in front of clinics offering abortions. The vast majority of the participants in these protests have been opposed to violence, but some have been willing to use more active efforts to limit the availability of abortions. Frequently, this activism has taken the form of vandalism and other damage to property. Glue is placed in locks, windows are broken, the automobiles of clinic workers are vandalized, and such like. This kind of vandalism and harassment is designed to make clinic operations more difficult. Some of the protesters have graduated from petty vandalism to the use of bombs, which are intended to cause only damage property, even though, at times, individuals have been seriously injured by accident. All of these activities that have damaged property have been effective to some extent. Clinics have closed or the hours of operation have been limited. Insurance costs for clinics providing abortions have risen so much that some doctors have ceased to provide the procedure. In other cases, landlords have refused to renew leases for clinics and offices where abortions are performed or even where abortion counseling is offered because of the fear of damage to their property (Perlstein 1997: 544). Thus, the property attacks have achieved some of the goals of the groups. The bombings may have been the most important in this regard since such attacks are the ones most likely to lead to increased costs and generate fear amongst the relevant property owners.

In a few cases, the violence has escalated to assaults on individuals. Doctors and other clinic workers have been attacked or murdered. The target audience for these attacks have been the other doctors and workers in the clinics where abortions could be obtained (Kydd and Walter 2006: 53). In other cases, the militants threatened the doctors and others and their family members. The violence and the threats have proven to be effective. Some individuals stopped working at the clinics, while others would only perform abortions at out-of-town locations. Other doctors were effectively deterred from entering into the practice (Wilson and Lynxwiler 1988: 266–7). This type of violence has been relatively rare, and, when it has occurred, it has usually been committed by individuals or small groups rather than large organizations, but the actions have clearly instilled the intended fear. The persons thought to be involved in such attacks or murders have frequently been difficult to capture, even when they have been identified. It took seven years to capture Eric Rudolph, who was responsible for attacks on abortion clinics—as well as a gay bar and the Atlanta Olympics (Heymann 2003: 81). It has been apparent in the United States that there have been groups that have been willing to aid the activists in escaping from punishment for the assaults and murders.

The Army of God was one group in the anti-abortion movement that used violence. It was a rather shadowy organization in that was apparently founded by the Reverend Mike Bray. The group has claimed responsibility for a number of bombings of abortion clinics. Bray himself was involved in some of the bombings and seems to have initiated the use of the term Army of God. He may also be the author of an underground manual on anti-abortion activities with that title, which has been distributed to activist groups. In addition, he has provided justifications for the use of violence to stop abortions, and he has defended bombings, assaults, attempted murders, and murders undertaken to achieve this goal. Several persons associated with Bray have been involved in murders or attempted murders. He has indicated that one important goal of the violent attacks is that they dissuade persons from offering abortions. The violence should not be considered retribution but should be intended as a deterrent to future actions (Juergensmeyer 2000: 21–4). The Army of God wanted to provoke violence against abortion providers by other individuals as well, and it was somewhat successful in stimulating these attacks (Chalk 1999: 157). There is no doubt that he has hoped to encourage violence against abortion clinics and providers, and there is a great deal of evidence that he has been successful. There seem to be many anti-abortion activists who have volunteered to serve in the Army of God and who have adopted the terminology. Of course, no formal membership has been required to join. The network of like-minded individuals associated with the Army of God has become a form of leaderless resistance. There are indications of links between the Army of God and more formal organizations. In addition, the impression of an organization that is active gives greater weight to activities and encourages a belief that the group is larger and better supported than it actually might be. Ultimately the activities of the Army of God and other violent activists have been effective since abortions have become much more difficult to obtain in some parts of the United States (Laqueur 1999: 229).

The anti-abortion movement activities have frequently not been included in any terrorism statistics for the United States. Many of the attacks are property attacks without violence to people, even though the intent is to induce terror in a target audience. While the attacks are violent, they may not be seen as terrorism since the targets of the violence are not governmental. Probably more important is the fact that labeling the persons involved as terrorists would create image problems for organizations opposed to abortion. As a consequence, while these activities have been considered as crimes they have usually avoided have the much more negative label of terrorism attached to them.

CASE STUDY 5.6   OSAMA BIN LADEN AND THE AL QAEDA NETWORK

Osama bin Laden and his Al Qaeda (the Base) network have become very prominent actors in the international terrorist scene. The organization is multinational in terms of its makeup, and there are organizations in many countries that are linked to the network while still operating at the national level. Al Qaeda is relatively unique compared to earlier groups because of its fluid organization, its recruitment across national boundaries, its funding, and its use of modern communications (Cronin 2006: 32). The Al Qaeda organization has been flexible. There is an inner circle of members dedicated to bin Laden, a second, broader group of Muslims from many countries with whom he has had contact, and a third, outer group that has been inspired by him and that considers him a hero but which has lacked direct contacts (Burke 2003: 127). It is estimated that there are between 5,000 and 12,000 members in at least twenty-four different groups. In addition to undertaking joint operations, the groups share resources, provide local contacts for each other, and aid in money laundering (Abuza 2002: 428–9). The organizational capabilities of this network and the financial resources that it has available have been impressive. The various individuals associated with the network have also displayed extreme dedication, especially among those who have carried out the attacks planned by the group. At the higher levels it is believed that there is a council that reviews and proposes terrorist activities around the globe. Bin Laden has provided important centralized leadership and streamlined the decision-making process (Nedoroscik 2002: 72). Bin Laden was also successful in focusing the attention of various groups on the threat that Western supremacy represented. By orchestrating a confrontation with the West, moreover, he was able to unite groups that had previously been divided by their more localized agendas (Burke 2003: 150). He may also have hoped that the 9/11 attacks would provoke a violent US response that would further unify the Muslim world against the United States and the West (Kydd and Walter 2006: 50, 71). Bin Laden has brought a number of important resources to his terrorism campaign that has made him and the network so dangerous. His personal wealth brought considerable financial resources to his violent political activities. Not only has he provided funding, he has had access to financial channels that have permitted wealthy supporters that are sympathetic to the activities of the Al Qaeda network to transfer funds to the organization. Bin Laden obviously has impressive organizational skills to keep the network of groups in the Middle East functioning and cooperating. The coordination required, and the major attacks attributed to bin Laden, are clear proof of the abilities in this area. Among the other resources that bin Laden has brought to his activities are the face-to-face contacts that he had made in previous years while in Afghanistan that have been so critical to facilitating activities among the different organizations and groups in the network. The network also would appear to use modern technology in terms of the internet and computer access to maintain contact with each other (Ranstorp 1998: 323). Such modern technology obviously has permitted anti-government groups to work together without necessarily always coming together. One other advantage that this particular group has is its loose organization. Destruction of one part by local security forces will not threaten the overall viability of the network. The network is unlikely to be compromised by any single penetration by security forces or informers.

Al Qaeda has been responsible for many terrorist actions. It supported the Somali groups that attacked US forces in 1993, although there is no evidence it had any direct role in those attacks. It apparently had some role in the bombing of the US barracks in Dharan, Saudi Arabia in 1996 that killed nineteen US service personnel and wounded over 500, and it was clearly involved in the suicide attack on the US destroyer *Cole* in 2000 in Aden harbor that killed seventeen service personnel and wounded thirty-nine others. Bin Laden's network was also responsible for the attacks in 1998 on the US embassies in Nairobi, Kenya and Dar-es-Salaam, Tanzania, which resulted in the deaths of over 200 people and the wounding of thousands, most of whom were the nationals of these countries. Of course, the most deadly attack was the use of the hijacked airliners against the World Trade Center towers and the Pentagon on September 11th, 2001. These attacks were effective in gaining major attention for Al Qaeda, publicizing its issues and the motives behind the attacks, and gaining global prominence (Nacos 2003: 8). Al Qaeda has also targeted Israeli tourists in Kenya, including an attempt to shoot down an airliner and a suicide car bomb attack at a tourist hotel (Schweitzer 2006: 143). Groups with some links to Al Qaeda undertook the bombings that targeted tourist areas in Bali in 2002. Al Qaeda operatives were involved in the attacks on the Madrid commuter trains in 2004 (Rabasa *et al.* 2006: 122–3). There is no evidence, however, of any link between Al Qaeda and the attacks in 2005 on the London transit system. The militants involved in these attacks were undoubtedly inspired by bin Laden and Al Qaeda. In fact, leaderless resistance kinds of attacks such as these can be more dangerous, and they are harder to detect since there are no organizational ties to monitor. Cells belonging to the network have been discovered in many countries, and local intelligence agencies, security forces, or the police have prevented the planned actions in a number of other locations. One of the characteristics of al Qaeda is that unlike other dissident groups it has no set style of action. The various attacks have been innovative, harder to detect, and deadly, making the group much more dangerous (Hoffman 2002b: 309).

The genesis of the network goes back to the struggles in Afghanistan against the local Communists and the Soviet Union. Bin Laden was one of the many Muslims from around the world who went to Afghanistan to fight on the side of the Afghans. At this time, many countries were supplying arms and funds to the Afghan guerrillas, including Muslim countries out of religious solidarity and the United States as the primary Cold War opponent of the Soviet Union. Recruits from Muslim countries all over the world made their way to Afghanistan. There were somewhere between 7,000 and 10,000 such Muslim volunteers (Ranstorp 1998: 321). Many of these fighters received training in camps covertly supported by the United States. Bin Laden was able to meet a substantial number of committed Muslims from many countries—the "Arab Afghans." Such face-to-face contacts are extremely important in Middle Eastern cultures, and the opportunities to interact with such committed Muslims from different countries provided a basis for the network that developed. Many other militants were trained in camps in Afghanistan after the Soviet withdrawal as part of a coordinated effort to prepare them for conflicts in their home countries. Many of the fighters in Afghanistan and the members of groups in Al Qaeda and other networks from are middle- or upper-class backgrounds and recruited from the Arab or Muslim diaspora in Europe (Friedman 2001: 98, 101). When the former guerrillas returned to their home countries, they frequently became disenchanted with the political policies and activities of their governments, and they joined local Islamic groups seeking changes in policies or leaders, while in other cases they were attracted to struggles by local Muslims opposed to non-Muslim rulers (Fuller 2002: 53). The linkages that had been formed in Afghanistan have permitted continued cooperation and support among groups in different countries.

After the Soviet withdrawal from Afghanistan, bin Laden saw the West, especially the United States, as the greatest threat to Islam. His negative opinion of US policy had a number of causes. The United States was the primary source for cultural contamination of the Islamic world (Robbins 2002: 355). Members of the Al Qaeda network see themselves as fighting against the evil influences represented by the secular cultures of the West. Bin Laden and others see the United States as being responsible for attacks on Muslim populations in many parts of the world, including Bosnia, Lebanon, and Chechnya (Doran 2002: 28–9). In their eyes, the United States avoided involvement in Bosnia for so long so that the Christian Serbs could gain ground at the expense of the local Muslims (Pillar 2001: 68). He has also been concerned about US policies that favor the Israelis over the Palestinians. The Persian Gulf conflict that arose after the Iraqi occupation of Kuwait became the trigger in bin Laden's turn against the United States. He opposed the UN sanctions against Iraq as one of his concerns with US policy as well as the presence of Western troops on the soil of Saudi Arabia where the holy cities of Mecca and Medina are located. Bin Laden has seen all of these activities as part of a Christian–Judeo conspiracy, led by the United States, to weaken Islam. The holy places of Islam are targeted for occupation by the Western forces, a process already begun by the Israeli occupation of East

Jerusalem in 1967, which contains the Mosque of the Dome of the Rock, considered to be the third holiest site in Islam (Ranstorp 1998: 325). These issues seemed to have coalesced to lead bin Laden toward seeking a reinvigorated Muslim community, one that could deal with threats to its holy sites, including those from the West, and which could defend itself.

There is some evidence that bin Laden attempted to acquire weapons of mass destruction. He used Chechen contacts to try to acquire a nuclear device in the former Soviet Union (McCaffrey and Basso 2002: 215). Such weapons would have made threats and demands upon the United States and its allies more effective and credible (Cameron 1999). Clearly, had an opportunity to acquire chemical, biological, or even nuclear weapons presented itself, bin Laden would have taken it. The financial resources available to him would have made such an acquisition eminently possible. Their use would have been quite probable as well given the willingness already demonstrated to use deadly conventional weapons to cause mass casualties (Wilkinson 2003: 124).

Al Qaeda has become the symbolic center of what is increasingly called the global jihadist movement involving Muslims from many lands. Bin Laden sees Al Qaeda waging a global guerrilla war against the West (Ramakrishna 2002: 209). Further, bin Laden and others in the group see the United States as a key sponsor of local regimes that prevent them from controlling local societies (Neumann and Smith 2005: 579). More recently extremist groups have gained recruits from the *madrassas* (literally schools, but generally the term refers to religious schools that teach intolerance and encourage violent attacks on enemies of Islam). Saudi Arabia and other Arab states as well as private donors have funded many of these Islamic schools. The *madrassas* have spread more fundamentalist ideas. In some, but hardly all, cases they advocate launching holy wars against foreigners and secular governments (Burke 2003: 88). At least some of the individuals studying in these schools have often become terrorists and members of the global jihadist movement. The movement has generated support from Muslim communities in Europe that have not been assimilated (Leiken 2005). These Muslims in Europe have become radicalized from their stay abroad, in part because they often have faced a loss of social status and in part because they have been influenced by the existing leftist tradition that has emphasized Western exploitation of the developing world (Roy 2006: 163).

The various components of Al Qaeda and the jihadist movement all include fundamentalist groups within individual countries, including the Islamic opposition groups in Egypt and Algeria as well as links with a number of groups in the Philippines and Indonesia (Abuza 2005). The targets for the group have included Western countries and their citizens as symbols of outside contamination of Islam and the local governments and citizens that cooperate with the intrinsically evil outsiders. Attacks on the West are designed to bring about changes in foreign policy. They would like to see the United States and other Western countries withdraw from the Middle East, end support for Israel, and stop aiding the local governments that do not meet with the favor of the organization. The withdrawal would permit the re-establishing of Islamic values and governments. The governments of secular authoritarian states such as Egypt, Algeria, and Iraq would be replaced. The conservative monarchies in the Arabian Peninsula, whose Islamic credentials are somewhat suspect, might also be in line for replacement. The resulting Islamic governments in various parts of the Middle East might even combine into the historical ideal of a unified Muslim community that incorporates believers of different languages, nationalities, and ethnic heritages. Islamic principles and laws would then govern this community. Al Qaeda and the global jihadist movement have been successful in drawing in individuals in the Islamic Salifiyyah movements that seek to unite all Muslims in a single caliphate (Azra 2003: 51). The Salafiyyah ideas have been particularly important for attracting recruits from the Muslim diaspora in places such as Europe (Post 2006: 24).

The religious views of the network also explain why the militantly religious Taliban regime in Afghanistan had cooperated with al Qaeda and bin Laden. Al Qaeda and other militant groups are not going to disappear even if bin Laden is captured or killed. Some militant dissident groups have been destroyed by security forces only to be replaced by others. Revivalist Islamic movements provide recruits for dissident groups, and as long as existing governments in the Middle East continue to repress opposition groups, including Islamic ones, dissidents will be able to attract the disaffected as well (Khashan 1997: 17). The US and allied attacks against the Taliban regime in Afghanistan destroyed the safe haven of Al Qaeda, and the losses sustained in the battles in Afghanistan have clearly hurt. Al Qaeda was destroyed as a hierarchical organization and led to the development of a decentralized network structure (Hegghammer 2006: 14). Many of the key elements are now overseas, operating in their home countries or other areas. There are some indications that many of the surviving leaders of the group have relocated to Southeast Asian countries where there have become increasingly active (Chalk 1998a: 127). Al Qaeda has been quite effective in connecting with existing Islamic groups in the region rather than creating them (Abuza 2003b: 81). The US intervention in Iraq, on the other hand, has provided additional opportunities for attacks from groups connected to Al Qaeda. While hurt by the expulsion from Afghanistan, Al Qaeda has continued to operate on a global basis. The flexible network structure has served the group well.

BOX 5.3 ABU SAYYAF GROUP

The Abu Sayyaf group in the Philippines is one of the local Muslim terrorist groups with links to Al Qaeda. Various Muslim dissident groups have appeared seeking autonomy or independence from central authority over the years using both terrorism and guerrilla tactics (Rodell 2007). Somewhere between 300 and 500 Filipinos fought in Afghanistan with the Islamic opposition (Abuza 2002: 440). Returning fighters formed the core of the Abu Sayyaf group. Bin Laden provided organization support and training for the members in the use of kidnapping and extortion (Tan 2003: 108). The southern part of the Philippines has a significant concentration of Muslims in a largely Christian country. Abu Sayyaf is one of the latest groups to appear. It is more extreme than some other dissident groups such as the Moro National Liberation Front that has been willing to negotiate with the central government to achieve greater local autonomy. The Abu Sayyaf group has kidnapped foreign tourists in the Philippines and surrounding countries. Many of the victims have been ransomed, providing funds for the organization. The group has been virulently anti-Christian and has launched attacks against clergy, churches, and the Filipino Christians in general. The group has frequently targeted Catholic clergy in its attacks (Thayer 2005: 88). The group has suffered numerous casualties in its operations, including the death of key leaders, but it has managed to gain new recruits and to continue the struggle (Rodell 2007: 234). The group to some extent has degenerated into a criminal organization, focusing more on the profits to be made from kidnapping than achieving political objectives, but it does continue to use terrorist actions with political goals. In 2004 it was responsible for the bombing of a Manila ferry that killed more than a hundred persons (Tan 2006: 116–17). The group continues to operate throughout the southern Philippines, taking advantage of weak governmental structures, difficult terrain, a population hostile or indifferent to the government officials, and the availability of aid from abroad as a consequence of linkages with other Islamic dissident groups.

SUMMARY

The cases indicate that the use of terror and violence had mixed results for the dissidents. The Sikhs and the efforts of Aum Shinrikyo failed. The dissidents involved in the previous violence, however, have not been eliminated from the scene in their respective countries. Aum has reorganized, and it might again be able to rekindle the global conflagration that it sees as necessary for the triumph of the sect. Similarly, the Sikhs may again attempt to create an independent Khalistan. If Hindu majoritarian efforts at dominance increase, such an outbreak could become more likely. The Zealots came close to achieving their goal of independence, and they might have been victorious under more auspicious circumstances, such as more severe disruptions elsewhere in the Roman Empire. The successes that they achieved led to Roman decisions to punish the rebels and make additional revolts more difficult. Such a response by the state in the case of Japan and India, however, has not been possible. Japan cannot really eliminate or disperse a religious sect, and any effort by the Indian government to scatter the Sikh population throughout the country would probably lead to an outbreak of the violence that such dispersal would be seeking to avoid. The violent anti-abortion groups in the United States have been partially successful since abortions have become more difficult to obtain. For the Muslim dissidents in Algeria it is too soon to judge the long-term effectiveness of their attacks. It is possible that the regime could still be toppled by violence, but a more likely outcome is some continued role in the government for religious groups such as the FIS. If changes do occur, then the violence will have been partially successful.

The US response to the attacks of September 11th, 2001 has hurt the Al Qaeda network. The safe haven in Afghanistan was eliminated, although it has maintained enough organization cohesion to continue to operate and to exist as a functioning group in the border areas between Afghanistan and Pakistan. Segments of the network have found themselves targets for police forces and intelligence agencies and have had to deal with greater repression. The success of the attacks, such as the bombings of the East African embassies and of the destruction on September 11th, however, can serve to mobilize support in the future. The attacks have demonstrated what is possible to those seeking a Muslim resurgence and assaults against the West. Revenge attacks for other US policies could be more likely in the future. If the United States had withdrawn from the Middle East as desired by the attackers, violence against Israel and other governments in the region that the dissidents disliked would have increased. In addition, groups in other regions might have sought to undertake similar spectacular attacks to change US policies that they disliked (Reinares 1998: 355). The launching of the war on terrorism, the efforts to find bin Laden and to destroy Al Qaeda, the destruction of the Taliban regime in Afghanistan, and the recent invasion of Iraq may increase the chances of revenge attacks, including suicide bombings.

In none of the six cases surveyed was foreign support especially important. The Jewish rebels operated with no external support. Beyond the activities of the former Taliban regime, there has been little indication of external state sponsorship of bin Laden and Al Qaeda, in part because bin Laden's own financial resources precluded the need for such sponsorship (Cameron 1999: 282). There has been no evidence of links between Iraq, Syria, or the Hizballah organization with bin Laden, even though these actors have all been involved in some acts of terrorism (Posen 2001/2: 54). Al Qaeda and bin Laden had the safe haven in Afghanistan and what support the Taliban regime could provide, but the group had enough resources of its own. There has been increasing cooperation among Islamic groups around the world—facilitating travel, obtaining false documents, and the provision of other support (Pillar 2001: 52). The anti-abortion movement in the United States, including the violent components, was homegrown with no international connections. Aum Shinrikyo attempted to purchase biological and chemical weapons abroad, but it was unsuccessful. Foreign governments were unwilling to support the group even when there was a financial profit involved. The Sikhs had some assistance from Pakistan in various periods, but never on a massive scale. The Sikh diaspora population was a more important source of support. The Algerian dissidents would appear to have had the most foreign support of any of the case studies.

Casualties from the terrorist attacks and related violence were substantial in the case studies. The example of the Jewish Zealots is one of the oldest known, but the leaders of the revolt dealt with opponents summarily when they were plotting the revolt and continued to do so once in power. The resulting deaths were substantial in number. The death toll from Aum Shinrikyo was small, but the intent of the cult was to cause massive casualties in the population. The terrorist actions of the Sikhs, the Algerian dissidents, and Osama bin Laden have also resulted in significant death counts. It appears that the carnage from the 9/11 attacks exceeded bin Laden's expectations, but he was pleased by the extent of the destruction (Hoffman 2006: 134). It would appear that suggestions that religious groups are more likely to seek to inflict high casualties have been supported by the above cases.

There are some indications that religious terrorism occurs in agreement with Huntington's thesis that the clash of cultures and civilizations is likely to generate violence of a more severe kind. The various revolts of the Jews involved a definite antipathy towards foreign cultures. The monotheistic Jewish believers feared the pantheon of gods and the associated Greek culture that were part of the Roman Empire. In the revolts that occurred, the rebels frequently attacked Greeks and Hellenized Jews, and Greek temples were often destroyed as well (Josephus 1981: 168–9; Rapoport 1984: 669). When Jewish rebels captured Salamis in Cyprus during the second revolt, they slaughtered the Greek inhabitants of the city (Fuks 1961: 99). The Muslim dissidents involved in Al Qaeda could succeed in the long run if there is indeed a clash of civilizations between the Western culture and the Islamic culture. Osama bin Laden and the Al Qaeda network clearly have sought to prevent the intrusion of external cultural values and the contamination of an outside civilization in the Middle East. Bin Laden sought to create such a clash; he expected an American counterattack in the wake of 9/11 that would lead to destruction and that would help to rally Muslims everywhere to support the agenda of Al Qaeda (Chipman 2003: 165). Indeed, if Muslim extremists choose to wage war against Western civilization, than a clash of civilizations is already occurring (Howell 2003: 160). The clash of cultures was also evident in the violence in Algeria as the Muslim dissidents, especially the GIA, have sought to drive out Western influences. The example of Aum Shinrikyo is less clear. The sect's origin was in part a reaction to modernity, but the violence was within the same cultural area. The violence between Sikhs and Hindus clearly does not fit within this context of clashing cultures. Sikhism and Hinduism are closely related; thus, this prolonged violence has occurred within the same civilization. Thus, not all religiously inspired terrorism occurs along the borders of religiously based cultural areas.

Terrorism and violence grounded in the religious beliefs of groups has been present in the world in many circumstances. Such actions are likely to continue. In addition to having millenarian visions, they are often unwilling to compromise or reach accommodations with their opponents (Kelly 1998: 27). Such compromises are not possible since the agreements would run the danger of violating key religious beliefs held by the dissidents. The violence results from the view of some religious groups that the social and moral pillars of society have collapsed and they must be re-established (Juergensmeyer 1996: 20). To the extent that such violence is a reaction to changes in the world, it will continue because change will continue. Change and globalization will challenge religions throughout the world, and violence is one form of response to these challenges. The clash of civilizations idea has relevance as well, and the differences between different areas are unlikely to disappear in the immediate future. The fact that state sponsorship has been limited in at least some cases is one positive sign that might indicate that there will be at least a reduced level of violence in the future.

TERMS

Abu Sayyaf group	Islamic Salvation Front (FIS)
Akali Dal	Jewish Defense League (JDL)
Al Qaeda	jihad
Army of God	Meir Kahane
Shoko Asahara	Khalistan
Assassin sect	madrassa
Aum Shinrikyo	Operation Black Thunder
Ayodhya	Operation Blue Star
Bharatiya Janata Party	Yitzak Rabin
Sant Jarnail Singh Bhindranwale	Rashtriya Swayamsevak Sangh
Osama bin Laden	(RSS—National Patriotism Organization)
Indira Gandhi	sarin
global jihad	Sharia
Gush Emunim	Shia Muslim
Hinduvata	Sicarri
Hizballah	Sikhs
Iron Guard	Sunni Muslim
Islamic Army Group (GIA)	Taliban
Islamic Movement Army (MIA)	Zealots

FURTHER READING

Burke, J. (2003) *Al-Qaeda: Casting a Shadow of Terror*, London: I. B. Tauris.

Huntington, S. P. (1996) *The Clash of Civilizations and the Remaking of World Order*, New York: Simon & Schuster.

Lifton, R. J. (2000) *Destroying the World To Save It: Aum Shinrikyo, Apocalyptic Violence, and the New Global Terrorism*, New York: Henry Holt.

Rapoport, D. C. (1990) "Religion and Terror: Thugs, Assassins, and Zealots," in C. W. Kegley, Jr (ed.) *International Terrorism: Characteristics, Causes, Controls*, New York: St Martin's Press, 146–57.

Stone, M. (1997) *The Agony of Algeria*, New York: Columbia University Press.

Wallace, P. (1995) "Political Violence and Terrorism in India: The Crisis of Identity," in M. Crenshaw (ed.) *Terrorism in Context*, University Park, PA: Pennsylvania State University Press, 352–409.

CHAPTER 6

Ethnic and National Bases of Terrorism

While the popular image of terrorism today is that of a religiously motivated suicide bomber, much of the violence that actually occurs in the world is based in disagreements and dissidence in ethnic and national communities. Ethnic and nationalist violence was one of the basic causes for increased levels of terrorism in the world in recent years (Chalk 1999: 152). Ethnic confrontations have become more numerous as groups have sought autonomy or independence or the right to attach themselves to some other country. In multicultural societies where ethnic populations intermingle, communal violence has become more common with opposing groups defining themselves ethnically or racially. Ethnic conflicts have the additional characteristic of being quite persistent and lasting for long periods of time (Tan 2000: 268).

While nationalism does not date back to the first century CE in the conventional sense as an inspiration for violence, it is also not totally new. There were indications of national feeling in the struggles of the Welsh, Irish, and Scots against the English monarchs. Persians, Turks, and Arabs did not always peacefully coexist in various Islamic states. Most conflicts in the first millennium CE and beyond, however, had a religious base rather than national ones or represented struggles between various kings, princes, sultans, dukes, and others. By the eighteenth century, the stage was finally set for nationalism to become an important force as the ideas of nations began to become more important. Both the American Revolution and the French Revolution clearly involved the development of national feelings and popular mobilization. Once peoples began to see themselves as nations, the possibility of political violence rooted in feelings of nationalism became more likely. The practice of terrorism then became one of the potential tools for any nationalist group seeking to achieve some sort of political autonomy or independence. Changes in government policies remained among the objectives of such nationalist groups, but local self-governance was often a key. These new nationalist feelings were often based on a distinctive language, but national feelings could also rely on perceptions of ethnic differences and a cultural or political history, including former golden ages as much as language (Tan 2000: 270). For example, the Scandinavian kingdoms of Denmark, Norway, and Sweden developed with distinctive identities based on their histories. Their languages were similar, their ethnic backgrounds not tremendously different, all three were overwhelmingly Lutheran, and their cultures had much in common, yet they perceived themselves as separate. The end result was different national identities for these territories, even though provinces could change hands and the populations could be readily assimilated into different kingdoms given enough time.

MODERNITY AND ETHNIC CONFLICT

With modernity, nationalism has emerged more forcibly. It would be useful, of course, to have a clear and precise definition of what constitutes an ethnic or national group, but such precision is not possible. Ultimately, ethnicity or national identification will be self-defined by the groups in question. All that is necessary is that a group sees itself as being unique. And, if a group perceives that it faces disabilities because of ethnic or national differences, the potential for violence, and terrorism, exists. In modern times, the use of terrorism by nationalists has often been associated with national liberation struggles against colonial powers. Terrorism may be the first step in efforts to create the national feeling necessary to force the occupying colonial power to consider giving up control of the territory. In a colony the indigenous inhabitants are almost by definition weaker than the colonizing power, making terrorism one of the few violent techniques available if the colonial power ignores peaceful efforts to change colonial polices. When European colonial empires were being challenged after World War II, nationalist movements lacked the military power to directly confront the European military and security forces, so they had to rely on guerrilla warfare and terrorism.

There were some significant confrontations as the colonial empires were ending. The fighting at times was accompanied by terrorist campaigns. Beginning in 1954, the French in Algeria faced such a conflict. The French were determined to stay in Algeria in part due to the large number of French settlers who had migrated to the area over the years. Thus, part of the struggle was between local French settlers (colons), a million strong and about 10 percent of the population, and the Muslim inhabitants of Algeria (O'Ballance 1967: 24–5). While the Algerian National Liberation Front used a guerrilla insurgency to force France to begin the negotiations that led to independence, an urban terrorism campaign was an important part of the early campaigns against the French. Attacks with knives and guns as well as bombs were directed at police, local government officials, Algerian collaborators, businesses, and the European colon population in general. The French had to bring in military reinforcements when the civilian officials were unable to control the city and eventually managed to win the "Battle of Algiers." In the process, however, large segments of the Muslim population were alienated from the colonial administration and France, a goal consciously sought by some of the Algerian leaders. The cycle of bombings and retaliations was designed to eliminate any possibility of compromise and to alienate a majority of Algerian Muslims from the French (Crenshaw 1995a: 487). The struggle for independence had increasing support among the Muslim population. After the Battle of Algiers the insurgents continued to use terrorist attacks to supplement guerrilla attacks in the countryside. While the urban terrorism campaign failed in the short run to oust the French, the battle for the city did ultimately contribute to independence. The French defeated the Algerian insurgents militarily, but the continued urban terrorism created insecurity for the colon population and led the French leaders to conclude that continued control of Algeria would be costly and incomplete (Crenshaw 1995a: 499).

The British also had to face terrorism in their colonial empire. In many colonies peaceful demonstrations sufficed to bring about the negotiations leading to independence. In some cases, however, the nationalists resorted to violence to convince them to leave. In the case of the British mandate in Palestine, the colonial administration faced a particularly difficult situation. There was fighting between the Arab and Jewish communities in the mandate before World War II, and the colonial administration became a target for terrorist actions by Jewish groups that were seeking to establish a national state. This three-sided battle continued after the end of the war. Later, Count Folke Bernadotte, a UN peace mediator from Sweden, was assassinated by members of the Stern Gang, a Jewish terrorist organization, for suggesting that Palestinian Arab refugees be allowed to return to their homes as part of a peace settlement (Cooley 2000: 11). Many Jewish groups viewed the colonial administration as being more favorably disposed to the Arab interests and felt that continued British rule would eventually be to their detriment. The attacks eventually convinced the British to withdraw from the Palestinian mandate since the cost was too high for any benefits that were received from the colonial position. The British withdrawal led to fighting between the Arabs and the Jews and the establishment of the state of Israel. The attacks on the British were successful in their goal of forcing a withdrawal that was probably favorable to the Jewish community. A few years later the British faced a guerrilla and terrorist uprising in Kenya in the 1950s, the Mau Mau Rebellion. This revolt was less successful. The British committed sufficient resources and effectively utilized local self-defense groups to defeat the rebels (Beckett 2001: 124–7). Independence came to Kenya as part of the broader decolonialization movement in Africa, although it is possible that the Mau Mau uprising did speed up the British decision to grant independence to Kenya and other African colonies (Walton 1984: 130). In the mid-1950s the British also faced violent nationalism in Cyprus as the Greek inhabitants of the island colony sought union with Greece. The nationalist movement focused on an urban terrorism campaign rather than a rural guerrilla campaign in part because the urban terrorism gave the nationalists access to the media and the resultant publicity for the cause of the Greek Cypriots (Hoffman 2006: 54–5). The attacks caused enough casualties and problems for the British that independence was negotiated, although the desired union with Greece was not achieved when the British were careful to protect the rights of the Turkish minority on Cyprus that did not desire union with Greece. The terrorism campaign and the resulting cost to the British to maintain the colony had led to the decision to withdraw. The decision to leave Cyprus was strengthened by the fact that Egypt had earlier gained its independence and then had assumed control over the Suez Canal, and Cyprus thus became less useful as a military base.

While colonial national liberation struggles have frequently resulted in terrorism, other kinds of ethnic or nationalist violence exist. Separatist movements have appeared in a variety of other circumstances. A group that somehow sees itself as distinctive will wish to separate from the larger country. It is not surprisingly, consequently, that terrorist violence has been more likely in multiethnic countries (Engene 2004: 41). French-speaking inhabitants of Quebec wish for a Quebec that is not part of an English-speaking Canada, and a few of them have been involved in rare instances of terrorist violence (see Box 6.1). Corsican nationalists have mounted a campaign of terrorism in an effort to separate their island from France. They have been careful

BOX 6.1 THE QUEBEC LIBERATION FRONT (FLQ)

Canada experienced a brief period of separatist terrorism in the late 1960s and early 1970s. The Quebec Liberation Front (FLQ) sought to separate French-speaking Quebec from the rest of Canada. The FLQ developed links with Algeria and Cuba, and some of the members of the group even trained with Palestinians in camps in the Middle East (Ross 1995). The group conducted a small number of terrorist attacks in an effort to obtain independence. In 1970, a British official and member of the provincial cabinet in Quebec were kidnapped. The Canadian government implemented heightened security measures, and in retaliation the FLQ killed the provincial minister. The murder resulted in public outrage and in an increase in support for government security measures designed to deal with the terrorist threat. The members of the group holding the British official decided to release him in exchange for safe passage to Cuba (Gurr 2003: 208–9). This violent campaign for an independent Quebec quickly collapsed. Public opposition to the violent methods of the FLQ and the fact that the Canadian political system permitted parties advocating independence for Quebec to compete in elections and to win a considerable number of seats limited the appeal of this violent approach. In fact, the strength of the Quebec separatist parties suggests that normal political activities may be all that will be necessary to achieve the goal of an independent Quebec at some time in the future. The political strength of the separatists has been too great for many of them to actively consider a technique of the weak, such as terrorism. Should political support for independence in the province decline or should the Canadian government prevent secession by extraordinary means, a reliance on terror could reoccur.

to avoid casualties, but they have been responsible for a substantial number of all the terrorist incidents in Europe (Engene 2004: 120, 125). The United States has faced terrorist attacks from Puerto Rican nationalist groups seeking independence for the island. A variety of nationalist groups have been responsible for bombings on the island and the mainland through the years since World War II, and they made two attempts to assassinate President Harry Truman (Gurr 1989: 217). Separatist movements of all kinds can lead to terrorist campaigns or other types of political violence. Kurds in Turkey and Iraq, Croats in Yugoslavia before World War II, various non-Burmese groups in Myanmar, and many others have sought independence, relying on political violence and terror to achieve their aims. Dissidents in these circumstances may engage in terrorism in an effort to force a harsh government response against one community, further dividing the society and creating additional support for the dissidents (Gurr and Cole 2000: 89). All these national groups have sought to gain greater autonomy or to become independent, and the active members of the struggles have regarded themselves as fighters in liberation struggles. Many of the nationalist struggles current in the world also have a strong religious element that strengthens the national feeling, but the dominant political goals of the groups are separatist or involve efforts to be united with fellow members of their ethnic group (Hoffman 1995: 272). The struggles of the Jewish settlers in Palestine were nationalist even though religion separated the Jews from the Arabs and the British. Similarly, the Muslim Algerians and Greek Orthodox Cypriots had nationalist political goals, not religious ones.

Ethnic movements may seek to join themselves to some neighboring country that is populated by members of the same ethnic group, as was the initial goal for the Greek Cypriots. Such movements may invite support from groups or the government of this neighboring country. These irredentist movements do not seek independence or autonomy but absorption into some other country. The German minority in Czechoslovakia engaged in provocative acts in their efforts to be attached to Germany, and the Austrian Nazi Party and other groups used terror to try to attach their state to Hitler's Germany. Similarly, Somalis in Kenya and parts of Ethiopia in the 1970s and 1980s, Armenians in the Soviet successor state of Azerbajain, and Serbs in Bosnia and Croatia have all sought to be united to some neighboring state. These groups have been willing to use violence and at times terrorism to attempt to achieve the goal of joining their fellow nationals in some neighboring state.

Violence can occur within a state between different communities as different groups compete for control in regions where they are intermingled. The majority may seek to repress the minority and may even try to ban the use of the minority language and to forcibly assimilate the minority groups. The minority group may be seen as being potentially disloyal elements. Ironically, the efforts at repression or assimilation frequently encourage the outbreak of the disloyalty that the actions were designed to avoid. The minority may resort to violence to safeguard its position in the society that is under threat. Elements of the majority may then use violence as well, leading to outbreaks of violence between different linguistic, national, or ethnic groups. The entire minority community may then come to be seen as legitimate targets for terrorist actions (C. Drake 1998: 65). Of course, the minority community comes to see the entire majority community as legitimate targets as well. Violence among intermingled populations has often broken out. Hutu and Tutsi in Rwanda and Burundi intermingled throughout the long history of the two groups. The intermingling of the populations has exacerbated the periods of communal violence between these ethnic groups. South Africa with black African, white, Asian, and coloured (persons of mixed race) populations intermingled was in a similar situation. Geographical separation of the different groups was not ultimately possible, although the apartheid system established by the white minority regime was designed to achieve social separation. As a consequence, when violence did occur it was likely to be communal in nature. Obviously outbreaks of violence in ethnically mixed countries remain possible in the future and related terrorist campaigns will be possible as well.

It has been suggested that the end of the Cold War and the decline of ideological confrontations have led to the increased salience of ethnic confrontations and possible outbreaks of violence and terrorism. With the end of the conflict between the United States and the Soviet Union, governments in some countries are no longer being propped up by one of the superpowers as worthwhile allies. Violence has become more likely since the governments of former allies or satellite countries no longer have the essential external support to deal with local ethnic groups seeking independence or autonomy. Similarly, the break up of the German, Russian, Austro-Hungarian, and Ottoman Empires in the aftermath of World War I led to a significant number of ethnic conflicts and outbreaks of violence. Violence within the successor states often had ethnic elements since the intermingling of populations meant that any effort to draw borders on ethnic or linguistic lines was impossible. Population exchanges were at times a possibility, but more frequently assimilation, expulsions, or violence resulted. The break up of European colonial empires created such problems. The dismantling of the Spanish Empire in Latin America has led to boundary disputes that in some cases have still not been resolved. Most of the boundaries in Africa have been arbitrary and represent borders of convenience for

BOX 6.2 TERRORISM AND ARMENIAN HISTORY LESSONS

Ethnic violence and terrorism can even occur in unusual circumstances where neither control of a state nor separation is desired. Among the more unusual terrorist groups to appear after World War II were the Armenian Army for the Secret Liberation of Armenia (ASALA) and the Justice Commandos of the Armenian Genocide (JCAG). While the two groups differed in their political ideologies, they shared the same goals, all related to the attempt of the Ottoman Turks to commit genocide against the Armenians during World War I. Eventually over a million Armenians (two-thirds of the population of the Ottoman Empire) perished during this time (Fein 1979: 16). Members of these two organizations sought revenge for the genocide. They wanted the Turkish government to acknowledge the genocide—something no Turkish government had done, and they also wanted the Turkish government to pay reparations. Although the two groups operated separately, they often chose the same types of targets. Both groups undertook a number of assaults against Turkish diplomatic personal and their families (Hoffman 2006: 72). Both ASALA and JCAG were seeking to publicize the past rather than to create an Armenian state or an autonomous Armenian region in Turkey since the Turkish massacres had destroyed the potential territorial base for a nation. Those who were not killed were scattered throughout the Middle East and the world. The Armenian extremists assassinated thirty individuals, attempted to kill sixteen others, engaged in over a hundred bombings, and seized three embassies (Pluchinsky 2006: 49–50). While the activities of the two groups did generate greater awareness of the fate of the Armenians, none of their demands were realized. By the end of the 1980s, the groups had ceased to operate. The appearance of an independent Armenia as one of the successors of the old Soviet Union has given the Armenians around the world a new focus for their attention. A revival of terrorist campaigns against Turkey does not currently appear likely barring the outbreak of international disputes between Turkey and the new Armenian state.

the former European colonizers. As a consequence, many countries became agglomerations of different language groups, ethnic affiliations, or former pre-colonial states. In many cases such groups have been divided by these borders, leaving groups in one state that may hope to rejoin their fellow nationals in some unified country. The former Belgian Congo (variously known as Congo-Kinshasa and Zaire) has threatened to break apart on numerous occasions and currently is the scene of separatist efforts in many areas and interventions by its neighbors. The difficulties in the West African countries of Liberia, Sierra Leone, and Guinea have been exacerbated as a consequence of the presence of boundaries that have divided different ethnic groups. The Dutch Empire in the East Indies was essentially a combination of different states and cultures that was held together by the colonial administration. The government of Indonesia today is still wrestling with problems resulting from the removal of Dutch control over the entire area.

The Soviet Union was no exception to the possibility of increased ethnic or national conflict that comes from the break up of previous empires. The end of the USSR and the collapse of Communism in Eastern Europe both led to ethnic conflict. In the case of Eastern Europe the collapse of communism removed the strong governments that had held ethnic conflict in check.

For example, in Czechoslovakia the antipathy between Czechs and Slovaks resulted in the peaceful separation of the two groups. In the case of Yugoslavia, the ending of the external threat represented by Soviet-style Communism resulted in an outbreak of ethnic violence and the splintering of the state along those ethnic lines. The sometimes arbitrary boundaries between republics in the old Soviet Union have left virtually all the successor states facing significant problems with minority populations. The revolt of the Chechens is one of the more dramatic examples. In addition, there has been violence and fighting in Georgia, Azerbajain, and former Soviet Central Asia among others (Chalk 1999: 153). The successor states have all been less able to deal with these tensions and violence than the old Soviet system. Before the collapse of Communism, ethnic outbreaks were dealt with quickly and severely. None of the new states, either in Eastern Europe or the territory of the old USSR, has yet been able to match the capabilities that were present before 1990. It has even been suggested that parts of the former Soviet Union could even replace the Middle East as future generators of violence and terrorism (Pluchinsky 1998: 140).

CASE STUDIES

Terrorism based on ethnicity or nationality has been common. The cases examined in detail below indicate the range that such violence can take. The cases include the attacks on property exemplified by the Boston Tea Party prior to the outbreak of active warfare between colonists and the British, the ongoing struggle of the Basques in Spain for autonomy and even independence, communal violence in Borneo in Indonesia, the efforts of the Albanians in Kosovo and Macedonia to achieve greater control of these regions or greater input into the government, and the continuing Palestinian struggle to create a nation.

CASE STUDY 6.1   THE BOSTON TEA PARTY

The prelude to open warfare between the British Crown and the colonialists during the American Revolution was a period that was filled with high levels of political conflict, including occasional instances of violence. The eventual war itself was an early example of a national liberation struggle. The actual war contained some examples of efforts to instill fear in those on the other side and some instances of cruel and inappropriate actions taken against the military and civilian opponents. There were, however, examples of non-lethal terrorism prior to the outbreak of hostilities at Lexington and Concord. The Boston Tea Party is the best known, but hardly the only example of the type of activities that occurred.

The actions in Boston built upon early actions designed to negate British policies. The colonists consistently resisted taxes on trade. On the rare occasions when smugglers were actually caught, convictions in colonial courts were almost impossible to obtain (Morgan and Morgan 1962: 61–2). When local activists burned a British revenue cutter (used to intercept smugglers) off Rhode Island, no witnesses could be found to testify in court (Schlesinger 1955: 248). Because of a fear of violence, customs officials had frequently been afraid to enforce British trade policies or to actively pursue those guilty of smuggling (Bobrick 1997: 62). In 1765 the British parliament passed the Stamp Act to raise money to pay off the debts incurred in the recent wars with France. The colonists were opposed to these taxes, in part because they were levied without the consent of the colonial legislatures. They then organized to resist. Many officials appointed to collect the tax resigned in the face of popular disapproval. Mobs, often organized by the Sons of Liberty, threatened those who did not immediately resign. They were assaulted and their property was destroyed. Anyone obeying the law and using the stamps also became a target for the intimidation and violence (Morgan and Morgan 1962: Chap. 8). The opposition to the Stamp Act was so effective that by the time parliament finally repealed the law, it had already become "completely meaningless" (Hollon 1974: 10). The political objective of the organized violence had been achieved. "In short, terrorism implemented by dissident Americans was used to force a fundamental redirection of British policy" (Davis 1996: 224).

During these protests the militants developed a set of effective techniques for dealing with their opponents. Many of the attacks were directed against the property of supporters of the monarchy in colonial America (Division of Archives 1926: 33). Officials and supporters of the Crown were hanged in effigy and their homes and property were attacked (Bobrick 1997: 75). Supporters of the Crown were also tarred and feathered with some frequency (Rapoport 2003: 37–8). The personal attacks were daunting, of course, but all these actions served to indicate that financial losses could occur for supporting the wrong side. Crown supporters in Boston—and elsewhere—were put on notice that their property was at risk if they continued to oppose the goals of the American "freedom fighters" or supported British efforts to deal with the colonial "terrorists." When parliament attempted to collect revenues from the sale of tea, the Sons of Liberty became active again and the same techniques were used. Agents for the sale of the British tea were similarly induced to resign their positions (Leckie 1992: 79). Tea on a ship in the Hudson River was thrown overboard by a group of "Mohawk" Indians (Division of Archives 1926: 33). Patriots in Maryland also boarded a ship and threw the tea overboard while in Pennsylvania a local pilot was persuaded not to navigate a ship carrying tea into the port of Philadelphia (Bobrick 1997: 89, 92).

The dumping of tea into Boston harbor is simply the best known of the attacks against the laws passed by parliament. The planners of the Boston Tea Party had a number of objectives. First, the dumping of the tea was a clear protest against British laws. The tax on tea and the limitations on trade contained in British regulations (which required that tea be purchased from the East India Company) were seen as illegal and oppressive acts of the Crown. The tea was a highly symbolic target, and attacks on it served to represent colonial dissatisfaction with other policies. Second, the planners were likely hoping that the provocation would lead to a response from the Crown that would further unify the colonies. The closing of Boston Harbor and the sending of troops to the city rallied supporters throughout the colonies, especially as many colonialists viewed the punishment as an overreaction. The third objective was to intimidate those Americans who were supportive of the English authorities, which included many persons of some wealth and property. While political discussions and debates over the appropriate course of action that the colonies should take continued with a remarkable level of toleration given the heightened feelings in the colonies, the Boston Tea Party and other actions elsewhere formed an important prelude to the coming battles and kept the loyalists in the colonies on edge and probably silenced them on some occasions.

The Boston Tea Party and the other actions are examples of terrorist actions undertaken largely against property. It is important to note that most of the actions protesting British policies were not isolated efforts, and they were not spontaneous. They were "part of a carefully executed *campaign* of violent politics" (Hollon 1974: 10, emphasis added). The activities were non-lethal but effective. The dissidents "trusted to horror rather than homicide" (Scheslinger 1955: 246). In the final analysis the Boston Tea Party was a successful terrorist act. Local supporters were cowed, and the British authorities were provoked into retaliation. When General Gage sought workers to build barracks for the British troops stationed in Boston to cow the colonists, no one dared to come forward to work for him (Leckie 1992: 92). Closing Boston Harbor to trade led to greater colonial unity, and the increased tensions in Massachusetts contributed to the outbreak of hostilities. The British government, of course, had little choice but to respond to the dumping of the tea. Doing nothing would have encouraged the colonial dissidents and completely undercut the possibility of gaining support from those elements favorable to continuation of the colonial administration. Britain had been backed into a corner and had to make a choice from among a number of poor options.

CASE STUDY 6.2 BASQUE NATIONALISTS IN SPAIN

The Basques in northern Spain bordering on the Bay of Biscay and France have always been somewhat distinct from other groups in the country. The Basque language is unrelated to Spanish and probably represents the modern version of the language of the original inhabitants of the Iberian Peninsula before the arrival of the Celts or the Romans. This distinctive language has always served to set apart the Basque people from other regions in Spain. In the early days of the Spanish state the language difference was not an important one since states and allegiances were not defined on the basis of language but rather on loyalty to the dynasty or ruler. The Basque region did have special rules (the *furores*) that reflected special privileges that they received from the Spanish Crown for their support of the state through the centuries. By the twentieth century the Basques had developed strong regional feelings based on their language and culture. The Basque region also remained a stronghold of Catholicism, which placed the region at odds with the more secularizing elements of the Spanish state. When the Spanish Civil War broke out between the supporters of the Second Republic and the conservative forces (the Nationalists) led by Francisco Franco, the Basques sided with the Republicans against the nationalists despite the strong anti-clerical stance of the Republicans. The Basque country, however, was separated from the other Republican areas, and it was one of the first areas conquered by the Nationalists. When Franco came to power at the end of the Civil War he eliminated the special regional status of the Basque region and other areas while imposing a strong centralized structure for Spain. The Basque language was even banned as the Franco regime refused to countenance any weakening of the central state and any possibility of autonomy for the Basque region (or other areas of Spain).

More recent Basque opposition to the Franco regime became organized when the Euzkadi ta Askatasuna (ETA)—Basque Homeland and Freedom (in Euskara, the Basque language)—was formed in 1959 to contest the centralization policies of the Spanish government (Corrado 1997: 572). While some ETA members were leftist in their ideology and hoped to unite the Basque and Spanish members of the working class, most were nationalists who hoped to unite Basques of all classes while implicitly or explicitly excluding those of non-Basque background. Notwithstanding the leftist rhetoric sometimes associated with ETA, most of the members of this dissident group joined because of their nationalist feelings and desire for an independent Basque state (Jimenez 1992: 111). Differences have continued to exist to the present time, and splits within the nationalist camp have been frequent, but ETA continued to be the major violent dissident organization for the Basques. The divisions within the nationalist camp have weakened the Basques at times, but they have also provided the region the opportunity to pursue more than one path to autonomy or special rights by providing the government in Madrid, in effect, with a number of options at various time periods. While a majority of the Basques support nationalism in either the form of independence or autonomy, the majority has not supported terrorism as such (Khatami 1997: 408).

ETA did not initially favor the use of violence against the Franco government, but increasing repression in the Basque region in the 1960s led to the decision to resort to violent tactics. The ultimate goal of ETA is independence for the Basque region, including Euskara-speaking inhabitants across the border in France. During the Franco period, ETA frequently targeted members of the political establishment and the security forces. ETA even managed to pull off one of the more spectacular assassinations in the 1970s by killing Franco's prime minister. The attacks in the Basque region itself provoked a violent reaction by the state, resulting in the arrest, imprisonment, and torture of many Basques by the central authorities. One result was that new recruits were attracted to ETA in response to the state repression (Woodworth 2001: 6). In this case the state security forces could not eliminate the violence and actually contributed to violence in the future by helping to alienate segments of the population.

The Franco regime had not succeeded in repressing Basque nationalism when it was replaced with a democratic government. With the appearance of a democratic regime in Spain, nationalist activity did not cease. ETA violence was especially great while the political system was in transition. Since the nationalists were no longer fighting against a dictatorship, their appeal to public opinion was weaker. It could easily be argued that ETA no longer had any reason to continue the struggle. Nevertheless, ETA did continue, arguing in part that the situation of the Basque region still reflected a situation of oppression by the majority (the Spanish) over the minority (the Basques) in their own homeland. As a consequence, ETA was now attempting to end this system of internal colonialism and provide true freedom for the Basque region.

ETA continued its struggle against the Spanish state attempting a variety of maneuvers to increase its appeal among the Basque population and to justify its existence as a dissident organization representing the region and its interests. ETA has generally tried to avoid casualties among civilians, and it has been extremely careful to avoid such casualties in the aftermath of 9/11 (Pluchinsky 2006: 53). ETA, however, has continued its campaign of "systematic murder" of state officials (Brunn 1982: 123). Attacks were still often focused on the security forces in an effort to provoke the state into massive repression that would be likely to push other individuals into the ranks of ETA (Corrado 1997: 572–3). The Spanish government normally has, however, refrained from taking the bait and not adopted dramatically repressive policies (Shabad and Ramo 1995). From 1983 to 1987, however, the Spanish authorities did utilize a special, unofficial squad, the Anti-Liberation Terrorist Group (GAL), to track down and kill Basques, many in France, suspected of being involved with the different dissident groups or supporting them. When the activities of this group came to light, however, it was discontinued. These extra-legal activities do not seem to have benefited the Spanish government in any significant way in the drive against the dissidents, especially once it was discovered that the group was operating. They even gave some credence for many Basques to the idea that the democratic system, like the Franco regime before it, was determined to repress and control the Basque region (Woodworth 2001: 7). Ironically, arrests, trials, and subsequent punishment of ETA activists within the context of normal legal processes often generated public support for the dissidents as martyrs for the cause of Basque freedom. On the other hand, the more successful dissident actions involving violence often alienated the more moderate Basques and drove them away from the group (Byman 1998: 154). Over the years the restraint generally shown by the democratic government has weakened support for ETA and other violent nationalists. ETA has shifted to other themes in order to gain support in the Basque region. It has opposed the creation of nuclear power plants and other environmentally harmful projects (Khatami 1997: 398). ETA has also launched attacks against foreign tourists, attempting to economically damage the state and to reduce the inflow of income from tourism (Chalk 1998b: 380). Since Spain is a major destination for European tourists, when such attacks reduce revenue, it is noticed. This type of economic warfare was quite successful at times, as there were clear downturns in the number of tourist visits after attacks by ETA (Enders and Sandler 1991). Similarly, terrorist attacks have negatively affected levels of foreign direct investment in Spain, particularly in the Basque region (Abadie and Gardeazabal 2003). Since ETA in particular and other Basque dissidents groups in general were the major source of terrorist actions, the Basque dissidents were most responsible for this lower level of investment from outside countries. Ultimately, these efforts have all failed to increase support for the group.

ETA did not have any direct source of foreign support. ETA dissidents had some contacts with the PLO and some members trained in their camps, and there were rare opportunities to interact with other nationalist dissidents from other countries. In the 1980s when the control of the border by the French authorities became more effective, ETA lost a valuable sanctuary (Wilkinson 2006: 162). Financial support for the movement was largely self-generated. Members of the Basque community in Spain and France as well as Basques in other countries supplied financial support. ETA also raised funds through some of the traditional means available to dissidents, including kidnappings. In some cases ETA collected very substantial ransoms in return for the release of prominent, wealthy individuals (Jimenez 1992: 188). ETA also relied on revolutionary taxes levied on Basques and others to support the cause, and punishment attacks were sometimes undertaken against those who failed to contribute or pay the taxes. The successful kidnappings and the punishment attacks against individuals who did not contribute to the nationalist cause made it relatively easy for ETA to blackmail industrialists and business persons for funds. In some cases the punishment for failing to provide the requested funds was death (Albin 1989: 202).

ETA has continued to have at least some local support. While the majority of the Basques oppose violence, they are also frequently unwilling to cooperate with the authorities in apprehending members of ETA. ETA has also in a way managed to help the Basque region. While the demands of ETA have not been met, the central government has granted greater autonomy and local control to the regional government. In effect, the Spanish government and local politicians have used the threat of ETA violence to negotiate for more local control (Shabad and Ramo 1995: 468). Some splinter groups from ETA have been reconciled with the system as a consequence of these concessions. It is unlikely that the government would have conceded as much local autonomy if there had not been the implied threat that more Basques would have joined ETA or some other violent nationalist organization. Notwithstanding its indirect successes in helping the region to achieve greater autonomy, ETA has not gained its ultimate goal of independence. For ETA other rights granted by the democratic Spanish government are meaningless without independence (Woodworth 2001: 3). Such an outcome is not likely in the future. The Basques no longer constitute a majority in their own region. As little as 25 percent of the population can write in Basque, although many more speak it (Brunn 1982: 117). In some ways the identity loss has fueled the concern of the nationalists as they see the local language and culture being overwhelmed by their outsiders (Dingley and Kirk-Smith 2002).

Changing circumstances do not appear to have affected ETA. There have been times when there were indications that ETA might be willing to settle for a negotiated solution to the future of the Basque region (Newman 2000: 37). This willingness to negotiate, however, has not yet lasted and the nationalist attacks have always begun again. To some extent the core of ETA may have become wedded to the violence that it inflicts. Members have become so immersed in a culture of violence that they cannot give up the struggle. Terrorism can become "an end in itself, both a way of life and a lifestyle for the terrorists" (Reinares 2005: 128). ETA demonstrates that terrorist groups, once established, can survive for a long time with small levels of support, and that it is virtually impossible in the short term to undermine a well-established terrorist organization by negotiation or destroy it completely by police, security, and military measures.

CASE STUDY 6.3   DAYAKS AND MIGRANTS IN BORNEO

Communal violence can occur in response to government policies without the attacks being directed against the government. The violence can be more directly focused on members of an ethnic community by another group or groups that see the first group as a threat. Such a situation has occurred in the Indonesian provinces on the island, of Borneo or Kalimantan (see Map 2). The Dayaks, the local inhabitants of the island, have reacted negatively to the government-supported migration of Madurese to the Indonesian portions of the island. There has been a great deal of pressure on the land in many portions of Indonesia. The land densities in some portions of the country are extremely high, creating situations where migration to less densely supported areas of the country has been seen as a viable option. The island of Java in particular has faced severe overpopulation. As a consequence, the government has encouraged and fostered migration to other areas (the outer islands from a Javanese perspective) where land has been available (Peluso and Harwell 2001: 84). This policy has led to local dissatisfaction in a variety of areas as the migrants have clashed with the local inhabitants. The local dissatisfaction was held pretty much in check while the authoritarian Suharto regime was in power. The return to a more democratic system of government has created a system in transition that is more vulnerable to violent activities than a firmly established governmental system. Javanese migrants have faced opposition from the local populations in Sumatra, including Aceh in the northern portion of that island where a low-level guerrilla insurgency has been ongoing for many years (Tan 2000). The migration also was a factor leading to the religious violence that occurred in Sulawesi and the Moloccus. It has also led to communal massacres in Kalimantan where large number of Madurese had migrated from an island just off the coast of Java.

The Madurese with the government support were taking over land and establishing farms in territory that the local Dayak inhabitants naturally regarded as their own. The new migrants in at least some cases were in better positions to dominate commercial relationships in the areas. The indigenous groups have had difficulties competing economically with the Madurese (Schiller and Garang 2002: 248). The differences between the two communities were exacerbated in this case by the fact that many Dayaks are Christian while most of the Madurese are Muslim like the vast majority of the population of Indonesia. The attacks do not appear to be religiously motivated since the other Muslim residents of the island have not been attacked; the violence has been limited to the Madurese. Other government sponsored migrants from Java, largely Muslim, were ignored as were Chinese (Peluso and Harwell 2001: 90). With the loosened control by the central government that came with the demise of the military regime and the creation of a more democratic system, the Dayaks began to attack the Madurese migrants. The violence at first was not noticeably organized and reflected antagonisms between the two communities, and the Madurese fought back in many cases or were even responsible for initiating some of the violence (Peluso and Harwell 2001: 87–8). Eventually, however, the attacks came to include a larger element of direction and defined purposes. The attacks on Madurese at times resulted in the massacre of the outsiders by the Dayaks. The loss of life has been significant. In 1997, 500 Madurese

Map 2 Indonesia

died and 25,000 were driven off by the Dayaks. In 1999 other natives of the island, mostly Muslim, joined with the Dayaks in the violence. These attacks drove off another 30,000 and left 200 dead. In 2001, Dayak attacks in the cities killed 400 and forced 50,000 to flee (Malley 2003: 208). The Dayaks, however, have not attacked Madurese fleeing from their areas of settlement. The goal of the attacks has been the forced flight of the migrants, not their extermination. The target audience for the violence has extended beyond the immediate victims to the other migrants. The goal has been the expulsion of the whole migrant community. Survivors of the massacres have been the necessary medium to transmit the message of the locals to the Madurese, both on Borneo and Java.

The government has not supported the attacks on the migrants, especially since the migration itself has been a government supported policy. In a country that is largely Muslim, the government would be more likely to favor the Muslim migrants, especially in a democratic society where the political parties with a strong, Islamic, religious orientation have been especially important for the governments in power. The government, however, has been ill-prepared to deal with the violence. Security forces, the police, and the military were present in small numbers and not up to the task of protecting the Madurese. The absence of large security forces has been due in part to the problems in other areas of the country—the need for the military to maintain control for the government in Aceh, the requirements to keep order in East Timor for many years, separatist feelings in Irian Jaya (the Indonesian portion of New Guinea), and the communal violence in Sulawesi and the Moloccus. Police officers have been overwhelmed in the face of the attacks and unable to defend the migrants even if they had desired to do so. The involvement of the other groups native to the island has also meant that the Madurese were facing a united front from the local inhabitants. Such local unity would make intervention by the local police to protect an unpopular group more difficult. Providing security for isolated farms is clearly beyond the means of the government when there are insufficient resources to protect the migrants in the towns. The government would have to devote major resources, which have been stretched, to provide even minimal protection in the region. Since the violence has not yet moved toward opposition to the central government as the appropriate political authority on Kalimantan, the government is unlikely to provoke a strong local response and generate even more separatism in the country given the significant demands on government resources that already exist.

The campaign of terror against the Madurese was quite successful in leading to ethnic cleansing. At least 100,000 migrants, virtually the entire Madurese community fled (Mann 2005: 495). New migrants have been discouraged, notwithstanding population pressure on the land and local poverty on Madura. For the government to successfully counteract these local successes requires resources unlikely to be available in the near future. At some point in time the consolidation of the democratic system may permit a new attempt at colonization, but in a democracy local politicians might be able to prevent the resumption of large-scale migration. If local issues in Aceh, Sulawesi, or Irian Jaya are dealt with, the government may eventually be able to provide the necessary security for such a policy. Of course, if the democratic consolidation means more local autonomy for various provinces, the Dayaks may even prove to have been very successful not only in the short term but in the long term as well in preserving their land for themselves.

CASE STUDY 6.4 ALBANIANS IN KOSOVA AND MACEDONIA

Kosovo is in the Serbian part of what remained of Yugoslavia after the break up of that country. The outbreaks of ethnic violence in the area represent some of the classic ethnic issues that generate conflict. The violence also illustrates the very effective use of tactics and techniques by the Albanian dissidents to further their cause. After the violence in Kosovo, the Albanian minority in Macedonia, another successor state from the old Yugoslavia, began to use some of these same techniques and tactics. The similarity of tactics would suggest that the Albanians in Macedonia were quick learners, had advice from their fellow Albanians in Kosovo, or indeed that some of the same people were involved in the activities in both areas.

For the Serbian population of Yugoslavia the Kosovo region has always had special significance. It was the heartland of the original Serb state and the later Serbian Empire. It was also the site of two of the most important military defeats suffered by the Serbs at the hands of the Ottoman Turks. The first battle of Kosovo destroyed the Serbian Empire, leading to its subjugation by the Ottomans. The somewhat later second battle of Kosovo resulted in the defeat of the attempt to re-establish Serb independence, which led to the incorporation of the region in the Ottoman Empire for centuries. The Albanians are a non-Slavic people, differing from the Serbs and Macedonians, and their language is not Slavic, so it is easily distinguishable from Serbo-Croat. Although some Albanians were Greek Orthodox, large numbers converted to Islam under Ottoman rule, adding a cultural divide to the linguistic and ethnic one. While religious practices of all kinds were discouraged to some extent in Communist Yugoslavia, the cultural milieu that Islam provided for most Albanians set them apart from the cultural setting and history of the Greek Orthodox Serbs.

With the establishment of the Kingdom of Yugoslavia after World War I, Kosovo became an integral part of the new country. In this period the central government encouraged the movement of Serbs into Kosovo (and Macedonia) to change the ethnic balance. Albanians were encouraged to either emigrate or assimilate (Vickers 1995: 127–8). Both before and after World War II the economic centers of Yugoslavia were in Slovenia, Croatia, and the area around the capital of Belgrade (see Map 3). As a consequence of the greater economic opportunities in these regions, Serbs in Kosovo began to leave in increasingly larger numbers. The Albanian population in the area grew both in an absolute sense and as a proportion of the total regional population. By the time the unified Yugoslavia had begun to disintegrate with the collapse of Communism, the Albanians had become an overwhelming majority in the Kosovo region.

When Yugoslavia was still united under the Communist government headed by Marshal Tito, power was decentralized to a surprising extent for cultural and educational purposes. There were six republics in the federal Yugoslavia—Slovenia, Croatia, Bosnia and Herzegovina, Serbia, Montenegro, and Macedonia. In addition, within the Serbian Republic there were two autonomous provinces in Serbia with special powers—Kosovo with its Albanian majority and Vojvodina (the Banat), which has a Serb majority but large Hungarian and German minorities. Local party organizations were important in governing

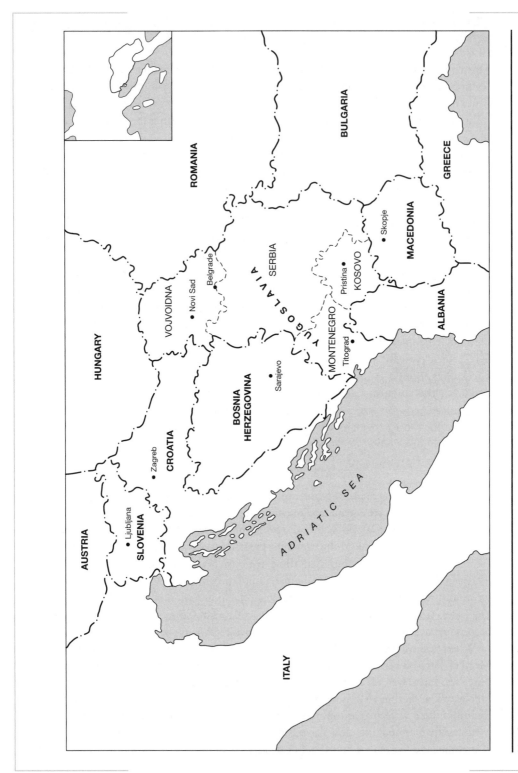

Map 3   Former Yugoslavia

the six republics and the two autonomous provinces, and the largest ethnic and cultural group invariably dominated the local parties. Thus, local ethnic leaders, even if they were Communists, had the opportunity to establish themselves in the various regions, and they catered to the ethnic concerns of local populations to some extent. Even while the Communists still ruled in a unified Yugoslavia, tensions appeared between the Albanians and the local Serb population. The Albanians felt like the dominant Serbs treated them poorly. The local Serbian population, on the other hand, felt that the Albanians were doing everything in their power to force out the remaining Serbs from the province and to take over completely. These tensions generated riots and difficulties, despite a strong Communist government in power (Vickers 1995: 205–6).

With the break up of the country, the surviving territory of Yugoslavia consisted of Montenegro and Serbia, which still included Vojvodina and Kosovo. The Serbs were a clear majority, while the Albanians were the largest remaining minority. Under the government of Slobodan Milošević, a Communist turned Serbian nationalist, but authoritarian by nature regardless of ideology, the situation in Kosovo deteriorated. Albanians were treated harshly, and the Yugoslav government sought to repress Albanian aspirations. Local autonomy was withdrawn, while the government encouraged Serbs to migrate back to Kosovo to change the ethnic balance in the province. Albanian dissidents eventually coalesced into the Kosovo Liberation Army (KLA), which began to fight back using both guerrilla and terrorist tactics. Attacks were directed against police, Serb civilians, and Albanians considered to be collaborating with the Yugoslav government (Judah 2000: 137). The Albanian dissidents quickly decided to attempt to provoke an excessive response from the local Yugoslav (i.e., Serb) authorities. They hoped that retaliation would fall upon the local Albanians, alienating them even more from a repressive state and driving them into the arms of the dissident movement. Army or police patrols would be fired upon from Albanian villages to encourage local security forces to return fire on the villages indiscriminately. Frequently, these tactics were successful. Further, bombs were set off, and assassinations undertaken, including attacks against the local Serb civilian minority. These attacks were successful in provoking retaliation. Other methods used by the dissidents to drive a wedge between the local population and the security forces included the torture of prisoners from the security forces or the mutilation of the dead. Serbian police were, in fact, one of the major targets for terrorist attacks (Chalk 1999: 152). It reached the point where Serb police came to regard a transfer or assignment to Kosovo as a virtual death sentence (Macgregor 2001: 97). These techniques were successful in provoking government forces to be increasingly repressive, to be high-handed in their techniques, and to regard the entire Albanian community as suspect, creating a situation of ongoing and continuous ethnic tensions. The KLA attacks and Serbian responses led to the alienation of most of the population from the government (Bieber 2003: 47).

Since it could not control the territory or the Albanian population, eventually the Yugoslav government decided to attempt to force large segments of the Albanian population out of Kosovo altogether. The government line was that it was expelling post-war migrants and their descendants from Kosovo (Judah 2000: 151–2). Army units, police, and paramilitary groups entered villages, shooting some inhabitants and terrorizing others (Mann 2005: 397). A large number of the Albanians took the warnings to heart and became refugees, attempting to flee to Montenegrin territory, Albania itself, or Macedonia. The ruthlessness with which the Serbs pursued this policy of forced emigration was ultimately counterproductive. It had extremely negative effects on public opinion in Europe and the United States. The Serbian government was warned to cease its efforts to expel the Albanians or face a military response. When the government failed to yield to the pressure and to withdraw military units from Kosovo, Yugoslavia was subjected to an aerial bombing campaign launched by the United States and other Western countries. The attacks targeted military units, lines of communications, and economic facilities in Serbia proper. Eventually the Yugoslav military forces were withdrawn from Kosovo, and peacekeeping forces were introduced to protect the Albanians against further repression by the central government.

The violent activities of the KLA were successful since Kosovo is now independent, and Serbian efforts to drive out many Albanians was defeated. Nagging questions about the future of the province remain. The Albanian dissidents would have preferred total independence or unity with Albania, options which would still be opposed by the central government. Since the withdrawal of the Serbian police and military units, the Albanians in power in Kosovo have also not acquitted themselves particularly well. They have used violence against the remaining Serbs in Kosovo and the Gypsies who are assumed to be pro-Serbian. The goal has been to drive both groups out of the province (Judah 2000: 286–90). More than 100,000 Gypsies have fled the province as a consequence of the pressure (Cooper 2001/2: 71). By 1999 it was obvious that an organized campaign of murder and terror was taking place in an effort to drive out the small number of Serb civilians that had remained in Kosovo (Macgregor 2001: 103). Some of these activities might be based on vengeance for past wrongs, but if the remaining Serbs are forced out, independence or unity with Albania becomes a much easier proposition to sell elsewhere in Europe.

There is no indication that there was any external state support for the Albanian dissidents although the KLA took advantage of a weak government in Albania to freely cross the border, to obtain arms and to maintain supply bases (Pavkovic 2000: 190). It was relatively easy for arms and other forms of support to cross the border between Albania and Kosovo (Judah 2000: 172–3) even if such movements were not part of any organized state effort. The Albanians in Kosovo and Macedonia also benefited from the support of the Albanian disapora communities in the United States and Western Europe (Pluchinsky 2006: 50–1).

Once the Serbs had been forced to relinquish control of Kosovo, violence broke out in Macedonia. The Albanian minority in that country began to seek policy changes and greater autonomy for themselves. The National Liberation Army (NLA) was set up to represent the Albanian population. Armed Albanian dissidents began to fire on police patrols, and then on the military, from ethnic Albanian villages. The goal again appeared to be an effort to provoke a violent response by the Macedonian majority and to drive a wedge between the government and the Slavic Macedonian majority on the one hand and the Albanian minority on the other hand. The tactics that worked in Kosovo were tried again in Macedonia, a not surprising circumstance since the leader of the NLA had previously been active with the KLA in Kosovo (Ash 2003: 63). The situation in Macedonia, however, did not deteriorate as quickly, even though antagonisms between

Albanians and Macedonians did increase. Peacekeeping forces that had been sent to Kosovo to deter the government in Belgrade and other peacekeeping troops that were sent to Macedonia were able to provide security in the border areas before the outbreak of trouble with the Albanian minority. Somewhat ironically from the perspective of the Albanian dissidents, the forces initially on the border between Macedonia and Kosovo to help the refugees created by the Serbian efforts as expulsion have provided a deterrent to increased Albanian dissident activities in Macedonia.

To date the success of the dissidents operating in Macedonia has not matched that of the KLA. The Albanians gained some recognition as a group, and the government agreed to some concessions and changes, but on the negative side inter-ethnic tensions have been increased. In this case, the Albanians have been less able to mobilize European or American public opinion on their behalf in the case of Macedonia as was true for Kosovo. While Milošević had already weakened his position vis-à-vis public opinion by his support for Serbs in their attacks in Bosnia and Croatia and by his own hard line within Yugoslavia, the Macedonian government was democratically elected, and did not have the negative image associated with the Milošević government. Also, in the case of Kosovo, the Albanians were very much the majority of the province. The segment of Macedonia that is clearly Albanian has awkward geographic outlines. Activities by dissidents in Macedonia are unlikely to aim toward independence, only toward local autonomy or greater rights for the Albanians. Union with an independent Kosovo or Albania might be a goal for the future, but that is a solution that rewards the dissidents for increasing tensions within Macedonia. At least for the moment tensions in Macedonia have eased considerably, and representatives of the government and the Albanian community have reached a peaceful agreement (Pluchinsky 2006: 51).

CASE STUDY 6.5   THE PALESTINIAN LIBERATION ORGANIZATION AND THE STRUGGLE WITH ISRAEL

The British mandated territory of Palestine was the scene of violence and terrorism in the days prior to World War II and in the years from the outbreak of World War II to the creation of the state of Israel in 1948 by force of arms. Israel defeated the local Arab militias and then the armies of the neighboring states. The Palestinian Liberation Organization (PLO) was a nationalist response to the loss of territory. The PLO's main objective was creating an independent secular state for the Palestinian Arabs. While the PLO has not been the first reasonably successful user of terrorism, among modern-day political groups that made terror an integral part of their programs for a significant period of time, the PLO has been one of the more successful and longest-lasting organizations of nationalist dissidents.

The PLO, founded in 1964, itself was an umbrella organization that has included through the years many separate groups. Fatah, the group that Yasser Arafat led, was one of the most important groups, and his chairmanship of the umbrella group was one indication of the importance of his organization. At times in the decades since the formation of the PLO groups have dropped out or been expelled for failure to agree with PLO policies. Since the PLO has been composed of many groups and factions, it has sometimes been difficult for it to truly speak with a unified voice. The PLO by conscious choice also has maintained itself as a secular organization, appealing to Muslim, Christian, and non-religious Palestinians. The organization has never stressed Islam as an integral part of the principles of the group. In fact, the failure to stress Islam is one of the things that has led to conflict between the PLO and Hamas.

The PLO was formed as many Palestinians became disenchanted with the prospects of the liberation of their homeland by conventional armed forces of the Arab countries. Israel had defeated the armies of Egypt, Jordan, Syria, Lebanon, and Iraq in 1948, and in 1956 the Israeli army easily dealt with the Egyptian forces in the Sinai. The Palestinians initially formed guerrilla groups to conduct raids and to complement conventional military action by the Arab armies. In the Six Day War in 1967, the Israeli Defense Force decisively defeated the armies of Egypt, Jordan, and Syria, and Israel occupied the West Bank, the Gaza Strip, the Golan Heights, and the Sinai Peninsula. The occupation of Gaza, formerly administered by Egypt, and the West Bank, which had been part of the Kingdom of Jordan, brought many Palestinian Arabs under direct Israeli rule. The governments of the defeated Arab states now naturally became much more concerned about controlling any Palestinian guerrilla operations in order to avoid military engagements with Israel. As might be expected, they placed their national interests ahead of the Palestinian objective of reclaiming their homeland.

In the aftermath of 1967, the PLO and its component units opted to resort to terrorism. It should be noted that while the PLO was almost always "blamed" or "credited" for terrorist actions, not all terrorist actions have been under the control of the PLO. The PLO did at times organize or sanction terrorist attacks. On other occasions it seems reasonably clear that some other independent Palestinian groups undertook actions on their own, contrary to the desires of the PLO leadership. In more ambiguous cases, it would appear that separate organizations undertook actions with the tacit approval or at least the knowledge of the PLO leadership. The leadership had the option, however, of denying involvement if such a denial was beneficial. In general in the period from 1968 to the early 1980s, the PLO was actively undertaking or encouraging terrorist activities as a means of weakening the state of Israel and attracting international attention.

In July 1968, three members of the Popular Front for the Liberation of Palestine (PFLP), a group within the PLO, hijacked an El Al plane en route from Rome to Tel Aviv. El Al as the national airline of Israel was an appropriate target for the Palestinians. The hijackers offered to trade the passengers on the flight for the release of Palestinians imprisoned by the Israelis (Hoffman 2006: 63). The publicity that the effort received indicated to the PLO that such operations could generate significant media attention and publicize the cause of the Palestinian people in a way that was not otherwise possible. In fact, the successful hijacking of the plane generated more media attention that any of the battles fought by the Palestinians with the Israeli security forces in their guerrilla incursions (Cooley 1997: 299). The aftermath of this operation convinced the Palestinians to engage in additional acts of terrorism. In 1969, Yasser Arafat was elected chairman, making it clear that this approach had become the policy of the PLO (Sayigh 1997: 29). While some attacks continued to occur inside Israel, other attacks shifted to other locations. The 1972 Munich Olympics provided an ideal forum to publicize the Palestinian cause when the Black September organization captured Israeli athletes and held them hostage. For days world attention was focused on the hostage situation in Munich, and everyone was aware of the failed attempt by the West Germans to rescue the hostages that resulted in the death of all the Palestinians and the Israeli athletes and coaches. These attacks continued throughout the 1970s and 1980s. Some of the activities were relatively spectacular, such as the simultaneous hijacking of four airliners, while other actions included property attacks on Israeli targets in the United States and Western Europe, with El Al being a frequent target. There were also assassination attempts against Israeli diplomats abroad. Ultimately, all of these activities generated a tremendous amount of publicity for the Palestinian cause and ultimately for the PLO as well. All of the international attacks and hijackings resulted in a limited number of deaths compared to the attacks within Israel or the Occupied Territories or the Gaza Strip or the West Bank.

The publicity that resulted from these international activities was essential to the Palestinian cause in a number of ways. Every success attracted new recruits from the Palestinians living in the refugee camps and from Palestinians living abroad. The successful attacks also brought in financial support from the Palestinian diaspora. Palestinians in Europe and the United States have been especially important as sources of funds for the PLO and other groups (Kushner 1996: 333). The successes of the PLO also meant that it received financial support from other Arab states including the oil rich monarchies that found it expedient to supply funds to their fellow Arabs. The flow of funds from Kuwait or Saudi Arabia neutralized any dangers of dissident activity from Palestinians residing in their territories and also neutralized criticism from non-monarchial Arab states such as Syria and Egypt. The publicity also brought the situation of the Palestinians to world attention and generated sympathy for a people without a land. Prior to these attacks, "few outside the region took any notice of, much less cared about the Palestinians" (Hoffman 2006: 66). The PLO was successful in having the future of the Palestinians become a permanent issue for the international agenda (Gal-Or 1994: 143). The PLO was ultimately successful to some extent in equating the situation of the Palestinians as a people without a land to that of the Jewish population of the world in 1948 as a people without a land. If the establishment of a Jewish state in Palestine was acceptable, then the establishment of a Palestinian state in the area had gained validity as well.

The PLO survived and grew as the nationalist organization seen to represent Palestinian interests in the Occupied Territories for the Palestinian diaspora. The PLO, unlike most dissident groups, developed a complex organizational structure and developed its own sources of support. The PLO was recognized in an official or semi-official capacity by many governments. In effect, the organization served as an unofficial government-in-exile for the Palestinian people, and it had more diplomatic contacts than the state of Israel at one point in time (Hoffman 2006: 70). The PLO even had observer status at the UN. Funds from the diaspora, the oil states, and its own businesses permitted the PLO to develop its own financial base.

The PLO did have important external state support at various times in its organizational history. The Soviet Union frequently provided aid, training, and weapons. Soviet support was always conditional and related to some extent to Soviet foreign policy objectives (Kushner 1998a: 5). Most other Arab states provided financing or training, bases for striking against Israel, diplomatic contacts, and a variety of other assistance that allowed the organization to grow and prosper. The PLO in turn supported other dissident and terrorists groups. PLO training camps in Lebanon were used by more than forty different terrorist organizations (Kushner 1998b: 14). The PLO also frequently had differences with its sponsor states as indicated by the fighting between the PLO and the Jordanian army in September of 1971 (the source of the name for the Black September organization that became one of the more notorious Palestinian terrorist groups) or the PLO's participation in the fighting in Lebanon during that country's long civil war.

Slowly the PLO changed its tactics in terms of the confrontation with Israel. The group moved away from its stance of non-recognition of the right of Israel to exist and slowly conceded that the presence of the state of Israel was a fact of life that had to be recognized. The PLO eventually also opened the door for negotiations with the state of Israel and announced its intention to forgo further terrorist attacks while still keeping its options open for operations against the Israeli military. The shift toward negotiations had costs. Some groups such as the PFLP left the PLO, and Palestinian extremists assassinated moderates in the PLO (Rolef 1997: 260). The PLO consolidated its position as the recognized representative for the Palestinian people. When the *intifada,* the uprising against the Israeli occupation of the West Bank and the Gaza Strip, broke out the PLO was the logical and accepted political representative for the local inhabitants. The uprising with stone throwing, civil disobedience, riots, and low-level violence resulted from local Palestinian dissatisfaction and distaste for the military occupation. While the PLO did not organize the uprising, it supported it, and an overwhelming majority of the Palestinians considered the PLO to be their representative. The effects of the *intifada* clearly played a role in the eventual negotiations between Israel and the PLO that led to the creation of the Palestinian Authority with some governmental roles in parts of the West Bank and the Gaza Strip.

The establishment of the Palestinian Authority was in effect the PLO transformed into a governmental body, even if it was one with limited authority under Israeli oversight. The PLO has moved from being a dissident organization to a political actor that had to be consulted on at least some issues regarding the Occupied Territories. The PLO has achieved one of its major objectives that it had long fought for. It was recognized as the body representing the Palestinian people and had achieved the status where it could negotiate with Israel (Kushner 1998b: 21–2). Events in 2001, 2002, and 2003 have led some to argue that the PLO is still a terrorist organization because of continuing terrorist attacks on Israeli targets by some Palestinians. The PLO was being held responsible for the actions of its citizens as any other state actor might be. Of course, the PLO as former terrorist organization was being held to a higher standard, but the continuing terrorism could not be conclusively linked to the PLO as an organization. With the death of Arafat and the victory of Hamas in elections for the Palestinian Authority, the PLO has lost much of its cohesion. Fatah reappeared as the successor to the old PLO. Even though Fatah used religious appeals more than in the past, it still remained basically a secular group (Frisch

2005). The Al Asqa Brigades, a part of Fatah, have resumed terrorism, including suicide missions. The use of suicide attacks by the secular Palestinian groups is a consequence of efforts to retain popular support and compete with Hamas for the political loyalty of the Palestinians (Bloom 2004). The suicide attacks also represent an effort to create a balance of terror between the Palestinian community and the militarily superior Israeli state (Ahmed 2005: 92).

The PLO ultimately is an example of a dissident organization that used terrorism successfully to change the balance of power. When it was first formed, the Palestinians were clearly a weaker element in the Middle East equation. They were much weaker militarily than Israel, and the supporting Arab states were quite willing to use them as they saw fit and to sacrifice Palestinian interests for the national interests of the state in question. With the passage of time, the PLO became the representative of the Palestinian people with a sufficient increase in its power and influence to become one of the negotiators of the future rather than a pawn in someone else's game. Public opinion in the world changed to a view more favorable of the goals of the Palestinians. While many persons in the United States or Europe would continue to favor the interests of Israel, they were now more willing to concede that the Palestinians demands had at least some merit. (Others, of course, continued to favor Israel or the Palestinians unequivocally.) With greater international support for the Palestinian cause, the Israelis faced greater pressure to at least consider Palestinian demands. It is highly unlikely that these changes in relative positions would have occurred without the resort to terrorism. It is also instructive that when the PLO was at its weakest it chose to use terrorism but once it had gained political leverage it was in a position to dispense with it. As a consequence, it is not surprising that the PLO became a model for other ethnic and nationalist groups in other areas that sought to improve their situation or achieve independence (Hoffman 2006: 71–4). The actions of the PLO may yet fail to lead to the creation of a Palestinian state, but even with the violence in the region today, there is a chance that such a state may yet appear.

BOX 6.3 HAMAS

Hamas (an Arabic acronym for Islamic Resistance Movement) is a Palestinian organization that combines both religious and nationalist appeals. The major objective of the group is an independent Palestinian state that will be an Islamic republic. The focus on Islam places it at odds with the PLO, which is more secular in its orientation. Israeli authorities actually initially provided some support to Hamas in an effort to weaken the PLO (Kimmerling 1997: 235). Hamas has also expressed its commitment to a Palestinian state that includes all the territory of the old British mandate—Israel, the Gaza Strip, and the West Bank. It has refused to recognize the legality of the existence of the state of Israel. The platform of Hamas also calls for the return of the Palestinian refugees and the descendants of the refugees who were forced out in 1948 and 1967 and the expulsion of many of the Jewish inhabitants of Israel. Hamas has gained considerable strength among the Palestinians in the Occupied Territories, especially in the Gaza Strip. This increased strength and the uncompromising objectives of the organization quickly led Israel to withdraw support from the group. Hamas has become an increasingly important political actor in Israel/Palestine, and it has at least temporarily replaced the PLO as the leading Palestinian political group. Hamas, along with Islamic Jihad, has attempted to disrupt various peace proposals or negotiations between Israel and the PLO at various times (Kydd and Walter 2006: 74). Both groups initiated attacks by suicide bombers to inflict casualties on the Israeli population and to upset peace talks. At other times, however, the group has been more pragmatic. It has tacitly cooperated with the PLO at times, and it has indicated a willingness to accept truces while negotiations are ongoing. Such pragmatism may reflect a desire to gain some rights for the Palestinian people or even an independent state, where there might be opportunities for political gains in the future.

SUMMARY

Ethno-nationalist terrorism and violence based on language differences have been quite prevalent in recent years. While nationalism first became a dramatic force for change with the American and French Revolutions, it did not immediately result in notable increases in terrorism, even though it was quite important as a prelude to the American Revolution. The levels of military technology may have been a factor in the relative lack of terrorist violence in the 1700s and into the 1800s. Arms were not tremendously complicated and could be procured with relative ease. The French revolutionary leaders enrolled mass armies and provided muskets that could be used in large numbers to at least have a chance of defeating the more professional and disciplined armies of the other European states. It thus became possible for hastily assembled and sometimes even poorly equipped citizens' armies to defeat the professional regiments. The possibilities for victory were aptly demonstrated by the ultimate victory of the American colonialists, by the early victories of the French revolutionary armies, and even some of the success of the Irish and Scottish Highlanders in their uprisings against English rule. The lack of sophisticated weaponry in the hands of the national armies meant that the weapons of the weak were conventional arms, sometimes used in set-piece battles with the government forces and sometimes used with guerrilla tactics. Since nationalist causes could usually command widespread popular support, there was little need to resort to terrorism to challenge a foreign, occupying power.

In the twentieth century national groups began to rely much more on terrorism as a tactic to challenge an occupying force. By this time the weapons available to central governments or colonial powers had advanced and become much more deadly. Aircraft, armored cars, and heavy artillery were much less likely to be available to any dissident nationalist group engaging in conventional war. Such weapons, even if captured, require constant maintenance and spare parts and fuel and specialized ammunition. The break up of the German, Russian, Austro-Hungarian, and Ottoman Empires after World War I resulted in boundaries that were questioned and contested by groups that found themselves on the "wrong" side of a border or groups that thought their nation should have been granted independence. Resorts to terrorism increased after World War II as colonial empires in Asia, Africa, and the Middle East began to collapse. Dissidents seeking independence began to rely on terrorism when confronted with the weaponry of European troops or European-led local troops. The Greek Cypriots and the Algerians in their wars of independence are some examples of groups forced to rely on terrorism at least in part. Terrorism, sometimes in combination with guerrilla warfare, became the appropriate weapon of the weak.

Problems that came with the end of the colonial empires continue. The Soviet Union and Yugoslavia collapsed, and disputes over boundaries and national affiliations continue to plague the successor states. The ethnic conflicts in the former Yugoslavia resurfaced after more than four decades of firm, centralized rule, indicating that ethnically-based violence can indeed persist for lengthy periods of time. The problems in the Balkans today, including those in the former Yugoslavia, can even be seen as the final stages of conflicts that started with the break up of the Ottoman Empire (Cronin 2002/3: 36). Ethnic tensions in the Soviet Union resurfaced after more than seven decades of firm control. Successor states to empires continue to face problems as well. The United Kingdom provided unity to India, but that unity collapsed with the separation of Pakistan in 1948, and India has faced other violence since then as well. Indonesia is in jeopardy of losing the unity that was provided by the Dutch. All of these examples indicate that ethnic or nationalist violence can indeed last for long periods of time. Once violence has occurred and communal trust has been broken, like Humpty Dumpty it would seem that not all the king's horses or all the king's men can put it together again.

Terrorism helped convince European powers to abandon many of their colonies. The Albanians in Kosovo and perhaps in Macedonia as well in the future have been successful in achieving at least some of their political objectives. Even the activities of ETA in Spain seem to have led the central government to grant a larger measure of autonomy to the region than it might otherwise have been willing to concede. The Dayaks in Borneo managed to reverse a government policy fostering immigration, at least for the immediate future. Finally, the PLO and its related groups have used terrorism to create a situation where the possibility of a Palestinian state is at least being considered. The successful Algerian war of independence was a model for Fatah and the PLO (Sayigh 1997: 26). In sum, nationalist or ethnic terrorism will continue because it is encouraged by the past successes of groups.

External state support has not been essential for the success of the nationalist dissidents, even if it has been helpful. In none of the case studies were the dissidents under foreign control. The property terrorism of the colonials in America prior to the actual rebellion also lacked any foreign assistance but was successful in achieving its goals. The Dayaks in Borneo accomplished their major objectives without any external aid. The Basque effort had mixed results in terms of objectives achieved, but there has never been any indication that there was external assistance for ETA or any of its breakaway groups. The KLA and Albanian dissidents also did not have any major foreign backers, although the Albanian diaspora provided important external support. Similarly, Jewish settler terrorists groups that attacked the British in Palestine received support from the Jewish diaspora (Wilkinson 1975: 92). Only the PLO had major external support for part of its history. The foreign backers were a mixed blessing since they would often attempt to rein in the Palestinians, and at times were successful in doing so. The fact that the PLO was driven out of Jordan by the Jordanian armed forces and then out of Lebanon by Syria and its local allies is one indication of the ambiguous nature of the foreign linkages. Given the strong roots of various groups in Palestinian society, the foreign support was not essential. The PLO or some representative of the Palestinians (such as Hamas) was going to exist, and as an initially weak organization in the last half of the twentieth century it would have been likely to use terrorism as a weapon. While foreign links could be important, they were not essential. External influences, however, were important in another way. There is some evidence that globalization played a role in some outbreaks of ethnic terrorism. Modernity had provided greater opportunities for migration, and the Dayaks and the Basques have been defending their lands and cultures from foreign intruders that were threatening their way of life. For the moment the Dayaks would appear to have met the threat while the Basques have continued to lose ground.

TERMS

Al Asqa Brigades	Judea and Samaria
Anti-Liberation Terrorist Group (GAL)	Justice Commandos of the Armenian
Armenian Secret Army for the	Genocide (JCAG)
Liberation of Armenia (ASALA)	Kosovo
Count Folke Bernadotte	Kosovo Liberation Army (KLA)
Black September	Kurds
Chechnya	Mau Mau
colons	Slobodan Milošević
Dayaks	National Liberation Army (NLA)
Euzkadi ta Askatasuna (ETA)	Occupied Territories
Fatah	Palestinian Authority
Francisco Franco	Palestinian Liberation Organization (PLO)
furores	Popular Front for the Liberation of Palestine (PFLP)
Gaza Strip	Quebec Liberation Front (FLQ)
Hamas	Stern Gang
Hutu (Bahutu)	General Suharto
intifada	Tutsi (Watutsi)

FURTHER READING

Battle of Algiers (film—1965)

Ahmed, H. H. (2005) "Palestinian Resistance and 'Suicide Bombing': Causes and Consequences," in T. Bjorgo (ed.) *Root Causes of Terrorism: Myths, Reality and Ways Forward*, London: Routledge, 87–102.

Byman, D. (1998) "The Logic of Ethnic Terrorism," *Studies in Conflict and Terrorism*, 21, 2: 149–69.

Judah, T. (2000) *Kosovo: War and Revenge*, New Haven: Yale University Press.

Scheslinger, A. M. (1955) "Political Mobs and the American Revolution, 1765–1776," *Proceedings of the American Philosophical Society*, 99, 4: 244–50.

Woodworth, P. (2001) "Why Do They Kill? The Basque Conflict in Spain," *World Policy Journal*, 18, 1: 1–12.

CHAPTER 7

Terrorism and Ideologies of the Left

The two previous chapters dealt with dissident organizations linked with religion and ethnicity—two of the most basic forms of identification available to individuals. Ethnic or national identity is generally difficult to change. Even if one becomes a naturalized citizen, one may still be regarded as foreign, or perhaps just different. In states where communal violence has occurred, shared citizenship has not prevented violence between groups that are perceived to be different. Similarly, religion has formed one of the more basic identifiers for members of a society. While some individuals can and do change religions, most individuals do not. Personal, family, and peer groups may reinforce the religious identity to a sufficient degree as to make conversion relatively rare. Even if individuals are not particularly active in the religion of their group, they will still often have a cultural identification with that religion and be affected by the values that are inherent within it. Of the religious groups discussed in Chapter 5, Aum Shinrikyo was the one exception in this regard since its members voluntarily chose to join and become devoted to the sect and its leader. The followers of Islam, Judaism, Christianity, or Sikhism, on the other hand, are much less likely to be composed of converts or persons who have recently joined, and in religious groups of long-standing members, the newcomers will usually be obvious.

Unlike religion and ethnicity, ideological affiliation involves a much more conscious choice for the followers of the set of political beliefs. Individuals can choose which set of political ideas to value and support, and they can even change their views without necessarily changing other aspects of their lives, such as language or ethnicity. Individuals may even consider these political ideas and values to be worth fighting for. Obviously, if the political ideas are in general agreement with the structure and practices of the governmental system in power, individuals are unlikely to become violent dissidents. On the other hand, if the government in power seems to be antithetical to the cherished ideological concepts and hopes, violence becomes possible for firm believers.

IDEOLOGY AND BELIEFS

Ideologies cover virtually all possible political views, solutions to problems or perceived problems, and perspectives. For the most part, political movements that do not involve religious or ethno-nationalist elements can be broadly grouped into left and right categories. Leftist ideologies generally proclaim that their ideal state will include the establishment of greater equality and the reduction or destruction of privilege and rank. They are frequently universalistic in that they claim to apply to many, if not all, the peoples and societies of the world. Rightist ideologies usually stress the need for order and hierarchy and the presence of some form of natural ordering of groups in political systems. They may even define some natural elite (with definitions varying substantially) that should govern. They can even suggest that there is great value in differences and even in the presence of inequalities. Inequality is considered to be a principle of nature (Bjorgo 1995b: 3). Ideologies of the right often, but clearly not always, involve elements of nationalism, meaning that in many cases they are not really universalistic in their applications. Their prescriptions are seen as being relevant for a particular society or particular group of societies rather than most or all of the societies of the world.

Almost any ideology can be used to support the use of violence and terrorism in the appropriate circumstances. The government may be, or perceived to be, controlled by an elite following a different or even contradictory ideology. The end result is the followers of one ideology will become dissidents, and just as religious or nationalist dissidents may feel compelled to resort to violence if their views are not being heard or are being ignored, ideological dissidents may feel the need to resort to violence to make their points about policies or the political system. The government in power may also be seen as repressive, and of course it may in fact be a very repressive government. If the government views a particular ideology as being dangerous in terms of circulating ideas that are contrary to the government policy or the structure of the government itself, the groups in power could resort to repression to control the dissidents and generate the violence and the danger that they are seeking to avoid. A dissident group may also resort to violence if it feels there are questions of basic fairness involved in the dispute between themselves and the government. If government policies are seen to be unfairly rewarding one group or penalizing some portion of the population, the unfairness could be used as a justification for violence. If other means of political activity fail to generate the appropriate policies in an ideological sense, groups may resort to violence if their beliefs are strong enough, and the beliefs may be strengthened by the presence of a well-developed political ideology that explains why the unfairness is present.

DISSATISFACTION FROM THE LEFT

While ideological conflict, like nationalism, is often seen as a nineteenth- or twentieth-century phenomenon, there have been occurrences of political violence and even terrorism in the past that have some of the hallmarks of ideological attacks. Politics in the Roman Republic up to the time of Julius Caesar was often quite violent. Aspirants to public office often used groups of supporters or even paid mobs to intimidate opponents and even to coerce voters. Assassinations were not unknown, and the politicians of Rome often felt that it was necessary to maintain armed retainers and to have bodyguards when traveling in the streets of the city. The assassinations that did occur at times were intended in at least some of the cases not only to remove a political leader who was a threat but also to send a message to an opposing group. While the various groups in these internal struggles did not think of themselves as being left or right in terms of their ideologies, some of the leaders sought to extend privileges to a larger group of citizens and to reduce the advantages and privileges of the nobility (B. Lutz and J. Lutz 2006).

Other examples of violence in centuries past that drew on ideas and concepts that are related to current leftist ideologies were the peasant rebellions that occurred in Europe in the late Middle Ages, the early Renaissance, and at other times as well. The peasant rebellions usually involved violence against the local minor nobility, agents of the upper classes, and other officials. These peasant revolts in the second millennium CE had elements of equalitarian violence, and even included acts of terrorism (J. Lutz and B. Lutz 2005: 31). The early days of the French Revolution involved political violence and terrorism that took place in urban areas as well as rural ones. The Reign of Terror will be discussed in some detail as a case study in Chapter 10. Much of the violence and intimidation in this case was linked to the more radical groups supporting the revolution, which hoped to change the political system of France even more. Opposition to monarchies and aristocracies was not limited to France. Movements by the middle classes and lower classes to limit the powers of the governing noble and royal elites in other countries would qualify as movements based on at least implicit ideologies of the left. These movements were opposed to privilege and sought a more equitable distribution of political power (and wealth), even if they did not seek equal political rights for all.

The most important source for ideologies of the left, of course, appeared with the writings of Marx and Engels, followed by the writings of later communists such as Lenin and Mao Tse-tung. The detailed ideology that developed in the initial writings of Marx provided a critique of the inequality and limitations present in the capitalist societies that existed in nineteenth-century Europe, and the ideology provided a blueprint for a better future. Marx's writings also performed the extremely useful purpose of helping to demonize the existing system and providing at least an initial basis to serve as a justification for violence. While theoretical disputes have raged and will continue to rage about whether Marxism is correct, about whether Marxism has ever really been put into effect (Communism being considered by many to be a major aberration from what Marx intended), and whether various interpretations and additions to Marx's writings are correct, the ultimate importance of his writings and of others that elaborated and supported his theories is that they have been believed by many adherents. The believers and supporters of anarchism, Marxism, Marxism-Leninism, Maoism, and other variations have been motivated by the theories and have used the theories to encourage others to undertake actions against capitalist political systems or other non-Marxist systems. The theory and its ideals have served to fuel dissidence, and the dissidents have in many cases eventually opted to use violence and terrorism as the only means of defeating exploitive, non-Marxist political systems.

Leftist dissident groups are unlikely to simply seek a change of political leaders when they resort to political violence. Ideologies of the left are usually economically deterministic and indicate that the evils of modern-day societies occur when a particular class dominates the system. As a consequence, for the leftists changing leaders without changing the underlying system is unlikely to make much of a difference. Changes of policies at the very least are likely to be sought by leftist dissidents who resort to violence. The dissidents may seek better conditions for workers, changes in the tax structure so that the wealthy contribute more to society, modifications of economic policies to discourage investment by foreign multinationals and to favor domestic business, changes in trade policy, the end to foreign military alliances or other changes in foreign policy, land reform, or better social services. All of these desired policy changes would reflect the leftist ideology and various Marxist interpretations of what ails society. If such changes in policy occur, the dissidents might actually end their opposition and their reliance on violence. Even though changes in policy to remedy injustice may be sought, leftist groups are more likely to seek structural changes in the government, society, and economy. True policy reform cannot occur without more far-reaching reforms in the society. The capitalist ruling class needs to be deprived of its opportunity to dominate and control the political system. In order for this domination to end, the power base of the class must be destroyed and political institutions changed to permit continued control by the appropriate classes in society.

The fact that leftist dissidents often see connections between domestic classes and similar groups in other countries can affect their choice of targets. Since both domestic and foreign capitalist groups are in league to perpetuate the dominance of the local and global system by international capitalism, they both are appropriate targets for violent attack. While dissident leftists may focus more on domestic targets because they are more important for the local population or they are more accessible, they can also select targets that are in other countries. The United States as the center of the capitalist system can always be seen as a legitimate symbolic target and as a key supporter of the local capitalist ruling class. Attacks against foreign interests abroad may do little to mobilize support at home, so dissident groups may have to focus upon targets in their own countries if they hope to mobilize the local population to support them and their objectives. These local targets can include foreign operations in the country. In fact, attacks against foreigners by local leftists instead of native citizens are often very popular with the local population and may generate additional support for the group (Laqueur 2001: 223).

One of the first groups of leftists to opt for terrorism as a weapon in the struggle against the oppressive dominating class were the anarchists who began to operate in the nineteenth century. Anarchist doctrine suggested that the ruling classes would be overthrown as a result of a spontaneous uprising by the masses. The anarchists did believe, however, that the masses could be educated about the inferior position that they were relegated to and that they could be inspired to undertake the uprising. One method of informing the common people of their situation and of the need for change was by "propaganda of the word." (Propaganda as initially used simply meant to educate and thus did not originally have the negative connotation of biased information that goes with the term today.) The second form of inspiration and example that could be provided was "propaganda of the deed." The anarchists believed that actions including the violent ones could be used to mobilize the masses by indicating that the dominating classes and the supporting governmental structure were weak and vulnerable. The government would strike back with repression, driving opponents to more attacks, leading to more repression, and the eventual popular rebellion (Laqueur 2001: 50).

The deed that the anarchists hit upon to serve these purposes was assassination as part of a campaign rather than isolated actions unrelated to each other even though there was no central planning committee. The anarchists were an early version of a network of terrorist groups and also of a form of leaderless resistance to some extent since attacks were often spontaneous and uncoordinated. The particular individuals targeted were less important than their value as symbols of the ruling classes. While occasional attacks with bombs were made against legislative bodies, the most frequent targets were heads of state, who were symbolic of the political system. Among the casualties by anarchists were President Carnot of France in 1894, Spanish Prime Minister Canova del Castillo in 1897, Empress Elizabeth of Austria-Hungary in 1898, King Umberto of Italy in 1900, and President McKinley of the United States in 1901. Queen Victoria of Great Britain, King Louis Phillipe of France, and Kaiser Wilhelm I of Germany were also unsuccessfully targeted (Ford 1985: 208–9, 360). Like the current global jihadist groups that have drawn on immigrants in West Europe, the anarchists drew on immigrants, especially from Italy and France, for the personnel who launched attacks in Argentina, the United States, France, and Spain (Weinberg 2006: 52). All of these attacks were intended to disrupt the political system and to create the circumstances in which the anticipated popular uprising would occur. The targets themselves were not chosen for any particular actions that they had undertaken as indicated by the fact that the Empress Elizabeth was killed when the French Duke of Orleans failed to appear as expected (Ford 1985: 209). The anarchists were poorly trained and lacked external support, and they proved to be easy targets for infiltration and discovery by the security officials of the time (Carr 2002: 149–50). The anarchists did not believe that the assassinations alone would lead to the necessary changes in the political systems. They were designed to be catalysts for changes rather than the causes of the changes. In one sense the anarchists actually did have the catalyzing effect they were seeking, although not when anticipated. They served as an example and impetus for later leftist movements in the twentieth century.

The anarchist campaign of political assassinations became most extensive in Russia with the Will of the People (*Narodnaya I Volya*) organization. This group attempted to assassinate the Tsar and other high-ranking officials in the government. Over the course of years they managed to successfully assassinate ministers in the government, other officials, and Tsar Alexander II in 1881. The goal of this campaign of assassinations, like the anarchist attacks elsewhere, was to provide examples by propaganda of the deed to the general population and to provoke the government. The group did not believe that any one assassination would lead to measurable change in the political system. They were attempting to demystify authority in the Russian political system so that the general population could at least begin to think about attempting to change things (Rubenstein 1987: 145). The group was careful to avoid casualties among bystanders and those not directly connected to the government. In one case an assassin did not use a bomb at one point in the evening because the Grand Duke was in a carriage with his wife and a group of her nieces and nephews. He waited until later in the evening when he could assassinate the Grand Duke without killing the others (Combs 2000: 25). In the short term, these efforts by Russian anarchists failed. The police with the aid of informants managed to break the group, capturing and imprisoning those who were not killed. The autocratic government remained in power, and there was no popular uprising. Although the efforts of the Will of the People were not successful, the Social Revolutionaries that appeared in the early 1900s adopted the same tactics. They undertook campaigns of assassinations against both national and local officials (Laqueur 1999: 18). The groups also attempt to coordinate terrorism with industrial strikes and occupations of rural property in their efforts to create change (Perrie 1982: 72). The efforts of the Social Revolutionaries, like the anarchists before them, were contained by the Russian security forces. Of course, it is possible to argue that the repressive response of the government that was provoked by the assassinations did alienate the Russian people even more and did set the stage for the failed Revolution in 1905 and the Revolutions in February and October of 1917 (old calendar) that destroyed the Russian monarchy and the associated system of government (Enders and Sandler 2006: 15). For example, Vladimir Lenin's older brother Alexander had been executed following a plot against the life of Alexander III (Chamberlin 1935: 123). This defining event early in his life led Lenin to join the Bolshevik party, and his opposition to the regime eventually led to his participation in its overthrow and the establishment of the Soviet Union.

It is worth noting that Marx himself disagreed with the anarchists and their efforts to use propaganda of the deed to mobilize the masses. Marx felt that terrorism as a tactic was likely to be counterproductive in terms of achieving an ideal state in which the capitalist classes had been stripped of their power (Smith and Damphousse 1998: 140). While Marx may have been opposed to terrorism, after World War I, Marxist groups used terror, conspiracies, and mass uprisings interchangeably in efforts to overthrow existing governments. Lenin and Trotsky were practical; they used bombings and assassinations against the provisional government established in February 1917 and its middle-class supporters (Enders and Sandler 2006: 15). The creation of the Soviet Union as a Communist society provided local Marxist-Leninist parties and groups with external support for both election campaigns and clandestine underground activities. Some of these activities before World War II in effect became state sponsored and state controlled efforts by the Soviet Union to establish friendly regimes in different countries while in other cases the activities of local Communists were more autonomous. After World War II, left-wing ideologies served as the ideological basis for dissident groups in a variety of contexts, and these groups frequently resorted to the use of terrorism. These groups adapted variations of the theories of Marx and Lenin, sometimes claiming affinity with anarchist principles, the ideas of Leon Trotsky, or the ideas of Mao Tse-tung in China. Regardless of the variations in their particular theoretical principles, their justifications for political violence, including acts of terrorism, were usually similar.

While Marxist-Leninist ideologies have had very little scope for overlapping with dissident movements grounded in religion, the ideas have appeared as an element of national liberation movements since colonies and subject territories have often been seen as part of an international proletariat that is being exploited by the international capitalist classes. Marxist-Leninist groups have broken away from the mainstream nationalist groups to create parallel organizations seeking an independent, progressive, and working-class (Communist) state. The Vietnam War generated a great deal of political dissidence and activity in many countries, much of which was based on the premise of solidarity with the exploited Third World peoples, including the Vietnamese. Anti-war protests in the United States spawned groups like the Students for a Democratic Society (SDS). The most radical elements of the SDS in turn became the Weather Underground or the Weathermen that used terror attacks, usually confined to property, to challenge the system and US involvement in Southeast Asia. Groups, such as the Symbionese Liberation Army, grew out of the same protest culture of anti-government and anti-system feelings. Concern among leftists students in Europe and capitalism and exploitation of workers and the developing world and the war in Vietnam generated a wide variety of dissident groups that proved to be willing to use violence and terrorism to attempt to achieve their political goals of change in individual countries and the international system as a whole.

Leftist groups, have felt that the violence that they were undertaking could lead to victories for the working class in one of two ways. The first way in which they hoped to succeed was by destabilizing the state. If the government fails to deal effectively with the terrorists, popular

BOX 7.1 THE SYMBIONESE LIBERATION ARMY (SLA)

Even though the United States was normally seen as the center of the system of global capitalism and was also held responsible for the Vietnam conflict, domestic violence from the left was relatively subdued in the late 1960s and 1970s. The Weathermen or Weather Underground was not nearly as active as their European or Latin American counterparts. A number of isolated groups with elements of leftist ideology did appear, including the Symbionese Liberation Army (SLA). The SLA combined elements of the black community in the United States, individuals with criminal records, and a few white leftists. The SLA launched a series of violent attacks on US society and the political system, including bank robberies that helped to fund the group. The biggest coup for the organization was the kidnapping of heiress Patricia Hearst. As part of the ransom the SLA demanded that her family distribute food to the poor. This demand, as well as associated political communiqués, clearly established the leftist credentials and objectives of the group. Despite concessions and expenditures from the Hearst family, she was not released; instead, she became an active member of the SLA, either because of fear and intimidation, conversion, or a combination of both factors. Whether or not she was a willing participant in the group is still a matter of some controversy. When the police freed her from the SLA, she was placed under arrest and eventually tried for participating in a bank robbery. She was convicted, and sentenced to a term in jail. The life span of the SLA proved to be relatively short. Most of the members were either killed or captured by the police. A few surviving members of the group went into hiding, but they made no attempt to continue the revolutionary struggle. The SLA quickly became a thing of the past. The group would not have achieved the notoriety that it did except for the daring kidnapping of Hearst. The attention that came with the kidnapping gave the SLA tremendous publicity, but it may have been a double-edged sword since it focused special police attention on the SLA, which hastened its end.

support for the government will disappear. The resulting popular discontent could then bring about changes in the government. In such a period of change, the dissidents and progressive groups in the society would have an opportunity to gain power after which they could implement changes. A non-democratic government might be forced to open up the political process, presenting opportunities for the dissident leftists to gain greater power or even to seize control through some form of conspiratorial takeover (i.e., to replicate the Bolshevik seizure of power from a provisional government). The collapse of a parliamentary democratic system could also give a conspiratorial group or its legal allies an opportunity to gain power in order to establish a more ideal society.

A second type of objective that could result from such a terrorist campaign would be somewhat more indirect in its contribution toward undercutting a capitalist political system. A successful terrorist campaign, especially in a state that has the appearance of being a democratic country, could force the state and the ruling capitalist classes to reveal their true colors. Faced with popular violence and the threat to the security of the state and the ruling classes, the government will become more repressive in its activities as it seeks to destroy the terrorists that threaten to mobilize the population against the status quo. As the government becomes more repressive, it will trample upon the rights of the population. Protection of the interests of the ruling capitalist class will become more important than preserving the façade of democracy that was possible in more peaceful times. This resort to repression will make obvious to the population as a whole the true nature of the regime. If the population is alienated enough by the continued repression, a national uprising could be triggered. This more repressive state will undoubtedly make life for the dissidents much more difficult and hinder their pursuit of their political objectives in the short run, but according to this analysis the overthrow of the system becomes more likely when the people come to realize the true character of the government in power. A terrorist dissident group may even sacrifice itself in this situation since a more repressive state can sometimes better deal with terrorist violence, but it will be sacrificing itself to create a situation in which a population revolution becomes more likely. The assassination of Tsar Alexander II of Russia may have had such an effect since the state repression (along with other factors) may have increased popular dissatisfaction with the government.

It might appear to be a fantasy that a terror campaign could lead to the fall of a government and create a situation in which it would be replaced by a more repressive political system, yet such has indeed happened. The Tupamaros (officially the Movement of National Liberation) were a Marxist-Leninist group that appeared in Uruguay in 1964. This group, like European leftist groups was composed largely of students and other young idealists opposed to the inequities present in the supposedly democratic system. The dissidents robbed banks and even took over towns for a few hours to demonstrate their capabilities and to embarrass the politicians in power. They also used some of the funds they acquired to aid the poor in the fashion of latter-day Robin Hoods (Clutterbuck 1975: 36). With time the threat from the Tupamaros became more serious with kidnappings and increasing violence. The violence weakened early support that the dissidents had and eventually alienated the public that supported harsher measures for dealing with the terrorists (J. White 1998: 76). The activities of the Tupamaros called into question the competence of the government since the established politicians proved to be totally unable to deal with the situation. Eventually key military leaders intervened to overthrow the government and installed a military government. The Tupamaros had succeeded in creating the desired change of regime. This new regime opted for harsher and more repressive measures, in effect showing the true colors of the more powerful classes in Uruguay. This new government was much more effective than the previous democratic one, and the Tupamaros were defeated. Their members were arrested, imprisoned, and in some cases killed. While the predicted repressive government did appear, there was no mass uprising against it. Thus, their sacrifice was in vain. The Tupamaros did have another effect; European leftists admired them and were inspired by them (Sanchez-Cuenca 2006: 73). A democratic government in Turkey also fell as a consequence of terrorist violence. There was a wave of violence by leftist groups seeking to overthrow the government and establish a socialist state (Bal and Laciner 2001: 101). The leftist violence led to counterattacks by terrorist groups on the right. Thousands died in the resulting conflicts (Sayari and Hoffman 1994: 162). The high levels of violence led to intervention by the military in 1980. The new regime then successfully cracked down on the leftists (Bal and Laciner 2001).

Leftist ideologies have included Marxism-Leninism and anarchist strains among others. Terrorism and political violence have originated in social democratic and liberal democratic movements, which have targeted governments that were repressive or extremely conservative, could also be considered to be leftist. In 1878 in Japan, a senior government official was assassinated by a group seeking a *representative* national legislature (Angel 1990: 33). This action

BOX 7.2 JAPANESE RED ARMY (JRA)

The Japanese Red Army (JRA) attracted young leftists just as its European counterparts did. The group shared the general distaste of the left for global capitalism and joined in the general opposition to the economic and political policies of the United States. Unlike the Red Brigades or the Red Army Faction in Germany, this group undertook its most important attacks on foreign soil. Initially it attempted to launch campaigns in Japan, but these efforts were stymied by the Japanese authorities, who proved to be relatively efficient in tracking down and capturing or killing JRA members and other violent leftist dissidents in the country. As a consequence, the members of the JRA decided to undertake operations outside of the country where they would have some chance of surviving to continue the struggle. The group resorted to hijacking airliners flying out of Japan, it attacked embassies abroad as a means of furthering its Marxist-Leninist agenda, and it gained concessions from the Japanese government in return for releasing hostages (Wilkinson 2003: 117). Japan's willingness to pay ransoms or deal with the JRA contributed to terrorism becoming a global problem since the terrorists were rewarded for their actions (Heymann 2003: 124). The JRA has cooperated with a variety of other dissident organizations over the years. A group of members training in a camp in the Middle East joined with the PFLP to carry out an attack at Lod Airport in Tel Aviv, Israel in 1976. Twenty-five people were killed and seventy-six injured in the assault (Tan 2006: 177). The Japanese leftists found it much easier to smuggle weapons onto the flight than other individuals, especially since no intelligence agencies appear to have been aware of the involvement of Japanese leftists with Palestinian nationalists. This attack was basically a suicide mission since the members of the assault squad had no chance of avoiding death or capture once they opened fire with automatic weapons and grenades. Attacks have been rare in recent years, although the group has attempted to remain active, but like other leftist groups has gradually faded from prominence. Enough members or former members remain available for the core of a revived organization or for an alliance with other terrorist groups. Recently, members of the JRA have been in Colombia apparently to train leftists for an urban bombing campaign (Ortiz 2002: 139).

clearly was leftist in its political objectives given the existing political system. When the Shah was overthrown in Iran in 1979, the Muslim clerics and secular groups engaged in a contest for power in the government that was won by the clerics. The secular forces, which included both leftists and more centrist members of the middle class, launched a terrorist campaign against the clerics. Bombings and assassination took their toll of prominent officials and government supporters. It took the clerical government eighteen months to gain effective control and to defeat their opponents (Green 1995: 579–80). The target of the violence was a very conservative, religious regime; therefore, the attackers, including middle-class centrists, were attacking from the left. Any terrorist campaigns mounted by democratic forces against military dictators and personal tyrants would also be considered leftist in terms of the relative positions of the government and the dissidents. Not all political violence and terrorism based upon ideologies that are left of the government in power needs to be based on Marxist-Leninist concepts.

One additional kind of ideology that can be considered at least generally leftist involves views dealing with the preservation of the environment and animal rights. While such views are not Marxist in background, the views of the dissidents involved generally attack the political and theoretical premises of the political system from the left rather than the right. While Green parties and defenders of the position of animals in society as part of the necessary ecological balance do have clear differences with Marxist-Leninist groups, they also share some positions. Ecological groups, such as the Earth Liberation Front (ELF), are often concerned with fairness and the equitable distribution of resources to some extent, and ecological and environmental movements are almost inevitably anti-capitalist. Capitalism has hardly been environmentally benign, and pollution and destruction of the natural habitat has often been associated with capitalism. While Communist systems were more destructive of the environment, the Communist countries did not permit any meaningful environmental protests or resorts to violence. The Communist systems are now virtually gone, leaving only unrestrained capitalism to threaten environmental quality. There is a general distrust of big business, and especially of multinational corporations by environmentalists (Brannan 2006: 62). The idea that small is beautiful almost invariably runs counter to the idea that greater growth is valuable. Frustrated by the lack of progress in defending the environment, groups eventually resorted to violence and terror, and persons have been injured (Eagan 1996). There has been a recent increase in the use of violence, much of which has so far been directed against property targets, although people have been injured as well. Throwing paint on persons wearing furs or splashing corporate executives with the polluted water or earth from their companies' operations are not deadly acts. These types of activities have been designed to publicize the cause and to embarrass rather than to harm. There have also been attacks on ski resorts, new housing, recreational developments, and other property in the United States that threaten the national habitat in some way in the eyes of the attackers (Taylor 1998). More recently, large sport utility vehicles (SUVs) in the United States have even become targets for environmental violence. The Unabomber as an individual shared at least some of these concerns given his opposition to modernization and technology (Ackerman 2003). The increasing violence by environmental groups in the United States led to them being considered the most important domestic terrorist threat by officials in 2005 (Joosse 2007: 352).

CASE STUDIES

The following five case studies represent clear examples of dissident movements that have both been based on leftist ideologies and that have resorted to the use of terror. The cases include examples of two European countries that faced terrorist campaigns from the left in the latter half of the twentieth century, usually involving activities by dissident students. The activities of the Red Army Faction or Baader-Meinhof Gang in the former West Germany, and the Red Brigades in Italy are representative of activities by younger leftists. The other three cases are more varied. The Montoneros in Argentina, who were eventually destroyed by the military regime in power, were similar in many ways to the movements in Western Europe in the political goals that they sought. There have also been leftist groups in India that have long attempted to overthrow the government. The final case involves the Animal Liberation Front (ALF) in the United Kingdom that has indicated its willingness to use terror in its efforts to dissuade companies and individuals from violating the rights of animals.

CASE STUDY 7.1   THE BAADER–MEINHOF GANG IN WEST GERMANY

One of the most infamous of the Marxist-Leninist terrorist groups that appeared in Europe in the 1970s was the Baader–Meinhof Gang, which was also known as the Red Army Faction (RAF). While the group was not the most effective organization that appeared, it did catch the imagination of the press and public opinion. In this sense the group was very effective in broadcasting its message of opposition to the international capitalist system of which West Germany was a part. It developed a rather extensive support system within Western Europe, utilized contacts with East Germany and the Soviet Union to further its activities, and joined in some rather spectacular international efforts. The security forces effectively disrupted the original group, but the RAF was succeeded by the June 2nd Movement and the Red Cells as later generations of the same movement.

The RAF was formed in 1968 at the height of the student protests that were sweeping Europe and which seemed, even if only briefly, to have some chance of changing the political systems of the West. The particular motivation for the initial members of the RAF was the death of a student protester at the hands of the police. He died while protesting a visit of the Shah of Iran to Berlin in the midst of a struggle between protesters and the police authorities who were not prepared for the student demonstrations that had begun to appear (Otte 1997: 552). His death was seen as an integral part of the effort of the capitalists to maintain order and control in their home countries. The Shah was perceived to be a Third World leader who worked hand in glove with Western capitalism. The political system and government of West Germany was seen as a thinly disguised continuation of Nazi Germany by the young leftists (Crenshaw 1995b: 21). The founding members of the RAF drew upon Marxist-Leninist writings to explain current events. The war in Vietnam, the failure of student protests, the poverty in the Third World, and the failure of the Palestinians to achieve their rights were all seen as symptoms of the continuing domination of the world economic system by capitalists. Their ultimate goal was the destruction of international capitalism and imperialism (C. Drake 1998: 71).

The RAF selected a variety of targets in keeping with its anti-capitalist stance. The initial attacks launched by the group were relatively amateurish bombings of buildings, but the group quickly moved on to more violent and deadly attacks. A variety of businessmen, seen as representatives of the oppressive capitalist system, were chosen for personal attacks, letter bombs, kidnapping, or assassination. Other targets included bankers and the press and publishing industries. The group kidnapped reasonably prominent individuals in a number of efforts to gain the freedom of imprisoned comrades. American military personnel also became targets at times, and the RAF managed to detonate bombs on or near American military bases on a number of occasions. The RAF even attempted to assassinate General Alexander Haig, who was then the commander of the NATO forces in Europe (Pluchinsky 1992: 44). The RAF did threaten to launch a chemical attack on one occasion with mustard gas that it claimed to posses. This threat proved to be a hoax. The group apparently learned that the gas was missing and claimed to have acquired it in order to increase pressure on the West German government over an upcoming trial of RAF members. Ultimately, there was no evidence that the group ever did have the mustard gas (Claridge 2000a: 105). Since the RAF had already demonstrated its willingness to use violence to achieve its objectives, such a threat, however, could not be totally ignored.

The original members of the RAF turned out not to be very effective militants. Although they launched a number of successful attacks, and focused attention on the problems that they claimed were present within the system, they were all apprehended and sent to prison. These leaders of the RAF, however, were able to give directions to their followers while in prison, and, in fact, they were somewhat more effective from what would seem to have been a less than ideal location. From prison they served as an inspiration for other leftists to struggle against world capitalism by becoming symbols of the struggle against the status quo, and these new organizations even attempted some actions that were designed to free the imprisoned original members of the Baader–Meinhof Gang. These attempts included the kidnapping of a German industrialist and the hijacking of an airliner in 1977. When the hijackers were captured, three of the RAF leaders in prison committed suicide. The members on the outside were convinced that the three had been murdered, and the industrialist was killed in retaliation (Pluchinsky 1992: 46–7). Their suicides have continued to be considered suspicious by leftists in Germany and elsewhere in Europe, who have regarded them more as victims of the system.

The West German dissidents also developed strong connections with the Palestinian opposition groups. They received training in Palestinian camps, learning how to handle arms and weapons. The German dissidents and Palestinians cooperated in a number of major actions. At least one former or present RAF member was involved with the Palestinian groups that were responsible for the hostage situation involving the OPEC oil ministers in Vienna in December of 1975 (Otte 1997: 555). RAF members were also involved in the hijacking of the Air France flight that was eventually diverted to Entebbe in Uganda—only to be killed when the Israeli commandos struck and rescued the hostages. German and Palestinian terrorists were also involved in the hijacking of a Lufthansa airliner to Somalia in October of 1977. When special units of the German border police attacked the aircraft on the ground (with the permission of Somali authorities), the hostages were freed and the hijackers captured or killed (Pluchinsky 1992: 44). The failure of the hijackers to maintain control of the airliner and the hostages was the event that triggered the suicides of the three imprisoned RAF leaders.

One factor that made it possible for the RAF to survive and to continue to mount attacks was the presence of a substantial support network. While the active members of the various groups were relatively few in number, they depended upon a network of supporters to provide them with safe houses, information, to serve as couriers, and to scout locations for attacks. Surviving underground in West Germany was also an expensive proposition. It has been estimated that it cost $50,000 a year for one member of the RAF to survive in German society (Long 1990: 69). Such costs required a financial support network as well for the movement to be able to continue. Without the aid of other supporters of Marxist-Leninist ideologies, the German revolutionaries would have been much less effective than they were. The RAF was also very successful in its efforts to internationalize its activities. It undertook terrorist attacks, bank robberies, and engaged in confrontations with security forces in Sweden (where it seized the West German embassy), Belgium, Spain, Austria, Italy, Switzerland, the Netherlands, and France. Some of these effort involved coordination with other leftist dissident groups in these countries. The RAF was in fact the group most important in efforts at forming a broad, leftist, anti-capitalist front throughout Europe (Pluchinsky 1992: 44). This effort at international coordination was never as effective as the organizers hoped, but the combined efforts that did occur were indicative of the importance of the RAF. The RAF and its successors did have external support from East Germany and the Soviet Union. The external support was helpful but not essential for the survival of the group. The members of the RAF were capable of finding arms and building bombs on their own, and they did not have to rely on support from Communist countries, even though such help was useful. Probably the most important contribution made by the East Germans was to provide members of various groups with safe havens to relax without fear of arrest or discovery (Pluchinsky 1992: 81). Ten members of the RAF, including the leading surviving members of the RAF were discovered and arrested in East Germany in 1990 after the fall of the Communist government in that state (Laqueur 1999: 167).

The RAF that was relatively unique in one way. It was able to develop new generations of leaders as members of the current active group were caught or killed. The RAF was thus able to survive as a group even as its membership changed completely. It was able to overcome losses in personnel and leadership (Pluchinsky, 1992: 44). This continuity, which was due in significant measure to the well-developed support groups that supplied the active terrorists with material aid and information, was also able to supply recruits to replace the lost comrades. The RAF was able to bedevil the West German government for years. The RAF, however, was not prepared for the collapse of Communism in the Soviet Union and Eastern Europe (Merkl 1995b: 172–3). The Marxist goals and critiques of the capitalist system became more difficult to put forward with the disintegration of the system that the dissidents claimed to be their ultimate goal. There was a series of attacks and assassinations in 1991, but the group began to reconsider its whole campaign. In a series of communiqués in 1992, the surviving leftists indicated that they were ceasing their activities (Pluchinsky 1993).

BOX 7.3 POPULAR FRONT FOR THE LIBERATION OF PALESTINE (PFLP)

George Habash, who tied the cause of an independent Palestinian state to Marxist-Leninist theories and the battle against global capitalism, founded the Popular Front for the Liberation of Palestine (PFLP). He saw the struggle of the Palestinians as part of the broader struggle of colonial peoples and the working class against global capitalism. It joined the PLO when it was formed, but it never commanded the following of Fatah and Yasser Arafat. The group was very active in airline hijackings. In 1968 it successfully undertook a hijacking to popularize the cause of the Palestinians and to seek the release of imprisoned Palestinians (Hoffman 2006: 68). The group also took part in joint actions such as the hijacking of an Air France flight to Entebbe (with the RAF), the assault on oil ministers at an OPEC meeting in Vienna, the Lod Airport attack by the Japanese Red Army, and other attacks. Because of its leftist orientation it was able to develop effective ties with various leftist groups in Europe and Japan that saw the Palestinian struggle as part of a global battle between capitalism and the people.

The PFLP has been among the more intransigent Palestinian groups. It supported the *intifada* in the Occupied Territories when opposition to the Israelis broke out, joining forces with other local groups. When the PLO decided to renounce terrorism as a weapon, implicitly recognized the right of Israel to exist, and agreed to open negotiations with the government of Israel, the PFLP left the organization. It joined the "Rejectionist Front" with other groups that were opposed to any accommodation with Israel. Because of its Marxist-Leninist ideology the PFLP has become somewhat marginalized in the struggle with Israel. The ideology has prevented it from mobilizing on the basis of religion, and it has been less effective than the mainstream PLO groups in competing on the basis of Palestinian nationalism. Like other leftist groups it has suffered from the break up of the Soviet Union and the end of Communism in so many parts of the world, and like other leftist organizations it has suffered from internal differences and splits within the organization.

CASE STUDY 7.2   THE ITALIAN RED BRIGADES

The Baader–Meinhoff Gang/Red Army Faction managed to generate considerable publicity throughout Europe and the world without having had any major long-term successes in disrupting the German political system. The Italian Red Brigades, however, were a much more potent terrorist group. Their activities in the late 1960s, 1970s, and 1980s generated greater fear and disruptions. The total active membership of the Red Brigades or related groups reached levels that were considerably higher than the levels attained in West Germany. The Italian Red Brigades, however, concentrated almost totally on targets related to the domestic economic and political systems throughout their campaigns (although they did kidnap a US general assigned to NATO). The Red Brigades, as well as other leftists in Italy, regarded the parliamentary democratic system that was created after World War II to be simply a continuation of the Fascist regime in power under Benito Mussolini. There was a wide range of targets, including business leaders, judges, police officials, union personnel, party leaders, and politicians.

The Red Brigades grew out of the Italian university setting, and most of the members were young and idealistic. They could see the problems that were present with Western capitalism, and they were influenced by the purer versions of Marxism that were typically presented in the universities at the time. They sought to create the socialism of Lenin in the early years of Russia or of the Maoist revolution, not the version of socialism that existed in the USSR in the 1970s (Raufer 1993: 319). Flirtations with leftist ideologies were not unusual for university students in the late 1960s and early 1970s. Many Marxist theories also specified that the intelligentsia, including students, have a key role to play in preparing a society for revolution, so these theories had an additional attraction for young students since it potentially gave them a key role to play. These years were somewhat heady days for young Marxists with the appearance of student protests and demonstrations against the American involvement in Vietnam—and of the explicit or implicit support provided to the United States by its European allies. The leaders of the Red Brigades saw themselves as part of the vanguard of the proletariat. This intellectual vanguard was prepared to do battle with global system of capitalism in order to liberate the working classes. The Red Brigades were also able to attract recruits from students because an expansion of the university system had created many more graduates with expectations of careers than there were jobs to match these new aspirations (Waldmann 2005: 157).

The Marxist beliefs of the dissidents and their concern for the working class were obvious in the original choices of targets. The Red Brigades activities were clearly designed to discredit Italian business leaders. The first actions, while violent, were not lethal. Attacks were on company property and the possessions of local capitalists. Vehicles of prominent capitalists were vandalized or bombed. They undertook brief symbolic kidnappings of executives and labor leaders from the more conservative unions. In other cases they used kidnapping to fund their activities (Pisano 1987: 44). Bank robberies became another mechanism for attacking the system, as well as a means of funding their activities (Rimanelli 1989: 270). Eventually funding for the organization became easier when an Italian millionaire with a publishing firm, Franco Feltrinelli, joined the dissidents. His personal wealth funded the Red Brigades until he was accidentally killed while planting explosives on a tower for power lines (Rimanelli 1992: 160–1).

The early efforts of the Red Brigades had benefited from a shake up of the Italian security forces. Many key members of the intelligence services had been dismissed because of their links with members of the extreme right and because they were suspected of planning some sort of coup against the democratic government (Della Porta 1995: 117). As a consequence, the security forces were somewhat disorganized at the time that the Red Brigades became a threat. With the passage of time the Brigades escalated the violence and began the practice of kneecapping. They would approach targets, which included business executives, union leaders, and journalists who failed to report the truth as defined by the dissidents. The targets would then be shot in both knees. This intentional wounding of targets was a step towards greater violence, but it was still a technique that avoided killing the enemies of the people. Kneecapping was actually inherently more dangerous for the dissidents than simply killing targets, as could be done with a car bomb or letter bomb. Bombs could be detonated from a safe distance by remote control or activated by the pressure of the target entering a car or opening a package, whereas kneecapping required that a member of the organization had to be near enough to the target to be able to cause harm while also being able to avoid killing the target. The use of such a technique also demonstrated to the public at large not only the restraint of the dissidents in not killing their targets but also their nerve and their abilities in being able to get near enough to be successful. Kneecappings also demonstrated that the authorities were incapable of protecting persons who were supporters of the system, even though it was clearly impossible for the security forces to protect everyone who could be seen as a representative of the capitalist system. The decision to escalate to kneecapping was thus a very well-chosen tactic in many respects. It discredited the state in some ways, and it was effective in terms of instilling fear in a broad audience while limiting the possibility of alienating the general public by killing individuals in ways that virtually guaranteed that the deaths of innocent bystanders would not occur.

Notwithstanding the successes of kneecapping, the members of the Red Brigades graduated toward even more violent activities in efforts to liberate members who had been captured by the police or security forces, including some of the initial leaders of the group. When their trial was approaching in 1977, the Brigades concentrated on disrupting the judicial proceedings. In an effort to prevent the trial from taking place, they began to target judges, prosecutors, and the lawyers who were appointed to defend the captured members of the Red Brigades. They killed a judge, the president of the lawyers' association who had selected the public defenders, and members of the security forces. Their efforts were successful in disrupting the trial and forcing postponements because of the threats to the various participants in the proceedings. The legal system was almost paralyzed for a time. Jurors were afraid to serve because of the fear of retaliation, and not every judge was willing to be a hero (Laqueur 1999: 29). When the trials did resume, the public was treated to the spectacle of 8,000 security personnel being necessary to guard the courthouse in order for the judicial proceedings to begin anew (R. Drake 1997: 562). The Brigades had clearly demonstrated their capacity to undermine the system while demonstrating the inability of the system to function except through the use of massive defensive forces.

In 1978 the terrorist attacks of the Red Brigades became even more lethal. While kneecappings and other types of attacks continued, the dissidents were now much more likely to kill their victims. The highlight of the year came when members of the organization kidnapped the President of the Christian Democratic Party and former Prime Minister Aldo Moro in Rome, killing his five man security team in the process. He was held captive for almost two months while the authorities were unable to locate him despite massive efforts to do so. The Red Brigades then tried him for crimes against the people. He was convicted and was executed. His body left in the trunk of a car only a hundred yards from the Christian Democratic Party headquarters in Rome (R. Drake 1997: 562–3). The Moro kidnapping displayed the abilities of the dissidents, but his subsequent execution turned the political leadership in Italy and the general population against the group (Rimanelli 1992: 151). The Italian authorities now began to make even greater efforts to limit the Red Brigades. All the major political parties, including the Communist Party, cooperated in passing enhanced security laws that were designed to control the Red Brigades. Special units were set up to deal with the terrorists, and they proved to be more effective than the regular police. The government also began a policy of providing lighter sentences for members of the group who "repented" of their actions and demonstrated their repentance by providing information on the organization. The captured members were bribed with lighter sentences if they informed on others in the organization. This technique proved to be very effective once enough dissidents had been captured. When the first few opted to accept the reduced sentences, it became possible to capture others. By the mid-1980s the bulk of the members had been captured. The Red Brigades then became a negligible force that was no longer capable of matching the efforts of five years earlier, even though isolated attacks were still to occur. Early in 2002 the Italian Minister of Economics was assassinated by surviving members of the Red Brigades for suggesting that layoffs by companies should be made easier. The threat to political stability and the democratic system, however, had long since passed.

The Italian government ultimately managed to deal with the threat from these dissidents without major limitations on civil liberties. At least some members of the Red Brigades had hoped to force the Italian political elite to support a more repressive state. Greater repression would help the general public realize that the government fronted for the capitalists and their interests. In this effort they failed, although there was at least some evidence of at least one conspiracy by the extreme right to intervene against the democratic system and to establish a stronger government that would be able to deal more firmly with the leftist dissidents. When the security forces began to improve, the Red Brigades were further weakened by schisms within the movement. The lack of unity also means that it is harder for dissident groups to mobilize resources since to at least some extent they are competing with each other as well as with the government. The Brigades themselves were divided on the wisdom (or not) of killing Moro; thus, his death weakened the movement.

The Red Brigades had some external contacts and support. While the dissidents were organized within Italy and financed locally, there were some contacts with countries behind the Iron Curtain. In the case of Italy, Czechoslovakia served as the Soviet surrogate for providing assistance to the leftists. Training, some arms, and some financing were arranged through the Czech government. While logistical support was present from the Czechs, neither the Czechs nor the Soviet KGB played any role in developing the strategy and techniques utilized by the Red Brigades (Rimanelli 1989: 280). The Red Brigades also maintained contacts with other leftist groups in Europe, such as the Red Army Faction. Efforts to generate combined action among the various groups did not come to very much. Notwithstanding the contacts with outside supporters and groups, the Red Brigades remained very much a domestic Italian phenomenon drawing upon Italian circumstances.

The Red Brigades were one of the more successful dissident groups from the left that appeared in Europe. They were the only terrorist group in Italy that had sufficient organizational capabilities, personnel, and other resources to undertake complex actions (Rimanelli 1992: 149). The threat that they created to the stability of the Italian political system was very real. The fact that some groups on the Italian right were preparing to create a more authoritarian form of government indicates that the leftists had managed to at least create the possibility that Italian democracy would fall. The targets that they selected demonstrated their ability to attack the capitalist system in all its manifestations. The capitalist executives were among the first targets, and major business figures were always under threat. Targets went beyond the obvious to include journalists whose stories were less than flattering to the leftist goals or supportive of the government, union officials who were not active enough in challenging the system, and members of the major political parties that were correctly seen as being part of the system. The Red Brigades also demonstrated a progressive increase in the level of violence when their first attacks were insufficient to achieve their goals. They moved from the attacks on property and the symbolic kidnappings, to kneecapping and wounding targets, and finally to assassinations and murder. Even though the stability of the system was indeed challenged by the left, the attacks were not able to either bring the leftists to power, to change government policies in any significant factor, or to force the government to become extremely repressive as befitted a state that was simply fascist in disguise.

BOX 7.4 17 NOVEMBER REVOLUTIONARY ORGANIZATION

One of the leftist dissident terrorist groups in Europe that survived the longest was the 17 November Revolutionary Organization in Greece. The group initially was formed in opposition to the Greek military junta (the "Colonels' Regime") that was in power in the 1970s. It took its name from an incident in 1973 when security forces attacked pro-democracy protesters and killed at least thirty of them and injured more than 800 (Kassimeris 1995: 74–5). The military regime collapsed later in the 1970s after an ill-fated effort to join Cyprus to Greece, but the dissidents continued their attacks under the new democratic system that they saw as simply a front for capitalism and conservative interests. The dissidents continued their attacks for more than twenty-five years, targeting symbols of global capitalism—prominent conservative Greeks, multinational corporations, US and British military personnel, and the CIA section chief in Athens (Kassimeris 2001). These Greek dissidents also adopted the kneecapping techniques introduced by the Italian Red Brigades (Corsun 1992: 102). The group managed to avoid any security breaches, and the Greek security forces, even with the help of external agencies, could not identify any of the members of the group. They proved to be quite adept at avoiding identification. The group was finally broken when a bomb exploded prematurely in 2005 in the apartment of a member. He was injured, but did not die, and his capture permitted the Greek authorities to penetrate the group and capture many of the members. This group avoided detection for so many years because it was small. It would appear that the leaders intentionally limited the intake of recruits to individuals who could be trusted, and there was never any chance for government spies or informers to gain access (Kassimeris 2001: 150). While the small size of the group helped to ensure its anonymity and made it easier to avoid disruption by the security forces, it also meant that the group could never undertake an extensive campaign of terrorism on the same level that the Red Brigades were able to accomplish. While it launched well-planned, occasional attacks that could gain publicity and discomfort the authorities, it was never able to effectively challenge the Greek political system or those that were in power.

CASE STUDY 7.3 THE MONTONEROS IN ARGENTINA

The Montoneros were a left-wing movement that arose in Argentina in the late 1960s. The group was similar in some respects to the Marxist-Leninist movements that appeared in Europe at the same time, but there were distinctly Argentine elements that characterized the organization. The persons who joined the movement in the initial years were invariably young, middle-class idealists seeking greater equality and justice for all portions of the Argentine population, especially the working class. The government in power at the time of the group's formation was a military regime that had come to power in 1966. These dissidents maintained their opposition to at least some elements of government policies during a number of civilian and military regimes that followed. The Montoneros were initially supporters of former President Juan Peron. They were particularly in sympathy with the redistributive, populist, and nationalist policies that Peron and his wife, Evita, had supported while he was in power. Ironically, Peron himself had come to power through a military coup, although he later built a mass following from the civilian sector. His own policies while in power were a mixture of both conservative and progressive attributes. He did differ from other political leaders with a military background in South America in that he favored workers and labor unions, and some of his strongest support came from this sector, but he also worked closely with the military, business, and the Catholic Church. Peron was able to stay in power as long as his policies favoring the left did not become too irritating to the middle and upper classes, and as long as he was able to institute some policies that the more conservative interests desired. His nationalist policies that discriminated against European and American capital and businesses were popular with both the working classes and the middle classes. He was removed from power in a military coup in 1955 when he was no longer able to successfully balance all of these interests.

Although Peron was overthrown and left the country, he quickly became the most important Argentine political figure. From his exile in Spain he helped to direct his followers and appointed leaders of parties seeking his return. He chose other candidates for office that would be supported by his followers when various governments in Argentina prohibited parties openly supporting Peron from contesting elections. Peron's support was often essential for victory of the candidates, but any effort by civilian politicians to legalize the Peronista party or some version of it led to military intervention. The military would not permit supporters of Peron, or Peron himself, to govern, but the supporters of Peron were able to prevent any other party or president from governing effectively. Peron's followers continued to reflect the contradictions from the past since they included both the left and the right. Labor unions and leftists and conservative groups supported a return of Peron. These contradictions in the Peronista movement were not so obvious when it was in opposition. All the various groups could agree to be opposed to whatever civilian or military government was in power and assumed that if Peron did indeed return their preferred policies would be implemented. The Montoneros believed that if they were able to rid the country of the military government, they would be able to influence the supporters of Peron and Peron himself to follow the appropriate policies (Wynia 1986: 78–9).

The spark for the organization of the Montoneros from among the left-wing supporters of Peron was a popular uprising in the city of Cordoba in 1969 that united workers and students. The uprising was a protest against the austerity program implemented by the military government then in power (Holmes 2001: 143). The government was able to put down the uprising, but its suppression generated more opposition throughout the country. The Montoneros were one of the left-wing dissident organizations to appear, and they eventually became the largest one. In 1970 the small group of original members decided to begin violent political action directed against the military regime that was in power. They kidnapped a former president (and general) who had ruled immediately after Peron's ouster. After a trial for crimes committed while he was in office, he was executed for his misdeeds (Wynia 1986: 77–8). From this point, the battle lines between the Montoneros and other groups in Argentine society were clearly drawn.

While the government managed to capture most of the original members of the Montoneros, the organization had begun to expand and attract new recruits. It began a campaign against the government based on the use of terror. Efforts to undertake guerrilla insurgencies in Argentina in the past had failed, so the Montoneros, like the contemporary Tupameros in Uruguay, opted for an urban strategy using their attacks as examples of propaganda of the deed as part of an effort to influence the general public and to bring discredit upon the government (Wynia 1986: 79). The group relied on bombings, kidnappings, assassinations, and other tactics in cities as a means of promoting its political objectives, including the demand that Peronistas be allowed to participate in politics. The violence was not just directed against vulnerable civilians since the attacks included bombs and other attacks against the police and the military. Kidnappings of executives from multinational corporations became an especially effective way of financing the movement since a successful kidnapping not only displayed the ineptitude of the government but also generated the revenues for proceeding with the struggle. One leftist group accumulated $30 million from such kidnappings (Bell 1997b: 239).

The campaign of the Montoneros, the activities of the other supporters of Peron who were more conservative, and the attacks by the Peoples Revolutionary Army (ERP), a more clearly Marxist movement, were ultimately successful. The military government found it increasingly difficult to govern Argentina and eventually decided to hold free elections in 1973 that were open to all parties. A Peronist candidate won the presidency as a stand-in, and he immediately allowed Juan Peron to return in triumph. He then resigned so that Peron could run for President himself. Peron easily won the new election, completing his return to power. The successful election of Peron, however, brought the differences between the groups that were supporting him to the forefront. Violence between the supporters on the left and the right began (Holmes 2001: 145). Peron had to decide which group to favor. He initially moved against the ERP since that leftist group had never been supportive of him. The significance of the attacks should have been clear to the Montoneros in terms of Peron's ultimate choice between his own conservative backers and the more radical groups that had brought him to power. Restrictions were then placed on Montonero political activities, and Peron was clearly distancing himself from the Montoneros when he died in 1974 (Gillespie 1982: 150–1). The nature of the campaign against the Montoneros changed with Peron's death. His wife, Isabel, who had served as his vice-president, took power, but she quickly demonstrated that she was incapable of dealing with the complexities of governing, especially in a divided society facing assaults on the government from a variety of sources. Her advisers, who were among the most conservative of the Peronistas, used the security forces and paramilitary groups to launch attacks on the leftists (Poneman 1987: 33). Faced with repression, the Montoneros began assaults on government targets. Their attacks continued when Isabel Peron was replaced by a military coup in 1976, which was "the most predicted and well supported coup in Argentine history" (Holmes 2001: 146).

The new round of violence that had begun in 1974 was much more intense than the previous fighting. Both the Montoneros and the ERP began consciously targeting police and military officials. The Montoneros were especially careful to avoid innocent civilian casualties (Gillespie 1995: 214). When assassinations of members of the military increased, the security forces began to retaliate. When the military government took power in 1976, repression of dissidents became more determined. Previously, when members of the leftist groups were captured, they were often tortured for information before being released or imprisoned. With the new military government they were still tortured for information but then were killed. In addition, the security forces began to use death squads to kidnap and question suspected supporters of the leftist, and most of these persons died as well, becoming the "disappeared ones" from that era of Argentine history. The Montoneros and the ERP were crushed and destroyed as effective dissident organizations in two years. The death toll among the dissidents and other suspect members of the population has never been completely determined, since suspects were killed and no records kept or notifications made. One estimate for the total number of dead from the dissidents, presumed sympathizers, and others has been estimated to total somewhere between 15,000 and 30,000 individuals (Fagen 1992: 64). The survivors, few in number, fled the country. The terror campaign from the left had generated severe government repression as predicted, but that repression was more than adequate to deal with the challenges that the government faced. The deaths of sympathizers and even innocent persons, however, weakened support for the military regime, and popular dissatisfaction began to erode the public's willingness to acquiescence with the continuation in power of a military government. The seizure of the Falkland Islands by Argentine forces was an effort by the military regime in power to restore public support. The successful seizure was quite popular throughout Argentina, but the failure to prevent the British recapture of the islands resulted in the military turning power over to civilians.

The use of terror by the Montoneros and the other leftist organizations in Argentina had mixed results in terms of their political objectives. They were quite successful in helping to destabilize the military regime that was in power in the early 1970s. As a consequence, their efforts had indeed helped to bring about free elections and the return of Peron. Peron's return, however, did not result in the adoption of their desired policies. Thus, while they were successful in bringing down the old regime, they lacked sufficient support to establish the government and policies that they desired. Once Juan Peron died, the struggle became more intense, and the security forces and the military defeated the Montoneros. Ironically, the Montoneros were not one of the Marxist-Leninist movements that sought to force the government to become more repressive to demonstrate its true character. The Argentine circumstances did not adapt themselves to that approach, and the frequent presence of military regimes in power was a sufficient indication to most that the Argentine government was responsive to conservative and business interests. The terrorism of the Argentine dissident groups, however, did indicate that such campaigns could indeed result in a government adopting measures involving massive repression as theorists had predicted. In this case the repression decimated the dissident organizations. Ultimately, it could be argued that the campaign by the Montoneros and the resulting repression did actually shorten the life of the military regime and that it helped to set the stage for the resumption of free elections and democratic rule, but it came at a high cost.

CASE STUDY 7.4 NAXALITES IN INDIA

The collapse of Communism in Eastern Europe and the Soviet Union undercut the appeal of Marxism-Leninism for leftist groups in many parts of the world since it had become much harder to argue that Communism was the wave of the future. North Korea remained a rigid Communist state, but its economic problems were clear to most observers. While China and Vietnam were more successful in maintaining their Communist systems, Marxism had still been discredited in many areas. Notwithstanding the apparent failure of Communism in the European states, leftist groups opposed to their governments and the actual or perceived unequal economic systems remained. These groups continued to be willing to use peaceful means or violent ones in their efforts to generate reform. There have been leftist guerrillas and terrorist groups active in parts of Latin America, including Mexico (Wrighte 2002), but some of the most persistent Marxist-Leninist organizations have been operating in India and Nepal.

There has been popular support for the left in India since independence. There are two Communist parties that have been active in the party system, one affiliated more closely with the Soviet Union (when it existed) and one that was Maoist in orientation and more supportive of Chinese practices and ideologies. Both of the parties contested elections and have regularly won seats in the national and state legislatures, and they have served in governing coalition cabinets, although neither one has ever been strong enough to be the dominant party in any of these coalitions. Both parties have attempted to appeal to voters in both the urban and rural areas. Rural poverty and inequality have been important problems in many areas of India; consequently, the radical left parties have been able to attract supports. Leftist groups had been associated with violent acts at times in the past, but the Naxalite movement came to be one of the more important outbreaks in the late 1960s since the issues raised and the example set have carried forward. Tensions and problems appeared in the town of Naxalbari in Bengal, and the movement derived its name from this location. The original uprising by rural residents in this area mobilized the support of many Indian citizens discontented with the system and the violence has since become a model for action that has been emulated by other groups elsewhere in India. The term Naxalite has come to be used as a generic term for a variety of leftist movements that have mobilized members of the lower classes and the poor who have become dissatisfied with the economic and political system (Banerjee 1984: 92).

In rural areas there were many kinds of inequality. Over the course of time landlords and moneylenders had gained control over much of the land, and many of the peasants in Naxalbari were landless and had become sharecroppers on larger holdings. The landlords were invariably members of upper caste groups. Although the caste system was officially abolished at independence, its deep roots in Indian society meant that the influence of this system of unequal social status did not quickly disappear. Social discrimination against those who were members of lower castes, and especially the former untouchable castes, continued. The social dominance of the higher caste landlords contributed to their ability to exploit the peasants and sharecroppers. In addition, in some areas there were members of tribal groups who represented the original inhabitants of the Indian subcontinent, and like indigenous peoples elsewhere in the world they had progressively lost their land to new groups of people moving into their areas. They were often even more economically disadvantaged than lower caste Indians in dealing with landlords and other members of the local elites. The situation for peasants and sharecroppers steadily declined in the Naxalbari area. The landlords expected their tenants to provide free labor on a variety of projects; furthermore, the landlords frequently imposed special fees or other demands on the resources of tenants (Banerjee 1984: 4). In many parts of the world, landlord–peasant relationships are reciprocal where there are duties and responsibilities that the landlords must meet. Such duties have often included provision of seeds, agricultural implements, and other materials, as well as providing for the security of their tenants in adverse circumstances. Members of the local rural elites, especially newer ones, often ignored the traditional practices that had helped to make the system of landholding and sharecropping workable (Duyker 1987: 61). In theory, national legislation provided protections and safeguards for the poorer peasants—there were legal limits on the percentage of crops that landlords could claim and other guaranteed rights. While the protections written into law were significant on paper, they were often not applied at the local level. The local power structure reflected the higher social and economic position of the landlords. Not surprisingly local officials usually supported the landlords. Judgments in courts against the landlords or their agencies were not enforced, and when criminal charges were brought against them, they and their employees were often acquitted (Banerjee 1984: 86, 103). The landlords organized and armed gangs of retainers to maintain control of their own lands and to intimidate peasants and sharecroppers, and the local peasants usually lost in confrontations with these gangs. These armed gangs were able to attack the poorer sections of the population while the local administration looked the other way (Nauriya 1996: 301). The gangs became in many ways extensions of the state. They clearly could not have operated with relative impunity without the acquiescence of the local officials (Nathan 1996: 165). The basic economic and political inequality present in the countryside provided the circumstances in which a violent outbreak was more likely.

The situation in the Naxalbari area was exacerbated by other factors. A United Front government came into power in the state of Bengal, and the government attempted to implement a land reform program that would have put land into the hands of many peasants. The new program gave hope to the landless that they could actually own land for the first time or regain control of land that had been lost to moneylenders or others. The government efforts at land reform, however, were not successful. The larger landlords managed to avoid losing their lands. They were especially adept at using the law and the court system to frustrate the distribution of the land (Banerjee 2002: 126). The Indian court system has faced huge backlogs of cases, and it is often in the interest of one side to prolong the proceedings as long as possible. The backlog and legal maneuvers meant that any real distribution of land from the larger landlords was years in the future. This effort at reform ended up pitting small landlords against the landless rather than uniting these groups in their common interests against the larger landholders (Duyker 1987: 63–4). The second factor that helped to spark the violence was the presence of Communist party members. Members of the Communist parties have been active in the region since the 1950s (Banerjee 2002: 125). They had contacts with the local peasants and were supportive of the demands of the poor in the rural areas, and they eventually provided leaders for the struggle, and the more radical distrusted elections and the likelihood of meaningful reform resulting from actions of the government. These party workers became disenchanted with the failure of land reform and other policies of the United Front government and even formed another Communist party to support the rural poor and to distance themselves from the parties in the United Front government. These activists were able to provide organizational skills and political leadership for the violence that followed (Banerjee 1984: 122).

The killing of two peasants and the failure of the local administration to provide protection was the spark to the outbreak of violence in Naxalbari in 1967. Many of the local poor peasants organized and began to use guerrilla and terrorist tactics against the local elites, their gangs, and the police. The landlords and their employees, as well as moneylenders, became one of the key targets for violence (Nathan 1996: 156). Many of them fled the areas where the Naxalites operated while others changed practices that were considered objectionable (Oommen 2005: 138). Minor officials and police officers were often targets as well (Banerjee 1996: 224). While the dissidents initially were successful in threatening the local power structure, taking over land and seizing crops, the arrival of military and police reinforcements turned the tide against them. The local dissidents lacked the military resources to challenge the army. Local groups were rounded up by the military or the local police caught individual dissidents and arrested them. While a few scattered groups survived, the uprising had been defeated. Similar outbreaks, however, began to appear elsewhere in India.

Support for these disadvantaged dissidents came from a number of sources. In the case of the uprising in Naxalbari, many supporters were Santals, a tribal group in the region that had increasingly lost control of their land to outside groups (Duyker 1987). The movement here, and outbreaks elsewhere, also attracted support from lower-caste Hindus who also suffered under the local economic, social, and political system (Nathan 1996: 156). Prospects of upward mobility or access to land were limited for both groups because of the disadvantages that they faced. In addition, changing economic conditions that had come with the integration of the Indian economy into the global market were creating difficulties for local artisans. The village artisans who produced local handicrafts had in many cases lost their economic position in society. These artisans were often members of lower level castes; therefore, the loss of economic position created even greater problems for them (Duyker 1987: 140). The lower-caste Hindus, the members of tribal groups, the sharecroppers, and the artisans provided a group of discontented citizens willing to turn to violence in efforts to redress the inequality that they faced and the prospects of continuing exploitation, unrelieved even by the United Front government in the state capital.

India has continued to face a series of small leftist outbreaks in different parts of the country. None of the violence has led to a major challenge for the state, but collectively they have diverted resources away from other programs. The difficulties they have created have probably been worsened by the fact that India has faced more serious outbreaks of violence with the Sikhs in the Punjab and groups in Kashmir. As a consequence, it has been more difficult for the government to focus its resources and attention on relatively minor situations of unrest that have not reached the same threat level as the Punjab and Kashmir. What is important for an understanding of leftist violence in India is that these kinds of outbreaks continue, and leftist groups relying on political violence, including terrorism, have not disappeared from the scene.

Neighboring Nepal has faced a similar, but more serious, situation in regard to leftist dissidents. The Nepalese government was initially concerned that the Naxalbari uprising would spill over into its lands (Oommen 2005: 127). Nepal has, in fact, faced a major leftist insurgency in recent years, which undoubtedly drew at least some inspiration from this earlier uprising. The Marxist dissidents have used both guerrilla tactics in the countryside and terrorist attacks against the elite in the urban areas to change the government (Tan 2006: 142–3). The rebels have gained effective control of some of the more remote areas of the state and represent a serious threat. The monarchy in this Himalayan kingdom has also faced peaceful protests from political parties and groups seeking a more democratic system. So far, the government has not been able to defeat the Marxist-Leninist dissidents, and it appears to be losing ground. The monarchy was weakened when a member of the royal family killed the ruling king (who exercised real power) and other members of the royal family before taking his own life. The attack does not appear to have had any political motivation; it was apparently due to mental problems on the part of the attacker. The consequences for political stability in the country have been negative. The leftist insurgents may eventually force policy changes by the government or may remain a continuing threat, but their example cannot help but encourage other leftist groups—in India, elsewhere in Asia, or even further aboard.

CASE STUDY 7.5   THE ANIMAL LIBERATION FRONT AND THE ANIMAL RIGHTS MILITIA

Various organizations have appeared in the Western industrialized countries that have been opposed to using animals as test subjects in situations leading to death or injury. Some groups are opposed to using animals as a food source. While there have been differences among the persons involved in these groups, most of them have been opposed to the killing animals simply to provide fur that can be made into more stylish coats. Animal rights activists have also been opposed to the use of animals as subjects for tests of cosmetics for potential problems or for research on other products where the animals serve as convenient test subjects. Most activists oppose using animals in cases where it is simply cheaper and more convenient to use animals instead of more expensive lab processes. Some opponents have extended their activities to attempt to prevent the use of animal subjects for medical research. Such research will involve pain since the animals will suffer as they are injured or infected with diseases in order for the necessary tests and research to occur. Not all persons concerned with the welfare of animals, however, share this view since such medical research prolongs human life and helps to facilitate medical breakthroughs. The maximum goal for some of the activists in animal rights groups is the hope that eventually it will be possible to prevent the eating of any meat and require vegetarianism as a matter of state policy, although they realize this objective is unlikely to be achieved at any point in time in the near future.

Persons in favor of animal rights have already had an impact on the activities of private companies and have influenced government policies through peaceful means. Boycotts of cosmetic firms using animals for experiments have led many of them to discontinue the practice and to publicize their commitment to not using animals for such research. Public pressure has resulted in the passage of laws in many countries that prohibit cruelty to animals. Cruel owners can be fined or imprisoned, and their animals taken into protective care. There are international treaties and conventions prohibiting trade in endangered species or products obtained from endangered species (such as ivory from elephants). In the private sector standards have been established for using animals in films and TV productions, for appropriate care for animals that are used in racing—such as horse and dogs, and for housing animals in zoos and similar situations. Groups seeking to protect animals, however, have felt that such peaceful actions have been either too slow or not successful enough and, as a consequence, have resorted to the use of violence to achieve their objectives. One very active group has sunk at least eight whaling ships and rammed others in efforts to protect sea life (Eagan 1996: 5).

Another group that has resorted to violence has been the Animal Liberation Front (ALF) in the United Kingdom. The initiative for the ALF originated in the early 1970s with groups that were opposed to hunts, especially fox hunting, and the attendant cruelty to animals involved in such activities (Monaghan 2000: 160). Sabotage of hunts by friends of animals has a long history in the United Kingdom and a logical connection with a concern for animal rights. The ALF as an organization drew on this tradition of concern and has focused on both short-term and long-term goals in its ongoing struggle for animals. The basic short-term goal has been to prevent obvious animal abuse in its various forms, while the ultimate goal has been an effort to end all animal suffering and abuse and to force the recognition that the rights of animals cannot be sacrificed to meet human needs. In order to achieve both goals, the ALF has sought to drive companies and individuals profiting from abuse of animals out of business (Monaghan 1997: 110). The ALF, like many animal rights groups, very early on was willing to attack property as a means of achieving its goals. What has been somewhat different about ALF and the animal rights movement in general is that the targets have not usually included the government or any of its agencies. These groups target individuals and firms that are in the private sector for the most part. While the government and its policies and personnel have not been seen as the main enemy, governments are usually on the business side of this policy debate since they attempt to protect the targets that are attacked or to prosecute the perpetrators when they are caught.

ALF members have broken into labs to free test animals and destroy the results of the previous research, raising the cost of animal research to such levels that it could become prohibitive. They have also vandalized cars and buildings, set fires, poured glue into locks, and used similar tactics available to groups that seek to intimidate individuals and businesses. The disruptions to business that have resulted from the attacks have cost hundreds of millions of dollars. Fur sales in particular have suffered a dramatic decline because of the peaceful and violent actions of such animal rights groups (Knickerbocker 1997: 5). The vandalism has extended to the homes of persons working in research institutions as a means of heightening the cost of continuing such research and frightening employees (Dodge 1997: 201). Many operations using animals or supplying animals for research have shut down as a consequence of the attacks (Loder 2000: 3). In one case activists stole the body of the mother of a farm owner who bred animals for experimentation as part of an effort to close down the operation (Jones *et al.* 2007: 258). The ALF has been causing more than six million pounds annually in damage to businesses (Liddick 2006: 41). The animal rights groups have often been effective in using the media to publicize their cause and to send a message to all similar kinds of businesses operating elsewhere in the country and even abroad. The end result of such attacks has been changes in business practices as companies have sought to avoid the extra costs of being targeted. The groups have been successful in part because their actions have been directed against the economic interests of the companies involved (J. Lutz and B. Lutz 2006b: 15). Animal rights groups have also raised the cost of food production and therefore the final costs for consumers (Tweeten 2003: 184). Of course, the activists would regard higher costs for animal products as a positive benefit that would effectively limit consumption.

Notwithstanding the successes, which have been achieved with the property attacks, violence escalated to actions directed against people. There have, in fact, been some indications that animal rights militants (and environmental activists) have been increasingly likely to resort to violence (Ackerman 2003). A group called the Animal Rights Militia (ARM) has appeared, and it has been willing to use violence against people to prevent the abuse of animals. The number of violent attacks by animal rights activists have been particularly large in Great Britain (Liddick 2006: 75). The attacks against people have included car bombs, letter bombs, and personal assaults that have resulted in severe beatings (Dodge 1997: 201). There have been physical attacks on hunters as well (Taylor 1998: 27). Letter bombs were sent to the leaders of the four major political parties in 1982 to publicize the cause (Monaghan 2000: 161). The ARM and its members have clearly progressed to the point where they feel that their political objectives are important enough to justify violence against human beings. The threatening nature of the animals rights groups has extended to hoaxes involving products coming from companies that continue to utilize animals in inappropriate ways. The hoaxes have indicated that certain products have been contaminated, and the perpetrators have introduced foreign substances of a non-harmful nature or written notes to indicate what they could do. There have, however, been some instances of actual product tampering and the inclusion of harmful substances (Dodge 1997: 201). Such product scares have expanded the target audience to include the public at large as the militants sought to generate additional adverse public reactions to the continued use of animals for experiments. The trend in recent years has been for an escalation of the violence or threatened violence. These more violent kinds of activities suggest that in the future there might be a significantly greater danger for persons who are considered to be abusing the rights of animals. Once individuals accept that there is moral duty to break the law in pursuit of a higher principle, violence becomes more likely (Monaghan 1997: 114). While injuries to date cannot compare with the casualties involved in many other terrorist groups, the potential for such violence could increase in the future.

It is not clear whether the ARM is a group that is really different from the ALF. Leftist dissidents in other countries that have engaged in violence have often credited fictitious organizations with violence in order to confuse the authorities and avoid recriminations for actions that have not been popular with the public. The ALF could have copied this tactic. The statements of the ARM make it clear that it seeks the same goals as the ALF, but this organizational separation permits the ALF to deflect negative opinion from itself while the ARM generates greater fear and pressure upon those who would continue to violate the rights of animals. It is very probable that there is some crossover between the personnel in the two groups, and there have even some suggestions that the ARM is simply representative of the more violent wing of the ALF. If such is the case, the ALF may simply have invented the ARM to provide cover for the more violent activities (Monaghan 2000: 165).

The ALF, like other violent environmental groups, has demonstrated another very modern characteristic of terrorist organizations by adopting the leaderless resistance style of operations (Joosse 2007: 352). The ALF lacks firm membership rolls, since maintaining them could make it easier for the government to track down members who may be responsible for property attacks or violence against individuals. It has extended notational or honorary membership to any individual who agrees with its goals. The ALF has also published newsletters and maintained web sites identifying possible targets, opponents of the movement, or members or former members who have provided information to the authorities. While the ALF has disseminated the information, it cannot be held responsible for the actions of isolated groups of individuals who act on their own to protect the rights of animals, even though provoking such attacks is the intent of the published lists (Monaghan 2000: 165). This organizational method has been very effective in permitting the ALF to present a non-violent image to the general public while still facilitating actions that are effective in shutting down the activities that the group opposes. Government prosecutions are also hindered as well since there is no hierarchical organization involved.

Animal rights groups have been successful in even achieving policies changes by governments in power. Fox hunting has recently been banned in the United Kingdom; the animal rights groups have thus achieved one of their initial objectives. While the Labour government in power may have banned fox hunting for a number of reasons, it is possible that one intent of the ban was a desire to weaken support for the ALF, ARM, and kindred groups by removing one source of contention and mobilization. It is possible, however, that the limit for such policy changes can be quickly reached. It is unlikely that any new major changes are on the horizon for countries that have already enacted basic legislation. Protests and demonstrations and other pressures on law-makers have achieved most of what they can. Violence against property has been successful as well. The activists have forced changes in practices by raising costs for the individuals or businesses involved. Many companies now forgo the use of animal experimentation (or one might suspect that they contract it out to braver souls in some cases) because of the costs involved from vandalism and other attacks. As a consequence, such attacks are likely to continue against groups that persist in using animals in ways that are unacceptable to the ALF and ARM. Some businesses, however, are not likely to give up the current practices, meaning that more personal violence may appear to be justified for animal rights activists in the future.

SUMMARY

Except for the campaigns of assassinations of the anarchists in the late 1800s and early 1900s, Marxist-Leninist groups usually avoided terrorism as a weapon before World War II. Major terrorist activities by leftists have been concentrated in the years after the war. Leftist dissidents engaged in other kinds of political violence prior to World War II. Revolution and uprising were the preferred courses of action. The Communists under Mao Tse-tung's leadership in China opted for guerrilla insurgency based in the countryside. Even though uprisings and insurgencies as the preferred tactics of the left usually failed in this era, the emphasis on these particular techniques does explain the relative scarcity of examples of terrorism from the left in these decades.

After World War II, and especially in the latter part of the 1960s, terrorist groups from the left did appear with regularity. Students in many Western countries were attracted to such groups such as the Weathermen, the Red Brigades, the Red Army Faction, the Montoneros, the Tupamaros, and others. Most of these organizations had great attractions for the young, particularly in the 1960s when demonstrations and youthful protests appeared to have weakened the capitalist democracies and set the stage for even more progressive groups from the left to dominate in their countries. Opposition to the war in Vietnam, both as a specific event and as a representative event of Western domination and control of the developing world, furthered the mobilization of students to question the status quo. Since these movements were disproportionately movements of the young, however, they were at least initially also going to be movements of the weak. Mass membership was usually not possible. The terrorist movements in Italy, Germany, India, and Argentina started out small, and in Germany they remained small. In addition, dissident movements had to use violence to acquire financing for their activities unless they could enlist the support of a wealthy member or sympathizer or foreign funds. Unless an organization had already proven itself, however, it was unlikely to receive such infusions of outside money. Revolutionary expropriation will work up to a point, but robbing banks to finance a revolution means that scarce resources actually have to be utilized in efforts to acquire more resources, and any robbery, even if successful, exposes the organizations to additional risks. Given the weaknesses of most leftist groups, at least initially, terrorism was one of the few methods of violence that was available to them. Popular uprisings, guerrilla warfare, insurrections, and even civil war might be the ultimate goals, but the radicals had to depend upon propaganda of the deed as a means of attempting to mobilize the populations of their countries.

These efforts by the left had mixed results. Some attempts to generate popular dissatisfaction with the governments in power were relatively successful. The Montoneros, partially because of their alliance with the Peronists, accomplished the most in this regard. Once Peron turned against the leftists, their influence waned and they were unable to recreate their early success. The military intervention then doomed the dissidents and their organizations. The changes in government structures wrought by the leftist in Argentina, and Uruguay as well, were significant ones, but they did not result in the improvements that the leftists had expected. The Red Army Faction in Germany was troublesome for the government, but it was never able to generate any kind of meaningful threat to the government. The leftists in India remain a threat, and their activities have grown over time. The 17 November Movement in Greece had similarly limited results in its attacks upon various governments and the Greek political system. Its small size was important for a long time in preventing the government from penetrating the organization, but its size also limited the extent of the damage that it could do. The Red Brigades presented a greater threat to the stability of the Italian political system, but they eventually failed as well. Finally, animal rights groups, as well as some environmentalist organizations, that have been willing to use violence have been less concerned with mobilizing the public to change the form of the governments in the countries where they operate. Of all the dissident groups described in this chapter, they have been most interested in influencing policies of governments or especially the practices of some businesses rather than changing governments.

While these various leftist movements failed to generate the major changes that they sought in their societies, it is more difficult to measure the long-term effects that they might have had. The activities of the Montoneros (and other groups) did help Peron to return to power; he was seen as the only leader who could control the violence (Holmes 2001: 152). His return, the resurgence of terrorism, the military coup against Isabel Peron, and the deadly suppression for dissidents were all linked. In Germany and Italy the leftist attacks eventually led to increased competency in the security forces, but few other ongoing changes occurred. No leftist group would consider improvement in the quality of the security services to be a worthwhile result. In neither of these cases did massive violations of civil rights of the populations result from the campaigns as was hoped. In India the Marxist rebels have not generated repressive tactics by the government, although the methods used in the Punjab and Kashmir have been used here as well. The efforts of the more violent animal rights groups in the long term are difficult to predict. The fact that their violence to date has been effective in achieving some objectives is likely to provide a spur to additional actions. A major ecological disaster, however, could stimulate both the animal rights groups and the environmentalists to greater activity, and perhaps more violent activity.

None of the case studies involved movements that had major external support. The animal rights groups have cross-national contacts, but there is no indication of external government support. The Montoneros had some outside contacts, but there was no major foreign state backer for their efforts. Cuba was a sanctuary and an ideological beacon for many Latin American leftists, but it was too far away to offer practical support to dissidents in Argentina or Uruguay. The Naxalites have no doubt had external contacts, but there is no indication of massive external support. The Red Brigades and Red Army Faction did receive some external supports, especially from Czechoslovakia and East Germany respectively. This support was helpful to the groups, but it was never essential for their survival when they were at the height of their activities. The various leftist groups in Europe did attempt to form some international linkages. The RAF was generally in the center of these efforts, and the German dissidents were able to coordinate actions with Spanish, Belgian, and French dissident groups. While contacts with the Red Brigades were frequent, attempts to coordinate between the Italians and Germans were not as successful due to theoretical differences. The Italians focused on their domestic enemies in Italy while the RAF was more concerned with the exploitation created by the international capitalist system (Merkl 1995b: 166–8). Cooperation of the RAF with the PFLP was more effective as demonstrated by the joint airline hijackings.

Much of the dissident terrorism from the left has largely has disappeared with the exception of the environmental and animal rights groups. The collapse of Communism in East Europe and the Soviet Union with publicity about mistakes, torture, false arrests, and other deviations from ideological purity further undercut the appeal of leftist ideologies. The loss of models of future utopias was more devastating than the loss of the limited external support that came from these sources. Dissident movements based in Marxist ideologies, however, could reappear in the future. With time, the extremes of Communism in power will fade as opponents of capitalism look for answers to the problems that come with that system. Marxism in one of its many forms could once again appeal to idealists seeking to deal with the inequities of the world. The passage of time has unfortunately weakened memories of Nazi atrocities to the extent that some give credence to denials of the Holocaust, and a similar pattern could appear with Marxism. At some point there will be those who will deny the failures of Communism and think that the negative images that have been publicized will have been the result of capitalist propaganda campaigns. Leftist ideologies will remain strong in some areas of the developing world where populations still face repressive regimes that continue to deny basic rights. In these situations, the left can encompass many different groups that are opposed to conservative and authoritarian governments. Naxalite groups remain active in India, and Nepal is facing a serious insurgency from violent Maoist dissidents who have been using both guerrilla and terrorist tactics. Small, violent leftists groups are still present in parts of Latin America. Marxism in many of its varieties can still provide a critique of the evils that can come with globalization and modernization, which today are inevitably accompanied by capitalism. It would be premature, and even dangerous, to assume that the terrorist threat from the left has disappeared (Wilkinson 2003: 119). Anarchists, for example, have become involved in environmental groups, providing a more intense ideological component to the activities of some groups (Taylor 2003: 181). Thus, do not be surprised if leftist ideologies resurface and again become the basis for dissident groups, ones that could choose violence.

▍ TERMS

anarchism	Isabel Peron
Animal Liberation Front (ALF)	Juan Peron
Animal Rights Militia (ARM)	Popular Front for the Liberation of Palestine (PFLP)
Baader–Meinhof Gang	propaganda of the deed
"disappeared ones"	propaganda of the word
Earth Liberation Front (ELF)	Red Army Faction (RAF)
Frederich Engels	Red Brigades
Franco Feltrinelli	Red Cells
Japanese Red Army	Reign of Terror
June 2nd Movement	Rejectionist Front
kneecapping	17 November Organization
leaderless resistance	Social Revolutionaries
left-wing ideology	Students for a Democratic Society (SDS)
Vladimir Lenin	Symbionese Liberation Army (SLA)
Karl Marx	Leon Trotsky
Montoneros	Mao Tse-tung (Mao Zedong)
Aldo Moro	Tupamaros
Benito Mussolini	Weathermen
Naxalites	Will of the People
Peoples Revolutionary Army (ERP)	

FURTHER READING

State of Siege (film—1973)

Drake, R. (1989) *The Revolutionary Mystique and Terrorism in Contemporary Italy*, Bloomington, IN: Indiana University Press.

Gillespie, R. (1982) *Soldiers of Peron: Argentina's Montoneros*, Oxford: Clarendon Press.

Kassimeris, G. (2001) *Europe's Last Red Terrorists: The Revolutionary Organization 17 November*, New York: New York University Press.

Monaghan, R. (2000) "Terrorism in the Name of Animal Rights," in M. Taylor and J. Horgan (eds) *The Future of Terrorism*, London: Frank Cass, 159–69.

Pluchinsky, D. A. (1992) "An Organizational and Operational Analysis of Germany's Red Army Faction Terrorist Group (1972–91)," in Y. Alexander and D. A. Pluchinsky (eds) *European Terrorism: Today & Tomorrow*, Washington: Brassey's, 43–92.

Taylor, B. (1998) "Religion, Violence and Radical Environmentalism: From Earth First! to the Unabomber to the Earth Liberation Front," *Terrorism and Political Violence*, 10, 4: 1–42.

CHAPTER 8

Terrorism and Ideologies of the Right

Ideologies of the right, just like left-wing ideologies, have served as a basis or justification for terrorist acts. Right-wing groups usually seek to conserve what exists or seek to return to some recent or distant past situation that should have been conserved. If the golden era is far enough in the past or different enough (the Nazi goals in Hitler's Germany), the changes being sought can be revolutionary rather than simply conservative. These groups will often seek to support the existing institutions in society and the ruling elites or to return these elites to power and re-establish institutions. As a consequence, these ideologies have gained strength as a result of some of the changes that appeared with modernization and globalization that threatened existing institutions and patterns of governance. Initially the ideologies of the right were reactive since they are often opposed to changes sought by the left. When no group was threatening to bring about change, there was little need for groups supporting the status quo to become active. Groups seeking the restoration of monarchies could not appear until monarchies had been overthrown or were under threat. Similarly, right-wing ideologies frequently had to wait for left-wing ideologies to appear. Without the threat to government and other institutions that left-wing ideologies represented for some groups, there was no need for a defense against the left or for a reversal of changes already accomplished by the left. The use of terrorism by the right lagged behind that of left-wing groups because prior to World War I the ideologies of the right were in power as the political establishment (Laqueur 1999: 12).

Right-wing ideologies and associated violence go back to the days of the Roman Republic. The forces supporting the status quo were involved in the turbulent policies of the Republican era. The lesser nobles that opted to lead the commoners (or more precisely the upper middle-classes and lower nobility) were particular targets for the aristocracy. The Gracchi brothers were both assassinated at different times for advocating changes that would have provided increased power to some of the middle class groups in Rome. Tiberius Gracchus challenged the powers of the Senate and his supporters were threatening opponents when a group of Senators and their followers attacked. They killed Tiberius and many of his followers. Thirteen years later his brother Gaius was killed for again challenging the privileged position of the Senate and ruling groups (Ford 1985: 55–8). In the second case the establishment forces attempted to eliminate the threat from Gaius and his supporters more thoroughly through a campaign of repression (B. Lutz and J. Lutz 2006: 501). Such threats to the status quo were obviously taken quite seriously by the nobles, especially the great Senatorial families. The deaths of Tiberius and Gaius Gracchus and some of their followers as well indicated that costs could come with opposition. Challenges to the system were obviously not going to be tolerated. The message that challenges to the system would be met with violence by the opposition forces was clear.

During the early days of the French Revolution, violent reactions from opponents generally came in the form of rebellion or insurrections rather than through campaigns of terror. The Vendee was a classic conservative rural uprising directed against the revolutionary regime with peasant groups fighting for God and the king. There was no effort to use terror to undercut the republican forces in France. In addition, the returns of monarchs to power in the seventeenth and eighteenth centuries did not involve terror. The Bourbons and other royal families were returned to power in France after the defeat of Napoleon and his armies by the allied powers of Europe. No resort to domestic violence to support the restoration was necessary.

RIGHT-WING DISSATISFACTION: MARXISM AND MINORITIES

In large measure it was the appearance of Marxist doctrines that stimulated the appearance of violent rightist groups. These groups from the right were committed to preventing the Marxists from seizing power. Karl Marx thus unwittingly was the source for two types of ideologies that were willing to use violence and terror, even though Marx himself felt that terror was normally counterproductive. Dissidents from the right have been willing to use violence to keep leftist groups from obtaining power in a number of ways. They targeted adherents of the left directly. Perhaps the first such groups to appear in the defense of the status quo was the Black Hundred in Russia at the beginning of the twentieth century. This group targeted Jews and liberals who sought to challenge the monarchy and traditional society in Czarist Russia (Laqueur 1999: 21). After World War I, supporters of right-wing groups and parties were often mobilized to attack party rallies, buildings, or newspapers of the Marxists and other leftists. These assaults were designed to weaken the parties of the left in their competition for power. Right-wing groups were more likely to resort to paramilitary violence than their leftist opponents in this period (Mann 2005: 65). Benito Mussolini's Fascists in Italy took to the streets to do battle with the socialists and the Communists. The intent of the Fascists was to fight fire with fire and defeat the relatively mild violence, demonstrations, and agitation from the left with counterviolence from the right. As it turned out, the street battles helped to promote the Fascists as the best alternative for preventing the socialists from disrupting the Italian political and economic systems or even of seizing power—a possibility that conservative groups wanted to prevent at all costs. The Fascists used the street battles to announce their political goals, and the violence was an effective means of communication and propaganda that did not rely on the media in a society where illiteracy was still high (Lyttelton 1982: 259, 266). It was the socialist agitation that permitted the Fascists to organize and gain support from the middle classes and other groups in Italy. The Fascist violence and intimidation in Italy did weaken the left. Mussolini actually needed the socialist threat to give him the chance to gain political power for himself and his Fascist Party.

Another way in which forces of the right sought to battle the left followed a more indirect approach to achieving the desired goals. Marxist dissidents were considered to be much more likely to be able to seize power if the state was weak; consequently, fascists and other conservatives in the 1920s and 1930s considered weak states to be an open invitation to Marxist plots, disruptions, and takeovers. They felt that parliamentary democracies were vulnerable because they gave too many rights to those who were unwilling to support the state. Further, democracies invited dissent and disagreement, weakening the state, perhaps fatally. They had before them the examples of the Bolshevik takeover in Russia, as well as the short lived communist regimes in Bavaria and Hungary, and attempted seizures of governments elsewhere to heighten their fears. The best way to avoid dangerous attacks and the threats of takeovers from the left would be to take over the state and create a strong, authoritarian government that could and would deal with any plot from the left quickly and severely or even pre-emptively by banning the left entirely. Mussolini's assumption of power in Italy followed this path. Similar street fighting and violence was present in Austria and Romania where attacks on political opponents by right-wing activists occurred with great regularity in the 1930s (Berend 1998: 303, 337). The Romanian Iron Guard adopted the practices of the anarchists by emphasizing propaganda of the deed in their struggles to support conservative causes in that country (Laqueur 2001: 73). The Romanian fascists paid a heavy price for their efforts as more than 500 died in attacks against opponents and the political system (Barbu 1968: 157). A direct takeover by a right-wing dissident group, like the Fascists in Italy, was not always possible. A number of right-wing groups had other objectives. The violence was used to create a need for a conservative authoritarian system to replace a democratic one. The violence was designed to expose the weaknesses of the democratic systems and their replacement by a government that emphasized law and order. The political objective of the right, therefore, was to create a crisis situation that would force the government to become stronger in self-defense, enacting sufficient measures to protect the country, doing away with weak democratic practices, and transforming the country into an authoritarian government that would be able to defeat any threats coming from the left. While this stronger government would also be able to deal better with threats from the right as well, the dissident groups were willing to accept this possibility since a stronger state is one of the principal goals that is being sought. Interestingly enough, there are thus circumstances where both left and right dissidents might seek to force a government to become more repressive. These two diametrically opposed groups, however, have drawn different conclusions from the prospect of a more authoritarian government. For the left the repressive regime would become an obvious defender of privilege and would lead to some kind of popular revolt against the ruling classes. For the right, the new government would also be more repressive, but it would be better able to deal with dissent. While both groups of dissidents have foreseen a similar process, they have anticipated dissimilar results.

Groups drawing upon right-wing ideologies may be content with policy changes by the government. If the government can be pushed to deal with leftist groups in an appropriate (i.e., repressive) fashion, the right-wing group may be satisfied. Such changes in policy, moreover, are likely to bring about basic structural changes in the government—more repression, a less democratic system, or a harsher authoritarian government. The sought-after policy changes are likely to breed structural changes. Similarly, the change in policies is likely to influence the type

BOX 8.1 THE NIVILLES GROUP

There was an outbreak of leftist violence in Belgium in the 1970s involving the Communist Combat Cells (CCC). It was similar to the Red Army Faction in Germany in its ideology, but it was never very effective. Another organization, the Nivilles Group, gave every appearance of being a leftist group by its pronouncements, but its tactics and targets were very unlike the normal choices of Marxist-Leninist dissidents. The attacks of the group resulted in the unnecessary deaths of bystanders and seemed especially geared toward alienating potential supporters of the left. As a consequence, it is thought that the group was more likely to have been composed of right-wing extremists, established by police or intelligence officials who were attempting to provoke a crisis situation that would lead the government to adopt more repressive policies in order to defend itself from these attacks from the left (P. Jenkins 1990: 300). The attacks were probably false flag attacks that were designed to force the government to crack down on leftist groups. This campaign failed to achieve this goal since the Belgian government did not adopt more repressive laws for dealing with terrorism. The relatively high casualties that occurred with these attacks in Belgium also suggest a source that was from the right. In this period of time right-wing dissident groups were generally weaker than leftist groups except in countries where the government was cooperating with and providing covert support to paramilitary groups. As a consequence, the rightist groups could mount fewer attacks. In order to have the desired impact of generating terror and publicizing a cause, the attacks that were undertaken by the right had to produce more casualties in order to have the desired effects on the population at large.

of leaders who will be governing. If the left is repressed, it will be unlikely that leftists will be included in the government. The elimination of leftist groups will then shift the balance in the political system to the right, making it more likely that political groups of the right will be more influential. Such a situation occurred in Turkey in the 1980s when the wave of right-wing violence occurred in response to the terrorism of the left. The right was able to create such tension that the military intervened and overthrew the democratic government. The military regime was more in sympathy with the Turkish right; thus, the terror strategy was relatively successful in leading to the defeat of the left and the establishment of a government more acceptable to the right (J. Lutz and B. Lutz 2005: 122).

Dissident groups depending upon ideologies of the right may have ethnic overtones, but these frequently are different from separatist movements or national liberation struggles. Right-wing ideologies may seek to force a government to attempt to acquire territory with related peoples or to intervene to protect the rights of an "oppressed" minority in a neighboring country. The Nazi Party in Germany before it was in power and obviously afterwards sought to incorporate the Germans in Czechoslovakia into a Greater Germany as well as seeking a union of Germany with Austria. Junior officers and fanatical civilians in Japan in the 1920s and 1930s were responsible for a number of attacks on civilian leaders. In this period the terrorists assassinated or attempted to assassinate prime ministers and other high-ranking officials when these leaders failed to follow policies that were nationalistic enough for the armed forces (Ford 1985: 256,

266–7). These assassinations effectively destroyed the developing system of parliamentary democracy in Japan (Havens *et al.* 1975: 31). It is worth noting that the assassins were widely admired by many in the population at large (Parry 1976: 441). The attempts and assassinations also sent clear messages to politicians of the dangers that would be present for opposing the nationalistic goals of the military, and Japan increasingly sought military solutions to its problems with reduced opposition from politicians.

While there are some more modern right wing groups that do not have racist overtones, many actually do (Bjorgo 1997: 21). Minority groups are despised, and they are targeted for attacks that are designed to inspire terror. The ethnic base of the terrorist group in these cases lies with the majority and does not reflect efforts of a minority to obtain equality or other goals. Such groups have become common. They have appeared in Eastern Europe and Russia where parties with fascist characteristics have appeared and have targeted ethnic minorities (Jackson 1999). Vladimir Zhirinovsky, an early leader of the Liberal Democrats, advocated extreme Russian nationalistic views, the reclamation of lost lands, and hostility to the ethnic minorities in Russia. Parties with very clear fascist trappings have appeared in Romania, and they have openly expressed their disdain for the ethnic minorities that reside in the country (Kurti 1998: 182). There have been attacks on Gypsies in Hungary and the Czech Republic and attempts to discriminate against Turks and Gypsies in Bulgaria (Wilkinson 1995). Attacks against the Gypsies began as soon as the restraining hand of Communism was removed in many countries (Cooper 2001/2: 71). Violence against migrant communities has even appeared elsewhere, such as Australia, albeit only rarely (Bessant 1995). The antipathy toward outsiders represents one facet of the need of the extreme right to create a stronger state. The outsiders and other minorities are seen as weakening the state because they create divisions in society (Hoffman 2006: 236). The ethnic exclusiveness of these dissidents frequently goes beyond migrants from other areas. It can include opposition to foreign ideas and influences of all kinds. All such potentially dangerous ideas must be kept out. The dissident groups are responding with violence to the challenges of globalization just as some religious groups have responded, and the increase of the radical right can be seen as one response to the problems that come with globalization (Betz 1994: 184). Religion can play a supportive role in reinforcing attitudes opposed to outside influences if there is a dominant religion associated with the national population.

Since right-wing dissidents appeared as a reaction to Marxism in its many variations, it would be logical to have expected violent groups on the right to decline after the collapse of Communism in Europe, but this has not happened. These ideologies have continued, and dissident groups subscribing to them have continued to use violence to achieve their aims. After the demise of Communist states in Europe terrorism from the left declined, and the initiative in the use of terror and violence passed to groups on the extreme right (Laqueur 2003: 151). The increasing attention paid to issues of race, ethnicity, and religion might have reflected shifts to the new enemy that was necessary with the disappearance of Marxism. Of course, to the extent that opposition to Marxism and its global ideology generated an earlier antipathy in the right toward change and globalization, other changes in society can play the same role today. There are indeed some indications that the conditions similar to the ones that led to the rise of fascism in Europe may now exist in at least some parts of the developing world (Jha 1994). The enemies are different, but they are still present, and democratic governments are seen as being just as weak and incapable of dealing with these threats as they were in the past. The underlying continuity in the justification for violence may not be these specific targets but the fear of change that exists for those attracted to the ideologies of the extreme right.

CASE STUDIES

There are five case studies presented. The violent groups from the right have often practiced leaderless resistance and have been involved in informal networks. As a consequence, it is difficult to discuss specific groups, so collections of related groups that are willing to use violence are considered together. The cases of the neo-Nazi groups in Germany and the patriot/militia movement in the United States that appear below discuss a number of related groups. Many paramilitary groups associated with the right wing and practicing terrorism have appeared in societies where they have received at least the covert support of the government in power in dealing with other political groups in the country. As such they provide examples of a form of governmental violence and terror, and these groups will be discussed in Chapter 10. The five cases presented below deal with the use of violence by the stormtroopers associated with the Nazi Party in Weimar Germany before (and shortly after) Hitler came to power, the activities of the revived Ku Klux Klan in the 1920s and 1930s, the efforts of neo-fascist groups in Italy to provoke the Italian government into adopting authoritarianism in the decades after World War II, the violent tendencies of the American militias and patriot groups in the United States that culminated in the bombing of the federal office building in Oklahoma City in April 1995, and the rise of the neo-Nazi groups in Germany and elsewhere in Europe.

CASE STUDY 8.1   STORMTROOPERS IN WEIMAR GERMANY

The German Empire collapsed in the final days of World War I when the Kaiser abdicated and a temporary government was put in place. The political leaders of the major parties created a new constitution, which was written in the town of Weimar. The new democratic system under this constitution has usually been referred to as the Weimar Republic. This initial attempt at democracy in Germany had a brief and troubled existence. The Republic finally ended when Hitler began to dismantle the democratic elements of the constitution after being appointed chancellor (prime minister) in 1933. The end of the Weimar Republic set Hitler and the Nazi Party firmly on the path that culminated in the Holocaust and the death and destruction of World War II. Violence and terrorism became an integral part of the history of the Weimar Republic. In its first years the new democracy faced an attempted coup by the radical elements of the Communist Party, an attempted takeover by forces of the right, and Hitler's abortive attempt in 1923 (the Beer Hall Putsch) to seize power in Bavaria—a seizure that was designed to signal a takeover by right-wing groups elsewhere in Germany. Hitler's failure to seize power in Munich and the lack of effort by other nationalist forces led him to rethink his options for assuming power. Hitler then chose an electoral approach, building the National Socialist Democratic Workers Party (NSDAP or Nazis) to the point where it was the single largest party in terms of votes received by the early 1930s. Hitler, however, did not give up on the use of violence to achieve the ends of the Nazi Party; it simply took new forms and became adjuncts to the electoral activities.

The violent arm of the Nazi Party included two groups. The minor organization in the period before the Nazis came to power was the Schutzstaffel (SS). The SS was Hitler's bodyguard that served with him at party meetings. In these years it was relatively small and played only a subordinate part in the violence associated with the party. The more important group was the Sturmabteilungen (SA), literally meaning storm sections but usually translated as stormtroopers. To confuse matters, the SS in later years were also sometimes referred to as stormtroopers, and the term has sometimes been used to include both groups when mention is being made of violence in conjunction with party and election activities. The SA, however, was a distinct organization that used street violence when the Nazi Party engaged in parliamentary politics (Bjorgo 1993: 32). The SS was actually part of the Nazi party while the SA was technically an independent organization that was associated with the party. Only Nazi Party members could belong to the SS, while party membership was not a prerequisite for joining the SA (Bucheim 1972). Hitler, however, made it very clear that the SA as an organization was to be subordinate to the leadership of the party (Pridham 1973: 39). Hitler was able to ensure this subordination because he simultaneously served as head of the party and the head of the SA. This joint leadership also ensured that potential challengers to his leadership of the movement would find it more difficult to succeed.

The SA was initially formed to provide protection for Nazi Party gatherings and campaign speeches against disruptions and assaults from members of other parties. Its activities quickly spread to include assaults on the activities of other parties. SA men would attempt to disrupt the gatherings and campaign speeches for other political parties, particularly those on the left. They would also attack leftist marchers when they were demonstrating or generate confrontations with leftist groups whenever possible (Shirer 1959: 43, 120). Newspaper offices and party reading rooms would be attacked, and eventually the violence extended to identifiable supporters of the opposition parties. Leftist groups in turn would sometimes provoke confrontations with the SA and the Nazi Party as well.

The SA was not an unusual political organization in Weimar Germany in the 1920s. There were many organizations that were nationalist in their orientations and which sought to influence the government and its policies. Many of them ultimately sought to create a stronger Germany to recover territory lost in World War I and to establish a strong central government capable of generating a return to national glory. These groups also engaged in street violence, as did supporters of left-wing parties. All of these groups placed pressure on the government in a variety of ways, including violence, and some of them even openly discussed the need to overthrow the democratic government of Germany. The organizations attracted younger Germans who had difficulties in finding employment, especially after the onset of the Great Depression. These younger Germans accepted the basic ideas inherent in the right-wing nationalism that was central to these paramilitary organizations (Merkl 1987: 202). The SA was also very effective in attracting both young rebels against authority (of all types) and young persons seeking action on the streets (Merkl 1986: 357–8). The SA was to become the strongest of these paramilitary organizations, and eventually all the others were disbanded after Hitler took power, and many of their members incorporated into various Nazi organizations.

Both left and right became very adept at provocation against the other, and these street battles were not one-sided affairs. The left organized its own groups and initiated some of the battles themselves, and left and right attacked each other and street brawls between the two sides became the order of the day (Bessel 1986: 138). The groups that probably suffered the most from these confrontations were supporters of the more middle-class parties in Germany whose supporters were less likely to take to the streets. The extremes progressively gained ground at the expense of the center groups, and many of the middle class and conservative groups in Germany came to prefer the Nazis to the socialists and Communists. The street battles created an atmosphere of tension that attracted people to the Nazi movement since it was frequently seen as a defense against dangers from the left (Merkl 1987: 171). Ultimately, the street battles probably proved more useful to the Nazis than to the Communists in this regard. The Nazi Party became very adept at utilizing violence to create publicity; thus, "a small and uninfluential group soon became nationally known" (Laqueur 2001: 72). While the use of violence by the Nazis and SA frightened off some potential supporters, there were many others that came to accept the Nazis as a viable political alternative for Germany because of their activities (Bessel 1986: 137).

The street brawls, the attacks on meetings of other parties, and attacks on individuals selected because of their political beliefs were designed to accomplish two basic purposes. On the one hand they were intended to terrorize and demoralize supporters of opposing political parties and the politicians themselves. It increasingly became more dangerous in at least some locales to openly support other parties at election where the Nazis or their sympathizers were dominant. This lack of outward support would progressively sap the strength of other parties as more and more individuals saw these parties as being less effective in terms of achieving policy goals or changes in government personnel. The second purpose of the street fighting and other violent activities was to serve as propaganda for the party, even if it was violent propaganda. The street actions provided demonstrations of the capabilities of the party and its level of support. The organized marches and military displays were designed to reinforce this propaganda by further demonstrating the strength of the Nazi Party (Merkl 1987: 105, 166). It was not even important for the SA to win the street battles or to control a certain section of a town or city; the propaganda purposes were served when the confrontation with the "enemy" occurred and the party and SA demonstrated their willingness to do battle (Merkl 1987: 164). Eventually, the Nazis came to be seen as the party most willing to defend Germany against the Communists and the socialists, and the party most likely to be able to do so. The SA did not target the police or the authorities. The violence of the SA in the streets was largely focused on members of the opposition. The Nazi Party almost always sought to avoid any direct assaults on state power by the violence in the streets (Bessel 1986: 135).

The SA and its use of violence to terrorize and as a propaganda device was effective in helping Hitler and the Nazi Party gain votes. By 1933, the NDSAP was seen as the one party most able to prevent the left from taking over the government. The violence and terrorism and street propaganda had weakened the parties in the center and even some on the right, leaving the Nazis as the clear alternative. Other options had fallen by the wayside. The SA and its tactics of street violence had been essential to creating these perceptions. Once Hitler was in power, however, the SA became something of a liability. Street violence became dysfunctional when the Nazis were the government. The leaders of the SA also had radical demands that Hitler as party leader was less interested in. He was also unwilling to alienate the regular army by integrating the SA into the armed forces (Merkl 1987: 181).

As a consequence, when Hitler moved in June of 1934 to eliminate threats to his leadership, many prominent leaders of the SA were among the 400 to 1,000 persons who were assassinated (Shirer 1959: 221–5). The SA was gradually demobilized with the members being transferred to the SS or other Nazi organizations for continuing service to the regime in power. Radical street fighters were valuable only in opposition, not as paramilitary extensions of the national government, especially once Hitler began to expand the regular armed forces.

CASE STUDY 8.2   THE KU KLUX KLAN (1920s AND 1930s)

The Ku Klux Klan (KKK) actually operated as a terrorist group in the United States on three separate occasions. It first appeared after the Civil War in the defeated states in the American South. It was a reaction to the changes that occurred as a consequence of the Civil War, and it was effective in using terror and intimidation to displace the former slaves and their supporters from positions of authority in state and local governments. Once the old elite was back in power, the KKK and similar groups disappeared since they were no longer needed. Government authorities could maintain social control of the former slaves, and a clandestine organization was no longer necessary (B. Lutz and J. Lutz 2007: 60–1). The Klan reappeared in 1915 when a local clergyman restarted the group. This version of the Klan became quite powerful in the 1920s in a number of states, but it eventually faded into relative obscurity by the start of World War II. The third version of the Klan appeared after the war as a reaction to the movement for racial equality and civil rights. The Klan regained some strength for a brief period, drawing in those who were opposed to racial equality. The KKK fell back into relative obscurity with the passage of the 1964 Civil Rights Act and the 1965 Voting Rights Act. Effective prosecution of various Klan members by the federal government also helped to weaken many chapters.

A local clergyman in Georgia appropriated the earlier name and re-established the Klan in 1915. He intended to establish the KKK as a fraternal organization. Almost from the outset the new KKK was willing to use violence in support of political goals. In the very first years, the group stressed patriotism, especially when the United States entered World War I on the side of the Allies. The Klan became a defender of the United States and opposed anyone who might weaken the country or the war effort. Unions became targets since strikes or agitation could threaten the war effort (Toy 1989: 135). Foreign residents were also under suspicion for holding radical ideas or being potentially disloyal (Chalmers 1965: 31). After the war there was a series of bombings attributed to foreign radicals— including anarchists, socialists, radicals, and Communists. The bombings and the general distrust of foreign radical ideas led to the Red Scare in the United States in which those with radical ideas and foreign roots were persecuted and harassed. Local Klan members were involved in many of the attacks on those suspected of being subversive or foreigners with the suspect ideas (Murray 1955: 87). While the patriotism and the fear of radical ideas displayed by the KKK in this period was genuine, these views probably also helped to attract new members to the group and aided in its spread and growth.

World War I, the Red Scare, and the superpatriotism of the organization influenced the development of the group and its views. This version of the KKK was, of course, anti-black, and it served as one mechanism for social control over blacks in the southern part of the United States. But the Klan did not consider black Americans to be the greatest threat to the country. In part, this view reflected the condescension of the white population that led them to dismiss the potential of the black population. This view, however, also reflected that fact that since they had long been part of the system and had not been contaminated by foreign ideas, they were also less of a threat to the American system or the unique American culture (Tucker 1991: 5).

This version of the KKK focused its energies on controlling the threats emanating from foreign sources. The group was anti-Catholic, anti-Semitic, anti-Chinese on the West Coast, and anti-immigrant in general. The Klan built upon the long-standing anti-Catholic tradition in the United States and the associated prejudices. The Klan was able to draw upon the fear held by many Protestants that Catholics and Catholics immigrants were seeking to destroy the United States. The anti-Catholicism provided the KKK with a powerful appeal in many areas of the country (Chalmers 1965: 33). Anti-Semitic views became more important at this time because there had been a significant influx of Jewish migrants in the last part of the twentieth century and the first part of the nineteenth century. Jewish migrants were now numerous enough to be considered a threat (Strong 1941: 14–15). The Klan even thought that there was a conspiracy between the Catholic Church and the Jews to destroy the United States (Murphy 1964: 72). Unlike the first Klan, which accepted white men of all religions, the new KKK was a Protestant organization. It often gained the support of local Protestant clergy who shared its view of foreign religions, and this version of the KKK became a group for white Protestants (Murphy 1964: 69). The KKK was loosely organized on the national level, and different state chapters gave greater attention to different threats according to local circumstances. Not all the local chapters were willing to resort to violence, intimidation, and terrorism, but many of them did. Catholics, Jews, and others were attacked and subjected to beatings, tarring and feathering, and murder, and in many cases the minority groups were driven out of local communities (Brown 1989: 41). In some areas the Klan drove out the foreign businessmen or blacks who threatened the economic position of local Protestant merchants (Gough 1997: 527).

The KKK also served as a form of social control in many areas of the country. In the South it was one of the groups that helped to keep blacks "in their place" through assaults and lynchings. Many of these racially motivated attacks were community-based and did not involved the KKK as an organization (although members of the Klan no doubt participated as individuals). The presence of the Klan as an organization clearly contributed to the atmosphere of fear present in the local black communities. Perhaps the clearest indication of the terrorist component of these local activities was the view that while it was preferable to punish the specific black American suspected of a crime or inappropriate social behavior, it was accepted to assault or murder *any* member of the local black community as a way of sending messages about acceptable behavior to blacks in general (Dollard 1978: 303). Such attacks were rarely punished. One study written in the early

1930s that dealt with lynchings of blacks found that of the thousands of persons who were involved or who were witnesses, there were only forty-nine indictments and only four convictions (Raper 1978: 294). The Klan also constituted a moral police force in some areas in keeping with the Protestant values of many of its members. Prostitutes, drinkers, adulterers, men who did not support their families, and others who transgressed the social and religious norms of local society were punished with beatings or assaults (Toy 1989: 133). The KKK normally limited these kinds of social control to the more marginal members of society; it usually avoided taking on any members of the local elite who transgressed the values upheld by the group (de la Roche 1996: 115).

The KKK had millions of members at its peak, but it did not survive at this level of strength for very long. In some areas it reached early limits because of the presence of large Catholic communities. A number of states passed laws prohibiting the wearing of masks (or hoods) during public parades or demonstrations. Members of local chapters who were no longer guaranteed anonymity left the organization rather than publicly affiliate with it. The organization also suffered from a series of financial and sexual scandals involving the national leadership and key individuals in some of the state chapters (Chalmers 1965: 167–70). Given the moralistic tone and values of the organizations for many of its members, it could not survive such scandals. As a consequence of these factors, the Klan gradually lost strength and by the 1930s was much weaker. It collapsed into a core area in parts of the South. There were relatively few Catholics and Jews in most states in the region and relatively few immigrants as well, so the group lacked a target that provided a stimulus for joining. Black Americans and their role in society were still concerns in the region, but even here the KKK was marginal. Local politics was still dominated by whites, and blacks were excluded for all practical purposes; therefore, there was little need for a strong Klan to provide social control. While local KKK chapters contributed to the prejudice and efforts at maintaining white superiority, they were not really essential for it. There was just enough concern and organizational viability to permit some Klan state chapters to survive in weakened form into the 1950s so that they were available to battle the civil rights movement (and lose).

CASE STUDY 8.3 NEO-FASCISM IN POSTWAR ITALY

Fascist ideologies of the right did not die with the defeat of Italy and Germany in World War II or with the deaths of Benito Mussolini and Adolf Hitler. Because the Fascists in Italy had never adopted the same extreme measures toward Jews and others as had the Nazis in Germany, the idea of fascism did not fall to the same level of disrepute in Italy, and fascist ideas survived defeat in World War II and have continued to be present in the political system. Arguments that violence and terrorism are a necessary means of saving the state from the wrong political forces that were heard in 1920 continue to be present today. There had been minor bombings, street violence that targeted groups on the left in the 1950s, and political intimidation of the left in Italy, but it was only in the later 1960s that more serious terrorism originating in right-wing groups appeared (Rimanelli 1989: 262). At this time there began a campaign of right-wing terrorism that has been considered the most severe that had been faced by any regime in Europe since World War II (Bale 1996: 132).

These right-wing efforts relied on many of the same themes that were important in the days before World War II and ideas current with other right-wing groups. The Italian neo-fascists were, however, much more concerned with the communist threat and less concerned with immigrant communities and minorities (Weinberg 1995: 222). These Italian dissidents were afraid that Communism would prevail in Italy, especially since a weak Italian state presented opportunities for the Communists to seize power. The strength of the Italian Communist Party (PCI), largest Communist party operating in democratic Western Europe, added to these concerns. The PCI did well enough in local elections, particularly in the areas around Bologna and other parts of central Italy, that it was able to dominate municipal governments and gain a reputation for honest and efficient local government—a relative rarity in Italy. The PCI was gaining increasing acceptance by Italian voters and other members of the political establishment. The extreme right regarded the PCI, despite its professed commitment to the democratic system, as a Trojan Horse that would permit a Communist coup in the country. The weak democratic system contributed to these opportunities for the left; thus, the right attacked not only the Communists as such but also the system of parliamentary democracy. Their goal was the creation of a strong government that would be able to deal with this threat from the left (Gurr and Cole 2000: 115). Some groups among the dissidents on the right engaged in terrorist attacks feared, in addition, that if Italy was not dominated by Communists it would be dominated by the United States. Thus, they sought a stronger state so that Italy could avoid being in a subordinate position vis-à-vis either the United States or the Soviet Union (Bale 1996: 132).

The dissidents hoped to achieve a number of different objectives by their actions. These groups sometimes used "false flag" attacks so that leftists would be blamed for the violence. They hoped to create a situation where the public would be willing to accept a *coup d'état* by the military to deal with the threat (Weinberg 1995: 232). An attack against a police station in Milan in 1973, for example, had the appearance of a left-wing terrorist action, but there is a wealth of information to suggest that the person responsible for the attack was at least manipulated by elements of the Italian intelligence agencies into making the assault in hopes of mobilizing support against the left (Bale 1996: 154). A somewhat different goal was the idea that outbreaks of violence would lead the general public to support the creation of a stronger government that would be able to deal with the increasing violence in the streets. The population could be terrorized into demanding or accepting more repressive security measures. Another possibility was that the left, including the PCI, might be provoked into overreacting to the violence, and the armed forces would be compelled to intervene in the government in order to deal with the violence and to establish a stronger state (Bale 1996: 132). In 1948, in fact, there had been serious rioting by leftists after an assassination attempt on the leader of the PCI (Pisano 1987: 34–5). The strategies of tension and attempting to have leftist groups blamed for violent actions were not mutually incompatible, so in a sense the dissidents did not have to make a conscious choice between the two in any irrevocable fashion. Either outcome might work to their advantage, and from their political perspective either outcome was also an improvement over the current situation.

The dissident groups initially relied on the methods utilized in Mussolini's rise to power. There were thousands of street actions involving attacks by the right against leftist targets, and battles where the rightists were defending against attacks from youthful leftist groups (Weinberg 1995: 231). These kinds of activities were designed to place greater pressure on the government to deal with the violence in the streets. In addition, the extreme right escalated the violence by mounting a number of significant attacks against the Italian state. There were urban guerrilla attacks in 1970 and 1971 in southern Italy. Bombings against crowded public areas included bombings in crowded squares, derailing of trains, and the detonation of a bomb in the crowded Bologna train station in 1980, as well as assassination of particular individual officials (Rimanelli 1989: 264–7). There has been evidence of connections between the intelligence agencies and the right-wing groups, and one judge was apparently assassinated by terrorists on the right for getting too close to the truth about these connections (R. Drake 1989: 22). While the public often blamed the left for many of these attacks, these incidents did not create the necessary tension to justify a takeover by the forces of the right. False flag attacks became unnecessary later when the real attacks from the left began in earnest.

There were indeed movements inside the Italian government, especially the intelligence agencies and parts of the military, that were considering strengthening the repressive capabilities of the state in order to be able to deal with any threat from the left. As it turned out, these efforts were stillborn when the maneuvering and plotting were exposed to the general public. The Red Brigades benefited when the security services were reorganized in the aftermath of publicity about plotting within government agencies that threatened the democratic system. In the final analysis, the terror from the right never matched that of the Red Brigades, even though it began earlier. The attacks from the right in some ways even weakened the security forces, so that they were less prepared to deal with the onset of the leftist violence that the right feared so much. Ultimately, not even these serious attacks from the left led to the harsh repressive measures that the right so greatly desired.

The evidence suggests that the various rightist dissident groups had at least some support within government agencies. There is no indication that any of the Italian parliamentary regimes actually supported the extreme right, but individuals in the security services most certainly appear to have done so. The shake ups within agencies and the discoveries of individuals linked to plots about government takeovers provide the best indication that the violence from the right was seen to be useful by these individuals and their political allies. The Italian rightists also had some external support for their activities. They had ties with other right-wing groups elsewhere in the world, the so-called Black International. Further, they received support, aid, and various other kinds of assistance from the security and intelligence services of conservative regimes in Spain, Portugal, Greece, and various Latin American countries (Bale 1996: 134). Members of various organizations on the right also received foreign training abroad in camps in Lebanon. Both Christian Phalangists (a right-wing militia group) and the Palestinians provided training at various times (Rimanelli 1989: 266).

Ultimately, the attacks from the right were not effective in bringing down the Italian system or in forcing it to become more repressive. One weakness of the extreme right was its division into many groups. The lack of unity, of course, in part represented competing ideological ideas and concepts, indicating that the right can be as badly divided in this regard as the left. The right-wing groups also lacked widespread popular support and apparently the ability to mount an extensive and continuing campaign against the democratic state. Notwithstanding the presence of domestic allies and foreign support, the Italian groups on the extreme right were tracked down and defeated by the Italian security forces, and most of the key leaders were killed or captured. During this same time period the political plotting was discovered and the potential internal threats to Italian democracy came to light and were dealt with. The plotters inside the government agencies were dismissed or forced into retirement, and the system went on to deal with other threats and problems. These terrorist attacks by the extreme right in Italy were significantly different from some of the other terrorist attacks carried out in Europe by nationalist groups and others opposed to foreign migrants. These attacks were not a short-term reaction to increasing immigration, an economic downturn, or the sudden appearance of members of a racial or religious minority (Weinberg 1995: 223). The efforts of the Italian terrorists of the right to destabilize the government continued for a significant period of time and had support from important groups in society, yet they did fail.

CASE STUDY 8.4   THE AMERICAN MILITIA/PATRIOT MOVEMENT

The extreme right wing in the United States become a more politically active in the 1970s. There have always been groups on the extreme right opposed to the political system and suspicious of minorities and foreign groups within the country. Many of these groups have been willing to use violence in pursuit of their political objectives (Smith and Damphousse 1998). The attack on the Murrah office building in Oklahoma City focused attention on this increased use of violence. Extreme right groups include a variety of racist organizations, including the surviving elements of the Ku Klux Klan and the Aryan Nations among others, dissident groups that have a more obvious religious orientation, tax resistors, those who fear a takeover of the United States by traitors who favor one world government, and some elements of the American militia movement and associated patriot groups. The extreme right in the United States is a rather disparate group. The Posse Comitatus, for example, believes that the highest official with constitutional authority is the county sheriff, and that a posse of citizens is the appropriate military authority. Of course, if the sheriff refuses to act in an appropriate fashion, he must be removed from office and replaced by someone who better represents the popular will. Alternatively, if he fails to lead the local citizens in the defense of their rights, the local posse can act on its own (Barkun 2000: 195–7). The members of this group believe that the federal courts, the Federal Reserve Bank, the income tax, and civil rights for minorities are not covered by the constitution

(Levin 1998: 108). Other groups that fall under the tax resistor category agree that the income tax is not constitutional and even argue that the IRS is not a true governmental agency. Many groups go even further and argue that gold is the only legal and official currency.

Some of these groups see the growth of government activity and increasing regulation as circumstances that will lead to an inevitable revolution. The militia movement itself is a diverse collection of organizations with varying ideologies and approaches to government, including many individuals who are very suspicious of the national government and its agencies. They see the government as the enemy, not as an ally (Pitcavage 2001: 959). This revolution in turn will give militia groups the opportunity to provide the framework for the new government (Mariani 1998: 131). Militia groups became more prevalent in the early 1990s. They generally attracted poorly educated men in jobs with limited opportunities and potential. These militia members also frequently take the view that government programs only aid minorities rather than more appropriate groups of Americans such as themselves (Freilich *et al.* 2001: 167–8). While there are many different groups with different ideas, the more extreme members of different groups move back and forth between different organizations, providing some connection and continuity to go with the shared ideas (Kaplan 1993: 34). Other organizations have in fact infiltrated the militia movement in search of recruits and wider support.

Most of the followers of extreme right groups subscribe to a variety of conspiracy theories to justify their existence and opposition to the government. These groups think that they must exist and remained armed to protect the true American people and their values against an insidious, clandestine takeover of the country by outsiders. They see these outside conspirators as cowards because they are unwilling to openly challenge the white American; thus, they have to sneak around in the shadows to accomplish their purposes. The various extremist groups generally agree on the elements of a generic conspiracy theory. There is an elite that operates through secret organizations. Its goal is world domination, and it will use the UN as one of its methods for taking over the United States. Special military forces (for some training in Canada with black helicopters) will strike when the time is right. In some versions of this conspiracy the Federal Emergency Management Agency (FEMA) has been building detention camps where the potential opponents to the takeover will be kept once they are rounded up (Barkun 1996: 51). While this conspiracy theory may not be logical, it is believed, and like all conspiracy theories, it can never be disproved. If there is no evidence that can be found to support it, the absence of evidence demonstrates that the conspirators are skillful indeed.

The various right-wing movements share some other basic views of the threat that faces the United States. They see the traditional values of the country being threatened by outsiders. The threats come from non-white immigrants who are disparaged, and the extreme right sees itself as defending the purity of the country, which usually also means the purity of the white race. These racist views are most obvious in groups such as the KKK and the Aryan Nations, but it is also implicit in most of the other groups as well. Even the general militia movement is noteworthy by the fact that its members are almost totally white. While hardcore racists are only a minority in the militia movement, they have been overrepresented in positions of leadership (Lee 1997: 346). Anti-Semitism almost inevitably complements this racism. Most of the organizations of the extreme right regard the government of the United States as being dominated by international Jewry, and their usual term for the national government is the Zionist Occupied Government (ZOG). The various components of the extreme right thus usually include Jews among the minority groups that are threats to the United States and enemies of the white race.

Members of virtually all of the extreme right-wing groups and the militias around the country are committed to what they see as their Second Amendment rights to have weapons. They are among those who believe that the Second Amendment refers to individuals rather than the rights of states to run militias, and they do not accept Supreme Court ruling over the centuries that limited the right to form militias to state authorities. The dissidents simply consider these rulings to be part of the plot to disarm citizens of the United States. The members of these organizations are also unwilling to accept regulation and control by state governments. These groups, as a consequence, have stockpiled arms and ammunition, including sophisticated weapons in many cases for the coming conflict with foreign invaders, and they are often better equipped than local police forces.

Various extremists draw upon the ideas present in William Pierce's *The Turner Diaries*, which proposes a strategy for undermining the government and advocates the leaderless resistance approach. His book is often seen as a blueprint for actions that will overthrow the government and preserve the true America from the negative outside influences. Before he died, Pierce was regarded by many as a leading ideologist by those on the right, and his writings continue to serve to spread the ideology of the extreme right. The internet and web sites have facilitated such a method of disseminating information while avoiding direct contact. The leaders have such mechanisms to advocate leaderless resistance to indicate who the real enemies are, thus providing direction for the members who are willing to actually undertake the terrorist violence. The leaders have been careful to avoid any organizational links with potential activists, they have not issued precise directions or orders, and they have avoided hierarchical organizations to prevent them from being convicted as conspirators in criminal actions or any of the violence that results from their suggestions (Smith 2000: 59). The leaders continue to provide information on the legal means of obtaining weapons, on finding directions for preparing bombs, and praising actions undertaken by individuals. This style of leadership may be especially useful for the extreme right-wing groups in the United States since there is no centralized direction among the many groups. Lone wolf terrorists, who operate as individuals and who identify with the goals of one or the other of these organizations, can also be directed by the availability of literature and ideas (Kaplan 1993: 39). Individuals involved in right-wing violence can get support from others in the broad movement. Eric Rudolph, who was responsible for anti-abortion and anti-gay violence and the bombs at the Atlanta Olympics, lasted on the run for seven years (Heymann 2003: 81). There can be little doubt that he had at least intermittent support of other activists. The resistance fighters know the general targets and can operate accordingly. It is difficult for law enforcement agencies to infiltrate such amorphous groups since they are so fluid and unorganized (Kushner 1998a: 15). The groups also often appeal to persons who are socially isolated and lack education (Whitsel 2001: 98). They can belong by self-enlistment as soldiers in the crusade against evil in the United States—and the world. These freelance terrorists operating within this kind of loose organizational structure may be the greatest continuing threat to the security of the United States in the future (Kushner 1998b: 92).

Some groups have lacked such religious justifications, but extreme views of Christianity have been associated with the racist attitudes of a number of the violent groups on the extreme right (Michael 2006). Some groups are part of what has been called the Christian Identity movement, which sees the attack from the outside being an attack on a white, Christian nation. Their defense of the United States against non-Christian values thus has both a religious and ethnic themes (Wilkinson 2000b: 57). Most of the people identified with the Christian Identity movement favor withdrawal and quietism rather than violence, but a small portion of the persons affiliated with these groups does engage in violence (Kaplan 1993). Some extreme versions of Christian Identity have gone so far as to maintain the idea that the real people of Israel, and hence Jesus Christ, were actually white Aryans. The Jews have been falsely claiming to be the Chosen People, further justifying anti-Semitic postures (Kaplan 1995: 51). Jews are actually portrayed as the killers of Christ and the "offspring of Satan" (Smith 2000: 56). Such a religious belief increases the potential for anti-Semitism and reinforces the need to struggle against the ZOG. The religious themes have also provided a justification for attacks on homosexuals (Gurr and Cole 2000: 148). They also justify disobedience to laws and state authorities when there is a conflict with God's law since the believers are bound to obey God's laws (Pitcavage 2001: 960). Even those extreme right groups that are basically non-religious frequently have millenarian views in which they seek a perfect world (Whitsel 2001: 91). These groups, however, can coexist with the more religious portions of the extreme right, and they will regard foreign religions such as Islam or Buddhism—or Judaism—to be threatening to their vision of America as well.

The negative vision of the national government was increased by the incident at Ruby Ridge in Idaho in 1992 and the one with the Branch Davidians in Waco, Texas on April 19, 1993 (Lee 1997: 347). In Ruby Ridge a standoff developed between Randy Weaver and federal authorities over a relatively minor weapons offense. The extreme right saw this episode as an attempt by the government to begin the process of taking away the rights of Americans to own guns. Before the standoff was resolved, Weaver's wife, his son, and a federal marshal had been killed. The militants saw this as proof that the government would attack citizens seeking to defend their rights. The events at Waco that resulted in the deaths of many of the followers of David Koresh and some federal agents provided further fuel to the belief by the right that the government was willing to attack its own citizens. Groups on the right normally ignored the unusual religious beliefs of this cult and focused on the fact that issues of illegal weapon possession were involved. Thus, the Waco situation also was proof that the government would disarm its own citizens and even kill them for being different (Pitcavage 2001: 961). Both incidents provided important propaganda for the extreme right. At best, the officials on the scene mishandled the situation at Ruby Ridge. There will always be a debate about Waco, even though it seems that the deaths of the members of the group resulted from a desire for martyrdom on the part of Koresh since the fires that killed so many were started internally. The extreme right, supported by some more mainstream conservative groups, has claimed that government forces were directly responsible for the deaths. While the hardcore of the extreme right was already opposed to the ZOG and to government in general, these incidents provided them with opportunities to gain additional recruits and built their strength.

Members of the extreme right have also been willing to resort to violence. Members from a variety of different groups have killed police officers in confrontations over speeding stops and subpoenas for relatively minor offenses. The paranoia of the extreme right wing, of course, could lead individuals to assume that any arrest is the excuse to send them to the detention camps that are ready. These groups have often demonstrated an attraction for chemical and biological weapons. Four members of the Minnesota Patriots Council, a tax resistors group, processed and accumulated ricin, a deadly poison. While ricin is, in fact, quite deadly, it is not useful for inflicting mass casualties. The group intended to use the poison against local and federal law enforcement and judicial officials, but they were caught before they had a chance to implement their plans (Tucker and Pate 2000: 159). Another group, the Covenant, the Sword, and the Arm of the Lord (CSA) had plans to poison municipal water supplies. It wanted to inflict mass casualties that would start the conflagration that would hasten the second coming of the Messiah (Stern 2000a). This fascination with such weapons indicates that at least some elements in the extreme American right would be willing to cause mass casualties and would also use the weapons against government targets. Concentrations of federal workers, including those in Washington DC would seem to be prime targets for these groups (Post 2000: 288). The presence of a large minority population in Washington DC would also seem to make it a very inviting target for these groups.

Timothy McVeigh and Terry Nichols were both marginally involved with the Michigan Militia, one of the larger such groups in the country. McVeigh and Nichols, of course, gained support for their views of the oppressive government that led them to become involved in the bombing of the Murrah office building in Oklahoma City. The choice of April 19th, the anniversary of the FBI assault on the Branch Davidian compound in Waco was not a coincidence; it was apparently chosen to represent a counterattack against the government by those on the extreme right. While no other domestic terrorist attack in the United States so far has matched the death toll from Oklahoma City with 168 fatalities, members of various militias and patriot groups, racist organizations, and other elements of the extreme right continue to support the idea of attacks on the government and minorities and other outsiders. The attack in Oklahoma City demonstrated what the extreme right was capable of undertaking. Some members of militia movements have refused to believe to this day that a white American from their group would undertake the attack. They prefer to believe that the federal government undertook the attacks as a means of discrediting the militia movement and other American patriots and setting the stage for government repression (Hamilton 1996: 45).

Efforts to unify the various elements of the extreme right have so far failed since the different groups have differences in doctrines. Ideological differences of opinion have separated the extreme right in the United States just as such differences have often divided the left in Europe, the Middle East, and Latin America. It is also apparent that the leaders of various individual groups are not willing to submerge their identities in some umbrella organizations, even when they are willing to cooperate. The extremes represented by the militia movement and other groups still remain in the United States. They have not disappeared, nor have they changed their views on the presence of a ZOG and the negative influences represented by outsiders and non-white elements. Extremist actions in the United States tend to come in waves, and it is quite possible for there to be a resurgence of militia and right-wing violence in the future (Whitsel 1995: 134). Attacks against blacks, homosexuals, Asians, and other minorities have continued in the years after Oklahoma City. In at least some cases the attackers have been motivated by links with the extreme right or propaganda emanating from those groups. The militia movement lost a lot of its members in the wake of the Oklahoma City bombing, but the hardcore, dedicated members of the right-wing ideological groups remain committed to their cause. The militia movement has provided a stepping-stone for the most militant individuals involved to join other extremist groups (Pitcavage 2001: 962). The attacks on the World Trade Center in New York on September 11th were evidence of a foreign threat. Those attacks have also provided a cover for continuing attacks against at least some outsiders and may have produced an important recruiting tool for various groups on the extreme right and militias that purport to be prepared to defend the United States.

BOX 8.2 THE SILENT BROTHERHOOD (THE ORDER)

The Order, which operated in the Pacific Northwest, was formed by Robert Mathews in 1983. It was one of the few radical right-wing groups in the United States to actually launch a campaign of terrorism against the government. He found inspiration in the writings of William Pierce for this campaign. He copied the terrorist tactics used by the left in the 1960s in his efforts to change the political system (Kaplan 1997: 61). The group was overtly racist, anti-Semitic, and anti-government. In 1983 it launched a series of attacks on Jewish and minority individuals and businesses. The group relied on bank and armored car robberies to finance its operations. These robberies netted more than $4 million for the group (Michael 2003: 98). A year and a half later local police officials effectively destroyed the group. Mathews was killed in a gun battle with police, and many other members of the group were convicted of various crimes and sent to prison (George and Wilcox 1996: 341). Most of the money stolen by The Order was never recovered. It is believed that the unrecovered proceeds from the bank robberies had been channeled to other groups on the far right, including the one headed by William Pierce before he died (Michael 2003: 103). Mathews' efforts were designed not only to attack the ZOG, as he and his followers saw it, but to inspire right-wing groups all over the United States to join in that attack against the government. His efforts in this regard obviously failed since similar groups did not join the offensive against the government. Even though he failed to inspire an uprising, he became a hero and a martyr to the extreme right, both in the United States and in Europe (Kaplan 1997: 66).

CASE STUDY 8.5   NEO-NAZIS AND SKINHEADS IN EUROPE

Right-wing neo-Nazi violence has been on the increase since the 1990s. This violence has often been directed against migrants or anything that is considered foreign. Groups linked with neo-Nazi or other racist organizations have appeared in most European countries. Attacks against immigrants and minorities in a number of countries came to total more than a thousand per year in some European countries by the 1990s (Merkl 1995a: 103–6). Many of these European extreme right movements focus on preserving their national cultures. They fear that their countries will become like the United States with its great ethnic and cultural diversity, a fate they are fanatically seeking to avoid (Weinberg 1996: 85). This result would suggest that violence would continue even in good economic times, and programs by the government to compensate those who cannot benefit from the good society may not be the answer to the problems. Domestic organizations or the government agencies that are seen as aiding foreign intrusion or contamination have also become targets. Germany has been one of the countries most affected by the appearance of these groups and the violence that has been associated with them.

After World War II, there were always some groups that maintained emotional and political ties to the Nazi past. These individuals formed groups, some clandestine and some more open, that provided support for the members and even hopes that the Nazi form of government could be resurrected. Parties that directly linked themselves to the Nazi past, of course, were limited. Such groups were either outlawed outright in West Germany and some other countries or would have generated so much opposition that they would have had little hope of success. As a consequence, the more open groups that clearly aligned themselves with some portions of Nazi doctrine made it a point to proclaim their support of democracy even if their ultimate goal was to replace the democratic system with a right-wing authoritarian system. It might have been expected that as former Nazis and others associated with the old system died out and that these types of organizations would disappear. In point of fact, while time removed most of the die-hard Nazis from the scene, the passing of the Nazi generation did not mean the end of the threat to governments and citizens from groups on the extreme right willing to use violence to achieve their political goals. Europe has seen the appearance of new neo-Nazi movements ("neo" since they lack the direct link to the old Nazi Party) and other groups, such as Skinheads, which identify with these extreme right organizations.

There are a variety of neo-Nazi groups that have appeared in Germany and elsewhere in Europe. These groups have been different from their American counterparts in one respect. They do not fear a strong centralized government, and, in fact, they seek to strengthen it (Weinberg 1996: 82). The right continues to see strong governments as essential to provide protection to the state and its people. The state only becomes a target when it seeks to aid the victims of the neo-Nazi violence (Gurr and Cole 2000: 144). In Germany such groups have become even more active since unification of the two Germanys, even though they existed in West Germany before the collapse of Communism in the East. In the mid-1990s it was estimated that there were over eighty extreme right groups in Germany with 42,000 members, 6,200 of which were involved in violent activities (Wilkinson 2003: 119). The number of violent attacks increased in the later part of the 1990s (Heitmeyer 2005: 142). These neo-Nazi groups share certain common ideological themes. They oppose the idea of democratic government that they see as corrupt, they are opposed to any form of ethnic pluralism, and they seek the creation of strong national state in which the leader will determine the course of action to be taken by the state. The neo-Nazi groups have also been active in the Holocaust denial industry, in claiming that the death camps did not exist. The various groups also retain the anti-Semitism that was so much a part of the original Nazi party.

The violence and appeal of the neo-Nazi groups increased after German unification for a number of reasons. Right-wing terrorism in Germany as elsewhere has often attracted those who have not benefited from changes in society. The young and unemployed often viewed the state as part of the problem for their lack of status and opportunity. Their educational attainments were insufficient to arrange for decent jobs, and government services and programs were geared toward other groups. The conservative, free market type of parties supported policies that provided few benefits since they could not aspire to good jobs, and the parties of the left provided services that benefited other groups; consequently, neither major ideological wing of the German party system offered any advantage or hope for improvement. Unemployed youths have been attracted to these groups, providing the activists who participate in actions against those they consider to be undesirable (Laqueur 1999: 124). Unification increased tensions within parts of Germany and provided a recruiting ground for the extreme right. Citizens of the former German Democratic Republic (East Germany) found themselves at obvious disadvantages with citizens from the western parts of the unified country. Their education, including the required dosages of Marxist-Leninist theory, was often less useful and less relevant than the education received in the west. The factories in the east were not as competitive as those in the west, and many of them ended up closing, leaving persons in the east unemployed. Reunification also meant a reduction in government services, programs, and agencies, resulting in additional unemployment and fewer benefits. The end result was an increase in dissatisfaction for many of the people in the east.

The collapse of Communism in Eastern Europe and the Soviet Union led to increases in the number of persons seeking to immigrate to Germany in hopes of a better life. The newcomers increased pressures on public services and were potential competitors for jobs. In addition, Germany had also received refugees elsewhere in the world who were seeking safety and asylum. Persons fleeing conflicts in the Middle East, Bosnia, Sri Lanka, and Indonesia, as well as persons from all over the world seeking employment and the basic necessities had entered the country. These outside groups were added to an existing population of guest workers, many of them Turkish, who had been brought to West Germany. These guest workers provided labor in areas where there was a labor shortage as well as being willing to do work that because of its menial nature or hardship most Germans (or other Europeans) would not do. As a consequence, unemployed youth saw not only a scarcity of jobs and an absence of government programs but also a whole group of outsiders who were using resources that should have been devoted to "real" Germans. The mix was a rather explosive one, and provided extreme right groups with many new recruits. It is important to note, however, that only a portion of the persons engaged in right-wing violence in Germany were unemployed. Many, in fact, did have jobs. Most, however, whether employed or unemployed, were of working-class backgrounds and had lower levels of education (Willems 1995). The fear of unemployment or of resources being diverted to foreign groups provides some indication as to why the individuals with jobs participated.

Given the greater pressure on resources in the eastern part of Germany, it is probably not surprising that many of the attacks by the extreme right against the outsiders have occurred in this area of the country (Husbands 1995: 331, 334). To some extent, local factors contributed to the problems. It is important to note, however, that it has not just been persons from the east who have participated in the attacks, and many of the leaders of the neo-Nazi groups are from the west. Much of this violence has been directed against foreigners, including attacks on housing for migrants, guest workers, and those seeking asylum. Perhaps more disturbing than the attacks themselves have been the obvious support from local populations that the right-wing activists have received. News of the initial attacks against migrants, guest workers, and other outsiders prompted additional assaults as others were encouraged to adopt violence (Heitmeyer 2005: 147). The public support has encouraged the activists and given hope to the leaders of the groups that there could even be an increase in public support in the future. One other disturbing aspect about the violence is the fact that at least one analysis of the outbreaks of violence in Germany found that unemployment had little effect on the violence directed against foreigners. While the number of attacks declined in later years, the potential for violence is still present. The number of foreigners present in an area has been associated with attacks in the past; thus, in difficult economic times the mere presence of foreigners is sufficient for attacks to occur (McLaren 1999).

While the violence in Germany to date has included many violent actions, the number of deaths has so far been limited. Of course, as groups see little change in their circumstances or in the problems that they perceive to be present, the violence could escalate as it has for so many other groups willing to resort to terror. The target for many of the attacks are the "foreign" elements that the right-wing groups would like to see leave the country. If one injury can persuade some to leave, then increased violence may be likely to persuade other members of foreign communities to flee as well. Many of the activists engaging in street violence may not share the ultimate right-wing goals of the leaders, but there is no indication that all the stormtroopers in the SA in the 1920s and 1930s shared the political ideas of the Nazi Party leadership. In this regard, the extreme right groups have also been recruiting Skinheads for violent activity. While the Skinheads are difficult to organize, extremist groups have made the effort to use them for their own purposes, being successful often enough to indicate that this discontented segment of society is available for participation in violent activities (Sprinzak 1995: 36–7). The Skinheads themselves represent another manifestation of unrest by the young members of the working class or unemployed members of the working class countercultural protest (Laqueur 1999: 125–6). The ideological commitment of these groups is probably not great, but it is violence from the right that provides them with an outlet for aggression, and members of the right have consciously sought to utilize these rebellious elements of German society to further their own extreme political agendas.

Germany has not been very effective in dealing with violence from the extreme right in many cases (Pedahzur 2001a: 352). The leadership of the groups retains a certain amount of separation from the street actions of the activists while providing funds and other support for the street activists, which can be quite important. Various extreme right political parties and political associations have been banned under the German law and the German constitution, which permit banning political groups seeking to undermine a democratic government. These efforts have been largely fruitless since the groups reappear under new names with the same leaders in relatively short order. Even when activists have been arrested, the sentences handed down have been relatively light, especially when compared to jail terms for leftists of the Red Army Faction. Part of the reason for the leniency was the youth of the right-wing activists (Anderson 1995: 44). Also, since the right-wing violence has not usually resulted in fatalities, the offenses in question would not lead to severe jail sentences. In the short term, however, the absence of long prison terms has probably made the costs of action bearable by the activists on the street.

The appearance of extreme right groups has not been restricted by any means to Germany. Such groups have appeared in most other European countries. They all share virtually the same ideology, including anti-Semitism, fear of that which is foreign, and a willingness to use violence. Some Swedish groups on the extreme right have even adopted the concept of a ZOG as being responsible for the problems of their society (Bjorgo 1993: 36). In some other countries the targeted outsiders have been Muslim migrants, and the right-wing groups see themselves as fighting "the Muslim invasion" (Bjorgo 1997: 314). In the Netherlands there have been attacks on Turks and other foreigners as well as bombings of mosques, coffeehouses that are frequented by Muslims, and the living quarters of the migrants (Merkl 1995a: 102). European countries have proven to be unable to either absorb or assimilate the Muslim migrants and their children (Leiken 2005: 133–4). A wide variety of small groups that exist in the Scandinavian countries have launched many attacks on foreigners and refugees living in their countries. As is the case in Germany, the activists are young while the organizers and supporters are older and more ideologically committed (Bjorgo 1997: 102). In some cases the attacks and violence have been broader. Not only have foreigners been attacked, but targets have included "national traitors"—such as politicians, journalists, political officials, and supporters of the migrants (Bjorgo 1995a: 202). In Sweden in some years as many as half the non-European migrants have been threatened or assaulted (Bjorgo 1997: 42).

The attacks by the extreme right in Europe have actually had some important successes for the dissidents. A number of establishment parties have increasingly supported and argued for greater limitations on immigration and the granting of asylum (Leiken 2005). In general the ability to secure the status of asylum or to be allowed to enter many European countries has become much more difficult. As a consequence, it is now harder to migrate to many European countries, meaning that the violence and attacks by neo-Nazis, racists, and Skinheads has been successful at least in part. Governments have limited migration in an effort to reduce the violence and the appeal of the parties of the far right by these policy modifications, indicating their desire to limit the extreme right. Even so, the violence and terror has been successful, and these modifications of immigration policies run the risk of encouraging future violence since past violence has been rewarded.

While many of the groups have been very nationalistic and focused on their own countries, many of them have developed international ties. The extreme right in Europe has availed itself of modern technology to coordinate activity. Internet access and networks have been established among the various groups. International gatherings are fairly common, especially on important dates such as Hitler's birthday. The ideologically committed core of many of the groups is quite small, and in their own countries they may feel like isolated elements. The international gatherings provide them with positive reinforcement for their ideas by permitting them to meet with fellow extremists from other countries. Electronic bulletin boards have increasingly been used to provide information on rallies and demonstrations (Lee 1997: 273). The international contacts also provide the groups with some ways around national laws and restrictions. For example, Nazi material and some neo-Nazi material is banned in Germany, but such restrictions are not in place in other countries. Such items can be ordered by Germans and other Europeans from a websites in countries such as Denmark that have fewer restrictions on political paraphernalia or unpopular ideas (Bjorgo 1997: 84).

In Germany and elsewhere, while the actual violence may wane at particular points in time, the breeding ground for right-wing terrorism continues to exist (Laqueur 1999: 124). As is true in the United States, such attacks tend to come in waves, but after each wave the level of violence is at higher levels than before the wave (Bjorgo 1997: 312). The potential for violence obviously remains. Just as religious fundamentalism may be a reaction to changes in the international system and the intrusion of foreign ideas, right-wing groups seem to gain strength in times of societal difficulties. Globalization and external influences will continue to create problems for European societies. The 9/11 attacks, the Madrid train bombings, and the London transit attacks have all provided new impetus to the fears of alien cultures. These kinds of influences may have made at least some young people susceptible to extremist ideologies, such as the ones presented by the far right (Bessant 1995: 113–14). The passage of the original generation of Nazis has not led to a decline in the racist and anti-democratic ideas that were so much a part of that generation. Fascism and the Nazis may have originally appeared as a counter to communism, but the neo-Nazis and related groups no longer require a left-wing enemy to continue to operate. While the old enemy is dead, the right wing has been able to find other enemies to fight and groups to hate. The danger may lie dormant in the best of times and be much more active in the less than ideal times.

BOX 8.3 THE DANISH GREEN JACKETS

In the 1980s Denmark saw the emergence of a number of violent youth groups in Copenhagen. These youth groups adopted a racist and anti-immigrant attitude. One such group wore pilot jackets and became known as the Green Jackets. The term quickly came to be collectively applied to a variety of such groups, and many youth gangs accepted this collective designation. The members of the groups were often unemployed and were from broken homes, and they lived in high-rise state housing projects. Members of the gangs saw the migrants receiving apartments and other benefits at their expense. They proceeded to harass and attack immigrants, and they adopted symbols related to the Ku Klux Klan or neo-Nazi groups as well. The Green Jackets were actually successful to a degree in their use of violence. Immigrant families moved out of the neighborhoods, and local officials were careful to assign migrants to housing in other areas of the city. As a consequence, one result of the violence was the successful "cleansing" of foreign migrants from the area (Bjorgo 1997: 127–32). The Green Jackets faded from the scene by the late 1980s. As the members aged, they moved on to other interests and had less time for street activities. The concessions made by government officials had removed the impetus for their activities and probably also limited their ability to recruit new younger members into the organizations by removing the source of local tension. One interesting aspect of the Green Jacket activity is that it occurred in areas of Copenhagen where immigrants were a smaller percentage than in the capital as a whole. Both total number of migrants and those migrants who could readily be recognized as foreign were fewer than in many other areas (Bjorgo 1997: 92). The violence in this part of the city, therefore, was not directly triggered by a large concentration of foreigners. There may have been a threshold effect where a sufficient number of migrants were necessary to cause concern for groups that felt they were not receiving enough benefits from the state. It is also possible that members of the youth groups as a consequence of their movements around the city saw the local immigrant residents as a part of an increased foreign presence in Copenhagen in general and reacted accordingly. While the Green Jackets turned out to be a temporary phenomenon in Denmark, they demonstrate how quickly violent youth groups could appear and how they can become connected to other elements of the neo-Nazi dissident culture in Europe.

SUMMARY

Terrorism arising from right-wing ideologies has been most prevalent in the twentieth century. Conservative and authoritarian governments have often used violence to control their populations, and the Nazi regime was one of the most ruthless governments ever established in modern times. In the period before World War II, fascist parties and other movements subscribing to a variety of right-wing ideologies involving anti-socialist and anti-democratic themes utilized violence in their efforts to gain power. In some cases violence and intimidation played important roles in facilitating their increased prominence and even facilitated their eventual control of the government. Violenceon the streets was essential for the assumption of power by the Fascist Party in Italy and the Nazis in Germany. The street battles also attracted the support of other political groups and sectors of society opposed to the leftists.

Neither the Nazis nor the Italian Fascists had any external support in their struggles against other domestic parties and the democratic governments of their countries. Both movements grew out of the domestic discontents of populations within their own countries. Their finances and other support were provided by domestic groups that were fearful of the Communists and socialists or from domestic groups that favored the strongly nationalist agenda put forward by both Mussolini and Hitler. Once they were in power the two dictators eventually extended aid to other fascist parties and right-wing groups elsewhere in Europe. Thus, while neither the Fascists nor the Nazis received outside aid, they were to become key sources of support for right-wing dissident groups in other countries.

After World War II, right-wing ideologies became a basis for dissident terrorism in Europe and North America. The neo-fascists efforts in Italy after World War II were clearly a continuation of the fascist experiences from the years between the wars, and some of the techniques that were used were the same as well. In the case of right-wing groups elsewhere, terrorism against minorities in the United States had been present since the end of the Civil War in the case of the first appearance of the Ku Klux Klan. The KKK then reappeared during World War I. These early groups were not usually anti-government, but in the latter part of the twentieth century, however, officials and governments agencies have increasingly been targeted in the United States as agents of the ZOG. The bombing in Oklahoma City was simply a culmination of such assaults. In Europe as well attacks by right-wing dissidents have begun to include political figures and government officials who are seen as helping the immigrants and other outsiders (Bjorgo 1997: 313–14). Right-wing violence has become more threatening in Europe than leftist terrorism, and there are indications that the number of such movements is on the increase (Soeters 2005: 91). It is in the United States, however, that right-wing groups have displayed the greatest potential for violent actions (Hewitt 2003: 120).

The right-wing groups have had successes. Mussolini and Hitler took control of their governments. The KKK was part of the mechanisms for controlling blacks, immigrants, and at least some whites. The modern right-wing groups in the United States and Europe have made life difficult for minorities and others that they target. Immigration laws have been strengthened in many European countries and similar efforts are underway in other European states and the United States. Of course, at least some of the dissidents on the far right have had more far-reaching objectives than simply the limitation of foreign migrants. Anti-migrant actions have been a step towards grander political plans. It is possible that the immigration restrictions will lessen their appeal of these groups in the future since they will be less able to attract sympathizers from the population in general.

With the exception of the neo-fascists in Italy, there has been little evidence of outside support by governments for extreme right groups in Europe or North America. The extreme right groups in Europe and the United States have maintained links among themselves with modern technology, including the internet and web pages. Radical nationalism and intolerance have taken on a transnational character (Bjorgo 1997: 317). The international contacts also permit various dissident groups to maintain a presence even though a particular movement may be weak in a particular nation. To date, the various groups provide ideological support to each other but very little other assistance. At this point, the members of the extreme right groups do not appear to have developed any important cross-national linkages in planning terrorists attacks, but such cooperation could occur in the future. Al Qaeda has demonstrated the possibilities for such cooperation with modern technology, and right-wing groups could adapt to these technological possibilities as well. The presence of this technology would also explain why leaderless resistance and individual activities have become more common, not only in the United States, but also in Europe (Bjorgo 1997: 56–7).

There are some indications that right-wing dissidents have been more intent on causing casualties than their counterparts on the left. In France right-wing groups launched only 10 per cent of the attacks, but they were responsible for two-thirds of the deaths from such attacks (Engene 2004: 123). A comparison of deaths from left- and right-wing violence in Germany and Italy provides evidence to support this conclusion. The number of terrorist actions by right-wing dissidents in Germany from 1968 to 1987 was only a small fraction of left-wing attacks, but they resulted in considerably more fatalities (see Table 8.1). In the case of Italy, there is no breakdown on the number of attacks by the left and the right, but the Red Brigades were obviously much more active than the neo-fascist dissident groups, yet more people died in attacks by the extreme right. The single incident of the bombing of the Bologna train station inflated the death toll by the violent right, but even if this event is excluded, right-wing attacks were more likely to result in deaths than actions by the left. Increased fatalities have been more likely with right-wing violence for another reason. Some of the more racist groups even have genocidal goals that would require the infliction of mass casualties on a portion of the population (Gurr and Cole 2000: 113). When the targets are members of the minority groups that the dissidents dislike or hate casualties of course will not be a cause for concern and can even serve a purpose in terrorizing other members of the group. If minorities begin to feel uncomfortable and seek to leave, the terrorists have won. These dissidents, however, have also been responsible for attacks against the general population that have resulted in larger numbers of casualties among the general population. Oklahoma City and the Bologna train station attacks are prime examples. Since the objective of the right is to destabilize the government, higher casualty figures could better serve their purpose. The strategy of tension advocated by the right requires dead and wounded; attacks on empty buildings are less likely to be effective. Since the left often has sought to convert the general population, indiscriminate attacks on bystanders are counterproductive to the ultimate goal. Dissidents on the right may also have been more disposed toward more deadly attacks since in many countries they have had weaker popular support than the left has had. Since the right-wing dissidents could mount fewer attacks, they have had to be more spectacular. Should right-wing terrorism continue to occur in the future in industrialized countries or even increase, high casualty figures are likely to continue to be present.

TABLE 8.1 NUMBER OF DEATHS IN LEFT-WING AND RIGHT-WING ATTACKS IN WEST GERMANY AND ITALY, 1969–87

Country and terrorist groups	Incidents	Deaths
West Germany		
Left-wing groups	11,660	7
Right-wing groups	550	26
Italy		
Left-wing groups	n/a	148
Right-wing groups	n/a	193
External groups or unknown	n/a	78

Source: Jongman (1992).

TERMS

Aryan Nations
Beer Hall Putsch
Black International
Bologna train station bombing
Branch Davidians
Christian Identity
Communist Combat Cells (CCC)
false flag attacks
Fascist
Gracchi brothers
Green Jackets
Adolf Hitler
Iron Guard
Ku Klux Klan (KKK)
leaderless resistance
Timothy McVeigh
Minnesota Patriots Council
Murrah federal office building

Benito Mussolini
National Socialist Democratic Workers Party (NSDAP)
Terry Nichols
Nivilles Group
The Order
William Pierce
Posse Comitatus
Red Scare
ricin
Ruby Ridge
Schutzstaffel (SS)
Skinheads
Sturmabteilungen (SA)
The Turner Diaries
Vendee
Vladimir Zhirinovsky
Zionist Occupation Government (ZOG)

FURTHER READING

Bessel, R. (1986) "Violence as Propaganda: The Role of the Storm Troopers in the Rise of National Socialism," in T. Childers (ed.) *The Formation of the Nazi Constituency, 1919–1933*, Totowa, NJ: Barnes & Noble, 131–46.

Bjorgo, T. (1997) *Racist and Right-Wing Violence in Scandinavia: Patterns, Perpetrators, and Responses*, Oslo: Tano Aschehoug.

Chalmers, D. M. (1965) *Hooded Americanism: The History of the Ku Klux Klan*, New York: Quadrangle Books.

Merkl, P. H. (1987) *The Making of a Stormtrooper*, Boulder, CO: Westview.

Weinberg, L. (1995) "Italian Neo-Fascist Terrorism: A Comparative Perspective," in T. Bjorgo (ed.) *Terror from the Extreme Right*, London: Frank Cass, 221–38.

CHAPTER 9

Terrorism and Multiple Motivations

The preceding four chapters have focused on dissident groups and terrorist organizations that could be primarily categorized as being religious, ethnic/nationalist, or ideological. The examples and case studies in these four chapters were all discussed within the context of the dominant motivation for the dissidents and the political objectives that they were seeking. In a number of cases the dominant motivation for dissident groups was reinforced by other factors. National liberation movements, for example, occurred with populations that were often based in a different religious tradition than that of the colonial power. Elements of Marxist-Leninist ideology often appeared in the efforts of the colonial populations to free themselves from capitalist colonial powers. Basic concepts present in various leftist theories were easily applied to the situations of subject populations in colonial empires. Notwithstanding the addition of these ideological elements, the movements in question were still essentially ethnic and nationalist efforts directed to create a new independent state where a colony had been before.

TERRORIST CAMPAIGNS WITH COMPLEX CAUSES

There remain, however, examples of dissident violence that have proven to be extremely difficult to categorize as involving one dominant type of objective or only one basic motivation. Many different factors become involved in the motivations of terrorists (Fox 1998: 56). Any of the case studies included in this chapter could have been placed in one of the preceding four chapters, but they could also have been placed in more than one, which illustrates the complexity of causation and objectives. If they had been placed in any of the preceding chapters, they would have provided very unclear examples. As a consequence, it made more sense to deal with such complex cases separately. Further, the fact that these examples of terrorist activities include some of the most important and longest enduring campaigns of violence made it essential to include these cases in any discussion of terrorism in the world. Long campaigns may permit multiple objectives to develop within the dissident groups. Most movements that have been present for decades will necessarily have had to recruit new members to refresh the organization. Further, generational differences can appear and younger members of an organization may be more sensitive to different issues (such as discrimination in higher education) than older members who experienced different problems (attempts to extinguish cultural symbols, impose linguistic unity, or government repression). With the passage of time, dissident organizations may well have time to add ideological issues to nationalist or religious ones or to develop a regional base that in turn influences ideology. With time it is also possible for groups to splinter on ideological, ethnic, or religious grounds and, as a consequence, the battle between dissidents and governments will get more complex. The analysis of dissident groups that have been active for long periods of time may also suggest the future path that at least some ethnic, ideological, or religious groups that already exist may ultimately take.

Lebanon, especially during the civil war that began in the 1970s, supplies a clear example of complex causes underlying widespread violence, including various types of terrorism, including the taking of Western hostages. In this case, much of the complexity resulted from the fact that so many different groups relied on violence and terrorism in their efforts to achieve their political objectives. Christian–Muslim differences among the Arab population explained some of the violence, but there was also conflict among the Christians, within both the Sunni and Shia communities, and between Sunni, Shia, and Druze Muslims. At different times, groups of Christian or Muslims were in conflict with the PLO. Different groups of Palestinians also attacked each other at various times, and there were also Marxist-Leninist groups operating that sought to create a secular state that would be aligned with other radical states in the Middle East. Syria and Israel regularly intervened in Lebanon, in pursuit of their own goals, creating even more complex sets of conflicts, which in turn generated a different set of cleavages that reinforced the existing differences in the country. Groups could be anti-Christian, anti-Israeli, and anti-Syrian in their orientation or pro-PLO, pro-Syrian, and opposed to the traditional leadership patterns present in Lebanon (both Christian and Muslim). Hizballah, a Shiite group in Lebanon allied with Iran, was anti-Israeli, but it was also very involved in attempting to improve the position of the Shiite community, efforts that placed it at odds with Christian, Sunni, and the Druze political leaders at least part of the time. Other violent political organizations have had mixed causes. Immediately after World War II, the British in Malaya faced a guerrilla and terrorist movement that involved local communists who drew heavily upon the Chinese population of the country. While the dissidents were able to mobilize support among the Chinese by ethnic appeals, they had little appeal to other groups within Malaya (Desai and Eckstein 1990: 463). The Kurdish Workers Party that has operated in Turkey combined a militant leftist orientation with an ethnic appeal to the Kurdish population, especially in southeastern Turkey (see Box 9.1).

Another factor that has frequently complicated an understanding of terrorism in some countries or in some circumstances has been attacks by criminal groups. Criminal activity for financial gain, such as kidnappings or extortions, as noted in Chapter 2 are not acts of terrorism even though they are extremely frightening for the victims. Some attacks by criminal organizations, however, have only indirect relationships to motives of financial gain. The Mafia in Italy has assassinated judges, prosecutors, and other officials when they have been too efficient

BOX 9.1 KURDISH WORKERS PARTY

The Kurdish Workers Party (PKK), which has mounted terrorist operations in Turkey and against Turkish targets abroad, would appear at first glance to be an ethnic party that is seeking autonomy or independence for the Kurds. Somewhat surprisingly, however, the party under the leadership of Abdullah Ocalan has had strong Marxist-Leninist components that have influenced its activities. The party has clearly been striving not just for gains for Kurds in a Turkish state but to create a socialist community as well. The party, for example, has emphasized workers' rights and the need to eliminate colonialism and feudalism in Turkish society (Jongman 1992: 71–2). This ideological emphasis on the part of the PKK may reflect the fact that the Kurds are not as geographically concentrated in Turkey as they are in Iran or Iraq. While there is an area in southeastern Turkey that is overwhelmingly Kurdish, in nearby areas Kurds and Turks are intermingled. They are also large numbers of Kurds working in the major urban areas (Ergil 2000). Their location and occupations would make them obvious choices for a working-class appeal by a party instead of a solely ethnic one. Despite very real discrimination in the past, the Kurds are better integrated into the Turkish state than has been the case for Kurds in Iraq. In addition to ideology and ethnicity, there have been times when the PKK has emphasized Islamic themes in its propaganda, but these efforts appear to have been attempts to increase support among religious Kurds (and Turks) and have not represented a commitment to furthering a more religious political system (Criss 1995: 22–3).

The PKK has tried some unconventional attacks. In on case, it poisoned water tanks outside a Turkish military base, but the poison was discovered before anyone was affected (Cameron 2004: 81). The group has also had an element of fanaticism since it has utilized suicide attacks to achieve its goals. It was responsible for a number of suicide attacks. This fanaticism is related to the ideological beliefs of the attackers, not religion or ethnicity (Radu 2002: 280–1). These suicide attacks were designed to strengthen the morale of the group members after a series of defeats by Turkish forces (Dolnik 2003: 24). The Marxist-Leninist credentials of the PKK have made it possible for the party to cooperate with other leftist dissident groups in Europe. Its Kurdish base, on the other hand, has been a handicap since it has limited its ability to collaborate with other Turkish leftists. It has been even more difficult to cooperate with Armenian dissidents since the Kurds shared responsibility for the massacres that occurred in World War I. The PKK lost some of its willingness to persist in the struggle against the Turkish government when Ocalan was captured by Turkish commandos at the Greek embassy in Kenya. He ordered the movement to stand down, but Kurdish nationalist groups under a variety of new names have continued to challenge the government. While the leftist elements of the dissidents have been supplanted by Kurdish nationalism as the major mobilizing cause, the Marxism-Leninism of many members has not disappeared.

or too zealous in their investigative activities. While such deaths have the important goal of eliminating particular individuals who have constituted threats to the organization, there has been a broader target audience. Other officials have been warned of the dangers that can come from a too aggressive pursuit of certain criminals. These attacks were designed to force a modification of policy by the appropriate bureaucratic or police agencies (Wilkinson 2000b: 71). If other officials backed off from their investigations because of fear, the terrorism has been successful. In the 1950s and the 1960s, the Mafia was more likely to cooperate with the government to repress groups that were seen as dangerous to the Italian state, especially radical leftist ones. There were linkages between the Mafia and other criminal groups and right-wing terrorist organizations (Chubb 1989: 16, 43). Criminal organizations in the so-called "Triple Frontier" area where Brazil, Argentina, and Paraguay come together have cooperated with terrorist groups such as Hamas, and the terrorist groups have used the area for financing attacks and laundering money (Sverdlick 2005). In Southeast Asia, the laxity of banking laws and other conducive elements have also presented a nexus in which terrorist groups and criminal organizations can cooperate for their mutual benefit (Makarenko 2005). Much of the violence and the assassinations that have occurred in many of the successor states of the Soviet Union have elements of both criminal and terrorist activity. The background to individual deaths or attempted assassinations can be unclear to outsiders and the specific audiences that are being targeted may be difficult to identify (although members of the target audience will often surely know who they are). The individual victims may be chosen because of their political beliefs, but they could also have been attacked because they were interfering with criminal activities or even because they were demanding too much in the way of bribes or protection money. They could even have reneged on an arrangement they had already made with a criminal group (Pluchinsky 1998: 122). Some individuals in government or the police agencies in these states could even have angered both criminal and dissident groups at the same time. If the victim were killed for personal reasons as in the case of a criminal deal gone badly or disagreements about share of the profits from criminal activities, then the death would not be an example of terrorism. Similarly, if the target audience consisted of government officials taking bribes, the action would not have the requisite political goals to qualify as terrorism. The objective in this case would be financial gain rather than political changes. If the goal of the attacks were the reduction of active enforcement of existing laws, however, then the attack would be intended to bring about changes in government policies, or at least changes in the level of enforcement of the government policies. Journalists have become a special target in Russia, especially if they have been investigating corruption. More than half the journalists killed in the world in 1995 died in Russia (Stern 1999: 104). The message to other crusading journalists interested in investigating Russian criminal activity is obvious.

The drug trade and the use of narcotics have further muddied the waters for some dissident organizations and led to the idea of narcoterrrosim where dissident groups involve themselves directly or indirectly in the drug trade. Terrorist groups often have developed clandestine channels of communications and supply routes that are appealing to criminal organizations involved in smuggling drugs. Drug organizations in turn can provide financial support to the political dissidents in return for assistance in moving drugs into or out of a country. The dissidents and drug organizations have a shared goal in avoiding detection by security forces or the military. Opium producers in Afghanistan have supported one group or another in the various conflicts in that country. The Afghan rebels used drug profits to help finance their war against the Soviet Union (Miller and Damask 1996: 117). Drug producers have a common cause

BOX 9.2 RUSSIA'S CHECHNYA QUAGMIRE

Russia has faced major problems with an insurrection, complete with terrorist actions, in the province of Chechnya in the Caucasus mountain region of the country. The Chechens had been one of the most difficult groups in the region for Czarist Russia to subdue, and their loyalty to Russia and then the Soviet Union has been in doubt. Among the millions deported by Stalin during and after World War II for actual or suspected disloyalty were approximately 400,000 Chechens (Bell-Fialkoff 1999: 32). The present underlying hostility of the Muslim Chechens toward the Russians involves both ethnic and religious elements. The drive for independence has been fueled by the ethnic identification of the Chechens or their adherence to Islam. Many of the dissident Chechens have had contacts with Islamic groups in other countries and have adopted a basically Islamic orientation toward the struggle. They have been involved with Al Qaeda and have served in the Afghan campaigns on the side of the Taliban and al Qaeda. Chechens have been an important element in the Islamic Movement of Uzbekistan (Rashid 2002: 9, 174). Many Chechens have returned to do battle against Russian troops, and Muslims from other countries have supported them. Islamic extremists and elements of Al Qaeda have attempted to co-opt the Chechen independence movement and integrate the Chechen struggle in the global jihadist movement (Vidino 2005: 57).

While Islamic extremism has been important for some of the dissidents, there are many ethnic Chechens who have support the rebellion for nationalist reasons without adopting the Islamic values of the Muslim fundamentalist. Should an independent Chechnya appear, there could well be a struggle between the religious and nationalist elements for control of the new country. A third element in the Chechen struggle involves a criminal element that works with the religious and ethnic elements. Chechen gangs have been among the best-organized criminal groups in the successor states of the old Soviet Union, and they have established very profitable networks for their activities (Moore 2007: 309). These gangs have been involved in all kinds of criminal activities, including drug trafficking (Schmid 2000: 114). The criminal networks have also been important as a means of channeling contributions from the Chechen diaspora to the dissident groups inside Russia (Bowers et al. 2004: 274). For these Chechens, the establishment of strong central rule by Russia in the province could limit profits from criminal activity, whereas a weak government in an independent state would be more amenable to bribery and coercion. The three elements in the independence movement have not always cooperated. There have been clashes between Islamic groups and the more traditional nationalist ones (Williams 2001: 132).

The Chechen separatist groups have been involved in a variety of violent activities. They have fought pitched battles with Russian armed forces. By 2002 they had been forced out of the main cities and into the mountains, but Russian troops have been unable to control this difficult terrain, and the Chechen dissidents have continued to make guerrilla attacks. They have also launched all kinds of terrorist actions throughout Russia. There have been bombings of apartment buildings, car bombings, property attacks, and kidnappings (Chalk 1999: 153). Chechen dissidents have also been involved in a number of mass hostage situations, including the seizure of a large portion of the audience in a Moscow theater in 2002 and the hostage situation at the school in Breslan in 2004. There is some evidence that this bold attack in Moscow, which resulted in the capture of so many hostages in the capital of their adversary, was an effort to emulate the attacks of September 11th (Nacos 2003: 14). These hostage situations have resulted in many casualties, including the flawed rescue attempt of the Moscow theater hostages and the many deaths in Breslan among the children. The deadly nature of these terrorist attacks has been more disturbing since there have been indications that the Chechens have sought to obtain weapons of mass destruction (Cronin 2002/3: 48). A number of Chechen group have used suicide attacks against Russian troops in Chechnya and targets in Russia. Female Chechen suicide bombers, the so-called "Black Widows" who have lost their husbands or brothers or other relatives in the fighting, have been involved in a number of these attacks, including the destruction of two domestic airliners in flight (Vidino 2005: 61). Revenge for the loss of close family members, rather than religious feeling, appears to be the key factor in the decision to engage in a suicide attack (Bower *et al.* 2004: 267–8).

Regardless of the weapons used by the dissidents or their multiple motivations, Russia has been unable to defeat or control the dissidents. Russian military campaigns continue and the violence and terror by the dissidents is the response. Even if Russia were to grant Chechnya independence, terrorist violence from this source would be likely to continue given the international religious connections of some Chechens and the important role played by criminal organizations. One reason for the Russian determination to prevail is that there is the very real danger that the violence in Chechnya could ignite similar movements elsewhere in the region (Baev 2006: 5). Chechen groups have consciously sought to widen the conflict to other areas on a number of occasions (Moore 2007: 317–18).

with many dissident groups since they both want to avoid having an overly strong central government in power regardless of the religious, ethnic, or ideological complexion of that government. The Mafia in Italy has supplied arms to right-wing political groups in exchange for assistance in smuggling drugs (Schmid 1992b: 21). Islamic dissidents in Uzbekistan have been involved in the drug trade (Rashid 2002: 229). Kurdish dissident groups have also partially funded many of their activities with proceeds from drug smuggling (Radu 2002: 278), and the KLA in Kosovo developed links with drug smugglers (Macgregor 2001: 97, 103). Al Qaeda relied on drug money for some of its financing as well (Rabasa *et al.* 2006: 59). Connections between criminal groups and terrorist organizations have been so widespread because involvement with drug trafficking provides a much more effective and reliable source of finances for the terrorists than kidnappings or bank robberies (Chalk 1999: 12). While many different groups with various causes have availed themselves of this source of funding, ETA in Spain has been an exception. It has interfered with drug smugglers because some of the drugs have stayed in the Basque country (Khatami 1997: 399–401). Narcoterrorism involving drug producers and processors with dissident movements has also appear in Latin America in a variety of contexts as will be demonstrated in some of the following case studies. Conspiracy theorists put forward the argument that the Soviet Union was behind a global drug trafficking system that was designed to undermine Western democracies. There has been virtually no evidence that such a connection has ever existed (Miller and Damask 1996: 115). The decline of foreign countries as supporters of terrorist groups (discussed in Chapter 4) has accelerated this trend as terrorist organizations have increased their efforts to find new allies and new sources of funding (Jamieson 2005: 164). While narcoterrorism cannot realistically be considered to have been one aspect of the Cold War, it is a term that aptly describes alliances between dissident groups and drug operators.

CASE STUDIES

Examples of dissident groups that have used terrorism within a complex set of circumstances or objectives include the Shining Path movement in Peru, the IRA and other groups in Northern Ireland, the activities of dissidents in Colombia, and conflicts in Nigeria between different groups. The well-known struggles in Northern Ireland are normally seen as involving Catholic Irish on one side against the British and Protestants in power in the province. In reality, this struggle has been more complex, including ethnonationalist differences that have pitted Irish against the British, and ideological factors that have appeared over time as some dissident terrorist groups increasingly incorporated elements of Marxist-Leninist concepts and justifications. In the case of Peru and the Shining Path movement and the other dissident groups, leftist ideology has combined with a solid base in the Indian population. The Peruvian insurgents also had some links with drug producers and distributors. In neighboring Colombia, violence and terrorism has included leftist revolutionaries that have frequently operated in league with drug cartels. There was even an independent terrorist campaign against the government undertaken by one of the drug organizations. In the case of Nigeria, the conflicts have at times represented ethnic differences, but in other cases the dividing lines have been religious. In the case of problems in the oil-producing regions of the country, the conflicts have involved ideological conflicts, some related to terrorism in defense of the environment.

CASE STUDY 9.1   LEFTISTS AND INDIGENOUS POPULATIONS IN PERU

One of the most active terrorist and guerrilla organizations in Latin America in the 1980s and 1990s was the Shining Path group (Sendero Luminoso) in Peru. Abimael Guzman, a university professor at Ayacucho in the highlands of Peru, formed this organization in 1980. It had a clear leftist ideology and drew heavily upon Marxist-Leninist doctrines. Even though its ideology was leftist, it established itself in the rural areas by appealing to the discontents among the Indian population, which had traditionally been neglected by the central government. The movement thus came to represent not only objectives that were related to the ideology of the founders but also the ethnic grievances of a particular portion of the population as well. A similar movement, the Tupac Amaru Revolutionary Movement (MRTA), appeared nearby in the highlands of Peru. It was also leftist, and it drew upon Indian grievances over the continued dominance of Peruvian society by European and

Europeanized elements. The general failure of the government to provide much in the way of services or modernization to the rural area inhabited by Indians speaking local languages was present with supporters of this group as well. Further, both dissident organizations drew upon the resources available from local coca growers to help finance their campaigns against the government.

The Shining Path could appeal for support in the local Indian communities in its campaigns against the government since the rural areas had been neglected. The combination of leftist doctrine and ethnicity worked in the Peruvian context. The Indian population joined because of their traditional distaste with the government and lack of programs rather than as a result of any political commitment to a leftist ideology. The Shining Path was able to build up strength in the rural areas. Ayacucho, while not distant from Lima, is on the Amazon side of the Andes, and the region has been largely ignored by the central government. The government was weakly represented and was not very alert to this developing challenge (Barnhurst 1991: 82). The movement quickly began to build strength. The Shining Path combined guerrilla tactics, especially when battling with security forces, and terror. It first attacked local and government officials and the large landowners, who were hated by the peasants (Long 1990: 85). Local officials and clergy were assassinated as a warning against cooperating with the government. The Shining Path was so effective in the late 1980s that many candidates refused to run and officials resigned their offices in fear. Removing officials from their positions or threatening others who might take their places not only demonstrated the power of the movement but also limited the ability of the government to initiate programs that might have dealt with local grievances. Without local administrators, the ability to push through reforms was much more difficult.

The local peasant communities were also ruthlessly punished for not supporting the organization. Any local political, social, or economic groups that had any possibility of providing alternative leadership for the peasants were very quickly suppressed (Mason and Campany 1995: 161). The government security forces found it very difficult to control the areas for a long period of time, further reinforcing the need of local populations to cooperate with the dissidents if they wanted to survive. Further, the military and police in responding to the increasing attacks often resorted to repressive measures that drove more of the local population to support the dissidents (Palmer 1995: 301). The dissidents in Shining Path ultimately hoped to replicate the successes of the Chinese Communists by first controlling the countryside and eventually encircling the cities and capturing them by isolating them from the rural population (Rosenau 1994: 312). In pursuit of this goal Shining Path eventually began bombing campaigns in the cities. Specific individuals were targeted for assassination, including police and politicians. The group also sought to cause casualties among the general population to demonstrate that the government was impotent to deal with the threat that the dissidents have represented. It also wanted to increase insecurity among the social, economic, and political elite of Peru (Palmer 1992: 78). The shift to an urban campaign was an indication that the rural strategy had not been successful enough to destroy the system. The movement hoped that the urban attacks would force a military coup that would further polarize Peruvian society and increase the following of the dissidents (Hazleton and Woy-Hazleton 1988: 482). This dissident organization was clearly following the more or less classic left-wing strategy of attempting to force a more repressive government to appear in order to permit the rebels to mobilize the population against the government. The only difference from the same strategy of left-wing groups such as the Red Brigades or the Montoneros was the addition of a clearly ethnic element to the revolt against government authority in the rural areas. The movement was partially successful in that the guerrilla violence and terrorist assaults was one factor that led President Alberto Fujimoro to impose martial law and limit protections available to citizens in Peru. These harsher measures probably aided the government in dealing with the dissident groups in the country; therefore, the goal of forcing government repression to alienate the population was not successful.

The Shining Path and local drug groups were initially at odds with each other, and there was actually fighting between the traffickers and the dissidents in 1987 (Miller and Damask 1996: 125). The dissidents and drug groups, however, eventually began to cooperate. The Upper Huallaga Valley became a center of their strength. It had ideal climatic and soils for growing coca (Palmer 1992: 68). The Shining Path was willing to work with the local producers in Peru who were supplying cocaine to markets abroad (especially in the United States). The dissidents, growers, and the shippers had a common aversion to government interference in their activities. Coca production has been quite important to the peasant cultivators since it is by far the most profitable crop they can grow. In fact, coca has provided the first opportunity for many farmers to increase their standard of living (Mason and Campany 1995: 143). The Shining Path collected taxes from growers and charged fees for the small planes that carried coca paste to Colombia (Barnhurst 1991: 85). This alliance of convenience permitted Shining Path to finance arms purchases with the money received from the drug cartels. With these funds Shining Path militia units were quite well armed, and the Peruvian police and military forces were by comparison relatively under-equipped for a long time (Combs 2000: 100). While Shining Path supplied protection to the drug traffickers, it has also protected the peasants from abuse from the local drug cartels and forced higher payments to the peasants for the coca production (Mason and Campany 1995: 146).

The Shining Path lost some of its momentum when Guzman was arrested in 1992. At about the same time, most of the central leadership was captured as well. The dissidents were organized in cells and groups in the field and were largely self-sufficient, therefore, the organization was able to survive for a while in a weakened form. The existence of funding from the drug groups also meant the units in the areas of greatest strength could continue to finance themselves and to operate (Mason and Campany 1995: 166). Even so, the movement lost strength. Government forces eventually became more effective in gaining control of rural territory. Many of the dissidents accepted amnesties and peace offers, and their financial base disappeared when a fungus damaged the coca crop in one of their core areas of strength (Laqueur 1999: 187). Potential dissidents in the future, however, are all too aware of continuing corruption, discrimination, and a lack of commitment to real democracy in Peru (Zirakzadeh 2002: 89). The motivating cause for violence could again be ideological, given the previous experience, but it could also be even more directly rooted in the opposition of Indian groups to the government after decades of neglect and poor treatment.

MRTA was a more conventional Marxist group that drew upon Indian discontent. MRTA and Shining Path often operated in different regions, but they did not cooperate with each other. They even fought for control of the Upper Huallaga Valley. Like Shining Path this group formed a local alliance with drug producers and utilized financial support from the drug trade to aid in funding its activities. In 1993 many members of the group

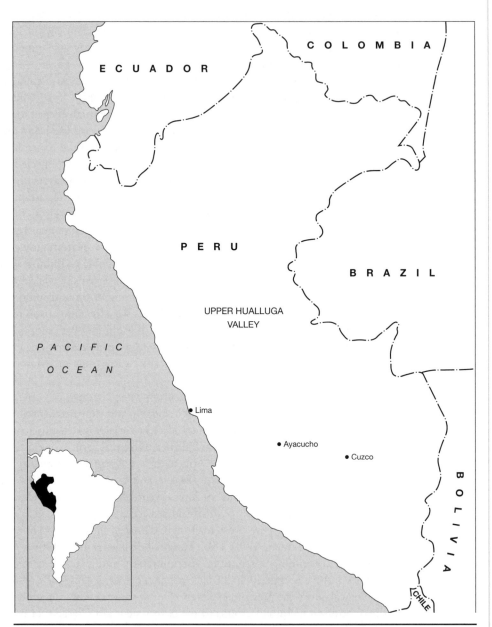

Map 4   Peru

either were captured by the government or surrendered, apparently ending the threat from this group of dissidents. The announcement of the group's demise, however, was rather premature since it was members of this organization (and not survivors of Shining Path) that seized the Japanese embassy in Lima in December of 1996 and held some of the guests hostages for many months. This was one of the most spectacular actions undertaken by any Peruvian dissident group, but it was in the nature of a last gasp gamble by a group that was in decline. The seizure ultimately failed to arouse public support or opposition to the government. When security forces attacked in a carefully controlled operation and recaptured the embassy, the crisis for the government was over.

The demise of the dissident violence in Peru has represented a victory for the government. The combination of terrorism and guerrilla insurgency, even when financed by drug money, had failed to bring down the government or even to force it into a permanent situation of authoritarian repression. The violence did result in the deaths of tens of thousands of Peruvians, many killed by Shining Path, but others killed by government forces in their efforts to deal with the violence. The death toll was significant since the two largest opposition groups lasted a little more than a decade. Other than the financing that has come from cooperation with the drug producers, there was no indication of any external support for the Shining Path movement. It was both anti-Soviet and anti-Chinese, and the group intentionally isolated itself from other movements, refusing to cooperate with the other local Marxist-Leninist and leftist groups that operated in Peru (Hazleton and Woy-Hazleton 1988: 481). MRTA did not have the same aversion to outside connections as Shining Path, but there are no indications that it received any external support beyond profits from the drug trade. The presence of some radical regime in the future in a neighboring country that favored the interests of the Indian population could stimulate dissidents inside Peru. Such a radical regime might provide a source of support for some future outbreak of violence. Even without a neighboring radical regime, however, violent opposition to the government remains possible. The needs of the Indian population are still largely unmet, and there have been some recent indications that remnants of Shining Path have again been linking up with drug traffickers and that the movement is becoming active once again in the more remote areas of rural Peru (Saavedra 2007: 184).

CASE STUDY 9.2 IRISH REPUBLICANISM

The battle of Irish dissidents seeking to unite the province of Northern Ireland or Ulster with the Republic of Ireland to the south has been an extremely long one. While the most recent round of violence began in 1969 Irish dissidents have a long history of opposing the British presence in the island. In the years after World War I, the Irish Republican Army (IRA) successfully used guerrilla attacks and terrorism to convince the British to negotiate the peaceful separation of most of Ireland from the United Kingdom. The six counties of Northern Ireland were separated from the twenty-six counties in the south that became the

Irish Free State and a dominion in the British Commonwealth. Many members of the IRA refused to accept the treaty and the loss of Ulster in the north. In fact, a civil war raged in the Irish Free State over this treaty. It was years before the violence in the south stopped. In the following years there were occasional efforts to launch attacks against the British position in the north, but they accomplished very little. They did, however, keep the spark of opposition alive (O'Day 1979: 125–6). The IRA remained organized and present in both the south and the north even though it eventually became relatively dormant.

In Northern Ireland, the Protestants were in a majority but felt that their position was insecure since there was a substantial Irish Catholic minority in Ulster and the over-whelmingly Catholic Republic just across the border. Any form of unification of the two parts of the island would result in the Protestants becoming a clear minority. One line of division between the two groups involved religion—Protestants divided from Catholics even if many of the Catholics and Protestants in question were not active churchgoers. The differences went beyond religion to include national identifications. Many of the Protestants were also descendants of Scottish settlers who had migrated to Ireland, and they clearly saw themselves as British. Catholics were more likely to consider themselves as Irish and less likely to think of themselves as British citizens. An economic element reinforced the differences between the two groups since the Protestants were in the domi-nant economic position in the province. While many Protestants were poor and faced unemployment, an even larger percentage of the Catholic population was likely to be in poor economic circumstances. The Protestants also actively discriminated against the Catholics in many ways. They dominated the political system so that government services disproportionately benefited the Protestant citizens in terms of employment opport-unities and housing (Clutterbuck 1974: 51–2). The Catholics, as a consequence, adopted a civil rights strategy to protest this treatment. The local government in Northern Ireland refused to grant the demands for greater equality and resorted to repression to deal with these demands. The failure of the government to respond to the civil rights effort gave opposition groups a chance to consider violence as an option in an effort to either support the Catholic community or to end British rule in the province. Repression led to confrontations, and the confrontations led to violence. In 1969 inter-communal violence broke out with Protestant groups attacking Catholic neighborhoods and isolated Protestant neighborhoods being attacked by Catholics. The police force and reserve police were overwhelmingly Protestant and offered relatively little real protection to the Catholic neighborhoods. The violence escalated to the point that units of the British army were sent to Ulster. Initially the Irish and Catholic population accepted the British troops sent to Northern Ireland since they offered projection against repression and discrimination by the majority.

The Official IRA had decided that violence was unlikely to work and thus chose to avoid a confrontation with the British. The unofficial IRA or Provisional IRA (hence the term Provos) was willing to continue to attempt to free Northern Ireland through the use of violence. The Provos were able to rally those who were ready for military action and attacks against the British, and most active members of the IRA sided with the Provos. The Provos felt that it was necessary to protect the Catholics from oppression by the local Protestants and then from the British troops. They undertook actions to increase confrontations with the British. IRA members would fire on police or military patrols, so that the troops entered Catholic areas in efforts to capture the IRA members. An essential part of the dissident program was to force the British to come into Catholic neighborhoods and undertake searches that alienated the local population. Usually the IRA members involved were able to escape, but the occasional IRA member who was caught or killed was a bearable price if the community rallied behind them. This increasing antagonism served the purposes of the Provos very well as more and more members of the minority were driven to support the IRA in its struggles against the majority and the British, and the British became more distrustful of the minority. The terrorist attacks by the Provos also aided in raising the morale of the Catholic community since the IRA was fighting back (O'Day 1979: 131). With time it became very difficult for members of the minority community to consider siding with the British against local heroes, and indeed it eventually became dangerous to do so.

As the violence continued, individuals in the Protestant community were targeted for assassination as warnings to broader groups in the majority community. Over time the car bombs increasingly became a favorite weapon. Sometimes the bombs were used against buildings or symbolic targets. In other cases they were left in areas where people would be in danger but warnings were given. The police were then forced to clear areas and search for bombs, and if they failed to find them, the explosions caused significant property damage. In other cases, however, cars loaded with explosives were left in shopping areas with no warning or insufficient warning being given. When they went off, there were many dead or wounded. The car bombs were usually left in Protestant neighborhoods or in shopping areas dominated by Protestant businesses. Most of the casualties were Protestants, and Protestants largely suffered the property damage. There was an associated campaign of economic disruption that at times involved the killing of business people and industrialists. This economic warfare was designed to weaken the economy, which was seen as catering to British rather than Irish interests (C. Drake 1998: 57).

The dissidents have also targeted the security forces whenever possible. They killed members of the police while they were on duty or off duty in their homes. They have launched attacks against police stations, often using car bombs to destroy the buildings and inflict casualties. The British army became targets as well. Off-duty soldiers were considered fair game. Snipers fired on patrols in urban areas. The IRA proved to be quite capable of creating intricate ambushes for British patrols, and it mined roads and set off the explosives when military vehicles approached. All of these IRA actions have been designed to put the police and the soldiers on edge, but they also served to drive a wedge between the security personnel and the minority population. Any off-duty soldier who was killed could increase the anger and anxiety of other soldiers and lead them to treat the Catholic population with suspicion and in a fashion that would further distance the security forces from the people. Creating even higher levels of distrust between the minority population and the security forces clearly worked to increase the support for the dissidents (Coogan 1993: 260–1). In addition to security personnel, informers and collaborators were targeted for death. While eliminating a particular informer removed a potential threat, the most obvious target audience was anyone else who might be tempted to inform. The dissidents have gone to great lengths to eliminate former informers, even when they have fled abroad in order to demonstrate the dangers of cooperating with state authorities. Attacks on individuals seen to be collaborating with the authorities also occurred. The IRA punishment for collaboration with the British or local authorities had a progressive scale of penalties. Punishment attacks against those suspected of collaborating with the officials have been a constant presence in Northern Ireland, and they even seem to have increased in periods when ceasefires have limited other forms of activities (Silke 1999).

The intimidation of members of the public has gone further. When many IRA suspects were in prison, the group began to target members of the prison staffs and their families in order to gain better treatment for their comrades. The staffs did modify their practices in order to keep from becoming targets, but the modifications also led to a reduction in security that benefited the IRA (Bates-Gaston 2003: 240–1). Anyone testifying in a court against the IRA or other dissident groups was subject to assassination, but the intimidation carried over even to members of juries in court proceedings. Jurors who voted to convict members of the IRA were subjected to retaliation after the trial. Needless to say, it became very difficult for the authorities to attain convictions of any IRA suspects that were arrested and charged. Without any real possibility of convictions it proved difficult to combat and restrain the IRA since the defendants would be acquitted or face a new trial because the jury could not reach a verdict. The British had to resort to the Diplock courts where IRA defendants were tried before a judge without a jury since honest jurors were at risk of death. These courts violated the basic rights of the British judicial system, but they did permit the British to at least try the defendants in a court of law. If the IRA had been using terror and violence with the intention of weakening the democratic principles of the British state, this expedient by the authorities would have been rated a success. This goal, however, was not one that was sought by the IRA and other dissidents, although it had propaganda value as an example of British repression.

The IRA also carried its campaign of violence and bombings outside of the territory of Northern Ireland. There were attacks or planned attacks on British military installations or soldiers in England, Germany, and Gibraltar. Three IRA members were actually killed by the Special Air Services (SAS) Regiment while planning an attack against a British military barracks in Gibraltar (Bell 1997a: 598–9). It is possible that the IRA chose targets in Europe because it was easier for the teams to operate there in place with less security (Warner 1994: 16). In 1979 a bomb on the boat of Lord Mountbatten killed this cousin of the Queen, his grandson, his daughter-in-law's mother, and a teenage Irish boat pilot (Bell 1997a: 450–2). The IRA also periodically undertook bombing attacks against sites in England. There were pub bombings in the mid-1970s in the London area and Birmingham as well as attacks on British military facilities in England, which were generally less well guarded than similar facilities in Northern Ireland. A Conservative member of the British parliament was assassinated, and there was the bombing of the hotel where the Conservative Party was holding its annual meeting. The IRA also mounted its remote control mortar attack against the prime minister's residence when John Major was the leader of government (Roberts 1997). Obviously, the reach of the IRA was quite extensive in terms of launching attacks against the British government in a wide variety of circumstances.

The violence from the IRA and other groups in the minority community generated counterviolence from Protestant paramilitary groups in return. A number of different organizations formed and sought to strike back with counterterrorist violence in an effort to intimidate the Catholic community or to force an end to the violence. The Protestant paramilitary groups even used terrorist attacks in the Republic of Ireland in retaliation for the IRA attacks in the north (Wilkinson 1983: 109). The Protestants could also rely upon the state for protection and action against the IRA and similar groups; thus their terrorism was basically defensive (O'Day 1979: 128). While the violence from this source has not been as extensive, it has contributed to insecurity in the province and made agreement on political solutions to the problems in the province much more difficult. There have been earlier examples of Ulster Protestants using terror attacks against Catholics to disrupt truces and negotiations (R. White 1993: 579). The increase in animosity between the two groups served the interests of the dissidents and the minority community.

While the Provisional IRA has been the key dissident group behind the violence in Northern Ireland, it has not been the only group involved, a fact that has complicated efforts directed at achieving peace. The Official IRA had taken on more of a Marxist perspective and this leftist orientation was part of the reason for the split between the Official IRA and the Provos. The efforts of the Officials to unite the working classes against the British capitalists, therefore, ran counter to the Provisional effort to mobilize the minority community. The Officials eventually focused on political work and on becoming a labor party (Dingley 2000: 453). Another group with a distinctive leftist orientation that operated at the same time as the Provos was the Irish National Liberation Army (INLA). This group was smaller but it conducted similar kinds of campaigns as the Provisional IRA, and the two groups cooperated at times. In addition to these long-standing groups, the various peace efforts between the Provisionals and the British resulted in breakaway groups from the Provos that refused to accept the idea that Northern Ireland would remain part of the United Kingdom under any circumstances. The Continuity IRA and the Real IRA were two such groups that sought to prevent any accommodation with the British. The Continuity IRA continued attacks when the Provos were beginning serious negotiations with the British to end the violence. There was hope that the attacks would derail the peace process (Gurr and Cole 2000: 154). The Real IRA has similar aims and was responsible for the bombing in Omagh in 1998 that killed 29 people and injured over 200 more. Apparently the car bomb was designed to destroy the courthouse as the symbol of British authority only after a warning was given, but confusion in the dissident ranks resulted in a late warning and the death and wounding of so many (Dingley 2000). The attack was intended to demonstrate the continuing intention of portions of the dissidents to battle the British until Ulster was reunited with the south. The IRA and the INLA both denounced this attack. The INLA even went so far as to support a ceasefire. The Real IRA eventually accepted the idea of a cease-fire in the aftermath of its miscalculation and the unexpected deaths at Omagh (Holland 1999: 222). The Real IRA, as well as the Continuity IRA, has continued its stance of opposition to negotiations that result in a solution short of reunification (Wilkinson 2000a: 77). Thus, it would appear that the danger of attacks from the hardliners would continue to be a threat in the future.

The IRA has had some important external support, although not often from other governments. Probably the most important source of support for the dissidents has been from Irish-Americans abroad. They have operated a number of organizations that channel funds to the dissidents, providing them with the financial resources to buy arms and to pay for the expenses of the groups. Noraid in the United States is one group that has collected funds for charitable purposes in Ulster that appears to have helped to finance the IRA (Roberts 1997: 584). Unlike some other groups supporting dissidents or terrorists in other regions or countries, the United States has failed to crack down on organizations with links to the IRA. The political clout of Irish-Americans sympathetic to the dissidents has been important in preventing the government from seeking to limit fundraising activities or to ban the organizations as is possible under US law. Government responses elsewhere in the world have also been relatively weak in terms of limiting fundraising amongst the Irish abroad. There has been some support among the population in the Republic to the south for the IRA, of course, but no Irish government has been supportive of the terrorist violence. Public opinion has gradually shifted toward a position of non-support for the IRA and even greater cooperation between the north and the south in dealing with the terrorist violence. The IRA has gotten occasional state support in the form of arms. Libya has at times aided the IRA in efforts to create as many difficulties for the British government as possible. While this aid pre-dated the American bombing of Libya in 1986, Qadaffi in Libya increased the shipments of arms to the IRA after the attacks as a form of retaliation for British support for the 1986 American attacks (Silke 2003b: 218). Irish dissidents have also received training in PLO camps.

The struggle in Northern Ireland has been going on for over thirty years in its latest manifestation. While there are prospects for real peace in the twenty-first century, the presence of extreme groups that have not given up on the idea of severing the tie between Ulster and the Great Britain does not bode well for future peace (Dingley 2000: 463). The north may even come to repeat the history of the south where disagreements about the degree of accommodation with the British generated violence within the ranks of the Republicans. The violence may continue because many in the IRA and other groups can argue that the violence has worked. The terrorism campaign was effective in bringing the British to the negotiating table (Alonso 2001: 142). It is unlikely that the British and moderate leaders in Northern Ireland would have been willing to negotiate with the dissidents if the decades of violence had not occurred. The hardliners in the majority community have been weakened, and much of the population of Northern Ireland is obviously weary of the violence. The attempts to disrupt the negotiations may yet succeed, and new problems could always appear, but there is at least some hope for the end to over three decades of violence.

Colombia has been a country long beset by violence, including civil wars, strikes with violence, and seizures of political power. Between 1948 and 1957 Colombia was wracked with violence that was an outgrowth of the long competition between the two major political parties in the country. Internal wars in the nineteenth century had resulted in regions where villages in Colombia were either entirely supporters of the Conservative Party or entirely supporters of the Liberal Party. In 1948 a leading Liberal leader was assassinated, sparking a round of violence between Liberals and Conservatives that continued for approximately a decade. Although the initial violence was in the cities, it spread to the countryside as security forces and Conservative paramilitary forces attacked rural areas that were Liberal Party strongholds. While figures on casualties are very imprecise, as least 200,000 people died in the ensuing violence (Walton 1984: 74, 91). The Colombian parties eventually ended the violence with an agreement that in effect led to power sharing and the alternation of their candidates in the presidency. The conflict from this period of violence, however, provided a source of discontent that the current dissidents have been able to draw upon. The violence destroyed governmental structures in many areas, giving alternative groups at least an opportunity to become more influential when they did appear (Ortiz 2002: 131). The power vacuum in the countryside was very helpful to the dissidents. Further, the period of *La Violencia* helped to prepare at least some communities to support more recent anti-government dissident groups.

In 1964 a new group of dissidents appeared. The Revolutionary Armed Forces of Colombia (FARC) was formed and began a guerrilla campaign against the government, drawing upon peasant discontent in some areas of the country and mobilizing at least some of those who had been involved in *La Violencia*. FARC has used guerrilla tactics and insurgency more than other types of violence. FARC as well as other leftist movements such as the National Liberation Army (ELN), the Popular Liberation Army (EPL), and the April 19 Movement (M-19) have utilized terrorism to further their cause. Bank robberies, kidnappings, and assaults on rich landowners and ranchers, as well as employees of large companies became common. There are significant areas of Colombia that came under the effective control of FARC or to the lesser degree the ELN. Government forces can only go into these areas at great risk. In areas that they control, the dissidents have supplied their own brand of law and order and have provided protection for peasants and others that had never been present when government forces were supposedly in control. On the other hand, FARC has also been known to kill and terrorize opponents in areas under its control (Ramirez 1997b: 432). FARC has also continued its systematic campaign of assassinations of politicians (Laqueur 1999: 214). More recently the FARC has dramatized its position in the country by kidnapping high-ranking political figures, including a presidential candidate of one of the smaller parties. Such incidents clearly illustrate the use of terrorism to demonstrate the power of the dissidents and the weaknesses of the government.

The other leftist movements have been weaker than the FARC. They have never controlled rural areas to the same extent as FARC, and they have had to rely more on terrorist attacks and less on any sustained guerrilla activities. These movements have been more urban in their activities. M-19 was able to mount some spectacular operations, including the occupation of the embassy of the Dominican Republican and the holding of fifty-seven hostages, including a number of ambassadors in 1980. The group also seized the Palace of Justice and captured hundreds of hostages in 1985, including most members of the Supreme Court. When the confrontation escalated to violence over 100 people were killed, including eleven judges of the Supreme Court (Rameriz 1997b: 430–1). After this confrontation with the security forces, support for M-19 weakened considerably. The media and propaganda advantages won by a daring action were dissipated when so many people died as a direct result of the attack. The various leftist movements that have operated in Colombia have derived some external state support. Castro's Cuba provided a positive example for the leftists and the hope that they could eventually triumph. Castro's regime supplied what support when it could to leftist guerrillas and dissidents in Venezuela and Colombia. Cuban support, however, ended long ago (Laqueur 1999: 212). It is perhaps not surprising that when the M-19 members took over the Dominican embassy in 1980 and they were granted safe passage out of the country, it was Cuba that was the chosen destination (Rameriz 1997b: 430). Even so, the Cuban aid has been relatively minor over the years, and FARC as well as the other groups has been able to mobilize support internally and to continue to operate primarily as a consequence of domestic factors.

If FARC has simply continued to be a leftist dissident movement practicing guerrilla warfare and terrorism against the government, it would have been less successful and might not have become as powerful as it is today. FARC, however, has formed a working alliance with various drug producers, who themselves have a history of practicing terrorism. Political leaders, judges, and other officials were assassinated for their efforts to attack the drug cartels. Journalists and academics who spoke out about the drug operations were killed as well (Manwaring 2002: 77) A Colombian airliner with 130 people was blown up so that informants on the plane would be eliminated (Quillen 2002: 282). The intent of this campaign of terror was to dissuade the government from active investigation and prosecution of the members of the drug cartels. Judges who were too aggressive in their investigations, for example, were murdered. More than 350 members of the judiciary were killed, including fifty judges. Not only were judicial officials or police threatened, but their families were threatened as well (Lassen 1990: 113, 116).

In the late 1980s the violence escalated as a drug cartel based in Medellin began a terrorist campaign against the government. The cartel launched this campaign to reverse a specific government policy. The Colombian government had agreed to permit the extradition of drug lords to the United States for trial and possible conviction. It hoped to avoid the domestic violence that would occur if the Colombians were tried in local courts, but Colombia still faced attacks as the cartel sought to reverse this decision (Manwaring 2002: 70). The presidential candidate of the Liberal Party was assassinated for supporting the arrangement (Jamieson 2005: 167). Car bombs went off in the streets of Bogotá, the capital, and other cities. The car bombs were designed to display to the population at large that the government was unable to protect them, and to suggest that it was the people who were suffering from the government attempts to challenge and destroy the drug cartels. The battle between the cartel and the police was a bloody one. Police officers were killed or wounded, and the police themselves frequently provided summary justice for captured members of the cartel or suspected members of the drug organizations (Thompson 1996: 63). The cartel eventually lost this confrontation, and the round of violence was effectively ended when Pablo Escobar, the leader of the largest drug group in Medellin was arrested in 1991. He escaped from prison in 1992, but was killed by police in 1993 (Thompson 1996: 55). While drug production and trafficking has continued in Colombia, there has been no other attempt by other drug cartels to actively attack the government. Other drug lords learned from the failure of this campaign and cooperated more closely with the leftists. The extradition policy, however, was changed with the new constitution approved in 1991 outlawed the extradition treaty that had sparked the violence (Jamieson 2005: 168).

With the at least partial defeat of their terrorist campaign, the cocaine producers shifted to cooperating with FARC and the ELN in certain areas. Their alliance with the leftist has proven to be more durable and profitable. The leftist areas of power were concentrated in the poorer areas of Colombia where coca could also be grown and where there were relatively few meaningful economic alternatives. The poverty also provided the social and economic background to permit the leftists to more successfully recruit support since previous governments had done little to ameliorate the problems of these areas (Laqueur 1999: 213). The dissidents and the producers also had a shared goal in terms of keeping government forces out of certain areas. The government and its security forces constituted a major threat to the economic goals of the producers and cartels as well as to the political objectives of the leftists.

Although collaboration has become the norm between producers and leftists, there have been examples of confrontation in the past. In areas that it controls, FARC has been able to increase the money that is paid to the peasants by the drug producers for the cocaine that is grown. More seriously for the alliance fighting between guerrilla forces and members of the drug cartels has occurred (Laqueur 1999: 213–14). The financing of the guerrillas by the drug cartels has been voluntary in some areas while in other areas it has constituted more of a form of protection money. The relative balance of power between the producers and the guerrillas has determined the level and type of support that has been present. In the areas that are dominated by FARC troops, the drug producers have relatively little choice in terms of paying "revolutionary taxes," even though they would probably support the guerrillas in any event. In areas where the FARC or ELN are weak, the payments are more voluntary, and one would assume relatively lower. One of the strengths of the FARC has been the financial base from drugs. The organization has been able to finance its activities from its own resources with payments from the drug cartels and revolutionary taxes in the areas it controls providing a secure base of funding. The movement has also invested in the legal economy to provide itself with a continuing flow of funds (Ortiz 2002: 137).

In recent years paramilitaries supporting the government, or at least opposed to the leftists, have appeared. In 1981 a paramilitary group known as Death to Kidnappers attempted to protect the citizens of Colombia from extortion and ransoms (Ramirez 1997a: 636). This group and later ones quickly began to attack and kill persons suspected of terrorist and criminal activities. The most active current group has been the Self Defense Forces of Colombia (AUC) that has targeted suspected leftists and their supporters, both in rural areas and in the cities. They have depopulated some rural areas by terrorizing the peasants and forcing them to flee to the cities. The government initially supported the paramilitary forces (Santina 1998/9). The paramilitary groups operating with at least tacit government support initially have reduced areas under control of the leftists. More recently the government has attempted to distance itself from these paramilitary groups given the increasing number of casualties that they have inflicted. The paramilitaries have not always been as harsh on the drug producers when they have entered a region since they seem to have been open to payments or bribes to look the other way. The money available to the drug producers has continued to permit them to buy protection from whichever groups happen to control a particular area (Manwaring 2002).

It is highly unlikely that there will be any immediate solution to the political violence in Colombia. Violence and murder has become so pervasive in Colombia that victims or their families fear reprisals and do not report crime, especially if there are armed groups—the military, guerrilla, paramilitary, or drug-related—in the area (Brauer *et al.* 2004: 447). Recent bombings in Colombian cities have indicated that terrorist violence is still possible, even though it was not clear which groups had actually set the bombs. The FARC has obviously been interested in expanding its activities to the cities. In 2002 three suspected members of the IRA were arrested. They had apparently come to Colombia to train FARC members in the building of bombs (Radu 2002: 283). Members of the Japanese Red Army have also been detected in Colombia. They had provided training that would permit the FARC to expand its operations into urban centers (Ortiz 2002: 139). The different participants in the violence in Colombia have clearly had different motives, but all that has been necessary in the short term is that the objectives of the drug producers and the leftists have not been directly contradictory. The sources of different types of terrorist violence are too diverse for easy solution and the pervasive influence of drug money in Colombia will remain. The wealth generated by the cocaine trade means that drug producers can buy protection from corrupt government officials or military officers, from the leftist guerrillas, and from the paramilitaries as needed (Manwaring 2002). The availability of the profits from the drug trade has also permitted the FARC and other dissidents to purchase arms and other supplies pretty much as needed. In the short term, any government of Colombia will be hard pressed to deal with the mixture of well-funded dissidents, private groups, and criminal elements.

CASE STUDY 9.4 NIGERIA: RELIGION AND REGION, ETHNICITY AND ENVIRONMENTALISM

Nigeria has had to deal with discontent and political violence in a variety of forms from a number of different groups since the country achieved its independence in 1959. Nigerian society is quite diverse with three major ethnic groups—the Hausa-Fulani in the north, the Yoruba in the west, and the Igbo (or Ibo) in the East—and more than 200 smaller communities. The country is also almost evenly divided between Muslims and other religions, mostly Christians (Suberu 2005: 139). There was a major civil war in the 1960s.

In addition, group hostilities between ethnic or religious groups have resulted in periodic outbursts of violence. The initial violence was primarily rooted in ethnic differences (with some religious overtones). The more recent outbreaks have involved both ethnic and religious components, and some of the violence in the oil-producing regions of the country has involved mixtures of ethnic concerns with class and environmental issues.

The first years of independence for Nigeria were stressful. The country was originally divided into three regions in a federal political system. The Northern Region was home to the Hausa-Fulani, was primarily Muslim, and had approximately half the population. The Eastern Region was dominated by the largely Christian Igbo. The Western Region's largest group was the Yoruba, who were both Muslim and Christian. During British colonial rule, the groups in the southern coastal regions had earlier and greater contact with Europeans and the colonial authorities, while the northern areas were incorporated into the colonial system later and were governed indirectly through local emirs (Muslim princes). One consequence of this different pattern of contact was that the southerners, particularly the Igbos, provided more attendees at mission schools, the personnel for the colonial bureaucracy, and members of the local middle class. Since they provided so many of the personnel, many Igbo civil servants and merchants worked in the Northern Region.

The first elections in an independent Nigeria occurred while ethnic tensions were simmering with each of the three major groups concerned about political control of the country. The elections were often violent and fraud was not uncommon. The inability of the politicians to deal with the discontents led to a military coup by junior officers in January 1966. While the coup was directed against all the leading politicians and some of the senior officers, the results of the military intervention were more deadly for those from the north. When the junior officers realized they were unprepared to actually govern the country, they turned power over to the surviving senior officer, General Ironsi, who as an Igbo. Many northerners concluded that the coup had really been a southern plot to gain control of the government. In May attacks against Igbos and other southerners in the Northern Region began to occur (Williams and Turner 1978: 144). In July there was a second coup in which General Ironsi was killed. One result of the second coup was a diminished Igbo influence in the government. Attacks on Igbos in the north, however, continued. In some cases local authorities were unable to provide protection, but in other parts of the region soldiers joined the mobs and some local political leaders encouraged the attacks. At least 10,000, and perhaps as many as 30,000, were killed while another million Igbos and southerners became refugees fleeing to the south, especially into the Eastern Region (Hatch 1970: 284; Williams and Turner 1978: 146).

After the civil war, Nigeria had a series of governments. The military continued to play a key role with military regimes often alternating with civilian ones. The three large regions in the federal system were broken down into a number of smaller states (a total of thirty-six by 1999) as various governments attempted to reduce the influence of the three large ethnic groups by creating states dominated by other smaller groups or with enough diversity so that no single ethnic group dominated the state. Despite the efforts to defuse tensions, there have been periodic outbreaks of violence between groups. The trigger for the violence has often been the movement of peoples from the Muslim north into areas populated by non-Muslims and non-Hausa-Fulani groups. While not all the internal migrations have been opposed, many have. The indigenous groups already in these border areas sought to maintain their control of the arable land and to keep out the "foreign" groups (Harnischfeger 2004: 436). The conflicts and violence between the indigenous groups and the settlers have increasingly had religious overtones. The religious elements in the conflicts became more serious when the governments of some of the largely Muslim states in the north began imposing Muslim Sharia law as the law of the land in their states. Initially this religious law only applied to Muslims, but in some cases it has been extended to non-Muslim groups as well. Further, the police or Islamic militias have enforced the Sharia provisions on non-Muslim individuals (Harnischfeger 2004: 432). The extension of the religious law to non-Muslims also provoked ethno-religious violence that left many dead and led to an exodus of southerners, mainly Christian Igbos, from the north (Suberu 2001: 5). The violence in the north led to retaliation by ethnic militias in the south (Harnischfeger 2004: 435). The violence in the north creates additional problems because the fear in areas with settlers became a concern that not only would the settler groups threaten political control by the local ethnic groups but also that alien religions could be imposed as well (Harnischfeger 2004: 444). The violence has been quite severe in some cases. In the city of Jos, ethnic confrontations "turned into a religious confrontation" and led to street battles that left 3,000 dead (Harnischfeger 2004: 446). In this case the violence led to the departure of most of the Muslim population of the city. The violence in at least some cases has resulted in examples of successful ethnic cleansing, and the continuing violence has threatened the continued viability of Nigeria.

The oil-producing region of Nigeria has provided another area where outbreaks of terrorist violence have occurred. Some of the problems that have appeared are related to the ethnic and religious differences between the north and the south since the vast majority (as much as 97 percent) of the revenues from the oil fields go to the central government for redistribution to the states (Watts 2004: 60). In fact some of the poorer northern states have relied on oil revenues for up to 99 percent of their total budgets (Suberu 2005: 147). The states with the oil fields have effectively been subsidizing other parts of the country. The local leaders in the oil-producing areas have tried to form new states in efforts to gain some control over revenues to have more of the money from the industry stay with local government, but not surprisingly, they have not been very successful. The financial consequences are probably heightened by the fact that corruption has been a problem in government circles; therefore, some of the oil funds that have gone to the national government have ended up in private hands. Disputes over the allocation of the benefits from the exploitation of natural resources have introduced a class element into the arguments.

There has been an additional set of circumstances that has been involved with terrorist attacks in the oil region. The oil drilling, the pipelines, and the pumping stations have all had negative effects on the local environment. The local inhabitants have found their agricultural lands contaminated by pollution, and local fisheries have been destroyed as well (Osaghae 2003: 57). Thus, the local residents have seen their livelihoods endangered or destroyed, but they have not received any compensation from the oil revenues. Local groups initially complained, but the government and the multinational oil companies were generally seen as being insensitive or indifferent to the adverse effects that the oil operations had (Ikelegbe 2005: 152–3). A varsity of dissident organizations appeared, and they began to more vigorously protest the damage that was occurring. They launched attacks on the property of the oil companies, including the drilling installations, and they regularly sabotaged pipelines (Olojede *et al.* 2000: 10). The government in turn responded with force and repression rather than concessions. Security forces attempted to deal with the dissidents, but often relied on reprisals against villages that were thought to be sympathetic to the dissidents (Osaghae 2003: 58). This approach has led to escalating violence between the dissidents and the security forces (Watts 2004: 70). The dissident groups have responded with more attacks and they have increasingly resorted to kidnapping foreign workers in the oil fields to protest the situation and to gain international attention for their grievances (Osaghae 2003: 69). The kidnapped workers have usually been released unharmed, but the potential for a greater escalation of violence has clearly been present.

The violence in the oil region has been somewhat successful. At one point the major firms closed down operations as a consequence of the actions and the threats of the militants (Watts 2004: 51). The government has not made any meaningful concessions to the dissidents. Part of the reasons for the government intransigence is that the oil revenues have been an important resource to prop up the ruling elites, both military and civilian over the years. The oil revenues also supply a source of funds that can be used to appease groups in society, and they are a mechanism that can be used to ameliorate some of the ethnic and religious tensions in the country. One of the reasons that the government has kept most of the revenues in a central fund is that it cannot afford to give up the advantages that come with central control. While the government has generally refused to change policies, some of the oil companies have actually modified their practices to more environmentally sound ones as a consequence of the attacks by the dissidents (Watts 2004: 63). The actions of the dissidents have hurt profits; thus, the private sector has responded as a consequence of a profit and loss calculus. In at least some circumstances such economic terrorism is more likely to be effective than political terrorism (J. Lutz and B. Lutz 2006b: 15).

The situation in Nigeria holds the potential for increasing disruption in the country. Conflicts among the Yoruba, Igbo, and Hausa-Fulani are the most threatening because they combine ethnicity, religion, and regionalism (Osaghae 2003: 62). The violence between other groups, however, also has added to the problems. These tensions may provide openings for Islamic extremists and those who hope to extend the global jihad to Nigeria. There have been extremist, anti-Western Muslim clerics preaching in the country, and the imposition of Islamic law has not helped resolve the differences between communities. The conflicts over oil revenues and ecological damages are not totally separate from these issues, and the general background of communal and ethnic tensions has influenced the setting for the conflicts. The environmental issues have clearly added an ideological element to the violence, and these environmental concerns place the dissidents at least partly in the same category as the ELF. Nigeria has faced increasing criminal violence. So far, the criminal groups do not seem to have developed any connections with the dissident terrorists in any part of the country. Some of the actions against the oil companies, however, have the trademark of extortion and the provision of protection services rather than being politically motivated (Watts 2004: 65). It is possible, therefore, that terrorism in Nigeria could become an even more complex phenomenon in the future.

SUMMARY

The above four cases and others like them indicate that insurgency and terrorist movements with long histories can indeed have complex motivations that play a role in the activities of dissidents. Of the four cases analyzed above, three had elements of ethnic or nationalist feeling involved in the violence—Irish versus British, Peruvian Indian versus European or Europeanized citizens, and the conflicts in Nigeria. The violence in Chechnya had ethnic components as well. The endemic violence in Colombia lacks any such component, and the era of great violence in Lebanon also did not involve any ethnic considerations since virtually all the combatants were Arab. Thus, ethnicity or nationalism is not necessarily a common overriding theme in long-standing campaigns of political violence such as the ones discussed in this chapter even if it was important in some cases.

Religion also failed to be a common link in all the cases. There have been no religious issues involved in the cases of Columbia and Peru. Admittedly the leftist guerrillas may have been atheistic and generally opposed to religion. They appear to have considered the Catholic Church to be one of the instruments of oppression for the elites in both of these countries, but they have not put forward another religion nor have they mobilized their supporters on any religious basis. While Catholicism is the dominant religion in these two countries, it can hardly be claimed that the government and the political elite provided a front for organized religion or that they were especially religious. Religion, as a consequence, does not appear to have been a major theme in the violence in these two countries. Liberation theology in Latin America has also meant that at least some Catholic clergy have been sympathetic to leftist dissidents or have supported them. Nor did religion play a major role in the Malayan insurgency. Religion, however, clearly was a contributing factor in the case of Northern Ireland. The family religion, at least in a cultural sense, was important in drawing the battle lines between Irish and British. Mobilization on the basis of religious ideas has been a major element in the violence that occurred in Lebanon, Nigeria, and Chechnya.

Criminal activity has become important in some dissident movements, including links with drug trafficking and other kinds of illegal criminal ventures, but again such links were not consistently present. Money from the drug trade was important in Peru. Narcoterrorism was more obvious in Colombia with both the direct attacks of the drug cartels on government officials and their alliance with the leftist dissidents in the country. Criminal groups also have contributed to the violence in Chechnya. The partnership of criminal elements with terrorists was absent in Nigeria or Northern Ireland. Drug production and export and criminal organization can provide very important sources of funding for violent dissident groups that do exist, but the presence of criminal activity cannot generate popular opposition to governments nor effectively seek broad political objectives on its own. The failure of the drug cartels in Colombia to achieve any political objectives when they operated alone is a good illustration of the limitations of criminal organizations as groups seeking political objectives. The government was ultimately able to defeat this more direct attack of narcoterrorism. Once the cartels joined with the FARC, an existing dissident group, they have become more successful in pursuing their "business" activities unimpeded by the government. Cooperation between criminal groups and terrorist organizations has been increasing, making both groups more dangerous and harder to detect, especially since they increasingly rely on networks instead of hierarchical organizations (Dishman 2005).

Ideology would appear to be a more consistent confounding element in cases of violence with complex motivations for the dissident groups and their allies, and it has been ideologies from the left rather than those of the right that have been the most relevant. Leftist doctrines combined with Indian ethnicity in Peru, and leftist ideologies were present with narcoterrorism in Colombia. The presence of Marxist-Leninist views has also become involved somewhat peripherally with the violence in Northern Ireland. Nigeria has seen some ideological elements in the terrorism in the oil fields. It would seem that on the whole leftist ideologies appear to have been a contributing factor in the long-standing complex examples of dissident uses of violence. The leftist ideology may actually serve to provide one additional rationale for the use of violence by the dissidents and may be effective in helping to portray the targets for the violence less as innocent bystanders and more as individuals involved in supporting the system. Right-wing groups did appear in Colombia as a reaction to the activities of the left, adding an additional complication in that state.

Assistance from foreign states was not a particularly important element in any of the four cases that were analyzed in depth. The violence in Nigeria seems to have occurred with little external support so far. There was limited early assistance by Cuba for some of the leftist dissidents in Colombia, but FARC was never dependent on such aid. Elsewhere in Latin America, there was little indication that Shining Path or MRTA received any outside state support. The IRA and INLA occasionally received some aid from foreign governments, especially Libya for a period. What was of much greater importance to the dissidents in Peru, Colombia, and Northern Ireland, and what permitted them to continue the struggles, was the external support from non-state actors. In the case of Peru and Colombia the key source of support was funding from drug cartels. The pervasiveness of drug money in Colombia has corrupted the political system, the leftist revolutionaries, and the right-wing vigilantes (Manwaring 2002). The armed groups operating in Colombia have become more concerned with protecting their resources in the form of drug-producing areas and less concerned about political objectives (Brauer *et al.* 2004). For the dissidents in Northern Ireland, it was Irish migrants and descendants of Irish migrants abroad who were important in channeling funds to the IRA and other groups. The funds from these sources have helped to keep the IRA active in its campaigns in the north. The Chechen groups have also benefited from the support of Chechens abroad, as well as some possible support from groups associated with Al Qaeda. While the money contributed by or extracted from drug cartels may be greater than the amount that can be raised from sympathizers abroad, it is not as secure in the long run. The dissident sympathizers living aboard may be able to supply less money, but they are also likely to be more loyal supporters and contributors. Drug cartels can always revert to bribing government officials to survive—a process that could be less expensive than paying taxes or making contributions to a dissident movement or guerrilla organization. It could also prove to be much more difficult for governments to interdict the flow of funds from such supporters than would be the case with funds coming from more organized actors such as drug cartels and foreign states. The routes for funds from the diaspora community to help their embattled compatriots will be multiple ones and highly varied.

It could be possible that dissident organizations able to mobilize support based on more than one element or characteristic might be more successful than other groups, but the success of the groups analyzed above was not particularly greater than other dissident groups considered in earlier chapters. The insurrection in Malaya failed, notwithstanding ideological and ethnic supports. In Peru, the combination of leftist ideology, Indian discontent, and drug money was insufficient to maintain the active campaigns against the government, although the drug cartels may be re-associating themselves with the remnants of Shining Path in a new alliance against the government. In Colombia FARC has been able to survive and even prosper in the territory under its control, it currently does not appear to have the resources to actually force the collapse of the government or to bring about major policy shifts. FARC may have accepted a role as a de facto regional government or alternative government in some areas, a situation not unusual in Colombia with its history of regionalism influence. In any event, FARC does not currently seem to possess the necessary resources to actually replace the government of Colombia with one more amenable to its purported ideological objectives. In Nigeria while some attacks against settlers or outsiders have failed, there have been some successes for groups that engaged in local ethnic cleansing, and the groups operating in the oil fields gained some concessions from the oil companies. The case of Northern Ireland is one where the dissidents have had some clear political successes. There have been changes in the government structures in Northern Ireland, and the Catholic community is treated more fairly and has a greater political role to play than it did twenty-five years earlier.

TERMS

April 19 Movement (M-19)	narcoterrorism
Black Widows	National Liberation Army (ELN)
Chechnya	Noraid
Continuity IRA	Abdullah Ocalan
Diplock courts	Official IRA
Pablo Escobar	Popular Liberation Army (EPL)
ethnic cleansing	Provisional IRA
Alberto Fujimoro	Real IRA
Abimael Guzman	Revolutionary Armed Forces of Colombia (FARC)
Hausa-Fulani	Self Defense Forces of Colombia (AUC)
Hizballah	Shining Path (Sendero Luminoso)
Igbo	Special Air Services (SAS) Regiment
Irish National Liberation Army (INLA)	Triple Frontier region
Irish Republican Army (IRA)	Tupac Amaru Revolutionary Movement (MRTA)
Kurdish Workers Party (PKK)	*La Violencia*
Medellin Cartel	Yoruba

FURTHER READING

Bell, J. B. (1997) *The Secret Army: The IRA*, revised 3rd edition, New Brunswick, NJ: Transaction Books.

Dishman, C. (2005) "The Leaderless Nexus: When Crime and Terror Converge," *Studies in Conflict and Terrorism*, 28, 3: 237–52.

Mason, T. D. and Campany, C. (1995) "Guerrillas, Drugs and Peasants: The Rational Peasant and the War on Drugs in Peru," *Terrorism and Political Violence*, 7, 4: 140–70.

Ortiz, R. D. (2002) "Insurgent Strategies in the Post-Cold War: The Case of the Revolutionary Armed Forces of Colombia," *Studies in Conflict and Terrorism*, 25, 2: 127–43.

Osaghae, E. E. (2003) "Explaining the Changing Patterns of Ethnic Politics in Nigeria," *Nationalism and Ethnic Politics*, 9, 3: 54–73.

CHAPTER 10

State Use of Domestic Terrorism and Repression

One issue that is frequently raised with the analysis of terrorism concerns the need to deal with state activities that qualify within the definition of such violence. The definition utilized in Chapter 2 and all the following chapters required that at least one of the actors involved in the terrorism either as a perpetrator or a target be a non-state group. Covert attacks by one state against another were thus excluded, as were actions undertaken by nations and intelligence agencies during wartime, although state support of existing terrorist groups was not excluded. Government activities that seek to generate terror against its own citizens, however, remain an important concern. The types of activities that might qualify would include the intentional use of secret police and the apparatus of the state to induce fear and compliance in a population, government complicity in the activities of death squads and other vigilante groups, and government involvement in genocide and ethnic cleansing.

It has indeed been suggested that governments do practice internal terrorism against their own citizens, and that such uses of violence logically should be included in any discussion of the prevalence of terrorism in the world. The inclusion of state violence in terrorism definitions does involve political questions and reflects the political agendas and motives of those seeking to include state actions (Sproat 1991: 20). Even so, states can and do encourage violence against domestic groups in a variety of ways, and the internal terrorism has as one goal the intimidation of the population (Raymond 2003: 71). While state practices involving the use of violence for control purposes can be included within a discussion of terrorism, it is necessary to do so with clear definitions that will provide as much clarity as possible. If terrorism by definition is restricted to non-state groups, then countries by definition cannot be considered terrorists in terms of dealing with their own citizens. The state and non-state distinction is obviously an important one, especially when used by the general public or in government pronouncements. In point of fact, at least some types of government actions or government supported actions undertaken in a domestic context can fall within a working definition of terrorism. If the state has a target audience beyond the victims and a political objective, the action could qualify as terrorism. One key for distinguishing terrorism by the state from repression is that with repression individuals in the society have a chance to know the law and thus to avoid violations that would lead to punishment (Sproat 1991: 24). The laws can be repressive but will not constitute terrorism if the citizen has an opportunity to modify his or her behavior and be immune to government action while with terrorism the danger of violence will be unavoidable for some.

GOVERNMENT INDUCED FEAR AND COMPLIANCE

It has been suggested that analysts ignore terrorism undertaken by government because this violence is often in support of Western objectives (George 1991). Social scientists, however, have long been interested in the use of violence by governments. Authoritarian and totalitarian governments that rely on the use of repression and force in controlling their populations have been widely studied. Definitions of totalitarianism have even included the use of secret police and terror as one of the necessary characteristics of this type of regime (Neumann 1968: 183). Authoritarian governments are also likely to use repressive measures for controlling their populations and extraordinary mechanisms for dealing with dissidents and other opponents. In any event, while government use of force may not have been discussed with direct reference to terrorist practices, such practices have been analyzed in great depth.

A government action can be considered terrorism when the target group is the general population and the government is attempting to influence or control the population. In order for this approach at control to be effective, the government actions will have to be relatively open in order to have the desired results with the target population. A covert termination of an opponent via poison or a traffic accident (i.e., death by natural causes) will not constitute terrorism since there is no attempt to influence an audience. Labeling the death of an opponent or dissident as being due to natural causes keeps alive the fiction that the rule of law is still in operation. In this case the death cannot cause the necessary terror since it is disguised. If the death is passed off being due to criminal action or a personal grudge, then it also cannot be considered terrorism. When the police or secret police openly come to arrest individuals for political crimes or when it is widely known that individuals have been arrested for expressing the "wrong" opinions, however, then a government is obviously attempting to cow others in the population into submission. The Gestapo in Nazi Germany was a gray presence everywhere ready to detect any trace of treason or anti-government activity. Some of the terror under Stalin in the Soviet Union had random elements involved in terms of which members of target groups were actually arrested. Group membership rather than individual activities was the basis for arrests because the secret police could not consistently identify individual suspects with reliability (Herreros 2006). The weakness of the state surveillance apparatus resulted in a less discriminating approach to potential dissidents. The arrests and trials were designed to instill terror. The NKVD (predecessor to the KGB) in Stalin's Russia came in the middle of the night to arrest people, but coming at night with the dreaded knock on the door was not to hide what was happening but to make the whole event more terrifying (Fitzpatrick 1999: 209). "Manipulation of various forms of terror and the threat of terror became the dominant characteristic of the Soviet art of government" (Henze 1996: 390). Arrests in Iraq under the regime of the Ba'ath Party and Saddam Hussein were equally obvious so that other potential opponents would be intimidated (al-Khalil 1989: 1–21). Iraqi specialists were forced to work at government biological or chemical facilities. Sometimes they would be called into work in the middle of the night, perhaps because of a special need for their services but sometimes so that the security forces could "reinforce the fact that the scientists were at the beck and call of the authorities" (Tucker 2006: 251). The persons arrested in Nazi Germany, the Soviet Union, Iraq, and elsewhere were often specific individuals who had run afoul of the authorities, but the arrests and punishments were also designed to have a deterrent effect on opposition tendencies within the rest of the population. These examples do indicate that governments as a matter of conscious policy can intend to terrorize their populations, but it is clearly a special kind of terrorism since it has the weight of the state behind it and is undertaken within some kind of legal framework, however arbitrarily the laws may be applied.

GOVERNMENT COMPLICITY IN TERRORISM BY NON-STATE GROUPS

Governments have frequently acquiesced in violent activities that have targeted certain groups in their societies because of their unpopularity with the general population. The record of governments attempting to deal with domestic violence against women has been highly mixed, and in some countries such violence is virtually ignored. Unpopular minorities—cultural, religious, racial or ethnic, or groups identified by sexual preference—may be targets for such violence and government indifference as well. Continuing attacks on women, minorities, and homosexuals are ongoing examples of terrorism that can be present in a country, especially when such attacks are largely ignored by the authorities and the public (Grosscup 2000: 83). The government may fail to prosecute the attackers even when they are caught. The end result may be that the victims are terrorized and persons in similar situations begin to fear as well, in part because they know the government will not do anything to protect them. In some cases the government could be ignoring the problem because the minorities are indeed unpopular and the attacks have been deflecting public attention from other problems in the society, but such inaction still constitutes complicity. While the government's failure to react to injustice clearly contributed to the problem and is manifestly unfair, it is at best a marginal example of terrorism, especially when the victims are selected as individuals rather than as members of a group.

Assailants, however, have clearly directed some attacks toward influencing a wider audience. As the Ottoman Empire receded, local Christians used ethnic cleansing against Muslims in the new Christian states that were formed. As many as five million died and another 5.5 million became refugees (Mann 2005: 113). The new governments either acquiesced in this violence or supported it. In Germany shortly after World War I paramilitary groups often used force against the left while the government did little to stop the violence (Brenner 2000: 60). In Poland before World War II, the government tolerated attacks on Jewish property by members of the Polish Nationalist Party. These attacks were not intended to kill the Jews who owned the property but to encourage them to migrate to Palestine (Schuddekopf 1973: 169). Similarly, in Germany before Hitler came to power, the police frequently did not interfere with attacks by the stormtroopers against leftist political activities. Further, the courts were more likely to punish Communists for violence that did occur than the Nazis (Lepsius 1978: 68). More recently, anti-Gypsy activities in Romania after the fall of communism have not been undertaken by the state, but local authorities have done virtually nothing to protect this minority or to arrest attackers

(Merkl 1995a: 101). Similarly, in Russia local and provincial authorities have supported some of the attacks against ethnic minorities that have occurred since the break up of the Soviet Union (Jackson 1999). In Sweden in 1990 the police and authorities often failed to respond when neo-Nazi groups were assaulted by the left-wing groups that have been opposed to their racist views (Bjorgo 1995a: 202). In all these cases the government or the local police gave positive signals to the groups using violence, indicating approval and acquiescence in the attacks.

Governments may participate in terrorism when they permit and even support paramilitary groups, vigilante organizations, and semi-official groups that use violence in efforts to support government policies. The government may wish to have these private groups target dissident elements in the population when government persecution may be difficult or unwise. Shortly after Hitler came to power in Germany, members of the SA and the Nazi Party were used to attack Jewish businesses in the country when a German diplomat in Paris had been killed by a German Jew to protest against Nazi anti-Semitism. The government organized the attacks, although they were supposedly a spontaneous outburst of anger by the German people, but the police did not intervene to prevent these attacks (Read and Fisher 1989). The use of the stormtroopers and the party members permitted the government to deny official responsibility abroad and to avoid the adverse publicity that would have come with official persecution. The unofficial groups that are supported by their governments have the additional advantage of being able to inflict more severe punishments, such as execution. After the attempted Communist coup in Indonesia in 1965–6, attacks that killed tens of thousands of local Chinese and known Communists were undertaken by local vigilantes, but they operated with the blessing and support of the state leaders (Cribb 2000: 184). In the Philippines, a number of Christian vigilante groups have been formed to oppose Muslim separatists. With at least the tacit support of local authorities, they have killed Muslims in retaliation for attacks by the separatists (Tan 2003: 105). Opposition by Christian militias and continued activities by these militias and Christian vigilantes have hampered efforts to achieve a compromise solution to the ongoing problems between Muslims and Christians (Tan 2007: 52–4).

The unofficial elimination of dissidents also avoids trials that can be used as a forum for propagating alternative views. Fair judicial proceedings can even become a test of strength between the government and the dissidents. Ultimately, many governments may find it useful to turn a blind eye to the activities of these groups while always being able to disavow their actions if necessary. When the private groups use the attacks to create fear in a target audience to obtain political objectives, it qualifies as terrorism, and when the state tolerates and even encourages such terrorism, it is an example of state terrorism.

One of the most deadly forms of state assisted terrorism has been the activities of death squads, especially those that have been formed by police and military personnel. These groups have operated with the knowledge of the state, and they have the advantages of targeting dissidents from information that can be gained from official files and records but without the restrictions that could be present in more open efforts to deal with government opponents. These death squads are covert, but they are not secret; they are designed not just to kill but to spread terror as well (Campbell 2000: 2, 4–5). Their activities have to be known in order to initmidate other opponents, but ultimate responsibility is not attributed to the government. In both of these cases the state has been instrumental in the formation of death squads and complicit in their activities (Campbell and Brenner 2000: xiv).

Death squads have been active in a number of countries. The Batista regime in power in Cuba in the 1950s executed suspected rebels clandestinely and left the bodies in busy areas as a warning to other dissidents (Piszkiewicz 2003: 3). The use of such groups by the government in Argentina was mentioned in the discussion of the destruction of the Montoneros and other leftist groups in that country. The terror by these death squads was so effective that friends, neighbors, public officials, lawyers, and others were unwilling to press investigations into the fate of those who disappeared for fear that they would become one of the victims (Calvert 1997: 631). Such groups in El Salvador accounted for only one-tenth of the deaths in the country, but their ability to operate with impunity from state investigations or prosecution increased the potential for their activities to instill terror in the population (Arnson 2000: 89). As noted in the previous chapter, the Colombian government tolerated the paramilitary groups that battled the FARC and other leftists. Elsewhere in Latin America the repression has often been undertaken by government forces, but sometimes the state has been assisted by less official groups. Death squads have not been just a Latin American phenomenon. They operated in South Africa when the apartheid system was in effect. Some of the groups existed within the security forces (unofficially, of course), while in other circumstances private vigilante groups operated as death squads in support of government policies. Over 1,000 deaths have been attributed to the activities of these groups between the 1969 and 1993 when the transition to a system of majority rule finally occurred (Gottschalk 2000: 232–3). The South African security forces often used former guerrillas from the African National Congress (ANC), and these former guerrillas also served in hit squads that eliminated opponents of white minority rule (Welsh 1995: 243).

BOX 10.1 DEATH SQUADS IN INDIA

Unofficial death squads and paramilitary groups have also operated in India in a number of conflicts. In Kashmir, the government adopted rather heavy-handed means of repression and tolerated beatings, torture, and rape by the security forces (Behera 2007: 422). When the government has been unwilling to use too much of such direct government violence in dealing with these threats as part of an effort to preserve its image, it has resorted to the unofficial groups (Campbell and Brenner 2000: xiii). The government actively permitted such activities in the struggle with the Sikhs in the Punjab and in dealing with guerrilla insurgents and terrorists in Kashmir. Not only were suspected terrorists and dissidents subjected to summary justice, but also individuals who protested against the deaths of suspects or otherwise opposed the harsh government practices have been killed or have disappeared without a trace. In both the Sikh area and Kashmir, the target audience has been both potential rebels and also those who might otherwise challenge the tactics of the government in dealing with these threats from separatists and religious minorities (Gossman 2000: 272–5). In the continuing struggle in Kashmir, Indian authorities have referred to the unofficial elimination of opposition members as the "Punjab" solution in reference to the employment of techniques that were first utilized against the Sikhs. Perhaps a more disturbing sign for the society has been the occurrence of similar violence by state affiliated groups against radical leftist dissidents and human rights activists in Andra Pradesh in central India (Gossman 2000: 262–3). The contagion of paramilitary violence and violation of individual civil rights may be spreading, and future Indian governments may be inclined to rely on this technique even more.

GENOCIDE AND ETHNIC CLEANSING

While death squads, vigilantes, and support for paramilitary groups have been relatively common as methods in which governments deal with dissidents, state violence has taken on more extreme forms. The most deadly type of violence directed against citizens of countries has been attempts at genocide intended to kill everyone in a particular group in the country. In the late nineteenth century and the early twentieth century there had been rare massacres of Armenians by local villagers or by the Ottoman authorities. While local authorities usually intervened, in at least some cases they did not or they did not punish the attackers (Mann 2005: 10). During World War I, however, the leaders of the Ottoman Empire decided to eliminate a large portion of the Armenian population. The Christian Armenians were seen as potential sympathizers with the Russian armies that were battling Ottoman forces on the frontier in the Caucasus region or with Western nations in general. The efforts to eliminate the Armenians involved direct executions in some cases and relied on encouraging local Turkish and Kurdish villagers to attack and kill the Armenians in other instances. Many of the deaths were a consequence of mass expulsions, deportations, and relocations of the Armenian population. The Armenians, including the elderly and children, were forced to march across arid terrain and deserts with inadequate food and water. As expected, and desired by the government officials, hundreds of thousands died in the process. When the attacks and deportations were over, almost two million Armenians had died (Fein 1979: 12–17).

The attempt of the Nazis in Germany to exterminate the Jews in Europe during the Holocaust clearly constitutes the worst example of government violence and genocide. The intent of the "Final Solution" was the death of the entire Jewish population in Europe, and by the end of World War II, the Holocaust had claimed the lives of six million Jews. There were also indications that the Nazis had intended a similar fate for other groups, such as the Gypsies (B. Lutz and J. Lutz 1995). The death camps that contained the Jews and others were clearly intended to kill the inmates. The fact that so few survived the death camps is clear evidence of the obvious intent of the Nazi government in Germany. The fact that any of the Jews in Nazi-controlled Europe survived was due to the efforts of individuals to rescue and hide Jews, the efforts of at least some of the governments of countries allied with Germany to protect their populations against Nazi collection and deportation to the death camps, and the activities of agents of some neutral countries to aid and shelter Jews when they could.

The initial assaults and persecutions against Jews by the Nazis and against Armenians by the Turks would qualify as terrorism since they seem to have been intended to overawe other members of the minority groups. The actual efforts at extermination do not constitute examples of government terrorism. The intent of the Ottoman Turks and the German Nazis and their collaborators was not to influence a target audience but to commit mass murder. To some extent both the German and Ottoman governments sought to hide the real objectives of the deportations from the intended victims to make them more compliant. Officials attempted to prevent fear from breaking out in the target populations. Eventually the intent of the governments became obvious and there were fewer pretenses involved in dealing with the persons who would be killed, but the creation of terror was not a goal of the efforts to concentrate and then to kill the Armenians and the Jews. While it is necessary to recognize the distinction between true genocide and other actions, it is even more important to recognize that the Holocaust did indeed occur, notwithstanding the Holocaust denial industry that seeks to downplay the number of Jewish victims in World War II or to claim that the Holocaust itself is a myth generated by Jewish populations in the world to gain political leverage in various countries.

Actions that are often labeled as genocide are more likely to qualify as examples of government sponsored or government supported terrorism. These actions—sometimes called ethnic cleansing—are better examples of the use of terror to achieve political objectives. Members of particular ethnic groups or religious groups will be attacked. Assaults, rapes, murders, and executions become weapons used against members of the target group. These actions, however, involve a target audience beyond the immediate victims. The real goal of the violence is to drive out members of the offending group, and the specific victims of the violence are chosen as a means of sending a message to the group. The target audience is more important than the immediate victims. The perpetrators of this type of violence, or at least the political leaders who instigate the violence, do not necessarily seek to eliminate all members of the target community. If they flee the country or the region, the political objective will have been obtained. Thus, for ethnic cleansing to work, it is important for the deaths and outrages to be communicated to the target population. Hiding the attacks from the community members would be counter-productive. It can even be in the interest of the government authorities to give extensive publicity to the events that occur, even while deploring the attacks and disavowing responsibility for the violence that has occurred. The ultimate goal of ethnic cleansing is designed to homogenize a population and to create opportunities for additional members of the dominant group to enter an area. The communal violence in India at independence between Muslims and Hindus was an implicit form of ethnic cleansing as the Muslim or Hindu majorities sought to drive the minorities out. More recently, Muslim rebels in Kashmir have practiced ethnic cleansing against Hindus in districts with Muslim majorities (Kumar 2002: 16). The goal of ethnic cleansing may be similar to the conquest in war in that some geographical area becomes available for control by a particular government or group. Conquest is no longer tolerated in the world, but actions within a state that generate violence against minorities often results in a more ambiguous response from other countries in the world community (Simons 1999: 14). An alternative to genocide or ethnic cleansing occurs when governments seek to forcibly assimilate a minority group into the dominant culture. The government may use force against educated members of the group to achieve this goal. The actions may involve the use of state supported terrorist attacks but such actions seek to eliminate a cultural identity rather than the whole group (Chalk and Jonassohn 1990: 23).

There have been other examples of efforts at ethnic cleansing. The Inquisition was a form of state supported, or at least state tolerated, terrorism directed at religious minorities (Cooley 2000: 8). The draconian laws applied by Oliver Cromwell in Ireland were an early version of ethnic cleansing. The Catholic Irish were to be expelled to the northwestern and western areas of the island. Ethnic cleansing also occurred in the early days of the independent United States when the Cherokees and other Indian tribes were forced to migrate to what is now Oklahoma through a combination of coercion state tolerated or supported vigilante attacks, and warfare (B. Lutz and J. Lutz 2007: 27–31). Relocation rather than extermination was the goal. Ethnic cleansing also has occurred in Tajikistan where some groups fled to neighboring countries to avoid persecution (Auten 1996: 203). The government of Yugoslavia (i.e., Serbia and Montenegro) in the 1990s sought to practice its own version of ethnic cleansing in Kosovo by driving out the Albanian population. The activities of government police, troops, and party militia were intended to clear the province of non-Serbs. The departure of over a million refugees to neighboring countries was an acceptable alternative for the government and the official and non-official groups attacking the Albanians. Such ethnic cleansing clearly has involved the use of terror by governments or governmental support of the use of terror by private groups,

BOX 10.2 THE UTASHE IN INDEPENDENT CROATIA (1941–5)

Ethnic cleansing and genocide have occurred in a variety of regions and time frames. In 1941 Germany and its allies invaded Yugoslavia and quickly defeated the armed forces of the country. The country was dismembered with Hungary, Germany, Italy, and Bulgaria directly acquiring territory. A German puppet state of Croatia was set up under the Croatian fascist and nationalist Utashe party. The Croatian nationalists had finally achieved their own state, and as an ally of Italy and Germany, one that included much of the territory that now constitutes most of Bosnia. There were Jewish and Gypsy minorities, and Serbs inhabited many of the areas in this new state. The government of Croatia under the leadership of Ante Pavelich practiced both genocide and ethnic cleansing. The Croatian state was a willing ally in the Nazi Holocaust, sending virtually the entire Jewish population of territory under its control to the death camps. Almost the entire pre-war population of Gypsies was exterminated as well (B. Lutz and J. Lutz 1995: 349, 353). The Utashe also attacked the Serbs who were located in its territory. While the atrocities against the Serbs were significant, there seems to have been no attempt at total extermination. Hundreds of thousands of Serbs were murdered, and many more fled from the violence and threats of violence. The Serbs who were killed were intended to be an example to force other Serbs to flee to other areas (Mann 2005: 296). These attacks constituted an early example of ethnic cleansing in the region.

paramilitary militias, or death squads. State violence can be considered terrorism when the actions of the government or its allies engages in violence that is systematic, has political objectives, is committed by the state or state proxies, is intended to generate fear and send a message to a wider audience, and is utilized against victims who are not armed at the time of the attacks (Claridge 1996: 52–3).

CASE STUDIES

The case studies considered below deal with a variety of activities that have been at the very least encouraged by governments. In some cases governments have even directly supported the violence and terror. Governments have by intention or lack of activity permitted, supported, and even organized terrorist actions, including examples of ethnic cleansing and mass murder. The first case considered deals with the use of violence and terror in the first years of the French Revolution, including the Reign of Terror, the event that ultimately supplied a name for the idea of inspiring fear to attain political goals. A second case considers the use of paramilitary groups and vigilante organizations by the government of Indonesia in East Timor in a failed attempt to eliminate opposition to continued Indonesian rule in that island. A third case deals with the use of militia of the government party and other informal groups in Zimbabwe to first dispossess white landowners of their property and then to weaken the opposition parties. The last three cases involve ethnic cleansing activities by the Serbs in Bosnia, the central government in the Sudan, and the massive loss of life in Rwanda as the Hutu population massacred members of the Tutsi group in that country.

The French Revolution was a very violent epoch in the history of that country. Mob violence played a role in the overthrow of the monarchy and the aristocracy, and the term terror was born during the Reign of Terror when the government sought out actual, suspected, and presumed enemies to eliminate before they could overthrow the state. The revolution even fed on its own as many of the first leaders of the revolt were executed. Initially, the more moderate members of the various national assemblies and legislative bodies that successively governed the country were forced out, and eventually many of the radical members were eliminated as well when the reaction to the violence set in. While much of the violence during this period was undertaken directly by the government, there were also activities by private groups that supported various factions in the government and thus constituted state support of private groups operating in conjunction with the activities of state officials.

The Reign of Terror itself was undertaken by the government to eliminate potential dissidents. The term referred to the government instilling terror in the population as a means of control as a conscious policy that originated with the radical Jacobins (Wilkinson 1975: 50). While persons who might be actively opposed to the government were eliminated, there was a target audience. Anyone thinking of conspiring against the revolution would have to deal with the threat of exposure and the likelihood of resulting execution. The revolutionary leaders were obsessed with the danger of treason and plots, especially by the nobility (Furet 1989: 147). Over 90 percent of the executions ordered by courts between the spring of 1792 and summer of 1794 were directed against individuals accused of conspiring with enemies of the revolutionary state (Tackett 2000: 692). Even successful generals in the revolutionary armies were sometimes executed because their noble birth led to suspicions that they had been disloyal or could be disloyal (Griffith 1998: Chap. 4). It is not surprising that many of the nobles who disagreed with the revolution and the new government or simply had some reservations about the new system chose to flee abroad rather than stay in the country and take a chance on a charge of disloyalty and possible death. Members of the clergy were another group that became a target for suspicion and arrests. Priests who refused to swear obedience to the new state as supreme over the church were targets as were those who were caught concealing members of the disloyal clergy or otherwise aiding them (Greer 1935: 16–17). While initially the executions were used against the nobles and presumed supporters of the old system, especially when Paris and France were threatened by armies of other European states, many individuals who were not members of the privileged classes also were executed for the flimsiest of reasons.

Once the immediate military threat ended, however, the guillotine and the executions became a method for political combat between different factions in the revolutionary government (Furet 1989: 148). Eventually, the more radical elements were able to triumph, at least temporarily. The Jacobin Clubs were among the strongest supporters of the radicals and they were generally associated with the more radical Montagnards who displaced the Girondins in the national legislature. The Clubs rallied public opinion against the moderates and at times organized demonstrations—including ones that led to violence—in their efforts to ensure that the new Republic was appropriately radical in its views. The Jacobins and other radicals also used the local Paris assemblies to achieve their goals. Riots were one mechanism used to pressure the various legislative bodies or their committees to undertake the appropriate actions (Griffith 1998: 62–3). The radicals eventually used the Parisian mobs to help them expel the more moderate Girondins from the legislature in 1793 (Rude 1959: 113). They proved to be especially adept at successfully branding all those that opposed them as being traitors and anti-revolutionary (Sydenham 1966: 166–7). The Law of Suspects permitted anyone to be detained on just the suspicion of treasonous activity (Wilkinson 1975: 51). Once the moderates had been expelled, the official executions increased tremendously as the radicals used the guillotine to intimidate groups that did not agree with them, including many former moderate members of the National Assembly. Surviving members of the Convention were so intimidated by the executions that they ceased to oppose the radicals (Parry 1976: 51). It is perhaps appropriate that when the radicals were finally displaced from their positions of power in the government, they were sent to the guillotine to share the fate that they had imposed on so many others.

While terror by the government was present in the first years of the revolution, there was also popular use of violence against individuals presumed to be enemies. The assembly utilized the presence of threats of popular violence, as well as actual violence, as one means of forcing concessions from the king and his supporters in the early days of the revolution (Rude 1959: 70–5). The general populace, and especially the sans-culottes militants, undertook violent actions on their own in many cases. The march on the Tuileries Palace to arrest the king that resulted in the massacre of most of the Swiss Guards was undertaken by the Parisians with the support of some of the representatives in the government, but not the government as such (Rude 1959: 104–5). Soon thereafter mobs murdered over a thousand persons being held in the prisons (Lucas 1994: 62). Similarly, the mob had arrested some members of the Ministry of War in 1792 when they occupied the building. There was a fear that they were aligned with the aristocracy and therefore disloyal. There were even calls for their execution, but they were more fortunate than many since they were just dismissed from their jobs (Griffith 1998: 67). Efforts to control the mob violence often failed, and the use of official executions that occurred later was another way to channel and control these popular passions (Furet 1989: 147). At one point the National Assembly even dissolved the local government in Paris, but it was forced to rescind the order due to massive popular pressure (Sydenham 1961: 117). Late in 1792 the lower middle classes began to purge local popular governing bodies of suspect individuals and began to round up suspects on their own. These actions were not part of any state repression designed to intimate opponents or to prevent treasonous activities. They were more the type of popular collective violence and executions "that enjoyed the tacit consent and support of the ruling power" (Baczko 1994: 25). These actions prompted the government to pass its own laws providing for the arrests of suspects, who came to eventually number some 300,000 persons (Sydenham 1966: 177).

The various factions also used the anger of the population and their willingness to use violence to advance themselves in the government. These attempts to gain advantages for one faction probably sped up the adoption of the official terror as opposed to street justice for suspects (Sydenham 1966: 174–8). The French Revolution was an event that was surrounded by violence in various forms. Much of the violent protest against the monarchy at the beginning of the revolution would qualify as left wing since the goals of the public and the leaders were definitely not conservative. The popular violence was also vaguely leftist in its targets. The whole revolutionary atmosphere also led to a situation in which disagreements among different groups bore the threat of eventual violence or elimination. The Montagnards did eliminate their enemies, and at least some of their enemies took up arms, especially in the outlying provinces, in protest against the radical policies in Paris. The radicals in one sense were correct in assuming that if they lost the political debate their lives would be forfeited, and indeed they were eventually executed.

CASE STUDY 10.2   PARAMILITARY MILITIAS IN EAST TIMOR

In 1975 the Portuguese pulled out of their remaining colonies around the world conceding independence to the local inhabitants. East Timor was the surviving remnant of Portuguese journeys of exploration and conquest to the Spice Islands. Parts of the island had remained Portuguese while the remainder of the island came to be governed by the Dutch and then part of the state of Indonesia when the Dutch East Indies became independent. While there had been little in the way of active opposition to Portuguese rule in East Timor, it was granted its freedom with the rest of the colonies in 1975, and the East Timorese proclaimed an independent republic. The Indonesian government claimed the territory was part of Indonesia, and a week later Indonesian troops occupied and formally annexed East Timor. The proponents of independence did not disappear, and an open rebellion occurred. For over twenty years the Indonesians remained in control, notwithstanding efforts of the East Timorese to assert their independence. Initially the new government always utilized regular security forces in their efforts to control the area, eventually the Indonesian regime came to utilize paramilitary groups and unofficial militias in its efforts to repress and intimidate the population.

After the initial occupation, a national liberation movement appeared to militarily contest control of the territory with the Indonesian forces that were present. The occupation and battle with the dissidents was often brutal, and the security forces and Indonesian military committed numerous atrocities in their battles with the guerrillas (Carey 2007: 381–3). The guerrillas were unable to defeat the Indonesian army, but the Indonesian army was unable to totally eliminate the independence groups. Over time, the Indonesian military forces became an army of occupation. The security forces were none too gentle with suspected dissidents, and torture and beatings by the security forces were not unusual. Rape also became a weapon against the indigenous population (Carey 2007: 382–3). The government also utilized other methods of disciplining potential dissidents or independence advocates, including dismissal from jobs, deportation to other provinces in the country, and loss of scholarships at universities (Salla 1994: 45). The Indonesian military and the militias also denied nationalists or suspected nationalists access to medical facilities as a weapon in their struggle to impose control and weaken support for independence (Stein and Ayotte 1999).

Indonesian rule was anything but beneficial for the original population of the area. Given the opposition of the native population, most of the government and professional posts went to Indonesians from elsewhere in the country, further antagonizing the local population. The province also suffered from poor health care and very high poverty rates. More than 100,000 migrants came to the area as part of a government plan to change the relative ethnic balance. Towards the end of the Indonesian occupation there were attacks by the East Timorese against these migrants from other parts of Indonesia. Most of these attacks were attacks on the property of the migrants, but they were clearly designed to suggest to the migrants that they should depart (Pateman 1998: 130).

While the regular military forces conducted operations in East Timor against the rebel forces and even used force against peaceful demonstrations by dissidents, paramilitary groups (ninjas) and militias were created to operate in the territory against those favoring independence. These groups, frequently trained and supported by military units, reflected the efforts of at least some within governing circles to maintain Indonesian control of the territory (K. Schulze 2001: 79). The national feeling of the East Timorese was buttressed in part by the fact that a large majority of the East Timorese was Roman Catholic, as opposed to largely Muslim Indonesia (Pateman 1998: 123). The paramilitary groups, as a consequence, targeted the Catholic clergy, who have often favored independence. Human rights activists were also targets for attacks by death squads or pro-Indonesian vigilantes (Zunes 2000: 329). These groups in conjunction with Indonesian soldiers and police in civilian clothes participated in attacks and murders in the province. Whatever was not looted was destroyed, leaving the inhabitants to attempt to survive without shelter or a means of livelihood (Traub 2000: 77–80). Many of the inhabitants of the province fled to West Timor for safety. The flight of a portion of the population to the Indonesian part of the island served the government's purpose. Support for the dissidents was weakened and the numerical advantage of the original inhabitants vis-à-vis the Indonesian migrants decreased. The government has acknowledged the presence of at least some of the violence perpetrated by the ninjas, but it claimed that the violence was either a result of conflicts between the pro-integration forces and independence groups or between different factions of the independence movement. The explanation advanced by the Indonesian government was that pro-independence groups undertook the violence to discredit the government and to gain foreign support for the idea of an independent East Timor (Claridge 1996: 60). The struggle in East Timor has been a bloody one. More than 200,000 people died, perhaps as much as one-quarter of the pre-annexation population of the country (Carey 2007: 389). The violence has often been called genocide, but neither the Indonesian government nor the militias operating with government blessings intended to eliminate the population of East Timor. The goal was assimilation rather than destruction as evidenced by the favorable treatment for those East Timorese willing to work with the Indonesians.

The efforts of the East Timorese to form their own nation were finally rewarded. A relatively impartial referendum of the population indicated that there was overwhelming support for the idea of independence, and East Timor attained independence. The final efforts by the militias and other groups supported by Indonesia to disrupt the referendum and to attempt to intimate the voters into supporting the continued association with Indonesia were unsuccessful. The decision to permit a referendum under international auspices in East Timor resulted from changing conditions within Indonesia itself when a more democratic regime replaced the military regime in power. The new government chose to accept the separation of East Timor and use its resources to deal with problems elsewhere in the country. For a long period of time the international community had accepted the incorporation of East Timor into Indonesia, but eventually, as the struggle of the East Timorese continued and the media became more aware of the occurrences in the country there was more concern for investigations and then support for the idea of independence for East Timor. International pressure did eventually play a role in forcing the Indonesian government to consider a referendum and even the possibility of independence when the atrocities committed by government forces became known (Jardine 1998: 199). The involvement of outside states coupled with the dramatic political changes in Indonesia helped the East Timorese to achieve their goal of independence.

CASE STUDY 10.3 FARM INVASIONS IN ZIMBABWE

In the early 1960s the colony of Southern Rhodesia had limited internal rule that favored the small white minority in the colony. When faced with the prospect that the British would create a political system incorporating the black African majority in 1965, the local leadership in Southern Rhodesia issued a unilateral declaration of independence, establishing a political system where the white minority continued to rule the new country of Rhodesia. The British opposed the unilateral declaration of independence and refused to recognize the new government. Economic sanctions were eventually imposed on the country. In 1971 a guerrilla movement appeared to contest for control of the country with the minority government. After eight years of guerrilla warfare the minority government conceded defeat and agreed to a transition to rule by the majority, resulting in the creation of a new political system. The new country then came to be known as Zimbabwe. Initially politics in Zimbabwe was a contest between the Zimbabwean African National Union-Popular Front (ZANU-PF) of Robert Mugabe and the Zimbabwean African Peoples Union (ZAPU). ZANU and Mugabe had greater popular support and triumphed in the electoral arena. Slowly but surely, however, the government began to place greater and greater restrictions on the opposition until Zimbabwe became a one party state and ZAPU was eliminated from the political scene and its leaders went into exile. Before the 1985 elections many elected officials and members of the opposition parties simply disappeared (Meredith 2002: 71). Even when many more states were adopting democracy in the late 1980s and early 1990s, Mugabe maintained one party rule under his leadership

While the one party state was being created, there was a related campaign directed against white settler farms. This campaign provides an example of government support for non-state actors that have practiced terrorism. The key agricultural sector for Zimbabwe consisted of the farms owned by whites; the farms were among the most productive in the country and provided both food surpluses for the local population and crops for export. Given the output from these farms, the ZANU government initially made no attempt to seize all the farms of the settler population since such seizures could have resulted in productivity declines. Great Britain funded farm acquisitions for a period, but such support ended because of corruption in the program (Taylor and Williams 2002: 550). There was some agitation by ZANU supporters and others in Zimbabwe to redistribute the land from these farms, in part because of a general land shortage in the country and in part because the white farmers had generally supported the white minority government during the guerrilla struggle. The white farm owners also became supporters of opposition parties instead of ZANU, providing the government with another grievance with them. While the government did not officially favor extensive land reform or expropriation, agitation by the ZANU militants continued. Part of the reason for the increasing levels of dissatisfaction by the veterans was their high level of unemployment and the fact that a government compensation fund had ceased making payments to them (Meredith 2002: 83, 133–4). Eventually these militants, especially the former guerrilla fighters, began to occupy the farms of the white settlers as part of a campaign to drive them out.

The farm occupations involved physical force and violence. If the owners of the lands resisted, there was damage to their property and even assaults. Some of the owners were killed while attempting to defend their farms from the unauthorized takeovers. The use of force by the owners inevitably led to the use of force by the militants who were attempting to take over the property. While the state did not officially back the militants, Mugabe's government was very tolerant of the land occupiers, and there was no effective protection offered to the farmers. Police were ordered not to enforce injunctions from the courts against the farm occupations (Rotberg 2000: 50). There were virtually no arrests of the persons who attempted to seize the farms, even in cases where violence was involved. At times it was the farmers who would be arrested and charged for using violence against the militants. The government did not accept the use of violence by the farmers, even in self-defense.

The inaction of the government was vital for this campaign of land occupations. Despite the protests of the government, it is clear that there has been secret support for the ZANU militants. To some extent it is possible that Mugabe could not afford to alienate the militants in his own party given his declining popular support. While the governing party and the veterans shared many objectives, there were differences as well. Mugabe could not automatically count on their support (McGregor 2002: 10). It is doubtful that he would have won a fair presidential election in 2002, and the absence of support within his own party could even have meant his replacement by a leader more willing to cater to the desires of the militants. Mugabe's weak political position coupled with white farmer support for the opposition may indeed explain his willingness to overlook the illegal occupations and the attacks. Of course, these policies were popular in many parts of Zimbabwe, and relatively few Zimbabweans were likely to feel much sympathy for the white landowners, even if they disapproved of the methods that were being used. While Mugabe may not have initially controlled the activities of the veterans, he was able to harness the violence and turn it to his own purposes (Hope 2003: 268–9). The government, of course, could have accomplished the same goals by an official policy of land reform and redistribution, even outright expropriation of the land held by the white owners, but such an official policy would have raised difficulties abroad with foreign countries whose aid or support Mugabe needed or desired. The unofficial nature of the farm invasions permitted the government to separate itself from the actions of the people while still benefiting from the popularity that the actions generated in at least parts of the population of Zimbabwe. More recently the government of Mugabe has felt itself strong enough to use land reform programs to take most of the remaining white farms for redistribution without compensation (Taylor and Williams 2002: 550). Virtually all the farms have passed out of white hands, even though the change in ownership has reduced the resources available to the government because of lower tax revenues and foreign currency earnings. In the short term, however, the government gained politically.

The campaign of farm invasions was in many ways a prelude to the resumption of extralegal violence against opposition parties. At the end of the 1990s opposition parties were permitted to form and present candidates for elections, but the government used both legal and illegal mechanisms to prevent these parties from having any realistic opportunity of winning. Opposition party gatherings were attacked, and the police provided no protection. Members of opposing parties were arrested and otherwise harassed. In the legislative elections of 2000 supporters of the opposition were beaten and several dozen killed while veterans of the independence struggle intimidated voters likely to favor the opposition. With increasing regularity members of the opposition were assaulted, killed, or simply disappeared (Meredith 2002: 177–9). The government also ordered hospitals and clinics to refuse treatment for supporters of the other parties (Rotberg 2000: 48). In 2002 there was a presidential election in which all of these types of tactics were again used by the veterans and militia, reinforced by other groups that favored Mugabe's reelection (McGregor 2002: 36–7). By this time the forces available to support Mugabe included not only the regular police and the security forces, but also a youth militia whose principle job was "to terrify people" (Hope 2003: 8). The outcome of the election, of course, was never in doubt. Mugabe was guaranteed a victory through rampant intimidation, manipulation of voting records, and rigging the final vote count.

CASE STUDY 10.4   ETHNIC CLEANSING IN BOSNIA AND HERZEGOVINA

The break up of Yugoslavia led to violence in many forms. The armed forces available to Croatia when it began its efforts to secede from Yugoslavia had to fight portions of the Yugoslav army. Later, when the Yugoslav army withdrew, parts of Croatia were held by separatist elements from among the local Serbian population for a significant period of time. The problems faced first by the Albanians in Kosovo and then the Serbs in that province have already been discussed in a previous case study in an earlier chapter. In addition, communal violence became the norm for many parts of Bosnia and Herzegovina as that new country sought to establish a government for itself and to gain control of its own territory (see Map 3). Many of the communal divisions that had undermined the unity of Yugoslavia were also present within Bosnia. Like Croatia, it faced intervention from what remained of the Yugoslav state (Serbia and Montenegro), and there was violence from Serbian separatist groups seeking to change their status within the state or to attach portions of Bosnia to what remained of Yugoslavia. Even democratization within Bosnia increased the level of confrontation since elections gave each communal group an opportunity to accurately gauge their share of support in the country. Further, the elections also provided an easy and relatively cost-free method for individuals to express their communal identification (Slack and Doyon 2001: 143). The murders and other violent actions undertaken by paramilitary groups to terrorize different portions of the population of Bosnia came to be termed ethnic cleansing, especially in areas where Serbs were present in large numbers as they sought to drive out Muslim and Croat populations.

Bosnia is the most heterogeneous of the successor states to the old unified Yugoslavia. The three largest groups in the country have been the Serbs, the Muslim Bosnians, and the Croats. All three groups speak Serbo-Croatian as a language, but their community identification is still distinct. The Croats, the smallest of the three groups, generally have an affiliation with the Roman Catholic Church and have looked to the west. The Serbs were originally the largest identifiable group in the country, but by the 1990s had come to be the second largest community. Their identification has basically been with the Greek Orthodox Church, and they have identified with their fellow Serbs in Serbia (the historic kingdom, the core of the Yugoslav monarchy, the republic in Communist Yugoslavia, and Serbia as the core of the current Yugoslavia). The Bosnian Muslims have become a self-identified communal group that has come to be the single largest community in the country. The Bosnian Muslims are the descendants of Catholic and Orthodox Serbs, as well as members of more unorthodox Christian sects, who converted when the area became part of the Ottoman Empire centuries ago. Thus, at independence the country had three distinct groups, with Muslim Bosnians being the most numerous, the Orthodox Serbs nearly as large, and a much smaller Catholic Croat population. The differences among the groups were religious in large measure rather than ethnic. The reaction of local Serbs to the Bosnian declaration of independence reflected their concern with their position as the second largest group in the country and one with a declining percentage of the population. As the second largest community the Serbs feared that they would face reduced employment opportunities and other disadvantages. The areas where the Serbian portion of the population had declined the most, thus endangering continued political control by the Serbs, were the areas where violence involving Serbian paramilitaries was to be the greatest (Slack and Doyon 2001). Both the Croats and Serbs in Bosnia could look to neighboring states (Croatia and the remainder of Yugoslavia respectively) where their community was a majority and which they might hope to join. The political leaders in both Croatia and Serbia also were prepared to incorporate Bosnian territory into their states if the opportunity presented itself (Mulaj 2005: 8). The situation of the Muslims differed from the other two groups, however, in that there was no neighboring state with which the Bosnian Muslims could hope to affiliate.

The preferred choice of many of the Serbs was incorporation into what remained of Yugoslavia. Local Serb paramilitary groups also wanted to capture enough territory to create secure land links with Serbia and to link areas in Croatia occupied by local Serbian groups with Serbia as well (Mulaj 2005: 12). The second choice was some form of greater autonomy within the Bosnian state for different areas organized on the basis of the predominant community in an area (Serb, Croat, or Muslim). Local governments would be dominated by the communal groups and would have a great deal of local power. The central government would be relatively weak and would have little opportunity to intervene in local affairs. Many plans were put forward incorporating this idea of local autonomy in one form or another. The dispersion of the population in Bosnia was such that the Serbs and the Croats tended to be concentrated in certain parts of the country, especially in the more rural locales. The Bosnian Muslims, on the other hand, were more concentrated in urban areas throughout the country. The fact that cities often had substantial Muslim populations made them special targets for Serbian military and paramilitary attacks (Simmons 2001). All of the decentralization plans put the largest communal group, the Muslims, at a disadvantage, but the presence of large numbers of Muslims in many areas of the country also meant that the Serbs (and the Croats) could not be absolutely sure of dominating their respective areas. The solution that was hit upon by the local Serbian political and military leaders was the policy of ethnic cleansing.

The ideas behind the policy of ethnic cleansing was to drive the Muslim populations, and in some cases Croats, out of particular areas and create relatively homogeneous communities. The departure of the Muslims increased the possibility that Serbs would then dominate these areas, and they would be able to detach the areas and incorporate them into Serbia. In these efforts the government of what remained of the Yugoslav state provided important assistance to the Bosnian Serbs, including arms and military personnel (Ron 2000: 286). In order to accomplish this goal, the Serbian militias in Bosnia supported by volunteers from rump Yugoslavia (who managed to volunteer with the equipment that was issued by the Yugoslav army) attacked areas where Bosnian Muslims were concentrated. Cities or the parts of cities with Muslim populations were shelled with tanks and heavy artillery and subjected to constant sniper fire. There has even been evidence that the shellings and sniper attacks intentionally targeted children as a means of increasing the terror value of the violence (Taylor and Horgan 2000: 87). Often escape routes were left open so that refugees could flee the places under attack, ultimately with many of them becoming concentrated in Sarajevo. Usually the Serb militias did not interfere with columns of Muslim refugees fleeing their homes for the presumed safety of Sarajevo or other cities where there was a UN presence since the departure of the Muslims was indeed the desired goal. The military equipment available to the central government of Bosnia was clearly incapable of dealing with these kinds of attacks, and local armed Muslim groups could not begin to match the firepower available to the Serb paramilitary and militia units.

The fighting in many parts of the country created many refugees. Serbs, Croats, and Muslims all used force to expel members of the other groups from territories that they controlled. Sometimes the expulsions were accomplished through the use of military units, but on other occasions the authorities permitted local vigilantes or criminal groups to force out members of the other groups. The homes and property of the expelled populations were then used to house and support refugees from other parts of Bosnia (Pavkovic 2000:

167). Many of the refugees had no desire to return to their original homes, and for the others returning was not an option. Local majorities have only tolerated the return of refugees from the other communities when the returnees are older and have no children, thus constituting no demographic threat to local control (Macgregor 2001: 96).

While more conventional military attacks were successful in some areas, the ethnic cleansing took on a more frightening form in some cases. Especially in rural areas, Serb militias would appear. Young men and boys (those of fighting age) were collected and marched off, usually never to be seen again. Other Muslims would be concentrated in makeshift camps and subjected to a variety of indignities. In some areas the Serb militias used mass rape as a method of achieving their political objectives. The violation of Muslim women was designed to humiliate them and their families and attach a stigma to the offspring. The threat of rape was intended to terrorize any Muslims who were considering remaining in areas dominated by the Serbs (Gavin 2001: 41). The vicious attacks of this type were designed not only to affect the immediate victims but a much wider target audience as well. The goal was to drive the Muslims from the area, and terror in different forms was the chosen weapon (Mulaj 2005: 14). It was not essential to kill all the Muslim men or rape the Muslim women. Selected but widespread atrocities would cause most of the Muslim population to flee on their own.

This example of ethnic cleansing is included in this chapter as government supported terrorization of a population because the Serb areas of Bosnia were in effect governed by local politicians supported by a foreign state in the form of what remained of Yugoslavia. While at some level the Serbian militias could be considered dissidents seeking freedom from the central government in Sarajevo, the conflict with the central government also had aspects of a civil war, and in this civil war the politicians associated with the militias were governing portions of the country. The Serbian paramilitary groups clearly saw themselves as members of a broader Serbian nation and regarded their actions as efforts to eliminate internal enemies (Ron 2000: 308). The Serbian political leaders in Bosnia and Yugoslavia never publicly called for ethnic cleansing as such, but they managed to indicate their support for the activities of the militias. The murders, shellings, and assaults—including the rapes—were tolerated and supported by the local Serbian politicians in Bosnia and the Yugoslavian government in Belgrade. The Bosnian Muslims were victims of governmentally supported vigilante and paramilitary operations.

The ethnic cleansing activities by the Serbs directed against the Muslims finally ended when external military forces by the United States and other NATO countries were brought into play, but not before hundreds of thousands had died in the violence and much of the rest of the population had been terrorized in some fashion. Eventually a relatively decentralized form of government was created with some areas controlled by the Croat–Muslim groups and other areas under Serb domination. The Serbs eventually came to control 49 percent of Bosnian territory compared to the Croats and Muslims (Pavkovic 2000: 169). The extent of the territorial control was disproportionate to the Serbian share of the population but it reflected the territory that the Serb groups had come to control by the time of the fighting ended. In effect the ethnic cleansing activities of the local Serbs and their external supporters had been successful in permitting political domination of more territory.

CASE STUDY 10.5   ETHNIC CLEANSING IN THE SUDAN

The Sudan has a history of state tolerated or supported terrorism against groups of its own citizens. The resort to terrorism by actors linked with the government reflects in part the cultural heterogeneity of the country. There are over 50 different ethnic groups and at least 114 different languages (Mann 2005: 429). The Sudanese central government has attempted to control different ethnic groups in the country. The inhabitants of the Nubian region were an early target. The government attempted to assimilate the Nubians into the dominant Islamic culture. Many Nubians have been relocated from their homeland and government supported militias were used to attack those that remained (O'Ballance 2000: 174). The actions were generally successful, and the relative success of this campaign may have encouraged various governments in the Sudan to make similar attempts elsewhere. The northern two-thirds of the country is culturally Arab and the population is overwhelmingly Islamic. The southern third of the country contains non-Arab and non-Muslim groups. The southerners are either Christians or followers of a variety of animist religions, and they are ethnically related to a variety of black sub-Saharan African ethnic groups. Since the Sudan attained independence in 1956 there has been a continuing struggle by the north to control the south. The south has sought greater autonomy and even independence, in part because southerners have always seen the government in Khartoum as only working for the northern part of the country (Soeters 2005: 103). During most of the years of independence the south has been in open rebellion. The forces of the central governments were never able to defeat the insurgents and completely control the region. The stakes of the conflict between the two regions increased when oil was discovered in fields that were partially in the south and partially in the north. Control of the southern region now had increased economic implications for the central government. More recently problems have appeared in Darfur in the western part of the country (see Map 5). The central government has supported ethnic cleansing and terrorist attacks against what it sees as threatening groups in the region.

The long-running civil war between the north and the south represented both ethnic and religious differences between the two regions. One important issue dividing the two sides was the role of Islamic law for the country. Northerners frequently proposed that Sharia law based in Islam should become the law of the land. Southerners regularly opposed such an idea. The Islamist strain in the government increased after a coup in 1989 that brought the National Islamic Front to power. Dr Hassan al-Turabi, the influential power in the government and leader of Islamist groups, successfully pushed for incorporating the Sharia into the national legal system for the whole country and for making Islam a larger component of government policies (Ousman 2004: 91–7). The imposition of the Sharia was important for the south because it represented a clear effort to force the entire country to assimilate into the dominant culture. Truces and agreements on power sharing between the two regions punctuated the long civil war, but none of them proved to be permanent. The war never had a clear winner. The army was always able to control the major towns, and during the dry season it was able to take over much of the countryside through the use of air power and armored units with significantly greater firepower than anything the

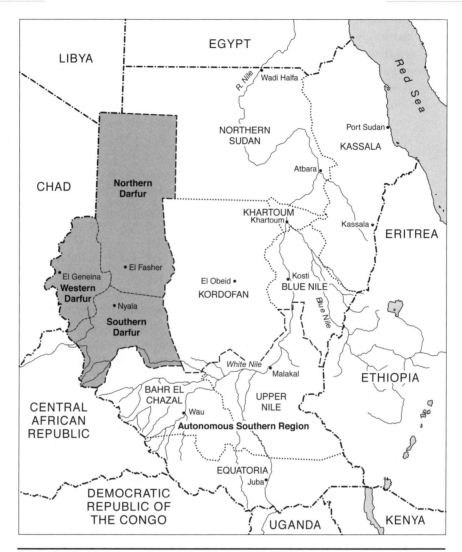

Map 5   The Sudan

rebels had. During the rainy season, however, the rebels regained control of much of the countryside and encircled the major towns, but they could never capture them. The southern dissidents had a strong popular base and could mobilize between 60,000 and 100,000 men for the conflict (Wilkinson 2006: 13). The fact that neither side could win the armed struggle increased the costs in human lives. More than 1.5 million died as a consequence of the violence (Tan 2006: 216). The inability of the regular army to defeat the rebellion eventually led the government to authorize the terrorism by northern militias against the south. These militias raided southern villages. They usually killed the adult males, stole the cattle, and carried off women and children as slaves (Mann 2005: 429).

The government not only tolerated these raids, but it also encouraged them. It was one way to weaken the resolve of the rebels and those that were supporting them by terrorizing the southern population. Apparently the government felt that if it could increase the costs of popular support for the insurgents, the dissidents would lose support and eventually either be defeated or brought to the bargaining table.

The discovery of the oil complicated the struggle. The possibility of increased revenues made independence or autonomy for the south more costly since at least some portion of the financial benefits of the oil would belong to the region. The availability of the oil and resulting revenues, moreover, increased the repressive capacity of the government (O'Ballance 2000: 205). The rebels recognized the importance of the oil fields and also realized that it presented an additional target. The southern dissidents attacked the oil operations and pipelines in an effort to deprive the government of this resource. While the attacks were troublesome, the government forces were able to keep the oil flowing (Glickman 2000). Somewhat surprisingly, the oil discoveries may ultimately have facilitated an arrangement between the north and the south that could last because both sides could now see benefits from an end to the fighting and the sharing of oil revenues. The two sides have agreed to a new power-sharing arrangement that has outlasted most of the previous ones. John Garang, the southern leader who was instrumental in the latest arrangement, died in airplane crash in 2006; thus, it is possible that new southern leaders could at some point in the future again result to violence, especially in the face of policies that fail to recognize the religious and ethnic differences between the two regions.

The central government has more recently been focused on repressing groups in Darfur that are opposed to the government or its policies. The agreement to grant autonomy to the southern region encouraged those who desired a similar status for Darfur (Howard-Hassmann 2005: 498). Faced with unrest, the central government first attempted to control the situation with security forces and the military, but the government forces were unable to gain effective control of the region. The government then began to use local allies in the struggle. The government took advantage of local ethnic and regional tensions between the herding tribes have viewed themselves as "Arab" while the farming communities that they have targeted have been seen as "African" (Howard-Hassmann 2005: 497). The government began to use local militias of the herding groups. For the militias the struggle is basically one over local resources. The cattle herders were competing with the local farmers and agriculturalists over water and land (Mann 2005: 429). The janjaweed militias attacked the local inhabitants killing and using rape to drive out those opposed to the government, and more than a million refugees have fled across the border into Chad. The militias have been willing collaborators in the ethnic cleansing. The government has suggested at times, like many governments relying on terrorism against their own citizens, that the militias are operating beyond official control and that the violence is due to local differences. These suggestions are not especially plausible since the militias have been supported at times by government air attacks.

The casualties from the campaign have left tens of thousands dead. The overall casualties are harder to calculate. While many have died as a result of direct violence, others have died as a consequence of being deprived of food or being forced to flee with no means of sustaining themselves. Those who have reached the refugee camps in Chad are often in poor health and susceptible to a variety of diseases. Those in camps in the Sudan face the danger of new attacks. The peacekeeping forces in the area are far too few to have any chance of offering adequate protection to the target population. While the actions of the government have been horrendous in their effects, the activities represent violent ethnic cleansing rather than genocide. The government and their local allies have been willing to see the opposing groups depart. The threat to the surviving inhabitants in the region is a continuing one. The government has limited foreign involvement in Darfur, in part because the status quo is working to support government policies to control the region. Perhaps one major concern for the government is that there could be another outbreak of dissident violence in the south that would take advantage of the unrest in Darfur and stretch government resources to the breaking point.

CASE STUDY 10.6   GENOCIDE IN RWANDA

The slaughter of members of the Tutsi (Watutsi) group in Rwanda by some portions of the majority Hutu (Bahutu) population constitutes the case of government supported or tolerated violence in recent times that most clearly could be considered genocide. The loss of life among the targeted group was quite significant, and the goal of the attackers was to rid the society of the minority that for centuries had formed a ruling class in the region. In this case the extremists were relatively successful in their goal. The relative isolation of Rwanda from the rest of the world meant that the violence was ignored in much of the rest of the world, much as was the case for the situation in East Timor, until it was too late for hundreds of thousands of victims. Both Rwanda and East Timor are small territories that are not in the public eye, in part because the Western media is normally not well represented in countries and places such as these.

Rwanda and neighboring Burundi are among the most densely populated areas in East Africa. The present territory generally corresponds to two indigenous kingdoms that were present when European explorers arrived in the area. Initially, these two kingdoms became part of German East Africa, and they then passed to Belgian rule after World War I. The Belgian spoils of war (or spoils of victory) were actually quite valuable since they provided an important manpower source that could be utilized, not only locally but in the much larger, neighboring Belgian Congo. By the time independence came to this part of Africa in the early 1960s, the populations had grown considerably due to Western medicine and better health care. What had been an initial advantage for the Belgians had now become a liability since the new states of Rwanda and Burundi were among the most densely populated in Africa and there was great pressure for access to farmland.

The Hutu had been the original inhabitants of the region, and they were basically farmers. The Tutsi arrived in the region later as invaders. Their weapons and organization permitted them to assume the role of a ruling aristocracy in the area, and eventually two kingdoms under Tutsi royal families developed. In the two kingdoms the Tutsi, who comprised approximately one-sixth of the population, became the ruling elite (Khan 2000: 3). The Hutu were co-opted to serve the Tutsi as herders and in other menial positions. Thus, the original society in the two kingdoms was stratified along ethnic lines, and the Germans and the Belgians did little to change the situation, preferring to work within the existing hierarchy when they governed the area. The reliance on traditional hierarchies meant that the Tutsi were relatively privileged. When the territories became independent as Rwanda and Burundi, the colonial administration considered establishing a hereditary monarchy for both states. Hutu politicians in Rwanda quickly eliminated any possibility of a monarchy in Rwanda, but Burundi actually did become a kingdom for a few years after independence.

Although both Burundi and Rwanda suffered from various kinds of violence between Hutus and Tutsis, they went in opposite directions with independence. The Tutsis continued to politically dominate Burundi, and a failed coup attempt in 1972, largely by Hutu officers, led to retaliation against the Hutu by the government. As many as 80,000 to 100,000 Hutu were killed in the massacres that followed, including virtually all the educated members of the Hutu majority (Shalom 2001: 45). Periodic outbursts of violence directed against the Hutu in Burundi by government security forces or Tutsi paramilitary groups have continued to occur, resulting in at least 300,000 deaths from the government violence (Cilliers 2003: 97). In Rwanda, on the other hand, the Hutu ruling groups discriminated against the Tutsi and limited their role in the political system. Many Tutsi fled the country, becoming refugees. The departure of the refugees had a positive benefit for the government and many landless Hutu since scarce land was now available for redistribution in this densely populated country (Mamdani 2001: 201). Some of these refugees eventually mounted raids into Rwanda seeking to overthrow the government. For almost thirty years the Rwandan government was able to deal with the incursions without too much difficulty, but each raid would then usually lead to violence against the remaining Tutsi (Khan 2000: 4). While more Tutsi then left Rwanda, becoming refugees or residents in neighboring countries, substantial numbers of Tutsi still remained in Rwanda. Thus, in 1990 the Tutsi were a minority governing in Burundi and a minority in Rwanda that was governed by the Hutu majority, who were not a monolithic group by any means.

In 1990 yet another invasion force of Tutsi entered the area and by 1993 had achieved some significant successes against the Rwandan armed forces, leading to increased tensions between the Hutus and Tutsis. As troops of the regular army suffered losses in the civil war with the rebels, political parties and other groups formed militias and self-defense units. These militias took on paramilitary functions and proliferated in Rwanda, providing troops that could be used in a variety of ways when the political system was in turmoil (Mamdani 2001: 206–7). The government utilized death squads, and massacres of Tutsis by militia groups such as Interahamwe and the Impuza Mugambi that were supported by at least some extreme members of the government (Langford 2005: 12). At this stage, the numbers of Tutsi deaths in these cases were relatively few, but the fact that the government tolerated terrorism was a symptom of what was to come. In addition, these groups and others had

Map 6   East Africa

already provoked confrontations with members of other parties and they had murdered members of opposition parties (Scherrer 2002: 107). The government of Rwanda with pressure from outside mediators agreed to a negotiated power-sharing arrangement with the rebels. Some elements within the governing elite, however, were unwilling to share power and risk the loss of influence that would occur. When it appeared that the government was giving in to the rebels, extremists shot down the president's plane in 1994 and took over the government. The extremists in the government gained support from the Hutus opposed to the Tutsi insurgents, including those who feared the loss of their farms or other possessions if the Tutsi were permitted to regain power (Mamdani 2001: 190–1).

The new interim government under control of the extremists began attacks against the Tutsis and others. The attackers included some elements of the armed forces and police, but the militias were dominant. The initial targets included the Tutsi political elite and leaders as well as moderate Hutus or members of the opposition parties (Khan 2000: 17). The militias then began to kill Tutsis wherever they could find them. Hutus who had fled from the government violence in Burundi frequently joined the militias in these attacks (Howard-Hassmann 2005: 493). As the genocide got underway, individuals caught alone had virtually no chance of survival. Groups of Tutsi who banded together to defend themselves fared better until soldiers or police used their weapons to give the Hutu mobs the edge when attacking buildings sheltering Tutsis. The attacks involved great savagery, and neither the elderly, women, nor children were spared. Many of the victims were tortured before they were killed or allowed to die. Within the span of less than four months the majority of the Tutsi population of Rwanda had been slaughtered. While local Hutus instigated some of the violence, the impetus for the larger scale massacres came from the interim government (Mamdani 2001: 194). Individual Hutus who refused to join in the violence also became targets for the extremists. Other Hutus were killed for attempting to protect Tutsi neighbors or refugees. Officials who refused to go along with the genocidal attacks were killed in order to intimidate other government personnel into cooperating (Scherrer 2002: 110). Anyone who did not participate in the killing faced the real possibility that he or she (and their families) would be killed. While some members of the clergy supported the genocidal attacks, other clergy were opposed, and many members of the clergy were among the casualties (Mamdani 2001: 219, 226). Not all Hutu, of course, participated in the massacres, but they lacked the means to prevent the massacres that occurred.

The killing eventually stopped when the rebel forces representing the Tutsi refugees were able to advance on the capital and defeat the troops that remained loyal to the government. While the government could organize massacres of civilians, it proved incapable of directing the organized military forces that it had available to defeat the rebels. The participation of the Rwandan armed forces in the massacres and violence in the areas that the government controlled probably weakened the ability of the government to fight the rebels since troops were diverted from the battles. Had the rebels not been victorious in driving the government from power, it is unlikely that any of the perpetrators would ever had been subjected to trial for their crimes (Snyder 2001: 446). Foreign peacekeeping forces also arrived on the scene, but by the time the rebels and foreign troops had arrived, the damage had been done and the extremists had achieved their goal of annihilation. Leaders of the slaughter of the Tutsis and many militia members fled from Rwanda to refugee camps in neighboring countries.

The death toll in Rwanda was indeed great in absolute and relative terms. One estimate is that 500,000 Tutsi in the country as well as perhaps as many as 100,000 Hutus were killed (Kuperman 2000: 101). Others have put the number of Tutsi deaths as high as 800,000 (Shalom 2001: 56). Well over half of the Tutsi population of Rwanda was slaughtered during the massacres. It is not just the magnitude of the loss of life that makes the events in Rwanda genocide. The fact that the government and other Rwandan groups attempted to hide the fact of the massacres from other Tutsi (and the outside world) while the killing was underway is an indication that the real goal was the elimination of the minority. When many Tutsi were killed early on in the attacks, the government hid the information so that outside intervention was less likely and so that Tutsi who were still alive were unaware of their probable fate (Kuperman 2000: 98).

The control of the state government was essential for the massacres to inflict such casualties on the Tutsi and to inflict them so quickly. State power not only facilitated the mass murder, but it also put a stamp of approval upon the proceedings (Mamdani 2001: 217–18). The Rwandan military units were invariably commanded by extremists, meaning that the units either participated in the massacres or they were neutralized and unable to intervene to protect Tutsis. The moderate officers and politicians simply had no troops at their disposal, and to attempt to prevent the massacres without troops would simply have exposed themselves to reprisals (Kuperman 2000: 111). Any Hutu opposition was simply too weak to prevent the deaths that occurred. While the massacres clearly provide an example of genocide, the earlier events are examples of the Rwandan governmental support for terrorism. The government ignored the activities of paramilitary groups, militias, and vigilantes that agreed with government policies. Assaults on opposition politicians and moderates before the death of the president were designed to intimidate those against the government. The use of death squads by the government and official toleration of the activities of the militias in the earlier periods were a prelude to genocide.

SUMMARY

Government repression and the use of terror by state agents against citizens have been fairly common throughout the world and throughout time. In some cases governments have tolerated the use of violence by security forces against dissidents and their supporters. The rights of dissidents and opponents of the government have been violated and transgressions overlooked by superiors with a wink and nod to subordinates, who have thus been encouraged to continue the activities. In other cases private groups such as vigilantes, paramilitary groups, and militias that have engaged in violence have not been prosecuted, and if offenders have actually been brought to trial, they are let off with a slap on the wrist. In the case of death squads, governments have been more actively involved in the use of terror against their own citizens while preserving the possibility of denying official participation. In the case of ethnic cleansing it is often government objectives that are being met and active government support is often present. Finally, with the occurrence of genocide government organization is essential to the elimination of the target population.

The various case studies in this chapter represented a range of terroristic activities directed against groups of citizens. The activities of the ZANU militants in Zimbabwe were designed to dispossess a portion of the population of valuable property. The government acquiesced in the dispossession of an unpopular group of citizens and made it clear that sanctions and legal remedies and restraining orders would not be applied against the offenders. The techniques that were used against the white farmers were also applied to opposition groups. In the case of the French Revolution and the Reign of Terror, the role of the government in violence was less consistent. In some cases the use of terror originated with the groups that were in power, which led to government by intimidation and fear. In other cases factions in the government supported violence against suspect groups or their political opponents to further their political goals and used terror to advance their political agendas. Finally, there were examples of popular outbreaks that did not originate with the government in Paris or local authorities and which basically took place beyond the control of the political leadership.

The cases of East Timor, Sudan, Bosnia, and Rwanda provide recent examples of the use or the increased use of ethnic cleansing tactics and even genocide. East Timor and Bosnia do not qualify as genocide, despite the death tolls, since the intent of the perpetrators was not physical elimination. The goal of the Indonesian government was the assimilation of East Timor and the suppression of the liberation movement. Thus, in both Bosnia and East Timor the target populations could survive by adopting the appropriate pattern of behavior (departure or assimilation). In Rwanda neither option of assimilation or departure was available, and a large portion of the Hutu population sought physical elimination of the Tutsis. The Holocaust required the active mobilization of millions of Germans and an even larger number of supporters in the German allies and occupied territories (Scherrer 2002: 124–5). Similarly, in Rwanda the massive death count could only have been achieved with the active participation of many members of the Hutu population, including the militias and paramilitary groups. In the Sudan there have been ethnic cleansing in the south and in Darfur, and the possibility for genocidal violence remains.

It has been suggested that ethnic warfare and ethnic cleansing are just cover terms for actions by thugs and marginal elements in society (Mueller 2000). Such a suggestion, however, overlooks the element of political direction supplied by governments or political leaders who encourage it. The key is the political objectives, not the personnel who carry out the terror. Security force members and paramilitary groups often attract those prone to violence or who enjoy it, but it is the organization that makes the groups more deadly and effective and more of a threat to a political system or a target group. The active involvement or support of governments contributes to the possibility for increased death tolls since the administrative apparatus of the state is available. Unlike non-state actors, it has been governments that have been able to use terror on a mass scale (Wilkinson 2006: 3). The casualty figures for Rwanda, Bosnia and Herzegovina, the Sudan, and East Timor were quite large, both in an absolute sense and in terms of percentage losses among the targeted group. Government violence led to high tolls in Argentina as well under the post-Peron military regime, and if there had not been outside intervention the deaths in Kosovo might have been very high. The loss of life in France during the Reign of Terror reached high levels as well. State terrorism and repression, however, does not always result in high body counts. The Tupameros were suppressed in Uruguay with relatively few deaths.

State supported or tolerated terrorism is one area where the presence of external support has largely been a non-issue. The vigilantes, paramilitary groups, and death squads generally have had sufficient domestic political support so that they did not have to look to external backers. Often in the case of government-supported terrorism, what outside involvement that does occur has been on behalf of the victims. In East Timor external pressures, domestic opposition, and the fall of the military regime in Indonesia all combined to lead to the independence referendum. In Bosnia and Kosovo the ethnic cleansing operations were eventually terminated when force was applied against the groups using terror and violence. The frequently ambivalent response of outside groups in areas where ethnic cleansing has been practiced, however, has encouraged such activities since punishment equal to the crime has been unlikely (Simons 1999: 15). Less than vigorous responses and prosecutions in effect have meant that ethnic cleansing has been allowed to be successful. In the case of large-scale attacks against targeted civilian population, intervention has to occur quickly if massive casualties are going to be prevented (Kuperman 2000: 117). In Rwanda, foreign involvement in the internal fighting in the country came far too late to do much good for the Tutsi victims. Similarly, foreign involvement has not yet proven to be very effective in the Sudan. In the case of the French Revolution the support from foreign countries for the old system was never very effective, but the outside pressure was strong enough to help initiate the Reign of Terror. Pressure on developing countries by foreign aid donors has led some authoritarian states to reduce the levels of official repression; however, they have then utilized paramilitaries and other private groups deal with opposition (Roessler 2005). The presence of outside observers in the case of Zimbabwe probably initially limited the violence directed against the white farmers and other opponents of the regime, but the restraint by the pro-government groups lessened over time. International public opinion was probably one factor that led to the use of party militants and veterans (rather than government security forces) in the land occupations and against the opposition.

One final, and unfortunate, point needs to be made in regard to the direct use or support of terror by governments against their own citizens. Since the persons applying the violence have had the government behind them and external interference is belated or non-existent, it is not surprising that this type of terrorism has often been successful in terms of achieving the goals of the perpetrators. State support of terror in whatever form is more likely to succeed than dissident terror. Violence and terror in France led to the destruction of the pillars of the old system before the revolution, and the political system was indeed transformed both in the short term and in the long term. Groups in Darfur opposed to the national government have suffered greatly. Robert Mugabe continues to govern as president in Zimbabwe, and at least some of the Zimbabweans continue to support him and his policies while the position of the few remaining white farm owners and opposition parties is not enviable. Serbs in Bosnia now control much more territory than they did before the violence and the political solution that has led to a federated political system in which they have been rewarded for the use of violence. Only in East Timor did the efforts to apply terror to intimidate the population fail to achieve any long-term results for those using the terror. East Timor has gained its independence notwithstanding the use of terror, but this failure has been more the exception than the rule. Elsewhere, government violence helped to destroy the Tupermaros in Uruguay, the Sikh dissidents, and the leftist groups in Argentina.

TERMS

African National Congress (ANC)	Montagnards
Hassan al-Turabi	Robert Mugabe
Oliver Cromwell	NKVD
Darfur	Nubia
ethnic cleansing	Ante Pavelich
genocide	"Punjab" solution
Gestapo	Reign of Terror
Girondins	Tutsi (Watutsi)
Hutu (Bahutu)	Utashe
Impuza Mugambi	Zimbabwean African National Union-Popular
Interahamwe	Front (ZANUPF)
Jacobin Clubs	Zimbabwean African Peoples Union (ZAPU)
janjaweed militias	

FURTHER READING

Claridge, D. (1996) "State Terrorism? Applying a Definitional Model," *Terrorism and Political Violence*, 8, 3: 47–63.

Furet, F. (1989) "Terror," in F. Furet and M. Ozouf (eds) *A Critical Dictionary of the French Revolution*, trans. A. Goldhammer, Cambridge, MA: Belknap Press, 137–50.

Mamdani, M. (2001) *When Victims become Killers: Colonialism, Nativism, and the Genocide in Rwanda*, Princeton, NJ: Princeton University Press.

Mann, M. (2005) *The Dark Side of Democracy: Explaining Ethnic Cleansing*, Cambridge: Cambridge University Press.

Pateman, R. (1998) "East Timor, Twenty Years After: *Resistir e Vencer* (To Resist Is to Win)," *Terrorism and Political Violence*, 10, 1: 119–32.

Rotberg, R. I. (2000) "Africa's Mess, Mugabe's Mayhem," *Foreign Affairs*, 79, 5: 47–61.

CHAPTER 11

Countries with Multiple Crises of Terrorism

Terrorism has been a recurring theme in some areas of the world, even when it has occurred in different contexts. While some countries have experienced a particular type of terrorist violence over the course of many years such as the activities of ETA in Spain, other countries seem to have been prone to terrorist activities by different groups seeking different objectives. In fact, there would appear to be a trend toward greater complexity wherein governments and populations in some regions are increasingly facing violent dissidents belonging to groups with entirely different motives (Wilkinson 2000b: 4). A number of countries have faced such waves of terrorist activity. Sri Lanka is one country that has suffered from terrorism used in efforts to achieve a variety of political objectives. It has faced crises in political terrorism—plural occurrences that go beyond the well-publicized violence and civil war between the two largest ethnic groups on the island. Iraq more recently has been afflicted with terrorism originating from multiple groups, often with different objectives, resulting in increasing turmoil in the country.

THE PREVALENCE OF MULTIPLE CRISES

The area that now constitutes Israel and the Occupied Territories (the old Palestinian Mandate) has also had waves of dissident terrorism. The Arab and Jewish communities attacked each other, and both sides utilized terrorist tactics in the conflict. Both sides at various times attempted to convince broader target audiences of Palestinian villagers or Jewish settlers to relocate. Terrorism also became an important weapon used by extremists among the Jewish nationalists (Zionists) in their successful efforts to convince the British to leave the territory. Leaders of the battles against the British and the Arabs in the period of the Mandate became heroes, especially to the right in Israel (Sprinzak 2000: 213). There have been the attacks by the PLO and more recently by Hamas, as well as attacks by Jewish extremist groups. The assassination of Prime Minister Yitzak Rabin did derail the peace process precisely as was hoped by the assassin and those who agreed with him. Palestinians have attempted to prevent negotiations as well. In the violence that began in 2001 (the second *intifada*), extremists on both sides have been able to weaken the peace process by resorting to violence. The Palestinian suicide bombers who have staged their attacks have consistently led to the postponement of peace talks and heightened tensions and suspicion (Kydd and Walter 2002).

What used to be Yugoslavia has suffered from a number of outbreaks of terrorist violence. After World War I, there were difficulties with the Croatian nationalists and Bulgarians in the Macedonian region, and the external meddling of Italy, Hungary, and Bulgaria. In the 1990s nationalist feelings resurfaced with the conflict in Kosovo and independent Macedonia where the Albanians used violence very effectively to mobilize the popular support for the cause of autonomy or independence. State terrorism and government supported violence also appeared with the Utashe regime in Croatia, the efforts to terrorize the Albanians in Kosovo by the regime of Slobodan Milošević, and the particularly vicious ethnic cleansing activities occurred in Bosnia and Herzegovina. In the case of this region the severity of the violence and its recurrence has often been increased by the fact that nationalist differences were reinforced by religious differences. Nationalism and religion have combined to strengthen communal antagonisms.

Indonesia is another country that has frequently been mentioned in the preceding pages. The demise of the Suharto regime and the movement toward establishing a functioning democracy under trying circumstances has meant that the political system has been in transition and is more vulnerable as a consequence. Indonesia as a multiethnic country has faced a variety of nationalist dissident groups. In Aceh in northern Sumatra violence has occurred not only between the dissidents and security forces; the dissidents have attacked Javanese migrants brought in by the government to solidify support for the nation (Schulze 2003: 261). The failed attempt to incorporate East Timor encouraged opposition groups in Irian Jaya, the Indonesian portion of New Guinea that was joined to Indonesia in 1963. The largely Christian population has particularly been opposed to the influx of more than a million Muslim migrants from Java (Tan 2006: 195). Ethnic conflict lay behind the violence on Borneo between Dayaks and Madurese. The cohesion of the Indonesian state has also been threatened by religious differences. Jemaah Islamiah was responsible for the simultaneous bombing of thirty Christian churches as part of this conflict (Gunaratna 2003: 126). The communal violence between Christians and Muslims in Sulawesi and Ambion in the Moluccas has involved religiously inspired terrorism. Laskar Jihad, a militant Islamic group with some ties to bin Laden, has sent members to the Moluccas to fight against the local Christians (Sholeh 2007: 151–2). Members of the armed forces and government civil servants facilitated the movement of these militant Muslims to the area (Hefner 2002: 760). Islamic militias have also gone to Irian Jaya to fight the rebels in that province with no interference from the government (Abuza 2003b: 196). Al Qaeda operatives have increasingly been active in this region of the world with links to groups in Indonesia, Singapore, Malaysia, and the Philippines (Chalk 1998a: 127–8). The bombings on Bali in 2002 and 2005 are recent examples. The presence of violent dissident groups in Indonesia has also affected the security forces. The use of terror by police and military personnel has been documented, and the government has tolerated attacks by paramilitary groups supporting the government, including the violence directed against the Chinese and Communists when the Suharto regime first came to power. Vigilantes trained and supported by the military were responsible for many of the deaths that occurred at this time (Cribb 2000: 184). Chinese merchants became targets in Java when Chinese shopping malls began to drive non-Chinese merchants out of business (Almonte 2003: 222). In the waning days of the weakened military regime, Chinese and Christians served as convenient scapegoats for the economic problems in 1997–8. Violence against the Chinese led to more than 100,000 fleeing the country (Hefner 2002: 759). The multiple tensions inherent in Indonesia, the limited size of the armed forces to deal with unrest in multiple—and often widely separated—locations, and the fragility of the new democratic system made the country especially vulnerable. The inability of the government to control the violence in Sulawsi, Ambion, and Borneo has dramatically demonstrated the vulnerability of the system, and the potential for a variety of domestic dissident groups to resort to violence and terrorism in the future would appear to be relatively high.

India is another country facing a variety of dissident groups and the use of violence to achieve political objectives. A large portion of the unrest is related to the multiethnic nature of the state and religious differences among the population, but ideological concerns have also played a role. India has also been notable in that civilians have been the targets so often. In terms of total casualties, India has been one of the "most terrorism battered countries in the world" (Chalk 1996: 15). The religious unrest manifested itself in the revolt of the Sikhs in the Punjab and unrest among the largely Muslim population of Kashmir. There have also been attacks against Christians, especially Western missionaries, as well as communal violence between Muslims and Hindus. The confrontation over the grounds at Ayodhya where Hindu militants have sought to reclaim the land and replace the mosque with a temple for their religion is a recent example of conflict. The Hindus have been at least partially successful in that the mosque Ayodhya was destroyed. Recent attacks on Hindus returning from the temple site (and the resulting retaliation by Hindus against Muslims elsewhere in India) and the bombings of commuter trains in Mumbai have resurrected tensions between the two communities (just as some Muslim and Hindu extremists hoped). Ethnic unrest has been present in India as well. Violence and terrorism have surfaced in Assam and other territories in the Northeast where the indigenous peoples fear the encroachment of outsiders, especially Bengalis (Wilson 1992). There have been signs of some unrest in Tamil Nadu in the southwest, related in part to the problems in Sri Lanka that will be discussed in detail below. Ideological groups on the left such as the Naxalites have resorted to violence, and the presence of a Marxist-Leninist insurgency complete with terror in neighboring Nepal could bode ill for India. Further, the fact that the government has tolerated the activities of death squads, vigilantes, and zealousness by security forces in dealing with many of these conflicts is another indication of the potential for terrorist violence in the future. In addition to the use of death squads, India has also had local governments that have tolerated communal violence. In Gujarat violence between Muslims and Hindis has been frequent. In 2002, however, the violence increased. More than 2,000 Muslims were killed in violence in Mumbai, including politicians, judges, intellectuals, and professionals (Oommen 2005: 120). In the rioting by Hindu mobs that targeted Muslims, the police were either absent or actively participated in the attacks (Soeters 2005: 26). While thousands were arrested for participating in the riots, most of the charges were dismissed and no one was ever brought to trial (Mann 2005: 484).

In Weimar Germany in the late 1920s and early 1930s both the Communists and the Nazis used violence and terror to bring down the democratic government. Once the Nazis were in power, they continued the use of violence by directing state terrorism against opponents, finally resorting to genocide in the case of the Holocaust and attacks on Gypsies. Later in the 1960s in West Germany there was the period of left-wing violence that continued until reunification.

With reunification there then was a clear increase in the level of violence by neo-Nazis, Skinheads, and associated groups. In effect, Germany has seen waves of dissident terrorism, and state terror in the case of Nazi Germany as well. Similarly, in Italy attacks from the left and right overlapped as both ideological groups sought to change government policies and leadership and to undermine the democratic system in that country. This violence after World War II was preceded by the use of street violence by the Fascists to obtain power under Mussolini early in the 1920s.

The United States is a country that has also had a rather substantial history of domestic terrorist violence, although not necessarily as organized or extensive as the political violence that has occurred in some other countries (B. Lutz and J. Lutz 2007). The Boston Tea Party was a prelude to a rebellion. The Indians were victims of ethnic cleansing. The KKK in various periods intimidated blacks and others. There was anarchist violence at the end of the nineteenth century, culminating in the assassination of President McKinley. The war in Vietnam generated left-wing dissent, which generated the generally low-level terrorism of the Weathermen and other groups of dissidents. Beginning in the 1980s violence and the use of terror increased in efforts to prevent abortions. Assaults on unpopular minorities occurred more frequently. Right-wing extremist groups have also used violence in efforts to achieve their political objectives with the bombing in Oklahoma City as the most deadly example. While domestic terrorism in the United States has usually been sporadic and many dissident groups have never reached the position of threatening the system, there still has been an undercurrent of strong political feelings and the presence of many dissident groups willing to use violence to intimidate or terrorize in efforts to bring about policy changes in the political system.

WAVES OF VIOLENCE AND TERRORISM IN SRI LANKA

Current analyses of terrorism in Sri Lanka today focus on the activities of the Tamil Tigers and their efforts to create an independent Tamil state in the northern and eastern parts of the island. Sri Lanka in its half century of independence, however, has experienced a series of violent dissident activities, many of which have included the use of terrorism. Sri Lanka is a diverse society in many respects. The largest identifiable group in the country is composed of the Sinhalese, who comprise a majority of the population. They speak Sinhala and are largely Buddhist. They also have been located in those portions of the island less influenced by the presence of European colonialism (first the Portuguese, then the Dutch, and finally the British). As a consequence, they have had the least exposure and access to European education and were relatively underrepresented in positions of authority and influence, first in the colony and then in the independent nation. The Tamils are the second largest group in Sri Lanka, comprising about a sixth of the population. There are actually many more Tamils just across the narrow straits from Sri Lanka in the Indian state of Tamil Nadu, but it is the proportion of Tamils in the Sri Lankan population that makes them important for the political stability of that country. These inhabitants speak Tamil and are largely Hindu or Christian. The Tamils interacted more with the colonial government, and they were more likely to know English. They eventually moved into positions in the British administration or professions in numbers greater than their proportion of the island's population (Kaarthikeyan 2005: 133). In addition, there is a small Muslim population, often Tamil, who were converted by Arab and Persian traders and merchants in the past. There is also a small Eurasian group. This group was the most overrepresented in positions of authority given the early linkages of its members with colonial administrations. As the violence in Sri Lanka increased, however, most left the country for safer locales (Crossette 2002: 271).

In the colonial period the major conflicts were religious, pitting Buddhists against the Christians and Muslims (Bell-Fialkoff 1999: 190). After independence, conflicts based in religion, ethnicity, and ideology appeared. The earliest symptom of problems in Sri Lanka occurred with an attempted *coup d'etat* by military officers and police officials, as well as a few civilians, in 1962. The plotters were arrested before they could move against the government. The coup itself reflected concern among many officers about increasing ethnic tensions in the country and the policies of the government for dealing with them. Sinhalese political leaders were seeking to increase the number of Sinhalese in the officer corps and command positions and to do the same in the bureaucracy and civilian sectors at the expense of the other groups. Tamils and the other minorities were overrepresented in the officer corps at independence, and this government policy obviously limited their career options in the future (Horowitz 1980: 21–30).

The next crisis that the political system faced came from the left. Sri Lanka had a strong and active leftist tradition, and at independence there was both a sizeable traditional Communist Party and a Trotskyite Party committed to its own version of Marxism (Laqueur 1999: 191). This strength led to young students creating another party, the Janatha Vimukthi Peramuna (JVP), to represent their Marxist-Leninist ideological views of the political system and its future. In order to free the country from these negative influences of global and local capitalism, the JVP organized an uprising to overthrow the government in 1971. They were sure that a one-day uprising in the cities would be sufficient to bring down the whole political system (Samaranayke 1999: 114). The attempt at a quick seizure of power in the country failed when the government and the political system were not nearly as fragile as the students had predicted. The JVP continued a guerrilla insurgency in the countryside for a few months, but the government security forces proved to be able to contain the threat without too much difficulty, and in less than a year the insurgency was over. There were only a few terrorist actions involved with this attempted insurgency, since the dissidents expected a quick takeover.

Continuation of policies favoring the Sinhalese, including the proclamation of Sinhala as the national language and the adoption of Buddhism as the national religion, threatened the Tamils and other minorities (Austin and Gupta 1990: 16). The two major Sinhalese parties competed for votes within the majority community by increasingly stressing their commitments to providing the native Sinhalese with their fair share of positions in government and additional educational opportunities. Although extreme views had been apparent as early as 1959 when two Sinhalese Bhuddist monks assassinated the prime minister because in their view he was not sufficiently nationalist in furthering the interests of the Sinhalese majority (Laqueur 1999: 191), extremism was now on the increase. At the same time, Tamil political parties found that they had to demand greater guarantees and more protection for the rights of the minorities in order to collect votes. Tamil demands thus increasingly included calls for greater local autonomy in areas where there were Tamil majorities. Eventually, some extreme groups even began to argue that an independent Tamil state on the island was the only way to prevent the Sinhalese from submerging the Tamils and their culture. This tension eventually led to the outbreak of violence between the communities, and this violence quickly generated terrorist actions in a variety of situations. Both government forces and Tamil dissidents became perpetrators.

The simmering tensions between the Tamils and Sinhalese broke into the open with an incident in July of 1983. Tamil rebels ambushed a small military patrol and killed the soldiers.

Sinhalese in various parts of the island proceeded to take part in anti-Tamil riots in retaliation for this attack. The government was slow to respond to the violence and waited days before restoring order and protecting the Tamils (Pape 2005: 141). The resulting mob violence killed 2,000 to 3,000 Tamils, and more than 100,000 became refugees (Kaarthikeyan 2005: 134). There were many indications that the government helped to organize and support the violence by Sinhalese mobs (Krishna 1992: 270). The mob attacks did not dissuade the Tamils from continued opposition; instead, it increased the support within the Tamil community for the use of violence to protect the position of their community and the interests of its members. A large number of Tamil political organizations appeared, ranging from moderates who still advocated some form of negotiated settlement with the Sinhalese parties in the government to those advocating complete independence for the Tamil areas of the island. The Liberation Tigers of Tamil Eelam (LTTE) or the Tamil Tigers became the most important of these dissident groups and the most powerful in terms of military resources that it could command and the types of actions that it could undertake.

Violence against the government by the Tigers and by other Tamil dissident groups initially began at a low level and gradually increased until it reached a full-scale civil war. Early in the struggle there were divisions among the Tamil dissidents. While the moderates were able to gain some government concessions on autonomy, the LTTE continued to hold out for independence for the Tamil areas of Sri Lanka and has, at least to date, managed to effectively short-circuit any meaningful implementation of compromises. Initially the Tigers fought against the government and other Tamil groups. The Tigers won out in their battles with the other Tamil groups, using measures as harsh as necessary to eliminate the competing organizations within the minority community. Leaders of other groups have been assassinated, both in Sri Lanka and abroad, and soldiers and guerrilla units of the other groups have been attacked inside Sri Lanka. The LTTE eliminated approximately thirty other Tamil dissident groups. Interestingly enough, there is a separate front organization that takes credit for the attacks against the other Tamil organizations, sparing the Tigers from the disrepute of attacking their own (Gunaratna 1997: 474). There is little doubt, however, that the LTTE has been behind these attacks.

The Tigers have used many of the standard mechanisms of dissident groups to battle the central government. Their overall approach has been one of guerrilla insurgency supported by extensive terrorist actions. Initial tactics included hit and run attacks against security forces and isolated military targets. The Tigers also attempted, with some success, to provoke harsh responses from the military against the Tamil population in general, making it more likely that larger numbers of Tamils would rally to the dissident side. With the passage of time the Tigers grew increasingly stronger and were able to field larger units and even to place some areas of the countryside under their effective control. There have been times when they have been strong enough to effectively control the major cities in the Tamil areas. The Sri Lankan military has not been able to control the entire countryside continuously, and any attempts to do so would simply open up government forces to the types of ambushes and hit and run tactics at which guerrilla forces excel. Eventually, the Sri Lankan military forces in the north, especially in the Jaffna Peninsula, were restricted to their military bases and could only venture into the countryside or even the cities if they sent out large forces. In 1996 the Tigers overran and captured a military base, killing all 1,200 military personnel stationed there. The death of the entire garrison was designed to further inflame differences between the Sinhalese and Tamils since some of the troops on the base were undoubtedly captured or wounded during the attack. In another daring action underwater frogmen penetrated the main naval base in Sri Lanka and sank two of the larger ships in the Sri Lankan navy (Laqueur 1999: 193–4). Another attack at the main airport and military base near the capital damaged military aircraft and destroyed half of the planes in the national airline (Crossette 2002: 31). By the 1980s, the battles between the LTTE and the government forces often reached the scale of civil war. The civil war has continued as the Tigers have not been able to defeat the government, and the government has been unable to eliminate the rebels.

In addition to the guerrilla strikes, the Tamil Tigers have utilized terrorism in their causes. The Tigers have practiced assassinations against key government officials with great regularity. Victims have included a president of Sri Lanka, a defense minister, a minister of national security, and the head of the naval forces (Joshi 1996: 19). The attacks, however, have extended beyond key individuals in positions of national authority or prominence. The Tigers attacked government officials in general to frighten other government officials into leaving threatened areas. When these officials flee, government control is weakened. Tamils seen to be cooperating with the government have also become targets. Cooperation has been defined as a willingness to accept government positions. Politicians who have advocated compromise or some form of settlement that falls far short of the goals of the Tigers have also become targets (Hoglund 2005: 164). Ultimately, if these kinds of attacks intimidate large sections of the population of Sri Lanka, they may achieve their objective of establishing regional autonomy or independence for the Tamil areas.

The Tigers have also launched attacks on the general population, particularly in areas that are predominately Sinhalese or where most of the casualties would be Sinhalese or pro-government Tamils. They have detonated bombs that have killed hundreds, and the bombs have obviously been placed to inflict significant casualties. They have destroyed an airliner and killed all the passengers on board (Long 1990: 55). The Tigers also began to use suicide attacks when other measures failed to achieve their goals (Pape 2005: 140). Suicide bombers have driven explosive-laden trucks into targets or had otherwise set off explosives that they were carrying when they were close enough to their targets. In fact, the Tamil Tigers have the highest rates of the use of suicide missions of any dissident organization in the world. These attacks have been both deadly and sophisticated (Dolnik 2003: 24). Captured members of the organization have also frequently committed suicide while in custody to demonstrate their dedication and the strength of the dissidents (Pape 2005: 143).

The Tigers have also practiced their own version of ethnic cleansing by targeting non-Tamil groups such as Sinhalese and Muslims. When insurgent forces were able to occupy villages in areas that the Tamils hoped to incorporate into either an autonomous region or an independent state, all the non-Tamils in the village would be killed. In other cases the insurgents would set up roadblocks. When buses were stopped, the Tamils would be released and the others would be killed. Muslims were often special targets because the Tigers feared that they might be a group that would cooperate with the government (Samaranayke 1997: 116–17). One consequence of this campaign, favorable to the other objectives of the dissidents, was that the government forces were now more likely to use indiscriminate artillery shelling and air attacks against areas that had been cleansed of all but the Tamil inhabitants, further alienating the Tamils in the area and driving them to side with the dissidents. The attacks against Sinhalese and Muslim civilians have also served to send another form of warning to potential and actual government supporters that the military and security forces of the state were not capable of protecting them on a daily basis.

The Tamil Tigers developed a sophisticated and extensive support network for their battles with the government. The LTTE maintained contacts with various Palestinian organizations and trained in their camps (Joshi 1996: 21). The Tigers also developed links with various criminal groups that operated in Sri Lanka. Smuggling, including drugs, between Sri Lanka and nearby India has always been common and difficult to stop. While the Tigers may not have been directly involved in the smuggling of drugs, the organization has tolerated the activity and has undoubtedly profited from it in the form of taxes, contributions, payments, and for access to the smuggling routes in order to ship arms from India to Sri Lanka (Laqueur 1999: 194–5). The LTTE has also created its own companies, both to generate profits and to provide cover for various activities such as purchasing and transporting arms. The Tigers have also received funds from Tamils living abroad. The long conflict has meant that many Tamils in the diaspora have had relatives killed or injured in the violence on the island, leading to their financial support (Fair 2005: 139). Since their struggle has been reasonably popular with many Tamils in foreign lands, some of the money has been voluntarily contributed to the liberation cause. There have also been indications that some of the contributions have been coerced by the LTTE (Laqueur 1999: 194). As a result of this foreign fund raising, business activities, criminal activities, and even some foreign government support, the Tamil Tigers have been able to purchase arms pretty much at will. The end of the Cold War has meant that there are major arms surpluses on the clandestine global market. The surpluses have meant that armaments are available at lower costs, a situation that clearly benefits well-to-do dissident groups such as the LTTE.

One surprising early source of foreign support for the Tamil Tigers for a period of time was India. India has always been concerned that a successful Tamil rebellion in Sri Lanka could spill over to southern India where over 50 million Tamils live. Should the LTTE or other groups be successful in creating an independent Tamil state, it might set an example that would encourage the Tamils of India to seek independence and that could lead to the break up of multiethnic India. As a consequence, support for the Tamil rebels would at first glance make no sense. The options for the Indian government in dealing with the violence in Sri Lanka, however, were somewhat limited. When Indira Gandhi was prime minister, she had to provide at least some diplomatic support to the Tamils in their demands in order to woo the Tamil voters in India. Openly siding with the Sri Lankan government could have triggered the very unrest in India that the government was seeking to avoid (Crenshaw 2000: 139). The seats won by local Tamil state parties have also been important at times for providing for a legislative majority to control the national government, and various prime ministers have had no choice but to take into account the responses of voters in Tamil Nadu to actions in Sri Lanka. There is clear evidence that the Indian political leaders and the Indian intelligence services felt that they could manipulate the Sri Lankan rebellion to the advantage of India. In retrospect it is obvious that this was a major miscalculation, since the guerrillas proved to be uncontrollable and the LTTE was able to use the Indian support to further its own goals rather than the reverse (Joshi 1996: 21). As the independence of the organization became very obvious, Indian support declined.

In 1987 India made a major effort to help broker a peace settlement in Sri Lanka between the government and the Tamils. The arrangement called for the Indian army to monitor the disengagement of the LTTE guerrillas and the Sri Lankan armed forces and provide a setting wherein an autonomy arrangement between the government and the rebels could be implemented. The Sri Lankan military withdrew and India sent troops as a peacekeeping force. The Tamil Tigers turned in a few weapons in the early stages of the arrangement, but this cooperation soon ended. Ultimately, this peace effort failed. Most of the LTTE still wanted an independent state rather than autonomy, and it appears that it had no intention of honoring the arrangement. Their short-term tactical objective in agreeing to the disengagement was to bring about the withdrawal of the Sri Lankan armed forces to give the Tigers an opportunity to regroup and consolidate their support among the Tamil population in Sri Lanka. Soon, Tamil guerrillas began to attack the Indian troops, and the attacks eventually provoked the peace-keepers into retaliation. The guerrillas managed to lead the Indian military forces into situations in which they retaliated indiscriminately and alienated the local Tamil civilian population, undercutting any chance of local support (Pape 2005: 152). The Indian armed forces then became involved in the fighting on the side of the government but proved to be no more effective in dealing with the rebels than the Sri Lankan army had been. The military options for the Indian army were limited since the presence of so many Tamils in India made it difficult for the Indian military to follow any consistent strategy in trying to deal with the LTTE (Crenshaw 2000:156). The Indian forces never really had the option of employing sufficient force to defeat the LTTE. Eventually the Indian peacekeeping effort was ended and the troops were withdrawn.

The violence that India feared all along did spill over from the Sri Lankan conflict. There have been a few attacks against supporters of the central government in Tamil Nadu and indications that the success of the LTTE has inspired some Indian Tamils. The pattern of attacks has been similar to those in Sri Lanka in that the targets have often been those individuals who have been pushing for the establishment of Hindi as the sole national language to the exclusion of other languages such as Tamil (Joshi 1996: 34). The most spectacular attack in India, however, had a different target—it was directed against former Prime Minister Rajiv Gandhi. He had been in power when the peacekeeping effort was undertaken, and he was held responsible for the fact that the Indian military had ended up fighting against the Tigers. While he was campaigning for his party in Tamil Nadu in 1991, he was killed by a suicide bomber with links to the LTTE. The assassination demonstrated the power of the LTTE, but it may have had some negative consequences for the LTTE. Adverse reactions in India gave the central government more freedom to deal with the Sri Lankan conflict. The Indian security and military forces became more effective in interrupting communications and supplies crossing the narrow straight between northern Sri Lanka and Tamil Nadu.

There have been a number of truces and ceasefires in Sri Lanka in addition to the one brokered by India. None of these has put an end to the violence. The LTTE either sought too much or the government was willing to yield too little. The tsunami of 2005 did severe damage to many areas of Sri Lanka in contention between the two sides. There was a brief period of cooperation between the two sides, but disagreements broke out over who would distribute the foreign aid that was coming in. Neither side could afford to let the other get credit for the aid distribution. Unlike Aceh where cooperation followed in the wake of natural disaster, in Sri Lanka the natural disaster provided another point of disagreement and another truce that failed.

While the struggle with the Tamil dissidents was ongoing, the Sri Lankan government faced a renewed assault from the left. The JVP revitalized itself and in 1987 launched a second violent effort to create a socialist political system in the country. Unlike its earlier effort at seizing power, this attack was based on the idea of a long-term insurrection. This attack relied on a strategy of relying on both terrorism and guerrilla strikes. Attacks were launched against government officials of all types, including politicians, members of the parties in the government and those in opposition, political supporters of these parties, and even members of their families. University personnel, journalists, and religious leaders became targets as well. The goal of the assassination campaign was to paralyze the government leaving the JVP as the only alternative for governing the state (Samaranayke 1999: 115; Samaranayke 1997: 114). There was, in fact, a period in which government officials and leaders were in danger of assassination by either the

JVP or the LTTE. The JVP undertook bloody terrorist actions in the cities to demonstrate the general vulnerability of the governments and its supporters. The battle against the JVP continued for two years before the government was able to defeat the leftists. The government did derive a benefit from the presence of the Indian military units during this period. Since Indian troops were dealing with the Tamils in the north, the government was able to mobilize larger forces to deal with the threat by the JVP (Crenshaw 2000: 143). Even so, tens of thousands of Sri Lankans died before the violence was contained. The JVP made no attempt to cooperate with the LTTE since the JVP unequivocally opposed the separation of the Tamil areas from the country. Unlike the Tamil insurgents, the JVP had no external support network. In fact, the JVP prided itself on having no external ties. The JVP also vehemently opposed the presence of the Indian peacekeepers on Sri Lankan soil as a matter of principle (Samaranayke 1997: 108). After this second defeat the JVP has transformed itself (again) into a conventional political party, and it has denounced the use of terror and violence to achieve political objectives.

Yet another type of terror has appeared in Sri Lanka. There have been increasing examples of the use of violence and terror by government forces or groups supported by the government. The indirect government support for the Sinhalese mobs in the earlier anti-Tamil riots was one example. The security forces at various times have been overzealous in dealing with the Tamil rebels and other dissidents as well as their supporters or suspected supporters. It would be amazing if such a long civil war did not result in at least some atrocities by the security forces or the military, especially when the dissidents have done everything in their power to stimulate or to encourage such overreactions on the part of the government forces. The Sri Lankan government has also used death squads, torture, and counterterror as a matter of policy, especially in the struggle against the JVP. Sympathizers with the leftists were targeted for government violence, not just the active dissidents (Samaranayke 1999: 117). Government personnel have also been involved in attacks against Tamil cultural activities and symbols of the Tamil culture (Krishna 1992: 270). In addition, Sinhalese Buddhist activists have on occasion attacked Christians in the country with little official interference, and there has been a general increase in religious intolerance in the country (Crossette 2002: 34). Overall, polarization among the ethnic and religious communities in the country has increased.

The discussion of Sri Lanka in some detail has illustrated that different types of terrorist violence can afflict a country at virtually the same time. The political system has been sorely tested with the deadly civil war with the LTTE and the battles with the left. The second JVP campaign would qualify as one of the bloodier examples of internal violence except when it is compared to the battles between the government and the Tamils. The government itself has resorted to the use of terror as well. Further, there have even been a few examples of right-wing terrorism and the attempted military coup. The Sri Lankan violence clearly spilled over into neighboring India as well. What is surprising is that in the midst of this violence the Sinhalese majority has been able to maintain a reasonably democratic political system. While the government has not been overthrown by any of the dissident groups, the LTTE is still in effective control of a significant portion of the country, and threats from the left, or even the right, could reappear.

TERRORISM AND INSURGENCY IN IRAQ

Prior to the US invasion in 2003, Iraq was not a country that was heavily involved in terrorism. The regime of Saddam Hussein and the Ba'athist Party, like other totalitarian systems, was largely immune to domestic terrorist attacks. While Iraq has been accused of sponsoring foreign groups, it was not particularly active in this area. Like virtually all the other Arab countries, Iraq supported selected Palestinian groups. When the Ba'ath (Arab Socialist Renaissance) Party came to power via a military coup, the new regime sent assassination teams to eliminate Iraqi dissidents abroad (Sciolino 1991: 91–2). The foreign military adventures undertaken by Iraq under the leadership of Hussein also involved support for other terrorist groups. In the long war with Iran, Iraq supported the dissident groups in that country, particularly the leftist Mujahedin-e-Khalq (MEK), which had fought to overthrow the new clerical regime. The invasion of Kuwait by Iraqi forces and the pressure from the United States and others to withdraw led to threats from Saddam Hussein to unleash campaigns of terrorism if force were used. The subsequent defeat of Iraq by the military forces led by the United States did lead to additional terrorist attacks. There were over 200 terrorist incidents during the Gulf crisis, mostly against businesses associated with the countries that had joined the coalition to force Iraq out of Kuwait. Some of these incidents probably involved Iraqi agents, some involved groups supported by Iraq, and others resulted from the independent actions of groups that favored Iraq in this conflict. Iraqi efforts to support these kinds of terrorist actions, however, were more inept than similar activities by other national intelligence agencies (such as the CIA or the old KGB) or even well-established terrorist groups (Pillar 2001: 57).

The defeat in Kuwait led Hussein to re-emphasize terrorism as a weapon to be used against countries that opposed him. The most daring plan was an attempt to assassinate former President George Bush, Sr in apparent retaliation for the US attempt to eliminate Saddam Hussein with smart bombs during the war to liberate Kuwait (Richelson 2002: 252). The 1993 attempt involved the assistance of MEK operatives, but it was detected before it could be launched (Mylroie 2000: 114). There were some other attacks after the liberation of Kuwait but the threat of increased terrorism was largely negated by additional preparation in the countries that were potential targets (Wilkinson 2006: 166–7). Iraqi dissidents abroad, however, remained targets. By 2003, however, there was little evidence of any major Iraqi involvement with other foreign terrorist group, and there was never any credible evidence of any link with Al Qaeda.

Saddam Hussein survived the Iran–Iraq War and the liberation of Kuwait. Because of no-fly zones, the Kurdish regions in Iraq were able to achieve some autonomy, but the Ba'athist regime was able to control the rest of the country. While Iraq had previously developed (and used) chemical weapons, and possibly biological ones, these weapons were destroyed after Kuwait was liberated. Saddam Hussein's pretense that he might still have such weapons was apparently intended to intimidate neighboring countries. This pretense turned out to be a costly one. The fear that such weapons actually existed and could fall into the hands of terrorist groups was unfounded, but it was a factor of some importance in the US decision to invade Iraq in 2003. Perhaps the greatest problem that comes with the previous efforts to develop biological and chemical weapons is the possibility that the expertise necessary for such weapons that Iraqi scientists have developed could now spread to other countries or terrorist groups (Cronin 2004: 318).

The invasion by the United States and its allies and the overthrow of Saddam Hussein created a new set of circumstances for outbreaks of terrorist activities from a variety of sources. Iraq has faced waves of terrorist and insurgent attacks with the occupation. The terrorist violence in Iraq is complex for another set of reasons. Some of the violence reflects antagonisms between political leaders as they jockey for position, but many of the attacks reflect domestic divisions in Iraqi society. The Arab Shia inhabitants of the south form an absolute majority of the population. The Sunni Kurds in the north and the Sunni Arabs in the center of the country each form about 20 percent of the population. These divisions between the Sunni and Shia Arab communities have lead to deadly sectarian violence. Sunni Arabs were the bulk of the elite under the Ottoman Empire, and they dominated every government in the country since its creation after World War I. The Sunnis now fear the consequences of a government that for the first time in recent history would favor the Shia majority. In addition, both Sunni and Shia Arabs have often looked down upon the Kurds.

There are quite distinct groups involved in the terrorist violence. One of the things that makes the situation so chaotic is that different groups with different agendas have chosen different or similar targets, and a variety of groups have also made use of suicide attacks. The attacks against the US and other military personnel are not recorded as terrorist incidents; they are guerrilla or insurgent attacks against regular military forces. There is, moreover, more than one group involved in these attacks. Islamic jihadists associated with or encouraged by Al Qaeda are behind a number of the attacks. The invasion of Iraq had actually given the global jihadists a new focal point for their struggle with the West (Hegghammer 2006: 31–2). Nationalist Iraqi groups, including remnants of the Ba'athist Party, have also targeted the coalition military forces as a foreign occupation. Some Shia groups have attacked the military targets as well because they see the US presence as interfering with their political goals for dominating a future Iraq since the United States has been supporting broad-based coalitions (including Sunnis) or preventing the Shia majority from dominating the new political system (Brigham 2006: 58).

The same groups have also been responsible for many of the terrorist attacks in Iraq. Politicians, government offices and bureaucrats, and others involved in the political system have become frequent targets. Recruiting centers for the police, security forces, and the military have often been the scenes of bombings and suicide attacks. If recruits can be dissuaded from joining the police or the military, the government will be weakened, perhaps fatally so. Sunni activists, probably including former Ba'athists, have attacked the new state because they see that the new government could ultimately serve the interests of the Shia majority. If the government is forced into a more authoritarian style of rule, the Sunnis may hope that they will be able to retain a measure of their power. Those groups linked to the global jihadist movement and Al Qaeda have opposed the government as well since they see it as an ally or puppet of the United States in their greater, global struggle. The United States suffers when these attacks are successful since it is blamed for its inability to provide protection for those Iraqis willing to cooperate with the new regime (Neumann and Smith 2005: 578). Further, if the attacks are successful in undercutting the democratic system that the United States wants to create, the attackers will have weakened the influence of the West. Elements from the Shia majority would have the same reasons for attacking the central government as they do for attacking US troops—it could be an obstacle to assuming more complete control of the country.

The attacks against foreign aid organizations in Iraq have much the same goals as the terrorist attacks against the other targets, and the same groups are probably responsible. One early attack against the UN headquarters in Baghdad was quite effective and may have been an Al Qaeda operation (Rabasa *et al.* 2006: 138). It killed UN personnel in the country and basically led to the UN to abandon its efforts in Iraq aimed at helping to re-build and stabilize the country. The UN could have served as an important buffer between the United States and Iraqis, and any programs administered by the UN would have had at least the potential for greater neutrality, especially if the UN had been able to use personnel and experts from the Middle East or other non-Western countries. The departure of UN personnel and other aid workers from the country was a victory for the groups opposed to the United States, the new government, and a stable Iraq. As is the case with most terrorist attacks, the choice of the UN facilities was quite purposeful and reflected careful consideration in the choice of targets.

Sectarian differences explain some of the terrorist violence. The Sunni terrorists have attacked Shia targets and the government, apparently hoping to retain at least some influence in the government by demonstrating their ability to disrupt the political system. Attacks from the Shia community have different objectives. Some of the attacks may be retaliatory and designed to force the Sunnis to accept Shia dominance. The Shia community is not unified, however, and Shi'ites have battled each other (Tan 2006: 136–7). Some of the Shia attacks may be designed to drive an even greater wedge between the two communities. Greater communal animosity would make it difficult for any important Shia leader to collaborate with the Sunnis. Eliminating the possibility of coalitions between Sunnis and moderate Shias obviously favors the more militant factions in the Shia community. The potential of such militant groups to dominate the government and to then implement their desired ideological or religious programs would be increased if cooperation across sectarian lines is diminished. It is also possible that the global jihadists have sought to increase Sunni–Shia tensions to make the establishment of a successful, stable, pro-US regime more difficult (Tan 2006: 166).

To date the Kurds have managed to avoid being targets for much of the endemic violence that has plagued the rest of the country. While there have been some terrorist and insurgent attacks, they have not been at the same level as for the Arab portions of the state. The two main Kurdish factions, the Kurdish Democratic Party (KDP) and the Patriotic Union of Kurdistan (PUK) have fought each other at times in efforts to control the region. An extremist Kurdish religious group, Ansar al-Islam, which has links with Al Qaeda, appeared in 2001 (Rabasa *et al.* 2006: 138). It began to attack the more secular parties, especially the PUK (Tan 2006: 130). The group has been driven out of the Kurdish region, but it remains a potential threat in the future. If Iraq disintegrates into component Kurdish, Sunni, and Shia areas, more violence among the Kurdish groups is likely. Since the Shia would dominate a unified Iraq by sheer numbers, they are opposed to Kurdish separatism (Stansfield 2005: 144). Violence between Arabs and Kurds in efforts to control the oil fields in the north would be almost inevitable if Iraq disintegrates. In addition, if Iraq manages to remain unified, it is possible that the Kurdish groups could be drawn into confrontations between different factions and that the terrorist violence targeting them could increase significantly.

The presence of the new, weak government in Iraq has made the situation worse for the country. The destruction or demobilization of the military, security forces, and police that served the Ba'athist regime left the occupation government and then the new Iraqi government in a very weak position. The resulting regime has provided a classic example of weak system in transition that became vulnerable to terrorist assaults. The military forces of the United States, Great Britain, and other countries were not in a position to deal as effectively with local dissidents as local security personnel would be. The new government, a system in transition, has lacked the resources of the old system, and it has not been able to build up new resources since it has been under constant assault. The disunity and variety of the local political forces has also kept the system weak, especially since many of the key leaders of different groups appear to hope to gain from a situation of instability.

The situation in Iraq has been complicated by the activities of foreign countries. US troops and other personnel have become a magnet for attacks. The chaos in Iraq has provided an opportunity for many groups opposed to US objectives to launch attacks there. It is likely that Iran has been providing at least some assistance to selected Shia groups in the country. It would be in Iran's interest, of course, to have a friendly regime in power in Baghdad, although it might be even more in Iran's interest to have a weak (and non-threatening) Iraq as a neighbor. If Iraq become three states, they might present opportunities for Iran as well, although a Kurdish state would be a potent draw for Iran's own Kurdish minority. What is clearly not in Iran's interests at the current time is a strong Iraqi government allied to the United States or pro-Western in its orientation. Syria has also been accused of furthering the insurgency and terrorism in Iraq. The benefits to Syria from this involvement are not as clear as for Iran, although if the United States is bogged down in Iraq it is less likely to being pressure to bear on Syria on other regional issues (such as the Golan Heights or Lebanon). Of course, one of the most important external actors is not a state but Al Qaeda and groups associated with it. These groups have been assisting the various insurgents and terrorists and sending volunteers into the country. The borders between Iraq and its neighbors have been porous enough for the foreign volunteers to slip into the country. There is obviously a support network available to them inside the country since they are not routinely killed or captured upon arrival. While there has been a great deal of attention paid to these foreign volunteers, they appear to make up less than 5 percent of the dissidents (Pape 2005: 246). Further, while the global jihadists are responsible for some of the suicide attacks that have occurred, they are clearly not behind all of them (Merari 2005: 73–4). Although much of the terrorist violence occurring within the country has been related to domestic issues, connections with foreign elements have contributed to the violence and instability.

As of 2007 it would appear that the various terrorist groups operating in the country have been successful in preventing the establishment of an effective government. A strong government that represented most Iraqi groups in some fashion would make achievement of many of their ethnic, political, or religious goals of the violent groups—whether domestic or international— more difficult. What is apparent after analysis that the terrorist violence in Iraq has been effective in a negative fashion. The violence has prevented opponents from achieving key goals. The United States has *not* been able to establish a friendly, democratic regime, the Shias have *not* dominated a strong national government, and the Sunni minority has *not* maintained itself in power. The terrorist violence, however, has not resulted in any groups achieving other, more positive objectives. The eventual US withdrawal, hastened by insurgent attacks and terrorism, will create a new political matrix in which sooner or later some group or groups will come to dominate either a united Iraq or the components of a dismembered country. Whether the victorious groups are linked to the current dissident factions or which factions remain to be seen.

SUMMARY

In some cases there is evidence that one type of terrorist violence does indeed lead to others. There are many countries, however, which have faced terrorist violence but have not experienced waves of terrorism. The Scandinavian countries have had to deal with right-wing radicalism but virtually no other form of terrorism. Greece has faced leftist violence for over twenty-five years, but no new waves of terrorism from other sources have appeared. Canada has had a brief flurry of ethnic violence in Quebec, and in Nepal there is continued violence associated with a leftist insurrection complete including terrorism even after a peace agreement that was negotiated in 2006. Clearly one form of terrorism need not lead to or inspire other dissidents in these nations to use the same methods. Even long campaigns such as ETA in Spain have not led other dissident groups to adopt the same approach. Terror does not always beget terror.

Sri Lanka has suffered so much violence because it is a divided society and because it has been a political system in transition, and systems in transition are most vulnerable to such violence. The movement from colonial status to independent democracy started out well, but the transition was complicated by the ethnic differences. The relative lack of repression gave the JVP what seemed like an excellent opportunity to seize control of the country, both in the case of the first attempt and even the second. Many of the other countries suffering waves of violence such as Indonesia and Yugoslavia have also had political systems in transition or political systems that qualify as democracies or weaker authoritarian systems. Another commonality among the countries facing waves of terrorism is their status as successor states to empire. India, Sri Lanka as Ceylon, and Indonesia were colonial creations that brought together diverse populations. Unity in India only occurred within the context of empires, the last of which was British India. British India did not survive to independence with Pakistan breaking off at independence, and disputes over borders and places such as Kashmir continuing to be important issues. The constant concerns about the boundaries of the country, which are present in Indian political discussions, are a symptom of anxieties related to the colonial period (Weiss 2001: 39). Indonesia is comparable to India in being a former colonial empire composed of disparate parts. Yugoslavia was also the product of the breakup of empires, and its own break up in the 1990s provides a similar example of imperial decline. Yugoslavia was a small multiethnic empire, but the problems faced by Croatia, Bosnia, and Macedonia, as well as Serbia in Kosovo, are similar to the problems faced by the successor states of larger empires or former colonies. Iraq is both a system in transition and a reflection of absorption in two previous empires (Ottoman and British). While Iraq had some involvement with terrorism in the past, the current situation is unique in that a variety of groups using terrorism as a technique have simultaneously been pursuing different, and even contradictory, objectives. The new government and the United States presence have been assailed from many directions, and different groups in the general population have become targets as well. The diversity of the successor states to the USSR suggests that terrorism will be a continuing problem in that area of the world as well. The empire is gone, and the new governments clearly qualify as political systems in transition.

Even though political systems in transition, and perhaps especially successor states of empires, are most vulnerable, not every country that has faced waves of terror qualifies on these counts. The United States has not been a political system in transition for a long time nor is it a successor state to an empire. Germany in the 1970s would no longer qualify either—although the Weimar Republic was a very good example of a vulnerable system in transition in an earlier period. Some countries will suffer from multiple types of terrorism despite having had long-established political systems and histories as independent countries within the same general boundaries. Terrorists do learn from each other, and it is possible for dissidents in the same country to borrow the tactics of others. National vulnerabilities are different, and no one type of country is doomed to face terrorist violence while only the totalitarian and very strong authoritarian seem to be immune to serious terrorist threats. To some extent the presence of previous terrorist actions does not always indicate there will be future campaigns, and the absence of previous terrorism cannot guarantee a terrorism-free future.

TERMS

Aceh	Kashmir
Ansar al-Islam	Kurdish Democratic Party (KDP)
Assam	Laskar Jihad
Ayodhya	Liberation Tigers of Tamil Eelam (LTTE)
Ba'ath Party	Mujahedin-e-Khalq (MEK)
Rajiv Gandhi	Patriotic Union of Kurdistan (PUK)
global jihadist	Saddam Hussein
Hamas	Tamil Nadu
Irian Jaya (Western Papua)	Tamil Tigers
Janatha Vimukthi Peramuna (JVP)	Zionists

FURTHER READING

Crenshaw, M. (2000) "Democracy, Commitment Problems and Managing Ethnic Violence: The Case of India and Sri Lanka," *Terrorism and Political Violence*, 12, 3/4: 135–59.

Joshi, M. (1996) "On the Razor's Edge: The Liberation Tigers of Tamil Eelam," *Studies in Conflict and Terrorism*, 19, 1: 19–42.

Malley, M. (2003) "Indonesia: The Erosion of State Capacity," in R. Rotberg (ed.) *State Failure and State Weakness in a Time of Terror*, Cambridge, MA, and Washington DC: World Peace Foundation and Brookings Institution Press, 183–218.

Stansfield, G. (2005) "The Transition to Democracy in Iraq: Historical Legacies, Resurgent Identities and Reactionary Tendencies," in A. Danchev and J. MacMillan (eds) *The Iraq War and Democratic Politics*, London: Routledge, 134–59.

CHAPTER 12

Counterterrorism

The previous chapters said relatively little about what measures might be effective in dealing with terrorist movements, although the successful responses were fairly obvious in some of the case studies. Potential solutions to terrorism in the world will be discussed below. Programs to counter terrorism run the gamut from detection and prevention of violent dissident activities by police, security agencies, and military forces to more involved efforts to eliminate support within society for the dissident groups. The techniques are available to all kinds of governments, although in some cases different regimes will find some approaches more in keeping with their style of governance. How governments attempt to deal with terrorist threats will influence the future of the dissident organizations and their societies. Some actions may defeat dissidents, but failures could strengthen the terrorist groups. Even short-term successes could have negative consequences if they sow the seeds of future problems.

TECHNIQUES OF COUNTERTERRORISM

It is important to recognize from the outset that no one solution exists for dealing with all types of dissident groups. What works in one place or time could fail in another place or time. Terrorism is far too complex for one solution to be effective in dealing with all the possible threats. Among the more obvious possible responses to the threat of terrorism are the provision of greater security, better detection and prevention: disrupting fiances; repression; retaliation or punishment for foreign supporters of dissident groups; pre-emptive action; special counter-terrorism units; granting concessions, actually granting concessions and instituting reforms; and diplomatic appraoches and international cooperation.

Increased security

Increased security, especially around critical targets or personnel, is one solution to the terrorist threat. Remove the targets that provide dissident groups with so much publicity, and the incentive to launch attacks may be eliminated. Greater security can help, but there are far too many targets for security measures to be effective. If the potential targets include any government or party official or any member of the security forces, no defense is completely effective. If the entire population or a substantial portion of the population is the target, there will always be someone who is vulnerable. Car bombs are too easy to create and use, and there are far too many offices, monuments, buildings, schools, places of worship, and other structures to defend. In an environment that is rich with potential targets, terrorists can always avoid heavily defended targets and find easier alternatives (Raymond 2003: 76). For example, Hizballah operatives bombed the Israeli embassy in Buenos Aires in 1992 and a Jewish cultural center in 1994 in the same city in retaliation for Israeli actions in the Middle East. Buenos Aires was apparently chosen for the attacks because Hizballah had a support network in the area and because Argentina lacked a rigorous security apparatus (at this time); Argentina as a country had no special significance beyond convenience (Pillar 2001: 59). The 1998 attacks against the US embassies in Nairobi and Dar-es-Salaam were similarly a matter of convenience, including the fact that Kenya and Tanzania had weaker security than many other countries. Even in countries with high levels of security, it is possible for terrorists to find targets. Israel is as security conscious as any country in the world and is as experienced in detecting terrorists as any nation, yet suicide bombers and other attackers have been able to almost routinely penetrate into many parts of the country and launch their attacks.

Of course, the fact that absolute security is impossible to achieve does not mean that improved security is not worthwhile. Physical security can save lives and limit the damage of the attacks that do occur (Pillar 2001: 37–8). Improvements in airport security over the decades meant that many hijackings were avoided, although not those of the September 11th attacks. Total airport security has never been possible, and it would probably be foolish to expect it to be so in the immediate future. Metal detectors in buildings have deterred some assaults but have failed to detect weapons in other cases. Bombs still get through, as do armed terrorists; it is just much more difficult to accomplish. Key personnel can vary their routines or take suitable precautions to prevent kidnappings or assaults. Such actions are eminently wise, but they cannot grant immunity. Any measure "that would preclude every possible attack by every possible terrorist group for every possible motive is not even theoretically conceivable" (Hoffman 1997: 10). Enhanced security and prevention can limit the damage that attacks will generate, but they cannot currently eliminate all danger of such attacks. Further, it is possible that enhanced security will only have temporary effects in reducing attacks. Groups will be willing to lie low until security is relaxed (Gurr 2003: 212). Such increased security, however, can have a down side. The widespread use of metal detectors in airports led to more deadly attacks with bombs against airliners (Silke 2003b: 219). The so-called substitution effect can be present in other ways as well. When the embassies of major countries, especially the United States, became more difficult targets for Latin American terrorist groups because of increased security, the terrorists switched to the embassies of smaller countries that were more vulnerable (B. Jenkins 1981: 21). More recently, protective actions by developed countries after September 11th led to terrorist groups transferring attacks to weakly protected areas in developing countries (Enders and Sandler 2006: 2). When Germany was able to reduce terrorist attacks from within its own borders, it inadvertently increased the chances that such attacks would occur elsewhere (Katzenstein 2003: 754).

Enhanced security measures will increase the costs to the government and private companies and groups. Resources will be diverted away from other purposes toward providing protection. While the security measures might pay for themselves in terms of the death and destruction that are prevented, there are still the opportunity costs that come from not being able to use the resources elsewhere (Davis and Jenkins 2002: 36–7). If security forces, police, or the military have to be expanded then the money and resources have to be taken from other sectors of the economy. If one of the goals of the dissident group is to cause economic dislocation and hardships by launching attacks, they will have already succeeded when extra security measures go into effect. It is even possible in extreme cases that the resulting strains on the economy could eventually lead to the downfall of the government in power or even a change in the political system.

Intelligence gathering—detection and prevention

Prevention via intelligence gathering and infiltration of dissident groups is another possible solution in the battle against terrorism. In the wake of the 2001 attacks on the World Trade Center and the Pentagon, the CIA and other US intelligence agencies were faulted for not having discovered what was about to happen or for not having recognized the value of information that was available to them. Intelligence agencies obviously did not take the threat represented by Al Qaeda seriously enough (Betts 2002b: 22). Hindsight, of course, is almost always nearly perfect. The existence of a multitude of targets in any country makes effective detection of terrorist plans much more difficult and all the potential targets cannot be protected. Even if the intelligence agencies had known an attack was coming, they would not have known the method that was going to be used. Generals have often been accused of preparing to fight the last war, and intelligence agencies are likely to focus on preventing reprises of successful attacks such as car bombs, not new methods. Since even the old methods can succeed barring very precise information of tactics and targets, prevention via intelligence gathering is difficult. Without someone inside the planning group itself or the chance to interrogate someone involved in the planning, information is not likely to be precise enough to provide the details necessary for effective prevention from normal intelligence sources. The great multitude of potential targets that terrorists have makes prevention very difficult. US intelligence services are also handicapped by the devotion of intelligence resources for fifty years to Cold War enemies. Resources were directed toward gaining information on the Soviet Union, China, and their allies, not to countries and regions where many terrorist organizations now have their headquarters and recruit members (L. Johnson 2003). US intelligence gathering also increasingly came to rely on technology rather than human resources (Ilardi 2004: 219). While such an emphasis was effective during a cold war against a technologically sophisticated opponent, the reliance on technology has been less effective for dealing with non-state, terrorist groups. Russian efforts to deal with the Chechen insurgents and terrorists have been hampered for many of the same intelligence limitations (Kramer 2004/5: 55–6). In addition, the CIA has had the disadvantage of not really controlling intelligence gathering. There are competing agencies—including the FBI, the military services, and the National Security Administration. The CIA actually only controls about 15 percent of the overall intelligence budget (Zegart 2005: 99–100).

Effective intelligence requires allies whose national police forces can gather the essential raw data for analysis. US intelligence agencies, for example, cannot be as effective working alone, even with greater resources (Posen 2001/2: 46). Both US agencies and other intelligence services need to recruit and train local agents to supply them with information, but these kinds of efforts take time. While intelligence agencies *should* be able to predict which areas will become trouble spots, they cannot really do so with any certainty. It would have been very unlikely in September 1991 for the CIA to correctly perceive the danger that a Saudi billionaire headquartered in Afghanistan would constitute for the United States ten years later, and that it would be necessary to train or recruit Pathan-speaking operatives to be ready in the future. Had a CIA operative actually suggested such a scenario, in all likelihood he or she probably would have been in danger of losing his or her job.

Security services have some advantages when fighting domestic dissident groups as opposed to foreign ones. Potential operatives or agents will know the language and local culture and will not need advance training to attempt to penetrate groups or gather information. But even in the domestic area, security services may still have difficulties. The United States has not done particularly well over the years in dealing with local right-wing extremist groups. Even though the FBI suspected that Eric Rudolph was responsible for bombings at abortion clinics and the Atlanta Olympics, it took seven years to capture him (Heymann 2003: 81). French domestic intelligence gathering, on the other hand, improved over time after being relatively ineffective. The security agencies were ill prepared when they had to face terrorist attacks in the 1980s. The government and agencies did not predict the attacks, and they were unable to catch the perpetrators. By the 1990s French authorities proved to be much more capable in gathering information on terrorist groups associated with the rebels in Algeria and then Al Qaeda in later years (Shapiro and Suzan 2003: 80, 86–7). They learned by experience, albeit experience of failure. Improved capabilities are thus possible, but they have to be learned over time, and new types of threats are likely to require new capabilities, meaning that learning curves for intelligence agencies will always be present since the initiative for attacks almost always lies with the dissident groups.

Intelligence operations are likely to be more effective against larger organizations that are more vulnerable to penetration and gathering of information (O'Neil 2003). Difficulties with detection, and therefore prevention, are increased when the dissident group is small. When all the members know each other on a face-to-face basis, the infiltration of informers is extremely unlikely. The 17 November Movement in Greece survived for as long as it did because of its small size. Constant efforts to penetrate dissident groups or discover facts about them should eventually succeed, but it may take years or decades. Leaderless resistance type of operations further complicate the task of intelligence agencies in detecting planned assaults since the potential terrorists undertaking the attack have no direct organizational link with the planners or ideological leaders. Discovering the plans of these kinds of terrorists or other ad hoc groups formed for particular actions will be quite difficult. There are far too many groups to monitor effectively, especially since some groups may never get beyond the stage of talking about violent resistance. Yet some of these groups will actually launch attacks. Detecting and monitoring all such groups will be beyond the scope of any country facing any significant dissatisfaction. Keeping tabs on such groups when their headquarters is abroad raises additional complications. US security agencies cannot operate in every country at will, any more than British, Israeli, or Russian intelligence operatives are free to gather information in the United States.

It is only when a new terrorist group strikes that the real threat becomes obvious. Many potential terrorist groups never actually attempt an attack, and others are caught before they can do any real damage. The Minnesota Patriots Council was caught stockpiling ricin poison before they had a chance to use it. In Iran under the Shah leftist groups were routinely infiltrated and destroyed. Al Qaeda cells have been discovered in many parts of the world. Yet some groups will not be detected until they strike. One of the great difficulties for intelligence services is keeping track of all potentially violent dissident groups that a society may have to deal with. Some will inevitably escape notice. Others may attack in unexpected places and in unexpected ways. Ultimately, "no strategy for a war against terror can bank on prevention" (Betts 2002a: 59). India's intelligence services have mounted a number of sophisticated clandestine operations that have detected and defeated terrorist groups (Raufer 2000: 49). Notwithstanding these successes, India has suffered from frequent terrorist attacks. The failure of the Israeli security forces to detect and prevent Palestinian bombings, including suicide attacks, is further testimony to the fact that prevention is not always possible. The Israeli intelligence agencies have proven their worth many times over, and they have a wealth of experience in dealing with Palestinian dissident groups, yet they have not detected all the attacks or provided information on all aspects of the leadership and planning groups of all the varied Palestinian nationalist groups that are currently willing to use violence as well as which groups *may* be willing to use violence. The Israeli security services also seem to have been ineffective in detecting attacks by Jewish extremist groups, probably because they were focusing almost all their resources on Palestinian threats. The very nature of terrorism means that the group that is responsible for disasters that occur is the group that went undetected (Imai 2002: 99).

Disrupting finances

A special area where intelligence can be combined with other efforts that come into play involves attempts to limit or eliminate the flow of financial support to terrorist organizations. This financial support has been important for many terrorist groups. Some financial aid was direct and in other cases it was indirect. Money can come from foreign governments, but it can also come from private sources. The United States government encouraged individuals to provide funds for the Contras in Nicaragua when official funding was limited. Fertinelli eased financial problems for the Red Brigades. Osama bin Laden's wealth and support from other Muslim contributors has helped to make Al Qaeda as dangerous as it has become. The PLO set up various businesses and developed its own sources of income to complement support from Arab governments. Diaspora populations have provided funding for many dissident groups. Collaboration with criminal groups and profits from the drug trade have become very important for a number of other dissident groups. Whatever the source, money has been important for either maintaining the dissident groups or making them more dangerous. When the financial sources of the groups can be stopped, their ability to mount attacks is reduced even if not eliminated, and the groups become less dangerous. Governments can attempt to disrupt the financial operations of these groups. Intelligence agencies can identity dummy corporations, charities, or other groups that are used to channel funds to the terrorists. There are national laws that prohibit contributions to terrorist groups or money laundering, and some of these financial flows can be tracked and stopped. Accountants and government auditors may also be able to discover connections between supporters of dissidents and attacks that are planned or that are going to be launched by following the money trail. One advantage of focusing on the financial base of terrorist groups is that those involved in the financial operations may be less committed to the organization (Trager and Zagorcheva 2005/6: 96–7).

Unfortunately, success in closing off financial support for violent dissident organizations has been limited. The first US efforts to seize assets of terrorist organizations had only minimal results (Pillar 2001: 261). Contributions for Noraid (and the IRA) continued in the United States with little interruption for many years. Terrorists have access to alternative means of financing their activities (Gurr 2006: 98). There have been some suggestions that Al Qaeda's financing has been severely curtailed (Rudner 2004: 222). Overall, efforts to disrupt the financial resources and links of the group have proven to be quite difficult. The initial efforts of either accountants or intelligence operatives to find or track the funding sources for Al Qaeda have met with only limited success, and only a small percentage of Al Qaeda funds have been stopped (Cronin 2006: 37). Al Qaeda has been successful using both modern technology and more traditional and personal financial networks—such as the *hawla* (Feldman 2006). It has also tapped into Islamic charities, operated its own businesses, become involved in criminal activities, and found other ways of raising funds (Abuza 2003a: 171). The organization has apparently been able to move some of its financial resources into commodities such as precious stones and gold that are more difficult to trace (Raphaeli 2003: 74–5). Al Qaeda has taken advantage of chaotic conditions in Africa to buy and market diamonds as a means of funding its activities (Lyman and Morrison 2004: 84). Governments in many countries have passed new banking laws and regulations to attempt to stop financing, but such laws are difficult to implement successfully (Abuza 2003b: 21, 211). The failure of governments around the world to effectively find profits from the drug trade, whether the money was funding dissident groups or criminal organizations, is another indication of the difficulties involved. Most drug money gets laundered successfully. Drug cartels match the sophistication of large multinational corporations in their ability to use the international banking system with relative secrecy and impunity from indictment and conviction (Klare 2003: 28). A group such as Al Qaeda is organized like international criminal groups and is as effective (Schneider and Schneider 2002). Many dissident groups have become quite adept at using offshore banking systems, numbered accounts, dummy corporations, and other mechanisms to hide their transactions and to make purchases. The same banking systems that provide benefits to multinational corporations, wealthy individuals, and criminal organizations in terms of laundering and secrecy can also serve the more sophisticated dissident groups. The funds involved with terrorist groups are probably more difficult to detect since they are only a fraction of the amounts that are moved by criminal organizations (Cronin 2002/3: 50). Al Qaeda operations have gravitated toward Southeast Asia as a region for transferring funds and hiding assets given weak government surveillance of banking operations (Abuza 2003a: 170). Even when there are laws on the books, implementation has been problematic at best (Raphaeli 2003: 79).

While interfering with financial flows is not easy, at least some governments have the resources in place to make the attempt. In addition to looking for criminal profits or persons or companies dodging taxes, government tax agencies can now also look for money being channeled to dissident groups. These efforts to interrupt financial flows will also not require major expenditures on the part of the developed countries. While the success in blocking the flow of financial support has been limited, any successes do contribute to a weakening of such groups. If they have to allocate resources (money, time) to more carefully cover their financial tracks, the resources used in this fashion are not available for lethal attacks. Terrorist organizations can have opportunity costs too!

Repression

One factor that has made a difference for the occurrence of non-state terrorism, or its absence, has been the presence of a totalitarian political system or a powerful authoritarian state. These types of states are likely to have very effective intelligence agencies as part of their control mechanisms (Heymann 2001/2: 34). Since totalitarian governments have a great deal of control over society, they have managed to avoid many terrorist threats because of their ability to eliminate dissidents or potential dissidents before they can organize. Ruthlessness is often a hallmark of such governments, and they can strike at not only the dissidents themselves but also at their family members or friends. Democratic states, on the other hand, pay a price in terms of vulnerability to attacks by domestic dissident groups or foreign ones that find it convenient to launch attacks on their soil. The benefit of a democratic system for the citizens is that they do not have to worry about arbitrary arrests, contrived prison sentences in concentration camps or gulags, or execution without cause. State imposed or state supported terrorism on the national soil is not normally present in a democratic system, although democratic governments at times have looked the other way when unpopular groups were the victims of vigilante violence or mob action (B. Lutz and J. Lutz 2007). While democracy may have a price that must be paid in terms of the loss of life because of greater susceptibility to terrorist attacks, the loss is normally less than what could occur in a strong authoritarian system or a totalitarian one. Even in the case of efforts to deal with terrorist attacks, democracy as a system of government would appear to still have more advantages than disadvantages.

Repression of violent groups is an option for all states including democracies. In fact, virtually every state facing the threat of terrorist violence will chose repression if such a course of action seems likely to succeed. The regular police or security forces defeat most dissident groups that resort to terror before they actually constitute a real threat to a state by creating major disruptions. The successful defeat of these groups depends on luck, the use of intelligence sources, and normal police investigatory methods for discovering perpetrators of criminal or terrorist actions. The detection and arrest of members of violent dissident groups is fairly common in democracies, weak and strong authoritarian systems, totalitarian states, and even political systems in transition. Even terrorist groups that successfully launch more serious attacks on the political system can usually be contained with the usual police routines. Timothy McVeigh in the United States was caught after the attack in Oklahoma City. The Red Brigades in Italy and the Red Army Faction in Germany were eventually defeated by the state *without* any major reduction in democratic practices and protections of civil liberties. Various right-wing groups in the United States have been uncovered and their members arrested by the police without resorting to extraordinary laws.

There is no guarantee that repression will be successful. In Colombia the government has failed to regain control of its territory by concessions to the leftists. To date the efforts at repression have been noticeably ineffective. Continued efforts at repression have failed in Sri Lanka with the Tamil Tigers (although not the JVP), in the Basque region with ETA, and elsewhere. Israel has used great force and an extensive and sophisticated intelligence-gathering network in efforts to control the Palestinians in the Occupied Territories without defeating the nationalist and religious groups involved. Repression alone will not end the terrorism that Israel has been facing. Repression can even be counterproductive since terrorism "can provoke government repression, which in turn stimulates further terrorism, which provokes more repression" (Crenshaw 1983: 6). Thus, repression can result in new recruits joining the dissident groups; one factor that explains the willingness of new recruits to join terrorist groups is the injury to or death of a family member or close friend (Silke 2005: 245). The repression practiced by Indian forces in Kashmir alienated the previously apolitical population (Behera 2007: 422). IRA recruitment dramatically increased in some periods when the British were vigorous in dealing with suspects (Heymann 2001/2: 29). Repression in Russia and Romania in the past has had similar perverse results (Laqueur 2001: 12). Regimes in transition may be less able to use repression if the regular police or security forces are in disarray. New groups can appear to threaten a state in these times as well. Even when repression does work, the elimination of the terrorist threat may be a long and costly battle. The struggle of the Italian government with the Red Brigades resulted in the deaths of thousands. In Algeria, over 100,000 have died in the battles between the secular government and the Muslim dissidents, and there was no guarantee that the Muslim rebels would not succeed in overthrowing or bringing about a major transformation of the state.

State terrorism is an extreme form of repression for dealing with violent dissidents, although not all state terrorism is designed as counterterrorist strategy. The ethnic cleansing in Bosnia and attacks on white farmers in Zimbabwe were not responses to terrorist attacks. In the case of East Timor, Sudan, and Rwanda, the state support for terrorist militias and death squads was to some degree a consequence of guerrilla campaigns, but ones that did not involve significant terrorist activity. In other cases, however, governments have chosen to use extra-legal violence to search out and destroy opponents. Just as government repression and terror may trigger the formation of violent dissident groups, dissident terrorism may lead to governmental use of terror as a counterterrorist weapon (Wilkinson 2003: 108). These kinds of efforts have proven to be effective in the short term in many cases. The initial Algerian uprising for independence from France led to local authorities and the military using torture, indefinite detention, and other techniques to acquire information. The French were able to destroy the National Liberation Front's organization in the cities and weaken it in the countryside as well. The military regimes in Uruguay and Argentina were able to defeat their domestic leftist groups by using state terror. Governments in many other parts of the world have resorted to these techniques as well. Giving free rein to vigilantes and death squads, however, does not always destroy the opposition. In El Salvador and South Africa the dissidents survived, East Timor became independent, and India is not in effective control Kashmir.

Retaliation or punishment

Striking back is an obvious counterterrorism option, and one that is often popular, but it is a choice fraught with difficulties. Countries retaliate when there is evidence of support for domestic terrorists by another country. It has also been argued that security alone cannot prevent terrorist attacks; it is also necessary to go after nations that harbor terrorists (Chellaney 2001/2: 99). During the Cold War, direct military incursions by the superpowers were limited since the two antagonists were roughly equal in capabilities. Soviet support for dissidents in a Western ally of the United States often resulted in Western support for rebels in a pro-Soviet state. US aid for the *mujahedin* in Afghanistan repaid the Soviet Union for its support for national liberation struggles in Latin America, Asia, and Africa. The aid did not really end the Soviet support for terrorism by dissident groups, but it did make it potentially more costly. Retaliation provides an immediate response to terrorist attacks. Many countries have felt free to bomb or attack guerrilla and terrorist camps in other states—the United States in the case of Libya and the attacks against Al Qaeda camps in Afghanistan when President Clinton was in power, Israeli attacks into Lebanon and Jordan, and South African incursions into Angola during the struggle for control over Southwest Africa (Namibia). South Africa made sure that any state that offered sanctuary to the exiled ANC knew it could expect either attacks against ANC bases or pursuit of guerrilla forces into its territory (Welsh 1995: 243). Turkish forces have engaged Kurdish insurgents in northern Iraq. Indian artillery has regularly fired on presumed guerrilla camps and positions in that portion of Kashmir under the control of Pakistan. The attack by the United States and its allies on the Taliban regime in Afghanistan for supporting the Al Qaeda network is simply a recent and massive example of military retaliation against a government supporting terrorist attacks. One explanation for the rarity of attacks on US soil by foreign terrorists is that such attacks would have resulted in retaliation against the governments of the countries (such as Iran, Iraq, or Syria) that supported the terrorist groups in question (Heymann 2001/2: 25). Such self-imposed limitations are less relevant to loosely connected networks of terrorist groups such as Al Qaeda. Of course, retaliation is not even a realistic option when the local dissidents are supported by a stronger state. Nicaragua, for example, could not do much to retaliate for American support for the Contras.

Retaliation can take forms other than military action. Economic sanctions can be applied against the country suspected of encouraging terrorism. Potential sanctions can include a virtual trade embargo, such as was imposed on Cuba by the United States. The economic sanctions can also be subtler or less obvious. The country harboring or supporting terrorists may not be able to get loans or only get them at higher interest rates. Foreign investors may not receive guarantees or aid from their home governments for doing business in a given country, reducing the incentives for them to invest. Arms sales to the country may be curtailed. The US unilateral sanctions against Iran ultimately limited the ability of the Islamic Republic to purchase arms and thus weakened that country's military capacity. The sanctions, however, had little effect on Iranian support for foreign terrorist groups since that support did not depend on a strong Iranian military establishment (Pillar 2001: 168). Membership in international economic organizations or other groups may be denied. Tourist visas for visits to the country that supports a terrorist group may not be issued. None of these less obvious pressures were readily available to the United States in the case of the Taliban in Afghanistan. The regime in power was virtually uninterested in tourists, foreign aid, foreign investment, or even trade. Libya faced many of these types of sanctions in the 1980s in response to its reported support of terrorists. Sanctions like these supported by the United Nations and the United States were eventually effective in reducing Libyan support for terrorism (Crenshaw 2003b: 165). Ultimately, the change in Libyan attitudes was a reflection of a combination of reciprocal concessions, multilateral sanctions, and the willingness of the United States to use force (Jentleson and Whytock 2005/6). Syria has managed to have itself removed from the list of countries that have supported terrorism by taking appropriate actions. Even Iraq was relatively quiet in supporting dissident groups in other countries after the first Persian Gulf War with the United States and its allies. The military defeat and continuing military and economic sanctions had an impact on that country's actions or lack of actions. Japan in dealing with terrorist incidents abroad has encouraged further attacks by concessions and by failing to retaliate (Angel 1990: 41). It has been suggested that terrorists see India as a soft target because the government imposes no costs on them or their foreign supporters for their activities (Chellaney 2001/2: 99). Further, the withdrawal of Western peacekeeping forces from Lebanon in 1983 after the attacks on the US marines and French paratroopers, the withdrawal from Somalia in 1993, and the Israeli withdrawal from Lebanon in 2000 were all seen as victories for the terrorists. The absence of an appropriate show of force can be seen as counterproductive in these cases (Heymann 2003: 165).

Retaliation can also be attempted against terrorist organizations. Some groups, such as Hizballah, are simply too large to be destroyed by a few well-conceived attacks, even if they can be weakened (Pillar 2001: 33–4). Israel has frequently retaliated against suspected Palestinian militants when faced with suicide bombings and other attacks. To date the retaliation seems to have kept a cycle of violence going where Palestinian groups feel bound to retaliate in turn. Indiscriminate retaliation against presumed supporters has largely failed to prevent increased support for terrorists. The events with the Israelis indicate that the deterrent effect of retaliatory strikes is more likely to be effective against state actors, not dissident groups (Chyba 2002: 129). The US attack and invasion of Afghanistan did disrupt Al Qaeda, and it is possible that bin Laden would not have carried out the 9/11 attacks if he had foreseen this result (Merari 2005: 84). Some dissident groups, however, are more difficult to target than others. If military action fails to damage an elusive terrorist group, the effort could be counterproductive. The launching of expensive missiles that miss their targets may increase the publicity for the groups responsible for attacks and even increase the prominence of its cause (Pillar 2001: 105). Retaliation against dissident groups may be counterproductive if splinter groups are involved in the attacks. An assault against the main body may lead these groups to restart a campaign of terror if they were not involved in the attack launched by a splinter group. Breakaway groups have been real enough as demonstrated by the Real IRA and Continuity IRA, the departure of groups from the PLO for its conciliatory policies, splits within ETA, and the divisions among the Algerian dissidents battling their government. It has been argued that some splits within dissident organizations are basically tactical. The "militants" leave, vowing to continue to use terrorism while the "moderates" declare a truce and negotiate. Unfortunately for counterterrorist campaigns, it is often difficult to determine which splits represent real differences and which ones are fictitious divisions. Uncertainty, however, does make effective retaliation more difficult, and retaliating against the wrong group would generate new attacks. The Albanians in Kosovo and Macedonia proved to be very effective in generating such retaliation and then taking advantage of the anger against the government to recruit additional support. There is even the possibility of some outside organization mounting false flag attacks as a means of forcing governments to crack down on a dissident organization rather than negotiating with it. Failure to retaliate, moreover, may hold costs for states suffering from terrorist attacks. The inability or unwillingness to strike back may encourage terrorists to continue attacks just as retaliation or the threat to retaliate *may* convince them to cease their operations in at least a specific locale. The lack of punishment or retaliation simply encourages renewed attacks. Of course, the Indian intelligence services have been willing to use death squads and other forms of repression against domestic groups that are within their reach. The Indian case thus provides an example of both successful retaliation and the lack of such activities with different consequences.

Of course, one ultimate aim of retaliatory attacks designed to punish terrorist groups or their supporters is to deter attacks in the future. The air raids on Libya initially had a perverse effect. Libyan support for attacks increased in the aftermath of the raids before returning to their original levels (Enders and Sandler 2004: 132). Other actions in addition to the threat of retaliation were important for the eventual change in Libyan policies. One analysis of Israeli retaliation has found that it had only temporary effects on the level of terrorism. In the long term, the level of violence returned to the usual levels (Brophy-Baermann and Conybeare 1994: 209). In later years Israeli retaliation has similarly not stopped terrorist attacks. The Palestinians in many periods increased their attacks in size and strength in the aftermath of such attempts at retaliation (Silke 2003b: 220–1). Overall, there has been a consistent finding "that major military retaliation had never led to a reduction of terrorism" (Silke 2003b: 216). There is the possibility that selective deterrence, however, may work. If the costs of cooperating with Al Qaeda become prohibitive, local groups may avoid contact with the organization (Trager and Zagorcheva 2005/6: 122). The overall record for retaliation as a deterrent against further attacks suggests that such attacks are not likely to work.

Pre-emptive action

A country can attempt a pre-emptive strike; pre-emption may in fact be a necessary strategy if the threat of retaliation has no deterrent effect (Richelson 2002: 246). Strikes can be against training camps of the terrorist group or against state supporters. The 2002 attack against Al Qaeda and the Taliban in Afghanistan was both retaliation and an attempt to pre-empt additional attacks. If such strikes work, pre-emption is an ideal strategy for threatened states since it will limit the number and intensity of future terrorist operations, at least in the short run. While pre-emptive action will work in some circumstances, it is highly unlikely that such attacks will be successful enough to eliminate the threat for terrorist organizations (Sederberg 2003: 274). Pre-emptive action, of course, requires excellent intelligence gathering in order to be effective. Without detailed knowledge of the activities of the terrorist groups and the whereabouts of their personnel, it will not be possible to identify targets with enough precision. It is also necessary to detect those groups that have the potential to strike some time in the future. Not all groups in the process of forming are equally dangerous. Only a handful will pose a serious threat, and by the time they do so, the responses are likely to be one of retaliation rather than pre-emption. While strong authoritarian states might be able to eliminate most potential threats through an extensive security apparatus, at the present time, it seems unlikely that a democratic state can consistently pre-empt dissidents who might use violence and still remain democratic.

Pre-emption against dissidents who become violent will also be even more difficult when terrorist groups rely on organizational attributes such as leaderless resistance. Targeting members is difficult in the best of circumstances. Loosely connected networks like Al Qaeda are difficult to attack in any pre-emptive fashion in order to prevent future attacks. Linkages among the groups often only become apparent *after* the attacks have occurred, such as the Al Qaeda groups that were present in Southeast Asia. Once such attacks have occurred, normally police and intelligence methods will often be sufficient to track down the individuals involved and their support network. Pre-emptive attacks against state supporters of terrorist groups have similar limitations. True state support may be difficult to prove, and rallying support for pre-emptive actions can be difficult as evidenced by the situation of Saddam Hussein's regime in Iraq. Even successful pre-emption against a state might have negative diplomatic consequences elsewhere in the international system. The threat of pre-emption or the attack itself might even stimulate the actions that the military attack was designed to avoid (Posen 2001/2: 54). Even if there are no immediate negative political, military, or diplomatic consequences, the seeds may be sown for the formation of new groups willing to use violence in the future.

BOX 12.1 ASSASSINATION

Governments can undertake assassinations as a form of retaliation or as an effort at pre-emption. The Assassins demonstrated the deterrent effect that could occur with this technique against government officials, and it could serve the same purpose with dissident leaders. Assassination could serve a preventative function if the death of a leader or leaders leads to a disruption of the organization. Like other forms of pre-emption, successful assassination requires high-quality intelligence efforts to locate the targets. The death of leaders is unlikely to affect large organizations since they have the capacity to replace individuals who may be killed. Smaller organizations are more vulnerable to this type of action, but then these are the groups for which it is harder for authorities or security forces to gain information. The death of Osama bin Laden would undoubtedly disrupt Al Qaeda, at least for a period, given his organizational talents, but his death would not be crippling. The organization would not disappear over-night (Pillar 2001: 56), and the threat from the component parts would continue since the important linkages already exist. While assassinations can disrupt or even deter in some cases, they can also create martyrs and lead to increased recruitment for terrorist groups (Heymann 2003: 48). The assassination of bin Laden, for example, would make him a martyr in Arab and Muslim eyes and could increase support for terrorist groups at least in the short term (Nacos 2003: 2).

There have been some efforts to assassinate leaders and key members of various groups, but the results have suggested that these efforts are not likely to be very successful. Israel has frequently targeted specific members of Palestinian groups for death. Even when the assassins have been successful, the result has often been an upsurge of support for the PLO or the Palestinian cause. Israeli 'targeted killings" (i.e., assassinations) have not been very effective in disrupting the Palestinian opposition (Byman 2006). Assassinating Palestinian militants in the more recent confrontations has simply resulted in retaliation and more Israeli casualties (Luft 2003: 3). The PLO and Hamas are not dependent on any one individual to survive, and provocations by Israel may even strengthen their hand. Assassinations can also be tricky. The assassinations also seem to have had absolutely no deterrent effect. In 1985, the CIA attempted to kill a Hizballah leader considered responsible for attacks on the United States. He survived, although ninety-two others were killed and hundreds injured. He later changed his anti-US tactics in return for $2 million in Saudi aid for his followers (Piszkiewicz 2003: 55–6). In 1984 when the United States bombed Libya in retaliation for supporting terrorist attacks on US soldiers in Germany, one of the targets was the palace where Qadaffi was presumed to be sleeping, clearly with the intent to remove him from political power as a casualty in a conventional attack. Similarly, efforts were made in both 1991 and 2003 to eliminate Saddam Hussein in choosing targets in Iraq. The obvious intent of the targeting in Libya and Iraq was to take out the key leaders of the group in a conventional retaliatory strike.

Special counterterrorism units

Many countries have trained special units to deal with terrorist situations. These forces can play a role in rescues but can also serve for retaliation and for preemptive actions. The presence of special forces can change the contexts in which terrorism can occur and can modify the options available to governments in dealing with violent dissident groups. The creation of such forces, however, is a tacit admission that terrorist incidents cannot always be prevented and that there could be situations where there is a need for such forces. These units can be used either in a domestic situation or as part of effort to rescue hostages held abroad. If such units are frequently successful in rescuing hostages or retaking buildings, they will have a positive deterrent effect on terrorist organizations in at least some cases. Planned dissident operations will appear to be more costly since members of the organization are more likely to be killed or captured (although such forces are not much of a deterrent to suicide attacks). Successes by the special forces also could make the dissident group appear to be more vulnerable and less able to achieve its objectives.

The record of special units has been a mixed one. When members of M-19 captured the Ministry of Justice in the Colombian capital of Bogota, the effort to retake the building resulted in over a hundred dead among the hostages, terrorists, and troops involved in the assault. Colombia lacked any special units trained for such a situation. On the other hand, Peruvian troops were very successful in recapturing the Japanese embassy in Lima from MRTA dissidents. In this case, the lengthy period that the crisis lasted served the government and security agencies well since the assaulting troops had ample time to rehearse the assault and observers could discover patterns being used by the dissidents in control of the embassy. These two cases from neighboring countries demonstrate how well things can go as well as how badly they can go.

The 1972 Munich Olympics provides another example of a failed rescue attempt. West Germany at that time lacked a trained counterterrorism force, and the effort to rescue the hostages resulted in the deaths of all the Israeli athletes. The German government learned from the experience and trained a special unit for possible use in the future. When a hijacked Lufthansa airliner was taken to Mogadishu in Somalia, West Germany received permission from the Somali government to attempt a rescue. The special unit successfully undertook an assault on the plane. Egyptian commandos also successfully rescued hostages on an airliner in Luxor (Enders and Sandler 2006: 168). A later effort by Egyptian commandos to emulate the German success in Mogadishu with a hijacked plane in Malta, however, resulted in the deaths of sixty of the ninety-eight passengers and crew (Pillar 2001: 98). The Russian "rescue" of theatergoers held by Chechen rebels in 2002 was another costly failure when the immobilizing agent that was used resulted in the death of many of the hostages. The crisis at the school in Breslan is another example of a less than successful Russian effort to release hostages. The United States has a variety of special operations units divided among the different branches of the armed forces. The closest they came to a hostage rescue attempt was the effort to release the hostages at the American embassy in Tehran in 1980, but the rescuers never reached the target area after mishaps in a staging area in the desert in Iran. Despite the failures, it is possible that the presence of such units may deter some situations and the absence of special units might encourage hostage taking by terrorist groups.

The British SAS is perhaps the special military unit with the greatest training for anti-terrorist operations, and probably the most experienced as well. The SAS was long involved in operations against the IRA units in Northern Ireland, often but not always successfully. It has also been called upon to deal with special situations, such as the occupation of the Iranian embassy in London by dissidents. Even with its training and its operations experience, it has not always been successful in its missions. Israeli special units also have had a great deal of experience with hostage cases and similar situations. Most people are aware of the spectacular successes such as the raid on Entebbe in Uganda that freed virtually of the hostages being held by German leftists and Palestinians. There have been other examples of successful rescues inside of Israel. On the negative side, however, many such situations have resulted in the deaths of many hostages. The record for Israel has been very mixed, indicating that even special units with extensive field experience will often fail to achieve their objectives.

Concessions and reform

Another potential approach to dealing with terrorism takes a dramatically different tact. When faced with active dissident groups, a government could recognize that the terrorism is a result of existing problems in the country. An ethnic minority, religious group, or ideological faction may have been neglected or faced discrimination as a matter of routine. As a consequence, dissident violence has resulted due to the increasing frustration felt by the group. While the government could continue to use repression, detection, and security measures to deal with the dissidents, it could also seek to change policies in order to address the issues that led to the dissident violence (Crenshaw 1995b: 23). It "is widely believed that giving in to terrorist's demands encourages them to continue their activities, but evidence for this proposition is weak" (Crenshaw 1998: 225). Concessions may be made as part of an effort to reduce support for the dissidents among those likely to favor their cause or the government may make policy changes because there is a real problem that needs to be addressed. Reforms thus become a response to the presence of terrorism in the society. Realistically, reform efforts may dissuade new members from joining dissident organizations or supporting the violence, but such efforts are unlikely to get active members to leave the groups (Gurr 2003: 210). Efforts at concession could fail if the grievances that fueled terrorist actions are multicausal rather than deriving from just one factor (Ross 1993). It may also be true that it will be difficult in at least some cases to find changes in policies that will be acceptable to the dissidents. Elements of a society supporting dissidents, even if small, have objectives that extend well beyond acceptable reforms (Gurr 2003: 212). For example, in Sri Lanka by the time the government was willing to discuss autonomy for Tamil regions, many of the Tamil rebels were unwilling to accept anything less than independence.

Of course, concessions are not always a realistic option for a government, even if the dissidents are willing to listen. Democracies cannot banish racial minorities targeted by right-wing terrorist groups. Further, a democratic government may find it difficult to establish the majority religion as a state religion. It is possible that the proposed domestic policy changes required by the dissidents or even changes in the government structure could lead to violent opposition by other groups. Groups such as al Qaeda that are interest in polarization rather than compromise are unlikely to be amenable to concessions (Schmid 2005: 226). There are no changes in US foreign policy that the United States could make to reduce Al Qaeda's hatred (Jervis 2002: 44). Settler populations in Algeria in the 1960s and the West Bank resorted to violence when the governments in power were negotiating with the Algerian Muslims and the Palestinians (Sederberg 2003: 281). If the terrorism originates from a group located abroad, foreign policy changes may not be possible, or the changes in foreign policy could even be unwise. The original groups could even add new demands to their list once the initial concessions were gained. Countries can also be caught in the middle of foreign conflicts. Taking no action could be deemed offensive by the losing side, while any action favoring one side could lead to violence from the other. A country can be condemned for interfering where it has no interests or it can be condemned for indifference and abdication of responsibility, all in regard to the same conflict (Ajami 2001: 10). For example, one of Al Qaeda's criticisms of the US and Western foreign policy was that for years there was no intervention in Bosnia to protect the Muslim population from attack from local Christians.

Concessions in some cases would appear to have worked as a response to violence by dissidents. The ultimate concession in colonial situations has been to grant independence to the territory where the violence is occurring. The British left Cyprus and Palestine, while the French gave Algeria its independence. In the Basque region, the activities of ETA led to concessions by the Spanish government in terms of regional autonomy that have limited the level of support for ETA. British negotiations with the IRA have offered the hope of peace after more than three decades of violence. In Algeria the government released the FIS leaders from prison and began negotiations for permitting fair elections, leading to a decline in the level of violence. A number of European governments have tightened up immigration policies in an effort to deprive their domestic extremists on the right of a focus for the agitation and violence. The Indonesian government did not choose to continue its policy of encouraging Madurese to settle in Borneo. Israel eventually agreed to negotiate with the PLO, and there is now a Palestinian National Authority that has some governmental power. The decision to grant concessions, however, can create a dilemma for governments. Reform efforts to deal with grievances after a terrorist attack run the danger of suggesting to the terrorists (and other dissidents) that they have been successful, encouraging further demands and the possibility of escalating violence (Heymann 2001/2: 28). Failure to undertake reform, however, could also lead to continued or escalating violence.

Another type of reform could include government programs to address the concerns of that portion of the population supporting the dissidents. Socioeconomic reform programs have been considered to be the best antidote against terrorism from the left or the right (Wilkinson 2000a: 82). Economic development, education, and political participation are potential long-term solutions to religious terrorism in the Middle East (Gurr 2003: 215). While it has been suggested that the spread of democracy would be an appropriate reform, it is not an immediate solution to the problem of terrorism since it takes time for democracy to become established. In addition, democratic regimes in transition are vulnerable to terrorism (Bjorgo 2005b: 9). Of course, establishing democracies will mean that change must occur, and any groups that experience negative effects from such changes may resort to their own forms of violence to protect what they have or to protest what they have lost. Concessions and government programs may also not be able to address all or even some of the underlying issues of dislocation due to modernization. Further, to the extent that the terrorism has weakened the economy and limited the resources available to the government, such corrective programs become more difficult. Efforts at reform can be quite costly. If attempts are going to be made to eliminate the root causes of terrorism, especially in poor countries, it will be expensive. If reforms are designed to deal with the problems that come with globalization and modernization that contribute to the rise of terrorist groups, it will require extensive sums. It would require significantly greater levels of foreign aid from the United States, for example, than that country has been willing to spend— in the neighborhood of $5 billion a year (McCaffrey and Basso 2002: 218). Changes in policies and concessions will work in some circumstances, but short of total surrender to dissidents this option is not always one that can be pursued.

Diplomatic approaches

International agreements achieved through diplomacy are an additional possibility to complement efforts at dealing with terrorism. Cooperation among nations in terms of dealing with terrorism has increased, providing some hope that this approach can help (B. Jenkins 2001: 323). The UN has been able to draft at least a dozen multilateral agreements that help to counter specific terrorist acts (Joyner 2004). Major problems, however, still remain for using diplomatic approaches for ending terrorism. Some countries will avoid signing such conventions since they currently do not face any terrorist threats and since signing and abiding by such conventions may lead to retaliation by terrorist groups (Wilkinson 2000b: 200). In other cases, the problem of definition once again becomes important (Richardson 2000: 203). Governments will need some form of legal definition of terrorism in order to agree to an international convention. Does a murder or assassination of a political figure by a dissident constitute terrorism or a political act? If it is terrorism, can the person be extradited? In the case of a murder without a political motive, extradition would be likely, but once politics becomes involved, issues become less clear cut. It would have been hard to imagine the United States extraditing an individual to Iraq for the assassination or attempted assassination of Saddam Hussein, yet a formal treaty might in theory require such an action. Many states prefer to have flexibility in defining unacceptable violence, and determining on a case by case basis whether or not to cooperate in dealing with cases involving persons accused of terrorism. Conventions and supposed international rules can still be ignored when states choose to do so (Crelinsten 2000: 174). Diplomatic conventions and resolutions, even vague statements and platitudes, can be useful. They help to reinforce international norms against accepting and supporting terrorism (Pillar 2001: 77). As such they may help to set the stage for more meaningful agreements.

There is always the possibility of reaching some limited agreements. For example, persons suspected of detonating bombs on civilian airliners may not be allowed to claim the status of a political refugee. In nineteenth-century Europe, most countries allowed asylum for individuals involved in political actions that were also normally criminal acts. An exception was made, however, for attacks against the heads of government (presidents, prime ministers, and monarchs) and members of their families. Attempted assassinations of these targets were not considered acceptable, and the assassins would not be granted asylum because by definition this kind of assassination would not be considered a political crime (Schreiber 1978: 152). Ultimately, international conventions and diplomatic approaches will be limited by the failure of the international community to arrive at a definition of terrorism and the failure to guarantee that persons identified as terrorists will be brought to trial (Dartnell 2000: 203–4). It may be possible, however, to develop less than global approaches to dealing with terrorism among nations. Countries with similar political systems—the United States and Great Britain as democracies or Argentina and Uruguay when they were both governed by military regimes—might reach formal or informal arrangements for returning suspected terrorists. Extradition of IRA suspects from the United States was difficult for a long period since the IRA was not on the official terrorist list. The United States and the United Kingdom signed a supplemental agreement in 1985 that made extradition of terrorist suspects much easier (Warner 1994: 34).

European countries have cooperated more in this area in recent years, and in the aftermath of September 11th, 2001, there has been improved coordination of efforts to arrest persons affiliated with Al Qaeda or organizations working with bin Laden. While such cooperation is unlikely to continue indefinitely, it does demonstrate what can be accomplished through international cooperation even when conventions and treaties are absent. While such limitations may be less than ideal, they are still one step closer to controlling terrorism.

WEAPONS OF MASS DESTRUCTION AND MASS CASUALTIES

Responses to the threat of weapons of mass destruction and other efforts to inflict large numbers of casualties, even by conventional means, deserve special attention. The same principles in terms of security, intelligence gathering, and diplomacy hold for these types of weapons, but repression and retaliation may have to be evaluated differently as options by government leaders and security agencies. In addition, there clearly has been a great deal of public and political concern about the possibility of biological, chemical, and nuclear terror attacks, leading governments to increase resources devoted to preventing such attacks or dealing with the aftermath of such attacks such as providing medical attention to large numbers of people.

In terms of the provision of enhanced security, potential targets that would directly contribute to the prospect of mass casualties should get top priority for greater protection. Nuclear power plants, biological labs dealing with contagious substances, storage facilities for chemicals, and similar sites should be protected against the possibility that they could be sabotaged or otherwise used to inflict death on a large scale. Security and monitoring of viruses and nerve gas obviously deserve high priority as well. It is also important to protect against conventional weapons of mass destruction designed to kill large numbers of people, but shopping areas, schools, stadiums, bridges and tunnels, and entertainment facilities are far too numerous for it to be possible to provide sufficient and effective protection against car bombs and other attacks. Depriving dissidents of chemical, biological, and nuclear weapons is important, but it will not eliminate the threat of mass deaths by other means. There may be political reasons to focus on the unconventional weapons in the case of the United States, but conventional terrorism is still likely to cause the most damage in the immediate future (Pillar 2001: 23). Oddly enough, one factor that may lead to the use of unconventional weapons of mass destruction is greater physical security and hardening of targets to conventional explosives. When bombs will no longer work, terrorists may expand their arsenals to include more unconventional weapons of mass destruction (Quillen 2002: 290).

Another issue for counterterrorist efforts related to the allocation of resources in terms of intelligence gathering, security, and other activities for weapons of mass destruction versus conventional weapons. Concern about nuclear weapons in the past lead to expending funds at levels out of proportion to the danger involved (Stern 2002/3: 121–2). The recent emphasis on possible biological and chemical attacks meant, in effect, that there were gaps in dealing with more conventional weapons (Hoffman 2002b: 306). These expenditures have occurred even though the successful use of such weapons has been unlikely. To date such weapons have not been especially deadly (Ivanova and Sandler 2006: 426). While such successful use is unlikely, one such attack could still kill thousands or tens of thousands. On the other hand, even discounting highly lethal conventional attacks such as September 11th, the continued use of conventional weapons by terrorists will take their toll slowly but surely. The number of dead from conflicts involving terrorism in Algeria, Sri Lanka, Colombia, Peru, and the Punjab have all exceeded the death toll of September 11th or even the likely death toll of the sarin gas released by Aum Shinrikyo in the Tokyo subway had it been more successful. If governments focus too many resources on the threat of weapons of mass destruction, they may permit the continuation of conventional attacks where death totals steadily mount. If they ignore the threat of weapons of mass destruction, they risk a major catastrophe. It is surely not an easy choice, and it is also one where the correct choice can only be known after the fact. One advantage for government security agencies is that it is only the largest groups that are likely to be able to acquire such weapons or to be able to successfully create their own weapons with sophisticated production facilities, and these groups are more susceptible to effective penetration or intelligence gathering by security agencies than smaller groups (O'Neil 2003).

Weapons of mass destruction create special concerns for efforts at countering terrorism. While the same mechanisms that work with other terrorist weapons apply to a certain extent, any groups with these weapons must be handled with more care given the potential for mass casualties. Even the most hardline government might consider concessions or negotiations under these circumstances. Other governments might be more tempted to undertake pre-emptive actions in these cases if success seems likely. Repression could trigger the use of such weapons. A group facing detection and destruction might utilize such a weapon as a last-ditch measure for protection or in a final effort to inflict as much destruction on the enemy as possible. Aum Shinrikyo used the sarin gas when it feared increasing scrutiny by Japanese authorities. Such a reaction might occur with other groups in the future. On the other hand, fear of retaliation has been present with terrorist groups. Foreign countries are unlikely to risk retaliatory strikes if they are discovered to have been accomplices in attacks killing large numbers of people. Even terrorist groups have balked at the possibility of using such weapons. Hamas has indicated that chemical weapons have not been used because of a fear of reprisals (Dolnik and Bhattacharjee 2002: 121). Weapons of mass destruction clearly complicate the options for both governments and terrorist groups.

SUMMARY

There is no one counterterrorist technique that surfaces as the solution to the challenges provided by violent dissident groups in the world. Effective intelligence (when such is possible), of course, is invariably useful, but once the information has been gained, decisions will have to be made on the appropriate course of action to be taken. Heightened security, while expensive in some cases, is likely to play a role, but not all attacks can be prevented. Governments will have to decide, often on a case-by-case basis, what mix of repression, retaliation, pre-emption, diplomacy, reforms and concessions, and negotiations to pursue when dealing with terrorist groups. An effective strategy will require dealing with both the causes and the actions of the groups (von Hippel 2002: 25). Negotiations with a group that controls a weapon of mass destruction may be necessary even if the government would normally prefer some other tactic. If special commando teams are available, they may work in some hostage situations or building seizures but may be less advisable in others. Not only is there no one technique that works, but also there is no equation that provides the exact amount of repression and reform that will eliminate a terrorist threat.

The counterterrorist techniques available are accessible to all types of governments just as terrorist techniques are available to all kinds of dissident groups. Democracies and authoritarian societies can use the same mechanisms, although the mix might vary among different kinds of political regimes. It has been suggested that the defeat of Al Qaeda and the global jihadist movement requires both defeating the terrorists *and* dealing with the sources of unrest (Davis and Jenkins 2002: 28). Strategies that work to defeat domestic extremists or foreign attackers in a democracy may work equally well in an authoritarian system by a government determined to repress local democratic dissidents or to keep an ethnic or religious minority suppressed. A minority government can even use control techniques to keep itself in power. Effective intelligence gathering may serve to destroy a dissident movement seeking democratic reforms just as much as it can undermine a religious cult seeking to trigger the apocalypse. On the other hand, the same techniques may not work equally well against different terrorist groups. Normal police investigations in France worked well against leftist terrorists but have failed to defeat separatist violence in Corsica (Wieviorka 1990: 77).

Sederberg (2003) has suggested that there are three approaches to combating terrorism. The conflict can be viewed as one of war—the approach taken by the United States after September 11th, 2001, with the declaration of a "Global War on Terrorism." Framing a crisis involving terrorism as one of war also means that the maintenance of civil liberties could be seen as

BOX 12.2 THE ISSUE OF CIVIL LIBERTIES

It is worth emphasizing that counterterrorist techniques may threaten the presence of civil liberties in a society. There is a constant tension between freedom and safety although the two are not mutually exclusive except at the extremes. A totally free society is very vulnerable. Europe has become more vulnerable, in fact, as the European agreements have removed many border controls (Chalk 1996: 3). Even if the country itself is not a target for domestic groups because of religious, ethnic, or ideological reasons and not a target for foreign groups due to national foreign policy, the country will still be a convenient location for attacks on embassies or offices of foreign corporations by activities of terrorist groups in other countries. Strong authoritarian governments and totalitarian regimes, on the other hand, avoid the problem of civil liberties interfering with efforts to repress violent dissident groups. Democracies and even many mildly authoritarian states that have a concern for the rule of law and providing civil liberties (if not political liberties) will find balancing the tension to be difficult. A democracy that does not implement stringent enough safeguards faces the danger of attacks. A government that makes sure that terrorists are rooted out and dealt with faces the danger of transforming the political system from a democracy into something much less free.

The loss of civil liberties may be most severe for certain segments of the population. The United Kingdom placed limits on civil liberties in Northern Ireland. The government used the SAS and special courts and other limitations on civil liberties to control the activities of the IRA and to prevent a victory for the nationalists. The Irish became a suspect community in England because of the IRA and its activities (Hillyard 1993). France has recently been effective in limiting terrorism as a result of greater government ability to monitor and detect dissident groups. The increased counterterrorist ability did not result from a peculiarly French civic culture that tolerated the greater government intrusion into personal lives, it was "born of a necessity revealed by an inability to combat terrorism in other ways" (Shapiro and Suzan 2003: 92). Israel has used martial law and other mechanisms in efforts to eliminate the threat from Palestinian nationalists, but the government has avoided the extreme measures necessary to make prevention more effective. Suicide bombings in Israel have been as effective as they are because they can only be prevented with extreme suppression of the rights of the Israeli population as well as the Palestinian population (Dolnick and Bhattacharjee 2002: 116).

Prior to the devastation of the recent terrorist attacks in the United States, it was acceptable to let guilty individuals go free to avoid falsely convicting the innocent. The fear of terrorism however, has led to a reversal of this view (Betts 2002b: 31). In the aftermath of the September 11th attacks more extraordinary measures have been taken in the United States that have affected some citizens and residents, and there have been suggestions of the necessity of even greater latitude for government surveillance and detention of suspicious individuals. The reaction among European democracies led to changes in anti-terrorism laws and restrictions on civil liberties. Britain, France, and Germany joined the United States and Canada as the most restrictive of individual rights among democracies (Haubrich 2003: 7). In Germany, it became easier to prosecute individuals for supporting terrorist groups or for criminal intent (Katzenstein 2003: 741). Muslims and persons from the Middle East have increasingly become suspect communities in the United States and parts of Europe just as the Irish became one in the United Kingdom. The passage of the Patriot Act provided the government in the United States with greater opportunities for the surveillance of citizens and residents. It also provides a clear example of how civil liberties can be traded away for security in the aftermath of a major terrorist attack (Enders and Sandler 2006: 228). In the United States Homeland Security Institutes at universities and in the private sector have rushed to provide better methods of increasing security, monitoring activities, and searching out terrorists in the country with more regard for the technical possibilities than for the rights of citizens. Bin Laden himself recognized that one positive outcome (for him) of his campaign would be a reduction of civil liberties and freedom in the United States (Nacos 2003: 6). It is even possible that increased security and limitations on civil liberties will not only weaken democracy but also such actions might even lead to an increase of internal dissidence that could increase the likelihood of terrorism in the future (Sederberg 2003: 273). Democracies, however, can win without drastic changes. The real challenge is not to just stop terrorism but to do so in a fashion consistent with democratic values (Heymann 2003: 159). Europeans and Israelis, who have had to face terrorism for years, usually accommodated themselves to the dangers with only occasional abridgements of civil liberties (Malkin and Elizur 2002: 67). Spanish democracy has been able to contain ETA, although the brief experimentation with a death squad as a significant aberration from normal democratic practice. Similarly, the Scandinavian countries have been able to control their right-wing extremists that have targeted minorities and immigrants without resorting to dictatorial methods. Even Sri Lanka's hard-pressed democratic government has managed to prevent a victory by the Tamil Tigers without imposing an authoritarian system of government. India, which has used extra-constitutional violence with some regularity, still remains largely democratic. Thus, it is not surprising that democracies still have a generally better record in the area of protecting civil liberties than less democratic states (Landman 2006).

providing "opportunities for the enemy" (Baker 2003: 563). As a consequence, the war reference may create greater stress on civil liberties. A second approach treats terrorism as crime and relies on the police and the judicial system to deal with the violence. This approach was the one taken by the British authorities in the aftermath of the London transit bombings in 2005 (Landman 2006: 143). The third approach treats terrorism as a disease, where the goal is to treat the causes of terrorism—and also to deal with the symptoms. Of course, no government only follows one approach. The attack against the Taliban regime in Afghanistan was clearly in keeping with the war approach, but few disagreed with the need to neutralize the threat that the Taliban cooperating with Al Qaeda represented (Heymann 2003: 15). The war approach relies on intelligence, retaliation, assassination, and pre-emption more than other methods. Before 9/11, the United States, and most other countries dealt with terrorism as crime, relying on intelligence, repression, retaliation, and diplomacy (to arrange extraditions). Since the United States was attacked from the outside on 9/11, it resorted to a war approach, whereas countries suffering from domestic violence are more likely to continue to rely on police techniques (Katzenstein 2003: 735). The disease analogy, of course, pays the most attention to reform and concessions, but it would rely on some other tactics as well. In the final analysis, however, the government cannot really rely on just one approach since each terrorist group is different. A military response alone is not likely to be a successful counterterrorist strategy (de Castro 2004: 198). If the global jihadist movement is going to be defeated, not only do the militants need to be found and defeated but also their supporters need to be provided with the benefits, as opposed to the disadvantages, of globalization and modernization (Kilcullen 2005: 612). While the United States may need to deal with Al Qaeda with a military option, it would continue to regard right-wing extremists as a criminal matter and seek to deal with some issues involving potentially violent minorities through reform.

One final point that needs to be emphasized in any analysis of counterterrorist techniques is that there will be an ongoing need for such efforts. There are too many groups and too many causes for terrorist activity around the world for attacks and violence to disappear any time in the immediate future. Even if international terrorist activity is eliminated from the scene, there were still be eruptions of domestic terrorism, and sooner or later such domestic terrorism is likely to overflow into the international system and involve other countries. Fighting terrorism is usually more akin to fighting crime than it is to fighting a war. In wars one can hope to win and achieve final victory by defeating an enemy. When governments fight crime, they realize that the battle is an ongoing one—that crime can be dealt with but not eliminated. Unlike war, the "struggle against terrorism, however, is never-ending" (Hoffman 2002b: 314). As a consequence, the concern about counterterrorist tactics and techniques is one that will remain important for the immediate future.

TERMS

African National Congress (ANC)	KGB
CIA	Special Air Services Regiment (SAS)
false flag attacks	suspect community
hawla	weapons of mass destruction

FURTHER READING

Silke, A. (2003) "Retaliating against Terrorism," in A. Silke (ed.), *Terrorists, Victims and Society: Psychological Perspectives on Terrorism and Its Consequences*, Chichester: Wiley, 215–31.

Pillar, P. R. (2001) *Terrorism and U.S. Foreign Policy*, Washington DC: Brookings Institution.

Raphaeli, N. (2003) "Financing of Terrorism: Sources, Methods, and Channels," *Terrorism and Political Violence*, 15, 4: 59–82.

Sederberg, P. C. (2003) "Global Terrorism: Problems of Challenge and Response," in C. W. Kegley, Jr (ed.) *The New Global Terrorism: Characteristics, Causes, Controls*, Upper Saddle River, NJ: Prentice Hall, 267–84.

CHAPTER 13

Terrorism: A continuing phenomenon

The discussions in the previous chapter indicated that terrorism is not likely to disappear anytime soon. The United States announced that it was beginning a war against terrorism, a war that would be prosecuted as vigorously as possible. This is not the first time a war against terrorism had been declared. In September 1901 President Theodore Roosevelt called for a campaign to exterminate terrorism in the aftermath of the assassination of President McKinley by an anarchist (Rapoport 2003: 36). Needless to say, terrorism was not eliminated in the century that followed the McKinley assassination. Notwithstanding the hopes of some in the West, it is also not likely to disappear anytime in the immediate future. Terrorism has been common throughout history, and it would be contrary to past experience to expect it to disappear in the current century (Davis and Jenkins 2002: 3–4). Frustrations among those not in power, the effects of globalization, ethnic and religious animosities, and the continuing effects from the break up of empires and states will continue to fuel problems and violence. Trouble spots in various parts of the world will continue to be present and contribute to circumstances that are conducive to political violence.

The discussions in the previous chapters clearly demonstrate that violent attacks by dissident groups have not just been a recent phenomenon. Terrorism did not begin with the attacks of September 11th, 2001 in New York City and Washington DC, or in April 1995 with the bombing in Oklahoma City, or with the hostage taking at the Munich Olympics in 1972. Nor did terrorism begin with the Cold War or the establishment of the Soviet Union after World War I. Nor has terrorism been restricted to activities by groups from the Middle East or those parts of the world with large Muslim populations. Terrorism has been a nearly universal phenomenon. The Red Brigades were a threat to Italy. Violence and terror have continued for decades in Sri Lanka. The Boston Tea Party was a successful prelude to the American War of

Independence. Right-wing groups have resorted to violence in the United States and Europe. Ethnic cleansing has occurred all too widely, practiced by both governments and dissidents. Rwanda was a late twentieth-century example of genocide. Al Qaeda and Osama bin Laden have had no connection with most of this modern violence even though global jihadist directly or indirectly linked with Al Qaeda have become a major threat. Terrorism has been present in many locations and many different time periods, and it has involved a great many types of organizations and groups. Some have been religious, some ethnic, and some ideological. Some dissident groups have been successful, although most have failed to achieve their goals. We know more about the ones that became prominent, of course, than we do about the ones that failed and quickly disappeared. It would be extremely useful to know how many dissident groups have actually attempted terrorist violence, but the historical record is far too incomplete. As important as it would be, it is not possible to calculate the percentage of violent movements that actually survived long enough to have a major effect on a political system because it is impossible to document all these attempts that quickly failed. The overall ratio of successful terrorist operations to unsuccessful terrorist ones is probably a relatively small percentage of operations. The previous chapters have contained a bias since they have focused on those movements that became important enough to have some effects in a particular society or the world. While the percentage of successful movements may be relatively low, there have been enough of them to justify this book. If the past is prologue to the future, then terrorism will continue and will have at least some major effects on individual countries and maybe even the world at large.

WHY TERRORISM CONTINUES

There are three principal reasons why terrorism is likely to continue to be a problem for the immediate future. First, as was obvious from discussion in the previous chapter, there is no single counterterrorist technique that is likely to work to remove the threat. Nor is it likely that governments will be able to always find the correct mix of techniques to solve domestic terrorist problems. "Terrorism has existed for 2,000 years and owes its survival to an ability to adapt and adjust to challenges" (Hoffman 2002a: 46). Further, cooperation across international boundaries among countries will remain difficult at best, even when governments seek to help each other. The correct response for dealing with dissident groups using terrorism is only obvious in hindsight in many cases. Second, the events, circumstances, and issues that had fueled terrorism have not disappeared, nor is it likely they will be resolved any time soon. Third, while some would deny the possibility of successful terrorist campaigns, there are indications that such violence has indeed been successful.

Continuing causes of terrorism

One major reason that terrorism is likely to continue is that the issues underlying this kind of political violence have persisted. The difficult circumstances that often accompany the break up of empires and multiethnic states continue to plague the successor states. Problems also remain in countries that are not the remnants of empires. The threat of majority violence against religious or ethnic minorities has not disappeared, while minority ethnonationalist groups and some religious dissident groups are still seeking autonomy or separate status. While it is possible that some new states may appear in the future, thus pacifying separatist groups, it is not possible for all the disaffected minorities to create the independent states that they desire. Further, establishing boundaries for independent states or autonomous provinces will always face the challenge of intermingled populations. Even if the British had done a better job of drawing boundaries for Northern Ireland to separate Protestants from Catholics, the intermingling of the two populations would have been unavoidable. There would have been members of each group on the wrong side of the border. The problem was particularly problematic in Belfast with its Catholic and Protestant neighborhoods. When members of different groups end up on the "wrong" side of the borders the dangers of ethnic cleansing being the chosen option is always present. In Iraq, conflicts between Arabs and Kurds and between Sunnis and Shias are another example of the potential for terrorist violence between groups.

As noted in Chapter 12, no amount of reforms or concessions will be sufficient to meet the demands of some dissident groups. The state structure will not be changed to accommodate supporters of left-wing or right-wing ideologies, religious laws will not be revoked or created, districts with mixed populations will not be granted their independence, and ideally racial or religious minorities will not be persecuted or exiled to appease extremists in the society. When the demands of the dissidents conflict with the wishes of the majority, change will not occur, and the potential for violence by the dissatisfied dissidents will be present. The Baader–Meinhof Gang would only have been content with the end of capitalism in West Germany and the world, but most West Germans clearly did not desire such an outcome. As long as groups demand more than can possibly be achieved, it will be difficult to avoid terrorist violence. While democracies are vulnerable to terrorism because they are democracies, there is little doubt that government repression and state use or support of terror against its own citizens can generate violence. In an ideal world, the use of death squads and vigilante groups by governments would cease, but as long as the crown rests uneasy on the heads of the ruling elite, governments will be tempted to repress opposition groups. Such repression may also lay the groundwork for terrorism and other violence in the future.

The appearance of terrorism has also been a reaction to globalization and modernization, processes that place great stress upon societies and political systems. Globalization will continue to generate instability in societies. There will be winners and losers because of the changes, and the losers will be tempted to resort to violence. The various types of terrorism discussed in earlier chapters involve many cases of reaction to globalization. Religious groups frequently seek a return to a purer past and to purge society of outside influences. Both groups have opposed the intrusion of foreign cultures that were seen as threatening their societies. While Huntington's clash of civilizations does not explain all outbreaks of terrorism, it does appear on the mark as a factor for some outbreaks such as the conflicts in Bosnia, Chechnya, the activities of Al Qaeda, and others. This reaction was as true for the Jewish Zealots as it is for Al Qaeda. Many nationalist or ethnic dissidents also see their societies threatened by the outside world and foreign cultures. ETA is afraid that Spain will absorb the Basque cultural area, and the Dayaks in Borneo were seeking to avoid becoming a minority in their own land. Right-wing groups frequently have fought against changes that have come with globalization, including immigration of peoples of different racial stock or religious communities. Left-wing dissidents have battled against the evils that come in the train of global capitalism, sharing some of the same fears as religious groups and some ethnic groups (Mousseau 2002/3: 19). Globalization can also disrupt political systems and weaken states. Weak states do indeed provide opportunities for terrorists (von Hippel 2002: 31). Weak states clearly are a contributing factor in outbreaks of terrorism. The weaknesses of the Iraqi government in the wake of the US invasion have made terrorist attacks easier to mount. Government weaknesses in Colombia, revolutionary France, Indonesia, the Philippines, and elsewhere have also created opportunities for violent dissident groups. This weakness not only provides opportunities for terrorists but also for criminal groups (Makarenko 2005: 171). The resulting weaknesses in governments also make it easier for the terrorists and criminal groups to cooperate. Since greater global integration for the world is unlikely to disappear, the potential for violent reactions such as terrorist attacks is going to remain present.

Terrorism works

It has been argued that terrorism never works—that either in the short run or in the long run the resort to violence is counterproductive. Throughout history states relying on terror as a policy, both during war and in dealing with domestic opponents, and by dissident organizations using violence against governments always create enough negative consequences to suggest that it is an ineffective strategy (Carr 2002). Wilkinson (2000b: 13, 22) noted that terrorist groups could sometimes attain tactical objectives such as publicity or the release of imprisoned comrades, but that the overall track record of groups achieving their major goals was "abysmal." Abrahms (2006) concurs, suggesting that there is scant evidence that terrorism actually has worked in his analysis of twenty-eight terrorist groups. Many early Marxists and other leftists opposed the use of terror in their campaigns to gain power, and it was groups such as these that practiced restraint that have been the ones that normally survived and even flourished. In fact, however, the cases analyzed in this volume have demonstrated that terror can be a very effective technique for a group to use. The idea that terrorism is "a futile strategy" is one of the major erroneous images about this type of violence (Stohl 2003: 87). Most obviously, as noted in Chapter 10, state sanctioned terror often accomplishes the immediate goals of the government or its agents because the power of the state is behind the action, but terrorism by non-state actors has been successful as well.

There are a few obvious examples of successful terrorism that most analysts will accept. Terrorism was a successful technique in independence struggles (Crenshaw 1983: 7). The combination of urban terror and rural guerrilla attacks in Cyprus were important in convincing the British to give that colony its independence. The French gave up the battle for Algeria in the face of a guerrilla insurgency and continuing terrorist attacks. The French had defeated the rebels in Algeria through the use of torture and extra-legal means with the resulting cost in terms of civil liberties in Algeria and France. The French did not lose the battle militarily; they decided that the prize was no longer worth the battle (Crenshaw 1995a: 499). The departure of the British from Palestine under violent pressure from the Jewish settlers in the Mandate would generally constitute a third example for the successful use of terrorism (Wilkinson 2000b: 12). All of these cases, however, were colonial situations in which the occupying power had a home that served as a place for relocation. Surrender to the terrorist demands for independence may be painful, but the cost of surrender is not overwhelming. The colonialists simply retire, retreat if you like, to their own homeland. Not all anti-colonial campaigns relying on terrorism or terrorism and guerrilla tactics have worked. The Spanish "colonialists" are still present in the Basque country, while Muslim dissidents in the southern Philippines have yet to establish the independent state that they seek. Still there have been enough successful national liberation campaigns to provide an example to other groups in other countries that saw terrorism as a possible solution to their problems with governments or policies (Hoffman 2006: 61–2).

A more careful look at the track record of terrorism, moreover, suggests that such campaigns have been more successful than this focus on colonial struggles would suggest. The Jewish Zealots were very successful in eliminating opposition to the revolt that was being planned. Unifying the population behind the revolt was, in fact, the immediate objective of their attacks and violence. The Assassins were also very successful in protecting themselves against the Sunni majority and the leaders of nearby Muslim states and in preventing even more active persecution of the members of the Nizari sect for their beliefs. Their form of violence proved to be a very effective weapon of the weak in terms of achieving a very immediate goal for the sect—survival. The fact that the Assassins were ultimately defeated is less important than the fact that they survived as long as they did. Other cases in the preceding chapters also demonstrate relatively successful uses of terror by non-state actors. The Montoneros helped to bring down the military regime that was in power and to facilitate the return to power of Juan Peron. In the United States anti-abortion violence has been at least partially successful because it has indeed become more difficult to get an abortion. The Dayaks in Borneo persuaded the Madurese to leave and successfully negated the government policy on internal migration by terrorizing and killing the recent arrivals. Various Middle Eastern groups also perceive that violence has forced changes in US policies. The suicide attack on the USS *Cole* in Aden harbor saw the US navy humbled by two Arab men in a small boat (Ajami 2001: 9). It could even be argued that the September 11th attack and its aftermath effectively soured relations between the United States and Saudi Arabia and forced the Bush administration to place more pressure on Israel to compromise with the Palestinians (Nacos 2003: 11). Dissident groups feel that the attack against the US marines and French paratroopers in Beirut led to a withdrawal of these foreign forces as desired (Kydd and Walter 2006: 49). Even fewer casualties led to the end of US involvement in peacekeeping and humanitarian efforts in Somalia (Crenshaw 2003b: 172). Osama bin Laden, in fact, has used exactly these arguments of terrorist successes in his efforts to inspire continued attacks against the United States (Hoffman 2002b: 310). Mounting US casualties from terrorist and insurgent actions in the rebuilding of Iraq have led to pressure for an early US departure from that country, and clearly those who are calling for such attacks have accepted the theory that such actions will work.

There are also cases where terrorist groups have apparently failed, yet in the long run they may have been more successful than initially thought. The Croatian nationalists (Utashe) were not successful in maintaining the independent state that they wanted. The Macedonian nationalists were also unsuccessful in creating the independent nation that they desired. Yet, today, there is an independent Macedonia (even if it had to be called the Former Yugoslav Republic of Macedonia for a period of time) and an independent Croatia. Thus, it is possible that the earlier terrorist movements and their actions helped to maintain the idea of Croatia and Macedonia, and that ultimately these efforts may have contributed to the eventual creation of these countries (J. Lutz and B. Lutz 2005: 79). The future for places such as Kashmir and Chechnya may include eventual autonomy or independence. The efforts of the current insurgents and terrorists have prevented the consolidation of effective Indian and Russian control of the areas. If violent campaigns had not occurred, it is likely that Kashmir would have become more integrated with the Indian state. The inability of Russia to control Chechnya in the years since the break up of the Soviet Union has kept alive the idea of an independent nation for the residents of this area of the Caucasus. Even though there have been many failures among violent dissidents for each of the successes or possible successes, other dissidents are more interested in the successes from the past. An "*image* of success that recommends terrorism to groups who identify with the innovator" (Crenshaw 2003a: 98, emphasis added) may be more than sufficient to encourage other dissidents to resort to violence.

Evaluations of the success of terrorism can also be difficult because the criteria for success by the dissidents may be different than the criteria of governments or academics. Total success may not be necessary. For guerrillas and terrorists everywhere "not losing is winning" (Hoffman 2002b: 311). Survival holds forth the hope of future victory or concessions by the government—the presence of an independent Croatia and Macedonia are perhaps the most relevant examples. The newly independent Macedonia in turn has offered special programs and greater opportunities for its Albanian minority. The Albanian dissidents in Macedonia concluded that more was won by a few months of violence in Kosovo than in a decade of peaceful politics—a conclusion that led them to adopt the same tactics in Macedonia (Ash 2003: 63). In other cases, dissident groups have achieved partial successes through the use of violence. The PLO was not successful in creating a Palestinian state, but it became the recognized negotiating agent for the Palestinian people and the first government of the Palestinian Authority. The British similarly accepted the (Provisional) IRA, and the IRA's political wing, Sinn Fein, as appropriate organizations for involvement in negotiations on the future of Northern Ireland. The Italian Fascists and German Nazis used terror and intimidation as one technique in their rise to power. In the 1930s in Eastern and Central Europe, the other fascist parties using violence were successful in preventing the leftist parties from coming to power and aided in destroying parliamentary democracies, even when they did not take power themselves. The governments adopted other authoritarian styles of government to help them deal with that violence originating with these parties (Berend 1998: 301). ETA in Spain has not won the battle for an independent Basque homeland, but the region has much greater autonomy and there have been concessions to Basque culture that otherwise would not have been granted. European governments have made their immigration policies more restrictive in an effort to keep support for the far right from increasing. The violence in revolutionary France served the purposes of some of the political factions and permitted them to govern for at least a period of time. The Japanese extremists in the 1930s were able to undermine democracy in that country and to further the policies of the militarists and militant nationalists. While the conflict in Sri Lanka seems likely to continue, the Tamils have also been offered greater autonomy, and if any solution is reached in the near future, it is likely that the Tamils at the very least will have some guaranteed protections as a minority in a state with a Sinhalese majority. In all these cases, terror (combined with guerrilla activity as in Sri Lanka) has led to gains for the dissident groups that were unlikely to otherwise have been granted. Many of the above examples of reasonably complete or partial successes involved ethnic or religious organizations, but ideological groups relying on violence and terror had some successes as well.

Terrorist violence can be successful in the eyes of the practitioners for additional reasons, some of which may be tactical. Attacks can be designed to attract recruits. Groups may also attempt to get governments to overreact and alienate a portion of the population (Neumann and Smith 2005: 580). The KLA was effectively in creating this situation in Kosovo with the attacks against Serbian police and other officials. "Nothing radicalizes a people faster than the unleashing of undisciplined security forces" (Woodworth 2001: 7). Such provocation policies can be an intentional strategic and tactical goal of terrorist groups (Kydd and Walter 2006: 51). The violence could also be used to enhance group solidarity, not only within the dissident organization but also among a segment of the larger population. There could be an increase in communal identification as a consequence of the violence. In fact, terrorists may seek to polarize communities to make non-violent agreements more difficult to achieve (Gurr and Cole 2000: 89). The KLA was able to increase solidarity among the Albanians in Kosovo. Hindu nationalist groups have also been relatively successful in this regard. The same pattern can be observed in Bosnia among all the groups. Attacks by Kurdish dissidents against Turkish targets have undoubtedly been successful in slowing down the process of the assimilation of the Kurdish population into Turkish culture, an obvious acceptable intermediate goal for the dissident Kurdish organizations. The suicide attacks by the PKK (as well as the Tamil Tigers) have furthered group solidarity and improved morale within the group (Dolnik 2003: 21). In other cases terrorism may mobilize populations. The political direction that the mobilized populations will take may be unclear but the status quo can be threatened. The attacks of September 11th had major impacts around the world. Many Muslims in the Middle East and elsewhere may now perceive that it is possible to challenge the West (Ajami 2001: 9). Just as the United States will not be the same as a result of the attacks on the Pentagon and the World Trade Center towers, Muslim societies in many countries will be different as well. Some terrorist actions are counted as successes if they attract attention to the cause of the dissidents. The availability of the modern media and mass communications has actually encouraged dissident groups to use terrorist attacks to publicize their cause (Chalk 1996: 36).

Terrorist groups have also been successful in a negative sense. Attacks have been used to good effect (or to bad effect) to disrupt peace processes. In Israel/Palestine extremists on both sides have become adept at using violence to inflame public opinion and to make negotiations difficult or next to impossible. Hamas first used suicide attacks as part of an effort to derail the peace process (Moghadam 2003: 77). It also stepped up its attacks just prior to the elections in 1996 and 2001 to encourage election victories for the Likud Party since it was much less likely to implement the Oslo Peace Accords or reach a negotiated settlement (Kydd and Walter 2002: 74). This approach demonstrated considerable political sophistication and was quite successful. Splinter groups in the IRA have attempted to disrupt recent negotiations, and the IRA itself has used violence to undermine peace efforts that excluded it. The campaigns of the Contras in Nicaragua prevented the Sandinista government from consolidating its power and implementing many of its programs in the countryside. Violent attacks could also convince a government to continue to keep repressive legislation on the books and delay plans for democratization. If the dissidents are seeking the continuation of authoritarian measures as one policy objective, then the use of violence has prevented a course of action that the dissidents oppose. Another advantage with negative goals is that they can sometimes be easier to attain than more ambitious goals of changing current government policies, replacing the governing elite, or achieving an independent state. All of these examples indicate that terrorism can be an effective means for attaining goals, either completely or partially, either obtaining change or preventing change. The total successes and the partial successes all supply hope to other groups of dissidents that seek to redress power relationships by the use of terrorism.

WHAT WE KNOW FROM THE HISTORICAL EXPERIENCE

There are some obvious facts that have surfaced in regard to terrorism in the world. The most successful form of terrorism, and often the most deadly, is that involving the government. Direct state use of terrorism as occurred in Nazi Germany or Stalin's Soviet Union is more extreme but this form of terror needs to be acknowledged. When governments use terror against their own citizens or permit some groups to use violence, it is often effective in repressing those citizens. Terrorism is likely to continue to be used by non-state groups against the state not only because it has worked at least some of the time in the past but also because it may bring major results for a small investment in time and resources at least in terms of publicity. If properly managed, there may even be relatively little risk to the perpetrators (Chalk 1998a: 119). Of course, in some cases legal or political channels fail the dissidents because a popular majority disagrees with their position, not because the state is repressive. The disenchanted and frustrated minority, however, can still choose to resort to violence, explaining away the majority opposition as being due to lack of information, manipulation by elites, capitalist coercion, or other types of pressures. Terrorism will, consequently, continue to be used as a weapon of the weak because it has been used in the past, because there is the perception—at least partially accurate—that terrorism works, and because it is available to groups with limited resources.

There are very few final conclusions that can be reached with any certainty in a study of terrorism. It is a widely prevalent phenomenon. It is unlikely to disappear in the immediate future. Beyond these simple facts, conclusions become more difficult because the whole topic is a very complex one. Since terrorism and dissident violence cannot always be defeated, terrorism will continue. There have been just enough complete successes or major gains related to this kind of violence. Even in defeat dissidents can be partially successful, thus providing encouragement to potential terrorist in other countries and in the future. Inappropriate government responses and overreactions can add to the problems and contribute to the goals of terrorist groups. Most dissident groups, of course, never resort to the use of violence; instead, they seek change through non-violent means. Many of the groups willing to use violence or attempting to use violence are detected before they can act, and police or security forces quickly suppress others. Enough dissident groups, however, survive the initial period of vulnerability and become strong enough to pose a threat that will disrupt their societies. Some of these surviving movements are then defeated without creating the changes they seek. Others, however, manage to win some gains. Notwithstanding the long odds for dissident terrorists, as long as there is the possibility of success by organized dissident groups, the world will face the continued threat of violent terrorist attacks by the weak against the strong.

GLOSSARY

Abu Sayyaf group: This group has appeared claiming to represent the Muslim population of the southern Philippines. It is one of the more extreme Muslim dissident groups operating in that country, and it has links to al-Qaeda.

Aceh: This region is in the northernmost portion of the island of Sumatra in Indonesia. It was one of the last areas brought under the control by the Dutch in their colony. The population has long sought greater autonomy or even independence from the rest of Indonesia, and there has been simmering conflict between the central authorities and local population for decades.

African National Congress (ANC): This dissident organization in South Africa was in the forefront of the struggle of the black majority to achieve equal rights. It was largely non-violent in its opposition to the former white minority government.

Akali Dal: This is the largest Sikh political party in the province of Punjab and in India.

Al Asqa Brigades: The brigades are one of the more militant factions in Fatah. They appeared and engaged in terrorist attacks in the last days of Yasser Arafat. Although the brigades are a secular group, they have engaged in suicide attacks against Israeli targets as have the more militantly Islamic Palestinian groups.

Alexander of Yugoslavia, King: King Alexander attempted to unify the various ethnic groups in Yugoslavia after World War I. His assassination at the hands of Croat nationalists weakened the possibilities for creating a unified Yugoslav state.

Al Qaeda: This network of loosely organized extremist Muslim groups in various countries has been headed by Osama bin Laden.

al-Turabi, Hassan: Al-Turabi is the real power behind the government that came to power in a military coup in 1989 in the Sudan. He has sought to have Islamic values incorporated into the laws of the state.

anarchism: Practitioners of and adherents to this left-wing ideology believed that capitalism would be overthrown by a spontaneous uprising of the people. The anarchists tried to inspire the masses to begin this uprising through education or violent actions.

Animal Liberation Front (ALF): This animal rights organization in the United Kingdom (and other countries) has been heavily involved in the fight to protect animals. It has resorted to acts of violence, usually against property, in these efforts.

Animal Rights Militia (ARM): The ARM is an animal rights organization in the United Kingdom that has demonstrated its willingness to use violence, including attacks on people, in the pursuit of its political objectives. The group is supposedly an independent organization, but there are indications that the members are simply the hard-core members of the Animal Liberation Front using a different name as a cover for their more violent activities.

Ansar al-Islam: This group represents extremist Muslims amng the Kurdish population in Iraq. It has attacked the more secular political parties that have cooperated with the United States, and it is thought to have links to Al Qaeda.

anthrax: Anthrax is a biological weapon that is derived from cattle waste. It occurs naturally in nature and comes in many forms. Its most deadly forms can kill very quickly, but it is not contagious.

Anti-Liberation Terrorist Group (GAL): This cover name was used by a government death squad in Spain that targeted members of ETA and other Basque dissident groups. A number of dissidents were killed before the public learned of the activities of the group. The public awareness was a major embarrassment to the government, and the group was disbanded as a consequence.

April 19 Movement (M-19): This Colombian leftist movement was not the most powerful of the ideological dissident groups, but it did mount spectacular attacks against the Colombian state. Members took over the Ministry of Justice in 1985, holding over a hundred persons hostage. The group had links to the Castro regime in Cuba.

Armenian Secret Army for the Liberation of Armenia (ASALA): This Armenian group attempted to get the Turkish government to admit to the Armenian genocide during World War II. ASALA attacked Turkish diplomats and businesses around the world.

Army of God: This organization has been willing to use violence as part of efforts to end abortions in the United States. Little is known about the actual extent of the organization, and there are indications that this group relies on the idea of leaderless resistance.

Aryan Nations: This group is one of the racist organizations in the United States that has been increasingly opposed to the national government and programs for minorities. It has been linked with other right-wing organizations in the country that have been willing to use violence.

Asahara, Shoku: He was the founder of the apocalyptic Aum Shinrikyo sect.

Assam: This state in northeastern India has been the scene of communal violence and terrorism directed against recent migrants to the region. The Pakistani ISI has provided assistance to the dissidents.

Assassin sect: This unorthodox Shia Muslim group was present in the Middle East beginning in the eleventh century. The groups established bases in the Levant and Persia, and it used assassination as a weapon to prevent the more powerful Muslim states and empires from destroying the sect. It also targeted selected leaders in the Christian Crusader states.

Aum Shinrikyo: This Japanese sect believed that salvation for the world required the instigation of World War III. Its leader would then appear to rescue the world and create an ideal society. It was responsible for the sarin gas attack in the Tokyo subways.

Ayodhya: This town in northern India has been the center of religious conflict. It was the site of a Muslim mosque, but religious Hindus have claimed that it was an even earlier sacred site of the Hindu religion. Hindu extremists desecrated and then destroyed the mosque and have begun building a temple there. The controversy has led to communal violence between Hindus and Muslims on various occasions.

Baader–Meinhof Gang: This leftist dissident group, also know as the Red Army Faction, mounted many attacks in the 1970s and into the 1980s in West Germany. Members also cooperated with leftist groups elsewhere in Europe and with Palestinian groups.

Ba'ath Party (Arab Socialist Renaissance Party): The Ba'ath party has been a support for the ruling groups in both Syria and Iraq. The party has favored pan-Arabism and has advocated violence against Israel.

Bakhtiar, Shahpur: He was the last prime minister of Iran under the Shah. He was later assassinated in Paris where he was living in exile.

Beer Hall Putsch: This name has been given to the initial attempt of Adolf Hitler to seize power in Germany via an armed uprising in 1923. Hitler and others started the attempt in Munich, but it never attracted support elsewhere, and the local authorities were able to easily contain it.

Bekaa Valley: This area in Lebanon is a stronghold for Hizballah and the Shi'ite population.

Bernadotte, Count Folke: Count Bernadotte was a Swedish diplomat working for the United Nations. Jewish extremists in Israel assassinated him in 1948 for taking positions perceived to be favorable to the Palestinian refugees.

Bharatiya Janata Party: This large national party has supported the idea of officially recognizing the role Hinduism in India and even establishing it as the state religion.

Bhindranwale, Sant Jarnail Singh: He was a charismatic leader of the Sikh community who argued for political violence and whose followers were involved in some of the first terrorist actions designed to gain greater autonomy or independence for the Sikhs.

bin Laden, Osama: This Saudi Arabian millionaire has led and financed a group of Muslims dedicated to expelling Western influence from the areas where Islam is the dominant religion. Bin Laden's supporters were responsible for the devastating attacks on New York and Washington DC on September 11, 2001.

Black Hand: This organization of Serbs sought to unite all Southern Slavs in the Serbian kingdom. It included members of the Serbian military and supported the groups that assassinated Archduke Ferdinand of Austria–Hungary at Sarajevo in August 1914.

Black International: The occasional cooperation between various fascist, neo-fascist, and right-wing groups after World War II has been termed the Black International (as opposed to the various Socialist—or Red—internationals that existed). Authoritarian governments or their security agencies and intelligence ministries that at times provided aid to such groups were included in this cooperative network.

Black September: Black September was one of the more radical Palestinian liberation groups. It took is name from the battle with the Jordanian armed forces that led to the PLO being expelled from that country in 1970. Black September was responsible for some of the more spectacular terrorist actions undertaken against Israel and countries that supported Israel.

Black Widows: This term has been used for the widows of Chechen fighters killed by the Russians who have in turn served as suicide bombers.

blowback: Blowback is an expression that refers to the unintended consequences of providing support to violent dissident groups in other states. These groups, once they are successful, may turn on their former benefactors and create problems for them.

Bologna train station bombing: This attack on the train station in Bologna in 1980 was one of the single most deadly terrorist incidents in Italian history. The attack was undoubtedly undertaken by one of the neo-Fascist organizations, although there was an initial attempt to place the blame on leftist dissidents.

Branch Davidians: This group under the dominance of David Koresh established a compound near Waco, Texas where members of the cult could live. An effort to arrest members for weapons charges led to a shootout and long standoff for months between the authorities and the Davidians. An attempt by the FBI to gain control of the compound led the cult members to set fire to their compound resulting in the deaths of most of them.

Breslan: This town in southern Russia was the scene of a takeover of a school by Muslim extremists. The situation deteriorated and resulted in the deaths of many children and others.

Chechnya: This province in Russia has been the scene of guerrilla fighting and terrorist attacks as the Chechens have sought to obtain their independence. The Chechens are descendants of an Islamic culture and have gained support from other Islamic groups, including the Al Qaeda network.

Christian Identity: Many Christian Identity movements in the United States follow right-wing political prescriptions for solving the problems of the country. Most of the groups do not support violence against the government or other groups, but a few of them have been involved in right-wing terrorist actions.

CIA: The Central Intelligence Agency (CIA) is that branch of the US government charged with intelligence activities outside the United States. These activities have included supporting dissident groups in other countries.

colons: This name was given to the French in Algeria who had been long-term residents of the colony or descendants of settlers from earlier decades.

Communist Combat Cells (CCC): The CCC was a left-wing dissident group that appeared in Belgium in the 1970s. It undertook a few attacks but never achieved the prominence of other left-wing dissident groups in Europe.

Continuity IRA: This group is one that broke away from the Provisional IRA when it agreed to a ceasefire and negotiations over the future of Northern Ireland.

Contras: The US-supported opponents of the Sandinista were considered counter-revolutionaries by the new regime, hence the term Contras. Their battle against the Sandinista government involved both guerrilla insurgency and terrorism.

Cromwell, Oliver: Oliver Cromwell became the leader of the Puritan Revolution that overthrew the British monarchy. He served as Lord Protector of the Commonwealth after the monarchy was overthrown. His religious views led to the persecution of adherents of other religions, including Irish Catholics.

Darfur: In the twenty-first century this region of the Sudan has been subjected state terrorism in the form attacks and ethnic cleansing by groups that are tolerated and supported by the government.

Dayaks: The indigenous population in the Indonesian portion of Borneo (Kalimantan) consists largely of the Dayaks. They can be distinguished from other Indonesians, and the Dayaks are also frequently Christian, setting them apart from the vast majority of Indonesians who practice some version of Islam.

Diplock courts: These courts in Northern Ireland only had a judge for trying IRA defendants. The courts were established after local jurors in IRA trials were at risk for retaliation when they voted to convict members of the IRA.

dirty bombs: Dirty bombs are conventional bombs that are contaminated with radioactive material in order to extend the damage that they do and do contaminate bomb sites. To date, there have been very few cases involving the use of such bombs.

disappeared ones: This term was given to the individuals in Argentina who were abducted and killed by the death squads associated with the military and security forces in the country.

Duvalier, François: Duvalier was the long-term president of Haiti who organized a very effective security apparatus that terrorized the population of the country and kept him in power for decades.

Earth Liberation Front (ELF): The ELF is one of the more militant ecological groups that have at times been supportive of the use of violence in the pursuit of an improved environment.

Engels, Frederich: Engels was Karl Marx's closest companion and collaborator. He helped to write some of the key documents for what came to be Marxist theory and compiled much of Marx's later writings.

Escobar, Pablo: He was one of the leaders of the Medellin Cartel when it launched its terror campaign against the government of Colombia.

ethnic cleansing: This term refers to the efforts of governments and other groups to drive a particular ethnic or religious group out of an area. The usual method is to use violence against some members in order to create terror in others.

Euzkadi ta Askatasuna (ETA): ETA has been the longest lasting and most determined violent proponent of independence for the Basque region in Spain. There have been various splinter groups that have developed over the years, but ETA has consistently been considered the militant representative for Basque interests.

false flag attacks: This term is used when one type of dissident organization uses violence to discredit another group of dissidents. False flag attacks have frequently been undertaken by right-wing groups with the intent of having left-wing dissidents blamed for the violence.

fascist: This generic political term (as well as being the name of Benito Mussolini's Fascist Party in Italy) refers to political movements of the 1920s or later that were opposed to communists and socialists as well as the idea of parliamentary democracy. Fascist parties were often extremely nationalistic and often opposed to minority groups. Fascism as an ideology has not necessarily been anti-Semitic, although some parties following the ideology have adopted this view.

Fatah: Fatah is the largest component group in the former PLO. Yasser Arafat was the head of Fatah at the time that he assumed the chairmanship of the PLO. Given Arafat's position in the PLO, the identity of the two groups has tended to merge even though Fatah technically remained separate.

Feltrinelli, Franco: Feltrinelli was the very rich son of an Italian capitalist. He used his money to finance the Red Brigades in the early years of the organization.

Franco, Francisco: General Franco was the leader of the Nationalist side in the Spanish Civil War. With the victory of the Nationalists he became the ruler of Spain, serving as the Regent for the Bourbon monarchy until his death in 1975.

Fujimoro, Alberto: He was the elected president of Peru who authorized martial law and other harsh measures for dealing with Shining Path and MRTA dissidents. His harsh stance was successful, although Peruvian principles of democracy were weakened as a consequence.

furores: These documents were ancient grants to villages in the Basque country from Spanish monarchs, giving the local inhabitants a measure of autonomy in tax policy and local governance. The Nationalist government of Francisco Franco revoked them. The Basque separatists have always held them up as the ideal for the Basque region and as historical evidence of the distinctive character of the region.

Gandhi, Indira: She was the prime minister of India, assassinated by Sikh bodyguards after the assault on the Sikh Golden Temple of Amritsar in 1984 that killed many innocent religious Sikh pilgrims as well as the dissidents.

Gandhi, Rajiv: A suicide squad of Tamil nationalists from Sri Lanka assassinated Ghandi in 1991. He was targeted for death because of the assistance that India gave to the Sri Lankan government in its fight with Tamil dissidents.

Gaza Strip: The city of Gaza and the nearby shoreline on the Mediterranean was to be part of the Arab state of Palestine created after the end of the British Mandate since the population of the area was overwhelmingly Arab. In 1948, the Egyptian Army maintained control of the area, and it was under Egyptian administration until the Six Day War in 1967 when it was captured by Israel. The Gaza Strip is expected to eventually become part of the area governed by the Palestinian Authority.

genocide: Genocide is an effort, inevitably by a government, to totally wipe out particular ethnic or religious groups.

Gestapo: The Gestapo was the German secret police during the period of Nazi rule. The Gestapo was responsible for internal security in Germany and areas of Europe occupied by German forces.

Girondins: This term was applied to members of the national legislature in revolutionary France who were relatively moderate. They were displaced by more radical groups in the political infighting in the early years of the French Revolution.

globalization: Globalization refers to the general process wherein different parts of the world increasingly interact with each other. Increasing globalization has meant the more rapid penetration of societies by external economic, intellectual, religious, social, and political ideas and practices.

global jihadist: This term refers to those Muslim groups and individuals who see themselves involved in a global war against Western values and secularization. They are committed to an ongoing struggle to defend their faith against the onslaughts that have come with globalization.

Gracchi brothers: These brothers attempted to introduce reforms favoring the lower nobility in the Roman Republic. They were assassinated on separate occasions by the supporters of the status quo (and the upper classes).

Green Jackets: This group was a right-wing anti-immigrant organization that appeared in Copenhagen to protest what the members saw as preferential treatment for migrants from non-European areas of the world.

Gush Emunim: This group represents many of the settlers living in the West Bank territories of Judea and Samaria. It has demanded the incorporation of a maximum amount of territory on the West Bank or all of it into the state of Israel. Gush Emunim has been involved in a variety of violent activities to keep the territory as part of Israel.

Guzman, Abimael: Guzman was the founder and leader of the Shining Path group in Peru.

Hamas (Islamic Resistance Movement): This organization is based in the Occupied Territories of Israel, and opposes the existence of the state of Israel. It seeks instead to create an Islamic state in the area of Israel/Palestine. It has been responsible for many of the suicide attacks in Israel.

Harkat-ul-Mujahideen: This fundamentalist and militant group is based in Pakistan, and it has been important for training and aiding Islamic insurgents in Kashmir.

Hausa-Fulani: The Hausa-Fulani are the largest ethnic group in the northern half of Nigeria and in Nigeria as a whole. They are predominantly Muslim.

hawla: Hawla is a traditional way of transferring funds in many parts of the world. Terrorist groups such as Al Qaeda have used this mechanism for moving funds without detection.

Hinduvata: This term refers to the idea that basic tenets of Hinduism should become enshrined in the legal system of India.

Hitler, Adolf: Hitler was the leader of Germany from 1933 to 1945. His Nazi Party and allied organizations used violence and terror to help win elections. The Nazi Party under Hitler's leadership was also responsible for the Holocaust.

Hizballah: This Lebanese organization represents the Shia population of the country. It has received significant support from Iran and Syria and has engaged in at least some terrorist actions.

Hussein, Saddam: Hussein was the dictator of Iraq who was in power both at the time of the Iraqi invasion of Iran, the subsequent invasion of Kuwait, and until the US invasion in 2003. He was hanged for crimes against humanity in December 2006.

Hutu (Bahutu): The Hutu comprises the majority of the population of both Rwanda and Burundi. The political elite before independence in both countries was overwhelmingly comprised of members of the Tutsi community. Communal violence between the two groups was particularly pronounced in the 1990s in Rwanda.

Igbo: The Igbos were the dominant ethnic group in eastern Nigeria that attempted to set up the independent state of Biafra. They are predominantly Christian.

Impuza Mugambi: This Hutu paramilitary militia was one of the groups heavily involved in the genocide in Rwanda in the 1990s.

Interahamwe: This Hutu paramilitary group was associated with the radical wing of the ruling party in Rwanda. It was the largest paramilitary group and very active in the genocide against the Tutsi minority.

Inter-Services Intelligence (ISI): The major intelligence agencies of both Pakistan and India share this title. These agencies developed out of the intelligence sections of the British Indian Army during colonial days.

intifada: This is the Arabic term for the uprising in the West Bank and the Gaza Strip to protest against continuing Israeli military administration. It literally means "shaking off," including the idea of shaking off Israeli rule. The activities of the Palestinians were locally directed, but the Palestinian population in the two areas still looked to the PLO for leadership.

Irian Jaya (Western Papua): This Indonesian province occupies the western half of the island of New Guinea. Its population is ethnically quite distinct from the other groups in Indonesia and contains many Christians.

Irish National Liberation Army (INLA): The INLA was a much smaller dissident group in Northern Ireland seeking to end British rule by the use of violence. It had a much stronger Marxist-Leninist orientation than the Provisional IRA.

Irish Republican Army (IRA): The IRA was formed in the early 1900s to contest British rule of Ireland. After the Irish Free State was formed, the IRA eventually went into decline. It resurfaced in the 1960s in Northern Ireland. It has since split a number of times. The term currently is normally used interchangeably with the Provisional wing of the IRA.

Iron Guard: This fascist group in Rumania before World War II attempted to use terrorism as a means to gaining power. While briefly successful, the group's participation in government did not last very long.

Islamic Army Group (GIA): The GIA is one of the larger and most violent of the dissident organizations in Algeria that draws upon more fundamentalist Muslims for support.

Islamic Jihad (Palestine): This dissident group is opposed to the Israeli state and occupation of Palestine on both nationalist and religious grounds. It has sought to undercut various peace agreements between Israel and the PLO.

Islamic Movement Army (MIA): The MIA was one of the larger organizations composed of Muslim dissidents in Algeria. It had more connections with the FIS than some of the other rebel groups.

Islamic Salvation Front (FIS): The FIS was an electoral organization of Muslim groups that sought to bring about political reform in Algeria. The group also supported more reliance on Islamic tenets in the national law. Its initial success in the electoral process in Algeria resulted in the canceling of further elections and the eventual banning of the FIS.

Jacobin Clubs: These clubs attracted some of the more extreme elements involved in the French Revolution. The Jacobins supported more radical policies including the death of the king and other potential counterrevolutionaries.

Janatha Vimukthi Peramuna (JVP): This leftist party in Sri Lanka launched attempts to take over the government in 1971 and 1987. It was defeated both times.

janjaweed militias: These paramilitary groups have been used by the government of Sudan in a campaign to destroy dissident populations in the Darfur region of the country.

Japanese Red Army: Young Japanese leftists formed this group. It never became very effective within Japan itself, but it engaged in a number of actions outside of Japan, often in collaboration with other leftist or nationalist groups.

Jewish Defense League (JDL): This group was formed to help protect Jews in the United States from violent attacks. It also practiced terrorism against groups and countries that it saw as being hostile to Israel.

jihad: This Arabic word translates with a number of meanings. It literally means "striving" but it also has had the connotation of "holy war." Extreme Muslim groups tend to use it in the sense of holy war as an indication of their willingness to use violence, including acts of terror, to achieve their goals.

Judea and Samaria: Some Israelis refer to the West Bank occupied after the Israeli victory in the Six Day War in 1967 as Judea and Samaria to indicate the historical and biblical significance of the area.

June 2nd Movement: This group was one of the successors to the Baader–Meinhof Gang.

Justice Commandos of the Armenian Genocide (JCAG): This Armenian terrorist group has attempted to get the Turkish government to admit to the Armenian genocide during World War II by attacking Turkish interests around the world.

Kahane, Meir: This American Rabbi espoused an extreme version of Jewish nationalism, arguing that all Arab inhabitants of Israel and the Occupied Territories should be expelled. He also argued that virtually any violent actions against Palestinians were justified as a matter of self-defense.

Kashmir and Jammu: This Indian state has a Muslim majority but became part of India in 1948. It has been the scene of guerrilla fighting and terrorism at high or low levels of intensity for over half a century.

KGB: The KGB was the intelligence agency for the Soviet Union. It engaged in a variety of foreign espionage activities, including support for various kinds of dissident groups in the West.

Khalistan: This name is used for the independent Sikh homeland sought by terrorist groups in the Punjab.

kneecapping: This term applies to the practice utilized by the Red Brigades in Italy of approaching targets and shooting them in the knees or legs as punishment for their participation in the capitalist system or government. Wounding the victims more clearly demonstrated their vulnerability and the inability of the state to protect them than assassination.

Kosovo: Kosovo is a province in Serbia largely populated by Albanians. It has been a scene of tension between Serbs and Albanians and is now an independent state.

Kosovo Liberation Army (KLA): The KLA was the most important guerrilla and terrorist group that appeared to contest for control of Kosovo with the government of Serbia.

Ku Klux Klan (KKK): The KKK was first formed just after the Civil War in the United States to further the rights of former Confederate soldiers and officials who were disenfranchised. The KKK attempted (successfully) to intimidate former slaves in the South. With the advent of reconstruction and the dominance of white Southerners, the KKK became less prominent. It reappeared in the 1920s in the South and elsewhere in the United States. It was anti-black, anti-Jewish, anti-Catholic, and anti-immigrant. The KKK was responsible for attacks against black Americans and occasionally members of other groups in this period. Although now weaker, it has continued to be involved in violence against those groups it opposes.

Kurdish Democratic Party (KDP): The KDP is one of the major Kurdish parties that has sided with the United States during the occupation of Iraq and which is seeking either an autonomous Kurdistan or an independent state.

Kurdish Workers Party (PKK): The PKK was a Marxist-Leninist terrorist group operating in Turkey that also had a strong base in the Kurdish minority. The group was responsible for a campaign of suicide attacks.

Kurds: The Kurds are a non-Arabic people residing in areas of Turkey, Iraq, Syria, and Iran. They have sought an independent homeland since the end of World War I. Kurdish groups in Iraq, Iran, and Turkey have fought against their respective governments at various times, and independence movements or groups seeking greater autonomy have engaged in terrorist activities at times in all three of these countries.

Lashkar-i-Taiba: This group was formed to fight the Soviet forces and their local allies in Afghanistan. After the defeat of the Afghan Communists, the group has been sending guerrillas and fighters to Kashmir to fight against the Indian presence.

Laskar Jihad: This Indonesian Muslim organization sought to increase the influence of Islam within the country. It supplied arms and volunteers to areas of Indonesia where fighting between local Muslims and Christians had broken out.

leaderless resistance: Dissident groups that use violence, especially many groups in the extreme right in the United States, have adopted this organizational approach. The activists undertaking the violence do not have hierarchical links with the leaders. The leadership provides general guidelines and directions, but the persons involved in the violence chose the targets and the timing of the attacks.

left-wing ideologies: Ideologies of the left stress greater equality among different classes and less reliance on the free market to distribute resources.

Lenin, Vladimir: Lenin was the organizer of the successful Bolshevik takeover in Russia in 1917. His writings formed a key component of the Marxist-Leninist theory that forms the background of Communist theories.

Liberation Tigers of Tamil Eelam (LTTE): This dissident group has conducted a guerrilla and terrorist campaign to create an independent Tamil state on Sri Lanka for over twenty years.

Macedonia: This region was the southernmost part of the unified Yugoslavia, and is now an independent country. The traditional region of Macedonia included territory in present-day Bulgaria and Greece.

McVeigh, Timothy: McVeigh was arrested, convicted, and executed for setting off the bomb in Oklahoma City that destroyed the Murrah office building in 1995.

madrassas: These Islamic schools teach very fundamentalist beliefs and practices, and some of them support violent attacks against Muslims and others who do not share their views.

Marx, Karl: Marx is clearly the father of most strands of modern leftist theories. His writings from the nineteenth century have been modified and interpreted in many different ways explaining the diversity of latter-day left-wing ideologies.

Mau Mau: This term is applied to the Africans in Kenya who engaged in a rebellion against continued British rule and domination by white settlers in the 1950s.

Medellin Cartel: This Colombian drug organization attempted to force the Colombian government to stop extraditing drug lords by launching a terrorist campaign against the government in the 1980s. The cartel was defeated in this effort, but other drug producers have remained important in the country.

Milošević, Slobodan: Milošević was the ruler of Serbia when Yugoslavia fell apart. He adopted an extremely nationalistic posture for his government. He was put on trial for his support of ethnic cleansing and genocide in other parts of the formerly unified country but died before the end of the trial.

Minnesota Patriots Council: This right-wing US group was opposed a strong central government and any restrictions on the right to own guns. The group was stockpiling ricin to poison national and state officials. It was exposed in 1995 before it could take action and most of its members were convicted and sent to prison.

Montagnards: This term, meaning the mountain, was applied to the most radical elements present in revolutionary France. Leaders from this faction were responsible for much of the violence associated with the Reign of Terror.

Montoneros: The Montoneros were the largest leftist group that appeared in Argentina in the 1970s. They helped restore Juan Peron to power, but were destroyed by the military regime that eventually took power after Peron's death.

Moro, Aldo: Moro was a former Italian prime minister and leader of the Christian Democratic Party. He was kidnapped by the Red Brigades in a spectacular terrorist action and was later executed by them.

Mountbatten, Lord: Mountbatten rose to high rank in the British military during World War II and was a member of the royal family. His assassination by the IRA while on vacation in the Republic of Ireland was one of the more spectacular actions undertaken by this group.

Mugabe, Robert: Mugabe has been the president of Zimbabwe since the country gained its independence in 1980. He has rigged elections, and refuses to give up power. His supporters have used a variety of violent techniques to intimidate the opposition.

Mujahedin-e-Khalq (MEK): This group was composed of secular and leftist opponents of the Shah of Iran who were eased out of any share of political power by the Muslim clerics who came to power in 1979. They launched a number of successful terrorist actions against the regime before being decimated by countermeasures.

Munich Olympics (1972): Black September group seized Israeli athletes and coaches at the Olympic village in Munich to publicize the Palestinian cause. The terrorists and their hostages were all killed in a failed rescue attempted by West German police.

Murrah federal office building: This building in Oklahoma City was the target for Timothy McVeigh in 1995. The blast killed 168 people and wounded hundreds.

Mussolini, Benito: Mussolini was the Fascist dictator of Italy from 1922 to 1943. The Fascists used street violence against leftists to position themselves for support from conservative groups in Italy and to eventually take power.

narcoterrorism: This term has been applied to the idea that a Soviet led group of drug organizations were part of an effort to weaken the West. It has also been used to refer to cooperation among drug producers and violent dissident organizations.

National Liberation Army (ELN): This dissident group was formed in Colombia by leftist groups. It operated in the urban areas rather than rural locales.

National Liberation Army (NLA): The NLA was the organization that represented the Albanian minority in Macedonia. It used many of the same guerrilla and terrorist tactics as the Albanians in Kosovo.

National Socialist Democratic Workers Party (NSDAP): This party, usually referred to as the Nazi Party, was led by Adolf Hitler both before he came to power and when he ruled in Germany.

Nichols, Terry: Nichols was Timothy McVeigh's accomplice in the bombing of the Murrah federal office building in Oklahoma City.

Nivilles Group: This name was given to the terrorist group in Belgium in the 1980s that robbed banks and stores and was prone to killing members of the general public. The group gave the appearance of being a left-wing dissident group using terror, but it was generally thought to be a group on the extreme right seeking to make the left look bad.

NKVD: The NKVD was the official designation of the Soviet secret police when Stalin was in power. Its name was changed to the KGB, but the agency was not changed under the new title.

Noraid: This charity organization in the United States has collected funds for aid to persons in Northern Ireland. Much of the funding has apparently been used to support the IRA.

Nubia: This region in the northern part of the Sudan was effectively pacified by the government with the use of repression and attacks by militias loyal to the government.

Ocalan, Abdullah: Ocalan was the leader of the Kurdish Workers Party. After he was captured, he ordered the group to stop its attacks in exchange for a commutation of a death sentence into life imprisonment.

Occupied Territories: This term refers to the Gaza Strip and those areas of the West Bank that have not been incorporated within the boundaries of Israel. These territories have often been administered by the military with frequent reliance on martial law.

Official IRA: With the outbreak of violence in Northern Ireland in 1969, the leadership of the IRA followed a Marxist-Leninist line that was against the use of terrorism. The Officials became relatively insignificant when the Provisionals began a campaign of violence against continued British rule.

Operation Black Thunder: This military action against Sikh dissidents in the Golden Temple of Amritsar in 1988 was undertaken with great care to limit casualties among innocent civilians and to minimize damage to the temple grounds.

Operation Blue Star: This code name was used for the attack on the Golden Temple of Amritsar in 1984. Hundreds of innocent pilgrims were killed in the attack, and the temple itself was damaged.

Order, The: This far-right group operated for eighteen months in the Pacific Northwest. It began to rob banks in 1983 and even robbed an armored truck. Local police broke the organization, but most of the money taken in the robberies has never been recovered.

Palestinian Authority: This is the name give to the administrative agency that was headed by Yasser Arafat in the West Bank and Gaza Strip. The authority has had limited autonomy over those areas of the Occupied Territories where Israel has relinquished its responsibility for direct administration.

Palestinian Liberation Organization (PLO): This organization long represented the interests of the Palestinians in territories administered by Israel and in other countries. The PLO itself is an umbrella organization that is made of many different Palestinian groups. The PLO served as the basic unit for creating the Palestinian Authority in portions of the West Bank and Gaza Strip.

Patriotic Union of Kurdistan (PUK): The PUK is one of the major Kurdish parties that has sided with the United States during the occupation of Iraq and which is seeking either an autonomous Kurdistan or an independent state.

Pavelich, Ante: Pavelich was the leader of the Utashe, the Croatian fascist party that cooperated with Italy and Germany during World War II.

Peoples Revolutionary Army (ERP): The ERP was one of the leftist groups in Argentina that was opposed to the various military governments in power. There were under attack by the government of Juan Peron and then Isabel Peron and then destroyed by the military government that came into power in 1976.

Peron, Isabel: Isabel was the wife of Juan Peron when he returned to power in Argentina in the 1970s. She served as his vice-president and assumed office when he died. She proved to be an ineffective political leader.

Peron, Juan: Juan Peron was the ruler of Argentina in the 1940s and 1950s until overthrown. He became the focus of much of the opposition to governments in Argentina in ensuing years. Peron returned in triumph in 1973 and became president, but he died in 1974.

Pierce, William: Pierce wrote *The Turner Diaries* (1980), which he regarded as a blueprint for overthrowing the government of the United States. Many members of right-wing groups regarded Pierce, who died in 2002, as the leading ideologue for their groups.

Popular Front for the Liberation of Palestine (PFLP): This Palestinian nationalist group was formed by George Habash, a Greek Orthodox Arab. The organization's views incorporated a clearly leftist ideology and have long favored greater efforts to link the struggle of the Palestinians to class conflict.

Popular Front for the Liberation of Palestine-General Council (PFLP-GC): This Palestinian organization was an splinter group from the PFLP, and it has continued to espouse terrorism after the PLO modified its stance toward global attacks.

Popular Liberation Army (EPL): This organization was one of the smaller leftist dissident groups that operated in Colombia.

Posse Comitatus: This right-wing tax resister group in the United States believes that almost all levels of government are unconstitutional. They regard the county sheriff as the highest official to obey, and only if he or she is making the right decisions.

propaganda of the deed: Anarchists originated this term to describe violent attacks that were designed to educate the general public to the repressive nature of the governments in power. The demonstration of opposition by individuals was intended to inspire popular insurrections.

propaganda of the word: Anarchists considered educational activities to be propaganda of the word. Some anarchists believed that educational efforts would be sufficient to mobilize the public to oppose governments in power.

Provisional IRA: The Provisionals (Provos) have been synonymous with the use of the term IRA since the 1970s. They have formed the core of those opposed to continued British control of Northern Ireland.

"Punjab" solution: This term in India refers to the use of death squads for extra-legal executions of dissidents and guerrillas in a variety of areas. The term derives from the use of such squads in the Punjab during the fighting with the Sikh dissidents.

Quebec Liberation Front (FLQ): This separatist group wanted to create an independent Quebec nation and drew some support from French-speaking inhabitants of the province. It was active in the 1960s and early 1970s.

Rabin, Yitzak: Rabin was the prime minister of Israel assassinated by an Israeli Jew in 1995 for compromising with the Palestinians.

Rangoon bombing: In 1983 North Korean agents attempted to assassinate South Korea's president. While he survived, five members of the cabinet died in the bomb explosion.

Rashtriya Swayamsevak Sangh (National Patriotism Organization): This group was formed in the 1920s in India to protect Hindu culture against outside influences. In more recent times the group has practiced violence against non-Hindu groups in India.

Real IRA: This name has been adopted by a group of IRA members opposed to the peace initiatives between the IRA and the British government.

Red Army Faction (RAF): The official name of the Baader–Meinhoff Gang was the Red Army Faction, representing the leftist ideology of the members.

Red Brigades: The Red Brigades was the most important left-wing dissident group using terrorism in Italy in the 1960s, 1970s, and 1980s. The death toll attributed to the Red Brigades totaled thousands. The group was eventually defeated only after the Italian police upgraded their capabilities and after captured members were offered reduced sentences for informing on their fellow members.

Red Cells: This organization was one of the successor groups to the Baader–Meinhof Gang in Germany.

Red Scare: In the aftermath of World War I, the United States went through a period in which there was a fear that foreign radicals would overthrow the political system. Persons suspected of being radicals were persecuted or attacked.

Reign of Terror: This term refers to a period of the early years of the French Revolution when radicals gained control of the revolutionary government and used terror to control the population. Tens of thousands went to their deaths in Paris and elsewhere in the country, often through the use of the guillotine.

Rejectionist Front: This term was used for a group of Palestinian nationalist organizations that were opposed to PLO negotiations with Israel. They choose to continue the struggle against Israel and to continue to use terrorism.

Revolutionary Armed Forces of Colombia (FARC): This leftist group has provided long-lasting opposition to the government in Colombia. Its alliance with drug producers has given it the financial resources to arm itself and to battle the government for effective control of many rural areas.

Revolutionary Guards: This group of supporters of the Islamic Republic in Iran were formed to defend the regime and to deal with dissidents. The Guards have also provided personnel to staff terrorist training camps in Iran, Lebanon, and the Sudan.

ricin: This poison is made without too much difficulty from castor beans. Extreme right-wing groups in the United States have shown a great deal of interest in this particular poison.

Ruby Ridge: Ruby Ridge was the home of Randy Weaver, who failed to appear in federal court to face a weapons charge. Mishandling by the local federal officials resulted in the death of Weaver's wife and a federal officer in 1992. The situation provided right-wing groups with proof that the federal government was out to disarm individuals and was serving as a front for foreign interests.

Sandinistas: The opponents of the Somoza regime in Nicaragua took this name from an opponent of an earlier government in Nicaragua. They were successful in ousting Somoza and his supporters from power.

sarin: This nerve gas was used by Aum Shinrikyo in its efforts to cause mass casualties in the Japanese subway system in 1994.

Schutzstaffel (SS): The SS was originally formed to provide a personal bodyguard to Hitler as the leader of the Nazi Party. The SS provided the core of the personnel who operated the death camps during World War II.

Self Defense Forces of Colombia (AUC): This paramilitary group appeared to battle leftist forces in Colombia. It has generally supported the government, but its tactics have included efforts to terrorize presumed supporters of the leftist dissidents.

17 November Organization: This left-wing Greek dissident organization has been one of the most successful in avoiding any infiltration or exposure by official agencies. After almost thirty years of activity the Greek authorities finally captured members of the group.

Sharia: The guidelines and the directives of the Quran and the early life of the Prophet Muhammad form the Sharia and provide the basis for an Islamic legal system.

Shia (or Shi'a): This is a breakaway branch of Islam. Clerical leaders have somewhat greater weight in this version of Islam, which is practiced by most of the inhabitants of Iran. There are also significant Shia populations in Lebanon and Iraq.

Shining Path (Sendero Luminoso): This leftist group in Peru mounted a major challenge to the government, in large measure because it could draw upon dissatisfaction by the Indian population due to government policies that failed to help them.

Sicarri: These Jewish daggermen attacked supporters of Rome in Judea or those who were opposed to the idea of revolt in order to force consensus within the Jewish community in favor of the upcoming revolt.

Sikhs: Sikhs are followers of the Indian religion Sikhism, which has some similarities to Hinduism. It generally is considered to be a separate religion.

Skinheads: These groups of undereducated youth with limited job prospects have often joined in attacks against immigrant and foreign communities in Europe. They are frequently not part of right-wing organizations, but they provide personnel for many attacks undertaken by these right-wing groups.

Social Revolutionaries: The Social Revolutionaries were a Russian political party in the first decade of the twentieth century. They used both non-violent and violent means in their efforts to bring about major changes in the Russian political system. They adopted the anarchist tactic of targeted assassinations against high-ranking government officials.

Somoza, Anastacio: Somoza was the former dictator of Nicaragua who was overthrown by a popular uprising led by the Sandinistas. He was assassinated while in exile in Paraguay—apparently by Argentine leftists.

Special Air Services Regiment (SAS): This elite British military has been used in special operations to combat terrorists. Its rigorous training has meant that it has often been very successful in these efforts.

Stern Gang: This organization was composed of Jewish inhabitants of British Palestine. They used terrorism against both the British and the Arab inhabitants as part of their campaign to force the British to withdraw so that an independent Jewish state could be created.

Students for a Democratic Society (SDS): This student group formed in the 1960s in the United States to oppose the US involvement in the war in Vietnam. The students also used leftist ideology to attack capitalism and government practices. Members of the movement in small numbers did go on to engage in terrorist actions, but mostly limited themselves to symbolic property attacks.

Sturmabteilungen (SA): The SA, or stormtroopers, provided the Nazi Party in Germany with street fighters to intimidate the opposition and to protect Nazi Party rallies. The group was organizationally independent of the party, but Adolf Hitler was leader of the SA as well as the party. When the Nazis came to power, the SA was disbanded.

Suharto, General: General Suharto was the long time ruler of Indonesia who came to power through a coup in the 1960s. His resignation of the presidency and the return of at least partially democratic rule to Indonesia have been accompanied by increased communal violence between Muslims and Christians, ethnic fighting, and separatist movements in various parts of the nation.

Sunni: This is the orthodox version of Islam. The vast majority of Muslims in the world consider themselves to be Sunni.

suspect community: When members of a religious or ethnic group become automatic suspects of terrorist activity based on their membership, they are part of a suspect community. Members of such communities may face special disabilities or are more likely to be arrested or convicted of crimes.

Symbonese Liberation Army (SLA): The SLA was one of the more violent leftist groups that appeared out of the anti-war movement in the United States. It operated for a few years in California and is probably best known for the kidnapping of Patty Hearst.

Taliban: This group of Islamic fundamentalists eventually provided the leadership for most of Afghanistan after the withdrawal of Soviet troops. The Taliban leadership also provided a safe haven for Osama bin Laden and many of his operatives and supporters.

Tamil Nadu: This Indian state is near Sri Lanka, and it is populated by India's Tamil minority.

Tamil Tigers: This name if the one normally used by the members of the Liberation Tigers of Tamil Eelam (LTTE) who support the idea of independent Tamil state in Sri Lanka.

terrorism: Terrorism involves political aims and motives. It is violent or threatens violence. It is designed to generate fear in a target audience that extends beyond the immediate victims of the violence. The violence is conducted by an identifiable organization. The violence involves a non-state actor or actors as either the perpetrator, the victim of the violence, or both. Finally, the acts of violence are designed to create power in situations in which power previously had been lacking (i.e., the violence attempts to enhance the power base of the organization undertaking the actions).

Triple Frontier region: The Triple Frontier region is the area where Brazil, Argentina, and Paraguay share borders. It is known as an area where criminal organizations operate, and some terrorist groups are established there as well.

Trotsky, Leon: Trotsky was one of the leaders of the Bolshevik Revolution in Russia. He was a rival of Stalin and eventually forced to leave the country. Trotskyite versions of Communist place greater stress on participation by the rank and file of the party.

Mao Tse-tung (Mao Zedong): Mao was the leader of the Communist Party in China before, during, and after World War II. He successfully organized the party in the countryside and used peasant support to eventually overthrow the government. Maoist theories of Communism, as a consequence, frequently stress victory in the countryside as the means of acquiring power.

Tupac Amaru Revolutionary Movement (MRTA): This leftist movement in Peru was never as strong as Shining Path. It was largely eliminated as a threat to the government, but it was responsible for the takeover of the Japanese embassy during a Christmas celebration in 1996.

Tupamaros: The Tupamaros were a left-wing group in Uruguay opposed to the government in power. The Tupamaros attracted students from middle-class and upper-middle-class families.

The Turner Diaries: This book written by William Pierce (published in 1980) outlines a plan of action for its fictional hero to use to resist a dictatorial government in the United States and to return the country to its basic, democratic roots by defeating the Jewish and foreign groups that have conspired to destroy the country.

Tutsi (Watutsi): The political elite before independence in Rwanda and Burundi was overwhelmingly comprised of members of the Tutsi, who had formed the ruling class before the arrival of the Europeans. The Hutu comprise the majority of the population of both Rwanda and Burundi. Communal violence between the two groups was particularly pronounced in the 1990s.

Unabomber: This name was given to the then unknown individual who sent bombs to various individuals over ten years as part of a protest against modernization in the world. Theodore Kaczynski was finally identified as the Unabomber and caught.

USS *Cole*: This American destroyer was attacked in the harbor at Aden in Yemen. Two terrorists used a motorboat filled with explosives in a suicide attack that killed more than thirty crew members on the ship.

Utashe: This party contained the more extreme nationalist and fascist elements in the Croatian state created in 1941. Under the leadership of Ante Pavelich, the Croatian fascists attacked Jews, Gypsies, and Serbs. The victims numbered in the hundreds of thousands.

Vendee: The Vendee is a French region bordering on the Bay of Biscay north of Bordeaux. It is also the name given to a counterrevolutionary uprising that was opposed to the republic established by the French Revolution. The peasants in the uprising were fighting to restore the monarchy and the Catholic Church to their previous positions.

La Violencia: This term is applied to the violence between political factions in the late 1940s in Colombia.

weapons of mass destruction: These weapons are ones that are designed to cause massive causalities among target populations. Some biological weapons, chemical weapons, and nuclear devices are considered weapons of mass destruction.

weapons of mass disruption: These weapons are designed to disrupt the target society when used by terrorists or a state. Such weapons might disable communications networks or disrupt important computer systems. Such weapons would not necessarily directly cause major casualties in the target society.

Weathermen: This group, sometimes called the Weather Underground, was a radical offshoot of the Students for a Democratic Society. Protests against the war in Vietnam and capitalism in general led the group to adopt violent methods. The violence was largely restricted to attacks on property in efforts to change government policies.

Will of the People: This Russian anarchist group sought to inspire a popular rebellion by a campaign of assassinations against key officials and leaders, especially the Czar. The group was responsible for a number of successful assassinations, including Czar Alexander II.

Yoruba: The Yoruba are the largest ethnic group in the western part of Nigeria.

Zealots: This group of Jewish patriots in the Roman Empire instigated a revolt in CE 66 that was temporarily successful in liberating Judea from Roman rule.

Zhirinovsky, Vladimir: Zhirinovsky was the leader of the Liberal Democrats in Russia after the dissolution of the Soviet Union. The Liberal Democrats have been an extremely nationalistic party that had similarities to the fascist parties that appeared in Europe prior to World War II.

Zimbabwean African National Union (ZANU): ZANU was one of the major groups involved in the guerrilla struggle in Rhodesia. It is the party of President Mugabe, and has been in power since Zimbabwe gained its independence.

Zimbabwean African Peoples Union (ZAPU): ZAPU was the second largest group involved in the independence struggle in Rhodesia. The ruling party of independent Zimbabwe eventually banned ZAPU.

Zionist: This term is applied to Jewish nationalists who have desired the creation of a Jewish Homeland in Palestine (the land of Zion).

Zionist Occupation Government (ZOG): This term is used by extreme right-wing groups in the United States (and by some groups in Europe as well) to refer to their belief that Jewish financial interests control the government.

BIBLIOGRAPHY

Abadie, A., and Gardeazabal, J. (2003) "The Economic Costs of Conflict: A Case Study of the Basque Country," *American Economic Review*, 93, 1: 113–31.

Abrahams, R. (1988) *Vigilant Citizens: Vigilantism and the State*, Cambridge: Polity Press.

Abrahms, M. (2006) "Why Terrorism Does Not Work," *International Security*, 31, 2: 42–78.

Abuza, Z. (2005) "Al-Qaeda Comes to Southeast Asia," in P. J. Smith (ed.) *Terrorism and Violence in Southeast Asia: Transnational Challenges to States and Regional Stability*, Armonk, NY: M. E. Sharpe, 38–61.

—— (2003a) "Funding Terrorism in Southeast Asia: The Financial Network of Al Qaeda and Jemaah Islamiya," *Contemporary Southeast Asia*, 22, 2: 169–99.

—— (2003b) *Militant Islam in Southeast Asia: Crucible of Terror*, Boulder, CO: Lynne Rienner.

——(2002) "Tentacles of Terror: Al Qaeda's Southeast Asian Network," *Contemporary Southeast Asia: A Journal of International and Strategic Affairs*, 24, 3: 427–65.

Ackerman, G. A. (2003) "Beyond Arson? A Threat Assessment of the Earth Liberation Front," *Terrorism and Political Violence*, 15, 4: 143–70.

Ahmed, H. H. (2005) "Palestinian Resistance and 'Suicide Bombing': Causes and Consequences," in T. Bjorgo (ed.) *Root Causes of Terrorism: Myths, Reality and Ways Forward*, London: Routledge, 87–102.

Ajami, F. (2001) "The Sentry's Solitude," *Foreign Affairs*, 80, 6: 2–16.

Albin, C. (1989) "The Politics of Terrorism: A Contemporary Survey," in B. Rubin (ed.) *The Politics of Terrorism: Terror as a State and Revolutionary Strategy*, Washington, DC: Foreign Policy Institute, 183–234.

al-Khalil, S. (1989) *Republic of Fear: The Inside Story of Saddam's Iraq*, New York: Pantheon Books.

Allegro, J. M. (1972) *The Chosen People: A Study of Jewish History from the Time of the Exile until the Revolt of Bar Kocheba, Sixth Century B.C. to Second Century A.D.*, Garden City, NY: Doubleday.

Almonte, J. T. (2003) "Enhancing State Capacity and Legitimacy in the Counter-Terror War," in K. Ramakrishna and S. S. Tan (eds) *After Bali: The Threat of Terrorism in Southeast Asia*, Singapore: Institute of Defence ands Strategic Studies and World Scientific Publishing, 221–40.

Alonso, R. (2001) "The Modernization in Irish Republican Thinking toward the Utility of Violence," *Studies in Conflict and Terrorism*, 24, 2: 131–44.

Anderson, J. H. (1995) "The Neo-Nazi Menace in Germany," *Studies in Conflict and Terrorism*, 18, 1: 39–46.

Angel, R. C. (1990) "Japanese Terrorists and Japanese Countermeasures," in B. Rubin (ed.) *The Politics of Counterterrorism: The Ordeal of Democratic States*, Washington, DC: Foreign Policy Institute, 31–60.

Applebaum, S. (1971) "The Zealots: The Case for Revaluation," *Journal of Roman Studies*, 61: 155–70.

Apter, D. E. (1997) "Political Violence in Analytical Perspective," in D. E. Apter (ed.) *The Legitimization of Violence*, New York: New York University Press, 1–32.

Arian, A. (1998) *The Second Republic: Politics in Israel*, Chatham, NJ: Chatham House.

Arnson, C. J. (2000) "Window on the Past: A Declassified History of Death Squads in El Salvador," in B. D. Campbell and A. D. Brenner (eds) *Death Squads in Global Perspective: Murder with Deniability*, New York: St Martin's, 85–124.

Ash, T. G. (2003) "Is There a Good Terrorist?" in C. W. Kegley, Jr (ed.) *The New Global Terrorism: Characteristics, Causes, Controls*, Upper Saddle River, NJ: Prentice Hall, 60–70.

Austin, D., and Gupta, A. (1990) *The Politics of Violence in India and South Asia: Is Democracy an Endangered Species?* Conflict Studies 233, London: Research Institute for the Study of Conflict and Terrorism.

Auten, B. (1996) "Tajikistan Today," *Studies in Conflict and Terrorism*, 19, 2: 199–212.

Azam, J.-P. (2005), "Suicide-Bombing as Inter-Generational Investment," *Public Choice*, 122, 1/2: 177–98.

Azra, A. (2003) "Bali and Southeast Asian Islam: Debunking the Myths," in K. Ramakrishna and S. S. Tan (eds) *After Bali: The Threat of Terrorism in Southeast Asia*, Singapore: Institute of Defence and Strategic Studies and World Scientific Publishing, 39–57.

Baczko, B. (1994) "The Terror before the Terror? Conditions of Possibility, Logic of Realization," in K. M. Baker (ed.) *The French Revolution and the Creation of Modern Political Culture: Volume 4, The Terror*, Oxford: Pergamon, 19–38.

Badey, T. J. (1998) "Defining International Terrorism: A Pragmatic Approach," *Terrorism and Political Violence*, 10, 1: 90–107.

Baev, P. K. (2006) "Putin's Counter-Terrorism: The Parameters of a Strategic Dead-End," *Small Wars and Insurgencies*, 17, 1: 1–21.

Bajpai, K. S. (2003) "Untangling India and Pakistan," *Foreign Affairs*, 82, 3: 112–26.

Baker, N. V. (2003) "National Security versus Civil Liberties," *Presidential Studies Quarterly*, 33, 3: 547–67.

Bal, I., and Laciner, S. (2001) "The Challenge of Revolutionary Terrorism to Turkish Democracy, 1960–1980," *Terrorism and Political Violence*, 13, 4: 90–115.

Bale, J. M. (1996) "The May 1973 Terrorist Attack at Milan Police HQ: Anarchist 'Propaganda of the Deed' or 'False-Flag' Provocation," *Terrorism and Political Violence*, 8, 1: 132–66.

Banac, I. (1984) *The National Question in Yugoslavia: Origins, History, Politics*, Ithaca, NY: Cornell University Press.

Banerjee, S. (2002) "Naxalbari and the Left Movement," in G. Shah (ed.) *Social Movements and the State*, Readings in Indian Government and Politics, Vol. 4, New Delhi: Sage, 125–92.

—— (1996) "Strategy, Tactics, and Forms of Political Participation among Left Parties," in T. V. Sathyamurthy (ed.) *Class Formation and Political Transformation in Post-Colonial India*, Social Change and Political Discourse in India, Vol. 4, Dehli: Oxford University Press, 202–37.

—— (1984) *Indian's Simmering Revolution: The Naxalite Uprising*, London: Zed Books.

Barbu, Z. (1968) "Rumania," in S. J. Woolf (ed.) *European Fascism*, New York: Vintage Books, 146–66.

Barkun, M. (2000) "Violence in the Name of Democracy: Justifications for Separatism on the Radical Right," *Political Violence and Terrorism*, 12, 3/4: 193–208.

—— (1996) "Religion, Militias and Oklahoma City: The Mind of Conspiratorialists," *Terrorism and Political Violence*, 8, 1: 50–64.

Barnhurst, K. G. (1991) "Contemporary Terrorism in Peru: Sendero Luminoso and the Media," *Journal of Communication*, 41, 4: 75–89.

Barry, D., Vergara, R., and Castro, J. R. (1988) "'Low Intensity Warfare': The Counter-Insurgency Strategy for Central America," in N. Hamilton, J. A. Frieden, L. Fuller, and M. Pastor, Jr (eds) *Crisis in Central America: Regional Dynamics and U.S. Policy in the 1980s*, Boulder, CO: Westview, 77–96.

Bates-Gaston, J. (2003) "Terrorism and Imprisonment in Northern Ireland: A Psychological Perspective," in A. Silke (ed.) *Terrorists, Victims and Society: Psychological Perspectives on Terrorism and Its Consequences*, Chichester: Wiley, 233–55.

Beckett, I. F. W. (2001) *Modern Insurgencies and Counter-Insurgencies: Guerrillas and their Opponents since 1750*, London: Routledge.

Behera, N. C. (2007) "Kashmir: A Testing Ground," in J. McGuire and I. Copland (eds) *Hindu Nationalism and Governance*, New Delhi: Oxford University Press, 405–29.

Bell, J. B. (1997a) *The Secret Army: The IRA,* revised 3rd edition, New Brunswick, NJ: Transaction Books.

—— (1997b) "Terrorist Fundraising," in M. Crenshaw and J. Pimlott (eds) *Encyclopedia of World Terrorism*, Vol. 1, Armonk, NY: M. E. Sharpe, 239–40.

Bell-Fialkoff, A. (1999) *Ethnic Cleansing*, New York: St Martin's Griffin.

Berend, I. T. (1998) *Decades of Crisis: Central and Eastern Europe before World War II*, Berkeley, CA: University of California Press.

Bessant, J. (1995) "Political Crime and the Case of Young Neo-Nazis: A Question of Methodology," *Terrorism and Political Violence*, 7, 4: 94–116.

Bessel, R. (1986) "Violence as Propaganda: The Role of the Storm Troopers in the Rise of National Socialism," in T. Childers (ed.) *The Formation of the Nazi Constituency, 1919–1933*, Totowa, NJ: Barnes & Noble, 131–46.

Betts, R. K. (2002a) "Fixing Intelligence," *Foreign Affairs*, 81, 1: 43–59.

—— (2002b) "The Soft Underbelly of American Primacy: Tactical Advantages of Terror," *Political Science Quarterly* 117, 1: 19–36.

Betz, H.-G. (1994) *Radical Right-Wing Populism in Western Europe*, New York: St Martin's.

Bhatt, C. (2001) *Hindu Nationalism: Origins, Ideologies, and Modern Myths,* Oxford: Berg.

Bhatt, S. (2003) "State Terrorism vs. Jihad in Kashmir," *Journal of Contemporary Asia*, 33, 2: 215–24

Bieber, F. (2003) "Approaches to Political Violence and Terrorism in Former Yugoslavia," *Journal of Southern Europe and the Balkans*, 5, 3: 39–51.

Bjorgo, T. (2005a) "Conclusions," in T. Bjorgo (ed.) *Root Causes of Terrorism: Myths, Reality and Ways Forward*, London: Routledge, 256–64.

—— (2005b) "Introduction," in T. Bjorgo (ed.) *Root Causes of Terrorism: Myths, Reality and Ways Forward*, London: Routledge, 1–15.

—— (1997) *Racist and Right-Wing Violence in Scandinavia: Patterns, Perpetrators, and Responses*, Oslo: Tano Aschehougs.

—— (1995a) "Extreme Nationalism and Violent Discourses in Scandinavia: 'The Resistance,' 'Traitors,' and 'Foreign Invaders,'" in T. Bjorgo (ed.) *Terror from the Extreme Right*, London: Frank Cass, 182–220.

—— (1995b) "Introduction," in T. Bjorgo (ed.) *Terror from the Extreme Right*, London: Frank Cass, 1–16.

—— (1993) "Militant Neo-Nazism in Sweden," *Terrorism and Political Violence*, 5, 3: 28–57.

Bloom, M. M. (2004) "Palestinian Suicide Bombing: Public Support, Market Share, and Outbidding," *Political Science Quarterly*, 119, 1: 61–88.

Bobrick, B. (1997) *Angel in the Whirlwind: The Triumph of the American Revolution*, New York: Simon and Schuster.

Bouchat, C. J. (1996) "A Fundamentalist Islamic Threat to the West," *Studies in Conflict and Terrorism*, 19, 4: 339–52.

Bowers, S., Derrick, A. A., and Olimov, M. A. (2004) "Suicide Terrorism in the Former USSR," *Journal of Social, Political and Economic Studies*, 29, 3: 261–79.

Brannan, D. W. (2006) "Left- and Right-Wing Political Terrorism," in A. T. H. Tan (ed.) *The Politics of Terrorism: A Survey*. London: Routledge, 55–72.

Brauer, J., Gomez-Sorzano, A., and Sethuraman, S. (2004) "Decomposing Violence: Political Murder in Colombia, 1946–1999," *European Journal of Political Economy*, 20, 2: 447–61.

Brenner, A. D. (2000) "*Feme* Murder: Paramilitary 'Self-Justice' in Weimar Germany," in B. D. Campbell and A. D. Brenner (eds) *Death Squads in Global Perspective: Murder with Deniability*, New York: St Martin's, 57–83.

Brigham, R. K. (2006) *Is Iraq another Vietnam?* New York: Public Affairs.

Brophy-Baermann, B., and Conybeare, J. A. C. (1994) "Retaliating against Terrorism: Rational Expectations and the Optimality of Rules versus Discretion," *American Journal of Political Science*, 38, 1: 196–210.

Brown, R. M. (1989) "Historical Patterns of Violence," in T. R. Gurr (ed.) *Violence in America: Volume 2, Protest, Rebellion, Reform*, Newbury Park, CA: Sage Publications, 23–61.

Brownfield, A. C. (2000) "Jewish/Zionist Terrorism: A Continuing Threat to Peace," *Global Dialogue*, 2, 4: 107–17.

Brunn, G. (1982) "Nationalist Violence and Terror in the Spanish Border Provinces: ETA," in W. J. Mommsen and G. Hirschfeld (eds) *Social Protest, Violence, and Terror in Nineteenth- and Twentieth-Century Europe*, New York: St Martin's Press for the German Historical Institute, 112–36.

Bucheim, H. (1972) "The Position of the SS in the Third Reich," in H. Holborn (ed.) *Republic to Reich: The Making of the Nazi Revolution, Ten Essays*, New York: Pantheon Books, 251–97.

Bunker, R. J. (2000) "Weapons of Mass Disruption," *Terrorism and Political Violence*, 12, 1: 37–46.

Burke, J. (2003) *Al-Qaeda: Casting a Shadow of Terror*, London: I. B. Tauris.

Byman, D. (2006) "Do Targeted Killings Work?" *Foreign Affairs*, 85, 2: 95–111.

—— (1998) "The Logic of Ethnic Terrorism," *Studies in Conflict and Terrorism*, 21, 2: 149–69.

Calvert, P. (1997) "Argentine Government's Responses to Terrorism," in M. Crenshaw and J. Pimlott (eds) *Encyclopedia of World Terrorism*, Vol. 3, Armonk, NY: M. E. Sharpe, 629–31.

Cameron, G. (2004) "Weapons of Mass Destruction Terrorism Research: Past and Future," in A. Silke (ed.) *Research on Terrorism: Trends, Achievements and Failures*, London: Frank Cass, 72–90.

—— (1999) "Multi-Track Microproliferation: Lessons from Aum Shinrikyo and Al Qaida," *Studies in Conflict and Terrorism*, 22, 4: 277–309.

Campbell, B. D. (2000) "Death Squads: Definition, Problems, and Historical Context," in B. D. Campbell and A. D. Brenner (eds) *Death Squads in Global Perspective: Murder with Deniability*, New York: St Martin's, 1–26.

Campbell, B. D., and Brenner, A. D. (2000) "Preface," in B. D. Campbell and A. D. Brenner (eds) *Death Squads in Global Perspective: Murder with Deniability*, New York: St Martin's, vii–xvii.

Carey, P. (2007) "East Timor under Indonesian Occupation, 1975–99," in A. T. H. Tan (ed.), *A Handbook of Terrorism and Insurgency in Southeast Asia*, Cheltenham: Edward Elgar, 374–401.

Carr, C. (2002) *The Lessons of Terror: A History of Warfare against Civilians, Why It Has Failed and Why It Will Fail Again*, New York: Random House.

Carus, W. S. (2000) "The Rajneeshees," in J. B. Tucker (ed.) *Toxic Terror: Assessing Terrorist Use of Chemical and Biological Weapons*, Cambridge, MA: MIT Press, 115–37.

Chalk, F., and Johassohn, K. (1990) *The History and Sociology of Genocide: Analyses and Case Studies*, New Haven: Yale University Press.

Chalk, P. (1999) "The Evolving Dynamic of Terrorism in the 1990s," *Australian Journal of International Affairs*, 53, 2: 151–68.

—— (1998a) "Political Terrorism in South-East Asia," *Terrorism and Political Violence*, 10, 2: 118–34.

—— (1998b) "The Response to Terrorism as a Threat to Liberal Democracy," *Australian Journal of Politics and History*, 44, 3: 373–88.

—— (1996) *West European Terrorism and Counter-Terrorism: The Evolving Dynamic*, Basingstoke: Macmillan.

Chalmers, D. M. (1965) *Hooded Americanism: The History of the Ku Klux Klan*. New York: Quadrangle Books.

Chamberlin, W. H. (1935) *The Russian Revolution, 1917–1921: Vol. 1, 1917–1918, From the Overthrow of the Czar to the Assumption of Power by the Bolsheviks*, New York: Grosset & Dunlap, reprint edition, 1965.

Chandra, K. (1999) "Post-Congress Politics in Uttar Pradesh: The Ethnification of the Party System and Its Consequences," in R. Roy and P. Wallace (eds) *Indian Politics and the 1998 Election*, New Delhi: Sage Publications, 55–104.

Chellaney, B. (2001/2) "Fighting Terrorism in Southern Asia: The Lessons of History," *International Security*, 26, 3: 94–116.

Chima, J. S. (2002) "Back to the Future in 2002? A Model of Sikh Separatism in Punjab," *Studies in Conflict and Terrorism*, 25, 1: 19–39.

Chipman, D. P. (2003) "Osama bin Laden and Guerrilla War," *Studies in Conflict and Terrorism*, 26, 3: 163–70.

Chubb, J. (1989) *The Mafia and Politics; The Italian State under Siege*, Western Societies Program Occasional Paper No. 23, Ithaca, NY: Center for International Studies, Cornell University.

Chyba, C. F. (2002) "Toward Biological Security," *Foreign Affairs*, 81, 3: 122–36.

Cilliers, J. (2003) "Terrorism and Africa," *African Security Review*, 12, 4: 91–103.

Claridge, D. (2000a) "The Baader-Meinhof Gang (1975)," in J. B. Tucker (ed.) *Toxic Terror: Assessing Terrorist Use of Chemical and Biological Weapons*, Cambridge, MA: MIT Press, 95–106.

—— (2000b) "Exploding Myths of Superterrorism," in M. Taylor and J. Horgan (eds) *The Future of Terrorism*, London: Frank Cass, 133–48.

—— (1996) "State Terrorism? Applying a Definitional Model", *Terrorism and Political Violence*, 8, 3: 47–63.

Clutterbuck, R. (1975) *Living with Terrorism*, London: Faber and Faber.

—— (1974) *Protest and the Urban Guerrilla*, New York: Abelard-Schuman.

Combs, C. C. (2000) *Terrorism in the Twenty-First Century*, 2nd edition, Upper Saddle River, NJ: Prentice Hall.

Conroy, M. E., and Pastor, M., Jr. (1988) "The Nicaraguan Experiment: Characteristics of a New Economic Model," in N. Hamilton, J. A. Frieden, L. Fuller, and M. Pastor, Jr (eds) *Crisis in Central America: Regional Dynamics and U.S. Policy in the 1980s*, Boulder, CO: Westview, 207–25.

Coogan, T. P. (1993) *The IRA: A History*, Niwot, CO: Roberts Rineheart.

Cooley, J. K. (2000) "Terrorism: Continuity and Change in the New Century," *Global Dialogue*, 2, 4: 7–18.

—— (1997) "The Beginning of International Terrorism," in M. Crenshaw and J. Pimlott (eds) *Encyclopedia of World Terrorism*, Vol. 2, Armonk, NY: M. E. Sharpe, 298–300.

Cooper, B. (2001/2) "'We Have No Martin Luther King': Eastern Europe's Roma Minority," *World Policy Journal*, 18, 4: 69–78.

Corrado, R. R. (1997) "Basque Nationalist Terror: ETA," in M. Crenshaw and J. Pimlott (eds) *Encyclopedia of World Terrorism*, Vol. 3, Armonk, NY: M. E. Sharpe, 572–6.

Corsun, A. (1992) "Group Profile: The Revolutionary Organization 17 November in Greece (1975–1991)," in Y. Alexander and D. A. Pluchinsky (eds) *European Terrorism: Today and Tomorrow*, Washington: Brassey's, 93–125.

Crelinsten, R. D. (2000) "Terrorism and Counter-Terrorism in a Multi-Centric World: Challenges and Opportunities," in M. Taylor and J. Horgan (eds) *The Future of Terrorism*, London: Frank Cass, 170–96.

Crenshaw, M. (2003a) "The Causes of Terrorism," in C. W. Kegley, Jr (ed.) *The New Global Terrorism: Characteristics, Causes, Controls*, Upper Saddle River, NJ: Prentice Hall, 92–105.

—— (2003b) "Why is America the Primary Target? Terrorism as Globalized Civil War," in C. W. Kegley, Jr (ed.) *The New Global Terrorism: Characteristics, Causes, Controls*, Upper Saddle River, NJ: Prentice Hall, 160–72.

—— (2000) "Democracy, Commitment Problems and Managing Ethnic Violence: The Case of India and Sri Lanka," *Terrorism and Political Violence*, 12, 3/4: 135–59.

—— (1998) "Questions to be Answered, Research to be Done, Knowledge to be Applied," in W. Reich (ed.) *Origins of Terrorism: Psychologies, Ideologies, Theologies, States of Mind*, Washington, DC: Woodrow Wilson Center Press, 247–60.

—— (1995a) "The Effectiveness of Terrorism in the Algerian War," in M. Crenshaw (ed.) *Terrorism in Context*, University Park, PA: Pennsylvania State University Press, 473–513.

—— (1995b) "Thoughts on Relating Terrorism to Historical Contexts," in M. Crenshaw (ed.) *Terrorism in Context*, University Park, PA: Pennsylvania State University Press, 3–24.

—— (1994) "Political Violence in Algeria," *Terrorism and Political Violence*, 6, 3: 261–80.

—— (1983) "Introduction: Reflections on the Effects of Terrorism," in M. Crenshaw (ed.) *Terrorism, Legitimacy, and Power: The Consequences of Political Violence*, Middletown, CT: Wesleyan University Press, 1–37.

Crenshaw, M., and Pimlott, J. (eds), (1997) *Encyclopedia of World Terrorism*, Vols 1–3, Armonk, NY: M. E. Sharpe.

Cribb, R. (2000) "From Petrus to Ninja: Death Squads in Indonesia," in B. D. Campbell and A. D. Brenner (eds) *Death Squads in Global Perspective: Murder with Deniability*, New York: St Martin's, 181–202.

Criss, N. B. (1995) "The Nature of PKK Terrorism in Turkey," *Studies in Conflict and Terrorism*, 18, 1: 17–37.

Cronin, A. K. (2006). "How al-Qaida Ends: The Decline and Demise of Terrorist Groups," *International Security*, 31, 1: 7–48.

—— (2004) "Terrorist Motivations for Chemical and Biological Weapons Use: Placing the Threat in Context," *Defense & Security Analysis*, 20, 4: 313–20.

—— (2002/3) "Behind the Curve: Globalization and International Terrorism," *International Security*, 27, 3: 30–58.

Crossette, B. (2002) "Sri Lanka: In the Shadow of the Indian Elephant," *World Policy Journal*, 19, 1: 25–36.

Dale, S. F. (1988) "Religious Suicide in Islamic Asia: Anticolonial Terrorism in India, Indonesia, and the Philippines," *Journal of Conflict Resolution*, 32, 1: 37–59.

Dartnell, M. (2000) "A Legal Inter-Network for Terrorism: Issues of Globalization, Fragmentation and Legitimacy," in M. Taylor and J. Horgan (eds) *The Future of Terrorism*, London: Frank Cass, 197–208.

Davis, P. B. (1996) "American Experiences and the Contemporary Perception of Terrorism," *Small Wars and Insurgencies*, 7, 2: 220–42.

Davis, P. K., and Jenkins, B. M. (2002) *Deterrence & Influence in Counterterrorism: A Component in the War on al Qaeda*, Santa Monica, CA: RAND.

de Castro, R. C. (2004) "Addressing International Terrorism in Southeast Asia: A Matter of Strategic or Functional Approach," *Contemporary Southeast Asia*, 26, 2: 193–217.

de la Roche, R. S. (1996) "Collective Violence as Social Control," *Sociological Forum*, 11, 1: 97–128.

della Porta, D. (1995) "Left-Wing Terrorism in Italy," in M. Crenshaw (ed.) *Terrorism in Context*, University Park, PA: Pennsylvania State University Press, 105–59.

Desai, R., and Eckstein, H. (1990) "Insurgency: The Transformation of Peasant Rebellion," *World Politics*, 42, 4: 441–65.

Deutch, J. (1997) "Terrorism," *Foreign Policy*, 109: 10–22.

Dingley, J. (2000) "The Bombing of Omagh, 15 August 1998: The Bombers, Their Tactics, Strategy, and Purpose behind the Incident," *Studies in Conflict and Terrorism*, 24, 6: 451–5.

Dingley, J., and Kirk-Smith, M. (2002) "Symbolism and Sacrifice in Terrorism," *Small Wars and Insurgencies*, 13, 1: 102–28.

Dishman, C. (2005) "The Leaderless Nexus: When Crime and Terror Converge," *Studies in Conflict and Terrorism*, 28, 3: 237–52.

—— (2001) "Understanding Perspectives on WMD and Why They Are Important," *Studies in Conflict and Terrorism*, 24, 4: 303–14.

Division of Archives and History (State of New York) (1926) *The American Revolution in New York: Its Political, Social and Economic Significance*, Albany, NY: The University of the State of New York.

Dodge, T. (1997) "Single-Issue Group Terrorism," in M. Crenshaw and J. Pimlott (eds) *Encyclopedia of World Terrorism*, Vol. 1, Armonk, NY: M. E. Sharpe, 200–1.

Dollard, J. (1978) "Caste and Class in a Southern Town," in R. Lane and J. J. Turner, Jr (eds) *Riot, Rout, and Tumult: Readings in American Social and Political Violence*, Contributions in American History No. 69, Westport, CT: Greenwood Press, 299–306.

Dolnik, A. (2003) "Die and Let Die: Exploring Links between Suicide Terrorism and Terrorist Use of Chemical, Biological, Radiological, and Nuclear Weapons," *Studies in Conflict & Terrorism*, 26, 1: 17–35.

Dolnik, A., and Bhattacharjee, A. (2002) "Hamas: Suicide Bombings, Rockets, or WMD?" *Terrorism and Political Violence*, 14, 3: 109–28.

Dolnik, A., and Gunaratna, R. (2006) "On the Nature of Religious Terrorism," in A. T. H. Tan (ed.) *The Politics of Terrorism: A Survey*, London: Routledge, 80–8.

Doran, M. S. (2002) "Somebody Else's Civil War," *Foreign Affairs*, 81, 1: 22–42.

Drake, C. J. M. (1998) "The Role of Ideology in Terrorists' Target Selection," *Terrorism and Political Violence*, 10, 2: 53–85.

Drake, R. (1997) "Red Brigades," in M. Crenshaw and J. Pimlott (eds) *Encyclopedia of World Terrorism*, Vol. 3, Armonk, NY: M. E. Sharpe, 561–5.

—— (1989) *The Revolutionary Mystique and Terrorism in Contemporary Italy*, Bloomington, IN: Indiana University Press.

Duyker, E. (1987) *Tribal Guerrillas: The Santals of West Bengal and the Naxalite Movement*, Dehli: Oxford University Press.

Eagan, S. P. (1996) "From Spikes to Bombs: The Rise of Eco-Terrorism," *Studies in Conflict and Terrorism*, 19, 1: 1–18.

Eck, W. (1999) "The Bar Kokhba Revolt: The Roman Point of View," *Journal of Roman Studies*, 89, 76–89.

Ellingsen, T. (2005) "Toward a Revival of Religion and Religious Clashes?" *Terrorism and Political Violence*, 17, 2: 305–32.

Enders, W. and Sandler, T. (2006) *The Political Economy of Terrorism*, Cambridge: Cambridge University Press.

—— (2004) "What Do We Know about the Substitution Effect in Transnational Terrorism," in A. Silke (ed.) *Research on Terrorism: Trends, Achievements and Failures*, London: Frank Cass, 119–37.

—— (2000) "Is Transnational Terrorism Becoming More Threatening?" *Journal of Conflict Resolution*, 44, 3: 307–32.

—— (1999) "Transnational Terrorism in the Post-Cold War Era," *International Studies Quarterly*, 43, 1: 145–67.

—— (1996) "Terrorism and Foreign Direct Investment in Spain and Greece," *Kyklos*, 49, 3: 331–52.

—— (1991) "Causality between Transnational Terrorism and Tourism: The Case of Spain," *Terrorism*, 14, 1: 49–58.

Enders, W., Sachsida, A., and Sandler, T. (2006) "The Impact of Transnational Terrorism on U.S. Foreign Direct Investment," *Political Research Quarterly*, 59, 4: 517–31.

Enders, W., Sandler, T., and Parise, G. F. (1992) "An Econometric Analysis of the Impact of Terrorism on Tourism," *Kyklos*, 45, 4: 531–54.

Engene, J. O. (2004) *Terrorism in Western Europe: Explaining the Trends since 1950*, Cheltenham: Edward Elgar.

Ergil, D. (2000) "Suicide Terrorism in Turkey," *Civil Wars*, 3, 1: 37–54.

Fagen, P. W. (1992) "Repression and State Security," in J. E. Corradi, P. W. Fagen, and M. A. Garreton (eds) *Fear at the Edge: State Terror and Resistance in Latin America*, Berkeley, CA: University of California Press, 39–71.

Fair, C. C. (2005), "Diaspora Involvement in Insurgencies: Insights from the Khalistan and Tamil Eelam Movements," *Nationalism and Ethnic Politics*, 11, 1: 125–56.

Fein, H. (1979) *Accounting for Genocide: National Responses and Jewish Victimization during the Holocaust*, Chicago: University of Chicago Press.

Feldman, R. (2006) "Fund Transfers—African Terrorists Blend Old and New: Hawala and Satellite Telecommunications," *Small Wars and Insurgencies*, 17, 3: 356–66.

Fitzpatrick, S. (1999) *Everyday Stalinism: Ordinary Life in Extraordinary Times: Soviet Russia in the 1930s*, New York: Oxford University Press.

Ford, F. L. (1985) *Political Murder: From Tyrannicide to Terrorism*, Cambridge, MA: Harvard University Press.

Fox, J. (2004) "Religion and State Failure: An Examination of the Extent and Magnitude of Religious Conflict from 1950 to 1996," *International Political Science Review*, 25, 1: 55–76.

—— (1999) "Do Religious Institutions Support Violence or the Status Quo?" *Studies in Conflict and Terrorism*, 22, 2, 119–39.

—— (1998) "The Effects of Religion on Domestic Conflicts," *Terrorism and Political Violence*, 10, 4: 43–63.

Foxell, J. W., Jr. (2001) "Current Trends in Agroterrorism (Antilivestock, Anticrop, and Antisoil Bioagricultural Terrorism) and Their Potential Impact on Food Security," *Studies in Conflict and Terrorism*, 24, 2: 107–29.

Freilich, J. D., Pienik, J. A., and Howard, G. J. (2001) "Toward Comparative Studies of the U.S. Militia Movement," *International Journal of Comparative Sociology*, 42, 1: 163–210.

Friedman, J. (2001) "Impaired Empire," *Anthropological Quarterly*, 75, 1: 95–104.

Frisch, H. (2005) "Has the Israeli-Palestinian Conflict Become Islamic? Fatah, Islam and the Al-Aqsa Martyr's Brigade," *Terrorism and Political Violence*, 17, 3: 391–406.

Fuks, A. (1961) "Aspects of the Jewish Revolt in A.D. 115–117," *Journal of Roman Studies*, 51, 1/2: 98–104.

Fuller, G. E. (2002) "The Future of Political Islam," *Foreign Affairs*, 81, 2: 48–60.

—— (1996) *Algeria: The Next Fundamentalist State?*, Santa Monica, CA: RAND.

Furet, F. (1989) "Terror," in F. Furet and M. Ozouf (eds) *A Critical Dictionary of the French Revolution*, trans. A. Goldhammer, Cambridge, MA: Belknap Press, 137–50.

Gal-Or, N. (1994) "Countering Terrorism in Israel," in D. A. Charters (ed.) *The Deadly Sin of Terrorism: Its Effect on Democracy and Civil Liberty in Six Countries*, Westport, CT: Greenwood Press, 137–72.

Gavin, P. (2001) "Ethnic Cleansing in Bosnia-Herzegovina," in William Dudley (ed.) *Genocide*, San Diego: Greenhaven Press, 39–42.

Geiger, H. J. (2001) "Terrorism, Biological Weapons, and Bonanzas: Assessing the Real Threat to Public Health," *American Journal of Public Health*, 91, 5: 708–9.

George, A. (1991) "Introduction," in A. George (ed.) *Western State Terrorism*, Cambridge: Polity Press, 1–11.

George, J., and Wilcox, L. (1996) *American Extremists: Militias, Supremacists, Klansmen, Communists, and Others*, Amherst, NY: Prometheus Books.

Gillespie, R. (1995) "Political Violence in Argentina: Guerillas, Terrorists, and Carapintadas," in M. Crenshaw (ed.) *Terrorism in Context*, University Park, PA: Pennsylvania State University Press, 211–48.

—— (1982) *Soldiers of Peron: Argentina's Montoneros*, Oxford: Clarendon Press.

Glickman, H. (2000) "Islamism in Sudan's Civil War," *Orbis*, 44, 2: 267–81.

Gorenberg, G. (2000) *The End of Days: Fundamentalism and the Struggle for the Temple Mount*, Oxford: Oxford University Press.

Gossman, P. (2000) "India's Secret Armies," in B. D. Campbell and A. D. Brenner (eds) *Death Squads in Global Perspective: Murder with Deniability*, New York: St. Martin's, 261–86.

Gottschalk, K. (2000) "The Rise and Fall of Apartheid's Death Squads," in B. D. Campbell and A. D. Brenner (eds) *Death Squads in Global Perspective: Murder with Deniability*, New York: St Martin's, 229–59.

Gough, A. J. (1997) "Ku Klux Klan Terror," in M. Crenshaw and J. Pimlott (eds) *Encyclopedia of World Terrorism*, Vol. 3, Armonk, NY: M. E. Sharpe, 527–9.

Grant, M. (1974) *The Army of the Caesars*, New York: M. Evans.

Green, J. D. (1995) "Terrorism and Politics in Iran," in M. Crenshaw (ed.) *Terrorism in Context*, University Park, PA: Pennsylvania State University Press, 553–94.

Greenway, H. D. S. (2001) "Hindu Nationalism Clouds the Face of India," *World Policy Journal*, 18, 1: 89–93.

Greer, D. (1935) *The Incidence of Terror during the French Revolution: A Statistical Interpretation*, Cambridge: Harvard University Press.

Griffith, P. (1998) *The Art of War of Revolutionary France, 1789–1802*, London: Greenhill Books.

Grosscup, B. (2000) "Terrorism-at-a-Distance: The Imagery that Serves US Power," *Global Dialogue*, 2, 4: 74–87.

Gunaratna, R. (2003) "Understanding al Qaeda and its Network in Southeast Asia," in K. Ramakrishna and S. S. Tan (eds) *After Bali: The Threat of Terrorism in Southeast Asia*, Singapore: Institute of Defence ands Strategic Studies and World Scientific Publishing, 117–32.

—— (1997) "Tamil Tiger Terror in Sri Lanka," in M. Crenshaw and J. Pimlott (eds) *Encyclopedia of World Terrorism*, Vol. 2, Armonk, NY: M. E. Sharpe, 472–7.

Gurr, N., and Cole, B. (2000) *The New Face of Terrorism: Threats from Weapons of Mass Destruction*, London: I. B. Tauris.

Gurr, T. R. (2006) "Economic Factors," in L. Richardson (ed.), *The Roots of Terrorism*, New York: Routledge, 85–101.

—— (2003) "Terrorism in Democracies: When It Occurs, Why It Fails," in C. W. Kegley, Jr (ed.) *The New Global Terrorism: Characteristics, Causes, Controls*, Upper Saddle River, NJ: Prentice Hall, 202–15.

—— (1989) "Political Terrorism: Historical Antecedents and Contemporary Trends," in T. R. Gurr (ed.), *Violence in America: Volume 2, Protest, Rebellion, Reform*, Newbury Park, CA: Sage Publications, 201–30.

—— (1970) *Why Men Rebel*, Princeton, NJ: Princeton University Press.

Hamilton, N. A. (1996) *Militias in America: A Reference Handbook*, Santa Barbara, CA: ABC-CLIO.

Hanauer, L. S. (1995) "The Path to Redemption: Fundamentalist Judaism, Territory, and Jewish Settler Violence in the West Bank," *Studies in Conflict and Terrorism*, 18, 4: 245–70.

Harmon, C. C. (2000) *Terrorism Today*, London: Frank Cass.

Harnischfeger, J. (2004), "Sharia and Control over Territory: Conflicts between 'Settlers' and 'Indigenes' in Nigeria," *African Affairs*, 103, 412: 431–52.

Hatch, J. (1970) *Nigeria: Seeds of Disaster*, Chicago: Henry Regnery.

Haubrich, D. (2003) "September 11th, Anti-Terror Laws and Civil Liberties: Britain, France and Germany Compared," *Government and Opposition*, 38, 1: 3–28.

Havens, M. C., Leiden, C., and Schmitt, K. M. (1975) *Assassination and Terrorism: Their Modern Dimensions*, Manchaca, TX: Sterling Swift.

Hazleton, W. A., and Woy-Hazleton, S. (1988) "Terrorism and the Marxist Left: Peru's Struggle against Sendero Luminoso," *Terrorism*, 11, 6: 471–90.

Hefner, R. W. (2002) "Global Violence and Indonesian Muslim Politics," *American Anthropologist*, 104, 3: 766–75.

Hegghammer, T. (2006) "Global Jihadism after the Iraq War," *Middle East Journal*, 60, 1: 11–32.

Heitmeyer, W. (2005) "Right-Wing Terrorism," in T. Bjorgo (ed.), *Root Causes of Terrorism: Myths, Reality and Ways Forward*, London: Routledge, 141–53.

Henze, P. B. (1996) "Russia and the Caucasus," *Studies in Conflict and Terrorism*, 19, 4: 389–402.

Herreros, F. (2006) "The Full Weight of the State: The Logic of State-Sanctioned Violence," *Journal of Peace Research*, 43, 6: 671–89.

Hewitt, C. (2003) *Understanding Terrorism in America: From the Klan to Al Qaeda*, London: Routledge.

—— (2000) "Patterns of American Terrorism 1995–1998: An Historical Perspective on Terrorism-Related Fatalities," *Terrorism and Political Violence*, 12, 1: 1–14.

Heymann, P. B. (2003) *Terrorism, Freedom, and Security*, Cambridge, MA: MIT Press.

—— (2001/2) "Dealing with Terrorism: An Overview," *International Security*, 26, 3: 24–38.

Hillyard, P. (1993) *Suspect Community: People's Experience of the Prevention of Terrorism Acts in Britain*, London: Pluto Press.

Hoffman, B. (2006) *Inside Terrorism*, revised and expanded edition, New York: Columbia University Press.

—— (2002a) "The Emergence of the New Terrorism," in A. Tan and K. Ramakrishna (eds) *The New Terrorism: Anatomy, Trends and Counter-Strategies*, Singapore: Eastern Universities Press, 30–49.

—— (2002b) "Rethinking Terrorism and Counterterrorism since 9/11," *Studies in Conflict and Terrorism*, 25, 5: 303–16.

—— (2001) "Change and Continuity in Terrorism," *Studies in Conflict and Terrorism*, 24, 5: 417–28

—— (1998) *Inside Terrorism*, New York: Columbia University Press.

—— (1997) "The Confluence of International and Domestic Trends in Terrorism," *Terrorism and Political Violence*, 19, 2: 1–15.

—— (1995) "'Holy Terror': The Implications of Terrorism Motivated by a Religious Imperative," *Studies in Conflict and Terrorism*, 18, 4: 271–84.

Hoffman, B., and McCormick, G. H. (2004) "Terrorism, Signaling, and Suicide Attack," *Studies in Conflict & Terrorism*, 27, 4: 243–81.

Hoffmann, S. (2002) "Clash of Globalizations," *Foreign Affairs*, 84, 1: 104–15.

Hoglund, K. (2005) "Violence and the Peace Process in Sri Lanka," *Civil Wars*, 7, 2: 156–70.

Holland, J. (1999) *Hope Against History: The Course of Conflict in Northern Ireland*, New York: Henry Holt.

Hollon, W. E. (1974) *Frontier Violence: Another Look*, New York: Oxford University Press.

Holmes, J. (2001) "Political Violence and Regime Change in Argentina: 1965–1976," *Terrorism and Political Violence*, 13, 1: 134–54.

Hope, C. (2003) *Brothers under the Skin: Travels in Tyranny*, Basingstoke: Macmillan.

Hoptner, J. B. (1962) *Yugoslavia in Crisis: 1934–1941*, New York: Columbia University Press.

Horgan, J. (2003) "The Search for the Terrorist Personality," in A. Silke (ed.) *Terrorists, Victims and Society: Psychological Perspectives on Terrorism and Its Consequences*, Chichester: Wiley, 3–27.

Horowitz, D. L. (1980) *Coup Theories and Officers' Motives: Sri Lanka in Comparative Perspective*, Princeton, NJ: Princeton University Press.

Howard-Hassmann, R. E. (2005) "Genocide and State-Induced Famine: Global Ethics and Western Responsibility for Mass Atrocities in Africa," *Perspectives on Global Development and Technology*, 4, 3/4: 487–516.

Howell, L. D. (2003) "Is the New Global Terrorism a Clash of Civilizations? Evaluating Terrorism's Multiple Sources," in C. W. Kegley, Jr. (ed.) *The New Global Terrorism: Characteristics, Causes, Controls*, Upper Saddle River, NJ: Prentice Hall, 173–84.

Huntington, S. P. (1996) *The Clash of Civilizations and the Remaking of World Order*, New York: Simon & Schuster.

Husbands, C. T. (1995) "Militant Neo-Nazism in Germany," in L. Cheles, R. Ferguson, and M. Vaughan (eds) *The Far Right in Western and Eastern Europe*, 2nd edition, London: Longman, 327–53.

Ikelegbe, A. (2005) "Encounters of Insurgent Youth Associations with the State in the Oil Rich Niger Delta Region of Nigeria," *Journal of Third World Studies*, 22, 1: 151–81.

Ilardi, G. J. (2004) "Redefining the Issues: The Future of Terrorism Research and the Search for Empathy," in A. Silke (ed.) *Research on Terrorism: Trends, Achievement and Failures*, London: Frank Cass, 214–28.

Imai, R. (2002) "Weapons of Mass Destruction: Major Wars, Regional Conflicts, and Terrorism," *Asia-Pacific Review*, 9, 1: 88–99.

Iordachi, C. (2004) "Charisma, Religion, and Ideology: Romania's Interwar Legion of the Archangel Michael," in M. R. Lampe and M. Mazower (eds), *Ideologies and National Identities: The Case of Twentieth Century Southeastern Europe*, Budapest: Central European University Press, 19–53.

Ivanova, K., and Sandler, T. (2006) "CBRN Incidents: Political Regimes, Perpetrators, and Targets," *Terrorism and Political Violence*, 18, 3: 423–48.

Jackson, W. D. (1999) "Fascism, Vigilantism, and the State: The Russian National Unity Movement," *Problems of Post-Communism*, 46, 1: 34–42.

Jamieson, A. (2005) "The Use of Terrorism by Organized Crime: An Italian Case Study," in T. Bjorgo (ed.) *Root Causes of Terrorism: Myths, Reality and Ways Forward*, London: Routledge, 164–77.

Jardine, M. (1998) "Power and Principle in East Timor," *Peace Review*, 10, 2: 195–202.

Jenkins, B. M. (2003) "International Terrorism: The Other World War," in C. W. Kegley, Jr (ed.) *The New Global Terrorism: Characteristics, Causes, Controls*, Upper Saddle River, NJ: Prentice Hall, 15–26.

—— (2001) "Terrorism and Beyond: A 21st Century Perspective," *Studies in Conflict and Terrorism*, 24, 5: 321–7.

—— (1998) "Will Terrorists Go Nuclear?: A Reappraisal," in H. W. Kushner (ed.) *The Future of Terrorism: Violence in the New Millennium*, Thousand Oaks, CA: Sage, 225–49.

—— (1990) "International Terrorism: The Other World War," in C. W. Kegley, Jr (ed.) *International Terrorism: Characteristics, Causes, Controls*, New York: St Martin's, 27–38.

—— (1981) *Embassies under Siege: A Review of 48 Embassy Takeovers, 1971–1980*, Santa Monica, CA: RAND.

Jenkins, P. (2003) *Images of Terror: What We Can and Can't Know about Terrorism*, New York: Aldine de Gruyter.

—— (1990) "Strategy of Tension: The Belgian Terrorist Crisis 1982–1986," *Terrorism*, 13, 4/5: 299–309.

Jentleson, B. W., and Whytock, C. A. (2005/6) "Who Won Libya? The Force-Diplomacy Debate and Its Implications for Theory and Policy," *International Security*, 30, 3: 47–86.

Jervis, R. (2002) "An Interim Assessment of September 11th: What Has Changed and What Has Not?" *Political Science Quarterly*, 117, 1: 37–47.

Jha, P. S. (1994) "The Fascist Impulse in Developing Countries: Two Case Studies," *Studies in Conflict and Terrorism*, 17, 3: 229–74.

Jimenez, F. (1992) "Spain: The Terrorist Challenge and the Government's Response," *Terrorism and Political Violence*, 4, 4: 110–30.

Johnson, C. (2003) "American Militarism and Blowback," in C. Boggs (ed.) *Masters of War: Militarism and Blowback in the Era of American Empire*, London: Routledge, 111–29.

Johnson, L. K. (2003) "Strategic Intelligence: The Weakest Link in the War against World Terrorism," in C. W. Kegley, Jr (ed.) *The New Global Terrorism: Characteristics, Causes, Controls*, Upper Saddle River, NJ: Prentice Hall, 239–52.

Jones, B., Kavanagh, D., Moran, M., and Norton, P. (2007), *Politics UK*, 6th edition, Harlow: Pearson.

Jongman, A. J. (1992) "Trends in International and Domestic Terrorism in Western Europe, 1968–1988," *Terrorism and Political Violence*, 4, 4: 26–76.

Joosse, P. (2007) "Leaderless Resistance and Ideological Inclusion: The Case of the Earth Liberation Front," *Terrorism and Political Violence*, 19, 3: 351–68.

Josephus (1981) *The Jewish War*, trans. G. A. Williamson, New York: Dorset Press.

Joshi, M. (1996) "On the Razor's Edge: The Liberation Tigers of Tamil Eelam," *Studies in Conflict and Terrorism*, 19, 1: 19–42.

Joyner, C. C. (2004) "The United Nations and Terrorism: Rethinking Legal Tensions between National Security, Human Rights and Civil Liberties," *International Studies Perspectives*, 5, 2: 240–57.

Judah, T. (2000) *Kosovo: War and Revenge*, New Haven: Yale University Press.

Juergensmeyer, M. (2000) *Terror in the Mind of God: The Global Rise of Religious Violence*, Berkeley, CA: University of California Press.

—— (1997) "Terror Mandated by God," *Terrorism and Political Violence*, 9, 2: 16–23.

—— (1996) "The Worldwide Rise of Religious Nationalism," *Journal of International Affairs*, 50, 1: 1–20.

Justice, J. W. (2005) "Of Guns and Ballots: Attitudes towards Unconventional and Destructive Political Participation among *Sinn Fein* and *Herri Batasuna* Supporters," *Nationalism and Ethnic Politics*, 11, 3: 295–320.

Kaarthikeyan, S. D. R. (2005) "Root Causes of Terrorism? A Case Study of the Tamil Insurgency and the LTTE," in T. Bjorgo (ed.) *Root Causes of Terrorism: Myths, Reality and Ways Forward*, London: Routledge, 131–40.

Kaplan, D. E. (2000) "Aum Shinrikyo (1995)," in J. B. Tucker (ed.) *Toxic Terror: Assessing Terrorist Use of Chemical and Biological Weapons*, Cambridge, MA: MIT Press, 207–26.

Kaplan, J. (1997) *Radical Religion in America: Millenarian Movements from the Far Right to the Children of Noah*, Syracuse, NY: Syracuse University Press.

—— (1995) "Right Wing Violence in North America," in T. Bjorgo (ed.) *Terror from the Extreme Right*, London: Frank Cass, 44–95.

—— (1993) "The Context of American Millenarian Revolutionary Theology: The Case of the 'Identity Christian' Church of Israel," *Terrorism and Political Violence*, 5, 1: 30–82.

Kassimeris, G. (2001) *Europe's Last Red Terrorists: The Revolutionary Organization 17 November*, New York: New York University Press.

—— (1995) "Greece: Twenty Years of Political Terrorism," *Terrorism and Political Violence*, 7, 2: 74–92.

Katzenstein, P. J. (2003) "Same War-Different Views: Germany, Japan, and Counterterrorism," *International Organization*, 57, 4: 731–60.

Kegley, C. W. (ed.) (2003) *The New Global Terrorism: Characteristics, Causes, Controls*, Upper Saddle River, NJ: Prentice Hall.

Kelly, R. J. (1998) "Armed Prophets and Extremists: Islamic Fundamentalism," in H. W. Kushner (ed.) *The Future of Terrorism: Violence in the New Millennium*, Thousand Oaks, CA: Sage Publications, 21–32.

Kennedy, R. (1999) "Is One Person's Terrorist Another's Freedom Fighter: Western and Islamic Approaches to 'Just War' Compared," *Terrorism and Political Violence*, 11, 1: 1–21.

Khan, S. M. (2000) *The Shallow Graves of Rwanda*, London: I. B. Tauris.

Khashan, H. (1997) "The New World Order and the Tempo of Militant Islam," *British Journal of Middle Eastern Studies*, 24, 1: 5–24.

Khatami, S. (1997) "Between Class and Nation: Ideology and Radical Basque Ethnonationalism," *Studies in Conflict and Terrorism*, 20, 4: 395–417.

Kilcullen, D. J. (2005) "Countering Global Terrorism," *Journal of Strategic Studies*, 28, 4: 597–617.

Kimmerling, B. (1997) "The Power-Oriented Settlement: PLO-Israel—The Road to the Oslo Agreement and Back?" in A. Sela and M. Ma'oz (eds) *The PLO and Israel: From Armed Conflict to Political Solution, 1964–1994*, New York: St Martin's, 223–51.

Kirkbride, W. A. (1994) *North Korea's Undeclared War, 1953–*, Seoul: Hollym.

Klare, M. T. (2003) "The New Face of Combat: Terrorism and Irregular Warfare in the 21st Century," in C. W. Kegley, Jr (ed.) *The New Global Terrorism: Characteristics, Causes, Controls*, Upper Saddle River, NJ: Prentice Hall, 27–35.

Knickerbocker, B. (1997) "Mink Wars: Animal Rights Activists Get Violent," *Christian Science Monitor*, 89, 193: 5.

Kornbluh, P. (1987) "The Covert War," in T. W. Walker (ed.) *Reagan versus the Sandinistas: The Undeclared War on Nicaragua*, Boulder, CO: Westview, 21–38.

Kostiner, J. (1989) "War, Terror, Revolution: The Iran–Iraq Conflict," in B. Rubin (ed.) *The Politics of Terrorism: Terror as a State and Revolutionary Strategy*, Washington, DC: Foreign Policy Institute, 95–128.

Kramer, M. (2004/5) "The Perils of Counterinsurgency: Russia's War in Chechnya," *International Security*, 29, 3: 5–63.

Krishna, S. (1992) "India and Sri Lanka: A Fatal Convergence," *Studies in Conflict and Terrorism*, 15, 4: 267–81.

Kumar, R (2002) "Untying the Kashmir Knot," *World Policy Journal*, 19, 1: 11–24.

Kuperman, A. J. (2000) "Rwanda in Retrospect," *Foreign Affairs*, 79, 1: 94–118.

Kurti, L. (1998) "The Emergence of Postcommunist Youth Identities in Eastern Europe: From Communist Youth to Skinheads, to National Socialists and Beyond," in J. Kaplan and T. Bjorgo (eds) *Nation and Race: The Developing Euro-American Racist Subculture*, Boston: Northeastern University Press, 175–201.

Kushner, H. W. (1998a) "The New Terrorism," in H. W. Kushner (ed.) *The Future of Terrorism: Violence in the New Millennium*, Thousand Oaks, CA: Sage, 3–20.

—— (1998b) *Terrorism in America: A Structured Approach to Understanding the Terrorist Threat*, Springfield, IL: Charles C. Thomas.

—— (1996) "Suicide Bombers: Business as Usual," *Studies in Conflict and Terrorism*, 19, 4: 329–27.

Kuznar, L. A., and Lutz, J. M. (2007) "Risk Sensitivity and Terrorism," *Political Studies*, 55, 2: 341–61.

Kydd, A. H., and Walter, B. F. (2006) "The Strategies of Terrorism," *International Security*, 31, 1: 49–80.

—— (2002) "Sabotaging the Peace: The Politics of Extremist Violence," *International Organization*, 56, 2: 263–96.

Landau, S. (1993) *The Guerrilla Wars of Central America: Nicaragua, El Salvador & Guatemala*, New York: St Martin's.

Landman, T. (2006) "Holding the Line: Human Rights Defenders in the Age of Terror," *British Journal of Politics and International Relations*, 8, 2: 123–47.

Langford, P. (2005) "The Rwandan Path to Genocide: The Genesis of the Capacity of the Rwandan Post-Colonial State to Organise and Unleash a Project of Extermination," *Civil Wars*, 7, 1: 1–27.

Laqueur, W. (2003) *No End to War: Terrorism in the Twenty-First Century*, New York: Continuum.

—— (2001) *A History of Terrorism*, New Brunswick, NJ: Transaction Publishers.

—— (1999) *The New Terrorism: Fanaticism and the Arms of Mass Destruction*, New York: Oxford University Press.

—— (1998) "Terror's New Face: The Radicalization and Escalation of Modern Terrorism," *Harvard International Review*, 20, 4: 48–51.

—— (1987) *The Age of Terrorism*, Boston: Little, Brown.

Lassen, S. B. D. (1990) "Drug Trafficking and Terrorism in Colombia," in B. Rubin (ed.) *The Politics of Counterterrorism: The Ordeal of Democratic States*, Washington, DC: Foreign Policy Institute, 107–36.

Leckie, R. (1992) *George Washington's War: The Saga of the American Revolution*, New York: Harper Collins.

Lee, M. A. (1997) *The Beast Reawakens*, Boston: Little, Brown.

Leiber, R. J., and Weisberg, R. E. (2002) "Globalization, Culture, and Identities in Crisis," *International Journal of Politics, Culture and Society*, 16, 2: 273–96.

Leiken, R. S. (2005) "Europe's Angry Muslims," *Foreign Affairs*, 84, 4: 120–35.

Leitenberg, M. (2000) "Aum Shinrikyo's Efforts to Produce Biological Weapons: A Case Study in the Serial Propagation of Misinformation," in M. Taylor and J. Horgan (eds) *The Future of Terrorism*, London: Frank Cass, 149–58.

Lepsius, M. R. (1978) "From Fragmented Party Democracy to Government by Emergency Decree and National Socialist Takeover: Germany," in J. L. Linz and A. Stephan (eds) *The Breakdown of Democratic Regimes: Europe*, Baltimore: Johns Hopkins University Press, 34–79.

Lesch, A. M. (2002) "Osama bin Laden: Embedded in the Middle East Crisis," *Middle East Policy*, 9, 2: 82–91.

Levin, B. (1998) "The Patriot Movement: Past, Present, and Future," in H. W. Kushner (ed.) *The Future of Terrorism: Violence in the New Millennium*, Thousand Oaks, CA: Sage, 97–131.

Liddick, D. R. (2006) *Eco-Terrorism: Radical Environmental and Animal Liberation Movements*, Westport, CT: Praeger.

Lifton, R. J. (2000) *Destroying the World To Save It: Aum Shinrikyo, Apocalyptic Violence, and the New Global Terrorism*, New York: Henry Holt.

Loder, N. (2000) "Britain May Boost Protection of Researchers from Intimidation," *Nature*, 407, 6800: 3.

Long, D. E. (1990) *The Anatomy of Terrorism*, New York: Free Press.

Lucas, C. (1994) "Revolutionary Violence, the People and the Terror," in K. M. Baker (ed.) *The French Revolution and the Creation of Modern Political Culture: Volume 4, The Terror*, Oxford: Pergamon, 57–80.

Luft, G. (2003) "The Logic of Israel's Targeted Killing," *Middle East Quarterly*, 10, 1: 3–8.

Lutz, B. J., and Lutz, J. M. (2007) *Terrorism in America*, New York: Palgrave.

—— (2006) "Political Violence in the Republic of Rome: Nothing New under the Sun," *Government and Opposition*, 41, 4: 491–511.

—— (1995) "Gypsies as Victims of the Holocaust," *Holocaust and Genocide Studies*, 9, 3: 346–59.

Lutz, B. J., Lutz, J. M., and Ulmschneider, G. W. (2002) "British Trials of Irish Nationalist Defendants: The Quality of Justice Strained," *Studies in Conflict and Terrorism*, 25, 4: 227–44.

Lutz, J. M., and Lutz, B. J. (2006a) "State Uses of Terrorism," in A. H. T. Tan (ed.) *The Politics of Terrorism: A Survey*, London: Routledge, 89–102.

—— (2006b) "Terrorism as Economic Warfare," *Global Economy Journal*, 6, 2: 1–20.

—— (2005) *Terrorism: Origins and Evolution*, New York: Palgrave.

Lyman, P. N., and Morrison, J. S. (2004) "The Terrorist Threat in Africa," *Foreign Affairs*, 83, 1: 75–86.

Lyttelton, A. (1982) "Fascism and Violence in Post-War Italy: Political Strategy and Social Conflict," in W. J. Mommsen and G. Hirschfeld (eds) *Social Protest, Violence and Terror in Nineteenth- and Twentieth-Century Europe*, New York: St. Martin's Press for the German Historical Institute, 257–74.

McCaffrey, B. R., and Basso, J. A. (2002) "Narcotics, Terrorism, and International Crime: The Convergence Phenomenon," in R. D. Howard and R. L. Sawyer (eds) *Terrorism and Counterterrorism: Understanding the New Security Environment, Readings and Interpretations*, Guilford, CT: McGraw-Hill/Duskin, 206–21.

Macgregor, D. A. (2001) "The Balkan Limits to Power and Principle," *Orbis*, 45, 1: 93–110.

McGregor, J. (2002) "The Politics of Disruption: War Veterans and the Local State in Zimbabwe," *African Affairs*, 101, 402: 9–37.

McLaren, L. M. (1999) "Explaining Right-Wing Violence in Germany: A Time Series Analysis," *Social Science Quarterly*, 80, 1: 166–80.

Maddy-Weitzman, B. (1997) "The Islamic Challenge in North Africa," in B. Maddy-Weitzman and E. Inbar (eds) *Religious Radicalism in the Greater Middle East*, London: Frank Cass, 171–88.

Makarenko, T. (2005) "Terrorism and Transnational Organized Crime: Tracing the Crime-Terror Nexus in Southeast Asia," in P. J. Smith (ed.) *Terrorism and Violence in Southeast Asia: Transnational Challenges to States and Regional Stability*, Armonk, NY: M. E. Sharpe, 169–87.

Maleckova, J. (2005) "Impoverished Terrorists: Stereotype or Reality?" in T. Bjorgo (ed.) *Root Causes of Terrorism: Myths, Reality and Ways Forward*, London: Routledge, 33–43.

Malka, H. (2003) "Must Innocents Die? The Islamic Debate over Suicide Attacks," *Middle East Quarterly*, 10, 2: 19–28.

Malkin, L., and Elizur, Y. (2002) "Terrorism's Money Trail," *World Policy Journal*, 19, 1: 60–70.

Malley, M. (2003) "Indonesia: The Erosion of State Capacity," in R. I. Rotberg (ed.) *State Failure and State Weakness in a Time of Terror*, Cambridge, MA, and Washington, DC: World Peace Foundation and Brookings Institution Press, 183–218.

Mamdani, M. (2001) *When Victims Become Killers: Colonialism, Nativism, and the Genocide in Rwanda*, Princeton, NJ: Princeton University Press.

Mann, M. (2005) *The Dark Side of Democracy: Explaining Ethnic Cleansing*, Cambridge: Cambridge University Press.

Manwaring, M. G. (2002) "Non-State Actors in Colombia: Threats to the State and to the Hemisphere," *Small Wars and Insurgencies*, 13, 2: 68–80.

Mariani, M. (1998) "The Michigan Militia: Political Engagement or Political Alienation?" *Terrorism and Political Violence*, 10, 4: 122–48.

Mason, T. D., and Campany, C. (1995) "Guerrillas, Drugs and Peasants: The Rational Peasant and the War on Drugs in Peru," *Terrorism and Political Violence*, 7, 4: 140–70.

Merari, A. (2005) "Social, Organizational and Psychological Factors in Suicide Terrorism," in T. Bjorgo (ed.) *Root Causes of Terrorism: Myths, Reality and Ways Forward*, London: Routledge, 70–86

Meredith, M. (2002) *Mugabe: Power and Plunder in Zimbabwe*, Oxford: Public Affairs.

Merkl, P. H. (1995a) "Radical Right Parties in Europe and Anti-Foreign Violence: A Comparative Essay," in T. Bjorgo (ed.) *Terror from the Extreme Right*, London: Frank Cass, 96–118.

—— (1995b) "West German Left-Wing Terrorism," in M. Crenshaw (ed.) *Terrorism in Context*, University Park, PA: Pennsylvania State University Press, 160–210.

—— (1987) *The Making of a Stormtrooper*, Boulder, CO: Westview Press.

—— (1986) "Conclusion: Collective Purposes and Individual Motives," in P. H. Merkl (ed.) *Political Violence and Terror*, Berkeley, CA: University of California Press, 335–74.

Michael, G. (2006) "RAHOWA! A History of the World Church of the Creator," *Terrorism and Political Violence*, 18, 4: 561–83.

—— (2003) *Confronting Right-Wing Extremism and Terrorism in the USA*, New York: Routledge.

Miller, A., and Damask, N. A. (1996) "The Dual Myths of 'Narco-Terrorism': How Myths Drive Policy," *Terrorism and Political Violence*, 8, 1: 114–31.

Moghadam, A. (2003) "Palestinian Suicide Terrorism in the Second Intifada: Motivations and Organizations Aspects," *Studies in Conflict & Terrorism*, 26, 2: 65–92.

Mohan, A. (1992) "The Historical Roots of the Kashmir Conflict," *Studies in Conflict and Terrorism*, 15, 4: 283–308.

Monaghan, R. (2000) "Terrorism in the Name of Animal Rights," in M. Taylor and J. Horgan (eds) *The Future of Terrorism*, London: Frank Cass, 159–69.

—— (1997) "Animal Rights and Violent Protest," *Terrorism and Political Violence*, 9, 4: 106–16.

Moore, C. (2007) "Combating Terrorism in Russia and Uzbekistan," *Cambridge Review of International Affairs*, 20, 2: 303–23.

Morgan, E. S., and Morgan, H. M. (1962) *The Stamp Act Crisis: Prologue to Revolution*, 2nd edition, New York: Collier Books.

Mousseau, D. Y. (2001) "Democratization with Ethnic Divisions: A Source of Conflict?" *Journal of Peace Research*, 38, 5: 547–67.

Mousseau, M. (2002/3) "Market Civilization and Its Clash with Terror," *International Security*, 27, 3: 5–29.

Mueller, J. (2000) "The Banality of 'Ethnic War'," *International Security*, 25, 1: 42–70.

Mulaj, K. (2005) "On Bosnia's Borders and Ethnic Cleansing: Internal and External Factors," *Nationalism and Ethnic Politics*, 11, 1: 1–24.

Murphy, P. L. (1964) "Sources and Nature of Intolerance in the 1920s," *Journal of American History*, 51, 1: 60–76.

Murray, R. K. (1955) *Red Scare: A Study in National Hysteria, 1919–1920*, Minneapolis, MN: University of Minnesota Press.

Mylroie, L. (2000) *Study of Revenge: Saddam Hussein's Unfinished War against America*, Washington, DC: AEI Press.

Nacos, B. L. (2003) "The Terrorist Calculus behind 9–11: A Model for Future Terrorism," *Studies in Conflict and Terrorism*, 26, 1: 1–16.

Nahm, A. C. (1988) *Korea, Tradition and Transformation: A History of the Korean People*, Elizabeth, NJ: Hollym.

Nandi, P. K. (1996) "Socio-Political Context of Sikh Militancy in India," *Journal of Asian and African Studies*, 31, 3/4: 178–90.

Nathan, D. (1996) "Agricultural Labour and the Poor Peasant Movement in Bihar," in T. V. Sathyamurthy (ed.) *Class Formation and Political Transformation in Post-Colonial India*, Social Change and Political Discourse in India, Vol. 4, Delhi: Oxford University Press, 151–78.

Nauriya, A. (1996) "Interception of Democratic Rights in India: Limits and Extent of the Constitutional Discourse," in T. V. Sathyamurthy (ed.) *Class Formation and Political Transformation in Post-Colonial India*, Social Change and Political Discourse in India, Vol. 4, Delhi: Oxford University Press, 258–320.

Nedoroscik, J. A. (2002) "Extremist Groups in Egypt," *Terrorism and Political Violence*, 14, 2: 47–76.

Neumann, F. L. (1968) "Notes on the Theory of Dictatorship," in R. Macridis and B. E. Brown (eds) *Comparative Politics: Notes and Readings*, 3rd edition, Homewood, IL: Dorsey Press, 178–88.

Neumann, P. R., and Smith, M. L. R. (2005) "Strategic Terrorism: The Framework and Its Fallacies," *Journal of Strategic Studies*, 28, 4: 571–95.

Newman, S. (2000) "Nationalism in Postindustrial Societies: Why States Still Matter," *Comparative Politics*, 33, 1: 21–42.

O'Ballance, E. (2000) *Sudan: Civil War and Terrorism, 1956–99*, New York: St Martin's.

—— (1967) *The Algerian Insurrection, 1954–62*, Hamden, CT: Archon Books.

O'Brien, S. P. (1996) "Foreign Policy Crises and the Resort to Terrorism: A Time-Series Analysis of Conflict Linkages," *Journal of Conflict Resolution*, 40, 2: 320–55.

O'Day, A. (1979) "Northern Ireland, Terrorism, and the British State," in Y. Alexander, D. Carlton, and P. Wilkinson (eds) *Terrorism: Theory and Practice*, Boulder, CO: Westview, 121–35.

O'Neil, A. (2003) "Terrorist Use of Weapons of Mass Destruction: How Serious Is the Threat?" *Australian Journal of International Affairs*, 57, 1: 99–112.

Olojede, I., Fajonyomi, B., Akhape, I., and Mudashiru, S. O. (2000) "Nigeria: Oil Pollution, Community Dissatisfaction and Threat to National Peace and Security," Occasional Paper Series, Vol. 4, No. 3, Lagos: Department of Political Science, Lagos State University.

Oommen, T. K. (2005) *Crisis and Contention in Indian Society*, New Dehli: Sage.

Ortiz, R. D. (2002) "Insurgent Strategies in the Post-Cold War: The Case of the Revolutionary Armed Forces of Colombia," *Studies in Conflict and Terrorism*, 25, 2: 127–43.

Osaghae, E. E. (2003) "Explaining the Changing Patterns of Ethnic Politics in Nigeria," *Nationalism and Ethnic Politics*, 9, 3: 54–73.

Otte, T. G. (1997) "Red Army Faction: The Baader-Meinhof Gang," in M. Crenshaw and J. Pimlott (eds) *Encyclopedia of World Terrorism*, Vol. 3, Armonk, NY: M. E. Sharpe, 552–6.

Ousman, A. (2004) "The Potential of Islamist Terrorism in Sub-Saharan Africa," *International Journal of Politics, Culture and Society*, 18, 1: 65–105.

Palmer, D. S. (1995) "The Revolutionary Terrorism of Peru's Shining Path," in M. Crenshaw (ed.) *Terrorism in Context*, University Park, PA: Pennsylvania State University Press, 249–308.

—— (1992) "Peru, the Drug Business and Shining Path: Between Scylla and Charybdis?" *Journal of Interamerican Studies and World Affairs*, 34, 3: 65–88.

Pape, R. A. (2005) *Dying to Win: The Logic of Suicide Terrorism*, New York: Random House.

Parachini, J. V. (2001) "Comparing Motives and Outcomes of Mass Casualty Terrorism Involving Conventional and Unconventional Weapons," *Studies in Conflict and Terrorism*, 24, 5: 389–406.

Parry, A. (1976) *From Robespierre to Arafat*, New York: Vanguard Press.

Pastor, R. (1987) *Condemned to Repetition: The United States and Nicaragua*, Princeton, NJ: Princeton University Press.

Pateman, R. (1998) "East Timor, Twenty Years After: *Resistir e Vencer* (To Resist Is to Win)," *Terrorism and Political Violence*, 10, 1: 119–32.

Pavkovic, A. (2000) *The Fragmentation of Yugoslavia: Nationalism and War in the Balkans*, 2nd edition, New York: Longman.

Pedahzur, A. (2001a) "Struggling with the Challenges of Right-Wing Extremism and Terrorism within Democratic Boundaries: A Comparative Analysis," *Studies in Conflict and Terrorism*, 24, 5: 339–59.

—— (2001b) "The Transformation of Israel's Extreme Right," *Studies in Conflict and Terrorism*, 24, 1: 25–42.

Pedahzur, A., and Perliger, A. (2006) "Introduction: Characteristics of Suicide Attacks," in A. Pedahzur (ed.) *Root Causes of Suicide Terrorism: The Globalization of Martyrdom*, London: Routledge, 1–12.

—— (2003) "The Causes of Vigilante Political Violence: The Case of Jewish Settlers," *Civil Wars*, 6, 3: 9–30.

Peluso, N. L., and Harwell, E. (2001) "Territory, Custom, and the Cultural Politics of Ethnic War in West Kalimantan, Indonesia," in N. L. Peluso and M. Watts (eds) *Violent Environments*, Ithaca, NY: Cornell University Press, 83–116.

Perlstein, G. R. (1997) "Anti-Abortion Activists' Terror Campaign," in M. Crenshaw and J. Pimlott (eds) *Encyclopedia of World Terrorism*, Vol. 3, Armonk, NY: M. E. Sharpe, 542–4.

Perrie, M. (1982) "Political and Economic Terror in the Tactics of the Russian Socialist-Revolutionary Party before 1914," in W. Mommsen and G. Hirschfeld (eds) *Social Protest, Violence and Terror in Nineteenth- and Twentieth-Century Europe*, New York: St Martin's Press for the German Historical Institute, 63–79.

Pettigrew, J. J. M. (1995) *The Sikhs of the Punjab: Unheard Voices of State and Guerrilla Violence*, London: Zed Books.

Pillar, P. R. (2001) *Terrorism and U.S. Foreign Policy*, Washington DC: Brookings Institution.

Pisano, V. S. (1987) *The Dynamics of Subversion and Violence in Contemporary Italy*, Stanford, CA: Hoover Press, Stanford University.

Piszkiewicz, D. (2003) *Terrorism's War with America: A History*, Westport, CT: Praeger.

Pitcavage, M. (2001) "Camouflage and Conspiracy: The Militia Movement from Ruby Ridge to Y2K," *American Behavioral Scientist*, 44, 6: 957–81.

Pizam, A., and Fleischer, A. (2002) "Severity versus Frequency of Acts of Terrorism: Which Has a Larger Impact on Tourism Demand," *Journal of Travel Research*, 40, 2: 337–9.

Pluchinsky, D. A. (2006) "Ethnic Terrorism: Themes and Variations," in A. T. H. Tan (ed.) *The Politics of Terrorism: A Survey*, London: Routledge, 40–54.

—— (1998) "Terrorism in the Former Soviet Union: A Primer, A Puzzle, A Prognosis," *Studies in Conflict and Terrorism*, 21, 2: 119–47.

—— (1993) "Germany's Red Army Faction: An Obituary," *Studies in Conflict and Terrorism*, 16, 1: 135–57.

—— (1992) "An Organizational and Operational Analysis of Germany's Red Army Faction Terrorist Group (1972–91)," in Y. Alexander and D. A. Pluchinsky (eds) *European Terrorism: Today and Tomorrow*, Washington, DC: Brassey's, 3–92.

Poneman, D. (1987) *Argentina: Democracy on Trial*, New York: Paragon House.

Posen, B. R. (2001/2) "The Struggle against Terrorism: Grand Strategy, Strategy, and Tactics," *International Security*, 26, 3: 39–55.

Post, J. M. (2006) "The Psychological Dynamics of Terrorism," in L. Richardson (ed.) *The Roots of Terrorism*, London: Routledge, 17–28.

—— (2000) "Psychological and Motivational Factors in Terrorist Decision-Making: Implications for CBW Terrorism," in J. B. Tucker (ed.) *Toxic Terror: Assessing Terrorist Use of Chemical and Biological Weapons*, Cambridge, MA: MIT Press, 271–89.

Poulton, H. (2000) *Who Are the Macedonians?* 2nd edition, Bloomington: Indiana University Press.

Pridham, G. (1973) *Hitler's Rise to Power: The Movement in Bavaria, 1923–1933*, New York: Harper and Row.

Putra, I. N. D., and Hitchcock, M. (2006) "The Bali Bombs and the Tourism Development Cycle," *Progress in Development Studies*, 6, 2: 156–66.

Quillen, C. (2002) "A Historical Analysis of Mass Casualty Bombers," *Studies in Conflict and Terrorism*, 25, 5: 279–92.

Rabasa, A., Chalk, P., Cragin, K., Daly, S. A., Gregg, H. S. *et al.* (2006) *Beyond al-Qaeda: Part 1, The Global Jihadist Movement*, Santa Monica, CA: RAND.

Radu, M. (2002) "Terrorism after the Cold War," *Orbis*, 46, 2: 275–87.

Rajendram, L. (2002) "Does the Clash of Civilizations Paradigm Provide a Persuasive Explanation of International Politics after September 11th?" *Cambridge Review of International Affairs*, 15, 2: 217–32.

Ramakrishna, K. (2002) "Countering the New Terrorism of Al Qaeda without Generating Civilizational Conflict: The Need for an Indirect Strategy," in A. Tan and K. Ramakrishna (eds) *The New Terrorism: Anatomy, Trends and Counter-Strategies*, Singapore: Eastern Universities Press, 207–32.

Ramirez, J. (1997a) "Colombian Government's Responses to Terrorism," in M. Crenshaw and J. Pimlott (eds) *Encyclopedia of World Terrorism*, Vol. 3, Armonk, NY: M. E. Sharpe, 636–7.

—— (1997b) "Terrorism in Colombia," in M. Crenshaw and J. Pimlott (eds) *Encyclopedia of World Terrorism*, Vol. 2, Armonk, NY: M. E. Sharpe, 430–3.

Ranstorp, M. (1998) "Interpreting the Broader Context and Meaning of Bin-Laden's *Fatwa*," *Studies in Conflict and Terrorism*, 21, 4: 321–30.

—— (1996) "Terrorism in the Name of Religion," *Journal of International Affairs*, 50, 1: 42–62.

Raper, A. R. (1978) "The Tragedy of Lynching," in R. Lane and J. J. Turner, Jr (eds) *Riot, Rout, and Tumult: Readings in American Social and Political Violence*, Contributions in American History No. 69, Westport, CT: Greenwood Press (excerpt from material originally published in 1935), 292–9.

Raphaeli, N. (2003) "Financing of Terrorism: Sources, Methods, and Channels," *Terrorism and Political Violence*, 15, 4: 59–82.

Rapoport, D. C. (2003) "The Four Waves of Rebel Terror and September 11th," in C. W. Kegley, Jr (ed.) *The New Global Terrorism: Characteristics, Causes, Controls*, Upper Saddle River, NJ: Prentice Hall, 36–52.

—— (1998) "Sacred Terror: A Contemporary Example from Islam," in W. Reich (ed.), *Origins of Terrorism: Psychologies, Ideologies, Theologies, States of Mind*, Washington, DC: Woodrow Wilson Center Press, 103–30.

—— (1990) "Religion and Terror: Thugs, Assassins, and Zealots," in C. W. Kegley, Jr. (ed.) *International Terrorism: Characteristics, Causes, Controls*, New York: St. Martin's, 146–57.

—— (1984) "Fear and Trembling: Terrorism in Three Religious Traditions," *American Political Science Review*, 78, 3: 658–77.

Rashid, A. (2002) *Jihad: The Rise of Militant Islam in Central Asia*, New Haven: Yale University Press.

Rathmell, A. (1997a) "Iranian Sponsorship of Terrorism," in M. Crenshaw and J. Pimlott (eds) *Encyclopedia of World Terrorism*, Vol. 2, Armonk, NY: M. E. Sharpe, 392–5.

—— (1997b) "State Sponsored Terrorism," in M. Crenshaw and J. Pimlott (eds) *Encyclopedia of World Terrorism*, Vol. 3, Armonk, NY: M. E. Sharpe, 652–6.

Raufer, X. (2000) "New World Disorder, New Terrorisms: New Threats for Europe and the Western World," in M. Taylor and J. Horgan (eds) *The Future of Terrorism*, London: Frank Cass, 30–51.

—— (1993) "The Red Brigades: Farewell to Arms," *Studies in Conflict and Terrorism*, 16, 4: 315–25.

Raymond, G. A. (2003) "The Evolving Strategies of Political Terrorism," in C. W. Kegley, Jr (ed.) *The New Global Terrorism: Characteristics, Causes, Controls*, Upper Saddle River, NJ: Prentice Hall, 71–83.

Read, A., and Fisher, D. (1989) *Kristallnacht: The Unleashing of the Holocaust*, New York: Peter Bedrick Books.

Reich, W. (1998) "Understanding Terrorist Behaviour: The Limits and Opportunities of Psychological Inquiry," in W. Reich (ed.) *Origins of Terrorism: Psychologies, Ideologies, Theologies, States of Mind*, Washington, DC: Woodrow Wilson Center Press, 261–79.

Reinares, F. (2005) "Nationalist Separatism and Terrorism in Comparative Perspective," in T. Bjorgo (ed.) *Root Causes of Terrorism: Myths, Reality and Ways Forward*, London: Routledge, 119–30.

—— (1998) "Democratic Regimes, Internal Security Policy and the Threat of Terrorism," *Australian Journal of Politics and History*, 44, 3: 351–71.

Richardson, L. (2005) "State Sponsorship: A Root Cause of Terrorism?" in T. Bjorgo (ed.) *Root Causes of Terrorism: Myths, Reality and Ways Forward*, London: Routledge, 189–97.

—— (2000) "Terrorists as Transnational Actors," in M. Taylor and J. Horgan (eds) *The Future of Terrorism*, London: Frank Cass, 209–19.

Richelson, J. T. (2002) "When Kindness Fails: Assassination as a National Security Option," *International Journal of Intelligence and Counterintelligence*, 15, 2: 243–74.

Rimanelli, M. (1992) "Foreign Comrades in Arms: Italian Terrorism and International Ties (1968–91)," in Y. Alexander and D. A. Pluchinsky (eds) *European Terrorism: Today and Tomorrow*, Washington, DC: Brassey's, 127–80.

—— (1989) "Italian Terrorism and Society, 1940s-1980s: Roots, Ideologies, Evolution, and International Connections," *Terrorism*, 12, 4: 249–96.

Robbins, J. S. (2002) "Bin Laden's War," in R. D. Howard and R. L. Sawyer (eds) *Terrorism and Counterterrorism: Understanding the New Security Environment, Readings and Interpretations*, Guilford, CT: McGraw-Hill/Duskin, 354–66.

Roberts, B. (1997) "Nationalist Terror in Northern Ireland, 1976–1996," in M. Crenshaw and J. Pimlott (eds) *Encyclopedia of World Terrorism*, Vol. 3, Armonk, NY: M. E. Sharpe, 581–5.

Roberts, H. (1995) "The Islamists, the Democratic Opposition and the Search for a Political Solution in Algeria," *Review of African Political Economy*, 22, 64: 237–44.

Rodell, P. A. (2007) "Separatist Insurgency in the Southern Philippines," in A. T. H. Tan (ed.) *A Handbook of Terrorism and Insurgency in Southeast Asia*, Cheltenham: Edward Elgar, 225–47.

Roessler, P. G. (2005) "Donor-Induced Democratization and Privatization of State Violence in Kenya and Rwanda," *Comparative Politics*, 37, 2: 207–27.

Rohde, D. (2001) "Indonesia Unravelling," *Foreign Affairs*, 80, 4: 110–24.

Rolef, S. H. (1997) "Israel's Policy Toward the PLO: From Rejection to Recognition," in A. Sela and M. Ma'oz (eds) *The PLO and Israel: From Armed Conflict to Political Solution, 1964–1994*, New York: St Martin's, 253–72.

Ron, J. (2000) "Territoriality and Plausible Deniability: Serbian Paramilitaries in the Bosnian War," in B. D. Campbell and A. D. Brenner (eds) *Death Squads in Global Perspective: Murder with Deniability*, New York: St. Martin's, 286–312.

Rosenau, W. (2001) "Aum Shinrikyo's Biological Weapons Program: Why Did It Fail?" *Studies in Conflict and Terrorism*, 24, 4: 289–301.

—— (1994) "Is the Shining Path the 'New Khmer Rouge'?" *Studies in Conflict and Terrorism*, 17, 4: 305–22.

Ross, J. I. (1995) "The Rise and Fall of Quebecois Separatist Terrorism: A Qualitative Application of Factors from Two Models," *Studies in Conflict and Terrorism*, 18, 4: 285–97.

—— (1993) "Structural Causes of Oppositional Political Terrorism: Towards a Causal Model," *Journal of Peace Research*, 30, 3: 317–29.

Rotberg, R. I. (2000) "Africa's Mess, Mugabe's Mayhem," *Foreign Affairs*, 79, 5: 47–61.

Roy, O. (2006) "Terrorism and Deculturation," in L. Richardson (ed.) *The Roots of Terrorism*, New York: Routledge, 159–70.

Rubenstein, R. E. (1987) *Alchemists of Revolution: Terrorism in the Modern World*, New York: Basic Books.

Rude, G. (1959) *The Crowd in the French Revolution*, Oxford: The Clarendon Press.

Rudner, M. (2004) "Hunters and Gatherers: The Intelligence Coalition against Islamic Terrorism," *International Journal of Intelligence and Counterintelligence*, 17, 2: 193–230.

Saavedra, B. (2007) "Confronting Terrorism in Latin America: Building Cooperation in the Andean Region," in A. Aldis and G. P. Herd (eds) *The Ideological War on Terror: Worldwide Strategies for Counter-Terrorism*, London: Routledge, 163–78.

Saikia, J. (2002) "The ISI Reaches East: Anatomy of a Conspiracy," *Studies in Conflict and Terrorism*, 25, 3: 185–97.

Salla, M. E. (1994) "East Timor's Clandestine Resistance to Indonesian Integration," *Social Alternatives*, 13, 1: 44–7.

Samaranayake, G. (1999) "Patterns of Political Violence and Responses of the Government in Sri Lanka, 1971–1996," *Terrorism and Political Violence*, 11, 1: 110–22.

—— (1997) "Political Violence in Sri Lanka: A Diagnostic Approach," *Terrorism and Political Violence*, 9, 2: 99–119.

Sanchez-Cuenca, I. (2006) "The Causes of Revolutionary Terrorism," in L. Richardson (ed.) *The Roots of Terrorism*, London: Routledge, 71–82.

Sandler, S. (1997) "Religious Zionism and the State: Political Accommodation and Religious Radicalism in Israel," in B. Maddy-Weitzman and E. Inbar (eds) *Religious Radicalism in the Greater Middle East*, London: Frank Cass, 133–54.

Santina, P. (1998/9) "Army of Terror," *Harvard International Review*, 21, 1: 40–3.

Sayari, S., and Hoffman, B. (1994) "Urbanisation and Insurgency: The Turkish Case, 1976–1980," *Small Wars and Insurgencies*, 5, 2: 162–79.

Sayigh, Y. (1997) "The Armed Struggle and Palestinian Nationalism," in A. Sela and M. Ma'oz (eds) *The PLO and Israel: From Armed Conflict to Political Solution, 1964–1994*, New York: St Martin's, 23–35.

Scherrer, C. P. (2002) *Genocide and Crisis in Central Africa: Conflict Roots, Mass Violence, and Regional War*, Westport, CT: Praeger.

Scheslinger, A. M. (1955) "Political Mobs and the American Revolution, 1765–1776," *Proceedings of the American Philosophical Society*, 99, 4: 244–50.

Schiller, A., and Garang, B. (2002) "Religion and Inter-Ethnic Violence in Indonesia," *Journal of Contemporary Asia*, 32, 2: 244–54.

Schmid, A. P. (2005) "Prevention of Terrorism: Towards a Multi-Pronged Approach," in T. Bjorgo (ed.) *Root Causes of Terrorism: Myths, Reality and Ways Forward*, London: Routledge, 223–40.

—— (2004) "Frameworks for Conceptualising Terrorism," *Terrorism and Political Violence*, 16, 2: 197–221.

—— (2000) "Terrorism and the Use of Weapons of Mass Destruction: From Where the Risk?" in M. Taylor and J. Horgan (eds) *The Future of Terrorism*, London: Frank Cass, 106–32.

—— (1992a) "The Response Problem as a Definition Problem," *Terrorism and Political Violence*, 4, 4: 7–13.

—— (1992b) "Terrorism and Democracy," *Terrorism and Political Violence*, 4, 4: 14–25.

—— (1983) *Political Terrorism: A Research Guide to Concepts, Theories, Data Bases, and Literature*, New Brunswick, NJ: Transaction Books.

Schneider, J., and Schneider, P. (2002) "The Mafia and al-Qaeda: Violent and Secretive Organizations in Comparative and Historical Perspective," *American Anthropologist*, 104, 3: 776–82.

Schreiber, J. (1978) *The Ultimate Weapon: Terrorists and World Order*, New York: William Morrow.

Schuddekopf, O.-E. (1973) *Revolutions of Our Time: Fascism*, New York: Praeger Publishers.

Schulze, F. (2004) "Breaking the Cycle: Empirical Research and Postgraduates Studies on Terrorism," in A. Silke (ed.) *Research on Terrorism: Trends, Achievement and Failures*, London: Frank Cass, 161–85.

Schulze, K. E. (2003) "The Struggle for an Independent Aceh: The Ideology, Capacity, and Strategy of GAM," *Studies in Conflict and Terrorism*, 26, 4: 241–71.

—— (2001) "The East Timor Referendum Crisis and Its Impact on Indonesian Politics," *Studies in Conflict and Terrorism*, 24, 1: 77–82.

Schweitzer, Y. (2006) "Al-Qaeda and the Epidemic of Suicide Attacks," in A. Pedahzur (ed.) *Root Causes of Suicide Terrorism: The Globalization of Martyrdom*, London: Routledge, 132–51.

Sciolino, E. (1991) *The Outlaw State: Saddam Hussein's Quest for Power and the Gulf Crisis*, New York: John Wiley & Sons.

Sederberg, P. C. (2003) "Global Terrorism: Problems of Challenge and Response," in C. W. Kegley, Jr (ed.) *The New Global Terrorism: Characteristics, Causes, Controls*, Upper Saddle River, NJ: Prentice Hall, 267–84.

Shabad, G., and Ramo, F. J. L. (1995) "Political Violence in a Democratic State: Basque Terrorism in Spain," in M. Crenshaw (ed.) *Terrorism in Context*, University Park, PA: Pennsylvania State University Press, 410–69.

Shalom, S. R. (2001) "Genocide in Rwanda," in W. Dudley (ed.) *Genocide*, San Diego, CA: Greenhaven Press, 43–58.

Shapiro, J., and Suzan, B. (2003) "The French Experience of Counter-Terrorism," *Survival*, 45, 1: 67–98.

Sheffer, G. (2006) "Diasporas and Terrorism," in L. Richardson (ed.) *The Roots of Terrorism*, New York: Routledge, 117–29.

Shirer, W. L. (1959) *The Rise and Fall of the Third Reich*, New York: MJF Books.

Sholeh, B. (2007) "Jihad in Maluku," in A. T. H. Tan (ed.) *A Handbook of Terrorism and Insurgency in Southeast Asia*, Cheltenham: Edward Elgar, 146–66.

Shultz, R. H., Jr. (1994) "Iranian Covert Aggression: Support for Radical Political Islamists Conducting Internal Subversion Against States in the Middle East/Southwest Asia Region," *Terrorism and Political Violence*, 6, 3: 281–302.

Sick, G. G. (1990) "The Political Underpinnings of Terrorism," in C. W. Kegley, Jr (ed.) *International Terrorism: Characteristics, Causes, Controls*, New York: St Martin's, 51–4.

Silke, A. (2005) "Fire of Iolaus: The Role of State Countermeasures in Causing Terrorism and What Needs to be Done," in T. Bjorgo (ed.) *Root Causes of Terrorism: Myths, Reality and Ways Forward*, London: Routledge, 241–55.

—— (2004) "An Introduction to Terrorism Research," in A. Silke (ed.) *Research on Terrorism: Trends, Achievements and Failures*, London: Frank Cass, 1–29.

—— (2003a) "The Psychology of Suicidal Terrorism," in A. Silke (ed.) *Terrorists, Victims and Society: Psychological Perspectives on Terrorism and Its Consequences*, Chichester: Wiley, 93–108.

—— (2003b) "Retaliating against Terrorism," in A. Silke (ed.) *Terrorists, Victims and Society: Psychological Perspectives on Terrorism and Its Consequences*, Chichester: Wiley, 215–31.

—— (1999) "Rebel's Dilemma: The Changing Relationship between the IRA, Sinn Fein and Paramilitary Vigilantism in Northern Ireland," *Terrorism and Political Violence*, 11, 1: 55–93.

Simmons, C. (2001) "Urbicide and the Myth of Sarajevo," *Partisan Review*, 68, 4: 624–30.

Simons, A. (1999) "Making Sense of Ethnic Cleansing," *Studies in Conflict and Terrorism*, 22, 1: 1–20.

Singh, J. (2002) "Kashmir, Pakistan and the War by Terror," *Small Wars and Insurgencies*, 13, 2: 81–94.

Slack, J. A., and Doyon, R. R. (2001) "Population Dynamics and Susceptibility for Ethnic Conflict: The Case of Bosnia and Herzegovina," *Journal of Peace Research*, 38, 2: 139–61.

Smith, B. L. (2000) "Moving to the Right: The Evolution of Modern American Terrorism," *Global Dialogue*, 2, 4: 52–63.

Smith, B. L., and Damphousse, K. R. (1998) "Two Decades of Terror: Characteristics, Trends, and Prospects for the Future of American Terrorism," in H. W. Kushner (ed.) *The Future of Terrorism: Violence in the New Millennium*, Thousand Oaks, CA: Sage, 132–54.

Snyder, J. T. (2001) "The Moral Imperative," *Peace Review*, 13, 3: 441–8.

Soeters, J. L. (2005) *Ethnic Conflict and Terrorism: The Origins and Dynamics of Civil Wars*, London: Routledge.

Sokolski, H. (2000) "Rethinking Bio-Chemical Dangers," *Orbis*, 44, 2: 207–19.

Sprinzak, E. (2000) "Extremism and Violence in Israeli Democracy," *Terrorism and Political Violence*, 12, 3/4: 209–36.

—— (1995) "Right-Wing Terrorism in a Comparative Perspective: The Case of Split Delegitmization," in T. Bjorgo (ed.) *Terror from the Extreme Right*, London: Frank Cass, 17–43.

Sprinzak, E., and Zertal, I. (2000) "Avenging Israel's Blood (1946)," in J. B. Tucker (ed.) *Toxic Terror: Assessing Terrorist Use of Chemical and Biological Weapons*, Cambridge, MA: MIT Press, 17–41.

Sproat, P. A. (1991) "Can the State be Terrorist?" *Terrorism*, 14, 1: 19–29.

Stansfield, G. (2005) "The Transition to Democracy in Iraq: Historical Legacies, Resurgent Identities and Reactionary Tendencies," in A. Danchev and J. MacMillan (eds) *The Iraq War and Democratic Politics*, London: Routledge, 134–59.

Stein, D., and Ayotte, B. (1999) "East Timor: Extreme Deprivation of Health and Human Rights," *The Lancet*, 354, 9195: 2075.

Stern, J. (2002/3) "Dreaded Risks and the Control of Biological Weapons," *International Security*, 27, 3: 89–123.

—— (2000a) "The Covenant, the Sword, and the Arm of the Lord (1985)," in J. B. Tucker (ed.) *Toxic Terror: Assessing Terrorist Use of Chemical and Biological Weapons*, Cambridge, MA: MIT Press, 139–57.

—— (2000b) "Pakistan's Jihad Culture," *Foreign Affairs*, 79, 6: 115–26.

—— (1999) *The Ultimate Terrorists*, Cambridge, MA: Harvard University Press.

—— (1993) "Will Terrorists Turn to Poison," *Orbis*, 37, 3: 393–410.

Stohl, M. (2003) "The Mystery of the New Global Terrorism: Old Myths, New Realities," in C. W. Kegley, Jr (ed.) *The New Global Terrorism: Characteristics, Causes, Controls*, Upper Saddle River, NJ: Prentice Hall, 84–91.

Stone, M. (1997) *The Agony of Algeria*, New York: Columbia University Press.

Strong, D. S. (1941) *Organized Anti-Semitism in America: The Rise of Group Prejudice during the Decade 1930–40*, Washington, DC: American Council on Public Affairs.

Suberu, R. T. (2005) "Reinventing the Architecture of Nigerian Federalism," *Brown Journal of World Affairs*, 12, 1: 139–54.

—— (2001) *Federalism and Ethnic Conflict in Nigeria*, Washington, DC: United States Institute of Peace Press.

Sverdlick, A. R. (2005) "Terrorists and Organized Crime Entrepreneurs in the 'Triple Frontier' among Argentina, Brazil, and Paraguay," *Trends in Organized Crime*, 9, 2: 84–93.

Sydenham, M. J. (1966) *The French Revolution*, New York: Capricorn Books.

—— (1961) *The Girondins*, Westport CT: Greenwood Press.

Szykowiak, K. and Steinhoff, P. G. (1995) "Wrapping Up in Something Long: Intimidation and Violence by Right-Wing Groups in Postwar Japan," in T. Bjorgo (ed.) *Terror from the Extreme Right*, London: Frank Cass, 265–98.

Tackett, T. (2000) "Conspiracy Obsession in Time of Revolution: French Elites and the Origins of the Terror, 1789–1792," *American Historical Review*, 105, 3, 691–713.

Takeyh, R. (2003) "Islamism in Algeria: A Struggle between Hope and Agony," *Middle East Policy*, 10, 2: 62–75.

Tan, A. T. H. (2007) "Old Terrorism in Southeast Asia: A Survey," in A. T. H. Tan (ed.) *A Handbook of Terrorism and Insurgency in Southeast Asia*, Cheltenham: Edward Elgar, 45–60.

—— (ed.) (2006) *The Politics of Terrorism: A Survey*, London: Routledge.

—— (2003) "The Indigenous Roots of Conflict in Southeast Asia: The Case of Mindanao," in K. Ramakrisna and S. S. Tan (eds) *After Bali: The Threat of Terrorism in Southeast Asia*, Singapore: Institute of Defence and Strategic Studies and World Scientific Publishing, 97–115.

—— (2000) "Armed Muslim Separatist Rebellion in Southeast Asia: Persistence, Prospects, and Implications," *Studies in Conflict and Terrorism*, 23, 4: 267–88.

Taylor, B. (2003) "Threat Assessments and Radical Environmentalism," *Terrorism and Political Violence*, 15, 4: 173–82.

—— (1998) "Religion, Violence and Radical Environmentalism: From Earth First! to the Unabomber to the Earth Liberation Front," *Terrorism and Political Violence*, 10, 4: 1–42.

Taylor, I., and Williams, P. (2002) "The Limits of Engagement: British Foreign Policy and the Crisis in Zimbabwe," *International Affairs*, 78, 3: 547–65.

Taylor, M., and Horgan, J. (2000) "Future Developments of Political Terrorism in Europe," in M. Taylor and J. Horgan (eds) *The Future of Terrorism*, London: Frank Cass, 83–93.

Testas, A. (2002) "The Roots of Algeria's Religious and Ethnic Violence," *Studies in Conflict and Terrorism*, 25, 3: 161–83.

Thayer, C. A. (2005) "Al-Qaeda and Political Terrorism in Southeast Asia," in P. J. Smith (ed.) *Terrorism and Violence in Southeast Asia: Transnational Challenges to States and Regional Stability*, Armonk, NY: M. E. Sharpe, 79–97.

Thompson, D. P. (1996) "Pablo Escobar, Drug Baron: His Surrender, Imprisonment, and Escape," *Studies in Conflict and Terrorism*, 19, 1: 55–91.

Tilly, C. (2004) "Terror, Terrorism, Terrorists," *Sociological Theory*, 22, 1: 5–13.

Toy, E. V., Jr. (1989) "Right-Wing Extremism from the Ku Klux Klan to the Order," in T. R. Gurr (ed.) *Violence in America: Volume 2, Protest, Rebellion, Reform*, (Newbury Park, CA: Sage Publications, 131–52.

Trager, R. F., and Zagorcheva, D. P. (2005/6) "Deterring Terrorism: It Can Be Done," *International Security*, 30, 3: 87–123.

Traub, J. (2000) "Inventing East Timor," *Foreign Affairs*, 79, 4: 74–89.

Tucker, J. B. (2006) *Wars of Nerves: Chemical Warfare from World War I to Al-Qaeda*, New York: Pantheon Books.

—— (2000a) "Lessons from the Case Studies," in J. B. Tucker (ed.) *Toxic Terror: Assessing Terrorist Use of Chemical and Biological Weapons*, Cambridge, MA: MIT Press, 249–69.

—— (ed.) (2000b) *Toxic Terror: Assessing Terrorist Use of Chemical and Biological Weapons*. Cambridge, MA: MIT Press.

—— (1996) "Chemical/Biological Terrorism: Coping with a New Threat," *Politics and the Life Sciences*, 15, 2: 167–83.

Tucker, J. B., and Pate, J. (2000) "The Minnesota Patriots Council," in J. B. Tucker (ed.) *Toxic Terror: Assessing Terrorist Use of Chemical and Biological Weapons*, Cambridge, MA: MIT Press, 159–83.

Tucker, R. K. (1991) *The Dragon and the Cross: The Rise and Fall of the Ku Klux Klan in Middle America*, Hamden, CT: Archon Books.

Tweeten, L. (2003) *Terrorism, Radicalism, and Populism in Agriculture*, Ames, IA: Iowa State Press.

Unnithan, N. P. (1995) "Explaining Collective Violence in India: Social Cleavages and their Consequences," *Studies in Conflict and Terrorism*, 18, 2: 93–109.

van Atta, D. (1998) "Carbombs & Cameras," *Harvard International Review*, 20, 4: 66–70.

Veitch, J. (2007) "Human Tragedy in Sulawesi Indonesia: 1998–2002," in A. T. H. Tan (ed.) *A Handbook of Terrorism and Insurgency in Southeast Asia*, Cheltenham: Edward Elgar, 122–45.

Veness, D. (2001) "Terrorism and Counterterrorism: An International Perspective," *Studies in Conflict and Terrorism*, 24, 5: 407–16.

Vickers, M. (1995) *The Albanians: A Modern History*, London: I. B. Tauris.

Vidino, L. (2005) "How Chechnya Became a Breeding Ground for Terror," *Middle East Quarterly*, 12, 3: 57–66.

Vinci, A. (2005) "The Strategic Use of Fear by the Lord's Resistance Army," *Small Wars and Insurgencies*, 16, 3: 360–81.

von Hippel, K. (2002) "The Roots of Terrorism: Probing the Myths," *Political Quarterly*, 73, S1: 25–39.

Waldmann, P. (2005) "Social Revolutionary Terrorism in Latin America and Europe," in T. Bjorgo (ed.) *Root Causes of Terrorism: Myths, Reality and Ways Forward*, London: Routledge, 154–63.

Wallace, P. (1995) "Political Violence and Terrorism in India: The Crisis of Identity," in M. Crenshaw (ed.) *Terrorism in Context*, University Park, PA: Pennsylvania State University Press, 352–409.

Walton, J. (1984) *Reluctant Rebels: Comparative Studies of Revolution and Underdevelopment*, New York: Columbia University Press.

Warner, B. W. (1994) "Great Britain and the Response to International Terrorism," in D. A. Charters (ed.) *The Deadly Sin of Terrorism: Its Effect on Democracy and Civil Liberty in Six Countries*, Westport, CT: Greenwood Press, 12–42.

Watanabe, M. (1998) "Religion and Violence in Japan Today: A Chronological and Doctrinal Analysis of Aum Shinrikyo," *Terrorism and Political Violence*, 10, 4: 80–100.

Watts, M. (2004) "Resource Curse? Governmentality, Oil and Power in the Niger Delta, Nigeria," *Geopolitics*, 9, 1: 50–80.

Weinberg, L. (2006) "Democracy and Terrorism," in L. Richardson (ed.) *The Roots of Terrorism*, New York: Routledge, 45–56.

—— (1996) "On Responding to Right-Wing Terrorism," *Terrorism and Political Violence*, 8, 1: 80–92.

—— (1995) "Italian Neo-Fascist Terrorism: A Comparative Perspective," in T. Bjorgo (ed.) *Terror from the Extreme Right*, London: Frank Cass, 221–38.

Weinberg, L., and Eubank, W. (2000) "Terrorism and the Shape of Things to Come," in M. Taylor and J. Horgan (eds) *The Future of Terrorism*, London: Frank Cass, 94–105.

—— (1998) "Terrorism and Democracy: What Recent Events Disclose," *Terrorism and Political Violence*, 10, 1: 108–18.

Weinberg, L., and Richardson, L. (2004) "Conflict Theory and the Trajectory of Terrorist Campaigns in Western Europe," in A. Silke (ed.) *Research on Terrorism: Trends, Achievements and Failures*, London: Frank Cass, 138–60.

Weiss, M. (2001) "The Body of the Nation: Terrorism and the Embodiment of Nationalism in Contemporary Israel," *Anthropological Quarterly*, 75, 1: 37–62.

Welsh, D. (1995) "Right-Wing Terrorism in South Africa," in T. Bjorgo (ed.) *Terror from the Extreme Right*, London: Frank Cass, 239–64.

White, J. R. (1998) *Terrorism: An Introduction*, 2nd edition, Belmont, CA: Wadsworth.

White, R. W. (1993) "On Measuring Political Violence: Northern Ireland, 1969 to 1980," *American Sociological Review*, 58, 4: 575–85.

Whitsel, B. (2001) "Ideological Mutation and Millennial Belief in the American Neo-Nazi Movement," *Studies in Conflict and Terrorism*, 24, 2: 89–106.

—— (1995) "Aryan Visions for the Future in the West Virginia Mountains," *Terrorism and Political Violence*, 7, 4: 117–39.

Wieviorka, M. (1990) "French Politics and Strategy on Terrorism," in B. Rubin (ed.) *The Politics of Counterterrorism: The Ordeal of Democratic States*, Washington, DC: Foreign Policy Institute, 61–90.

Wilkinson, P. (2006) *Terrorism versus Democracy: The Liberal State Response*, 2nd edition, London: Routledge.

—— (2003) "Why Modern Terrorism? Differentiating Types and Distinguishing Ideological Motivations," in C. W. Kegley, Jr (ed.) *The New Global Terrorism: Characteristics, Causes, Controls*, Upper Saddle River, NJ: Prentice Hall, 106–38.

—— (2000a) "Politics, Diplomacy and Peace Processes: Pathways out of Terrorism," in M. Taylor and J. Horgan (eds) *The Future of Terrorism*, London: Frank Cass, 66–82.

—— (2000b) *Terrorism versus Democracy: The Liberal State Response*, London: Frank Cass.

—— (1995) "Violence and Terror and the Extreme Right," *Terrorism and Political Violence*, 7, 4: 82–93.

—— (1983) "The Orange and the Green: Extremism in Northern Ireland," in M. Crenshaw (ed.) *Terrorism, Legitimacy, and Power: The Consequences of Political Violence*, Middletown, CT: Wesleyan University Press, 105–23.

—— (1975) *Political Terrorism*, New York: Halstead Press.

Willems, H. (1995) "Development, Patterns and Causes of Violence against Foreigners in Germany: Social and Biographical Characteristics of Perpetrators and the Process of Escalation," in Tore Bjorgo (ed.) *Terror from the Extreme Right*, London: Frank Cass, 162–81.

Williams, B. G. (2001) "The Russo-Chechen War: A Threat to Stability in the Middle East and Eurasia," *Middle East Policy*, 8, 1: 128–48.

Williams, G., and Turner, T. (1978) "Nigeria," in J. Dunn (ed.) *West African Sates: Failure and Promise: A Study in Comparative Politics*, African Studies Series 23, Cambridge: Cambridge University Press, 132–72.

Willis, M. (1997) *The Islamist Challenge in Algeria: A Political History*, New York: New York University Press.

Wilson, J. S. (1992) "Turmoil in Assam," *Studies in Conflict and Terrorism*, 15, 4: 251–66.

Wilson, M., and Lynxwiler, J. (1988) "Abortion Clinic Violence at Terrorism," *Terrorism*, 11, 4: 263–73.

Wirsing, R. (2002) "Kashmir in the Terrorist Shadow," *Asian Affairs*, 33, 1: 91–7.

Woodworth, P. (2001) "Why Do They Kill? The Basque Conflict in Spain," *World Policy Journal*, 18, 1: 1–12.

Wrighte, M. R. (2002) "The Real Mexican Terrorists: A Group Profile of the *Popular Revolutionary Army (EPR)*," *Studies in Conflict and Terrorism*, 25, 2: 207–25.

Wynia, G. W. (1986) *Argentina: Illusions and Realities*, New York: Holmes & Meier.

Yaeger, C. H. (1991) "Sikh Terrorism in the Struggle for Khalistan," *Terrorism*, 14, 4: 221–31.

Zegart, A. B. (2005) "September 11th and the Adaptation Failure of U.S. Intelligence Agencies," *International Security*, 29, 4: 78–111.

Zirakzadeh, C. E. (2002) "From Revolutionary Dreams to Organizational Fragmentation: Disputes over Violence within ETA and Sendero Luminoso," *Terrorism and Political Violence*, 14, 4: 66–92.

Zunes, S. (2000) "East Timor's Tragedy and Triumph," *Peace Review*, 12, 2: 329–35.

INDEX

abortion 71, 79, 91–3, 98, 99, 176, 247, 264, 287
Abu Sayyaf Group 97–8, 291
Aceh 114, 116, 246, 253, 291
Aden 2, 94, 287
Afghanistan 2, 64, 65, 66, 73, 87, 94, 95, 97, 99, 192, 193, 264, 268, 269, 270, 271, 281
African National Congress – see ANC
airline hijackings 1, 2, 3, 30
Akali Dal 82, 84, 291
Al Asqa brigades 125, 291
Albania, Albanians 55, 108, 117–21, 127, 222, 230, 246, 270, 288, 289
Alexander the Great 80
Alexander, King 16, 56, 291
ALF 138, 153–6, 291
Algeria 3, 30, 59, 79, 86–9, 96, 98, 99, 100, 103–4, 105, 127, 264, 268, 270, 274, 278; and French 88, 103–4, 268, 275, 286
al Qaeda 2, 30, 34, 64, 66, 79, 89, 93–7, 98, 99–100, 186, 193, 194, 213, 246, 255, 256, 257, 258, 263, 264, 265, 266, 269, 270, 271, 272, 274, 275, 277, 279, 281, 284, 285, 291
al-Turabi, Hasan 234, 291
Ambion 246, 247
American Revolution 102, 108–10, 126, 283
Amritsar 84–5
anarchists 20, 74, 131, 132–4, 136, 157, 159, 163, 169, 248, 283, 291
ANC 220, 269, 291
Angola 9, 269
Animal Liberation Front – see ALF
animal rights 138, 153–6, 158
Animal Rights Militia – see ARM
animists 234

Ansar al-Islam 257, 292
anthrax 3, 32, 292
anti-Catholic 170
anti-Chinese 170
anti-gay 70, 92, 176, 177, 179
Anti-Liberation Terrorist Group (GAL) 112, 292
anti-Semitism 170, 175–6, 177, 179, 181, 183, 219
apartheid 106, 220
April 19 Movement – see M-19
Arafat, Yassir 121, 123, 124, 141
Argentina 133, 138, 146–149, 157, 192, 220, 242, 243, 262, 268, 276
ARM 155–6, 291–2
Armenia 106, 107, 191, 221
Army for the Secret Liberation of Armenia (ASALA) 107, 292
Army of God 92–3, 292
Aryan Nations 174, 175, 292
Ashara, Shoko 89–91, 292
Assam 65, 247, 292
assassination 10, 27, 36–7, 45, 45–6, 49, 50, 72, 123, 124, 134, 136, 137, 139, 140, 141, 144, 145, 146, 148, 149, 172, 173, 192, 255, 272, 276, 281, 283; in Algeria 87–88; and anarchists 132–3, 157, 248; of Archduke Franz Ferdinand 52; of Bakhtiar 57; of Bernadotte, Count Folke 104; by Bulgarian secret service 50; Bush, George attempt 255; in Colombia 205, 206; of Croatian politicians 55; of Gandhi, Indira 84; of Gandhi, Rajiv 253; in Germany 169; in India 84, 85–6, 253; by IRA 201, 202; of Iranian exiles 57; by Israel 50, 66, 272; in Japan 164–5; in Judea (Roman) 80; of King

Alexander 16, 56; and Kosovo 119; by Mafia 190–1; of Rabin 71–2, 245; in Rome (ancient) 131, 161–2; by Shining Path 196; and Social Revolutionaries 133–4; of Somoza 61; and Spain 111; in Sri Lanka 249, 250, 251, 253–4; of Tsar Alexander III 134, 136

Assassins 72, 272, 287, 292

Atlanta Olympics 92, 176, 264

AUC (Self Defense Forces of Colombia) 207, 304

Aum Shinrikyo 79, 89–91, 98, 99, 100, 129, 278, 292

Australia 165

Austria 51, 106, 163, 164

Austria-Hungary 20, 55, 56, 106, 126, 133, 140, 141

authoritarianism 18, 21, 40–1, 44, 45–6, 96, 114, 119, 163, 166, 180, 185, 199, 217, 243, 256, 259, 267, 271, 278–9, 279, 280, 288, 289

Ayodhya 76, 247, 292

Azerbaijan 106

Baader-Meinhof Gang (see also Red Army Faction) 138, 139, 140, 142, 285, 292

Ba'ath Party 218, 254, 255, 256, 257, 293

Bahrain 58

Bakhtiar, Shahpur 57, 293

Bali 1, 38, 94, 246

Banat 55

Bangladesh 63, 65

bank robberies 10, 26, 28, 135, 179, 194, 206

Basques 108, 110–3, 127, 128, 267, 275, 285, 286

Bavaria 163, 166

Beer Hall Putsch 166, 293

Bekaa Valley 59, 293

Belgium 140, 158, 164, 237, 238

Bernadotte, Count Folke 104, 293

Bharatiya Janata Party 75, 293

Bhindranwale, Sant Jarnail Singh 82, 293

bin Laden, Osama 3, 30, 32, 79, 93–7, 99, 246, 265, 270, 272, 277, 280, 284, 287, 293

biological weapons 2, 25, 31, 32–5, 67, 78, 90, 91, 96, 99, 178, 255, 277

black Americans, as targets 169–71, 179, 248

Black Hand 51, 293

Black Hundred 162

Black International 173, 293

Black September 50, 123, 124, 293

Black Widows 194, 293

blowback 66, 293

Bologna train station bombing 173, 187, 293

Bolsheviks 20, 134, 135, 163

Borneo (Kalimitan) 108, 114–6, 127, 246, 247, 275, 285, 287

Bosnia (and Herzegovina) 55, 57, 79, 95, 106, 117, 121, 181, 223, 230–3, 242, 243, 246, 259, 268, 275, 285, 289

Boston Tea Party 108–10, 248, 283

Branch Davidians 177, 178, 293–4

Bray, Michael 92

Brazil 192

Buddhism 177, 248

Breslan 1, 27, 193, 194, 273, 294

Buddhist 248, 249, 254; extremists 74, 249

Bulgaria 16, 50, 54, 55, 56, 57, 165, 223, 246

Bull, Gerald 50

Burundi 237–8, 240; massacres of Hutus 238

Canada 104, 105, 175, 258, 280

capitalism 36, 46, 131, 132, 135, 137, 138, 139, 140, 141–2, 143, 145, 146, 157, 158, 189, 285

Catholics 70, 222, 227, 231

Chad 237

Chechnya, Chechens 3, 40, 95, 96, 108, 193–4, 212, 213, 263, 273, 285, 287, 294

chemical weapons 2, 25, 31, 32–5, 67, 78, 89, 90, 91, 96, 99, 178, 255, 277, 278; hoax 139

Chernobyl 32

Cherokees 222

China 150, 157, 199, 263

Christian Phalangists 173

Christians 70, 75, 79, 81, 91, 95, 129, 190, 208, 209, 219, 234, 246, 248, 275; extremists 77, 218; as targets 76, 77, 88, 97–8, 210, 234, 246, 247, 254

Christian Identity 177, 294

CIA 21, 46, 50, 61, 66, 146, 255, 263, 264, 272, 294

civil liberties 39, 46, 145, 158, 202, 267, 279–80, 281, 286

civil rights 174

Civil Rights Act, 1964 169

clash of civilizations 79, 99–100, 285
Cold War 21, 50, 53, 54, 66, 73, 95, 106, 195, 252, 263, 268, 283
Colombia 137, 195, 197, 205–8, 212, 213, 214, 220, 267, 273, 278, 286
colonialism 15, 17, 18, 103–4, 107, 189, 209, 259
colons 103, 104, 294
communism 20, 51, 169, 172, 184, 185, 196, 218, 247; collapse of 141, 142, 150, 158, 165, 180, 181, 218; in Weimar Germany 166–8
Communist Combat Cells (CCC) 164, 294
concessions 261, 267, 269, 274–5, 279, 281, 285
Concord 108
Continuity IRA 203, 270, 294
Contras 54, 61–3, 66, 265, 269, 289, 294
Copenhagen 184–5
Corsica 38, 104–5, 279
counterterrorism 21; in India 85
Covenant, the Sword, and the Arm of the Lord (CSA) 178
criminal organizations 190, 192, 193–4, 194, 206–8, 211, 212, 252, 265, 266, 286
Croatia, Croats 16, 55, 56, 57, 105, 106, 117, 121, 223, 230, 231, 232, 233, 246, 259, 287, 288
Cromwell, Oliver 222, 294
Cuba 9, 51–2, 61, 63, 105, 158, 206, 213, 219–20, 269
Cyprus 99, 104, 105, 106, 127, 146, 275, 286
Cyrene 81
Czechoslovakia 51, 106, 108, 145, 158, 164
Czech Republic 165

Dalmatia 55, 56, 57
Dar-es-Salaam, Tanzania 2, 43–4, 94, 262
Darfur 234, 236–7, 242, 243
Dayaks 114–6, 127, 128, 246, 283, 287, 294
Death to Kidnappers 207
death squads 13, 15, 216, 219, 221, 223, 241, 242, 268, 285; in Argentina 149, 220, 242; in Batista's Cuba 219; in East Timor 227, 268; in El Salvador 220; in India 85, 220, 247, 270; in Rwanda 238, 241, 268; in South Africa 220; in Spain 112, 280; in Sri Lanka 254
democratic governments 25, 275; as targets 39–47, 74, 267, 285; new 111, 114

Denmark 103, 184, 185
diaspora communities 52, 53, 54, 95, 96, 97, 213, 265; Albanian 120, 127; Algerians 89; Basque 113; Chechen 193, 213; and IRA 52–3, 204, 213; Jewish 127; Palestinian 52, 58, 123; Sikh 85, 99; Tamils 252
Diplock Courts 202, 294
dirty bombs 31–2, 294
"disappeared ones" 149, 295
Dominican Republic 206
drugs 26, 65, 192, 193, 194, 195, 197, 198–9, 206–8, 212, 213, 252, 265, 266
Druze 190
Duvalier, Francois 40, 295

Earth Liberation Front (ELF) 138, 211, 295
East Africa embassy bombings 2, 43–4, 45, 94, 98, 262
East Germany 139, 141, 158, 181
East Timor 116, 223, 226–8, 237, 242, 243, 246, 268
economic sanctions 269
Egypt 38, 41, 50, 51, 59, 71, 81, 96, 104, 112, 123, 273
El Al 122, 123
ELN (National Liberation Army) 205, 207, 301
El Salvador 61, 63, 220, 268
empires 259; dissolution of 20, 55, 106, 107–8, 126–7, 259, 283, 284
Engels, Friedrich 131, 295
Entebbe 140, 141, 274
environmental groups 138, 155, 158, 159, 195, 209, 210–1,
EPL (Popular Liberation Army) 205, 303
ERP – see Peoples Revolutionary Army
Escobar, Pablo 207, 295
ETA 111–3, 127, 194, 245, 259, 267, 270, 275, 280, 285, 288, 295
Ethiopia 106
ethnic cleansing 37, 216, 218, 221, 222, 241, 242, 284, 285, 295; in Borneo 116; in Bosnia 223, 231, 232, 233, 242, 246, 268; and Cherokees 222, 248; in Croatia 223; by East Timor guerrillas 227; in India 63; in Ireland 222; by Kashmir rebels 222; in Kosovo 119,

120, 222; in Nigeria 209, 210, 214; in
Rwanda 3, 223, 242 in Sudan 3, 223, 234,
237, 242; successful 242; in Tajikistan 222;
by Tamil Tigers 251; in Yugoslavia 3
ethnocentrism 169, 182, 183
extradition 14

Euzkadi ta Askasuna – see ETA
Falkland Islands 149
false flag attacks 270, 295; in Belgium 164;
in Egypt 50; in Italy 172, 173
FARC 205–8, 212, 213, 214, 220, 304
fascism 142, 162, 165, 184, 185, 288, 295;
in Croatia 56, 223; in Italy 56, 142, 162–3,
185, 186, 248, 288; in Romania 74, 162; in
Russia 165
Fatah 121, 124–5, 141, 295
February Revolution 134
Fertinelli, Franco 143, 265, 295
FBI 11, 46, 263, 264
Federal Bureau of Investigation – see FBI
FIS – see Islamic Salvation Front
food poisoning 33
foreign investment, as target 38, 88, 112,
211
foreign support 16, 49–67, 89, 99, 124, 127,
134, 139, 141, 145, 158, 186, 204, 206 ,
213, 232, 268–9; decline in support by
foreign governments 54, 100, 195
France 16, 19, 29, 30, 36, 38, 50, 53–4, 56,
75, 104–5, 109, 110, 111, 112, 113, 126,
131, 133, 140, 158, 186–7, 218, 224–6,
243, 269–70, 275, 279, 280, 286, 287,
288; and Algeria 86, 87, 88, 103–4, 268,
275, 286; and Reign of Terror 223, 224–6,
241–2
Franco, Francisco 110, 111, 112, 295
French Revolution 102, 126, 131, 162, 223,
224–6, 241, 243, 286, 288
Fujimoro, Alberto 197, 295
furores 110, 295–6

GAL – Anti-Liberation Terrorist Group
Gandhi, Indira 82, 84, 252, 296
Gandhi, Rajiv 253, 296
Gandhi, Mohandas 75

Garang, John 236
Gaza and West Bank (Occupied Territories) 58,
71, 122, 123, 124, 125–6, 142, 245, 267, 274,
296
genocide 187, 216, 221, 222, 227, 237, 241, 242,
247, 296; Armenian 107, 191, 221; in Croatia
223; by Nazis –see Holocaust; in Rwanda
237–41, 242, 284; in Sudan 242
Georgia 108
Germany, Germans 20, 33, 53, 56, 57, 106, 123,
126, 133, 138, 139–141, 142, 157, 158, 161,
164, 166, 187, 202, 219, 223, 237, 238,
247–8, 259, 262–3, 272, 273, 279, 285, 288;
and Holocaust 166, 221, 223, 242, 247; Nazi
period 19, 51, 70, 161, 164, 171, 185, 217,
218, 219, 248, 289; and neo-Nazis 34, 180–4;
and Red Army Faction 34, 267, 274; Weimar
period 166–8, 218, 247, 259
Gestapo 217, 296
GIA – see Islamic Army Group
Gibralter 202
Girondins 224, 225, 296
global jihad 96–7, 133, 193, 211, 256, 257, 258,
279, 281, 284, 296
Global War on Terrorism 23, 279
globalization 4, 18, 19, 36, 77, 100, 128, 152,
165, 184, 275, 281, 283, 285, 296
Golan Heights 122, 258
Goldstein, Baruch 71, 74
Gracchus, Gaius 162, 296
Gracchus, Tiberius 162, 296
Great Britain – see United Kingdom
Great Depression 19, 167
Greece 36, 104, 146, 157, 173, 258, 264; ancient
52, 74, 80, 99
Greek Orthodox 231
Green Jackets 184–5, 296
guerrillas 4, 11, 16, 20, 57, 62, 64–5, 79, 86,
87, 95, 103, 104, 114, 119, 122, 126, 127,
148, 150, 153, 157, 159, 212, 213, 256,
268–9, 286, 288; in Chechnya 193, 263; in
Colombia 205, 206, 207, 208, 212; in East
Timor 226; in Ireland 199; in Italy 173; in
Kashmir 220; in Malaya 190; in South Africa
220; in Sri Lanka 249, 250, 251, 252, 253; in
Venezuela 206

Guinea 107

Gush Emunim 71, 296

Gypsies 120, 165, 218, 221, 223, 247

Guzman, Abimael 195, 197, 296

Haig, General Alexander 139

Haiti 40

Hamas 58, 59, 74, 122, 124, 125–6, 127, 192, 246, 272, 278, 289, 296

Harkat-ul-Muhahideen 65, 297

Hausa-Fulani 208, 209, 211, 297

hawla 266, 297

Hearst, Patricia 135

hijacking 26–8, 49, 137, 140, 141, 262, 273

Hindus 63, 76, 70, 79, 82, 84, 86, 98, 100, 222, 247, 248; extremists 75–7, 247, 289; as targets 84, 247

Hinduvata 75, 297

Hitler, Adolf 19, 106, 161, 166–9, 171, 183, 1 86, 218, 219, 297

Hizballah 34, 58–9, 60, 75, 99, 190, 262, 270, 272, 297

Holocaust 159, 166, 221, 223, 242, 247; denial 181, 221; survivors 33

Homeland Security 46, 294

Honduras 61

hostages 27, 190, 193–4, 273, 274

Hungary 163, 165, 223; and Yugoslavia 54–7, 66, 246

Hussein, Saddam 58, 218, 254, 255, 271, 272, 276, 297

Hutu 106, 223, 237–41, 242

Ibo – see Igbo

Igbo 208, 209, 210, 211, 297

immigrants, opposition to 170, 175, 180, 182, 183, 184, 185, 186, 285, 288

imperialism 17

Impuza Mugambi 238, 297

India 3, 29, 36, 54, 75–7, 79, 127, 138, 150–3, 157, 158, 159, 222, 247, 252, 259, 265, 269, 270, 280; and caste system 150–1; and Kashmir 220, 247, 268, 287; and Pakistan 63–6; and Sikhs 81–6, 220, 247; and Sri Lanka 252, 253, 254

Indonesia 3, 38, 77, 96, 107, 108, 114–6, 127, 181, 246–7, 259, 275, 286; Chinese minority 247; and Communist coup 219; and East Timor 223, 226–8, 242, 246

Inquisition 222

Interahamwe 238, 297

International Court of Justice 63

international law 14, 63

Inter-Services Intelligence (ISI) 63, 297

intifada 124, 142, 297

intifada, second 246

IRA – see Irish Republican Army

Iran 57–60, 66, 67, 73, 75, 89, 137, 139, 190, 191, 265, 269, 273, 274; and Iraq 57, 58, 59, 60, 66, 75, 255, 258

Iraq 3, 11, 20, 50, 66, 95, 96, 99, 105, 122, 191, 217–8, 245, 254–8, 259, 269, 271, 272, 285, 287; and Iran 57, 58, 59, 60, 66, 75, 255; and United States 2, 59, 97, 99, 255–8, 286

Ireland, Irish 37, 102, 199–200, 203, 204, 212, 222

Irian Jaya 116, 246, 297

Irish National Liberation Army (INLA) 203, 213, 297

Irish Republican Army (IRA) 9, 31, 37, 52–3, 195, 199–204, 208, 213, 266, 268, 273, 275, 276, 279, 288, 289, 297; and diaspora 52–3, 204, 213

Iron Guard 74, 163, 298

Islam (see also Muslims) 129, 177

Islamic Army Group (GIA) 87, 88, 89, 100, 298

Islamic Call Party 58

Islamic Jihad (Palestine) 58, 126, 298

Islamic Movement Army (MIA) 87, 298

Islamic Movement of Uzbekistan 193

Islamic Republic for the Liberation of Bahrain 58

Islamic Salvation Front (FIS) 86–7, 88, 89, 98, 275, 298

Israel 2, 3, 30, 31, 53, 58, 67, 71, 79, 94, 95, 96, 98, 104, 121–6, 137, 140, 142, 190, 245, 246, 262, 264, 265, 267, 269, 270–1, 273, 274, 275, 280, 287, 289; and assassination 50, 66, 272

Italian Communist Party (PCI) 172

Italy 31, 36, 50, 54, 133, 138, 140, 142–5, 157, 158, 187, 190, 194, 223, 267, 268, 283; and fascism 56, 171, 185, 248, 288; and neo-fascism 166, 171–4, 186; and Yugoslavia 54–7, 66, 223, 246

Jacobins 224, 225, 298
Jammu and Kashmir – see Kashmir
Janatha Vimukthi Peramuna — JVP
janjaweed militias 236, 298
Japan 36, 79, 89–91, 98, 136, 137, 142, 164–5, 269, 288; Tokyo subway attack 3, 32, 33, 89
Japanese Red Army – see JRA
Jemaah Islamiah 246
Jews, 221, 223, 262; extremists 3, 71–2, 104, 245, 246, 265; nationalists 71, 286; as targets (see also anti-Semitism and Holocaust) 162, 171, 218, 219
Jewish Defense League (JDL) 72–3
Jewish Revolt 80–1
jihad 73, 298
Jordan 122, 124, 127, 269
JRA 137, 142, 208, 298
Judaism 129, 177
Judea and Samaria (West Bank) 71, 298
June 2 Movement 139, 298
Justice Commandos of the Armenian Genocide (JCAG) 107, 298
JVP 249, 253–4, 259, 267, 298

Kaczynski, Theodore 11–12
Kahane, Meir 71, 72–3, 298
Kalimantan – see Borneo
Kashmir 64–6, 152, 222, 247, 268, 269, 298
Kenya 2, 31, 43–4, 45, 94, 104, 106, 191, 262
KGB 21, 50, 66, 145, 217, 255, 299
Khalistan 83, 98
kidnapping 10, 26, 27, 28, 45, 46, 84, 97–8, 113, 135, 136, 139, 143, 147, 148, 190, 193, 194, 205, 207, 211, 262; symbolic 143, 145
KKK 166, 169–71, 174, 175, 185, 186, 248, 299
KLA 119, 120, 194, 288, 289, 299
kneecapping 26, 143–4, 145, 146, 299
Korea (South) 53
Koresh, David 177

Kosovo 108, 117–20, 121, 127, 194, 222, 230, 242, 246, 259, 270, 288, 289, 299
Kosovo Liberation Army – see KLA
Ku Klux Klan – see KKK
Kurdish Democratic Party (KDP) 257, 299
Kurdistan Workers Party – see PKK
Kurds 16, 31, 57, 105, 190, 191, 194, 221, 255, 256, 257, 258, 269, 285, 289, 299
Kuwait 123, 255

Lashkar-I-Taiba 65, 299
Laskar Jihad 246, 299
Law of Suspects 225
leaderless resistance 12, 94, 133, 156, 166, 176, 186, 264, 271, 299
Lebanon 29, 34, 41, 58–59, 60, 66, 67, 71, 74, 75, 95, 122, 124, 127, 173, 190, 212, 258, 269–70, 287
left-wing ideologies 300
Lenin, V. I. 20, 131, 134, 142, 300
Lexington 198
Liberation Tigers of Tamil Eelam (LTTE) – see Tamil Tigers
Liberia 107
Libya 50, 66, 204, 213, 269, 270, 272
Lockerbie, Scotland 50, 66
London transit system attacks 1, 94, 184, 281
Lord Mountbatten 37, 300
LTTE – see Tamil Tigers
lynching 171

McVeigh, Timothy 178, 267, 300
M-19 205, 206, 273, 292
Macedonia 54, 55, 56, 108, 117, 120–1, 127, 246, 259, 270, 287, 288
madrassas 96, 300
Madrid commuter train attacks 1, 94, 184
Madurese 114–6, 246, 275, 287
Mafia 190, 194
Malaya 190, 212, 213
Malaysia 246
Mao Tse-tung 131, 134, 142, 157, 306
Marx, Karl 131, 134, 162, 300
mass casualties 1, 2, 3, 31–5, 78–9, 96, 99, 178, 187, 277–8
Mathews, Robert 179

Mau Mau Rebellion 104, 300
Medellin Cartel 206–7, 300
media 3, 11, 21, 27, 32, 33, 36, 42, 46, 104, 122, 123, 139, 145, 155, 162, 206, 228, 237, 289; as targets 37, 87, 183, 192, 206, 253
Mexico 150
Michigan Militia 178
Middle East 3, 29, 41, 43, 54, 57
militia movement (United States) 174–9
Milosevic, Slobodan 119, 121, 246, 300
Minnesota Patriots Council 178, 265, 300
modernization 4, 11, 19, 36, 46, 78, 82, 86, 100, 103, 128, 138, 196, 275, 281, 285
Moluccas 77, 114, 116, 246
Montagnards 224, 226, 300
Montenegro 54–5, 117, 119, 120
Monteneros 138, 146–9, 157, 158, 197, 220, 287, 300
Moro, Aldo 144, 145, 300
Moro National Liberation Front 97
Moscow, Christmas theater takeover 193–4, 273
Mountbatten, Lord 202, 300
Mozambique 9
MRTA 195, 198–9, 213, 273, 306
Mugabe, Robert 228–30, 243, 301
Mujahedin-e-Khalq (MEK) 255, 301
Mumbai bombings 29, 65, 247
Munich Olympics 3, 50, 53, 123, 273, 283, 301
Murrah Federal Office Building 2, 174, 178, 301
Muslims 64, 77, 78, 79, 81, 190, 208, 209, 210, 222, 246, 247, 248, 265, 268, 272, 280, 289; as targets 63, 71, 77, 183, 218, 219, 222, 231–3, 251, 275, 286; in Bosnia 231–3; extremists 38, 66, 72–4, 77, 87–9, 93–7, 193, 211, 247
Mussolini, Benito 56, 142, 162–3, 171, 173, 186, 248, 301
Myanmar 53, 105

Nairobi, Kenya 2, 43–4, 94, 262
Napoleonic Wars 20
narcoterrorism 195, 212, 213, 301
Nasser 51

nationalism 20, 102, 103, 126
National Liberation Army, Colombia – see ELN
National Liberation Army, Macedonia (NLA) 120, 301
National Security Administration 263
NATO, in Bosnia 233
Naxalbari 150, 151, 152, 153
Naxalites 150–3, 158, 247
Nazis (National Socialist Democratic Workers Party) 8, 19, 33, 51, 106, 139, 159, 161, 164, 166–9, 171, 180, 182, 184, 185, 186, 217, 218, 221, 247, 288, 301
neo-fascists 166, 171–4, 186
neo-Nazis 34, 166, 180–4, 185, 219, 248
Nepal 150, 153, 159, 247, 259
nerve gas 277
Netherlands 107, 127, 140, 183, 226, 248
New York 1, 29, 32, 36, 283
Nicaragua 54, 60–3, 66, 265, 269, 289
Nichols, Terry 178, 301
Nigeria 79, 195, 208–11, 213, 214; and civil war 208–9; coup, January 1966 209; coup, July 1966 209; ethnic cleansing 209, 210, 214
Nivelles Group 164, 301
NKVD 217, 301
Noraid 204, 266
Northern Ireland 3, 29, 195, 199–204, 212, 213, 214, 273, 279, 285, 288
North Korea 53, 66, 67, 150
Norway 103
Nubia 234, 301
nuclear weapons 25, 31–2, 33, 53, 63, 64, 67, 96, 277

Ocalan, Abdullah 191, 301
Occupied Territories – see Gaza and West Bank 301
October Revolution 134
Official IRA 200, 203, 302
Oklahoma City 2, 23, 29, 43, 166, 174, 178, 179, 186, 187, 248, 267, 283
OPEC 140, 141
Operation Black Thunder 85, 302
Operation Blue Star 84, 302

Order, The 179, 302
Organization of the Islamic Revolution in the Arabian Peninsula 58
Oslo Accords 71, 289
Ottoman Empire 20, 55, 106, 107, 117, 126, 127, 218, 221, 231, 256, 259

Pakistan 30, 41, 54, 73, 98, 99, 127, 259, 269; and India 63–6
Palestine, Palestinians 2, 58, 67, 71, 74, 75, 95, 104, 105, 108, 121–6, 127, 137, 139, 140, 141–2, 173, 190, 245, 246, 251, 265, 267, 270, 271, 272, 274, 275, 280, 286, 287, 288, 289
Palestinian Authority 124, 275, 288, 302
Palestinian Liberation Organization – see PLO
Pan Am Flight 103 (Lockerbie) 50, 66
Paraguay 61, 192
paramilitary groups 119, 164, 167, 218, 219, 221, 223, 241, 242, 243, 246; in Bosnia 231–2, 233; in Burundi 238; in Colombia 205, 207–8, 220; in East Timor 226, 227, 268; in Nigeria 210; Protestant in Northern Ireland 203; in Rwanda 238–41, 242, 268; in the Sudan 235–6
Patriot Act 280
Patriotic Union of Kurdistan (PUK) 257, 302
patriot movement (United States) – see militia movement
Pavelich, Ante 56, 57, 223, 302
peasant rebellions 131
Peloponnesian Wars 52
Pentagon 1, 34, 36, 42, 94, 263, 289
Peoples Revolutionary Army (ERP) 148, 149, 302
Peron, Evita 147
Peron, Isabel 148, 158, 302
Peron, Juan 146–7, 148, 157, 158, 287, 302
Peru 26, 195–99, 212, 213–4, 278; Japanese embassy siege 199, 273
PFLP 122, 124, 137, 141–2, 158, 302
Philippines 96, 219, 246, 286
Pierce, William 176, 179, 302
PKK 34, 190, 191, 299
PLO 34, 53–4, 67, 141, 142, 112, 121–5, 127–8, 190, 246, 265, 270, 272, 275, 288; and diaspora 52, 58 123
Poland 218

Popular Front for the Liberation of Palestine — see PFLP
Popular Front for the Liberation of Palestine-General Command (PFLP-GC) 58, 303
Popular Liberation Army – see EPL
Portugal 173, 226, 247
Posse Comitatus 174, 303
propaganda of the deed 132, 133, 148, 157, 163, 303
propaganda of the word 132, 303
Provisional IRA (Provos) 200–1, 203, 303
Puerto Rico 105
Punjab 82, 84–5, 152, 220, 247, 278
Punjab solution 220, 303

Qadaffi 272
Quebec 104, 105, 259
Quebec Liberation Front (FLQ) 105, 303
Quran 73, 86

Rabin, Yitzak 71–2, 246, 303
racism 165, 175–6, 177, 178, 179, 183, 184, 187, 219
Radio Free Europe 50
radiological weapons 31–2, 78
RAF 139–41, 145, 157, 158, 164, 183, 267
Rangoon — see Yangoon
rape 220, 222, 226, 233, 236
Rashtriya Swayamsevak Sangh (RSS) 75, 76, 303
Real IRA 203, 270, 303
recession 4, 18–19
Red Army Faction – see RAF 303
Red Brigades 138, 142–5, 146, 157, 158, 173, 197, 265, 267, 268, 283, 303
Red Cells 139, 303
Red Scare 169, 170, 303
reforms 274–5, 278, 281, 285
Reign of Terror 131, 223, 224–5, 241–2, 243, 304
Rejectionist Front 137, 304
relative deprivation 17–18
Revolutionary Armed Forces of Colombia – see FARC
Revolutionary Guards 58, 59, 304
Rhodesia 31

ricin 50, 178, 265, 304

Rome under Empire 79, 80, 98, 99; as Republic 130–1, 161–2

Romania 74, 163, 165, 218, 268

Roosevelt, President Theodore 283

Ruby Ridge, Idaho 177, 304

Rudolph, Eric 176, 264

Russia 1, 20, 27, 36, 74, 79, 89, 90, 106, 126, 133–4, 162, 192, 193–4, 163, 165, 219, 263, 264, 268, 273, 287

Rwanda 3, 106, 223, 237–41, 242, 268, 284

SA 167–9, 182, 219, 305

Sandinistas 60–3, 289, 304

sans-cullottes 225

sarin nerve gas 89, 90, 91, 304

Saudi Arabia 58, 94, 95, 96, 123, 272, 287

Schutzstaffel – see SS

secular humanism 70, 78

Self Defense Forces of Colombia – see AUC

Sendero Luminoso – see Shining Path

Seoul Olympics 53

September 11th, 2001 (9/11) 1, 2, 4, 21, 22, 23, 30, 32, 64, 94, 98, 112, 179, 184, 194, 262, 270, 277, 278, 279, 280, 281, 283, 289

Serbia, Serbs 52, 54, 55, 56, 95, 106, 117–21, 222, 223, 231–3, 243, 259, 288

17 November Revolutionary Organization 146, 157, 264, 304

Sharia 73, 75, 218, 234, 305

Shia Muslims 57, 58–59, 60, 64, 66, 67, 72, 73, 190, 256, 257, 258, 285, 304

Shining Path 195–9, 213–4, 304

Sicarri 80, 305

Sierra Leone 107

Sikhs 63, 79, 81–6, 98, 99, 100, 129, 152, 243, 247, 305; as targets 84–5

Silent Brotherhood – see The Order

Sinai 122

Singapore 246

Sinhalese 248, 249, 250, 251, 254, 288

Sinn Fein 288

Six Day War 122

Skinheads 180, 182, 183, 247, 305

skyjackings – see hijackings

Slavonia 55

Slovenia 55, 117

Social Revolutionaries 133–4, 305

Somalia 106, 140, 270, 273, 287

Somoza, Anastacio 60, 61, 63, 305

Sons of Liberty 109

South Africa 9, 220, 268, 269

Southern Rhodesia – see Zimbabwe

South Korea – see Korea

Southwest Africa (Nambia) 269

Soviet Union 21, 31–2, 40, 41, 45, 51, 53, 61, 62, 63, 65, 87, 95, 96, 107–8, 124, 127, 134, 139, 141, 142, 145, 150, 158, 192, 172, 194, 199, 217, 218, 219, 259, 263, 283, 287, 289; and Afghanistan 95, 192; and Cold War 50, 53, 66, 73, 95, 106, 268; and Jewish Defense League 72–3

Spain 1, 106, 133, 140, 147, 158, 173, 259, 280, 285; and Basques 108, 110–3, 127, 194, 245, 286, 288

Sparta 52, 74

Special Air Services Regiment (SAS) 202, 273, 279, 305

Sri Lanka 3, 31, 74, 181, 245, 247, 248–54, 259, 267, 274, 278, 280, 283, 288; civil war 251, 254

SS 166–9, 304

Stalin 217, 289

Stamp Act 109

Stern Gang 104, 305

stormtroopers 167–9, 182, 218, 219

Students for a Democratic Society (SDS) 134, 305

Sturmabteilungen – see SA

successful terrorism 4, 5, 47–8, 74, 92–3, 98, 113, 116, 121, 125, 127, 148, 149, 155, 157, 158, 183, 185, 186, 202, 204, 206, 207, 211, 213–4, 233, 242, 243, 247, 258, 283, 284. 286–9

Sudan 3, 31, 59, 67, 73, 79, 89, 223, 234–7, 242, 243, 268; civil war 234–6; possibility of genocide 242

Suharto, General 114, 246, 305

suicide attacks 2, 3, 8, 29–30, 33–4, 41, 74, 88, 94, 99, 102, 137, 262, 273; by Chechens 194; in Iraq 256, 258; in Palestine/Israel 125, 126, 246, 265, 270, 280, 289; by PKK 191, 289; by Tamil Tigers 251, 253, 289

Sulawesi 77, 114, 116, 246, 247
Sumatra 114
Sunni Muslims 59, 64, 72, 73, 190, 256, 257, 258, 285, 287, 305
Nizari – see Assassins
Supreme Council for the Islamic Revolution 58
surface-to-air missiles (SAMs) 30–1
suspect community 279, 280, 305
Sweden 103, 140, 183, 219
Switzerland 140
Symbionese Liberation Army (SLA) 134, 135, 305
Syria 41, 59, 66, 99, 122, 123, 127, 190, 258, 269

Tajikistan 222
Taliban 64, 66, 73, 97, 99, 193, 269, 271, 281, 306
Tamil Nadu 247, 248, 252, 253, 306
Tamils 248, 249, 250, 251, 252, 253, 254, 274, 288
Tamil Tigers 248, 250–4, 267, 280, 289, 300, 306
Tanzania 2, 43–4, 45, 94, 262
tax resistors 174, 175
Thermopylae 74
Tito, Marshal 117
Tokyo subway attacks 3, 32, 33, 89, 90, 91, 278
totalitarianism 217, 254, 259, 267, 279
tourists as targets 38, 97, 112
transition, regimes in 41, 45, 111, 114, 246, 257, 259, 267, 268, 275
Triple Frontier region 192, 306
Trotsky, Leon 134. 306
Truman, President Harry 105
Tupac Amaru Revolutionary Movement – see MRTA
Tupameros 148, 136, 157, 242, 243, 306
Turkey, Turks 16, 31, 34, 59, 105, 107, 136, 164, 165, 181, 183, 190, 191, 221, 269, 289
Turner Diaries, The 176, 306
Tutsi 106, 223, 237–41, 242, 306

Ulster – see Northern Ireland
Uganda 140, 141, 274
UN 269, 276; as target 256–7
Unabomber 11, 138, 306
Union of Soviet Socialist Republics (USSR) – see Soviet Union

United Kingdom 9, 19, 37, 47, 50, 56, 133, 138, 146, 149, 154–6, 209, 248, 257, 259, 264, 276, 279, 280, 281; and American Revolution 108–10, 127; and Cyprus 104, 275, 286; and Kenya 104; and Malaya 190; and Northern Ireland 199–204, 212, 268, 285, 288; and Palestine 104, 121, 127, 245, 275, 286; and Zimbabwe 228, 229
United Nations – see UN
United States 1, 2, 3, 9, 19, 21, 29, 32, 33, 36, 42, 45, 50, 53, 60, 70, 75, 79, 94–7, 98, 99, 120, 123, 125, 132, 133, 136, 139, 142, 143, 146, 147, 169–71, 172, 180, 184, 204, 206, 222, 233, 248, 259, 262, 263, 264, 266, 269–70, 272, 273, 274, 275, 276, 277, 279, 280, 281, 283, 284, 287, 289; and abortion violence 91–3, 98, 99, 287; and Afghanistan 16, 64, 66, 95, 269, 270; and Civil War 169, 186; and Cold War 21, 53, 66, 95, 106, 268; and Contras 54, 60–3, 66, 265; and Cuba 51; and Iraq 2, 59, 97, 99, 255–8, 259, 286, 287; and Libya 204, 269, 272; and Puerto Rico 105; and militia movement 166, 174–9, 186; and Vietnam 134, 135, 143, 157, 248
Uruguay 136, 157, 158, 148, 242, 243, 268, 276
USS Cole 2, 94, 287, 307
Utashe 56, 223, 246, 287, 307
Uzbekistan 193, 194

Vendee 162, 307
Venezuela 206
Vietnam 150
Vietnam war 134, 135, 248
vigilantes 13, 71, 213, 216, 219, 220, 221, 222, 223, 227, 233, 241, 242, 246–7, 267, 268, 285
Violencia, La 205, 307
viruses 277
Vojvodina 117, 119
Voting Rights Act, 1965 169

Waco, Texas 177, 178
wars, as cause 19–20
Warsaw Ghetto 70
Washington DC 1, 32, 178, 283
waves of terrorism 20

weak states 20, 98, 120,172, 257, 259, 285–6
weapons of mass destruction 3, 25, 28, 31–5, 41, 67, 194, 277–8, 307
weapons of mass disruption 31, 307
Weathermen 134, 135, 157, 248, 307
Weather Underground 134, 135
Weaver, Randy 177
West Germany – see Germany
Will of the People 133, 307
World Trade Center 1, 23, 29, 30, 34, 36, 42, 43, 94, 263, 289
World War I 20, 52, 54, 55, 166, 167, 169, 170
World War II 37, 57, 166, 171, 221

xenophobia 70

Yangoon bombing 53, 303
Yoruba 208, 209, 211, 307
Yugoslavia 3, 16, 40, 54–7, 66, 105, 108, 117, 119, 120, 127, 222, 223, 230, 231, 246, 259

Zaire 107
Zealots 79, 80–1, 98, 99, 285, 287, 307
Zhirinovsky, Vladimir 165, 307
Zimbabwe 223, 228–30, 241, 268
Zimbabwean African National Union-Popular Front (ZANU-PF) 228, 229, 241, 243, 307
Zimbabwean African Peoples Union (ZAPU) 228, 307
Zionist 245, 307
Zionist Occupied Government (ZOG) 176, 177, 178, 179, 183, 186, 307